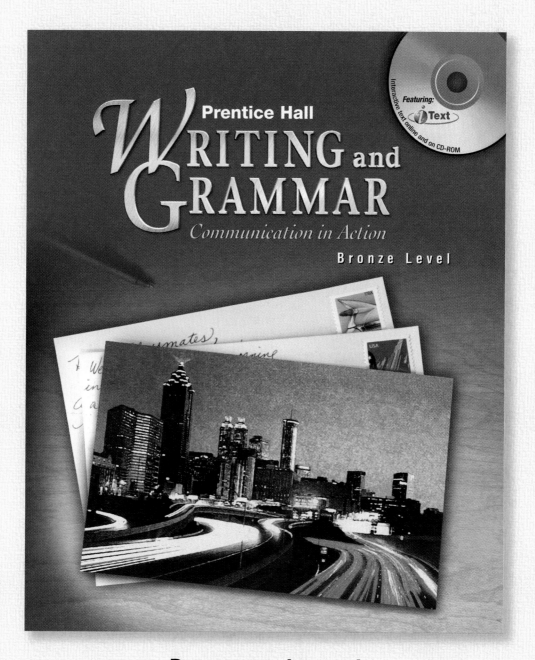

Prentice Hall

WRITING and GRAMMAR

Communication in Action

Bronze Level

Featuring: iText

Interactive text online and on CD-ROM

Bronze Level

PEARSON

Prentice Hall

Upper Saddle River, New Jersey
Needham, Massachusetts

WRITING and GRAMMAR

Communication in Action

Copper
Bronze
Silver
Gold
Platinum
Ruby
Diamond

ISBN 0-13-037492-X

8 9 10   09 08 07 06 05

Go Online
PHSchool.com

Use <i> Text *Writing and Grammar,* the interactive textbook!

(Includes every grammar exercise in this book!)

- instant feedback on interactive grammar exercises
- interactive writing tools and writing tutorials
- access to the *Prentice Hall Online Essay Scorer*

iText is also available on CD-ROM.

Go on-line to get instant help on the Writing and Grammar Web site!

- additional grammar practice opportunities
- scoring rubrics with scored student models for different modes of writing

Here's how to use the Writing and Grammar Web site:

Look for these Web Codes in your book:

> ebk-7001
> ebk-7002

Here's how to use Web Codes:

1. Go on-line. Enter URL: PHSchool.com

2. If you want instant feedback on interactive grammar exercises, enter Web Code: ebk-7002

   Choose the appropriate chapter from the menu that appears.

3. If you want to review writing rubrics and scored student models, enter Web Code: ebk-7001

   Choose the appropriate chapter from the menu that appears.

Program Authors

The program authors guided the direction and philosophy of *Prentice Hall Writing and Grammar: Communication in Action*. Working with the development team, they contributed to the pedagogical integrity of the program and to its relevance to today's teachers and students.

Joyce Armstrong Carroll

In her forty-year career, Joyce Armstrong Carroll, Ed.D., has taught on every grade level from primary to graduate school. In the past twenty years, she has trained teachers in the teaching of writing. A nationally known consultant, she has served as president of TCTE and on NCTE's Commission on Composition. More than fifty of her articles have appeared in journals such as *Curriculum Review, English Journal, Media & Methods, Southwest Philosophical Studies, Ohio English Journal, English in Texas,* and the *Florida English Journal.* With Edward E. Wilson, Dr. Carroll co-authored *Acts of Teaching: How to Teach Writing* and co-edited *Poetry After Lunch: Poems to Read Aloud.* Beyond her direct involvement with the writing pedagogy presented in this series, Dr. Carroll guided the development of the Hands-on Grammar feature. She co-directs the New Jersey Writing Project in Texas.

Edward E. Wilson

A former editor of *English in Texas*, Edward E. Wilson has served as a high-school English teacher and a writing consultant in school districts nationwide. Wilson has served on the Texas Teacher Professional Practices Commission and on NCTE's Commission on Composition. With Dr. Carroll, he co-wrote *Acts of Teaching: How to Teach Writing* and co-edited the award-winning *Poetry After Lunch: Poems to Read Aloud.* In addition to his direct involvement with the writing pedagogy presented in this series, Wilson provided inspiration for the Spotlight on Humanities feature. Wilson's poetry appears in Paul Janeczko's anthology *The Music of What Happens.* Wilson co-directs the New Jersey Writing Project in Texas.

Gary Forlini

Gary Forlini, a nationally known education consultant, developed the grammar, usage, and mechanics instruction and exercises in this series. After teaching in the Pelham, New York, schools for many years, he established Research in Media, an educational research agency that provides information for product developers, school staff developers, media companies, and arts organizations, as well as private-sector corporations and foundations. Mr. Forlini was co-author of the *S.A.T. Home Study* program and has written numerous industry reports on elementary, secondary, and post-secondary education markets.

National Advisory Panel

The teachers and administrators serving on the National Advisory Panel provided ongoing input into the development of *Prentice Hall Writing and Grammar: Communication in Action*. Their valuable insights ensure that the perspectives of teachers and students throughout the country are represented within the instruction in this series.

Dr. Pauline Bigby-Jenkins
Coordinator for Secondary English
  Language Arts
Ann Arbor Public Schools
Ann Arbor, Michigan

Lee Bromberger
English Department Chairperson
Mukwonago High School
Mukwonago, Wisconsin

Mary Chapman
Teacher of English
Free State High School
Lawrence, Kansas

Jim Deatherage
Language Arts Department
  Chairperson
Richland High School
Richland, Washington

Luis Dovalina
Teacher of English
La Joya High School
La Joya, Texas

JoAnn Giardino
Teacher of English
Centennial High School
Columbus, Ohio

Susan Goldberg
Teacher of English
Westlake Middle School
Thornwood, New York

Jean Hicks
Director, Louisville Writing Project
University of Louisville
Louisville, Kentucky

Karen Hurley
Teacher of Language Arts
Perry Meridian Middle School
Indianapolis, Indiana

Karen Lopez
Teacher of English
Hart High School
Newhall, California

Marianne Minshall
Teacher of Reading and Language Arts
Westmore Middle School
Columbus, Ohio

Nancy Monroe
English Department Chairperson
Bolton High School
Alexandria, Louisiana

Ken Spurlock
Assistant Principal
Boone County High School
Florence, Kentucky

Cynthia Katz Tyroff
Staff Development Specialist
  and Teacher of English
Northside Independent School District
San Antonio, Texas

Holly Ward
Teacher of Language Arts
Campbell Middle School
Daytona Beach, Florida

Grammar Review Team

The following teachers reviewed the grammar instruction in this series to ensure accuracy, clarity, and pedagogy.

Kathy Hamilton
Paul Hertzog
Daren Hoisington
Beverly Ladd

Karen Lopez
Dianna Louise Lund
Sean O'Brien

CONTENTS IN BRIEF

Chapters 1–13

Part 1: Writing 1

Chapter
1 The Writer in You 2
2 A Walk Through
   the Writing Process 12
3 Sentences, Paragraphs, and
   Compositions: Structure and Style . 28
4 Narration:
   Autobiographical Writing 48
5 Narration: Short Story 72
6 Description 98
7 Persuasion: Persuasive Essay . . . 124
8 Exposition:
   Comparison-and-Contrast Essay . 150
9 Exposition:
   Cause-and-Effect Essay 174
10 Exposition: How-to Essay 198
11 Research Report 222
12 Response to Literature 248
13 Writing for Assessment 274

Chapters 14–27

Part 2: Grammar, Usage, and Mechanics .. 292

Chapter 14 Nouns and Pronouns 294
15 Verbs. 314
16 Adjectives and Adverbs 334
17 Prepositions 360
18 Conjunctions and Interjections . . 374
19 Basic Sentence Parts 390
20 Phrases and Clauses 424
21 Effective Sentences 454
22 Using Verbs 490
23 Using Pronouns 518
24 Making Words Agree 532
25 Using Modifiers. 558
26 Punctuation 578
27 Capitalization 634

Chapters 28–31

Part 3: Academic and Workplace Skills .. 666

Chapter 28 Speaking, Listening, Viewing,
and Representing 668
29 Vocabulary and Spelling. 690
30 Reading Skills. 714
31 Study, Reference,
and Test-Taking Skills 736

Resources:

Styles for Business and Friendly Letters 758
Citing Sources and Preparing Manuscript 760
Penmanship Reference 760
Internet Research Handbook 765
Commonly Overused Words. 770
Commonly Misspelled Words 772
Abbreviations Guide 774
Proofreading Symbols Reference 778
Student Publications 779
Glossary 780
Index 788

CONTENTS
PART 1: WRITING

Chapter 1

The Writer in You 2

Writing in Everyday Life 2
Why Write? 3
Developing Your Writing Life 3
What Are the Qualities of Good Writing? 7
Reflecting on Your Writing 7

Chapter 2

A Walk Through the Writing Process .. 12

2.1 What Is Prewriting? 14
2.2 What Is Drafting? 18
2.3 What Is Revising? 19
2.4 What Are Editing and Proofreading? 22
2.5 What Are Publishing and Presenting? 23

Chapter 3

Sentences, Paragraphs, and Compositions
Structure and Style 28

3.1 Sentence Combining 29
Controlling Your Sentences 29
Inserting Words and Phrases 29
Using Compound Subjects or Verbs 30
Forming Compound Sentences 31
Using Subordination 32
3.2 Writing Effective Paragraphs 33
Stating the Main Idea in a Topic Sentence 33
Writing a Topic Sentence 34
Writing Supporting Sentences 35
Placing Your Topic Sentence 36
3.3 Paragraphs in Essays and Other Compositions . 37
Unity and Coherence 37
Understanding the Parts of a Composition 39
Recognizing Types of Paragraphs 40
3.4 Writing Style 42
Developing Style 42
Using Formal and Informal English 43

INTEGRATED SKILLS

▶ **Spotlight on the Humanities**
Analyzing How Meaning Is Communicated Through the Arts 8
▶ **Media and Technology Skills**
Making Technology Work for You
Activity: Identify Appropriate Technology 9
▶ **Standardized Test Preparation Workshop**
Writing for Standardized Tests 10

INTEGRATED SKILLS

▶ **Spotlight on the Humanities**
Recognizing Common Subjects in Art
Focus on Photography: Elliott Erwitt 24
▶ **Media and Technology Skills**
Using Technology for Writing
Activity: Build an Electronic Portfolio 25
▶ **Standardized Test Preparation Workshop**
Using the Writing Process to Respond to Writing Prompts. 26

INTEGRATED SKILLS

▶ **Spotlight on the Humanities**
Analyzing Artistic Composition
Focus on Dance: Anna Pavlova 44
▶ **Media and Technology Skills**
Evaluating Information Media
Activity: Comparing and Contrasting Newscasts. . . . 45
▶ **Standardized Test Preparation Workshop**
Analyzing Strategy, Organization, and Style . . . 46

Chapter 4 Narration
Autobiographical Writing 48

4.1 Model From Literature
"The Bike" by Gary Soto 50

4.2 Prewriting
Choosing Your Topic 52
    Freewriting 52
    Blueprinting 52
    Topic Bank 53
Narrowing Your Topic 54
    Use Looping to Narrow a Topic 54
Considering Your Audience and Purpose 55
    Analyze Your Purpose 55
Gathering Details 55
    List and Itemize 55

4.3 Drafting
Shaping Your Writing 56
    Create Tension 56
Providing Elaboration 57
    Characterize Through Details 57

4.4 Revising
Revising Your Overall Structure 58
    Revision Strategy: Identifying Connections
    to Conflict 58
Revising Your Paragraphs 59
    Revision Strategy: Coding for Coherence:
    "Weeding" Paragraphs 59
Revising Your Sentences 60
    Revision Strategy: Coding Events for Transitions . . . 60
Revising Your Word Choice 61
    Revision Strategy: Color-Coding Nouns for Precise
    Word Choice 61
Peer Review 62
    Highlight 62

4.5 Editing and Proofreading
Focusing on Capitalization 63

4.6 Publishing and Presenting
Building Your Portfolio 64
Reflecting on Your Writing 64
☑ **Rubric for Self-Assessment** 64

Connected Assignment: Firsthand Biography 67

Student Work
IN PROGRESS

Featured Work:
"To the Dogs"
by Emily Taylor Speer
Hildebrandt Intermediate
School
Spring, Texas

Blueprinting 52
Looping 54
Adding Characterizing
Details 57
Identifying Connections to
Conflict 58
Coding for Transitions . . . 60
Final Draft **65**

INTEGRATED SKILLS

▶ **Grammar in Your Writing**
Nouns 61
Capitalization of Proper
Nouns 63

▶ **Spotlight on the Humanities**
Use Visuals to Extend Meaning

Focus on Photography:
Berenice Abbott 68

▶ **Media and Technology Skills**
Produce Visuals to Make
Meaning

Activity: Create a Photo
Essay 69

▶ **Standardized Test
Preparation Workshop**
Using Narration to Respond to
Writing Prompts 70

Chapter 5 Narration

Short Story 72

5.1 Model From Literature
"Sarah Tops" by Isaac Asimov..................... 74

5.2 Prewriting
Choosing Your Topic 78
  Freewriting 78
  Magazine Flip-Through..................... 78
  Writing Round 78
  Topic Bank 79
Developing Narrative Elements 80
  Identify Conflict..................... 80
Considering Your Audience and Purpose 80
Gathering Details 81
  Use Listing and Itemizing..................... 81

5.3 Drafting
Shaping Your Writing 82
  Create a Plot..................... 82
Providing Elaboration 83
  Use Details to Define Character and Setting 83

5.4 Revising
Revising Your Overall Structure 84
  Revision Strategy: Using Clues to Evaluate Pacing .. 84
Revising Your Paragraphs 85
  Revision Strategy: Using Points to Illuminate...... 85
Revising Your Sentences 86
  Revision Strategy: Using a "Spy Camera" 86
Revising Your Word Choice 87
  Revision Strategy: Circling Verbs..................... 87
Peer Review 87
  Highlight Passages..................... 87

5.5 Editing and Proofreading
Focusing on Dialogue..................... 88

5.6 Publishing and Presenting
Building Your Portfolio..................... 89
Reflecting on Your Writing 89
  ☑ **Rubric for Self-Assessment** 89

Connected Assignment: Dramatic Scene 93

Student Work
IN PROGRESS

Featured Work:
"Showing Amanda the Ropes"
by Elisabeth Laskey
Gray-New Gloucester Middle
School
Gray, Maine

Writing Round 78
Adding Characterizing
Details............... 83
Using Points to Illuminate. 85
Final Draft.......... 90

INTEGRATED SKILLS

▶ **Grammar in Your Writing**
Identifying Action Verbs ... 87
Punctuating Dialogue 88

▶ **Spotlight on the Humanities**
Analyzing Themes Across
Cultures

Focus on Oral Tradition:
Scheherazade 94

▶ **Media and Technology Skills**
Analyzing Visual Meanings

Activity: Follow Events
in Animated Cartoons 95

▶ **Standardized Test
Preparation Workshop**
Responding to Prompts About
Short Stories........... 96

Chapter 6 — Description 98

6.1 Model From Literature
"Luke Baldwin's Vow" by Morley Callaghan 100

6.2 Prewriting
Choosing Your Topic 102
   Freewriting 102
   Drawing 102
   Timeline 102
   Topic Bank 103
Narrowing Your Topic 104
   Zoom In to Narrow a Topic 104
Considering Your Audience and Purpose 104
Gathering Details 105
   Use Cubing to Gather Details 105

6.3 Drafting
Shaping Your Writing 106
   Organize to Make Your Ideas Clear 106
   Create a Main Impression................. 106
Providing Elaboration...................... 107
   Build Upon Details....................... 107

6.4 Revising
Revising Your Overall Structure 108
   Revision Strategy: Cutting and Pasting for Order .. 108
   Revision Strategy: Circling Details
   to Strengthen a Main Impression 109
Revising Your Paragraphs.................... 110
   Revision Strategy: Adding Functional Paragraphs.. 110
Revising Your Sentences 111
   Revision Strategy: Color-Coding Clues
   to Eliminate Run-ons 111
Revising Your Word Choice 112
   Revision Strategy: Checkmarking Empty Words ... 112
Peer Review 113
   Analytic Talk 113

6.5 Editing and Proofreading
Focusing on Commas 114

6.6 Publishing and Presenting
Building Your Portfolio..................... 115
Reflecting on Your Writing.................. 115
   ✓ Rubric for Self-Assessment................ 115

Connected Assignment: Poem.................. 118

Student Work
IN PROGRESS

Featured Work:
"House of Memories"
by Kaitlin Crockett
Baypoint Middle School
St. Petersburg, Florida

Using a Personal Experience
Timeline to Choose a
Topic 102
Gathering Details Using
Cubing.............. 105
Depth-Charging to Build
Upon Sensory Details . . . 107
Circling Details to Strengthen
a Main Impression 109
Color-Coding Pauses to
Eliminate Run-ons 111
Checkmarking
Empty Words 112
Final Draft.......... 116

INTEGRATED SKILLS

▶ **Grammar in Your Writing**
Adjectives 113
Using Commas With Two or
More Adjectives 114

▶ **Spotlight on the Humanities**
Comparing Interpretations of
Nature
Focus on Fine Art: Georgia
O'Keeffe 120

▶ **Media and Technology Skills**
Analyzing Visual Meanings
Activity: Analyze Camera
Techniques in a Movie ... 121

▶ **Standardized Test Preparation Workshop**
Strategy, Organization, and
Style Skills 122

Chapter 7 Persuasion

Persuasive Essay 124

7.1 Model From Literature
"The Eternal Frontier" by Louis L'Amour 126

7.2 Prewriting
Choosing Your Topic 128
   Round Table 128
   Media Flip-Through 128
   Quicklist 128
   Topic Bank 129
Narrowing Your Topic 130
   "Funnel" Your Topic 130
Considering Your Audience and Purpose 130
Gathering Evidence 131
   Provide Support 131

7.3 Drafting
Shaping Your Writing 132
   Develop a Thesis Statement 132
   Organize to Emphasize 132
Providing Elaboration 133
   Layer Ideas Using SEE 133

7.4 Revising
Revising Your Overall Structure 134
   Revision Strategy: Highlighting Main Points 134
   Revision Strategy: Coding for Supporting Evidence . . 135
Revising Your Paragraphs 136
   Revision Strategy: Color-Coding the Connections . . 136
Revising Your Sentences 137
   Revision Strategy: Color-Coding Sentences That
   Express Related Ideas 137
Revising Your Word Choice 138
   Revision Strategy: Tagging Vague Words 138
Peer Review 138
   Analytic Talk 138

7.5 Editing and Proofreading
Focusing on End Marks 139

7.6 Publishing and Presenting
Building Your Portfolio 140
Reflecting on Your Writing 140
   ☑ **Rubric for Self-Assessment** 140

Connected Assignment: Persuasive Advertisement 144

Student Work IN PROGRESS

Featured Work:
"Learning to Speak Up:
the DCE"
by Josh McWhirter
College Station Junior High
College Station, Texas

Using a Quicklist 128
Using a T-Chart 131
Layering Ideas 133
Coding for Supporting
Evidence 135
Coding Connections
Between Paragraphs 136
Tagging Vague Words . . . 138
Final Draft **141**

INTEGRATED SKILLS

▶ **Grammar in Your Writing**
Compound Sentences . . . 137
End Marks 139

▶ **Spotlight on the Humanities**
Evaluating Performances

Focus on Music: Giacomo
Puccini and Opera 146

▶ **Media and Technology Skills**
Analyzing Bias in the Media

Activity: Evaluate Objectivity of
News Reports 147

▶ **Standardized Test
Preparation Workshop**
Responding to Persuasive
Writing Prompts. 148

Chapter 8

Exposition: *Comparison-and-Contrast Essay* 150

8.1 Model From Literature
"Bat Attacks?" by Laura Allen 152

8.2 Prewriting
Choosing Your Topic 154
    Quicklist 154
    BUT Chart 154
    Topic Bank 155
Narrowing Your Topic 156
    Use Cubing to Narrow a Topic 156
Considering Your Audience and Purpose 157
    Analyze Your Purpose 157
Gathering Details 157
    Use a Venn Diagram 157

8.3 Drafting
Shaping Your Writing 158
    Select an Effective Organization 158
Providing Elaboration 159
    Layer Ideas Using SEE 159

8.4 Revising
Revising Your Overall Structure 160
    Revision Strategy: Color-Coding Details
    for Effective Organization and Balance 160
    Revision Strategy: Tagging High Points 161
Revising Your Paragraphs 162
    Revision Strategy: Marking Paragraph Patterns . . . 162
Revising Your Sentences 163
    Revision Strategy: Circling Repetitious Sentences . . 163
Revising Your Word Choice 164
    Revision Strategy: Reading Aloud
    for Repeated Words 164
Peer Review 164
    Summarize 164

8.5 Editing and Proofreading
Focusing on Pronouns 165

8.6 Publishing and Presenting
Building Your Portfolio 166
Reflecting on Your Writing 166
   ☑ **Rubric for Self-Assessment** 166

Connected Assignment: Consumer Report 169

Student Work
IN PROGRESS

Featured Work:
"Skateboards for Success"
by Dylan Parker
Carr Lane VPA Middle School
St. Louis, Missouri

Using a BUT Chart 154
Using Cubing 156
Using Layering 159
Tagging High Points 161
Marking Paragraph
Patterns 162
Final Draft **167**

INTEGRATED SKILLS

▶ **Grammar in Your Writing**
Subject-Verb Agreement:
Compound Subjects 163
Pronoun-Antecedent
Agreement 165
▶ **Spotlight on the Humanities**
Evaluating Performances
Focus on Music: Gilbert &
Sullivan 170
▶ **Media and Technology Skills**
Comparing Media
Activity: Comparing Book and
Movie Versions 171
▶ **Standardized Test
Preparation Workshop**
Responding to Expository
Writing Prompts 172

Chapter 9

Exposition
Cause-and-Effect Essay 174

9.1 Model From Literature
"How Do Rainmakers Make It Rain?"
from *How in the World?* 176

9.2 Prewriting
Choosing Your Topic 178
    Brainstorming 178
    Blueprinting 178
    Media Flip-Through 178
    Topic Bank 179
Narrowing Your Topic 180
    Use Classical Invention to Narrow Your Topic 180
Considering Your Audience and Purpose 181
Gathering Details 181
    Do Research 181

9.3 Drafting
Shaping Your Writing 182
    Organize Logically 182
Providing Elaboration 183
    Elaborate Causal Connections 183

9.4 Revising
Revising Your Overall Structure 184
    Revision Strategy: Connecting the Steps 184
Revising Your Paragraphs 185
    Revision Strategy: Finding the "Tug" 185
    Revision Strategy: Coding Cause-and-Effect
    Connections. 185
Revising Your Sentences 186
    Revision Strategy: Circling Verbs in an
    Inconsistent Tense 186
Revising Your Word Choice 188
    Revision Strategy: Highlighting Key Events 188
Peer Review 188
    "Say Back". 188

9.5 Editing and Proofreading
Focusing on Prepositions 189

9.6 Publishing and Presenting
Building Your Portfolio. 190
Reflecting on Your Writing 190
    ☑ **Rubric for Self-Assessment** 190

Connected Assignment: Documentary Video Script . . . 193

Student Work
IN PROGRESS

Featured Work:
"Why Trains Are No Longer
Popular"
by Jake Sommer
Maplewood Middle School
Maplewood, New Jersey

Media Flip-Through 178
Asking Questions to
Narrow a Topic 180
Elaborating Causal
Connections 183
Connecting the Steps . . . 184
Circling Verbs in an
Inconsistent Tense 186
Final Draft. **191**

INTEGRATED SKILLS

▶ **Grammar in Your Writing**
Verb Tense 187
Prepositions 189

▶ **Spotlight on the Humanities**
Analyzing Ideas Represented in
Various Art Forms

Focus on Drama: A Broadway
Fairy Tale 194

▶ **Media and Technology Skills**
Analyzing Media Images

Activity: Caption
a Photograph. 195

▶ **Standardized Test
Preparation Workshop**
Responding to Expository
Writing Prompts. 196

Chapter 10 Exposition
How-to Essay 198

10.1 Model From Literature
"Moving Mountains" by Janice VanCleave 200

10.2 Prewriting
Choosing Your Topic 202
   Invisible Ink. 202
   List 202
   Topic Bank 203
Narrowing Your Topic 204
Considering Your Audience and Purpose 204
Gathering Details 205
   Itemize to Gather Details 205

10.3 Drafting
Shaping Your Writing 206
   Organize Details in Chronological Order 206
Providing Elaboration 207
   Add Details by "Exploding the Moment" 207

10.4 Revising
Revising Your Overall Structure 208
   Revision Strategy: Writing a Strong Lead 208
Revising Your Paragraphs 209
   Revision Strategy: Using Steps, Stacks, Chains,
   and Balances. 209
Revising Your Sentences 210
   Revision Strategy: Using Clues to Sentence
   Beginnings 210
Revising Your Word Choice 212
   Revision Strategy: Highlighting Repeated Words . . . 212
Peer Review 213
   Ask a Group to Try It Out. 213

10.5 Editing and Proofreading
Focusing on Commas 214

10.6 Publishing and Presenting
Building Your Portfolio 215
Reflecting on Your Writing 215
   ☑ **Rubric for Self-Assessment** 215

Connected Assignment: Problem-and-Solution Essay . . . 217

Student Work IN PROGRESS

Featured Work:
"Banana Cake"
by Felix Espinoza
Palo Alto Middle School
Killeen, Texas

Listing to Discover
a Topic. 202
Itemizing the Details 205
Exploding the Moment . . 207
Writing a Strong Lead . . . 208
Varying Sentence
Beginnings 210
Highlighting Repeated
Words 212
Final Draft **216**

INTEGRATED SKILLS

▶ **Grammar in Your Writing**
Adverb Clauses and Adverb
Phrases. 211
Using Commas to Separate
Items in a Series 214

▶ **Spotlight on the Humanities**
Comparing Media
Focus: Science Fiction
in Film 218

▶ **Media and Technology Skills**
Using Computer Technology
Activity: Getting "Help"
On-line 219

▶ **Standardized Test
Preparation Workshop**
Responding to Expository
Writing Prompts. 220

Chapter 11 Research Report . . . 222

11.1 Model From Literature
"Pandas" by Gillian Standring 224

11.2 Prewriting
Choosing Your Topic 228
   Listing 228
   Newswatch 228
   Self-Interview 228
   Topic Bank 229
Narrowing Your Topic 230
   Use Classical Invention 230
Considering Your Audience and Purpose 231
Gathering Details 231
   Use a Variety of Research Sources 231
   Take Notes 231

11.3 Drafting
Shaping Your Writing 232
   Develop a Main Idea or Thesis 232
   Make an Outline 232
Providing Elaboration 233
   Find Points for Clarification 233

11.4 Revising
Revising Your Overall Structure 234
   Revision Strategy: Matching Your Draft to Your
   Outline 234
Revising Your Paragraphs 235
   Revision Strategy: Finding the Glue Between
   Paragraphs 235
Revising Your Sentences 236
   Revision Strategy: Finding the Main Action
   in a Cluster 236
Revising Your Word Choice 237
   Revision Strategy: Color-Coding Technical Terms . . 237
Peer Review 238
   Summarize 238

11.5 Editing and Proofreading
Focusing on Citations 239

11.6 Publishing and Presenting
Building Your Portfolio 240
Reflecting on Your Writing 240
  ☑ **Rubric for Self-Assessment** 240

Connected Assignment: I-Search Report 243

Student Work
IN PROGRESS

Featured Work:
"Built to Survive: Whales"
by Jamie Barraclough
Los Alamos Middle School
Los Alamos, New Mexico

Conducting a
Self-Interview 228
Using Classical Invention . 230
Finding Points to Clarify . . 233
Finding the Glue Between
Paragraphs 235
Combining Short
Sentences 236
Final Draft **241**

INTEGRATED SKILLS

▶ **Grammar in Your Writing**
Participial Phrases 237
Quotation Marks and
Underlining With Titles
of Works 239

▶ **Spotlight on the Humanities**
Framing Questions to Direct
Research

Focus on Theater: *Oliver!* . 244

▶ **Media and Technology Skills**
Using On-line Sources in
Research

Activity: Find and Evaluate
On-line Sources 245

▶ **Standardized Test
Preparation Workshop**
Revising and Editing 246

Chapter 12 — Response to Literature 248

12.1 Model From Literature
"Making Fantasy Real" by Zena Sutherland 250

12.2 Prewriting
Choosing Your Topic 252
    Interview Yourself. 252
    Browsing. 252
    Topic Bank 253
Narrowing Your Topic 254
    Use a Pentad 254
Considering Your Audience and Purpose 255
Gathering Details 256
    Use Hexagonal Writing 256
    What to Look For 257

12.3 Drafting
Shaping Your Writing 258
    Define and Develop Your Focus 258
Providing Elaboration 259
    Provide Support 259

12.4 Revising
Revising Your Overall Structure 260
    Revision Strategy: Color-Coding Main Points
    and Support 260
    Revision Strategy: Circling the Strongest Point. ... 260
Revising Your Paragraphs 261
    Revision Strategy: Using Points to Illuminate
    to Add Support 261
Revising Your Sentences 262
    Revision Strategy: Highlighting Sentences
    That Explain Why 262
Revising Your Word Choice 263
    Revision Strategy: Color-Coding Value Words. 263
Peer Review 263
    Process Share 263

12.5 Editing and Proofreading
Focusing on Quotations 264

12.6 Publishing and Presenting
Building Your Portfolio. 265
Reflecting on Your Writing 265
    ☑ **Rubric for Self-Assessment** 265

Connected Assignment: Movie Review 269

Student Work IN PROGRESS

Featured Work:
"Frogs vs. Flowers"
by Jade Yamamoto
Calvary Lutheran School
Indianapolis, Indiana

Browsing 252
Using a Pentad 254
Using a Hexagon. 256
Providing Support. 259
Adding Support With
Points to Illuminate 261
Highlighting Sentences
That Explain Why 262
Final Draft. 266

INTEGRATED SKILLS

▶ **Grammar in Your Writing**
Combining Ideas in Complex
Sentences 263
Rules for Punctuating
Quotations 264

▶ **Spotlight on the Humanities**
Comparing Art With a Written
Story

Focus on Art: Henri
Matisse. 270

▶ **Media and Technology Skills**
Interpreting Literature in a
Variety of Media

Activity: Create a
Multimedia Interpretation . 271

▶ **Standardized Test
Preparation Workshop**
Responding to Literature-
Based Writing Prompts. ... 272

Chapter 13 Writing for Assessment 274

13.1 Prewriting
Choosing Your Topic 276
  Choosing a Writing Prompt 276
  Topic Bank 276
Narrowing Your Topic 277
  Identify the Topic and Purpose 277
Gathering Details 278

13.2 Drafting
Shaping Your Writing 279
  Find a Focus 279
  Plan Your Organization 279
Providing Elaboration 280

13.3 Revising
Revising Your Overall Structure 281
  Revision Strategy: Checking Your Introduction
  and Conclusion 281
Revising Your Paragraphs 281
  Revision Strategy: Checking Support 281
Revising Your Sentences 282
  Revision Strategy: Adding Transitions 282
Revising Your Word Choice 282
  Revision Strategy: "Show, Don't Tell" 282

13.4 Editing and Proofreading
Focusing on Complete Sentences 283

13.5 Publishing and Presenting
Building Your Portfolio 284
Reflecting on Your Writing 284
  ☑ **Rubric for Self-Assessment** 284

Connected Assignment: Open-Book Test 287

Student Work IN PROGRESS

Featured Work:
  "Air Pollution"
  by Brittany Wilson
  Stuart Middle School
  Louisville, Kentucky

Using a Topic Web to
Gather Details 278

Adding Supporting
Details to an Outline 280

Final Draft **285**

INTEGRATED SKILLS

▶ **Grammar in Your Writing**
Using Complete, Correct
Sentences 283

▶ **Spotlight on the Humanities**
Comparing and Contrasting
Print and Visual Media

Focus on Theater:
Kiss Me Kate 288

▶ **Media and Technology Skills**
Using Technology to Support
Learning

Activity: Explore Electronic
Tests 289

▶ **Standardized Test
Preparation Workshop**
Proofreading 290

PART 2: GRAMMAR, USAGE, AND MECHANICS

Chapter 14

Nouns and Pronouns 294

▶ **Diagnostic Test**. 295

14.1 Nouns 296
People, Places, Things, and Ideas 296
Collective Nouns 297
Compound Nouns 297
Common and Proper Nouns 298
▶ **Section Review**. 300

14.2 Pronouns. 301
Antecedents of Pronouns 302
Personal Pronouns. 303
Demonstrative Pronouns. 305
Interrogative Pronouns 306
Indefinite Pronouns 306
▶ **Hands-on Grammar**. 308
▶ **Section Review**. 309
▶ **Chapter Review** 310
▶ **Standardized Test Preparation Workshop** . 312

Chapter 15

Verbs 314

▶ **Diagnostic Test**. 315

15.1 Action Verbs 316
▶ **Hands-on Grammar**. 318
▶ **Section Review**. 319

15.2 Linking Verbs 320
▶ **Section Review** 325

15.3 Helping Verbs 326
▶ **Section Review**. 329
▶ **Chapter Review** 330
▶ **Standardized Test Preparation Workshop** . 332

Chapter 16

Adjectives and Adverbs.......334
- ▶ **Diagnostic Test**. 335
- 16.1 Adjectives 336
  - ▶ **Section Review**. 347
- 16.2 Adverbs 348
  - ▶ **Hands-on Grammar**. 354
  - ▶ **Section Review**. 355
  - ▶ **Chapter Review** 356
  - ▶ **Standardized Test Preparation Workshop** . 358

Chapter 17

Prepositions 360
- ▶ **Diagnostic Test**. 361
- 17.1 Recognizing Prepositions 362
  - ▶ **Section Review**. 365
- 17.2 Prepositions Used in Sentences 366
  - ▶ **Hands-on Grammar**. 368
  - ▶ **Section Review**. 369
  - ▶ **Chapter Review** 370
  - ▶ **Standardized Test Preparation Workshop** . 372

Chapter 18

Conjunctions and Interjections 374
- ▶ **Diagnostic Test**. 375
- 18.1 Conjunctions 376
  - ▶ **Section Review**. 380
- 18.2 Interjections 381
  - ▶ **Hands-on Grammar**. 383
  - ▶ **Section Review**. 384
  - ▶ **Chapter Review** 385
  - ▶ **Standardized Test Preparation Workshop** . 387

- ▶ <u>Cumulative Review</u> **Parts of Speech** 388

Chapter 19

Basic Sentence Parts. 390
- ▶ **Diagnostic Test**. 391
- 19.1 The Basic Sentence. 392
  - ▶ **Section Review**. 395
- 19.2 Complete Subjects and Predicates 396
  - ▶ **Hands-on Grammar**. 398
  - ▶ **Section Review**. 399
- 19.3 Compound Subjects and Compound Verbs. 400
  - ▶ **Section Review**. 404

Chapter 19

19.4 Special Problems With Subjects 405
  ▶ **Section Review** 409
19.5 Complements 410
  Recognizing Direct Objects 411
  Finding Direct Objects in Questions 413
  Recognizing Indirect Objects 414
  Recognizing Subject Complements 416
  ▶ **Section Review** 419
  ▶ **Chapter Review** 420
  ▶ **Standardized Test Preparation Workshop** . 422

Chapter 20

Phrases and Clauses 424
  ▶ **Diagnostic Test** 425
20.1 Phrases 426
  Recognizing Prepositional Phrases 426
  Recognizing Verbal Phrases 430
  Recognizing Appositive Phrases 434
  ▶ **Section Review** 436
20.2 Clauses 438
  Adjective Clauses 439
  Adverb Clauses 441
  Classifying Sentences by Structure 443
  ▶ **Hands-on Grammar** 448
  ▶ **Section Review** 449
  ▶ **Chapter Review** 450
  ▶ **Standardized Test Preparation Workshop** . 452

Chapter 21

Effective Sentences 454
  ▶ **Diagnostic Test** 455
21.1 Classifying the Four Functions
     of a Sentence 456
  ▶ **Section Review** 459
21.2 Sentence Combining 460
  ▶ **Section Review** 464
21.3 Varying Sentences 465
  ▶ **Section Review** 468
21.4 Avoiding Sentence Problems 469
  ▶ **Hands-on Grammar** 482
  ▶ **Section Review** 483
  ▶ **Chapter Review** 484
  ▶ **Standardized Test Preparation Workshop** . 486

▶ **Cumulative Review** Phrases, Clauses, and
                        Sentences 488

Chapter 22

Using Verbs 490

▶ **Diagnostic Test**. 491

22.1 The Four Principal Parts of Verbs 492

▶ **Section Review**. 499

22.2 The Tenses and Forms of Verbs. 500

▶ **Hands-on Grammar**. 506

▶ **Section Review**. 507

22.3 Troublesome Verbs 508

▶ **Section Review**. 513

▶ **Chapter Review** 514

▶ **Standardized Test Preparation Workshop** . 516

Chapter 23

Using Pronouns 518

▶ **Diagnostic Test**. 519

Identifying the Three Cases of Personal
Pronouns. 520

Using the Nominative Case 521

Using the Objective Case 523

Using the Possessive Case 525

▶ **Hands-on Grammar**. 527

▶ **Chapter Review** 528

▶ **Standardized Test Preparation Workshop** . 530

Chapter 24

Making Words Agree 532

▶ **Diagnostic Test**. 533

24.1 Agreement Between Subjects and Verbs . 534

▶ **Hands-on Grammar**. 546

▶ **Section Review**. 547

24.2 Agreement Between Pronouns
and Antecedents 548

▶ **Section Review**. 553

▶ **Chapter Review** 554

▶ **Standardized Test Preparation Workshop** . . 556

Chapter 25

Using Modifiers 558
▶ **Diagnostic Test.** 559
25.1 Comparison of Adjectives and Adverbs . 560
Regular Modifiers With One or Two Syllables . 560
Regular Modifiers With Three or More
Syllables 562
Irregular Adjectives and Adverbs 563
Comparative and Superlative Degrees 565
▶ **Section Review.** 566
25.2 Troublesome Adjectives and Adverbs . . 567
▶ **Hands-on Grammar.** 570
▶ **Section Review.** 571
▶ **Chapter Review** 572
▶ **Standardized Test Preparation Workshop** . 574

▶ <u>Cumulative Review</u> Usage 576

Chapter 26

Punctuation 578
▶ **Diagnostic Test.** 579
26.1 End Marks .580
▶ **Section Review.** 584
26.2 Commas. 585
▶ **Hands-on Grammar.** 598
▶ **Section Review.** 599
26.3 Semicolons and Colons 600
▶ **Section Review.** 605
26.4 Quotation Marks and Underlining 606
▶ **Section Review.** 617
26.5 Hyphens and Apostrophes 618
▶ **Section Review.** 629
▶ **Chapter Review** 630
▶ **Standardized Test Preparation Workshop** . 632

Chapter 27

Capitalization 634
▶ **Diagnostic Test.** 635
Using Capitals for Sentences and the Word *I* 636
Using Capitals for Proper Nouns 637
Using Capitals for Proper Adjectives 643
Using Capitals for Titles of People 644
Using Capitals for Titles of Things. 647
▶ **Hands-on Grammar.** 649
▶ **Chapter Review** 650
▶ **Standardized Test Preparation Workshop** . 652

▶ <u>Cumulative Review</u> Mechanics 654

▶ <u>Sentence Diagraming Workshop</u>. 656

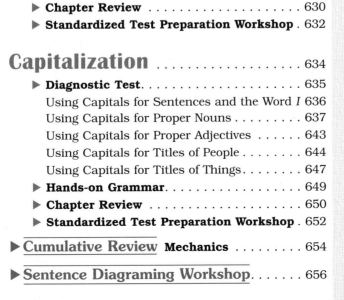

PART 3: ACADEMIC AND WORKPLACE SKILLS

Chapter 28

Speaking, Listening, Viewing, and Representing ... 668

28.1 Speaking and Listening Skills 669
Using Informal Speaking Skills 669
Using Formal Speaking Skills 671
Listening Effectively 673
28.2 Viewing and Representing Skills 675
Interpreting Maps, Graphs, and Photographs . 675
Viewing Information Media Critically 678
Viewing Fine Art Critically 680
Creating Graphic Organizers for Comprehension 681
Formatting to Create Effect............. 684
Developing a Multimedia Presentation 685
Creating a Video..................... 686
Performing or Interpreting 687
▶ **Standardized Test Preparation Workshop** . 688

Chapter 29

Vocabulary and Spelling 690

29.1 Developing Your Vocabulary 691
Recognizing Context Clues 692
Studying Meanings in the Content Areas... 693
Using "Possible Sentences" 694
29.2 Studying Words Systematically 695
Keeping a Vocabulary Notebook.......... 695
Studying New Words.................. 696
Using a Dictionary 697
Using Other Reference Aids............. 697
29.3 Studying Word Parts and Origins 698
Using Roots 698
Using Prefixes 699
Using Suffixes 700
Examining Word Origins............... 701
29.4 Improving Your Spelling............ 702
Starting a Personal Spelling List 702
Studying Your Spelling Words 703
Applying Spelling Rules 704
Adding Suffixes 705
Adding Prefixes 706
Using Memory Aids 706
Understanding the Influence of Other Languages and Cultures............... 707
Forming Plurals..................... 708
Spelling Homophones................. 710
Proofreading and Using References 711
▶ **Standardized Test Preparation Workshop** . 712

Chapter 30

Reading Skills 714

30.1 Reading Methods and Tools 715
30.2 Reading Nonfiction Critically 721
30.3 Reading Literary Writing 727
30.4 Reading From Varied Sources 732
▶ **Standardized Test Preparation Workshop** . 734

Chapter 31

Study, Reference, and Test-Taking Skills 736

31.1 Basic Study Skills 737
31.2 Reference Skills 740
31.3 Test-Taking Skills 751
▶ **Standardized Test Preparation Workshop** . 756

Resources

Styles for Business and Friendly Letters . . . 758
Citing Sources and Preparing Manuscript . . 760
Penmanship Reference 760
Internet Research Handbook 765
Commonly Overused Words 770
Commonly Misspelled Words 772
Abbreviations Guide 774
Proofreading Symbols Reference 778
Student Publications 779
Glossary 780
Index 788

PART
1

Writing

The Students, Eduard Von Gebhardt

The Writer in You

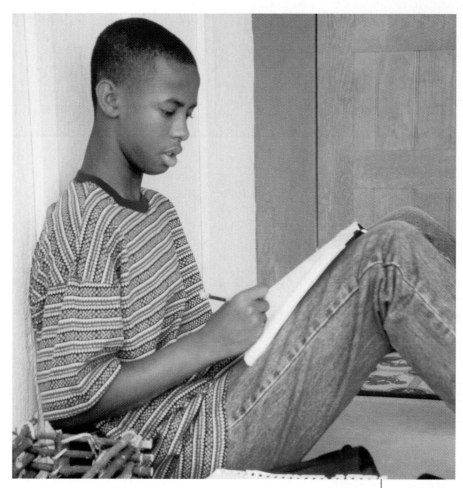

▲ **Critical Viewing**
Do you think this
student is writing to
himself or to some-
one else? Why?
[Speculate]

Which words describe you? You are a student, a friend, and
a reader. You might also be a dancer, a singer, a dog walker,
or a skater. There's one more word that describes you,
whether you realize it or not: You are a *writer*.

Writing in Everyday Life

You probably write every day. Think about all of the ways
you write. At school, you take notes and answer quiz questions. You write essays, poems, and stories. At home, you jot
down phone messages and shopping lists. You may send your
friends e-mail. You may even keep a journal. These are just a
few of the ways you write. You also write for special reasons.
Have you ever written a letter to complain about a product?
Maybe you have written an essay or a poem for a contest.

Why Write?

You write for the same reason you talk—to communicate. Through writing, you can communicate what you think, what you know, and how you feel. Furthermore, writing allows you to communicate—to yourself or to others—across time and space. You can write a postcard about a vacation adventure and send it to a friend three states away. A story you write could entertain many classmates over the course of the school year. The notes you write in class today will help you remember tonight what was discussed.

Developing Your Writing Life

Writing is already part of your life. By consciously choosing to develop your writing life, you will become a better writer and a better communicator.

Keep Track of Your Ideas

You probably come up with writing ideas all the time without even realizing it. Here are some strategies for keeping track of thoughts, feelings, and inspirations that you have, so that you can use them when you write:

Notebook or Journal Carry a small notebook wherever you go. Make a habit of writing down interesting facts and other tidbits. You might jot down an account of the day's events, make a quick sketch of a scene, or paste clippings from newspapers and magazines in your notebook.

Learning Log Writing about something can help you understand it. A learning log is a special tool that writers can use to think about information they collect. Open your learning log anytime you learn something new—from a fascinating historical fact to a new soccer play. Record the information you've acquired and write down your thoughts about it.

Keep Track of Your Writing and Reading

Writing Portfolio Maintaining a portfolio is one important way to become a more effective writer. Reviewing past work and strategies can help you make writing decisions that will work for you. Your portfolio can include finished writing as well as notes and drafts.

Reader's Journal Author Amy Tan advises writers to "read a lot and know what you like to read." You can use a reader's journal to keep track of your reading. Write down memorable quotations, reactions to characters, and responses to the message of a piece.

Writers in
ACTION

"Always write honestly and be true to what you need to write. . . . Don't ever try to copy anybody. Find out what is unique about the way you see the world and [realize] that only you can say it."

—*Amy Tan*

Try Different Approaches

Every writer is different. Develop your own personal approach to writing, one that reflects your tastes and preferences. Here are some ideas:

Getting Started How will you begin? You might decide to sit in a quiet place and just think. Perhaps music helps you get your ideas flowing. Another alternative is called *freewriting*. To freewrite, simply write whatever comes to mind. Don't stop to think or edit—just write.

Finding Ideas Ideas are all around you if you know where to look. You may get a great idea watching television or reading a magazine. If you keep a learning log or journal, you may turn to its pages to find inspiration for your writing.

Writing a Draft Some writers like to take their notes and write a complete first draft. They write in order from beginning to end. Other writers prefer to work out one idea at a time. They might begin in the middle or even at the end. Try both strategies to see which one you prefer.

Improving Your Work You may want to finish your draft and then go back and make changes, or you may make changes while you draft. You can draft on your own, or you can ask a classmate to help you find unclear passages or ideas that need support.

Sharing Your Work As you develop as a writer, you'll explore different ways of sharing your work. You may consider certain types of writing more personal and choose to keep them to yourself. On the other hand, you may write other pieces that you want to share not only with family and friends but with an even wider audience. There are many ways for you to share your work—student publications, Internet Web sites, and group readings, among others.

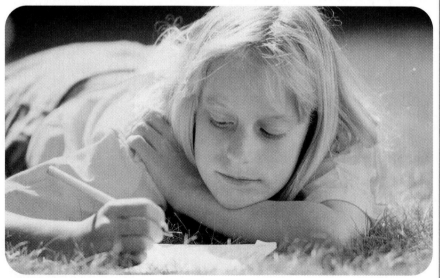

◀ **Critical Viewing** For what types of writing would the setting in which this girl is writing be appropriate? Explain. **[Analyze]**

Plan to Write

If you wanted to become a better inline skater, you would set aside time to skate every day. Make writing a part of your routine. Set aside some time every day to write in your notebook or journal. Choose a place where you are comfortable writing. When you have long-term writing assignments, create a plan and organize yourself so that you can focus on the writing, rather than on the deadline.

Choose the Right Spot Your surroundings can really affect the way you write. Pick a spot where you won't be interrupted. You might write in a quiet library or study area. You might prefer to work in your own room with music playing in the background.

Come Prepared It can be very frustrating to have to stop writing once your ideas are flowing, so gather your equipment before you begin. Make sure you have enough paper and a pen that works. In fact, bring along an extra pen, just in case. If you're using a computer, bring along a disk to back up your work.

Budget Your Time A deadline doesn't have to create stress. Writers can use deadlines to plan and budget their writing time. If you have a long-term goal, it's a good idea to divide it into several short deadlines. Use a calendar to help you plan your writing process. For example, suppose an essay is due on November 18. You can set deadlines for starting your research, writing a first draft, revising, and proofreading. Leave a little extra room in your schedule so that you can adjust the deadlines. Some tasks may take more or less time than you originally predicted.

▲ Critical Viewing How do the headings "Choose the Right Spot" and "Come Prepared" apply to inline skating as well as to writing? [Compare]

NOVEMBER

	1	**2** Choose biography subject and begin research	**3**	**4**	**5**	**6**
7	**8**	**9** Draft Biography	**10**	**11**	**12** Review draft with peer review team	**13** Revise
14 Finish revising	**15**	**16** Proofread biography	**17**	**18** Biography due	**19**	**20**

Work With Others

You don't have to write by yourself. Including other people in the writing process can help you grow as a writer.

Group Brainstorming Sometimes, the best way to get started is to bounce ideas around among a group of people. When you sit in a group and let ideas flow freely, building on them without stopping, you are brainstorming. A group might begin by brainstorming on a broad topic, such as pets or sports. Hearing other people's thoughts can help you come up with new, interesting ideas.

Collaborative and Cooperative Writing There are many ways that writers can work together on a project. A team of writers working on a poem might take turns suggesting lines. A team writing a research report might work differently, with each member writing a different section of the finished work. By working together, a group can benefit from the individual strengths of each writer.

Peer Reviewers It can be very helpful to ask another writer to help you review your work. A fresh pair of eyes may catch mistakes that you might have missed. A peer reviewer can help you see both strong and weak points in your writing.

Publish Your Work

There is nothing like finding an audience for your writing. You can find many publishing opportunities, including Web sites that accept student writing, writing contests, and the letters page of your local newspaper.

Writers in
ACTION

"Every time we work on our writing, it has more meaning. And it becomes something more beautiful."
—Denise Chávez

▼ **Critical Viewing** Do you think these students are brainstorming, drafting, or reviewing a draft? Why? **[Analyze]**

What Are the Qualities of Good Writing?

Ideas Good writing begins with interesting ideas. Explore topics that you find interesting and that you think will interest others. Focus on presenting information that will be new and fresh to readers.

Organization Organization refers to the way in which the ideas and details are arranged in a piece of writing. To enable readers to follow your ideas, choose an organization that makes sense for your topic, and stick with that organization throughout the piece of writing.

Voice Just as you have a distinctive way of expressing your-self when you speak, you can develop a distinctive voice as a writer. Your voice consists of the topics you choose, the atti-tude you express toward those topics, the words you use, and the rhythm of your sentences. By developing your own voice, you let your personality come through in your writing.

Word Choice Words are the building blocks of a piece of writing. By choosing precise and vivid words, you will add strength to your writing and enable readers to follow your ideas and picture the things that you describe.

Sentence Fluency In a piece of writing, it is important that the sentences flow well from one to another. By using a variety of sentences—different lengths and different struc-tures—and using transitions to connect them, you will create a smooth rhythm in your writing.

Conventions Conventions refer to the grammatical correct-ness of a piece of writing. Don't let errors in grammar, usage, mechanics, and spelling interfere with your message.

 Learn More

You'll take a closer look at the step-by-step process for achieving these qualities in Chapter 2, "A Walk Through the Writing Process," page 12.

Reflecting on Your Writing

You can learn a lot about your own writing by asking your-self a few questions. Try these for starters:

- What kinds of writing do you like to do?
- Where is your favorite place to write?
- What kind of writing would you like to learn to do?
- What would you say in a fan letter to your favorite author?

Share your responses with a partner, or record them in a writer's journal.

Spotlight on the Humanities

Analyzing How Meaning Is Communicated Through the Arts

Introducing the Spotlight on the Humanities

Writing is just one form of self-expression—there are many others. In the Spotlight on the Humanities features, you will learn about connections between different forms of creative expression in the arts. Photography, dance, music, fine art—these are just a few of the vast array of media that allow us to express ourselves. Each medium has its own unique characteristics.

- **Fine art** creates meaning through color, line, texture, and subject. Paintings, sketches, sculpture, and collage are just a few examples of the many types of fine art.

- **Photography** uses still images to create meaning. Although a photograph captures only still images on film, photographers express ideas through subject, composition, and lighting.

- **Theater** creates meaning through the performances of actors on a stage. Using props, scenery, sound effects, and lighting, drama brings a story to life. In some cases, music and dance are incorporated into the story line.

- **Film** captures ideas and stories through sound and motion. Like dramatic theater, most films tell stories and use setting, costumes, and characterization to develop them. A filmmaker can create a unique point of view using camera angles along with lighting and sound techniques.

- **Music** uses sound to create meaning. Whether presented as an oboe solo, an operatic aria, or a symphony, music can create moods or present variations on a theme.

- **Dance** creates meaning through organized movement. It can be performed by a single person, a pair, or larger groups.

▲ Critical Viewing This engraving is one artist's interpretation of a famous work of literature in which Dante, a medieval writer, is guided by Virgil, a writer from ancient Roman times. How does this artwork illustrate the connections between different time periods and art forms? [Interpret]

Writing Activity In a journal entry, consider which of these art forms is most familiar to you and which you would like to explore.

Media and Technology Skills

Making Technology Work for You

Activity: Identify Appropriate Technology

In the "old days," you probably would have handwritten all of your papers. If you wanted to share them with others, you would probably have had to read them aloud. Today, you have many more options for drafting, publishing, and presenting your work.

Learn About It Today's vast array of technology makes writing and other forms of communication faster and easier than ever before. Below are just some of the tools available.

- **Writing tools** Word-processing programs allow you to store and retrieve text as well as to create, draft, and edit a piece of writing. Desktop-publishing programs let you add pictures to your writing and customize the layout (appearance and arrangement) of your work.

- **Audiovisual tools** Several tools allow you to record images and sound. A video camera captures moving images as well as sound. A still camera records still images, which can be displayed on their own or projected in a series with a slide projector. A tape recorder can be used to take notes or to play background music or sound effects for a multimedia presentation.

- **Virtual resources** The Internet is an extensive computer network that allows you to access and to post information, pictures, and so on. E-mail is a way to send and receive messages nearly instantaneously over the Internet.

> **Available Technologies**
>
> **Writing Tools**
> - Word Processing
> - Desktop-publishing programs
>
> **Virtual Resources**
> - The Internet
> - E-mail
> - Electronic databases
>
> **Audiovisual Tools**
> - Video cameras
> - Still cameras
> - Slide projectors
> - Overhead projectors
> - Tape recorders

Report Title: _How to Grow Tomatoes_

Type of Technology	Advantages for My Report	Disadvantages for My Report
the Internet	• I can search gardening Web sites for information. • I can post my report on a Web page and invite people to give feedback. • I can e-mail an expert if I have a technical question.	• There might be too much information to review. • It may not always be clear how reliable the sources are.

Evaluate It Find out what technology tools are available in your school or local library. Talk to the librarian and other students who have used these tools. Ask for a demonstration and browse instruction manuals. Then, use a chart like the one above to plan how you might use these tools to produce or enhance a presentation or report. Compare your chart with the chart of a classmate who has also done this activity.

Standardized Test Preparation Workshop

Writing for Standardized Tests

As you have learned in this chapter, writing is an important part of your daily life. Your ability to communicate through writing is often measured when you respond to a writing prompt on a standardized test. When scorers evaluate your writing, they will look for evidence that you can

- respond directly to the prompt.
- make your writing thoughtful and interesting.
- organize your ideas so that they are clear and easy to follow.
- develop your ideas thoroughly by using appropriate details and precise language.
- stay focused on your purpose for writing by making sure that each sentence you write contributes to your composition as a whole.
- communicate effectively by using correct spelling, capitalization, punctuation, grammar, usage, and sentence structure.

The process of writing for a test, or any kind of writing, can be divided into stages. Plan to use a specific amount of time for prewriting, drafting, revising, and proofreading.

Following is an example of one type of writing prompt you might find on a standardized test. Use the suggestions on the next page to help you respond. The clocks next to each stage show a suggested plan for organizing your time.

> **Test Tip**
>
> Watch the clock. Try to keep within the time limits suggested so that you can complete your essay and revise it.

Sample Writing Situation

> Read the following quotation:
>
> "Find out what is unique about the way you see the world and [realize] that only you can say it."
> —Amy Tan
>
> What do you think Tan's advice means to student writers? Write an essay in which you explain the quotation. Support your interpretation with examples from your own experiences and from literature.

Prewriting

Allow approximately one fourth of your time for prewriting.

Identify Your Topic Explore the quotation by breaking it into parts. Write the quotation on a piece of paper. Circle the word in the quotation that is most meaningful to you. Freewrite on that word for two or three minutes. Reread the quotation and, using some words from your freewriting, restate the quotation in your own words. Write this sentence at the top of your paper.

Gather Details Begin listing experiences from your own writing life that show the truth of the quotation as you have restated it. Then, jot down the titles of stories and novels, as well as the names of authors, that can be used as examples.

Organize Details Group details into a few broad categories. Write a sentence about each category that explains what the details in the category have in common. For example, concerning one group of details, you might write that knowing about a topic makes it easier for you to write about it. For another group of details, you might write that the more interested you are in a subject, the more time you will be willing to spend writing about it. Use these sentences to plan the framework of your essay.

Drafting

Allow almost half of your time for drafting.

Write an Introduction Grab your reader's attention by beginning your introduction with a strong lead—an attention-getting first sentence. You might use a startling statement or an unusual observation that is related to the quotation. Then, give the quotation and explain how it is connected to your lead. Finally, give your interpretation in a sentence or two.

Support Your Interpretation Each supporting paragraph should begin with a topic sentence that supports your interpretation. Develop each topic sentence with details and examples.

Revising, Editing, and Proofreading

Allow just over a fourth of your time for revising. Use the last few minutes to proofread your work.

Review Details and Language Review your response for details that do not directly support your interpretation, and remove them. Make sure that you use language that is appropriate for a formal test response.

Make Corrections Check for errors in spelling, grammar, and punctuation. When making changes, place a line through text that you want to eliminate. Use a caret (^) to indicate places where you would like to add words.

A Walk Through the Writing Process

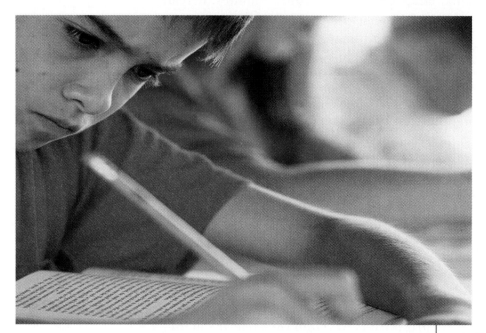

Whatever your final product, the writing process—a systematic approach to writing —can help you get there. From prewriting to publishing and presenting, knowing and using the stages of the writing process will help you do your best on any writing project.

▲ **Critical Viewing** How does your own writing process help or complicate your success as a writer? **[Relate]**

Types of Writing

One way to study types of writing is to analyze them by **mode**—the form or shape that writing takes. The list below shows the modes of writing you'll encounter in this book.

Another way to learn more about writing is to consider the source of the inspiration and the intended audience. For example, when you write **reflexively,** you choose what to write, what format to use, and whether to share your writing. Reflexive writing, such as a diary or a journal entry, is from yourself and for yourself. In contrast, when you write **extensively**, you are usually responding to a school assignment that will be read by a general audience. Extensive writing begins with others and is for others. It can take many forms, including poems, essays, and movie reviews.

MODES OF WRITING

Narration
Description
Persuasion
Exposition

Research
Response to Literature
Poems and Plays
Writing for Assessment

The Process of Writing

These are the stages of the writing process:

- **Prewriting** Freely exploring topics, choosing a topic, and beginning to gather and organize details before you write
- **Drafting** Getting your ideas down on paper roughly in the format you intend for the finished work
- **Revising** Correcting any major errors and improving the form and content of the writing
- **Editing and Proofreading** Polishing the writing and fixing errors in grammar, spelling, and mechanics
- **Publishing and Presenting** Sharing your writing with others

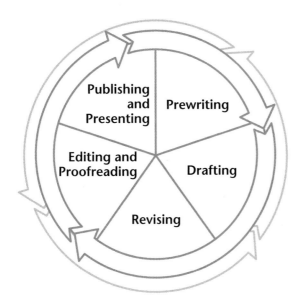

These steps may seem sequential, but writers often move among the various stages as they work. For example, as reporters draft news stories, they often discover that they must return to their prewriting work to gather more information.

A Guided Tour

Use this chapter as a guided tour to the writing process. Take a close look at the steps presented here. Learn new strategies, look at the way another writer has used them, and try them yourself. When you apply these strategies to your own writing process, the improved quality of your final draft may surprise you.

A blank piece of paper can challenge even the most seasoned writer. Writers may struggle over what to write, or they may wonder how much they can say about a topic. Prewriting helps to make the task less overwhelming. Just as athletes and musicians prepare for a performance by practicing and planning, you can warm up to write with your own set of strategies and routines.

Choosing Your Topic

Before you can begin writing, you need a topic. Generally, the best topics are those that you find interesting. That is why it is important to take time to explore ideas, issues, and experiences that are important to you. To generate a topic, you can use a wide variety of strategies. Try this sample strategy:

SAMPLE STRATEGY

Blueprinting Draw the floor plan of a place that is important to you. You might map out your home, your school, or a local park. Then, jot down memorable events that these places suggest. You can then review your list to choose a topic for your writing. In this sample, the writer listed ideas that the blueprint sparked. From that list, she highlighted a topic to develop.

BLUEPRINTING TO FIND A TOPIC

> **Learn More**
>
> For additional prewriting strategies suited to specific writing tasks, see Chapters 4-13.

Narrowing Your Topic

While you may initially be inspired to write on a broad topic like "museums" or "vacations," you'll quickly find that such an undertaking can be too much of a challenge. A topic that is too broad can force you to write a draft that is either too general or too long. Narrow your general topic into something more manageable. Look at these examples of broad and narrow topics. Then, try the listing strategy for narrowing a topic.

BROAD TOPIC:	Museums
NARROW TOPIC:	Boston's Museum of Fine Arts
NARROWER TOPIC:	The Impressionist exhibit at Boston's Museum of Fine Arts
BROAD TOPIC:	Vacations
NARROW TOPIC:	Vacations to take with your family
NARROWER TOPIC:	Enjoying a family vacation at the beach

SAMPLE STRATEGY

Listing To take a closer look at your subject and all the specific ideas it may include, jot down your broad topic at the top of a page. Then, list people, places, and things that may be associated with this broad topic. Finally, look for connections between items on your list. Choose a topic based on the connections you find.

Broad Topic: Friends		
People	**Places**	**Things**
Leslie	the mall	picnic table
Tara	school	bus
Mike	the park	phone
George		
Beth		
Narrow Topic: The lunch break Tara, Mike, and I enjoyed together at the mall		

Considering Your Audience and Purpose

Once you've pinpointed your topic, give yourself a little more direction. When you identify your **audience**—the people who will read your work—you can plan how you'll communicate with them. When you identify your **purpose**—the reason you are writing—you can plan what you'll communicate.

Consider Your Audience Tailor your draft to meet the needs of your audience. Avoid words that are too sophisticated, but don't "talk down" to your readers. Strike a balance by identifying your readers, their language level, and their knowledge. Keep this information in mind as you draft.

Consider Your Purpose Focus on why you are writing. You may want to entertain, persuade, or reflect on your experiences. This purpose will guide the kind of information you include.

Link Topic With Audience and Purpose You can use most topics to suit a variety of audiences and purposes. For instance, you might choose to write about a soccer game. If you are writing for parents, your purpose might be to encourage participation in team events. If you are writing for teammates, your purpose might be to inspire them. If you are writing for a local newspaper, your purpose might be to solicit businesses to support the team.

Gathering Details

Just as you assemble the ingredients you need before you bake, gather the materials you need before you write. Whether you want to tell a compelling story, describe an event clearly, or argue a position, collect as many relevant ideas and facts as you can to improve your writing. You may have to conduct research or talk to other people. The work you do in this phase will make the job of writing easier. Try these sample strategies:

SAMPLE STRATEGY

THE REPORTER'S FORMULA

Who did the action?

What was done?

Where did it happen?

When did it happen?

Why did it happen?

The Reporter's Formula To clarify the basics of your topic, use the first five questions most reporters ask. The Reporter's Formula is based on the five *W*s—the *who, what, where, when,* and *why* an event happened. After you have the simple answers, gather more details to round out your ideas.

SAMPLE STRATEGY

Hexagonal Writing When writing about literature, use a prewriting technique called hexagonal writing to focus your attention. Complete the six sides of the hexagon by following the directions in the diagram at right. The details and responses you create with this tool will help you give a thoughtful, thorough analysis. After you respond to each side of the hexagon, you may want to focus on a particular aspect of the novel, play, short story, or other literature you address.

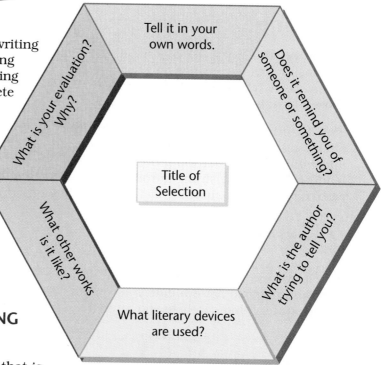

Tell it in your own words.

Does it remind you of someone or something?

What is your evaluation? Why?

Title of Selection

What is the author trying to tell you?

What other works is it like?

What literary devices are used?

▶ APPLYING THE PREWRITING STRATEGIES

1. Make a blueprint of a place that is important to you. Then, label your blueprint with the people, events, objects, and memories you associate with the place you blueprinted. Identify the topic you would choose based on this exercise.
2. Use the listing strategy to narrow your topic. Jot down people, places, things, and events you associate with the word you choose. Make connections between items on the list. Then, identify a topic narrow enough to address in an essay.
3. Identify two different audiences for a report you might write on a hobby. Then, create two different audience profiles.
4. For each audience and purpose listed below, identify three details you might include in an essay about traffic safety:
   a. To warn children about crossing the street
   b. To persuade town officials to install a traffic light
   c. To tell friends about a frightening personal experience.
5. Answer the Reporter's Formula questions to gather details for an account of a sporting event.
6. Complete a hexagon for a short story you have recently read.

What Is Drafting?

Shaping Your Writing

Focus on the Form Each form of writing has a specific aim: Persuasion has to convince, mystery has to surprise, and narration has to tell a story. As you draft, keep the aim of your chosen form in mind.

Pull Readers in With an Enticing Lead Pay special attention to the first paragraph of your writing. Start with an interesting opener that will provoke your audience to keep reading. To create a strong introduction, consider beginning with a quotation, a shocking fact, or a dazzling description.

Providing Elaboration

To make your writing as strong as it can be, add information to help readers imagine the action you describe, see the connections you make, or evaluate your opinion. The SEE method is one strategy that can help you strengthen your writing.

SAMPLE STRATEGY

Using the SEE Method

When you use the SEE method (Statement, Extension, Elaboration), you strengthen your writing by providing a greater depth of information. Begin with a statement that conveys a main idea. Write an extension by restating or explaining the first sentence. Elaborate further by providing even more details about the main idea. Look at this example:

STATEMENT: The space launch was a success.

EXTENSION: It was a picture-perfect start for the mission to Mars.

ELABORATION: The weather worked in the astronauts' favor, all systems worked well, and the engineers in Mission Control reported no problems as the shuttle escaped the Earth's atmosphere.

▶ **APPLYING THE DRAFTING STRATEGIES**

1. Write an exciting lead for a description of a sunrise.
2. Complete the sentences below. Then, using the SEE method, elaborate on each one.
   (a) The ___?___ is my favorite musical instrument.
   (b) If I had an extra hour every day, I would ___?___.

Learn More

Each writing chapter provides elaboration strategies suited to specific writing modes.

2.3 *What Is Revising?*

Color-Coding Clues for Revision

To use the stages of the writing process most effectively, devote full attention to the revision process. Focus your review by asking specific questions about your draft. The word **ratiocination** (rash´ ē äs´ ə nā´shen) means "thinking logically." Apply ratiocination to your writing by marking your draft with color-coded clues that will help you isolate specific problems and then make informed decisions about revising. These are sample revision strategies suited to color-coding:

- Circling vague words
- Bracketing transitions
- Highlighting topic sentences

Revision sections in Chapters 4–13 include strategies for revising structure, paragraphs, sentences, and word choice.

Revising Your Overall Structure

When you review the organization of your writing, make sure that ideas flow logically from start to finish. Consider reordering paragraphs to make the argument more logical or adding information to fill holes in organization.

SAMPLE STRATEGY

▶ **REVISION STRATEGY**
Highlighting Topic Sentences

To see the structure of your writing, use a highlighter to mark sentences that state the main idea of each body paragraph in your draft. Evaluate the order of the sentences you've highlighted, and rearrange the paragraphs as needed. In the example shown at right, the writer decided to switch the order of body paragraphs to make ideas flow more smoothly. Transitions help to make the structure more obvious to readers.

Writers in **ACTION**

William Zinsser, a writer on writing, says this about the act of revision: "The writer must . . . constantly ask himself: What am I trying to say? Surprisingly often, he doesn't know. Then he must look at what he has written and ask: Have I said it?"

Topic: The Internet is a great place to access timely information.

Most importantly,
Most newspapers and networks have Web sites to post updates to news stories. . . .

Ease of use is one feature.
You can use the Internet from the comfort of your home. . . .

Accessing daily information is another value of the Internet.
You can find almost anything you want online. Biographies, weather reports, and transcripts of Congressional hearings are available at the click of a mouse. . . .

Revising Your Paragraphs

Take a closer look at each paragraph in your writing. To make each element of your writing contribute successfully to the draft, you may have to change some of your paragraphs.

▶ **REVISION STRATEGY**
Making Paragraphs Apply

Once you've completed your first draft, analyze whether each paragraph is doing what you want it to do. Write the purpose or function of each paragraph on a piece of paper. Then, fill out the paragraph's qualifications. (You may want to copy the "application form" shown here.) If you find that a paragraph is missing an important point, look to see whether you can pull in a sentence from another paragraph near the one you are analyzing.

Paragraph Application

Job: _to show that walking is good exercise_

Qualifications:

1. _Example of someone who has benefited from walking_

2. _Fact that demonstrates walking is good_

Revising Your Sentences

When you focus on your writing at the sentence level, try to enliven it by breaking repetitive patterns. One way to find these patterns is to analyze sentence beginnings.

SAMPLE STRATEGY

▶ **REVISION STRATEGY**
Color-Coding to Vary Sentence Beginnings

To evaluate the variety of your sentence beginnings, use red to circle the first word of each sentence in your draft. Review the words to identify any pattern your draft includes. For example, you may have begun many sentences with the word *I* or *The.* To improve your draft, insert phrases or clauses that break the pattern. Look at this example:

START WITH *I*:	*I* like watching movies.
START WITH A PHRASE:	*On snow days,* I like watching movies.
START WITH A SUBORDINATING CONJUNCTION:	*Even though they sometimes scare me,* I like watching movies.

Revising Your Word Choice

Take a closer look at the language you have used to be sure that you express your ideas effectively. Look for places in your draft where an added detail can bring an idea to life or where an accurate or precise verb can replace a vague one.

▶**REVISION STRATEGY**
Circling "To Be" Verbs

"To be" verbs, such as *am, is, are, was, were, be, being,* and *been,* are often the words you choose first, but they don't provide the power that action verbs do. Circle the *to be* verbs in your draft, and then challenge yourself to change some of them to more vivid action verbs. You may need to rewrite the sentences when you change the verb. Look at these examples:

"TO BE" VERB: The stadium traffic *was* horrendous.

ACTION VERB: The traffic *inched* around the stadium.

Peer Review

During the revising stage, get someone else's opinion. A partner's fresh approach may reveal issues in your draft that you were too close to see.

Provide a Specific Task Ask your peer reviewer to discuss one part of your writing. Consider these focused options:

Focusing Peer Review	
Purpose	**Ask**
Evaluate introduction	What did the introduction suggest about the topic of the paper?
Check if more details are needed	What do you want to know more about?
Check which parts need to be clearer	Which parts were confusing? Why?

Make the Final Decision Consider your reviewer's responses to your writing, but do not feel obligated to make every suggested change. Make those revisions that you think will improve your draft.

▶ **APPLYING THE REVISION STRATEGIES**

Using the first draft of an essay or story you have recently written, try the revision strategies introduced in this chapter. When you have finished, identify the one that worked best for you.

🔵 **Learn More**

For extensive instruction on verbs see Chapter 15.

What Are Editing and Proofreading?

After you are satisfied with the content of your draft, edit and proofread your writing to make it presentable to readers. Whether you're correcting a letter to a friend, an application essay, or a brochure in support of a candidate, strive to make your writing error-free.

Focusing on Proofreading

Get in the habit of looking closely at your work. Each writing chapter offers a focus, providing closer instruction about a specific topic you can check in your draft. Use the suggestions you find there, but do not limit your proofreading to these topics. Instead, correct all errors you see. Following are the broad categories for proofreading:

Check Spelling To catch spelling errors, focus on each word separately. For this task, avoid getting distracted by content. Consider reading your paper last word to first.

Review Capitalization and Punctuation Check that you have properly capitalized proper nouns and words that begin sentences. Then, evaluate and correct your use of parentheses, quotation marks, commas, semicolons, colons, and other punctuation marks.

Confirm Grammar and Usage Use a usage handbook to correct troublesome language and grammatical structures. To start, confirm that you have written in complete sentences. Then, analyze agreement between subjects and verbs, and check pronoun references.

Check the Facts To be sure that the information you present is accurate, use an accuracy checklist like the one shown here. When necessary, consult encyclopedias and library sources to confirm the details you include.

Make It Legible If your work is handwritten, be sure that every word is readable. When you correct an error in your final draft, cross out the error and insert new information neatly.

> **Learn More**
>
> For extensive instruction on grammar, usage, and mechanics conventions, see Chapters 14–27.

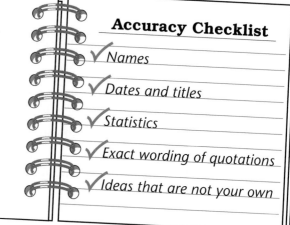

Accuracy Checklist

✓ *Names*

✓ *Dates and titles*

✓ *Statistics*

✓ *Exact wording of quotations*

✓ *Ideas that are not your own*

▶ **APPLYING THE EDITING AND PROOFREADING STRATEGIES**

Using a draft you have recently written, use the proofreading tips on this page. Circle your corrections in red, and note how many improvements careful proofreading generated.

2.5

What Are Publishing and Presenting?

Moving Forward

This walk through the writing process gives you just a taste of the strategies and techniques you can use as part of your writing process. Each of the chapters in Part 1 will teach you specific strategies suited to specific forms of writing.

Building Your Portfolio Keep your finished writing products in a folder, a box, or another safe, organized container. With all your work in one place, you can easily see your growth as a writer. You can also use your portfolio as a treasure chest of ideas. Set aside a section of your portfolio for prewriting activities, partly finished pieces of writing, and photographs that inspire ideas.

Reflecting on Your Writing Every time you write, you can learn from your experience. In addition to discovering information about your topic, take the time to consider what you gained from using the writing process. Questions at the end of each chapter will help you to reflect on your experiences.

Assessing Your Writing At the end of each chapter, you will find a *rubric,* or set of criteria, on which your work can be evaluated. Refer to the rubric throughout the writing process to make sure that you are addressing the main points of the particular mode you are using.

▶ **APPLYING THE PUBLISHING AND PRESENTING STRATEGIES**

1. Review the prewriting activities you used in this introductory walk-through. Select one or two, and put them in your portfolio as an inspiration for a later piece of writing. Talk with a partner about the activities you selected.
2. To begin reflecting on your own writing process, jot down a response to one of these questions. Save your writing in your portfolio.
   - What is your greatest strength as a writer?
   - Which writing experience in your life did you enjoy most? Why?

PORTFOLIO

Spotlight on the Humanities

Recognizing Common Subjects in Art

Focus on Photography: Elliott Erwitt

When you approach the writing process, you choose a topic, develop your idea, and decide how you want to present your work to your audience. Artists use similar processes to plan, create, and show their work. American photographer Elliott Erwitt was a photojournalist for such magazines as *Time* and *Life*, and he found inspiration in the objects and events around him. Erwitt has photographed people and places all over the world. In contrast to his work in the news media, Erwitt's dogs have provided a personal inspiration. Whenever he can, Erwitt adds a humorous touch to his pictures. He has had exhibitions all over the world, including the Museum of Modern Art in New York and the Art Institute of Chicago.

Literature Connection Dogs provide a common subject in the arts. Jack London (1876–1916) wrote *The Call of the Wild* (1903), narrating the adventures of a sled dog named Buck. After he is stolen from his home, Buck is forced to work in the Klondike. Eventually, the dog courageously journeys to freedom in the wild. London's story was originally serialized in *The Saturday Evening Post* from June 20 to July 18, 1903.

Film Connection Beyond photography and novels, dogs have also found their way onto the silver screen. *Old Yeller*, a classic motion picture created by media genius Walt Disney, was released in 1957. The film tells the story of a boy named Travis and the dog, Old Yeller, that he adopts. Set in Texas in the nineteenth century, the film starred Fess Parker, Dorothy Maguire, and Chuck Connors. Disney found his inspiration in the original story by Fred Gipson.

Writing Process Activity: Choosing a Topic Through Photograph Review

If the saying "every picture tells a story" is true, you probably have countless stories in photo albums and boxes. Choose a picture you like, and jot down several writing ideas that it brings to mind. Write a journal entry to explore your ideas, or keep the list in your portfolio for development later.

▲ **Critical Viewing**
What is your first reaction to this photograph by Elliott Erwitt? What detail created this response?
[Respond, Analyze]

Media and Technology Skills

Using Technology for Writing

Activity: Build an Electronic Portfolio

With today's word-processing software, you can effortlessly jot down, edit, save, and retrieve ideas. To make the most of writing on a word processor, build an electronic portfolio to store your work.

Learn About It Create a single folder for all your writing work. For each new project, create a subfolder. It can hold all your files for the project, including your prewriting notes, drafts, and revisions. Here are suggestions for arranging these files:

- **Prewriting** Create a subfolder for inspirations. Store freewriting notes, topic ideas, and miscellaneous notes here. Access these files when you want to begin a new writing project.

- **Drafting** The draft of a short essay may require only one file. In contrast, a research report may be better suited to several files—one for your introduction, one for the body of your work, and one for the conclusion. When you are ready to print a single draft, copy and paste the text into one main file. Store all the files in a folder that indicates the name or subject of the work.

- **Revising** Whenever you revise, save a new version of the file so that you can track the changes. An easy way to do this is to add a number to the end of the file name. Every time you create a new version, increase the number by one. Move your old drafts to a folder called Old Drafts.

🗀 my writing	
Name	**Date Modified**
▽ 🗀 Project 1 – Descriptive Essay	Oct 17
� 📄 Ideas	Oct 5
▽ 🗀 Old Drafts	Oct 14
📄 Rocky Mountain Park	Oct 9
📄 Rocky Mountain Park.1	Oct 14
📄 Rocky Mountain Park.2	Oct 17
▷ 🗀 Project 2 – Haiku Poem	Nov 11

Useful Functions

Editing
- Cut—deletes a selected section of text and stores it temporarily so that you can paste it elsewhere
- Copy—duplicates a selected section of text
- Paste—inserts previously cut or copied text

Saving
- Save—stores a file and any changes to it
- Save As—lets you save a new version of a file

Retrieving
- File Find—enables you to search for a file even if you remember only part of its name
- Text Find—helps you find specific text

Apply It Use this organizational plan for your next writing assignment. Then, get together with classmates to discuss the positive and negative features of storing your work electronically.

Standardized Test Preparation Workshop

Using the Writing Process to Respond to Writing Prompts

Many standardized tests include writing prompts that offer specific topics for you to address. Use the writing process to generate thoughtful, well-elaborated responses. You will be evaluated on your ability to do the following:

- Address the situation, problem, or question presented.

- Choose a logical, consistent organization for your ideas.

- Elaborate with the appropriate amount of detail for your specific audience and purpose.

- Use complete sentences and follow the rules of grammar.

- Use correct spelling and punctuation.

The process of writing for a test, or any kind of writing, can be divided into stages. Plan to use a specific amount of time for prewriting, drafting, revising, and proofreading.

Following is an example of one type of writing prompt that you might find on a standardized test. Use the suggestions on page 27 to help you respond. The clocks next to each stage show a suggested plan for organizing your time.

Test Tip

Although you won't have extensive time to devote to each stage of the writing process, take the time to prewrite and revise. Each of these steps will help you create a better final draft.

Sample Writing Situation

Your town has just received a grant to build a community center that would include a teen wing. Write a letter to the town council in which you explain what features you believe would most benefit teenagers in your community. Support your ideas with convincing reasons.

Prewriting

Allow about one fourth of your time for prewriting.

Focus Your Topic There are probably many things that you would like to see in a town teen center. List all the possibilities. Then, review them, eliminating those that are unrealistic, extremely costly, or too difficult to create. From this list, choose a few programs that you would like to see in the center.

Consider Audience and Purpose As you begin to gather details for your response, keep in mind the audience indicated in the prompt. Many of the members of the town council may not know what interests teens, and you may have to include details that will educate them. Be sure to include information that will persuade them to implement your ideas.

Choose an Organization To make your letter effective, organize ideas to make them easy to follow. For this assignment, identify the suggestions you will make, and plan to present them in order of increasing importance.

Drafting

Allow almost half your time for drafting.

Build Your Authority As a person who might visit the teen center, you are the perfect spokesperson for your interests. Start off with an introduction that shows your audience why they should consider your ideas. Then, devote a paragraph to each idea you suggest. End with a conclusion that politely encourages action.

Elaborate With Details An important part of your letter will be the details that you use to prove your points. Include examples or information that will help the council members understand your points. Use the SEE method to elaborate ideas in your writing. Review page 18 to see an example of this drafting technique.

Revising, Editing, and Proofreading

Allow about one fourth of your time for revising. Use whatever time remains to proofread your work.

Check Diction Your letter is addressed to a governing committee. Make sure that the words you have chosen reflect respect for your readers. Delete any slang and define any terms your audience may not know.

Make Corrections Review your paper for spelling and punctuation errors. Make all corrections neatly. Cross out text with a single line, and use a caret (^) to indicate insertions neatly.

Sentences, Paragraphs, and Compositions

Structure and Style

A **sentence** is a properly punctuated group of words that expresses a complete thought. To express an idea in writing, you must begin with a sentence. To explain or develop that idea, you must join sentences into a paragraph.

A **paragraph** is a unit of expression—a group of related sentences that focus on a main idea or thought. By using paragraphs when you write, you break information into logical, meaningful sections.

Groups of related paragraphs work together to form a **composition.** There are many kinds of compositions. They include various types of essays, research reports, and responses to literature. Even fictional works—not usually called compositions—depend on the logical use of paragraphs to present ideas. The specific types of compositions will be covered in the chapters that follow.

▲ **Critical Viewing**
Explain the ways in which constructing a building is like constructing an effective paragraph or composition.
[Connect]

3.1 *Sentence
Combining*

Controlling Your Sentences

Just as the paragraph is the basic building block of a composition, the sentence is the basic building block of a paragraph. By controlling the length and structure of your sentences, you can improve the variety and interest of each paragraph.

One way to develop that control is to practice sentence combining. By combining short sentences, you can

- avoid pointless repetition.
- show connections between events or ideas.
- stress important information.

Inserting Words and Phrases

One method of combining sentences is to take key information from one sentence and insert it into another, changing the form of the words and adding punctuation as needed. You should then eliminate the sentence from which you took the key information.

EXAMPLE: Icarus was the son of Daedalus. He flew on wings of wax and feathers.

COMBINED: Icarus, the son of Daedalus, **flew on wings of wax and feathers.**

EXAMPLE: Icarus flew above the waves. The waves were crashing on the beach.

COMBINED: Icarus flew above the waves **crashing on the beach.**

▶ **Exercise 1** Combining With Words and Phrases Combine each pair of sentences by inserting key information from one sentence into the other. Add commas as necessary.

1. The hydra was a monster in Greek mythology. The hydra was a nine-headed monster.
2. Hercules destroyed one of the hydra's heads. He destroyed the head with his mighty club.
3. The hydra grew two new heads. The new heads grew in place of the old one.
4. Hercules destroyed the hydra with the help of his nephew. His nephew was named Iolaus.
5. Hercules conquered other monsters in addition to the hydra. Hercules was a son of the god Zeus.

Using Compound Subjects or Verbs

Two or more sentences that have the same or similar verbs can be combined into one sentence having a **compound subject.** In a similar way, sentences that have the same subject can be combined into one sentence that has a **compound verb.** You can use conjunctions such as *or, and,* or *but* to make these compounds.

EXAMPLE:	Athens **was** a Greek city-state. Sparta **was** a Greek city-state.
COMPOUND SUBJECT:	**Athens and Sparta** were Greek city-states.
EXAMPLE:	**Athens** built a strong navy. **Athens** lost the Peloponnesian War to Sparta.
COMPOUND VERB:	Athens **built** a strong navy but **lost** the Peloponnesian War to Sparta.

🄿 Learn More

For additional information about compound subjects and verbs, see Section 19.3.

USING CONJUNCTIONS	
To show	**Use**
Equality	*and*
Contrast; difference	*but*
Choice; options	*or*

▸ **Exercise 2** Using Compound Subjects or Verbs Combine each pair of sentences using *or, and,* or *but* to create compound subjects or compound verbs as appropriate.

1. In the morning, an Athenian might stroll in the marketplace. An Athenian might exercise at the gym.
2. Athenian children were trained in music. Athenian children practiced sports.
3. Athenian citizens discussed political matters. Athenian citizens voted on important issues.
4. Athenian women received some education. Athenian women were not allowed to vote.
5. Persia gathered a mighty army. The Persian army invaded Greece.
6. Athens fought the Persians. Sparta fought the Persians.
7. The Athenians lost to the Persians on land. The Athenians won at sea.
8. The Greek city-states won the Persian Wars together. The Greek city-states did not form a united country.
9. Drama flourished in Athens after the Persian Wars. Philosophy also flourished in Athens during this period.
10. Pericles led Athens during its Golden Age. Pericles died in 429 B.C.

Forming Compound Sentences

When you wish to combine two short sentences that are equal in importance, you can create a **compound sentence** by using such words as *and, but, for, nor, or, so,* and *yet.*

Notice that by doing so, you are not simply linking two ideas: You are expressing a relationship between them. In the example below, *but* points out the difference between Odysseus' roles in two stories.

EXAMPLE: The hero Odysseus is one of the characters of the *Iliad.* He is the main character of the *Odyssey.*

COMPOUND   The hero Odysseus is one of the characters of the
SENTENCE: *Iliad,* but he is the main character of the *Odyssey.*

▶ **Exercise 3** **Forming Compound Sentences** Combine each pair of sentences using a comma and the appropriate coordinating conjunction to form a compound sentence.

1. Paris, a son of the king of Troy, kidnapped Helen. Helen's husband, Menelaus, was angry.
2. Paris' homeland was far from the homeland of Menelaus. Menelaus gathered together his fellow Achaean warriors and sailed to Troy.
3. The Achaeans, including Achilles, Odysseus, and Agamemnon, laid seige to Troy for years. The city did not surrender.
4. Achilles had a quarrel with Agamemnon. He sulked in his tent and refused to fight.
5. The mighty Achilles had to fight. The Greeks would lose.

▼ **Critical Viewing** Describe this scene from Hercules' adventure with the hydra, using a compound sentence. **[Analyze]**

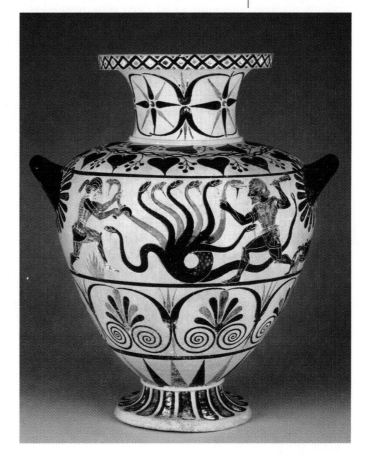

Using Subordination

A **subordinate clause** is a group of words that contains a subject and verb but does not express a complete thought.

Use Adjective Clauses To combine sentences, you can add more information about a noun or pronoun in one sentence by rewriting the other as an **adjective clause**—a subordinate clause that begins with *who, whom, whose, which,* or *that.*

EXAMPLE: Homer wrote the *Iliad* and the *Odyssey.* These works tell tales from the Trojan War.

COMBINED: Homer wrote the *Iliad* and the *Odyssey*, **which** tell tales from the Trojan War.

Use Adverb Clauses Alternatively, you can add more information about a verb, an adjective, or an adverb in one sentence by rewriting the other as an **adverb clause**—a subordinate clause that begins with a subordinating conjunction such as *although, after, because,* or *until.*

EXAMPLE: The Cyclops, a one-eyed giant, held Odysseus' men prisoner. Odysseus tricked the giant.

COMBINED: The Cyclops, a one-eyed giant, held Odysseus' men prisoner **until** Odysseus tricked the giant.

Learn More

For additional information about adjective and adverb clauses, see Section 20.2.

SOME SUBORDINATING CONJUNCTIONS	
after	so that
although	unless
as	until
because	when
before	where
if	while

Exercise 4 Combining by Using Clauses In each item, combine sentences by rewriting one as the type of clause indicated.
1. For years, Odysseus and his fellow Achaeans were unable to conquer Troy. The city's walls were massive. (adverb clause)
2. Odysseus suggested a trick using a giant wooden horse. Odysseus was well known for his cunning. (adjective clause)
3. The horse was hollow. Warriors could hide inside the horse. (adverb clause)
4. The Trojans saw the Achaean fleet sail away. They led the wooden horse inside the gates of their city. (adverb clause)
5. The Achaeans in the horse crept out and opened the gates for the rest of the Achaean army. The Achaean army was then able to conquer Troy. (adjective clause)

3.2 *Writing Effective Paragraphs*

Stating the Main Idea in a Topic Sentence

Most paragraphs have a main idea. Often, this main idea is directly stated in a single sentence called the **topic sentence.** The rest of the sentences in the paragraph support or explain the topic sentence, providing support through facts and details.

Sometimes, the main idea of a paragraph is implied. An **implied main idea** is not directly stated. Instead, the sentences communicate the main idea by working together to present the details and facts that allow the reader to infer the main idea.

WRITING MODELS

from **Melting Pot**
Anna Quindlen

Change comes hard in America, but it comes constantly. The butcher whose old shop is now an antiques store sits day after day outside the pizzeria here like a lost child. The old people across the street cluster together and discuss what kind of money they might be offered if the person who bought their building wants to turn it into condominiums. The greengrocer stocks yellow peppers and fresh rosemary for the gourmands, plum tomatoes and broadleaf parsley for the older Italians, mangoes for the Indians. He doesn't carry plantains, he says, because you can buy them in the bodega.

> In this passage, the stated topic sentence is shown in blue italics.

from **All Summer in a Day**
Ray Bradbury

Margot stood alone. She was a very frail girl who looked as if she had been lost in the rain for years and the rain had washed out the blue from her eyes and the red from her mouth and the yellow from her hair. She was an old photograph dusted from an album, whitened away, and if she spoke at all her voice would be a ghost. Now she stood, separate, staring at the rain and the loud wet world beyond the huge glass.

> In this passage, all the sentences work together to illustrate the implied main idea of the paragraph: Margot is a delicate, unhappy loner who is different from the others.

> **Exercise 5** Identifying a Stated Topic Sentence Identify the stated topic sentence of the following paragraph.

The first house I remember was kind of boxy and looked pretty much like its neighbors. However, because it was the house I grew up in, it seemed unique to me. I can still see the blue door with our house number on it, the lilac bushes my sister and I raided for bouquets each spring, and the driveway where we played hopscotch.

> **Exercise 6** Identifying an Implied Main Idea Identify the implied main idea of the following paragraph.

English is the first or official language of over sixty countries. In fact, one out of every seven people in the world understands or speaks English. Schoolchildren who live in countries where English is not the official language are often required to study it. More than half of the world's newspapers, books, magazines, radio programs, and mail are communicated in English.

Writing a Topic Sentence

When you outline a topic or plan an essay, you identify the main points you want to address. Each of these points can be written as a **topic sentence**—a statement of the main idea of a topical paragraph. You can organize your paragraph around the topic sentence.

A good topic sentence tells readers what the paragraph is about and the point the writer wants to make about the subject matter. The chart below offers some tips for writing a strong topic sentence.

Review details.

Group related details.

Write a statement that pulls the details together.

> **Exercise 7** Writing Topic Sentences Write a topic sentence for a paragraph on each of the following topics.
> 1. The condition of your locker
> 2. The typical weather in your area
> 3. How you are similar to or different from your best friend
> 4. Why the last movie you saw was or was not a good one
> 5. What makes your school unique

Writing Supporting Sentences

Whether your topic sentence is stated or implied, it guides the rest of the paragraph. The rest of the sentences in the paragraph will either develop, explain, or support that topic sentence.

You can support or develop the idea by using one or more of the following strategies:

Use Facts Facts are statements that can be proved. They support your key idea by providing proof.

TOPIC SENTENCE:	Our football team is tough to beat.
SUPPORTING FACT:	It wins almost all of its games.

Use Statistics A statistic is a fact, usually stated using numbers.

TOPIC SENTENCE:	Our football team is tough to beat.
SUPPORTING STATISTIC:	The football team's record is 10–1.

Use Examples, Illustrations, or Instances An example, illustration, or instance is a specific thing, person, or event that demonstrates a point.

TOPIC SENTENCE:	Our football team is tough to beat.
ILLUSTRATION:	Last week, the team beat the previously undefeated Tigers in an exciting upset game.

Use Details Details are the specifics—the parts of the whole. They make your point or main idea clear by showing how all the pieces fit together.

TOPIC SENTENCE:	Our football team is tough to beat.
DETAIL:	There were only seconds left in last week's game when the quarterback threw the winning pass.

▶ **Exercise 8** Writing Supporting Sentences Write two supporting sentences for each of the following topic sentences. Use a variety of types of support.

1. Good habits promote good health.
2. Everyone has a different style.
3. You get out of an experience what you put into it.
4. Doing well in school requires effort and a good attitude.
5. My favorite sport is fun to watch.

Placing Your Topic Sentence

Frequently, the topic sentence appears at the beginning of a paragraph. Topic sentences can, however, be placed at the beginning or at the end of the paragraph. Place your topic sentence at the beginning of a paragraph to focus readers' attention. Place your topic sentence in the middle of a paragraph when you must lead into your main idea. Place your topic sentence at the end of a paragraph to emphasize your main idea.

Paragraph Patterns Sentences in a paragraph can be arranged in several different patterns, depending on where you place your topic sentence. One common pattern is the TRI pattern (Topic, Restatement, Illustration).

- **T**opic sentence (State your main idea.)
- **R**estatement (Interpret your main idea; put it in other words.)
- **I**llustration (Support your main idea with facts and examples.)

T	Participating in after-school clubs is one of the ways you can meet new people. Getting involved in extracurricular
R	activities brings you in contact with a wide range of individuals. The drama club, for example, brings together
I	students from several different grades.

Variations on the TRI pattern include sentence arrangements such as TIR, TII, or ITR.

I	This month alone the service club at our high school delivered meals to thirty shut-ins.
I	In addition, members beautified the neighborhood with new plantings.
T	If any school-sponsored club deserves increased support, the service club does.

Exercise 9 Placing Topic Sentences Arrange the sentences below in a TRI pattern. Add transitions as needed. Include two additional details to support the topic sentence. Then, reorganize the sentences in a variation of TRI.

- Team sports teach cooperation.
- The player who passes the ball contributes as much to the team's success as the player who scores the goal.
- Working as part of a team, a player learns to work for a common goal, rather than a personal one.

3.3 Paragraphs in Essays and Other Compositions

Unity and Coherence
Achieve Unity

In a paragraph that has **unity,** all the sentences relate to the main idea. They either develop, support, or explain the main idea. To achieve unity in your paragraphs, refer to your topic sentence as you draft. Be sure that each point is related to your topic. When you revise a paragraph, strengthen unity by deleting any sentences or details that do not develop, support, or explain the main idea. In the following paragraph, one sentence is marked for deletion because it interferes with the unity of the paragraph.

WRITING MODEL

When choosing a pet, consider the space and time you have available. If you live in a small apartment and don't have a lot of extra time, you should not choose a pet that requires a lot of exercise and affection. A dog, for instance, is probably not the best choice if you don't have time to take it outside to walk and play. It's also expensive to take a dog to the veterinarian. A goldfish, on the other hand, is happy if you feed it once a day and keep its bowl clean.

> **Exercise 10** Revising for Unity On a separate sheet of paper, copy the following paragraph. Mark for deletion any sentences that interfere with the unity of the paragraph.

Orchestras consist of four main groups, or sections, of instruments. These sections are string, woodwind, brass, and percussion. The string section is made up of violins, violas, cellos, and basses. My sister plays the violin, and I play the cello. The woodwinds are flutes, oboes, clarinets, and bassoons. The oboe has a unique sound. The brass section contains trumpets, French horns, trombones, and tubas. Percussion instruments include drums, bells, cymbals, gongs, triangles, tambourines, and xylophones. Many schools offer programs in which students can learn one of these instruments.

Create Coherence

A paragraph has coherence when the ideas are arranged in a logical order and the sentences are connected so that it is clear to a reader how ideas are related. The type of organization you choose depends on your topic and purpose. When you draft, order the sentences in a paragraph so that one leads logically to the next. Use transitional words and phrases to indicate the connections between ideas.

TYPES OF ORGANIZATION

- **Chronological Order:** Details are arranged in order of time— what happens first, next, and last. This type of organization is useful for writing about events and explaining processes.

  Common transitions for indicating chronological relationships include *first, second, then, next, finally, before, after, at the same time, later, immediately, soon,* and *recently.*

- **Spatial Order:** Details are presented in order of how they relate to one another physically. This type of organization is frequently used in descriptions of places and things, and it may also be used in giving directions.

  Common transitions for indicating spatial relationships include *through, next to, above, below, in front of, behind, outside, inside, in the middle, near, past,* and *beyond.*

- **Order of Importance:** Details are presented in increasing or decreasing order of importance. This type of organization is especially effective in persuasive writing.

  Common transitions for indicating order of importance include *first, primarily, most important, in addition, also,* and *significantly.*

- **Cause-and-Effect Order:** Details are presented to show how one event or circumstance leads to or is the result of another. This type of organization is used to explain a process or the analysis of an event.

  Common transitions for indicating cause and effect include *therefore, because, if, then, due to, so,* and *thus.*

Exercise 11 Revising for Coherence On a separate sheet of paper, revise the following paragraph to create coherence. If necessary, reorder sentences. Add transitions to show connections.

If you have never been hiking, you should start with an easy trail. Some beginners have started off on a trail that is too difficult. They quickly become discouraged. Keep at it. You will build stamina and endurance. You will be able to tackle more difficult trails. Don't fall into the beginner's trap of thinking that hiking is easy. You need to become familiar with the woods. You need to know your own limitations.

Understanding the Parts of a Composition

To *compose* means to put the parts together—to create. Most often, *composing* refers to the creation of a musical or literary work—a composition. You may not think of the reports, essays, and test answers you write as literary works, but they are compositions. To write an effective composition, you must understand the parts.

The Introduction

The **introduction** does what its name suggests: It introduces the topic of your composition. An effective introduction begins with a strong **lead,** a first sentence that captures readers' interest. The lead is followed by the **thesis statement,** the key point of your composition. Usually, the thesis statement is followed by a few sentences that outline how you will make your key point.

The Body

The **body** of a composition consists of several paragraphs that develop, explain, and support the key idea expressed in the thesis statement. The body of an essay should be **unified** and **coherent.** In the same way that the sentences of a paragraph work together to support the topic sentence, the paragraphs in a composition work together to support the thesis statement. The topic of each paragraph should relate directly to the thesis statement and be arranged in a logical organization.

The Conclusion

The **conclusion** is the final paragraph of the essay. The conclusion restates the thesis and sums up the support. Often, the conclusion includes the writer's reflection or observation on the topic. An effective conclusion ends on a memorable note, with a quotation, a call to action, or a forceful statement.

> **Exercise 12** Planning a Composition On a separate sheet of paper, outline the parts of a composition on a topic that interests you. Write a thesis statement and a possible lead for the introduction. Write a topic sentence for each of several paragraphs that support your thesis statement. Then, choose a quotation or write a forceful statement that you might use in the conclusion.

Recognizing Types of Paragraphs

There are several types of paragraphs you can use in your compositions and creative writing.

Topical Paragraphs

A topical paragraph is a group of sentences that contains one key sentence or idea and several sentences that support or develop that key idea or topic sentence.

Functional Paragraphs

Functional paragraphs serve a specific purpose. They may not have a topic sentence, but they are unified and coherent because the sentences (if there is more than one) are clearly connected and follow a logical order. Functional paragraphs can be used for the following purposes:

- **To create emphasis** A very short paragraph of one or two sentences lends weight to what is being said because it breaks the reader's rhythm.

- **To indicate dialogue** One of the conventions of written dialogue is that a new paragraph begins each time the speaker changes.

- **To make a transition** A short paragraph can help readers move between the main ideas in two topical paragraphs.

WRITING MODEL

from **Winslow Homer: America's Greatest Painter**

H. N. Levitt

When he was six, the family moved to Cambridge, directly across the street from Harvard College. Sometimes Winslow's dad would suggest that the boy consider attending Harvard someday. But it was no use. All young Winslow wanted to do was fish and draw.

After a while, the family realized there was something special about Winslow, because that's all he would do—fish and draw, day in and day out, all year long.

But even if Homer had wanted to go to college, there would have been no money for it. When Homer was 13, his dad sold all and left to make his fortune in the California gold rush. He came back a few years later empty-handed.

The functional paragraph, highlighted in blue italics, provides a transition between Winslow's boyhood and teen years.

▶ **Exercise 13** Identifying Functional Paragraphs Skim a magazine or newspaper article to find one example of a functional paragraph that creates emphasis and one example of a functional paragraph that makes a transition. Explain to a partner how the paragraph works in the context of the longer piece of writing.

Paragraph Blocks

Sometimes, you may have so much information to support or develop a main idea that it "outgrows" a single paragraph. When a topic sentence or main idea requires extensive explanation or support, you can develop the idea in a paragraph block—several paragraphs that work together and function as a unit. Each paragraph in the block supports the key idea or topic sentence. By breaking the development of the idea into separate paragraphs, you make your ideas clearer.

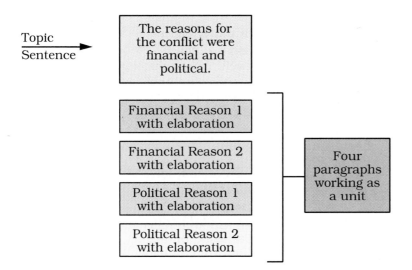

▶ **Exercise 14** Identifying Paragraph Blocks Look through magazine articles, factual reports, and short stories to find examples of paragraph blocks. Photocopy the works in which you find your example, and mark each block with a brace { }. Underline the topic sentence for the block. Next to each paragraph in the block, write a phrase describing its relationship to the main idea of the block.

3.4 *Writing Style*

Developing Style

Your style is the way you express yourself—in the clothes you wear, the music you listen to, and the way you fix your hair. Style also refers to the way you express yourself in writing. Several qualities contribute to the style of your writing.

Sentence Variety The different CDs in your music collection reflect your musical taste and style. You have a "collection" that contributes to your writing style as well. When you write, use a variety of sentence types, lengths, and structures. A paragraph or an essay composed of all short sentences will be choppy; too many long sentences will make a composition boring and difficult to follow. Vary sentences to create a rhythm and emphasize your most important points.

Diction *Diction* refers to the words you choose to use when you write. You can use words with positive connotations or associations for an upbeat style, or you can use words with negative connotations if you are trying to make a point about a problem or situation. The sounds of words can also contribute to the style of a paragraph.

Tone Tone is your attitude toward your subject. You may view your subject with fondness, disapproval, or humor. If you are writing an explanation of a process, your paragraphs will have a serious, formal tone. If you are writing a letter to a friend, your paragraphs will have a casual, friendly tone.

▶ **Exercise 15** **Writing a Paragraph** Read the two Writing Models on page 33. Study the sentence lengths and structures, the word choice, and the tone of each. Discuss with a partner how the styles of the two paragraphs are similar and different. Then, write a paragraph of your own, modeled on the style of one of the paragraphs you read.

Using Formal and Informal English

Standard English may be formal or informal. Use formal English when you want to discuss a subject in a serious way. Use informal English for casual writing or when you want your writing to resemble conversation.

The Conventions of Formal English

Use formal English for reports, persuasive essays, business letters, and most of your school assignments. When writing in formal English, observe the following conventions:

- Do not use contractions.
- Do not use slang.
- Use standard English usage and grammar.

Informal English

Informal English is the casual language you hear in everyday conversation. In writing, you may use informal English for friendly letters, casual notes, humorous writing, some narratives, and in dialogue. When writing in informal English, you can

- use contractions.
- use popular expressions and slang.

FORMAL ENGLISH: Please consider me for the position of lifeguard. I am well qualified and dependable.

INFORMAL ENGLISH: I'd love to land the lifeguard job. I'd be a super lifeguard. I'm dependable—my pals say they know they can count on me.

▶ **Exercise 16** Using Formal and Informal English On a separate sheet of paper, rewrite the following sentences. Use formal English for those written in informal English. Use informal English for those written in formal English.

1. Check out the show at seven.
2. This rule is such a drag.
3. I am writing to complain that you did not return my call.
4. My friends who participated were disappointed in the experience.
5. I can't believe that everyone isn't knocked out by how cool the movie is.

Spotlight on the Humanities

Analyzing Artistic Composition

Focus on Dance: Anna Pavlova

In a written composition, sentences and paragraphs work together to create a clear, unified piece of writing focused on a central idea. In dance, each movement contributes to the overall "composition." Each new step adds strength and beauty to the dance as a whole.

The ballet world produced a magnificent Russian dancer in Anna Pavlova (1881–1931). In 1907, she danced what was to become a signature piece for her called "The Dying Swan," with music by Camille Saint-Saëns. Pavlova toured the world and became an international ballet phenomenon. She continued to dance until illness prevented her from performing. She died of pneumonia, and reports were that on her death bed, she asked to have her swan costume brought to her. She felt unable to give up her love of dance.

Music Connection At the age of two, Frenchman Camille Saint-Saëns (1835–1921) began learning the piano, and by the time he was ten, he had memorized all of Beethoven's piano sonatas. Not only did he write the music for Anna Pavlova's signature dance, but he also wrote his Second Piano Concerto in seventeen days in 1868.

Photography Connection Known for her photographs of Anna Pavlova and other artists of her day, Doris Ullman (1882–1934) established herself as an important portrait photographer in the 1920's. Although her portraits of the famous were well published, Ullman spent most of her career photographing farm workers and street scenes.

Pavlova as Bacchante, Sir John Lavery, Glasgow Art Gallery and Museum, Scotland

▲ Critical Viewing Explain by referring to the painting the elements that a visual composition shares with a written composition. **[Analyze]**

Writing Activity: Analyze Composition

View a video of a group dance performance. Look for ways that the dancers work together to create a unified effect. For example, one dancer's outstretched arm may point toward another dancer in the group. Several dancers may perform the same step at different times. Identify specific examples of how the "parts" of the dance you view work together. Write notes on what you observe, and use your notes to give a presentation to your class or a small group. Show the video as part of your presentation.

Media and Technology Skills

Evaluating Information Media

Activity: Comparing and Contrasting Newscasts

Media is a general term used to label a broad range of communication delivery forms that provide the public with information, opinions, and ideas. One service provided by most kinds of media is to report and analyze world, national, and local events.

Think About It The types of information media differ in depth of coverage and in tone and method of presentation.

- **Print media** come in several formats, including newspapers and magazines. Newspapers may be distributed daily or weekly. Often, they provide ongoing coverage that is updated with each new publication. The tone is objective, except in sections that are specifically devoted to editorials and opinions. Magazines are usually published weekly or monthly. They may provide more depth of coverage than do broadcast media, but they cannot update information as frequently. Both newspapers and magazines use typefaces to stress headlines or key points. Photographs usually accompany articles.

- **Broadcast media** reach you by electronic means such as television or radio. Broadcast media combine elements of sound, images, and live narration to report the news. Television newscasts are broadcast several times daily and may show live coverage of an event while an anchor gives details and analysis. Although radio coverage provides verbal information only, it often provides the most frequent updates. The technology of the Internet allows users to access full coverage of any story at any time of day.

Types of Media

Print
- Books
- Magazines
- Newspapers
- Photography
- Print Advertisements

Broadcast
- Film
- Radio
- Television
- Internet Broadcasts

News story: _____

The New News

Print-Media Source: _____

Images: _____

Facts Included: _____

Most Memorable Detail: _____

Broadcast-Media Source: _____

Images: _____

Facts Included: _____

Most Memorable Detail: _____

Analyze It Using charts like these, compare the coverage of the same news story in a print-media source and in a broadcast-media source. Consider how the different approaches affect the way you view the information being presented.

Standardized Test Preparation Workshop

Analyzing Strategy, Organization, and Style

To measure your skill in writing an effective paragraph, standardized tests may feature items consisting of a paragraph in which each sentence is numbered. Specific questions based on the paragraph refer to the sentences by number. These test questions often ask about the writer's strategy, organization, sequence of sentences, and choice of words, and about the overall style of the paragraph. The following are three types of questions that you will need to answer:

- **Strategy questions** ask whether a given revision is appropriate in the context of the essay.

- **Organization questions** ask you to choose the most logical sequence of ideas or to decide whether a sentence should be added, deleted, or moved.

- **Style questions** focus on your analysis of the writer's point of view and the use of appropriate and effective language for the intended audience.

The sample test item will give you practice in answering questions on writing strategy, organization, and style.

Test Tip

Before reading the questions, read the paragraph, noting any places where the text does not flow or seems incorrect. Refer back to your notes as you answer the questions.

Sample Test Item	Answer and Explanation
Read the paragraph, and then answer the question that follows. (1) New members were welcomed at the meeting. (2) The year's first meeting of the school literary magazine was productive. (3) By the close of the meeting, each committee had several new and enthusiastic members. (4) Over thirty new students attended, expressing their interest in producing the magazine. Choose the most logical sentence sequence. **A** 2, 4, 1, 3 **B** 3, 1, 2, 4 **C** 2, 4, 3, 1 **D** Correct as is.	The correct answer is *A*. In order to arrange the information in the paragraph in a logical sequence, 2 should begin the paragraph as a topic sentence. 4, 1, and 3 must appear in this sequence to support the topic sentence and follow a logical order.

▶ **Practice 1** **Directions:** Read the passage, and then answer the questions that follow. Choose the letter of the best answer.

(1) Robert Frost explores humanity's shared experiences of life against a natural background in his poems. (2) Most frequently, Frost sets his work in the stark natural landscape of rural northern New England. (3) It is very cold in the winter here and the region often sees a great deal of snow. (4) There, isolated from America's bustling cities, Frost's speakers confront difficult and life-changing choices—which road to take, what commitments to honor, how connected each person should be to others. (5) This region is known for its natural beauty, harsh winters, and picture-postcard villages. (6) Frost likes to use these settings and themes for his poems.

1 Which of the following is the most logical sentence sequence for this paragraph?
 A 4, 5, 6, 1, 2, 3
 B 2, 3, 1, 5, 6, 4
 C 1, 2, 3, 5, 4, 6
 D 1, 4, 5, 6, 2, 3

2 Which of the following parts is irrelevant and could be deleted from the paragraph?
 F Part 5
 G Part 2
 H Part 3
 J Part 4

3 If the writer wanted to add more information about specific poems by Frost, which of the following would be most appropriate?
 A Frost has written several poems that can be found in his collections.
 B One such poem, "Stopping by Woods on a Snowy Evening," is an example of a man gaining insight into his life during a personal moment with nature.
 C Some poems describe working on the land.
 D One of Frost's most famous poems is "The Road Not Taken."

4 Which of the following sentences would best conclude the paragraph?
 F Sentence 6
 G By using these rural settings as a backdrop, Frost emphasizes the natural life processes that cause the narrator of the poem to make certain choices and confront challenges.
 H These settings are fitting for a writer from New England.
 J The stark beauty of New England is the theme of most of his works.

5 Which phrase BEST identifies the author's purpose?
 A To entertain
 B To inform
 C To criticize
 D To persuade

6 The tone of this passage can be described as—
 F persuasive
 G emotional
 H whimsical
 J admiring

Narration
Autobiographical Writing

Untitled, Pascal Milelli, Courtesy of the artist

Autobiographical Writing in Everyday Life

"Wait till you hear this!" Every day, you tell friends and family about events in your life. You might tell your parents about why it took so long to walk the dog. You might write a letter or send e-mail to friends, telling them about a trip you took last weekend.

Writing about the events in your life is a good way to share your life with others. It is also a way to discover more about yourself. When you start writing about events in your life, you may find yourself recalling details that you might otherwise have forgotten. Writers of all types use autobiographical writing as a way to understand themselves and their past.

▲ **Critical Viewing**
Name three events suggested by this painting. Which one do you think would make an interesting topic for an autobiographical narrative? Explain. **[Draw Conclusions]**

What Is Autobiographical Writing?

Autobiographical writing tells the story of an event or person in the writer's life. Writing autobiography is like showing a special object or photo to friends—it is a way of sharing your life. Writing autobiography is also like looking in the mirror—it is a way of asking and answering the question, "Who am I?" Autobiographical writing includes

- a clear sequence of events involving the writer.
- a problem or conflict, or a clear contrast between past and present viewpoints.
- vivid details portraying people and places.

To see the criteria on which your narrative may be judged, see the Rubric for Self-Assessment on page 64.

Types of Autobiographical Writing

These are a few types of autobiographical writing:

- **Autobiographical incidents,** which are also called **personal narratives,** tell the story of a specific event in your life.
- **Autobiographical narratives** or **sketches** describe a time or a group of events in your life, offering insight into them.
- **Reflective essays** recount an experience and give your thoughts on its meaning.
- **Memoirs** are the true story of your relationship with a person, place, or animal, including your thoughts and feelings about the relationship.

Writers in
ACTION

Gary Soto, author of short stories and poems, often writes about his past. He knows that good autobiographical writing cannot be a simple list of events but must engage the reader's interest. He arranges events in his autobiographical writing almost as if he were writing a short story:

"What I do as a memoirist or an essayist is that I try to slice up my life in a way that would be interesting to others. . . ."

PREVIEW
Student Work
IN PROGRESS

To create a piece of autobiographical writing, follow the models of the strategies in this lesson. You will trace the progress of Emily Taylor Speer, a student at Hildebrandt Intermediate School in Spring, Texas. As you'll see, Emily used featured prewriting, drafting, and revising techniques to develop her autobiographical essay, "To the Dogs." You can read her final piece at the end of the chapter.

4.1 **Model** *From* **Literature**

In this autobiographical account, short-story writer and poet Gary Soto (1952–) re-creates a memorable experience.

Reading Strategy:
Predict As you read "The Bike," **make predictions**. Come up with answers to the question, "What will probably happen next?" As you read further, compare your answers to what actually happens.

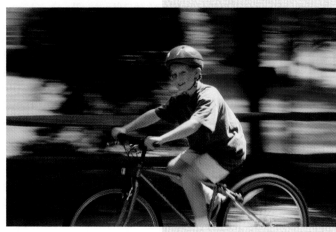

▲ **Critical Viewing**
What problems might a kid on a bike such as this one encounter? **[Speculate]**

The Bike

Gary Soto

My first bike got me nowhere, though the shadow I cast as I pedaled raced along my side. . . .

Going up and down the block was one thing, but taking the first curve, out of sight of Mom and the house, was another. I was scared of riding on Sarah Street. Mom said hungry dogs lived on that street, and red anger lived in their eyes. Their throats were hard with extra bones from biting kids on bikes, she said.

But I took the corner anyway. I didn't believe Mom. Once she had said that pointing at rainbows caused freckles, and after a rain had moved in and drenched the streets, after the sparrows flitted onto the lawn, a rainbow washed over the junkyard and reached the dark barrels of Coleman pickles. I stood at the window, looking out, amazed and devious, with the devilish horns of my butch haircut standing up. From behind the window, I let my finger slowly uncurl like a bean plant rising from earth. I uncurled it, then curled it back and made a fist. I should remember this day, I told myself.

I pedaled my squeaky bike around the curve onto Sarah Street, but returned immediately. I braked and looked back at where I had gone. My face was hot, my hair sweaty, but nothing scary seemed to happen. The street had looked like our street: parked cars, tall trees,

Soto's effective opener leaves readers curious to find out why the bike didn't get Soto anywhere. He also creates a conflict: He is afraid of riding around the corner, but he also wants to go there.

Details about Soto's mother, such as the stories she tells, help to characterize her—she is an imaginative woman.

Soto links each detail in this paragraph to the central conflict—his fear of biking around the corner.

a sprinkler hissing on a lawn, and an old woman bending over her garden. I started again, and again I rode the curve, my eyes open as wide as they could go. After a few circle eights I returned to our street. There ain't no dogs, I told myself. I began to think that maybe this was like one of those false rainbow warnings.

. . . I again tore my bike around the curve onto Sarah Street. I was free. The wind flicked my hair and cooled my ears. I did figure eights, rode up the curbs and onto lawns, bumped into trees, and rode over a garden hose a hundred times because I liked the way the water sprang up from the sprinkler after the pressure of my tires. I stopped when I saw a kid my age come down a porch. His machinery for getting around was a tricycle. Big baby, I thought, and said, "You can run over my leg with your trike if you want." I laid down on the sidewalk, and the kid, with fingers in his mouth, said, "OK."

He backed up and slowly, like a tank, advanced. I folded my arms behind my head and watched a jay swoop by with what looked like a cracker in its beak, when the tire climbed over my ankle and sparks of pain cut through my skin. I sat up quickly, my eyes flinging tears like a sprinkler.

The boy asked, "Did it hurt?"

"No," I said, almost crying.

The kid could see that it did. He could see my face strain to hold back a sob, two tears dropping like dimes into the dust. . . .

. . . I got on my bicycle and pedaled mostly with the good leg. The few tears still on my eyelashes evaporated as I rode. I realized I would live. I did nothing fancy on the way home, no figure eights, no wiggling of the handlebars, no hands in my pockets, no closed eye moments.

Then the sudden bark of a dog scared me, and my pants leg fed into the chain, the bike coming to an immediate stop. I tugged at the cuff, gnashed and oil-black, until ripping sounds made me quit trying. I fell to the ground, bike and all, and let the tears lather my face again. I then dragged the bike home with the pants leg in the chain. There was nothing to do except lie in the dirt because Mom saw me round the corner from Sarah Street. I laid down when she came out, . . . and I didn't blame the dog or the stupid rainbow.

LITERATURE

To read more of Gary Soto's reflections on his life, see the poem "Oranges" and the story "Seventh Grade." You can find these selections in *Prentice Hall Literature: Timeless Voices, Timeless Themes, Bronze.*

At the end of his autobiographical narrative, the conflict is resolved: Fear "wins," since Soto's overconfidence has gotten him into trouble.

Reading Writing Connection

Writing Strategy: Help Readers Make Predictions To help readers make predictions as they read your autobiographical narrative, include clues. For instance, Gary Soto leaves a clue about how his story ends when he writes "My first bike got me nowhere."

4.2 *Prewriting*

Choosing Your Topic

To choose a topic for autobiographical writing, think of times when you learned something, solved a problem, or gained an insight. Use these strategies to select a topic:

Strategies for Generating a Topic

1. **Freewriting** Write whatever comes to mind in response to the word *explore.* Then, reread what you have written, and circle the most interesting idea. Use the events connected to this idea as the inspiration for your topic.

2. **Blueprinting** Think of places that are important to you, such as your house or a place you go to with friends. Draw a map of this place, marking different areas. For each location, list connected memories. Choose a memory from this list as your topic.

Try it out! Use the interactive Blueprinting model in **Section 4.2,** on-line or on CD-ROM.

Student Work
IN PROGRESS

Name: Emily Taylor Speer
Hildebrandt Intermediate School
Spring, TX

Blueprinting
Here is how Emily used blueprinting to come up with a topic:

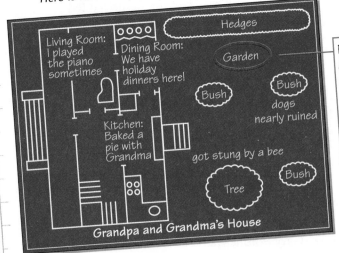

Emily decided to write about some of the events that had taken place in her Grandpa's garden.

TOPIC BANK

If you're having trouble finding a topic, consider the following possibilities:

1. **A Present That You Received** Think of a present you received that made you happy or proud or that disappointed you. Write about the occasion, the person who gave you the present, and your reaction to it.

2. **An Important Event** What happened and how did you feel the first time you went to the dentist? What was your experience the first time you went to a store by yourself? Write about one of these events, or choose a similar one.

Responding to Fine Art

March Wind, ©Robert Vickrey/Licensed by VAGA, New York, NY

3. Describe the weather in this painting and its overall mood. What might the girl be doing? Describe the details that lead you to answer as you do. Then, think of a day in your own life that had similar weather or a similar mood, or on which you felt as this girl might. Write about this day.

Responding to Literature

4. Read "A Day's Wait" by Ernest Hemingway. In this story, the main character's reaction to the situation is very different from the narrator's. After reading the story, write about a time when your reactions to an event or situation were very different from the reactions of other people. You can find "A Day's Wait" in *Prentice Hall Literature: Timeless Voices, Timeless Themes*, Bronze.

Cooperative Writing Opportunity

5. **Autobiography of a School Year** With a group, write about important or interesting events in the last school year. Each group member can write about a different aspect of school life: assemblies, school trips, sports, class projects, and so on. Artistic group members can draw pictures to illustrate the work. Assemble your work in a folder or binder and share it with others.

Narrowing Your Topic

Once you've chosen a topic, uncover the story that is hidden within it. For instance, the event of going to a concert includes many parts. The real story, however, might focus on the moment when you thought your friend had forgotten the tickets! Peel away details from your topic to include only points that create or enrich a story. Use the strategy of "looping."

Use Looping to Narrow a Topic

Here are the steps for looping:

1. Write freely on your topic for about five minutes.
2. Circle the most interesting or important word or phrase.
3. Write for five minutes on this main focus.
4. Circle your new main focus.

If the new focus is narrow enough, use it as your topic. Otherwise, continue looping until you find a narrow topic.

Student Work
IN PROGRESS

Name: Emily Taylor Speer
Hildebrandt Intermediate School
Spring, TX

Looping

Here is how Emily used looping to narrow a broad topic.

Grandpa and Grandma have a really big garden. It's got big bushes and trees as well as flowers. I used to hide in the bushes from my brother. Last time I was there, we found a big mess in the garden. Grandpa figured that the dogs must have gotten in, and used the garden as a pit stop.

Lots of dogs lived in the neighborhood. They come by Grandpa's house all the time. The man next door had Spanky, but Spanky is always on a leash. The woman across the street had Lucky and Buddy.

Focused Topic: There was the time Grandpa tried to stop the neighborhood dogs from messing up his lawn. I helped.

Considering Your Audience and Purpose

Your **audience**—the readers for whom you are writing—will determine how casual or formal your writing should be. Your **purpose** for writing should also affect your writing. Autobiographical writing can entertain, share an insight, or celebrate a person in your life. Before you draft, decide on your purpose.

Analyze Your Purpose

Use the following chart to see how your purpose should shape your writing.

If your purpose is to . . .	then organize your writing to . . .	Include details that . . .
tell an exciting, amusing, or moving story about yourself	build to a climax without giving away your ending.	create suspense, sympathy, or humor.
share an insight you have had	build up to the lesson you learned.	emphasize the contrast between your previous and your present points of view.
celebrate a person in your life	dramatically show the person's character, building up to the most revealing details.	reveal the character of this person.

Gathering Details

Next, find details to enrich your writing. For instance, if you were telling the story of the time your friend misplaced the tickets for a concert, you might describe the look of impatience on the usher's face as your friend looked through her pockets. Listing and itemizing will help you gather such details.

List and Itemize

Here are the steps for listing and itemizing:

1. Spend five minutes listing ideas connected to your topic.

2. Look over your list. Circle the most important items.

3. Look for connections among the phrases you've circled.

4. Highlight details that will add to the story you want to tell.

4.3 Drafting

Shaping Your Writing

Create Tension

Most stories, even incidents taken from life, create tension to keep readers interested. The most important form of tension is *conflict.*

Conflict A conflict is a struggle between opposing forces. If an obstacle prevents a character from getting what he or she wants, there is a conflict.

Contrasting Viewpoints Not every autobiographical piece has an obvious conflict. For example, your recollection of childhood games might not include a struggle. To keep your reader interested, though, you might write about the day when you realized that you were too old for some games. Here, the tension lies between your old and new ways of looking at the world.

Use a Conflict Map You can help focus your thoughts about conflict or other forms of tension by drawing a conflict map like the one below.

CONFLICT MAP

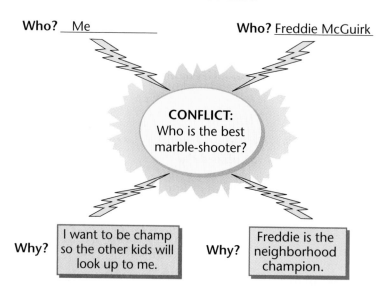

Create a Sequence of Events Arrange in sequence the events related to your conflict or change of viewpoint. These events should lead up to the point at which you solved the problem—the resolution of the conflict—or to the point at which your viewpoint changed—a moment of insight.

> **Technology Tip**
>
> You can use the "Table" feature of a word-processing program to track a conflict. Make a column for each character involved. In separate rows, list the reasons they are involved in the conflict. Then, make a new column for each new action that deepens or resolves the conflict. Enter each action in the same row as the reasons it involves.

Providing Elaboration

As you draft, you will realize you cannot say everything about your subject. One well-chosen detail, though, can conjure up an entire person or place.

Characterize Through Details

Characterizing details—Uncle Bob's laugh like a horse's whinny or Aunt Betty's careful way of walking—can create a strong, vivid image. For each important person in your autobiographical work, find a characterizing detail. Ask yourself these questions:

- What two details would I use to describe this person to a friend?
- What does this person look like?
- What is unique about this person's behavior?
- What kind of personality does this person have?
- How does this person sound?
- What expressions or words does this person frequently use?

As you draft, pause occasionally and review what you have written about other characters. Add any characterizing details that will help create a vivid picture for readers.

▲ **Critical Viewing** Describe two details in this photograph that could be used to characterize this man. **[Analyze]**

Student Work
IN PROGRESS

Name: *Emily Taylor Speer*
Hildebrandt Intermediate School
Spring , TX

Adding Characterizing Details

Look at the details Emily added to her draft to characterize her grandfather, painting a picture of a careful, meticulous person.

Grandfather was a good worker. We ~~tied the stuff~~, which looked like small, round balls, all over his bushes and trees. We followed the instructions and spaced them apart as the box directed.

spent hours

carefully tying the stuff

conscientiously exactly

Revising

Revising Your Overall Structure
Link Details to the Central Conflict

Keep your reader eager to read—right up to your final resolution or insight! Make sure the details in your autobiographical story are connected to the central conflict or tension.

▶ **REVISION STRATEGY**
Identifying Connections to Conflict

On an index card, write a sentence summing up your conflict or change of viewpoint. Run the card down your draft.
Read each paragraph and label it to show its connection with
the conflict or change. A connected paragraph may

- provide information necessary to understand the conflict.

- show events that make the conflict worse.

- show how the conflict is resolved or explain the insight.

If a paragraph is not clearly related to the central conflict,
rewrite it or consider deleting it.

⚙ Grammar and Style Tip

As you add and
delete material to
make your revisions,
make sure you
shape the material
into complete
sentences.

Student Work
IN PROGRESS

Name: *Emily Taylor Speer*
Hildebrandt Intermediate School
Spring, TX

Identifying Connections to Conflict
Emily decided to strengthen the connection of this paragraph to the conflict.

My grandfather was a ~~very tall man.~~ who always prized his lawn and shrubbery.
~~Everybody who met him liked him. He had a~~
~~garden.~~ Nearly all of the neighborhood agreed,
there was no lawn more ~~beautiful~~ well maintained than Bob
Speer's. It had the reputation of being the
best in the neighborhood. ~~My grandmother~~
~~worked in it, too, but it was mostly my grandfather's.~~

Conflict:
My grandfather
who wants
a neat lawn vs
the dogs, who
mess it up.
➡

NEEDED
INFORMATION

Revising Your Paragraphs

Strengthen Coherence

A paragraph should not be a clump of sentences that just happened to spring up in the same place. Like plants in an orderly garden, each sentence should clearly belong with the others in the paragraph. Check the connection of each sentence to the main idea of the paragraph by "weeding" paragraphs.

▶ **REVISION STRATEGY**
Coding for Coherence: "Weeding" Paragraphs

For each paragraph, jot a brief phrase on a sticky note summing up its main idea. Stick the note by the paragraph. (For a functional paragraph, identify the main function of the paragraph. See Chapter 3 for more on functional paragraphs.)

Go back over each paragraph. For each sentence in the paragraph, first read the phrase on the sticky note, then read the sentence. Place a check mark over any sentence that seems odd or out of place when read after your main idea.

When you are finished, review each checked sentence. Eliminate it if it does not belong in the paragraph, or rewrite it to make clear its connection to other sentences.

Get instant help! For additional help with coherent paragraphs, use the interactive Unity and Coherence Revision Checker, accessible from the menu bar, on-line or on CD-ROM.

WEEDING PARAGRAPHS

Revising Your Sentences

To help readers follow your story, make sure your sentences show the order of events and the connections between them. Add transitional words or phrases to clarify these connections.

Kinds of Transitions

Show Sequence	Identify Cause and Effect	Show Comparison and Contrast	Identify Conclusions
first, next, then, finally, before, after, soon	since, because, if	like, also, similarly, although, however, despite, but, on the other hand	therefore, thus, so, consequently, as a result

▶**REVISION STRATEGY**
Coding Events for Transitions

Select a paragraph in your draft. Circle each sentence that tells of an event. Number the circled sentences in the order of the events they narrate. Then, reread the paragraph. If the connection between circled sentences is clear, draw a link in a new color between the circles. If the connection is not clear, add a transition. You can use the transitions listed above.

Student Work
IN PROGRESS

Name: Emily Taylor Speer
Hildebrandt Intermediate School
Spring, Texas

Coding for Transitions

Emily coded events in this paragraph, and then added a few needed transitions.

① We conscientiously followed the instructions and spaced them apart exactly as the box directed. *Then, my* ~~My~~ grandfather

② and I led the dogs from their home and over to the testing site. *By that time, a* ~~A~~ neighborhood crowd had gathered around the

③ lawn, anticipating the dogs' reaction, for news spread quickly there. My grandfather and I carefully guided the

④ dogs to the bush most heavily covered in the artificial berries. *At the moment of truth, one* ~~One~~ of the animals leaned forward and began to

⑤ sniff the bush, and promptly took a bite out of it!

Revising Your Word Choice

Use Precise Nouns

Precise language helps a reader understand your ideas and picture the scenes you have described. A **precise noun** is a noun that stops readers from asking *what kind?* For instance, the word *dog* would leave a reader wondering, "What kind of dog? What does it look like?" A precise noun like *collie* or *poodle* gives the reader enough information.

VAGUE: There was a lot of **stuff** strewn about the garage.

PRECISE: Old **tires,** greasy **rags,** and crumpled **candy wrappers** were strewn about the garage.

GENERAL: At 9:00, I finished the **book** I was reading.

PRECISE: At 9:00, I finished the **mystery** I was reading.

▶**REVISION STRATEGY**
Color-Coding Nouns for Precise Word Choice

Using a red pencil, draw boxes around the first ten nouns in your draft. Evaluate whether these nouns are vague. If so, improve your word choice by replacing them with more precise nouns.

Research Tip

Look up a vague word in a thesaurus to find precise words with which you can replace it. (Always check the meaning of a synonym in a dictionary before using it.)

Grammar in Your Writing
Nouns

A **noun** is a part of speech that names a person, place, or thing (including a quality, an idea, or an action). Here are some examples of nouns:

People	Places	Things	Ideas/Qualities	Actions
teacher	Florida	bicycle	beauty	running
Dr. Cassidy	riverbank	childhood	kindness	hunting
sister	downtown	T-shirt	clarity	writing
Steven	Lake Erie	joy	freedom	relaxing

Notice that nouns can name concrete things (those that can be experienced with the five senses) or abstract things (periods of life like "childhood" or feelings like "joy").

Find It in Your Reading Review "The Bike" by Gary Soto on page 50. Find three examples of precise nouns.

Find It in Your Writing Identify the first ten nouns in your draft. For each, explain which of the five categories (above) it belongs to.

To learn more about nouns, see Chapter 14.

Peer Review

Highlight

After you've finished revising on your own, you can still use the help of other readers. Often, a classmate can see a possible improvement that you have overlooked.

Read your entire narrative to a small group. Group members should simply listen the first time. Then, read your narrative a second time. This time, listeners should write down the nouns you use that could be made more precise—nouns that leave them wondering *what kind?* or *which one?*

When you have finished reading, have listeners repeat back to you the nouns they wrote down. Highlight them on your paper. Consider changing the highlighted words to more precise nouns.

Collaborative Writing Tip

In a peer review session, express your criticisms as suggestions for improvement —not as negative comments.

▼ **Critical Viewing** Describe the mood of the girls in this picture. Explain what might be enjoyable about helping someone improve his or her draft. [**Hypothesize**]

4.5 Editing and Proofreading

Before you create your final draft, carefully check for errors in spelling, grammar, punctuation, and usage.

Focusing on Capitalization

As you check your work, ask yourself:
- Have I capitalized the first word of each sentence?
- Have I capitalized the names of people and places?

Clocking Form a circle with three classmates. Each student should pass his or her draft to the right. Then, each student should check the draft for correct capitalization, highlighting possible errors. Pass the papers again, and check for run-on sentences. Pass them again, and check for sentence fragments. Each writer should look over the highlights on his or her draft and correct any errors.

Grammar in Your Writing
Capitalization of Proper Nouns

Capitalize words when they serve as the name (or part of the name) by which someone or something is called.

I took a walk with Grandpa.
We went to the Rocky Mountains on vacation.

Do not capitalize words that do not serve as a name, unless they appear at the beginning of a sentence.

I took a walk with my grandfather.
We went to the mountains on vacation.

Find It in Your Reading Review "The Bike" by Gary Soto on page 50. Choose five capitalized words, ignoring words that start sentences and the title. For each word, explain whether it is the name of a specific person, place, or thing. If it is not, explain why the word has been capitalized.

Find It in Your Writing Choose five words in your draft that you have capitalized. Write down the reason you have capitalized each. Then, choose five words you have not capitalized, and write down why. Correct any mistakes you may discover in your draft.

To learn more about capitalization, see Chapter 27.

Publishing and Presenting

Building Your Portfolio

Here are some ideas for presenting your autobiographical writing:

1. **Perform a Dramatic Reading** Read your writing aloud to the class or to a group. Read expressively, matching your tone to the quality of the events that you are narrating—happy, sad, or funny.
2. **Send Your Story to a Magazine** Type your work neatly, and mail it to a magazine that publishes student writing. Include a brief letter that tells who you are and why you think your story should be published.

Reflecting on Your Writing

Reflect on your writing experience by answering the following questions in your writing journal or notebook:

- As you thought about and wrote about your topic, what new insights occurred to you?
- How did focusing on conflict help you structure your story?

 Internet Tip

To see an autobiographical narrative scored according to this rubric, go on-line: PHSchool.com Enter Web Code: ebk-7001

Rubric for Self-Assessment

Use the following criteria to evaluate your autobiographical piece.

	Score 4	Score 3	Score 2	Score 1
Audience and Purpose	Contains an engaging introduction; successfully entertains or presents a theme	Contains a somewhat engaging introduction; entertains or presents a theme	Contains an introduction; attempts to entertain or to present a theme	Begins abruptly or confusingly; leaves purpose unclear
Organization	Creates an interesting, clear narrative; told from a consistent point of view	Presents a clear sequence of events; told from a specific point of view	Presents a mostly clear sequence of events; contains inconsistent points of view	Presents events without logical order; lacks a consistent point of view
Elaboration	Provides insight into character; develops plot; contains dialogue	Contains details and dialogue that develop character and plot	Contains details that develop plot; contains some dialogue	Contains few or no details to develop characters or plot
Use of Language	Uses word choice and tone to reveal story's theme; contains no errors in grammar, punctuation, or spelling	Uses interesting and fresh word choices; contains few errors in grammar, punctuation, and spelling	Uses some clichés and trite expressions; contains some errors in grammar, punctuation, and spelling	Uses uninspired word choices; has many errors in grammar, punctuation, and spelling

4.7 Student Work
IN PROGRESS

FINAL DRAFT

To the Dogs

Emily Taylor Speer
Hildebrandt Intermediate School
Spring, Texas

My grandfather was a man who had always prized his lawn and shrubbery. Nearly all of the neighborhood agreed, there was no lawn more well maintained than Bob Speer's. It had the reputation of being the best in the neighborhood. One summer, several of the neighbors' dogs seemed to form a similar opinion. They flocked to his yard every day, using it as a pit stop. Being the creative man that he was, Grandpa asked for my help, and we began testing a series of methods to make his yard lose its appeal. We tried sprays, statues, plants, and even asked the owner of the most frequent pests, two huge, intimidating Dobermans, to reroute their morning walk. One attempt after the other failed.

Notice how Emily introduces the conflict between her grandfather and the dogs in the very first paragraph.

Ready to surrender, we were desperate when the answer appeared, a small ad for a "miracle repellent" at the bottom of the classifieds.

Grandpa was a perfectionist. We spent hours carefully tying the repellent, which looked like blueberries, around the vicinity of the house and yard, and all over the bushes and the trees. We conscientiously followed the instructions and spaced them apart exactly as the box directed. Then, my grandfather and I led the dogs from their home and over to the testing site. By that time, a neighborhood crowd had gathered around the lawn, anticipating the dogs' reaction, for news spread quickly there. My grandfather and I carefully guided the dogs to the bush most heavily covered in the artificial berries. At the moment of truth, one of the animals leaned forward and began to sniff the bush, and promptly took a bite out of it! The crowd was silent. Then the dog hiked its leg and clearly marked its territory!

I was devastated that the foolproof plan had failed, but Grandpa just shrugged and said, "Well, we've learned our lesson."

"What lesson?" I asked.

"Never succumb to the pull of an advertisement, however strong," he said." And, more important—let the dogs have their fun."

In the second paragraph, Emily heightens the tension by elaborating on the steps that she and her grandfather took. The reader asks: Will the plan work?

The conflict is resolved. The dogs "win." Note the final functional paragraph, in which Grandpa humorously accepts the resolution.

▼ **Critical Viewing**
Does this picture of a Doberman increase your appreciation of Emily and her grandfather's experiment? Explain.
[Evaluate]

Connected Assignment *Firsthand Biography*

A **firsthand biography** is your account of someone you know. It shares your unique perceptions of the person. To write a first-hand biography, focus on a series of events during your acquaintance with your subject. A firsthand biography includes

- use of the first-person point of view ("I").
- a well-organized retelling of events in the life of the subject.
- insights from the writer's perspective.

Prewriting List people who are important in your life—relatives, friends, teachers, coaches, and so on. Select one as your topic. Jot down impressions of your subject and your inter-actions with him or her.

Know	Want to Know	Learned
Ms. Grundy is a great English teacher. She makes the stories seem really important and alive.	• Did she read a lot as a kid? • Did she have a great English teacher like herself? • How did she become an English teacher?	

Then, arrange to talk with your subject. Ask questions about his or her life and the experiences you have shared. Use a K-W-L chart to help prepare these questions.

Drafting Organize the information you have gathered in logi-cal sequence. Determine the focus of your biography—your subject's most memorable personality trait or accomplish-ment—and organize your writing to develop that focus. Conclude with your strongest story about, or insight into, your focus. As you draft, elaborate on each main point with your own observations.

Revising and Editing When you have finished your first draft, review it. Make the following revisions:

- Rearrange paragraphs as necessary to make sure you nar-rate events in sequence. (If you tell an event out of sequence, make sure that you have good reason and that you handle the transition clearly to avoid confusion.)

- Check for places where you can clarify the order of events by adding transition words, such as *first, then, next,* and *after.*

- Then, look for places where you can elaborate on your main points. *Show* your subject's characteristics by adding descriptions, dialogue, and illustrative stories.

Publishing and Presenting After revising, proofread your biography. Consider presenting a copy of it to an organization to which your subject belongs, such as a school or civic group.

Spotlight on the Humanities

Use Visuals to Extend Meaning

Focus on Photography: Berenice Abbott

Just like an autobiographical narrative, a picture "tells a story." Photographer Berenice Abbott (1898–1991) used pictures to tell the story of a few artistic and literary figures who lived in Paris in the 1920's. James Joyce, the writer; Jean Cocteau, the filmmaker; and Eva Le Gallienne, the actress, are just a few of the luminaries she captured on film.

After living in Paris for many years, Abbott returned home to New York City in 1929 and began photographing the New York City landscape in all its variety. In the 1950's, Abbott merged photography with scientific principles and began photographing scientific subjects. She filled three high-school books on physics with these photographs.

Art Connection In 1927, Abbott photographed the famous fashion designer Coco Chanel (1883–1971). Born in France, Chanel was the leading fashion designer of her day, promoting necklaces and belts and short hairstyles for women. One early success was a loose-fitting sweater with a belted skirt. Chanel's revolutionary designs carried a feeling of simplicity, opposing the flamboyant styles popular in the early part of the twentieth century. Her influence on clothing design can still be seen in fashion today.

▲ **Critical Viewing** How does Abbott use Coco Chanel's pose in this photograph to suggest that Chanel is a creative woman with a vision? **[Interpret]**

Theater Connection Abbott also photographed actress, director, and producer Eva Le Gallienne (1899–1991). Cofounder of the American Repertory Theatre in 1946, Le Gallienne established herself as one of the leading American actresses of the twentieth century. Born in London, England, she lived in America throughout most of her professional career. She believed strongly in repertory theater and translated many of the works of classic playwright Henrik Ibsen.

Autobiographical Writing Activity: Photo Essay

Compile a collection of photographs that illustrate memorable moments in your life. Then, write a short paragraph to accompany each photograph so that you create an autobiographical photo essay of your life. Share your photo essay with your classmates.

Media and Technology Skills

Produce Visuals to Make Meaning
Activity: Create a Photo Essay

Like Berenice Abbott (previous page), you can use a camera to reveal something unique about a person. Learn more about taking photographs, and create your own photo essay.

Learn About It Read through the owner's manual of your camera to familiarize yourself with its features. If you are using a 35-mm camera, learn about the effects of film speed, f-stop, and aperture. Get the help of an experienced user of the camera if necessary.

Experiment To get to know your camera well, take lots of photos under different conditions—for example, pictures of an object at various distances in various lighting. Keep a log of the conditions under which you took each shot and the results they produced.

Creating Meanings Different uses of the camera create different meanings. For example, a picture taken on a sunny day creates a different effect from one taken on a cloudy day. See the sidebar for other ways in which pictures create meaning.

Apply It Take a series of photographs that reveal something about a family member or friend. Choose objects, places, and events that tell something about the person, and photograph the person in connection with them. Use a chart like the one below to plan your pictures. Display your results to the class.

Aspect of Person	Type of Photograph	Special Considerations
Dad coaches baseball.	Action Shot	• Take the picture on a sunny day. • Show players to make clear what the event is. • To make Dad's role clear, I should take a picture of him correcting somebody's batting stance.

Types of Images

Action Shot
A shot of a person performing a specific action. The photograph must include enough background to make the circumstances clear.

Portrait
A close-up of a person or his or her face. The person's pose can suggest a great deal about him or her. A person looking directly at the camera may appear frank and friendly; a person staring off to the side or out a window may appear thoughtful or moody.

Still Life
A shot of a group of objects. A still life is generally an exercise in composition (the arrangement of objects for effect). It can also be used to show something about the owner of the objects.

Standardized Test Preparation Workshop

Using Narration to Respond to Writing Prompts

The writing prompts on standardized tests often measure your ability to write a narrative or to use elements of narrative writing for a specific purpose. The following are the criteria upon which such writing will be evaluated:

- Organizes details in a meaningful and coherent sequence.

- Tailors word choice and style to the purpose and audience named in the response. For example, a letter to the school board should be more formal than one to a friend.

- Uses appropriate transitions to create a unified, coherent narrative.

- Elaborates on events with the effective use of description, characterization, and other details.

- Uses correct grammar, spelling, and punctuation.

Following is an example of a writing prompt that requires you to use elements of narrative writing. Use the suggestions on the following page to help you respond. The clocks show the suggested percentage of your test-taking time to devote to each stage.

Test Tip

Before drafting, jot down a list of supporting details. Then, choose the strongest details to include in your narrative.

Sample Writing Situation

> Extracurricular activities are an important part of middle school. Often, they require so much time and dedication that, if you are not careful, your grades can suffer. Think about your experiences balancing school work and outside commitments, and then respond to the following prompt.
>
> > Your school has just added your favorite extracurricular activity to the after-school program. You are already involved in two other activities but don't want to miss this opportunity. Your parents are concerned that you are involved in too many activities outside school. Write a letter to your parents in which you persuade them that you are responsible enough to participate in these activities and maintain good grades. To support your position, include accounts of past situations in which you successfully took on responsibility.

Prewriting

Allow close to one fourth of your time for prewriting.

Gather Details Begin to gather information about your experiences with responsibility. Using the strategy of listing and itemizing, focus on examples in which you successfully handled a few responsibilities at the same time. (To see the steps for listing and itemizing, refer to page 55.)

Consider Your Audience and Purpose As you begin to gather details for your narrative, keep in mind the audience and purpose indicated in the prompt—persuading your parents. A respectful tone is appropriate, but you may be less formal than if you were writing to a stranger.

Drafting

Allow almost half of your time for drafting.

Organization After you have gathered details, make an outline to organize them. Each story you tell to support your main idea should be organized in chronological order. Alternatively, you may introduce each story by summarizing the most important aspect, presenting less important details later. If you present more than one story, save the story that makes the strongest case for last.

Introduction, Body, and Conclusion After organizing details, begin drafting. Start off with an introductory paragraph that uses an example, an exaggeration, or another attention-grabbing device to establish your purpose in writing. In the body paragraphs, tell the stories that establish your capacity for responsibility. Connect each to your main purpose. Finally, sum up your letter by restating your evidence and what it supports.

Revising, Editing, and Proofreading

Allow almost one fourth of your time to revise and edit. Use the last few minutes to proofread your work.

Strengthen Your Case Review your draft. Neatly add in details to strengthen your persuasive case. Cross out any details that do not support your purpose. Change language that is inappropriately infomal for your audience. Add transitions where necessary to keep ideas flowing smoothly.

Make Corrections Check for errors in spelling, grammar, and punctuation. When making changes, place one line through text that you want to eliminate and enclose it in brackets. Use a caret (^) to indicate the places at which you want to add words.

Narration
Short Story

Early Carolina Morning, 1978, Romare Bearden, ©Romare Bearden Foundation/Licensed by VAGA, New York, NY

Short Stories in Everyday Life

Even if you've never *written* a story, you've probably *told* many stories. Perhaps you've made up a bedtime story to tell a younger brother. Maybe you've amused friends with the tale of the night you found a bat flying around your bedroom.

Storytelling comes naturally to us. The first stories were probably told around campfires, but these days stories are told around kitchen or cafeteria tables—or even passed around by e-mail. Every year, thousands of stories are published in books and magazines.

In this chapter, you'll learn strategies for writing a short story that captures your readers' interest—and may even take them somewhere they've never been before.

▲ **Critical Viewing**
What story do you imagine this painting is "telling"? **[Speculate]**

What Is a Short Story?

A **short story** is a brief, creative narrative— a retelling of events arranged to hold a reader's attention. From the Arctic tundra to a steamy rain forest, a short story can send you places you've never been. By letting you enter the lives of its characters, a short story reminds you that you can always be more than who you are today.

Most short stories include

- one or more characters (the people, animals, or other creatures involved in the story).

- a conflict or problem that keeps the reader asking, "What will happen next?"

- a beginning that introduces the characters and setting and establishes the conflict.

- a middle in which the story reaches a high point—usually, some type of conflict.

- an ending in which the conflict is resolved and loose ends are tied up.

To learn the criteria on which your short story may be evaluated, see the Rubric for Self-Assessment on page 89.

Types of Short Stories

The following are some of the different kinds of short stories:

- **Realistic stories** take place in familiar neighborhoods with people just like the ones you know.

- **Fantasy and science-fiction stories** take you to worlds that exist only in the mind—a far-off galaxy or a future Earth.

- **Adventure stories** immerse you in exciting action played out by larger-than-life heroes.

Writers in ACTION

Ray Bradbury has been writing science fiction since he was a high-school student in the 1930's and has published more than 500 short stories. Here is what he has said about how he gets the ideas for his stories:

"My stories run up and bite me in the leg—I respond by writing down everything that goes on during the bite. When I finish, the idea lets go and runs off."

PREVIEW Student Work IN PROGRESS

In this chapter, you'll see how Elisabeth Laskey, a student at Gray-New Gloucester Middle School in Gray, Maine, developed her short story "Showing Amanda the Ropes." You'll follow her work in progress, including the strategies she used to come up with a topic and revise her first draft. At the end of the chapter, you'll read her finished short story.

Isaac Asimov (1920–1992) was celebrated for his science-fiction and detective stories, as well as for his popular accounts of science.

Reading Writing Connection

Reading Strategy: Interpret

As you read, **interpret,** or restate the meaning of what you have read. Ask yourself: Why did this event happen? Why did the writer add that detail? For example, in "Sarah Tops," you might restate the significance of the narrator's decision not to linger at the museum as follows: The narrator is smart and responsible. You can also interpret the writer's decision to add this detail: He wants the reader to sympathize with the narrator.

▲ **Critical Viewing**
Citing details from this photograph, explain whether a museum seems a likely place for a crime. **[Infer]**

Sarah Tops

Isaac Asimov

I came out of the Museum of Natural History and was crossing the street on my way to the subway, when I saw the crowd about halfway down the block; and the police cars, too. I could hear the whine of an approaching ambulance.

For a minute I hesitated, but then I walked on. The crowds of the curious just get in the way of officials trying to save lives. My Dad, who's a detective on the force, complains about that all the time, and I wasn't going to add to the difficulty myself.

I just kept my mind on the term paper I was going to have to write on air-pollution for my seventh-grade class and mentally arranged the notes I had taken on the Museum program on the subject.

Of course, I knew I would read about it in the afternoon papers. Besides, I would ask Dad about it after dinner. Sometimes he

The opening paragraph draws the reader in by presenting signs of excitement without any explanation.

By revealing the narrator's thoughts, the writer shows the narrator's character —he is responsible and intelligent.

talked about cases without giving too much of the real security details. And Mom and I never talk about what we hear, anyway.

After I asked, Mom looked kind of funny and said, "He was in the museum at the very time."

I said, "I was working on my term paper. I was there first thing in the morning."

Mom looked worried. "There might have been shooting in the museum."

"Well, there wasn't," said Dad soothingly. "This man tried to lose himself in the museum and he didn't succeed."

"I would have," I said. "I know the museum, every inch."

Dad doesn't like me boasting, so he frowned at me. "The thugs who were after him didn't let him get away entirely. They caught up with him outside, knifed him, and got away. We'll catch them, though. We know who they are."

He nodded his head. "They're what's left of the gang that broke into that jewelry store two weeks ago. We managed to get the jewels back, but we didn't grab all the men. And not all the jewels either. One diamond was left. A big one—worth thirty thousand dollars."

"Maybe that's what the killers were after," I said.

"Very likely. The dead man was probably trying to cross the other two and get off with that one stone for himself. They turned out his pockets, practically ripped off his clothes, after they knifed him."

"Did they get the diamond?" I asked.

"How can we tell? The woman who reported the killing came on him when he was just barely able to breathe. She said he said three words to her, very slowly. 'Try. . . Sarah . . . Tops.' Then he died."

"Who is Sarah Tops?" asked Mom.

Dad shrugged. "I don't know. I don't even know if that's really what he said. The woman was pretty hysterical. If she's right and that's what he said, then maybe the killers didn't get the diamond. Maybe the dead man left it with Sarah Tops, whoever she is. Maybe he knew he was dying and wanted to give it back and have it off his conscience."

"Is there a Sarah Tops in the phone book, Dad?" I asked.

Dad said, "Did you think we didn't look? No Sarah Tops, either one *P* or two *P*'s. Nothing in the city directory. Nothing in our files. Nothing in the FBI files."

Mom said, "Maybe it's not a person. Maybe it's a firm. Sarah Tops Cakes or something."

"Could be," said Dad. "There's no Sarah Tops firm, but there are other kinds of Tops and they'll be checked out for anyone working there named Sarah. It'll take days of dull routine."

These paragraphs are part of the exposition: They introduce us to the characters.

The author uses dialogue to give information and move the story along.

These paragraphs establish the conflict: The police need to locate the missing diamond, but the only clue they have is mysterious and confusing.

L̲I̲T̲E̲R̲A̲T̲U̲R̲E̲

To read another short story involving a mystery, see "The Third Level" by Jack Finney. You can find this short story in *Prentice Hall Literature: Timeless Voices, Timeless Themes, Bronze.*

I got an idea suddenly and bubbled over. "Listen, Dad, maybe it isn't a firm either. Maybe it's a *thing*. Maybe the woman didn't hear 'Sarah Tops' but 'Sarah's top'; you know, a *top* that you spin. If the dead guy has a daughter named Sarah, maybe he gouged a bit out of her top and stashed the diamond inside and . . ."

Dad pointed his finger at me and grinned. "Very good, Larry," he said. "A nice idea. But he doesn't have a daughter named Sarah. Or any relative by that name as far as we know. We've searched where he lived and there's nothing reported there that can be called a top."

"Well," I said, sort of let down and disappointed, "I suppose that's not such a good idea anyway, because why should he say we ought to try it? He either hid it in Sarah's top or he didn't. He would know which. Why should he say we should *try* it?"

And then it hit me. What if . . .

Dad was just getting up, as if he were going to turn on television, and I said, "Dad, can you get into the museum this time of evening?"

"On police business? Sure."

"Dad," I said, kind of breathless, "I think we better go look. *Now.* Before the people start coming in again."

"Why?"

"I've got a silly idea. I . . . I . . . "

Dad didn't push me. He likes me to have my own ideas. He thinks maybe I'll be a detective, too, some day. He said, "All right. Let's follow up your lead whatever it is."

He called the museum, then we took a taxi and got there just when the last purple bit of twilight was turning to black. We were let in by a guard.

I'd never been in the museum when it was dark. It looked like a huge, underground cave, with the guard's flashlight seeming to make things even darker and more mysterious.

We took the elevator up to the fourth floor where the big shapes loomed in the bit of light that shone this way and that as the guard moved his flash.

▶ **Critical Viewing** Name each meaning of the word *top* discussed in the story. Explain how the discussion of different possible meanings catches readers' interest and builds suspense. **[Analyze]**

As the narrator asks his father questions, the conflict is deepened. A few explanations of the clue have been checked, but no answer has turned up.

The narrator's clever explanation helps increase the tension. The reader wants him to solve the crime but is disappointed at this first attempt.

At the turning point, or climax, of the story, the reader's suspense is at its greatest. The narrator's unfinished sentence "What if . . ." begins the falling action.

Details such as the guard's use of a flashlight and the description of the fossils give the reader a vivid sense of the setting.

◀ **Critical Viewing**
How does Asimov "spell out" the name of one of the dinosaurs in this picture without giving away the ending? **[Summarize]**

"Do you want me to put on the light in the room?" he asked.

"Yes, please," I said.

There they all were. Some in glass cases; but the big ones in the middle of the large room. Bones and teeth and spines of giants that ruled the earth hundreds of millions of years ago.

"I want to look close at that one," I said. "Is it all right if I climb over the railing?"

"Go ahead," said the guard. He helped me.

I leaned against the platform, looking at the grayish plaster material the skeleton was standing on.

"What's this?" I said. It didn't look much different in color from the plaster on which it was lying.

"Chewing gum," said the guard, frowning. "Those darn kids . . . "

"The guy was trying to get away and he saw his chance to throw this . . . keep it away from *them* . . . ." Before I could finish my sentence Dad took the gum from me. He squeezed it, then pulled it apart. Something inside caught the light and flashed. Dad put it in an envelope. "How did you know?" he asked me.

"Well, look at it," I said.

It was a magnificent skeleton. It had a large skull with bone stretching back over the neck vertebrae. It had two horns over the eyes, and a third one, just a bump, on the snout. The nameplate said *Triceratops*.

At the resolution of the story, the narrator finds the diamond.

The resolution is completed with the explanation of the dying man's last words.

Reading Writing Connection

Writing Application: Help Your Readers Interpret As you write your short story, emphasize details that will help readers interpret your characters' personalities and actions. You can emphasize a detail by discussing it at length, or by leaving out key information about it so that a reader's curiosity will be aroused.

Prewriting

Choosing Your Topic

Writers like Ray Bradbury may wait for a story idea to "bite them on the leg" (see page 73), but most of us need specific strategies for finding a topic, such as the following:

Strategies for Generating a Topic

1. **Freewriting** Set a timer for five minutes, and write down anything that comes to mind. Afterward, choose the most interesting idea for a story.

2. **Magazine Flip-Through** Grab a pile of magazines, and flip through them, looking for photographs, articles, or ads that spark your interest—or your scorn. Use sticky notes to mark your finds. Later, review the flagged pages, and take notes on the most promising ideas for your story.

3. **Writing Round** Form a circle with three or four class-mates. One student begins by saying the first sentence of a story, and then each student adds another sentence, with one student writing it all down. Afterward, one student should read the story aloud. Use one of the details in the group story as a springboard for your own story.

Try it out! Use the interactive Writing Round model in **Section 5.2**, on-line or on CD-ROM.

Student Work
IN PROGRESS

Name: Elisabeth Laskey
Gray-New Gloucester Middle School
Gray, ME

Writing Round

These are the notes from a writing-round session that helped Elisabeth come up with the topic for her story.

Sam: It was the first week of August.

Eleanor: My family was going on vacation.

Ahmed: I was looking forward to it, but I knew I was going to miss my friends.

Elisabeth: So I asked my parents if I could invite my best friend to come with us.

Talking about summer vacation made Elisabeth remember a weekend trip to her aunt's cottage with her friend Amanda, and she decided to write a story about something that had happened while they were there.

TOPIC BANK

If you're having trouble finding a topic, consider the following possibilities:

1. **Your Own Life** A short story can be based on your own experiences. Choose an object in your room that brings back memories of an event or a person in your life. Write a story about this object and the experience it evokes. You might even tell the story from the object's point of view.

2. **Your Own Community** Write a fantasy story set in your community or school in the future. As you plan your story, think about what will be different in the future and what will stay the same.

Responding to Fine Art

3. Write a story based on this painting. Your story might be the tale you imagine the storyteller is telling. Alternatively, your story might use the setting and characters depicted in the painting.

Storyteller, Velino Shije Herrera, National Museum of American Art, Washington, DC

Responding to Literature

4. Read the poem "Mother to Son" by Langston Hughes. Write a short story telling what happened either before or after this mother spoke these words to her son. You can find "Mother to Son," as well as background information on the poet, in *Prentice Hall Literature: Timeless Voices, Timeless Themes,* Bronze.

✍ Cooperative Writing Opportunity

5. **Collaborative Story** After participating in a writing-round session (see page 78), have each member complete the story the group has begun. Have a group discussion about the differences among the stories. Determine which were the most successful elements in each story. Afterward, illustrate the stories, and bind them in a collection. Present the collection to the school library for display.

Developing Narrative Elements

The best stories just fly along. As you read a well-written story, you might forget you are turning pages—they may seem to turn themselves! The secret of all this movement is a kind of "story motor"—the conflict. By finding the conflict inside your story idea, you can get your story moving.

Identify Conflict

A **conflict** is a struggle between two opposing forces. A character's conflict may be *external*, as when a sheriff has a conflict with an outlaw, or *internal*, as when an outlaw struggles with his conscience.

Using a Conflict Diagram To identify the conflict in a story, ask yourself these questions:

1 What does the main character want?
2. Who or what is preventing that character from getting what he or she wants?

Use a conflict diagram to find answers to these questions. Here's one based on "Sarah Tops" by Isaac Asimov (see page 74):

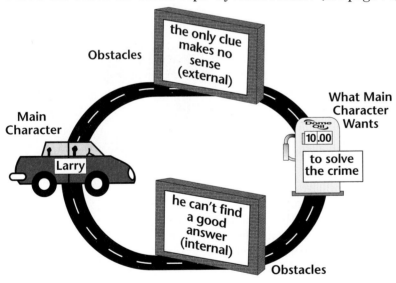

Considering Your Audience and Purpose

Your **audience**—who your readers are—should affect the details you include in your story. If your readers are other teenagers, they will probably understand a reference to a particular band. If you're writing for a wider audience, though, you will have to explain more about the band and its music.

Your **purpose** also affects the details you include. Consider whether you simply want to entertain or whether you also want to convey a theme—an insight or question about life.

Try it out! Use the interactive Conflict Diagram in **Section 5.2**, on-line or on CD-ROM.

Gathering Details

Your next step is to begin gathering details to include in your story. Here is a strategy that will help you get started:

Use Listing and Itemizing

To use the strategy of listing and itemizing, follow these steps:

1. Quickly jot down a list of everything that comes to mind about a general idea.
2. Circle the most interesting item on the list.
3. "Itemize" that item—create another list of everything that comes to mind about it.
4. After you've generated several lists in this way, look for connections among all the circled items on your lists. These connections will help you decide which details to include in your story.

▲ **Critical Viewing**
If this man was a character in a story, what kind of conflict— external or internal— do you imagine he would be experiencing? **[Analyze]**

LISTING AND ITEMIZING

a man is caught in a flood
a man is caught in a fire
a man is stranded on an island
a man is locked out of his house
a man is caught in an avalanche

the man nearly drowns
the man's dog nearly drowns
the man's house is nearly ruined

he's an inventor
he has invented something valuable
he has to finish building it before someone else creates it
the flood has destroyed most of his work

Drafting

Shaping Your Writing

Once you have come up with the main conflict in your story, you are ready to organize and draft.

Create a Plot

Begin by mapping out your plot. A **plot** is the arrangement of actions in the story, but it is more than a simple sequence. In most stories, the plot follows this pattern:

- The **exposition** introduces the main characters and their basic situation, including the central conflict.

- This **conflict** develops and intensifies during the rising action, which leads to

- the **climax** (the high point of suspense), followed by

- the story's **falling action,** which leads to

- the **resolution,** in which the conflict is resolved in some way (the good guy wins, a compromise is reached, and so on).

Using a Plot Diagram Map out the events in your story using a diagram like the one below. Refer to it as you draft.

Bland goes to the roof of Trampled Towers, where Dr. Morbid traps him in a giant net.

Dr. Morbid takes ad out in paper challenging Bland to a duel.

Introduce special agent Bland and setting (big city).

Just as the helicopter is dragging the net away, Bland appears by Dr. Morbid's side!

The two struggle.

Dr. Morbid makes his getaway, but not before Bland grabs his briefcase of secret plans.

Back at headquarters, Bland explains that he oiled himself thoroughly beforehand—he slipped right through the net!

Climax

Rising Action

Falling Action

Resolution

Exposition

← **Conflict Introduced**

Focusing on Conflict and Resolution As you write, make sure that the events you include help develop the story's conflict and create suspense about how that conflict will be resolved.

To help you work toward a resolution, expand the Conflict Diagram you created in the Prewriting section. Add a resolution box at the top. Brainstorm for an ending in which the main character overcomes or is defeated by the obstacle he or she faces.

Providing Elaboration
Use Details to Define Character and Setting

As you draft your story, try to make your characters and setting come to life by including vivid details.

Telling and Showing You can present setting or character traits and reactions directly by **telling** what a place or a character is like— "The ocean was pretty" or "Amanda was afraid."

It is often better to reveal characters and setting indirectly by **showing** what they are like. Instead of *telling* us that your character is happy, you can *show* that happiness through her light, skipping footsteps or her chirpy voice.

As you draft, pause occasionally, and review what you have written. Add details that reveal the mood of a place, what your characters look like, how they talk and act, what they think and feel, and how others react to them.

▼ Critical Viewing
Judging from this illustration, how is the conflict in this tall tale resolved? **[Interpret]**

from *Swamp Angel* by Anne Isaacs, illustrated by Paul O. Zelinsky, illustrations copyright ©1994 by Paul O. Zelinsky

Student Work
IN PROGRESS

Name: Elisabeth Laskey
Gray-New Gloucester Middle School
Gray, ME

Adding Characterizing Details
Elisabeth added characterizing details as she drafted.

"Of course! It'll be fun!" Amanda held the

worn rope in her hands.

"Okay, I'll just watch," I said, peering down

at the churning water far below.

Amanda's hands tightened on the rope as

she prepared to swing off. ~~Suddenly she was~~ Looking below, she gulped and hesitated.

~~afraid.~~ Now that we were on top, the bank

seemed higher and steeper, and a quick gust

of wind caused huge waves to crash toward

us.

Fear:
- gulping
- hesitation
- shaking

⑤.④ *Revising*

Revising Your Overall Structure

Build to a Climax

A good story builds to a single most exciting moment, called the **climax**. The secret of building to a climax is **pacing**—introducing important information or new twists at the right spots. To evaluate the pacing of your story, first consider this example:

SETTING THE RIGHT PACE

4. RESOLUTION: The two brothers defeat the thugs and return with the money and the thugs' treasure to their family.

3. CLIMAX: The family cannot pay the ransom. The young man worries that the thugs will soon find all the money. One of the thugs, though, is the hero's brother. He offers to help him.

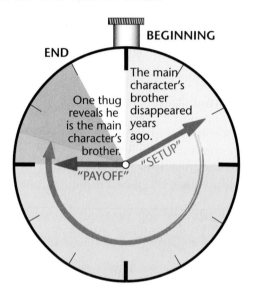

1. EXPOSITION: The hero must take all of his family's money out of the bank so the family can escape from a dangerous city. We learn that the hero's brother disappeared years ago.

2. RISING ACTION: On his way back from the bank, the hero is captured by thugs. The thugs hold him for ransom. He tries various ways to escape.

The reader learns at the beginning that the brother is missing. The early placement of this fact makes the ending believable. Notice, too, that the thug reveals his identity right at the climax. This placement adds surprise to the climax.

Evaluate the pacing of your own story, using this strategy:

▶ REVISION STRATEGY
Using Clues to Evaluate Pacing

To "time" the pacing of your story, take the following steps:
1. Mark the resolution of your story with the letter *R*.
2. Highlight the "setup" for the resolution (facts that make the resolution possible or believable—see diagram above).
3. In a second color, highlight the "payoff" (the point connecting the setup and the resolution—see diagram above).
4. Count paragraphs between the setup and the resolution. If there are too few, the setup may not seem believable.
5. Measure the distance between the payoff and the resolution. If it is too great, the story may drag.
6. Move your setup and payoff to the most effective spots.

Revising Your Paragraphs

Improve Characterization

Add details to bring characters to life. Use "Points to Illuminate" to find the best places to add information.

▶ **REVISION STRATEGY**
Using Points to Illuminate

Cut out a five-pointed star from construction paper. Label the points *appearance, actions, words, thoughts,* and *perceptions of others.*

Slide the star down your draft as you look for a place where your characters might "show themselves" more. Attach the star at such a place with a glue stick, and circle the point representing the kind of detail you will add. Repeat the process until you've read through your entire story. Then, go back and add the missing information.

Technology Tip

Your word-processing program may include a "track changes" function that highlights the inserts and cuts you've made. Use this function while revising, and you can decide later whether you want to "accept" or "reject" your first revisions.

Student Work IN PROGRESS

Name: *Elisabeth Laskey*
Gray-New Gloucester Middle School
Gray, ME

Using Points to Illuminate
Elisabeth used points to illuminate to improve her characterization of Amanda.

Suddenly two elderly couples appeared, one man holding a camera.

"Do you girls mind if we take a picture of you jumping from a rope?" asked the gentleman with the camera.

Amanda gave me a quick glance. ⋀"Sure, why not?" ~~Amanda said.~~ she quavered.⋀ The pressure was on.

She clutched the rope, and tension seemed to swell over her body. Every eye focused on her. She stood boldly, but⋀ I saw the fear in her eyes. A sidelong glance told me that she would welcome a way out.⋀

appearance
others *actions*
thoughts *words*

appearance
others *actions*
thoughts *words*

Revising Your Sentences

Combine Sentences for Variety

Writing too many short sentences in a row will produce a "choppy" effect. To avoid choppiness and create a smoother, more varied writing style, combine related sentences. Here are some simple techniques:

Add a coordinating conjunction (*and, but, for, nor, or,* or *yet*).

CHOPPY: I knew Cassie was my friend. I had no idea just how loyal she was.

COMBINED: I knew Cassie was my friend, **but** I had no idea just how loyal she was.

Use a subordinating conjunction, such as *when* or *because*.

CHOPPY: I heard the disappointment in Sam's voice. I knew he couldn't go to the movies.

COMBINED: **When** I heard the disappointment in Sam's voice, I knew he couldn't go to the movies.

Cross out repeated words and phrases.

CHOPPY: My mom said we could go to the park. ~~She said we could go to the park~~ in an hour.

COMBINED: My mom said we could go to the park in an hour.

Use a clause that begins with *who, which,* or *that*.

CHOPPY: We went to a beautiful beach. The beach has huge white dunes.

COMBINED: We went to a beautiful beach **that** has huge white dunes.

▶ **REVISION STRATEGY**
Using a "Spy Camera"

Cut a 1-inch by 2-inch window in an index card to create a "spy camera." Then, slide the camera around your draft, framing each paragraph in turn. Underline the sentences in each in alternating colors. Use the lengths of the lines to evaluate sentence length and revise as needed. Finally, think of a way to combine at least two of the sentences in each cluster.

Learn More

To learn more about subordinating conjunctions, see Chapter 20.

▼ **Critical Viewing**
In two short sentences, describe what's going on in this picture. Then, combine your sentences, using one of the techniques explained on this page. **[Analyze]**

Revising Your Word Choice
Use Vivid Verbs

You can keep your story exciting by using vivid verbs. Replace colorless verbs like *said*, *was*, and *went* with strong, colorful verbs like *quavered*, *radiated*, and *rocketed*.

▶ **REVISION STRATEGY**
Circling Verbs

Circle the first ten verbs in your story. Evaluate whether each verb vividly expresses your meaning. Replace any over-used verbs with vivid ones.

Peer Review

Highlight Passages

Read your draft aloud twice to a group of classmates, pausing after the first reading. Before the second reading, ask the group to write down any passages that they like or that they want to know more about. Afterward, take their comments. Underline passages they like, and highlight those they want to know more about. Consider their feedback as you revise.

Text

Get instant help! For more on action verbs, see the instruction in **Section 15.1**, on-line or on CD-ROM.

Grammar in Your Writing
Identifying Action Verbs

A **verb** is a word that expresses an action or a state of being. Every sentence includes at least one verb that tells us something about the subject of the sentence. An **action verb** tells what action the subject is doing.

Physical/Visible Actions		Mental Actions	
run	walk	remember	believe
jump	slide	wish	wonder
breathe	float	think	hope
hide	bang	want	worry
tremble	hug	study	dream

Find It in Your Reading Find three action verbs in "Sarah Tops" by Isaac Asimov on page 74. For each action verb, name the subject that is performing the action.

Find It in Your Writing Underline five action verbs in your story. If you can't find five different action verbs, consider whether you've overused certain verbs, and find replacements if necessary.

To learn more about verbs, see Chapter 15.

Editing
and Proofreading

Errors in spelling, punctuation, grammar, and usage are just as important to eliminate in a short story as they are in other forms of writing.

Focusing on Dialogue

As you proofread your story, pay close attention to the correct punctuation of **dialogue**—a character's speech.

Grammar in Your Writing
Punctuating Dialogue

When you write **dialogue,** you present words exactly as the character would say them. Here are some guidelines for punctuating dialogue:

Enclose dialogue in quotation marks.

"I'm taking an acting class on Thursdays," Yuki told me.

Don't use quotation marks when you report only the general meaning of a character's speech, not the exact words.

Yuki told me she was taking an acting class on Thursdays.

If dialogue comes *after* the words announcing speech, use a comma before the quote.

Max whispered, "I have no idea where the ruby ring could be."

If dialogue comes *before* the words announcing speech, use a comma, question mark, or exclamation point at the end of the quote—never a period.

"I have no idea where the ruby ring could be," whispered Max.

"I have no idea where the ruby ring could be!" screamed Max.

"Do you think Mr. Collins stole it?" asked Max.

Find It in Your Reading Find three examples of dialogue in "Sarah Tops" by Isaac Asimov on page 74. Explain why each is punctuated as it is.

Find It in Your Writing Highlight each instance of dialogue in your story, and circle the words announcing speech. Correct the punctuation if necessary.

To learn more about punctuating dialogue, see Chapter 26.

5.6 Publishing and Presenting

Building Your Portfolio

Here are some ideas for presenting your short story:

1. **Submit Your Story** Submit your story to a school literary magazine, a national publication, an on-line journal, or a contest. (See page 8 for suggestions, or ask your teacher or librarian.)

2. **Give a Reading** Read your story aloud to your class or to a group of friends. Prepare posters announcing your reading, and distribute signed copies of your story at the event.

Reflecting on Your Writing

Jot down your thoughts on the experience of writing a short story. Begin by answering these questions:

- Based on your own writing experience, what advice would you give another student who is about to write a story?

- Has writing your own short story changed your experience reading short stories written by others? Explain.

 Internet Tip

To read a short story scored according to this rubric, go on-line: PHSchool.com Enter Web Code: ebk-7001

Rubric for Self-Assessment

Use the following criteria to evaluate your short story.

	Score 4	Score 3	Score 2	Score 1
Audience and Purpose	Contains an engaging introduction; successfully entertains or presents a theme	Contains a somewhat engaging introduction; entertains or presents a theme	Contains an introduction; attempts to entertain or to present a theme	Begins abruptly or confusingly; leaves purpose unclear
Organization	Creates an interesting, clear narrative; told from a consistent point of view	Presents a clear sequence of events; told from a specific point of view	Presents a mostly clear sequence of events; contains inconsistent points of view	Presents events without logical order; lacks a consistent point of view
Elaboration	Provides insight into character; develops plot; contains dialogue	Contains details and dialogue that develop character and plot	Contains details that develop plot; contains some dialogue	Contains few or no details to develop characters or plot
Use of Language	Uses word choice and tone to reveal story's theme; contains no errors in grammar, punctuation, or spelling	Uses interesting and fresh word choices; contains few errors in grammar, punctuation, and spelling	Uses some clichés and trite expressions; contains some errors in grammar, punctuation, and spelling	Uses uninspired word choices; has many errors in grammar, punctuation, and spelling

FINAL DRAFT

View of Bear Island Harbor, c. 1950, Fairfield Porter, Courtesy Martha Parrish & James Reinish, Inc., New York

Showing Amanda the Ropes

Elisabeth Laskey
Gray-New Gloucester Middle School
Gray, Maine

Hopping off the boat, I skipped up the wharf ahead of my best friend, Amanda, eager to give her the experience of a lifetime. We were here on Bustin's Island to spend the weekend at my aunt's cottage. This was Amanda's first time on a Maine ocean island, but it wasn't mine. I had been here many times before, and I was prepared to show her the ropes.

Elisabeth's first paragraph grabs the reader's interest. It is also part of her exposition. She tells us who the two main characters are and establishes the story's setting.

Amanda had always been the quiet, shy type, but on that weekend I saw a different side of her. Who would have ever thought that Amanda would be teaching me the ropes?

It was late afternoon on our second day there, and the sun was beating down with fiery fists. Amanda and I were sitting on the dock, just listening to the calm lapping of waves against the shore. Suddenly, peals of laughter and loud splashing broke the serenity.

On the next beach, three teenage boys were taking turns swinging from a steep bank by a rope tied to an overhanging tree. At the farthest point from the shore, they would drop to the ocean at least ten feet below.

"Hey, that looks like fun!" Amanda exclaimed. She watched excitedly as a tall, lanky boy swayed in the breeze and hurtled toward the water with his arms and legs flailing wildly. I had to admit that it did look like a lot of fun. I knew it was safe, because my aunt had told my cousin he could jump there.

"Maybe they'll let us take a turn," Amanda said hopefully. She seemed fascinated by the whole idea. I didn't believe those boys would actually let us use their rope, but we could ask, anyway.

With swimsuits on, we made our way over to the next beach, but by the time we got there, the guys had left.

"Good! Now we have it all to ourselves," she said cheerfully. With that, she began climbing, and I followed her to the top of the bank.

"Are you sure you really want to do this?" I asked.

"Of course! It'll be fun!" Amanda held the worn rope in her hands.

"Okay, I'll just watch," I said, peering down at the churning water far below.

Amanda's hands tightened on the rope as she prepared to swing off. Looking below, she gulped and hesitated. Now that we were on top, the bank seemed higher and steeper, and a quick gust of wind caused huge waves to crash toward us.

Suddenly two elderly couples appeared, one man holding a camera.

"Do you girls mind if we take a picture of you jumping from the rope?" asked the gentleman with the camera.

Amanda gave me a quick glance. "Sure, why not?" she quavered. The pressure was on.

She clutched the rope, and tension seemed to swell over her body. Every eye focused on her. She stood boldly, but I saw the fear in her eyes. A sidelong glance told me that she would welcome a way out.

Here, the narrator's question helps "set up" the story's climax.

The vivid verb *beating*—and the image of the sun as an angry person—help the reader picture the scene.

These details of setting help create the story's conflict.

Elisabeth uses dialogue to show character and move the action along.

Here's the story's conflict: Amanda wants to jump but must first overcome her fear. Her conflict is internal. We also learn about her character: She appears easygoing but takes on more than she can handle.

The writer presents several details—including Amanda's appearance, speech, and the narrator's perceptions—that reveal her fear and her desire to seem bold.

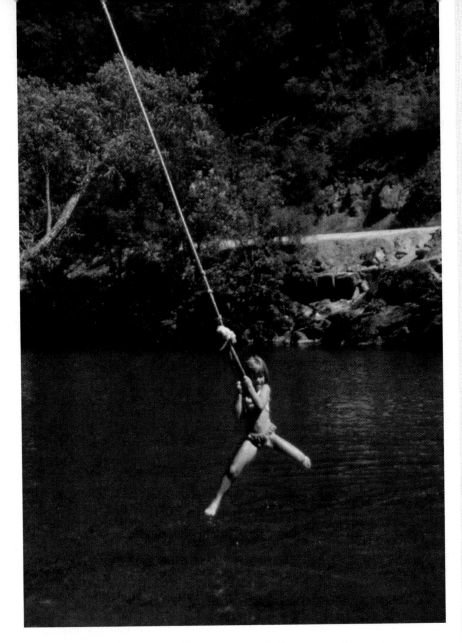

◄ **Critical Viewing**
How would you feel
in this situation?
Compare your prob-
able feelings with
Amanda's.
[Compare]

She froze. The awkward moments of silence made everyone uneasy. Finally the tourists grew impatient and began to walk away.

"Wait!" Amanda called to them.

In a sudden spring of action, she gripped the rope and glided off the rock. Sailing through the air, she held her head high. At just the right moment she let go of the rope and fell into the water with a mighty splash. When her head reappeared, I saw a smile of triumph spread across her face.

She did it! I couldn't help but smile. My timid friend had conquered her fear and taken the risk. Amanda had more courage than I had ever imagined, and I admired her.

Amanda's "frozen moment" heightens tension, building toward a climax.

Here, at the climax of the story, the reader's curiosity about what will happen next is highest. The resolution follows in the very next paragraph—Amanda jumps!

Connected Assignment *Dramatic Scene*

Like a short story, a drama presents a narrative. A dramatic script is a guide for actors to act out a story. Elements of drama include

• dialogue—or speech—for one or more characters.

• directions, when needed, for how the characters speak, where they are on stage, and what actions they perform.

Prewriting Imagine two characters who are in conflict. Write down important details about each character, and write a brief description of their conflict.

MODEL

from **The Monsters Are Due on Maple Street**
Rod Serling

In this passage, notice how stage directions and the identity of each speaker are set off from the spoken dialogue:

[*The people stare at* STEVE. *He stands for a moment by the car, then walks toward the group.*]

STEVE. I don't understand it. It was working fine before . . .

DON. Out of gas?

STEVE. [*Shakes his head*] I just had it filled up.

▲ **Critical Viewing** Are these men having a friendly conversation, or are they in conflict? Point out details justifying your answer. **[Evaluate]**

Drafting Note where your characters are and what activity they are engaged in. As you draft, "overhear" their conversation in your mind and write out what each says. Then, go back and add directions specifying how lines should be spoken; what the scenery is like; what actions characters perform, and so on.

Revising and Editing Read the draft of your scene aloud. Revise lines that do not sound as though your characters would say them, or that do not express the characters' situations and attitudes forcefully enough.

Publishing and Presenting With a classmate, act out your dialogue for the class.

Spotlight on the Humanities

Analyzing Themes Across Cultures

Focus on Oral Tradition: Scheherazade

You may have enjoyed writing one short story, but imagine having to tell a new one every night for a thousand and one nights! According to legend, Scheherazade does exactly that.

The sultan Shahriyar plans to execute Scheherazade. Scheherazade, though, tells the sultan a cliff-hanging story every night. Eager to hear the ending of the story, he puts off the execution by a day in exchange for Scheherazade's promise to continue the tale on the following night. In this way, Scheherazade saves her life (and shows the power of a good story). The tales she tells, as well as the story of her telling them, are known as *The Thousand and One Nights* or *The Arabian Nights' Entertainment.*

Scheherazade's colorful stories existed in the Middle East as early as the ninth century. Originally, they were passed from one teller to another. Eventually, they were copied down. Their origins vary: Indian, Persian, Egyptian, Arabian, and Turkish influences weave through the work. These tales have given the world such familiar characters as Sinbad the Sailor, Ali Baba and the forty thieves, and Aladdin and his magic lamp.

Ballet   Russian choreographer Michel Fokine created the ballet *Scheherazade* in 1910 for the famous producer of dance, Sergey Diaghilev.

Music   Composer Nikolay Rimsky-Korsakov of Russia created his symphonic suite *Scheherazade* in 1888. It is considered one of the most popular orchestral works ever written. Rimsky-Korsakov uses **leitmotif**—the repetition of melodic elements—to create his musical pictures.

Narrative Writing Activity: Tale for a Character

Listen to an excerpt from Rimsky-Korsakov's *Scheherazade*, taking notes on images it conjures up in your mind. Using these notes, write a tale involving a character from the tales.

▲ Critical Viewing
What mood does this painting of the ballet *Scheherazade* create? **[Interpret]**

▼ Critical Viewing
What themes in *The Arabian Nights' Entertainment* might have interested composer Rimsky-Korsakov? **[Speculate]**

Media and Technology Skills

Analyzing Visual Meanings

Activity: Follow Events in Animated Cartoons

A cartoon may be goofy, but it includes the same elements as a short story—character, setting, theme, and plot. To appreciate cartoons, learn about the storytelling techniques they use.

Think About It Cartoonists use many special storytelling devices to "jump" between events, including the following:

- **Cutting Between Viewpoints** A cartoon can create interest by making a sudden shift from one point of view to another. For example, a superhero rushes to save a child. Suddenly, the screen flashes to a villain leaving a bank with a large bag in his hand. The viewer realizes that while the hero was saving the child, she did not see the villain rob the bank.

- **Cliffhanger** Just at the moment when it appears that the hero is about to meet his doom, the screen flashes to show the search party looking for him. The viewer doesn't find out until later what happened to the hero. This device creates suspense.

- **Flashback** While a character in the present tells a story or reminisces about the past, the cartoon may "flashback" to the past, showing you past events as if they were occurring in the present.

- **Farcical Rhythm** Some cartoons jump from one scene to another in which a character tries to outwit a goofy hero and is instead outwitted. A cartoonist will generally "one-up" each scene with the next. That is, if the first scene involves a small explosion, the next will involve a larger explosion. The second scene might move at a faster pace than the first. In the zaniest cartoons, the final scenes take place at lightning speed, with characters trading places or moving from victory to defeat in dizzying alternation.

Your Turn As you watch a cartoon, complete a chart like the one shown. Then, using the chart, write an analysis explaining the storytelling devices the cartoon used. Evaluate the effectiveness of each.

Tips for Analyzing Events in a Cartoon
- Identify the relationship between characters. Which one is the hero and which is the villain? Which one is the frustrated hunter and which is the fool he or she never catches?
- In zany repetitive cartoons, pay attention to the differences between scenes. Does the frustration of one character build? Does the "cleverness" of his or her attacks increase? Does the pacing grow more frenzied?

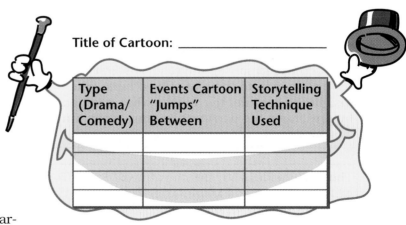

Title of Cartoon: _____

Type (Drama/ Comedy)	Events Cartoon "Jumps" Between	Storytelling Technique Used

Standardized Test Preparation Workshop

Responding to Prompts About Short Stories

Learning how the elements of a short story work together will help you write about short stories. Some standardized tests require you to write a short response to a story you have read. Before responding to a test prompt on a short story, think about the following elements of the story:

- **Plot** is the sequence of events in the story, arranged to catch your interest and maintain suspense.

- **Characters** are the people, animals, or other beings that take part in the story's action.

- **Setting** is the time and place in which the events occur.

- **Theme** is the message about life that the story conveys.

As you read the story, think about how each element helps create an effective short story. As you write, concentrate on creating a unified response in which you use details from the story to respond to the prompt.

Choose one of the following sample prompts for the short story "Sarah Tops" on page 74, and write a short response. Use the suggestions on the following page to help you respond. (The clocks show the suggested percentage of your test-taking time to devote to each stage.)

Test Tip

Look over the test questions before you read a passage. That way, you will know to which details you should pay special attention as you read.

Sample Writing Situation

In "Sarah Tops," the main interest of the plot is whether the narrator succeeds in solving the case. His first few guesses are wrong or have already been thought of by others. When he has his final insight, he does not tell anyone what it is right away. Explain how, by presenting the narrator's insight in this way, the author creates suspense.

The reader sides with the narrator of "Sarah Tops," hoping that he will solve the case. Explain what facts about the narrator make him an appealing character. Pay special attention to his relationship with his father. Explain how, if his attitude toward his father or his father's treatment of him were different, the reader might think he was just a "know-it-all."

Prewriting

Allow nearly one fourth of your time for prewriting.

Map Out Story Details Identify the element of the story on which the prompt focuses. Then, use a graphic organizer to gather details about this element. For instance, if the prompt asks about plot, use a plot diagram. (To see an example of a plot diagram, refer to page 82.) If the prompt asks about a character, you might use a cluster diagram.

Select Important Details Review your notes and reread the prompt. Then, circle details in your notes that will help you to respond. For instance, if you chose the prompt about the narrator's character, you might circle your note about his concern to stay out of the way of the police: It shows that he has self-control.

Drafting

Allow almost half of your time for drafting.

Outline Your Response Review your notes, and jot down a brief outline organizing your main points in logical order. If you are discussing plot, chronological order (the order in which events occur) might be the best choice. If you are discussing character, order of importance (from least to most important characteristics) might be an effective choice.

Elaborate After organizing details, begin drafting. Make sure that you state each of your main points clearly. For each main point, offer as many supporting illustrations or examples from the story as you can. At the same time, make sure you clearly show the connection of each detail to the prompt.

Revising, Editing, and Proofreading

Allow almost one fourth of your time to revise and edit. Use the last few minutes to proofread your work.

Strengthen Your Introduction and Conclusion Reread your introduction and conclusion. Make sure each includes a clear statement of the topic of your paper. This statement should reflect the prompt to which you are responding.

Strengthen Support Review each paragraph in your draft. Add any support you need to provide for each main point. Consider deleting paragraphs for which you cannot find supporting details.

Make Corrections Check for errors in spelling, grammar, and punctuation. When making changes, place one line through text you are deleting. Use a caret (^) to indicate where you are adding words.

Description

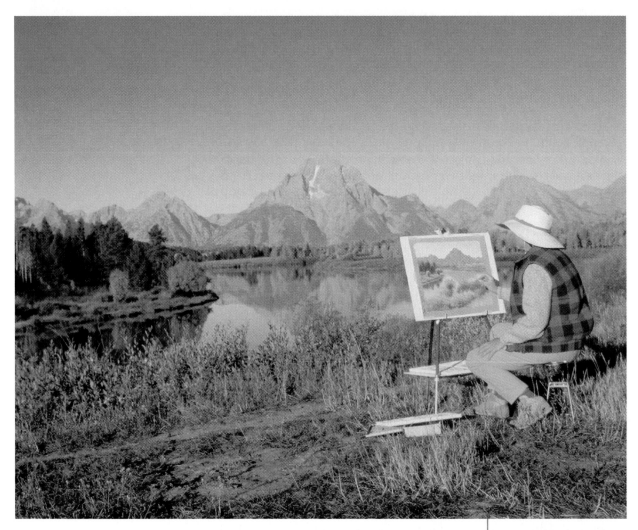

Description in Everyday Life

When you talk with your friends and family, you naturally describe things—a spectacular play on the soccer field, the sound of a musical group, the taste of a food you like or dislike, or the way the weather makes you feel.

As you talk, your words, gestures, and tone of voice blend together to create an impression of what you have seen, heard, tasted, touched, or smelled. When you write a description, however, you must rely on words alone. Just as an artist uses paint to create a picture, a writer uses words to create a description. By choosing your words well, you can help a reader to experience in his or her imagination what you have experienced in your own life.

▲ **Critical Viewing**
What words would you use to describe the scene that the artist is painting? **[Connect]**

What Is Descriptive Writing?

Descriptive writing creates a picture of a person, place, thing, or event. Like a painting, descriptive writing opens a door for a reader's imagination. Through that door might come the steam of savory dishes, the rattle of pot lids, or the "skritchy" rasp of a scouring pad. It might also let through a writer's wonder at a sunrise or gloom when it rains. Most descriptive writing includes

- vivid sensory details—details appealing to one or more of the five senses.
- a clear, consistent organization.
- links between sensory details and the feelings or thoughts they inspire.
- a main impression to which each detail adds.

To learn the criteria on which your description will be assessed, see the Rubric for Self-Assessment on page 115.

Types of Descriptive Writing

Your descriptive writing may be one of several types:

- **Descriptions of people or places** portray the physical appearance of a person or place and show readers why the subject is important or special.
- **Remembrances** capture a memorable experience in the writer's life; they may describe a specific moment or a longer period of time.
- **Observations** describe an event that the writer has personally witnessed.
- **Vignettes** capture a single moment in the writer's life, painting a picture with words.

Writers in
ACTION

Will Hobbs's novels, such as **Bearstone,** *are rich with descriptions of the outdoors. As he writes, Hobbs draws on his personal experiences hiking in the wild country of Alaska and in the mountains of Colorado and California. He realizes the power of using sensory details:*

"Descriptive writing is really using the five senses. When you write with the five senses, your description becomes real."

PREVIEW
Student Work
IN PROGRESS

Kaitlin Crockett, a student at Baypoint Middle School in St. Petersburg, Florida, wrote a description of her grandparents' house. In this chapter, you will see her work in progress, including the strategies she used to choose her topic, to organize details, and to revise her work. You'll find her finished description at the end of this chapter.

In his short story "Luke Baldwin's Vow," Morley Callaghan uses descriptive writing to create memorable characters. In this excerpt, Callaghan creates a picture of Uncle Henry using sensory details as well as descriptions of Henry's behavior and interactions with others.

▲ **Critical Viewing**
What details appealing to the senses would you include in a description of the place in this picture? **[Analyze]**

Reading Writing Connection

Reading Strategy: Infer A writer does not spell out all the information you need to know about a character. To understand a character fully, **make inferences,** or draw conclusions, based on the details the writer provides. For instance, knowing that Luke is mindful of his promise to his father, you might make the inference that he is a serious boy.

Luke Baldwin's Vow

Morley Callaghan

That summer when twelve-year-old Luke Baldwin came to live with his Uncle Henry in the house on the stream by the sawmill, he did not forget that he had promised his dying father he would try to learn things from his uncle: so he used to watch him very carefully.

Uncle Henry, who was the manager of the sawmill, was a big, burly man weighing more than two hundred and thirty pounds, and he had a rough-skinned, brick-colored face. He looked like a powerful man, but his health was not good. He had aches and pains in his back and shoulders which puzzled the doctor. The first thing Luke learned about Uncle Henry was that everybody

LITERATURE

For other examples of descriptive writing, see the poem "Fog" by Carl Sandburg and the poem "Four Skinny Trees" by Sandra Cisneros in *Prentice Hall Literature: Timeless Voices, Timeless Themes,* Bronze.

had great respect for him. The four men he employed in the sawmill were always polite and attentive when he spoke to them. His wife, Luke's Aunt Helen, a kindly, plump, straightforward woman, never argued with him. "You should try and be like your Uncle Henry," she would say to Luke. "He's so wonderfully practical. He takes care of everything in a sensible, easy way."

Luke used to trail around the sawmill after Uncle Henry not only because he liked the fresh clean smell of the newly cut wood and the big piles of sawdust, but because he was impressed by his uncle's precise, firm tone when he spoke to the men.

Sometimes Uncle Henry would stop and explain to Luke something about a piece of timber. "Always try and learn the essential facts, son," he would say. "If you've got the facts, you know what's useful and what isn't useful, and no one can fool you."

He showed Luke that nothing of value was ever wasted around the mill. Luke used to listen, and wonder if there was another man in the world who knew so well what was needed and what ought to be thrown away. Uncle Henry had known at once that Luke needed a bicycle to ride to his school, which was two miles away in town, and he bought him a good one. He knew that Luke needed good, serviceable clothes. He also knew exactly how much Aunt Helen needed to run the house, the price of everything, and how much a woman should be paid for doing the family washing. In the evenings Luke used to sit in the living room watching his uncle making notations in a black notebook which he always carried in his vest pocket, and he knew that he was assessing the value of the smallest transaction that had taken place during the day.

> *This description is organized in order of importance. It moves from physical details about Uncle Henry to deeper insights into his character.*

> *The writer links sensory details to the feelings they inspire in Luke.*

> *These details contribute to the reader's main impression—Uncle Henry is a strong, solid character, a little larger than life.*

◆ *Reading* ▶ *Writing* ◆ *Connection* **Writing Application: Help Your Readers Make Inferences** As you draft your description, include details that will help readers make inferences about the feelings you connect with the person, place, or object you describe.

▶ **Critical Viewing** Find two details in this photograph that match the description of Uncle Henry. **[Connect]**

6.2 Prewriting

Choosing Your Topic

You will find it easiest to describe an event, person, or place that has special meaning for you. To uncover your special topic, use these strategies:

Strategies for Generating a Topic

1. **Freewriting** Set a clock for five minutes. Then, write whatever comes to mind. You might want to start with a general idea, such as *friends*, *places*, or *holidays*. During freewriting, focus more on the flow of ideas than on spelling or punctuation. After five minutes, review your writing and choose as your topic an object, place, person, or event you mention.

2. **Drawing** Think about a general idea, such as *good times*, *adventures*, or *solving problems*. Draw the people, scenes, and places that come to mind. Don't worry about drawing well—just doodle! At the end of five minutes, review your drawings. Select the person, place, or event of which a drawing reminds you as your topic.

3. **Timeline** Make a timeline of events in your life. Then, choose a person or place associated with one event as the topic of your description.

Text

Try it out! Use the interactive Personal Experience Timeline in **Section 6.2**, on-line or on CD-ROM.

Student Work
IN PROGRESS

Name: Kaitlin Crockett
Baypoint Middle School
St. Petersburg, FL

Using a Personal Experience Timeline to Choose a Topic
Kaitlin used a timeline to note family visits. As she studied her timeline, she discovered that her first trip to her grandparents' house was a special memory.

TOPIC BANK

If you're having trouble finding a topic, consider these possibilities:

1. **Description of a Remarkable Place** Think of the most fascinating, most comfortable, or weirdest place you have ever visited. List qualities and features that give the place its special character. Then, write a description that will allow a reader to share your impressions of the place.

2. **Remembrance or Vignette** Describe a special moment or person in your life. (You might browse through family photo albums or videotapes for ideas.) Include details that show why the person or event is special to you.

Responding to Fine Art

3. Respond to this painting of Fort George Hill. Take notes on the scene it shows, describe the colors the artist uses, and note the mood these colors create. Also note the patterns or movement the objects in the painting create. Does space in the painting seem empty or full? Pull these details together in a written description.

Fort George Hill, 1915, Preston Dickinson, Munson-Williams-Proctor, Courtesy Martha Parrish & James Reinish, Inc., New York

Responding to Literature

4. Read Ray Bradbury's story "All Summer in a Day." Pay special attention to his descriptions of rain. Then, write a description of another kind of weather, such as a windy day. Following Bradbury's example, use musical language to make your description ring. You can find Bradbury's story in *Prentice Hall Literature: Timeless Voices, Timeless Themes,* Bronze.

☑ Cooperative Writing Opportunity

5. **Travel Brochure** With a group, create a travel brochure for your community. Brainstorm a list of places of interest, such as historic sites, libraries, museums, stores, and so on. Each group member should write a description of a different place on the list. Assemble the group's descriptions into a brochure illustrated with photographs and maps.

Narrowing Your Topic

Once you've chosen a topic, you may find that it is too broad to describe well. For instance, to describe your entire school building in detail, you would have to write many pages. "My school building" is too general a topic.

Narrow a broad topic by dividing it into parts and focusing on one of them. For instance, the topic "my school building" might be divided into such subtopics as "my homeroom," "the cafeteria," and so on. By focusing on one narrow topic, you can write a more effective description. Use an index-card "camera" to zoom in on just the right part of your topic.

Zoom in to Narrow a Topic

Cut a small hole in an index card to make a "camera." Look through the "camera lens" (the hole) at the subject or at a picture of the subject you wish to describe. (If you are describing a past event or a place or person you cannot revisit, draw pictures of your subject. Use your camera to zoom in on your drawings.) Focus first on one part of your subject and then another. Which details are specific to one part? Which are common to all parts? After observing various aspects of your subject, choose the most interesting one as your topic.

Considering Your Audience and Purpose

Your **audience**—those who will read your description—should affect the details you include. Before you begin drafting, think about how familiar your audience is with your topic. If your audience is unfamiliar with your topic, give basic details about it. If they are very familiar with your topic, focus on the details that show a unique or unexpected side of it.

Your **purpose** in writing a description is to let readers experience in their imaginations what you have experienced with your senses. You can best achieve your purpose by including vivid sensory details—details appealing to the senses—and by using colorful words and comparisons.

▲ Critical Viewing
Create an index-card camera as described on this page. Use it with this photograph. List two parts of this scene, and three details you notice for each part. [Analyze]

Gathering Details

Descriptive writing creates a vivid picture using sensory details. A sentence telling how something looks, smells, feels, sounds, or tastes gives a sensory detail, as in this example:

NO SENSORY DETAILS: The car turned the corner sharply.

ADDED SENSORY DETAILS: The flaming red car screeched around the corner, leaving only the stench of burning rubber.

Sensory details paint a scene. Other details, such as emotions, deepen a reader's experience of the scene. Use cubing to pull together different kinds of details to use in your description.

Use Cubing to Gather Details

Follow these steps to "cube" your subject:
1. **Describe it.** Explain how it looks, sounds, feels, tastes, or smells.
2. **Associate it.** List feelings or stories it calls to mind.
3. **Apply it.** Show how it can be used or what it does.
4. **Analyze it.** Divide it into parts.
5. **Compare and contrast it.** Compare it with a related subject.
6. **Argue for or against it.** Show its good and bad points.

☑ **Collaborative Writing Tip**

Practice cubing a topic with a group of classmates. Choose an object or place familiar to all, and name details for each side of the cube. Take special note of details your classmates contribute that you did not consider.

Student Work
IN PROGRESS

Name: *Kaitlin Crockett*
Baypoint Middle School
St. Petersburg, FL

Gathering Details Using Cubing

Kaitlin used cubing to gather details about her grandparents' house.

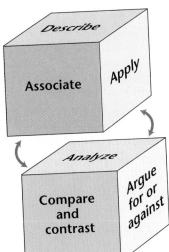

Describe:
2-story house
yellow and white
Associate:
big backyard
bedroom with quilt and photos
Apply:
it's fun and happy to be there
Analyze:
memories are part of the place
Compare/contrast:
new house is close to us
have memories from old house
Argue for or against:
miss the old house

Drafting

Shaping Your Writing

Once you have gathered the details you will use in your descriptive writing, you can begin drafting. Your descriptive writing will take your readers on a journey to see new places or people. To make sure they don't get lost, organize your details clearly.

Organize to Make Your Ideas Clear

The order in which you present details depends largely on the topic that you are describing. Using the following information, choose an organization plan that fits your topic.

Spatial Order
- Present details from left to right, front to back, or bottom to top.
- Use for descriptions of places or objects.

Chronological Order
- Present events in the order in which they occur.
- Use for a remembrance or other story.

Order of Importance
- Present least important details at the beginning and strongest observations at the end.
- Use to lead readers to your main impression.

▼ **Critical Viewing** Explain what main impression is created by this photograph. Describe two details that help create this impression. **[Apply]**

Create a Main Impression

Choose details for your description that will help create a main impression of your subject.

For instance, if you were describing a dog, you might want to leave readers with an impression of the dog as a small bundle of energy. To do so, you might describe its shaggy hair flying, its high-pitched yips, and its short legs blurring as it zips around. You might then tie these details together by calling the dog a "flying furball."

Providing Elaboration

Build Upon Details

By using sensory details, you create a clear picture of your subject. By elaborating on details as you draft, you bring your picture to life.

"Depth-charging" is one strategy you can use to build sensory impressions into a vivid picture.

Using Depth-Charging To depth-charge as you draft, pause at the end of a paragraph. Circle the detail in the paragraph that you find most compelling. It might be a word that suggests a strong feeling or a vivid sensory detail.

Next, draw an arrow from the circled word to a blank line. Write a new sentence telling more about the quality, action, or thing named by the circled word. Next, circle the most compelling word in your new sentence. Draw an arrow to a new line, and write a sentence giving more information about this second circled word. Review your paragraph, and decide whether it should include your new sentences.

Student Work
IN PROGRESS

Name: *Kaitlin Crockett*
Baypoint Middle School
St. Petersburg, FL

Depth-Charging to Build Upon Sensory Details
This is how Kaitlin used depth-charging to elaborate on her impressions of a toy village in her grandparents' home. Later, she incorporated these new details in her final draft.

The (village) children, dressed in their warm coats and bundled with scarves and mittens, enjoyed ice skating on the glimmering icy pond or building a snowman in the soft, white snow.

The village seemed so (cozy.)

When I was little, I used to wish I lived in one of those houses, happy and safe in their perfect little world.

Revising

After your first draft is done, it's time to review your description. As you reread your work, pretend that you are a reader who has never seen or experienced what you are describing. Consider first what changes to your organization would help such a reader experience what you describe.

Revising Your Overall Structure
Analyze Your Organization Plan

Review your entire description to be sure you used your chosen method of organization consistently. Group related details, rather than scattering them throughout your draft. Use cutting and pasting to move and regroup details as needed.

▶**REVISION STRATEGY**
Cutting and Pasting for Order

Make an extra printout or a photocopy of your draft. Reread your work, noting details that concern the same person, place, thing, or idea. If you find related details far apart in your draft, they may be in the wrong place. Consider putting them together. Cut each misplaced detail out of your photocopied draft and tape it to your original draft next to the related details with which it belongs.

⊙ Technology Tip

If you created your draft with a word processor, underline or highlight related details that are in different parts of your draft. Save a copy of your file under a different name, and cut and paste to rearrange details. If you want to restore a paragraph, you can always copy it from your original file.

CUTTING AND PASTING

Covered in hard scales from its head to its tail, a crocodile is like an armored tank. Its mouth bristles with sharp teeth. No other reptile seems quite as fierce.

A crocodile's mouth is its main weapon—for grabbing and tearing. A crocodile can also use its long, blunt head to knock an animal as big as a zebra off its feet. ~~It has long, sharp claws.~~

It has long, sharp claws.

Evaluate Your Main Impression

Consider whether each detail you have included supports a main impression. You may need to add or replace details to create or focus a main impression. Code details to make sure your main impression is strong.

▶ **REVISION STRATEGY**
Circling Details to Strengthen a Main Impression

On a note card, write down your main topic. Underneath, write down the main impression that you want your draft to provide. For instance, your topic might be "basketball" and the main impression might be "nonstop excitement."

Next, run your note card down your draft, stopping at each line in turn. At each line, ask yourself, "Does this detail support my main impression?" Circle in colored pencil those details that do not. Then, review your circled details.

If a circled detail does not add to your main impression and does not give information your reader needs, then either

• consider eliminating it, or

• consider rewording the detail using more vivid language. You might consider using the depth-charging strategy to elaborate on these details further (see page 107).

Student Work
IN PROGRESS

Name: *Kaitlin Crockett*
Baypoint Middle School
St. Petersburg, FL

Circling Details to Strengthen a Main Impression
Kaitlin identified a few details that did not clearly contribute to her main impression of her grandparents' house. She rewrote sentences, elaborated, and eliminated unnecessary details to strengthen her impression of a cheerful, well-kept house.

I remember how their two-story house looked. They lived there
It was freshly painted with light yellow and white paint.
a long time. It was yellow and white. My grandfather liked to
The newly mowed lawn was neatly trimmed, and bright flowers bloomed
work in the yard. He still gardens where they live now.
on the porch. Squash and other vegetables filled the garden.

Main Impression:
bright, cheery, well-kept home

Revising Your Paragraphs

Use Functional Paragraphs

A **topical paragraph** develops or supports one main idea. A **functional paragraph** adds emphasis or makes a transition. A functional paragraph may be one sentence or a series of sentences. It may be a character's words (dialogue), or it may be in the writer's voice. Although most of the paragraphs in your description are probably topical paragraphs, you can add functional paragraphs to "spice up" your writing. Here are some examples:

⊘ Learn More

To learn more about topical and functional paragraphs, see Chapter 3.

FUNCTIONAL PARAGRAPHS

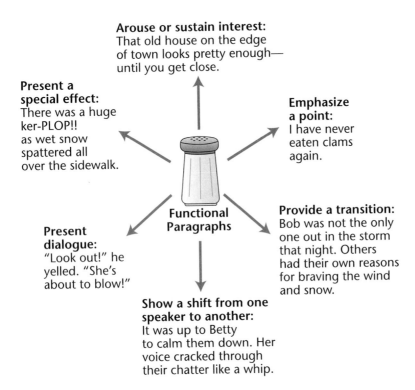

Arouse or sustain interest:
That old house on the edge of town looks pretty enough—until you get close.

Present a special effect:
There was a huge ker-PLOP!! as wet snow spattered all over the sidewalk.

Emphasize a point:
I have never eaten clams again.

Functional Paragraphs

Present dialogue:
"Look out!" he yelled. "She's about to blow!"

Provide a transition:
Bob was not the only one out in the storm that night. Others had their own reasons for braving the wind and snow.

Show a shift from one speaker to another:
It was up to Betty to calm them down. Her voice cracked through their chatter like a whip.

▶ REVISION STRATEGY
Adding Functional Paragraphs

As you reread your draft, look for surprising or especially interesting details. You can emphasize a surprising detail by writing a functional paragraph to introduce it. Look also for places where you need to make a transition. You can add a functional paragraph to guide a reader smoothly from one part of your description to another.

Revising Your Sentences

Eliminate Run-on Sentences

When writing a description, you'll probably want to pack sentences full of vivid details. It's easy to let these sentences become run-ons. A run-on sentence is two or more complete sentences written as though they were a single sentence.

RUN-ON:	I went to my grandma's, we ate then it was time to go.
POSSIBLE CORRECTION:	I went to my grandma's. We ate until we couldn't eat another bite. Soon it was time to go.

Get instant help! For additional practice eliminating run-on sentences, see **Section 21.4,** on-line or on CD-ROM.

▶ **REVISION STRATEGY**
Color-Coding Clues to Eliminate Run-ons

Read your draft aloud slowly. As you read, mark the places where you pause the longest with red dot stickers. Use yellow dots to mark shorter pauses. Review your draft. See whether you have written a period for each red sticker. Consider adding a period if the words before the dot express a complete thought. Capitalize the word following the period. For each yellow sticker, consider whether you need to add a comma.

Student Work
IN PROGRESS

Name: *Kaitlin Crockett*
Baypoint Middle School
St. Petersburg, FL

Color-Coding Pauses to Eliminate Run-ons
Here are some of the pauses Kaitlin marked in her writing. Notice where she added periods and commas.

There was a store with a red awning , and the train station was busy with travelers ● the *The* figures of people , placed along shelves, looked like they were busily working in the big city.

Revising Your Word Choice

Use Precise Words

You wouldn't want to buy a container of juice only to find that it was full of water. Don't give your readers a description full of watered-down words. For instance, *nice* is a watered-down adjective. Replace it with a precise adjective, such as *generous* or *helpful*—adjectives that describe a specific quality.

Sometimes, writers try to "juice up" their writing by using empty words and phrases such as *very* and *a lot.* None of these empty words, however, is as powerful as a precise one. If you use these empty words in your description, you need to eliminate them and use more precise words to express your meaning.

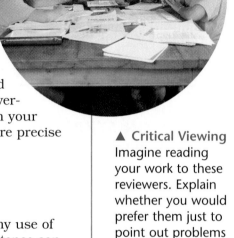

▲ **Critical Viewing** Imagine reading your work to these reviewers. Explain whether you would prefer them just to point out problems in your work or to suggest solutions as well. **[Relate]**

▶ **REVISION STRATEGY**
Checkmarking Empty Words

Reread your draft, and place a check mark over any use of the words *very, really,* or *a lot.* Next, reread each sentence containing a checked word. Think of the strong image or important information that you want the sentence to express. Choose a precise word or phrase to help convey that image or information, and use it in the sentence. Then, delete the empty word.

IN PROGRESS

Name: *Kaitlin Crockett*
Baypoint Middle School
St. Petersburg, FL

Checkmarking Empty Words

Kaitlin checkmarked her empty words and deleted them. Then, she found precise words to "juice up" her sentences. Notice the other replacements she considered.

curtained
~~large~~
A ~~really~~ big window almost filled the wall in the kitchen.

glistened
~~shone~~
Rays of sunshine ~~came~~ through the windowpanes ~~very~~

~~brightly.~~ Through the window you could see the great

expanse of the backyard where my grandfather and I used

every visit
to pick raspberries and play catch ~~a lot.~~

Grammar in Your Writing
Adjectives

If you use precise adjectives in your description, they will make your meaning clear. Adjectives are *modifiers*. **Adjectives** modify (slightly change) the meaning of a noun or pronoun by answering one of these four questions:

What Kind?	
oak table	*glimmering* pond

Which One?	
their house	*each* cottage

How Many?	
two shelves	*several* children

How Much?	
more time	*smaller* amount

Find It in Your Reading Review "Luke Baldwin's Vow" by Morley Callaghan on page 100. For each of the four questions—*What kind? Which one? How many? How much?*—identify one adjective used in the story to answer that question.

Find It in Your Writing Review your draft to identify seven nouns (words naming a person, place, or thing). Did you use adjectives to tell more about the thing each noun names? If not, evaluate whether the noun is precise enough or whether an adjective is needed.

For more on adjectives, see Chapter 16.

Peer Review
Analytic Talk

In a small group, read your revised draft twice. Ask the group members just to listen the first time you read. The second time, ask them to take notes on effective parts and on parts where they want to know more. Afterward, the group can discuss the description, responding to these questions:

1. What did I like in the beginning of the description? In the middle? In the end?

2. What did I want to hear more about? Did a lack of information make me feel as if I had been left hanging at the end?

Consider your peers' responses as you revise your draft further. Look for ways to improve parts they found unclear or ineffective.

Editing
and Proofreading

Proofread your description carefully to eliminate any errors in grammar, spelling, or punctuation. Errors can be distracting. For instance, missing commas may confuse readers.

Focusing on Commas

Commas signal readers to pause slightly. They are also used to prevent confusion. Color-code your draft to find places where you may need to add commas.

Color-Coding Clues for Commas

Using a colored pencil, circle adjectives wherever you use two or more of them in a row. Read the information below, and then review what you have circled. Add any commas you need.

Grammar in Your Writing
Using Commas With Two or More Adjectives

Adjectives are words that tell *what kind, which one, how many,* or *how much.* When two or more adjectives appear in front of the noun they modify, you may need to add a comma between them.

Use a comma to separate adjectives of equal rank. Adjectives of equal rank are those you can write before a noun in any order without changing the meaning of the phrase. For instance, "a colorful, handmade quilt" and "a handmade, colorful quilt" have the same meaning. *Colorful* and *handmade* are adjectives of equal rank. Separate them with a comma.

Do not use commas to separate adjectives that must stay in specific order. For instance, you should not use a comma between the adjectives *this* and *heavy* in the phrase "this heavy mug."

Find It in Your Reading Review "Luke Baldwin's Vow" by Morley Callaghan on page 100. Copy the sentence that describes Aunt Helen. Explain why the adjectives are separated by commas.

Find It in Your Writing Review your draft to find places where you use two or more adjectives before a noun. Determine whether the adjectives are of equal rank or whether they need to appear in a specific order. Be sure you have used commas to separate adjectives of equal rank.

For more information on commas, see Chapter 26.

6.6 Publishing and Presenting

Building Your Portfolio

1. **Publish in a Newspaper** If you've written a description of a person, place, or event in your school, submit your piece to the school newspaper or magazine.

2. **Create an Illustrated Booklet** You can make your description more interesting for readers by adding photos and drawings to illustrate specific details or your main impression. Find images in magazines or create your own. Assemble your words and pictures in a booklet.

Reflecting on Your Writing

Jot down your thoughts about what you learned from writing a description. Include a copy of this reflection in your portfolio. Begin by answering these questions:

- Did describing your subject lead you to new insights about it? Explain.

- Which strategy for revising might you recommend to a friend? Why?

 Internet Tip

To see examples of descriptive writing scored according to this rubric, go on-line:
PHSchool.com
Enter Web Code:
ebk-7001

Rubric for Self-Assessment

Use the following criteria to evaluate your description.

	Score 4	Score 3	Score 2	Score 1
Audience and Purpose	Creates a memorable main impression through effective use of details	Creates a main impression through use of details	Contains extraneous details that detract from main impression	Contains details that are unfocused and create no main impression
Organization	Is organized consistently, logically, and effectively	Is organized consistently	Is organized, but not consistently	Is disorganized and confusing
Elaboration	Contains rich sensory language that appeals to the five senses	Contains some rich sensory language	Contains some rich sensory language, but it appeals to only one or two of the senses	Contains only flat language
Use of Language	Uses vivid and precise adjectives; contains no errors in grammar, punctuation, or spelling	Uses some vivid and precise adjectives; contains few errors in grammar, punctuation, and spelling	Uses few vivid and precise adjectives; contains some errors in grammar, punctuation, and spelling	Uses no vivid adjectives; contains many errors in grammar, punctuation, and spelling

Student Work
IN PROGRESS

FINAL DRAFT

House of Memories

Kaitlin Crockett
Baypoint Middle School
St. Petersburg, Florida

When I think of my grandparents' old house, I remember a cheery atmosphere with lots of laughs and smiles filling the air. It was always a fun and happy place. When I found out my grandparents were selling their house, I was happy that they were going to be moving here. I was sad, though, that I would never see them in their old place again.

I remember how their two-story house looked. It was freshly painted with light yellow and white paint. My grandfather liked to work in the yard. The newly mowed lawn was neatly trimmed, and bright flowers bloomed on the porch. Squash and other vegetables filled the garden.

▲ **Critical Viewing**
What is your main impression of this house? Cite two details contributing to this impression. **[Analyze]**

In her introduction, Kaitlin starts to create a main impression of her grandparents' house—it had a "cheery atmosphere."

Kaitlin supports her main impression with phrases such as freshly painted, light yellow, *and* neatly trimmed.

A curtained window almost filled the wall of the kitchen. Rays of sunshine glistened through the windowpanes. Through the window you could see the broad expanse of the backyard where my grandfather and I used to pick raspberries and play catch every visit.

In the dining room, the big oak table was draped with a white lace tablecloth ruffling over the edge. The table was neatly set with flowered china and polished silver. Soon, the table would be filled with delicious homemade breads, piping hot dishes, and freshly baked apple pie. We were always ready to indulge. Next to the table, on two white wooden shelves, sat my grandmother's toy village. Each cottage was beautifully painted. There was a store with a red awning, and the train station was busy with travelers. The figures of people, placed along the shelves, looked as if they were busily working in the big city. The little children, dressed in their warm coats and bundled with scarves and mittens, smiled as they ice skated on the glimmering icy pond or built a snowman in the soft white snow. The village seemed so cozy. When I was little, I used to wish I lived in one of those houses, happy and safe in their perfect little world.

Downstairs in the basement a stone fireplace blazed with reds and oranges. A comfortable, overstuffed couch sat in a corner. Along the opposite wall, my grandfather's tools hung in shiny rows above his old wooden workbench. The smell of saw-dust and oil meant he kept busy fixing and building things.

Upstairs, on the second floor, a small bedroom nestled in the corner. The bed was covered with a colorful, handmade quilt, and old photographs filled the oak nightstand. This was the bedroom I stayed in during overnight visits. It was so exciting having a room of my own, like at home, but different.

My grandparents now live just around the corner from us. I enjoy spending time with them and get to see them more often. I still miss that house, but I will always remember the good times I had there with my grandparents.

Kaitlin uses spatial order, organizing her description of the house room by room.

Sensory details such as bundled with scarves and mittens *and rich adjectives like* glimmering *make the description of the village vivid.*

Kaitlin builds up her sensory description with her feelings and imaginings about the toy village.

Kaitlin concludes by exploring how her memories of her grandparents' old house make her feel.

▶ **Critical Viewing**
In what ways is this room similar to or different from the one described by Kaitlin? **[Compare]**

Connected Assignment
Poem

The best descriptions are often found in poems. While "poetry" may sound fancy, it is part of the beat of your life. Skip-rope chants, birthday greetings, television jingles, the latest rap single—wherever words mingle, chiming and rhyming, poetry is taking place.

A **poem** is a creation made of words chosen for their sound and associations—even their looks—as well as their meaning. It uses words to suggest strong images and feelings. Most poems include one or more of these features:

Early Houses, 1913, Lawren S. Harris, Robert and Signe McMichael, McMichael Canadian Art Collection

▲ **Critical Viewing** Find two musical-sounding phrases for this scene, drawing on the features the artist emphasizes. **[Apply]**

- words arranged for a rhythmical, visual, or musical effect
- figures of speech such as
    ‣ similes (comparisons of unlike things using *like* or *as)*
    ‣ metaphors (comparisons of unlike things that do not use *like* or *as)*
    ‣ personifications (descriptions of a nonhuman thing as if it were a person)
- a repeated pattern of lines and stanzas (groups of lines)

Write your own poem, using the strategies suggested below:

Prewriting Choose a topic to write a poem about. You might

- describe a place, object, animal, or person.
- tell a story, either one you have heard or one from your life.

Focus on one aspect of your topic—an event or a particular feature. Then, find a striking contrast between this aspect of your subject and another one. For instance, your poem might contrast a flower's timeless beauty with the short time it blooms. This contrast is your focused topic.

Next, use a web like this one to gather details. Write your topic in the middle. Use connecting circles to explore related details.

Drafting Once you have gathered details, choose a form in which you will present them. There are several forms from which you can choose, including those listed on page 119.

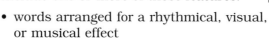

DARK

LIGHT

moves silently, quickly, like smoke

sunlight: like a pool of golden syrup

dark like smoke

likes lying in the sunlight

CONTRAST my cat: loves light, but he is dark and full of secrets

looks at me sometimes like he knows something I don't

sleepy

- **Rhyming poems** follow a regular pattern. Each line has a designated number of accented syllables (beats). Designated lines end with rhyming words. For instance, in "Pete at the Zoo" (below), Gwendolyn Brooks rhymes every other line. Her odd-numbered lines have four beats each. Her even-numbered lines have three.

- **Free-verse poems** do not rhyme and do not follow a regular pattern of beats. The poet must still pay close attention to the sounds and rhythms of the lines.

- **Haiku** are three-line poems in a traditional Japanese form. The first line contains five syllables, the second contains seven syllables, and the third has five syllables.

Look over poems you like, and choose one in order to copy its pattern of rhyming, rhythm, or repetition.

As you draft, incorporate details from your web and create the contrast you chose as your focus. Create strong images using figurative language such as metaphors and similes. Create musical effects by using words beginning with the same sound.

MODEL

Pete at the Zoo
Gwendolyn Brooks

I wonder if the elephant
Is lonely in his stall
When all the boys and girls are gone
And there's no shout at all,
5 And there's no one to stamp before,
No one to note his might.
Does he hunch up, as I do,
Against the dark of night?

Revising and Editing Once your first draft is on paper, go through your poem line by line. Focus on these revisions:

- **Replace vague words with precise ones.** Replace any worn-out expressions you have used with fresh ways of expressing your ideas.

- **Make sure that you have followed your chosen form.** Read your poem out loud, tapping as you go. Mark lines where there are too many or too few beats, or where the right rhythm is lacking. For a rhyming poem, check the last word of each line to make sure the right lines rhyme.

Publishing and Presenting Post a copy of your poem on a class bulletin board, or send it to a publication.

Spotlight on the Humanities

Comparing Interpretations of Nature

Focus on Fine Art: Georgia O'Keeffe

As you may have realized while writing a description, what your *mind* sees—the patterns you notice in things—is as important as what your *eye* sees. American artist Georgia O'Keeffe (1887–1986) excelled at seeing with her mind, finding new forms in nature.

O'Keeffe worked in oil paint and watercolors. Many of her paintings are nearly abstract—while they suggest particular scenes and objects, they also explore colors and shapes for their own sake. The paintings seem to discover something new about nature, expressing patterns lying behind the objects we ordinarily see.

O'Keeffe was one of a few women artists who achieved international recognition during her career. She is best known for her paintings of flowers and of natural forms found in the American Southwest.

Photography Connection Alfred Stieglitz (1864–1946), one of the masters of photography in the twentieth century, first brought O'Keeffe's work to the public when he showed it in his small Gallery 291 in New York. He later married O'Keeffe. One of his portraits of her is shown on this page (right).

Music Connection In 1931, Ferde Grofé composed his popular *Grand Canyon Suite*. His piece shares its title with a series of watercolors of Southwestern landscapes attributed to O'Keeffe. Like O'Keeffe, he was inspired by the elements of nature in the Southwest.

Descriptive Writing Activity: Comparison of Images in Music and Art

Listen to Grofé's *Grand Canyon Suite*. Then, view reproductions of O'Keeffe's paintings of the Southwest. Write an essay comparing the visions of this region that O'Keeffe and Grofé create.

Spring, ©1922, Georgia O'Keeffe, Frances Lehman Loeb Art Center, Vassar College, Poughkeepsie, New York

▲ **Critical Viewing** What natural objects can you discover in this painting? Describe how each is related to other forms in the painting. **[Synthesize]**

▶ **Critical Viewing** What do Georgia O'Keeffe's hands in this portrait suggest about her mood? **[Interpret]**

Media and Technology Skills

Analyzing Visual Meanings

Activity: Analyze Camera Techniques in a Movie

In a description, the details the writer chooses to include shape your idea of what is being described. Using a camera, a moviemaker can also shape your idea of a person, place, or event. Learn to identify the camera techniques used in movies and to recognize the effects they create.

Think About It Here are some important camera techniques:

Close-up Shots In a close-up shot, the person or thing filmed takes up most of the screen. The close-up shot tells you that what you are looking at is important. In a mystery movie, a director might use a close-up shot of someone's ring to let you know it is a clue. The shot also lets you see the ring in detail.

Zoom In When the camera zooms in on a person or thing, the image moves closer and closer. Like a close-up, a zoom shot tells you that you are looking at something important. It also increases the intensity or suspense of the moment. When the bad guys make a getaway, the camera might zoom in on their speeding car.

Zoom Out In zooming out, the camera begins with a tight focus on a single subject. Then, the image moves farther away and takes in more of the surrounding area. This shot shows how a person or thing fits into—or doesn't fit into—its environment. For example, an elderly person listening to a lecture may not seem unusual, but if the camera pulls away and shows him sitting among high school students, it might be funny, or touching.

Watch It Watch a movie, either on video or at the theater. Take notes on the camera techniques used. (Concentrate on the beginnings and endings of scenes and on moments of high drama.) Choose one example each of a close-up, a zoom in, and a zoom out. Describe the scene, and explain how the camera technique influenced your response to it.

Other Camera Techniques

Pan The camera moves from left to right over a person, place, or thing. A pan may be used to show the scope or full setting of something.

Aerial View The camera looks down from a point high above the subject. The shot gives a broad view of the setting and may emphasize the power of the camera—and the viewer—to see more than the characters can see.

Movie:_____

Close-up: Scene _____	Zoom In: Scene _____	Zoom Out: Scene _____
Effect _____	Effect _____	Effect _____

Standardized Test Preparation Workshop

Strategy, Organization, and Style Skills

To write a good description, you need to organize details effectively. Some standardized test items measure organizational abilities along with other writing skills. Such items consist of a passage followed by questions, which include:

- *strategy* questions, asking if a given revision is appropriate
- *organization* questions, focusing on logical sequence
- *style* questions, focusing on point of view and word choice.

Sample Test Items	Answers and Explanations

Read the passage, and then answer the questions that follow.
 	
(1) John cultivated the ground in preparation for planting. (2) He carefully placed a tulip bulb with the pointed side facing up in each hole. (3) He dug holes six inches deep and six inches apart. (4) He then buried each bulb.
 	
1 Choose the most logical sentence sequence.
  A 2, 4, 1, 3
  B 1, 3, 2, 4
  C 2, 1, 3, 4
  D Correct as is
	The correct answer is *B*. Part (2) must follow part (3) because John could not have placed the bulbs until he had dug the holes. Part (1) describes the first step in planting, and part (4) describes the last event that occurred.

2 Which of the following is the best way to write parts (2) and (3)?
 	
  A He dug holes six inches deep and six inches apart and placed a tulip bulb, pointed side up, in each.
 	
  B He dug holes six inches deep and six inches apart, and he carefully placed a tulip bulb with the pointed side facing up in each hole.
 	
  C He dug holes six inches deep and six inches apart, while carefully placing a tulip bulb with the pointed side facing up in each hole.
 	
  D Correct as is
	The correct answer is *A*. Although the other answers express similar meanings, this choice is the best way to combine the two sentences. It best conveys the order of steps without repeating words unnecessarily.

Practice 1 **Directions:** Read the passage, and then answer the questions that follow. Choose the letter of the best answer.

(1) After researching avocados, I found out that they are the fruit of a tropical American tree. (2) It is <u>oval</u> shaped. (3) It can have black or green skin. (4) It has a bland green pulp and a large seed. (5) I decided to use the seed to grow an avocado plant.

(6) My original assignment was simply to find out from where a food <u>item</u> in my refrigerator came. (7) I had chosen to find out more about an avocado because it is one of my favorite foods. (8) Was it grown on a vine, a tree, or a shrub? (9) Was it a fruit or a vegetable?

(10) First, I removed the seed from the avocado and placed it, wide end down, in a wide-mouthed jar. (11) It took a while before I saw roots, and a few weeks later the stem pushed its way through the <u>top</u> of the seed. (12) I added an inch of water. (13) I was then able to plant it in soil and watch it grow.

1 Which of the following is the best order for the paragraphs?
 A 1, 2, 3
 B 3, 2, 1
 C 1, 3, 2
 D 2, 1, 3

2 Which of the following would be the best way to write parts 2, 3, and 4 ?
 F It is oval shaped, can have black or green skin, has a bland green pulp, and contains a large seed.
 G It is oval shaped, and it can have black or green skin. It has a bland green pulp and a large seed.
 H It is oval shaped, and can have black or green skin. It also has a bland green pulp and a large seed.
 J An avocado has an oval shape, black or green skin, a bland green pulp, and a large seed.

3 Which of the following sentences should be inserted between parts 7 and 8?
 A I didn't know anything about avocados.
 B My choice was not a good one.
 C To complete my assignment, I needed to answer a few questions.
 D I had a lot of questions.

4 In part 7, which of the following should be deleted to eliminate irrelevant information?
 F because it is one of my favorite foods
 G about an avocado
 H I had chosen
 J to find out more about an avocado

5 If the author wanted to include scientific information about the growth of the avocado seed in paragraph 3, which of the following would be appropriate?
 A The roots looked like spaghetti hanging from the bottom of the seed.
 B I used toothpicks to hold the end of the avocado seed in the water.
 C It seemed to take forever before the roots began to grow.
 D The epicotyl, the upper part of the seed embryo, pushed the plumule, or leaf-bud, through the seed coat.

6 Choose the most logical sentence sequence for paragraph 3.
 F 10, 11, 12, 13
 G 10, 12, 11, 13
 H 13, 10, 11, 12
 J 12, 11, 13, 10

7 In which part should the underlined word be replaced by a more precise word?
 A Part 2
 B Part 6
 C Part 11
 D Correct as is

Chapter 7

Persuasion
Persuasive Essay

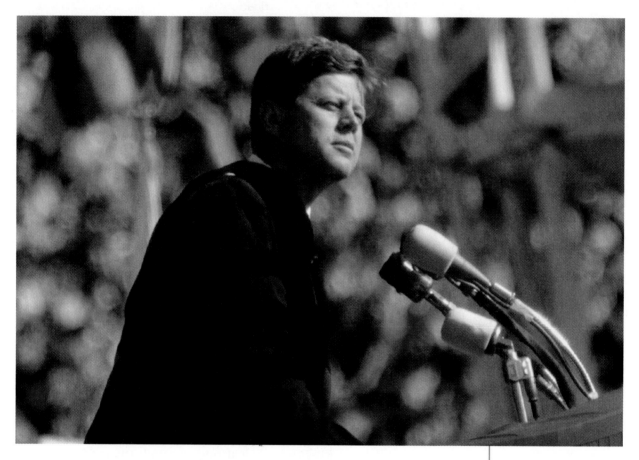

Persuasion in Everyday Life

A word is more than just a sound. "Words may be deeds," said Aesop, the ancient Greek fable writer. Said at the right time, they make things happen. Your words might persuade a friend to let you borrow her bike. They might encourage family members to watch a particular television show. When you use words to influence the actions and opinions of others, you are using **persuasion**.

You can find persuasion in writing all around you—in a magazine advertisement or a newspaper editorial, in a movie review or an advice column—even on a box of cereal. By encouraging action or changing people's views, persuasive writing turns words into deeds.

▲ **Critical Viewing** John F. Kennedy was famous for his use of persuasive words. Why might persuasive words like his be remembered for years after they were uttered? **[Speculate]**

What Is a Persuasive Essay?

A **persuasive essay** is a brief work in which a writer presents the case for or against a particular position. An effective persuasive essay includes

- a clear statement of the writer's position on an issue with more than one side.
- facts, examples, and other details supporting the writer's position.
- a clear organization.

To see the criteria on which your persuasive essay may be assessed, see the Rubric for Self-Assessment on page 140.

Writers in
ACTION

American history brims with powerful persuasive speakers. William Jennings Bryan (1860–1925), a politician and fiery speechmaker, knew that persuasion combines argument and emotion:

"An orator is a man who says what he thinks and feels what he says."

Types of Persuasive Writing

Here are a few other common types of persuasive writing:

- **Persuasive letters** are written to persuade a decision-maker to support a particular cause or measure.
- **Editorials** give and support an opinion on a current issue. They may appear in newspapers, magazines, or on television or the radio.
- **Political speeches** are delivered by a politician to win support for a policy or a position.
- **Public-service announcements** are radio or television commercials designed to persuade and educate the public.

PREVIEW
Student Work
IN PROGRESS

Use the sample strategies and tips in this lesson to improve your skills at writing persuasively. You'll follow the featured prewriting, drafting, and revising techniques used by Josh McWhirter, a student at College Station Junior High in College Station, Texas, to develop his persuasive essay. His final draft appears at the end of the chapter.

Novelist Louis L'Amour (1908–1988) set his action-packed bestsellers in the frontier days of the Old West. His fascination with the idea of the frontier also led him to write persuasively on the "New Frontier"—outer space.

Reading Writing Connection

Reading Strategy: Understand a Writer's Purpose A writer's **purpose**—to inform, to entertain, to argue for a position—affects the facts, arguments, and images he or she uses. When you read, formulate an idea of the writer's purpose. Test whether it is effectively achieved as you read. For instance, L'Amour's purpose is to encourage support for the space program. With this in mind, you can evaluate his comparison between those who oppose exploring space and babies clinging to their mothers.

The Eternal Frontier

Louis L'Amour

The question I am most often asked is, "Where is the frontier now?"

The answer should be obvious. Our frontier lies in outer space.

The moon, the asteroids, the planets, these are mere stepping stones, where we will test ourselves, learn needful lessons, and grow in knowledge before we attempt those frontiers beyond our solar system. Outer space is a frontier without end, the eternal frontier, an everlasting challenge to explorers not [only] of other planets and other solar systems but also of the mind of man.

All that has gone before was preliminary. We have been preparing ourselves mentally for what lies ahead. Many problems remain, but if we can avoid a devastating war we shall move with a rapidity scarcely to be believed. In the past seventy years we have developed the automobile, radio, television, transcontinental and transoceanic flight, and the electrification of the country, among a multitude of other such developments. In 1900 there were 144 miles of surfaced road in the United States. Now there are over 3,000,000. Paved roads and the development of the automobile have gone hand in hand, the automobile being civilized man's antidote to overpopulation.

▲ **Critical Viewing** Find a passage in the essay that captures the spirit of the photograph. **[Connect]**

The author begins with an attention-grabbing question—and a provocative answer. This answer is his thesis statement—the statement of his position.

L'Amour presents evidence in the form of facts and statistics to support his argument that we are ready for a new challenge.

What is needed now is leaders with perspective; we need leadership on a thousand fronts, but they must be men and women who can take the long view and help to shape the outlines of our future. There will always be the nay-sayers, those who cling to our lovely green planet as a baby clings to its mother, but there will be others like those who have taken us this far along the path to a limitless future.

We are a people born to the frontier. It has been a part of our thinking, waking, and sleeping since men first landed on this continent. The frontier is the line that separates the known from the unknown wherever it may be, and we have a driving need to see what lies beyond. . . .

A few years ago we moved into outer space. We landed men on the moon; we sent a vehicle beyond the limits of the solar system, a vehicle still moving farther and farther into that limitless distance. If our world were to die tomorrow, that tiny vehicle would go on and on forever, carrying its mighty message to the stars. Out there, someone, sometime, would know that once we existed, that we had the vision and we made the effort. Mankind is not bound by its atmospheric envelope or by its gravitational field, nor is the mind of man bound by any limits at all.

One might ask—why outer space, when so much remains to be done here? If that had been the spirit of man we would still be hunters and food gatherers, growling over the bones of carrion in a cave somewhere. It is our destiny to move out, to accept the challenge, to dare the unknown. It is our destiny to achieve.

Yet we must not forget that along the way to outer space whole industries are springing into being that did not exist before. The computer age has arisen in part from the space effort, which gave great impetus to the development of computing devices. Transistors, chips, integrated circuits, Teflon, new medicines, new ways of treating diseases, new ways of performing operations, all these and a multitude of other developments that enable man to live and to live better are linked to the space effort. Most of these developments have been so incorporated into our day-to-day life that they are taken for granted, their origin not considered.

If we are content to live in the past, we have no future. And today is the past.

L̲ITERATURE

To read another example of persuasive writing on a social theme, see the essay "I Am a Native of North America" by Chief Dan George in *Prentice Hall Literature: Timeless Voices, Timeless Themes,* Bronze.

With language such as "Out there, someone, sometime" and a dramatic contrast between the "tiny vehicle" and the "mighty message," L'Amour invites the reader to feel the heroic spirit of exploration.

L'Amour organizes his essay logically according to the different kinds of argument he uses. First, he makes an inspiring argument about the human spirit. Here, he adds a strong, practical argument.

He concludes with a stirring phrase summing up his main argument.

Writing Application: Help Readers Understand Your Purpose To help readers understand the purpose of your essay, begin with a statement of your issue and your position on it.

Prewriting

Choosing Your Topic

To create a powerful persuasive essay, write on an issue about which you care. Use the following strategies to choose a good topic. (Remember, your issue must have more than one side.)

Try it out! Use the interactive Quicklist in **Section 7.2**, on-line or on CD-ROM.

Strategies for Generating a Topic

1. **Round Table** With a group of classmates, hold a round-table discussion of problems in your school and community. Raise as many different issues as possible. Jot down topics on which you have strong feelings. Choose among these subjects for your essay topic.

2. **Media Flip-Through** Your city government announces a budget crisis. A slumping basketball team trades its key forward. Every day, controversies blare from newspapers and television sets. Over the course of a few days, flip through newspapers, watch TV, and listen to the radio for possible topics. Choose one that interests you.

3. **Quicklist** Fold a piece of paper lengthwise in three. In the first column, write a list of issues and ideas that interest you. In the second, write a descriptive word for each. In the third, give an example supporting that description. Review your list, and decide which topic interests you most.

Student Work
IN PROGRESS

Name: Josh McWhirter
College Station Junior High
College Station, TX

Using a Quicklist
Here's the quicklist Josh McWhirter used to choose his topic:

Topic	Descriptive Word	Examples
(After-school clubs)	helpful	Mr. Heisen's Math Club
Sports on TV	action-packed	table-tennis championships
Television comedies	stupid	Honey, I'm Home!
Mountain climbing	thrilling	weekend backpack trip with Dad
Computers	neat	program I wrote in Basic
Homelessness	sad	high rents
Global warming	scary	hole in the ozone over Australia

TOPIC BANK

If you're having trouble finding a topic, consider these possibilities:

1. **Editorial on School Issues** Choose an issue in your school, such as lunch quality or prices, class schedules, or transportation. Argue for the current policy or for a better one.

2. **Persuasive Essay on Kindness to Animals** Some argue that the laws protecting animals from unkind treatment should be expanded. Do research on the issue, and write an essay for or against new laws to protect animals.

Responding to Fine Art

3. Take notes on this painting to determine its mood—whether it captures the festive bustle of business or the confusing clamor of sales hype. Review your notes, and reflect on the advertisements that surround us. Should such advertising be reduced? Write a persuasive essay defending your views.

August Bargain Days, John Ward Lockwood, Collection of The McNay Art Museum

Responding to Literature

4. Read the Greek myth "Icarus and Daedalus." In the role of lawyer, write a statement either condemning or defending Daedalus for his role in Icarus' fall. You can find "Icarus and Daedalus" in *Prentice Hall Literature: Timeless Voices, Timeless Themes*, Bronze.

☑ Cooperative Writing Opportunity

5. **Radio Documentary on Required Courses** In a group, investigate which classes are required in your school and which are not. Divide the following tasks: analyzing the benefits and drawbacks of not requiring music, art, or drama courses; analyzing the benefits and drawbacks of requiring math, science, and foreign languages; and so on. Group members should each draft a section of the documentary. Tape the documentary, and play it for the class.

Narrowing Your Topic

Once you've chosen an issue, narrow your focus. For example, the topic "violence in the media" includes violence on news reports, in movies, on TV, and so on. To write an effective essay, you might focus on violence in television shows.

One strategy for narrowing your topic is the "funnel."

"Funnel" Your Topic

Here's how to "funnel" your topic. First, draw a funnel shape, as shown below. Then,

1. Write your general topic above the funnel mouth.
2. Off to the side, divide your topic into parts.
3. Select one part to focus on. Write it on the first line.
4. Note causes and effects connected with this subtopic.
5. Describe one cause or effect on the second line.
6. Formulate a narrowed topic based on the previous entries.

TOPIC FUNNEL

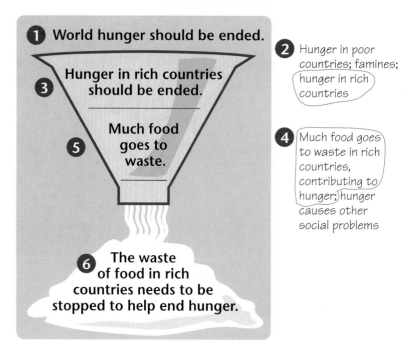

1. World hunger should be ended.

2. Hunger in poor countries; famines; hunger in rich countries

3. Hunger in rich countries should be ended.

5. Much food goes to waste.

4. Much food goes to waste in rich countries, contributing to hunger; hunger causes other social problems

6. The waste of food in rich countries needs to be stopped to help end hunger.

Considering Your Audience and Purpose

Your purpose in writing a persuasive essay is to convince readers. Knowing your audience will help achieve this purpose. As you gather details and draft, keep the following questions in mind: What will your readers think is important? To what kind of reasoning and language will your readers respond?

Gathering Evidence

Provide Support

To persuade readers, you must provide support for your position. Types of support include the following:

- **Logical arguments:** *The town needs money. A skating rink will bring in money. Therefore, we should build a rink.*

- **Statistics:** *Eighty percent of the voters support a rink.*

- **Expert opinions:** *Professor Irving Hud argues that public recreational facilities will improve business in our town.*

- **Personal observations:** *Every day, I see kids hanging out with nothing to do. A skating rink will give them an outlet.*

- **Charged language and striking images:** *Our "sleepy little town" is starting to wake up. We can turn over and go back to sleep—or we can get up and do what needs doing.*

Do research on your topic, and complete a T-chart to gather support for your position.

Completing a T-Chart Write your topic at the top of a sheet of paper. Fold the paper in half to create two columns. At the top of the first column, write "Pro," and jot down support for your position. At the top of the second column, write "Con," and jot down any evidence that might be used to argue against your idea.

Text

Try it out! Use the interactive T-Chart in **Section 7.2,** on-line or on CD-ROM.

Research Tip

To gather more evidence, ask your librarian for help using indexes to magazines and newspapers. Use these sources to find facts or statistics that will convince your reader.

Student Work
IN PROGRESS

Name: Josh McWhirter
College Station Junior High
College Station, TX

Using a T-Chart

In his T-Chart, Josh included several reasons for and against his idea for a debate club.

A Club That Discusses Current Events

Pro	Con
Gives experience speaking in front of others	May not be popular
Teaches students debating	Requires reading newspapers, watching news—extra work
Instills maturity	Might add expenses to school budget
Helps teach current events	

Drafting

Shaping Your Writing

Develop a Thesis Statement

The evidence you have gathered will support your position. To keep your position clearly before your readers, review your notes and develop a thesis statement—one clear sentence that sums up your argument. Include this statement in your introduction.

Organize to Emphasize

The ideas in a persuasive essay are like notes in a piece of music. Properly organized, they will build to a stirring climax.

To create a rhythm in your paper, identify the strongest point on your T-chart. Also, note the strongest arguments against your position. Then, consider using the following organization:

▲ **Critical Viewing**
Why is it important for a lawyer, such as the one in the photograph, to create a rhythm in his or her arguments before a jury? **[Analyze]**

CREATING A RHYTHM FOR YOUR ARGUMENTS

I. Introduction
- Open with a striking image or other attention grabber.
- Present your thesis statement.

II. First Set of Arguments
- Begin to win your reader over by presenting most of your arguments.

III. Acknowledging the Opposition
- Present the strong arguments against your position.
- Refute these arguments. Show that they are illogical or misstate facts, or that your ideas outweigh them.

IV. Strongest Argument
- Introduce the strongest argument for your position. You might note that even if your other arguments were bad, this argument alone would prove your case.
- Present your strongest argument.

V. Conclusion
- Summarize your arguments.
- Restate your thesis.
- Close with a memorable image, brief story, or phrase.

Providing Elaboration

Like a piece of music, a persuasive essay has a rhythm. If you make a point without providing support, though, it is as though you missed a beat. Supporting details include logical arguments, statistics, stories from personal experience, colorful images, and charged words and phrases.

As you draft, use the SEE technique to keep the beat and supply supporting details.

Layer Ideas Using SEE

To layer a paragraph, begin with the main idea. Then, create layer after layer to elaborate that idea. Follow these steps:

State the main idea for the paragraph.

Extend the idea. You might give your opinion on the idea, restate it with a new emphasis, or apply it to an example.

Elaborate on the idea in one or more sentences. Provide support for the idea or your view of it, referring to your T-chart.

Student Work
IN PROGRESS

Name: Josh McWhirter
College Station Junior High
College Station, TX

Layering Ideas

Josh wrote his essay on a debate club he called the "DCE." He elaborated on the main idea of the paragraph below by providing supporting details.

Statement: Finally, the DCE program will help students get over the fear of expressing their ideas aloud. **Extension:** Students need to find ways to conquer this fear. **Elaboration:** In classes, when I'm being graded, I often find myself shaking with fear. I also find that I can't think clearly about whatever subject I'm presenting. The best part about the DCE program is that it gives the student a chance to think about a subject and then discuss it in a nonpressured environment.

Josh states the main idea of his paragraph in the first sentence.

Josh's extension of his main idea emphasizes one aspect of it—students need help getting over their fear.

The support Josh provides includes: a reference to his personal experience ("I often find myself shaking with fear"); a logical argument (speaking in a setting without pressure will help students gain poise speaking before others); and instances of vivid or charged language ("shaking with fear").

Revising

Once you've written your first draft, look for ways to make it better. Start by reviewing the overall structure of your essay and paragraphs.

Revising Your Overall Structure
Analyze the Organization

As you reread your draft, look at the arrangement of your main points. Is it logical? Is it effective? Do your main points build toward a climax, with your strongest point last? Each point in your essay is like a rung in a ladder leading readers to your viewpoint—each must be in the proper position. To check your organization, highlight your main points.

▶ **REVISION STRATEGY**
Highlighting Main Points

Highlight the main points you have used to convince your readers. Then, number each in order. Next, look at the connections between your main points. For instance, will readers understand main point 3 if you haven't explained main point 4? If not, you should probably move point 4 before point 3. Write down any changes you need to make to the order of your points in the margin of your draft. Refer to this chart for more ideas about how points might connect.

💿 **Technology Tip**

If you are using a word processor, highlight or use boldface type for your main ideas so that you can more easily review your organization and supporting arguments.

Relation Between Main Points	Possible Revision
This main point is stronger than the others.	Save this main point until the very end of the essay.
This main point means the same thing as another.	If found in different paragraphs, combine the paragraphs.
This main point is related to, but different from, another.	Make sure that the paragraphs in which you discuss the two are next to each other.
The reader needs to know this main point before he or she can understand a second one.	Make sure the first main point comes before the second.

Check Support

Now that you've located your main points, make sure that they are well supported with evidence.

▶ **REVISION STRATEGY**
Coding for Supporting Evidence

Review each highlighted main point. Mark places where you might add supporting evidence using the following symbols:

▲ Specific example   ■ Expert opinion   ✳ Striking image

● Logical argument   ▼ Personal observation

▬ Measurable fact   ★ Charged language

Review your prewriting notes to find the supporting facts and other details you need to add.

Student Work
IN PROGRESS

Name: *Josh McWhirter*
College Station Junior High
College Station, TX

Coding for Supporting Evidence

Though Josh noted that he had strong support for the main idea of this paragraph, he found two places where he could add more. He added a specific example and a logical argument.

First of all, the program will teach students the art of debating. Adults and students should know how debating works. Important groups of people use debating to make decisions that affect you and me and everybody else.∧

▲ Let's say that someone has written a law to decrease the minimum driving age. Most likely, this law will never make it past the Senate, but it is still important to know that someone has written and proposed this law. And it's important for students to know how to debate and discuss this proposed law.

> To keep his reader's attention, Josh added an example of "decisions that affect you and me."

The DCE will teach students how to engage in a good argument, rather than a fight. They'll learn that they cannot debate current events by saying, "I think that's bad," or by engaging in unpleasant argument.∧

By teaching students to listen to each other and to respond to disagreements with reasoned arguments, debating will teach maturity.

> Josh added a logical argument supporting the idea that learning to debate is good. He also used the charged, positive word maturity.

Revising Your Paragraphs

Check Unity

Check the flow of your writing. The space between paragraphs is like a curve in a road. Readers need a sign showing which way the argument is turning. If the turn is not marked, the readers may go off the road! Code the connections between paragraphs. Then, mark turns by adding transitions.

▶ **REVISION STRATEGY**
Color-Coding the Connections

Highlight the sentence that expresses the main idea of each paragraph. In the margin, code the connection between each idea and the one before it, referring to the chart below. Then, add transitional words or sentences to signal the turns.

Code	Connection	Transition Words
A	**A**dds to, or elaborates on, the previous main idea	*for example, in one case, furthermore*
C	Offers a **c**ontrast, objection, exception	*in contrast, however*
N	Introduces a **n**ew idea	*in addition, finally, first (second, third), in the first place*
S	**S**ums up previous ideas	*in conclusion*

Student Work
IN PROGRESS

Name: Josh McWhirter
College Station Junior High
College Station, TX

Coding Connections Between Paragraphs

Josh discovered that this paragraph offered an objection to the position he defended in the previous paragraph. He added a needed transition.

 C

It's true that after-school

Afterschool programs can be difficult to set up and

keep going. Even if a club is popular at the

beginning, students can lose interest. . . .

Revising Your Sentences
Combine Sentences to Show Connections

A persuasive argument is composed of connected ideas. By combining sentences, you can show these connections clearly.

▶ **REVISION STRATEGY**
Color-Coding Sentences That Express Related Ideas

Reread each paragraph, looking for sentences that express ideas that add to each other. For instance, two sentences that support the same idea add to each other. Underline these sentences in blue. Underline in red any pairs of sentences that express opposing ideas. For instance, one sentence might give an objection to the other. Then, consider combining sentences underlined in the same color.

IDEAS THAT ADD TOGETHER:	The town already permits skating on the lake. We don't have the money to open a rink.
COMBINED:	The town already permits skating on the lake, **and** we don't have the money to open a rink.
OPPOSING IDEAS:	The town won't permit skating on the lake. We don't have the money to open a rink.
COMBINED:	The town won't permit skating on the lake, **but** we don't have the money to open a rink.

Grammar in Your Writing
Compound Sentences

To join two thoughts, you can create a **compound sentence**—a sentence containing two or more independent clauses.

An **independent clause** is a clause that can stand on its own as a complete sentence. Two independent clauses may be joined in a single sentence with a semicolon or with a comma followed by a coordinating conjunction: *and, but, or, for, so,* or *yet.*

┌──── independent clause ────┐ ┌──── independent clause ────┐
A skating rink is a good idea; we should open one now.

┌──── independent clause ────┐ ┌──────── independent clause ────────┐
A skating rink is a good idea, **yet** no one will vote to pay for one.

Find It in Your Reading Find a compound sentence in "The Eternal Frontier" by Louis L'Amour on page 126. Identify each independent clause.

Find It in Your Writing Circle three compound sentences in your draft. If you cannot find any, consider combining sentences.

For more on compound sentences, see Chapter 20.

Revising Your Word Choice

Use Persuasive Language

When you write to persuade, use precise words and phrases to point the readers in a clear direction. For instance, when you describe a "good" candidate, you may actually mean a *trustworthy, intelligent,* or *issue-oriented* one. A "bad" plan may be *poorly thought out, unfair,* or *unworkable.*

▶ **REVISION STRATEGY**
Tagging Vague Words

Use sticky notes to mark places in which you use general evaluative words like *good, bad, right,* and *wrong.* Ask, "Good or bad in what way?" to find more precise words.

Technology Tip

Use the thesaurus feature in your word-processing program to find specific alternatives to general words. (Always check the meaning of a new word in a dictionary before using it.)

Student Work
IN PROGRESS

Name: Josh McWhirter
College Station Junior High
College Station, TX

Tagging Vague Words

In an analytic talk session, Josh's peer reviewers noted a few places in which Josh used vague words. Josh made improvements based on their comments.

The DCE will teach students how to engage
                    civilized
in a ~~good~~ argument rather than a fight.

They'll learn that they cannot debate current

events by saying, "I think that idea is bad," or
                              aggressive and rude
by engaging in ~~unpleasant~~ argument.

> **good**
> In what way?
> – peaceful
> – civilized

> **unpleasant**
> In what way?
> – rude
> – aggressive
> – dangerous

Peer Review

Analytic Talk

Read your revised draft twice to a small group of peers. Before the second reading, ask listeners to jot down words or phrases to help them comment on some part of your draft. Listeners should use these questions as a guide:

1. Was the opening clear and interesting?
2. Did I get lost during the reading? If so, where?
3. What did I find most convincing? Least convincing?

7.5 Editing and Proofreading

You want your essay to persuade readers that your position is correct—not that your spelling needs improvement. Review your draft closely for errors in spelling, punctuation, grammar, and usage.

Get instant help! For more practice with punctuation, complete selected exercises in **Section 26.1**, on-line or on CD-ROM.

Focusing on End Marks

Persuasive writers use sentences to make statements, to ask questions, and to exclaim in the heat of an argument. Make sure that you use the correct end mark for each kind of sentence.

Grammar in Your Writing
End Marks

Sentences must be concluded with one of three **end marks:** the period (.), the question mark (?), or the exclamation mark (!).

- Use a **period** to indicate the end of a statement or a directive.

  Statement of fact Newspapers contain facts about current events.
  Directive Next, watch as many news programs as you can.

- Use a **question mark** to indicate the end of a direct question.

  Direct question Why shouldn't students learn in a relaxed setting?

- Use an **exclamation mark** to indicate strong feeling or urgency.

  Sentence with strong feeling There are only three days left!

  Urgent directive Give us a chance!

Find It in Your Reading Find two question marks in "The Eternal Frontier" by Louis L'Amour on page 126, and explain why the author uses them. Find a sentence for which an exclamation mark might be appropriate. Explain your choice.

Find It in Your Writing Read your draft aloud with expression. If your voice rises at the end of a sentence, check whether you need a question mark. If you emphasize a phrase, think about using an exclamation mark.

For more on end marks, see Chapter 26.

Publishing and Presenting

Building Your Portfolio

Give your persuasive essay a chance to change someone's mind—publish or present it! Consider these suggestions:

1. **Send a Letter** If you have written about a local problem, such as a dangerous traffic intersection, find a person or agency with authority over the situation. Then, send that authority your persuasive essay with a cover letter. Share your essay and any response with the class.

2. **Create a List-Serve** Encourage the exchange of ideas by making a list-serve, or discussion space, on the Internet or school server. Ask a teacher or administrator to help sponsor the list-serve. Post your essay, inviting responses.

Reflecting on Your Writing

Write out some of your thoughts about your experience writing a persuasive essay. Start off by answering these questions:

- What did you learn about your subject as you wrote?
- What part of the writing process seemed hardest for you?

Consider including this reflection in your portfolio.

 Internet Tip

To review persuasive essays scored according to this rubric, go on-line: PHSchool.com Enter Web Code: ebk-7001

Rubric for Self-Assessment

Evaluate your persuasive essay using the following criteria:

	Score 4	Score 3	Score 2	Score 1
Audience and Purpose	Provides arguments, illustrations, and words that forcefully appeal to the audience and effectively serve persuasive purpose	Provides arguments, illustrations, and words that appeal to the audience and serve the persuasive purpose	Provides some support that appeals to the audience and serves the persuasive purpose	Shows little attention to the audience or persuasive purpose
Organization	Uses clear, consistent organizational strategy	Uses clear organizational strategy with occasional inconsistencies	Uses inconsistent organizational strategy	Shows lack of organizational strategy; writing is confusing
Elaboration	Provides specific, well-elaborated support for the writer's position	Provides some elaborated support for the writer's position	Provides some support, but with little elaboration	Lacks support
Use of Language	Uses transitions to connect ideas smoothly; shows few mechanical errors	Uses some transitions; shows few mechanical errors	Uses few transitions; shows some mechanical errors	Shows little connection between ideas; shows many mechanical errors

Student Work
IN PROGRESS

FINAL DRAFT

◄ **Critical Viewing**
How might Josh caption this photograph to use it as supporting evidence for his position? **[Apply]**

Learning to Speak Up:
the DCE

Josh McWhirter
College Station Junior High
College Station, Texas

To start people talking, all it takes is the right question: Is it right for the United States to intervene in foreign conflicts? What is the role of government in education? Questions like these can set off endless controversy. They can also lead to real-life decisions that affect all of us. Discussing and debating are two very important activities in the United States and in the world. The Senate discusses and debates. The United Nations discusses and

This opening hooks readers with questions. It introduces the main topic and leads into the thesis statement.

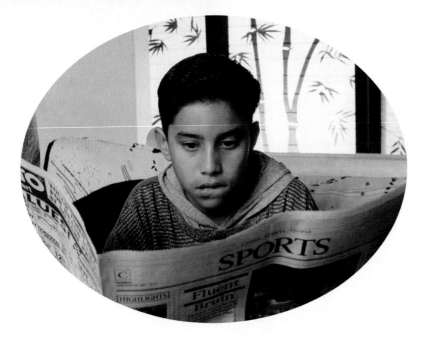

debates. Even families discuss and debate current events at the dinner table.

Realizing the importance of discussion and debate, I have come up with a great idea for an after-school program. I call it "DCE," or "Discussion of Current Events." Students will come after school to a room with a circular table, so everybody can see one another. As soon as students are ready and seated, the teacher running the program will select a student to bring up a current event. Each student will have a chance to express his or her views on the subject. I think this program would be great for the school and the students alike for several important reasons.

First of all, the program will teach students the art of debating. Adults and students should know how debating works. Important groups of people use debating to make decisions that affect you and me and everybody else. Let's say that someone has written a law to decrease the minimum driving age. Most likely, this law will never make it past the Senate, but it is still important to know that someone has written and proposed this law. And it's important for students to know how to debate and discuss this proposed law. The DCE will teach students how to engage in a civilized argument, rather than a fight. They'll learn that they cannot debate current events by saying, "I think that's bad," or by engaging in aggressive and rude argument. By teaching students to listen to each other and to respond to disagreements with reasoned arguments, debating will teach maturity.

Second, the DCE will make students more aware of current events. The program is based on discussing anything and everything in the news. Because students will have to know about current events, they will start reading newspapers and watching tele-

The second paragraph begins with Josh's thesis statement.

To support his argument, Josh presents the first of three main points.

Using the charged words civilized, *on the one hand, and* aggressive *and* rude, *on the other, Josh sets up a persuasive contrast.*

Josh uses a transition word, second, *to signal his turn to a new argument.*

vision news or listening to the radio to find out what's going on. Newspapers and television or radio news are great sources for current events in this country and around the world. In the DCE program, students will also learn about current events from other students. Remember, the biggest influence on the government is the people, and people must be informed.

Finally, the DCE program will help students get over the fear of expressing their ideas aloud. Students need to find ways to conquer this fear. In classes, when I'm being graded, I often find myself shaking with fear. I also find that I can't think clearly about whatever subject I'm presenting. The best part about the DCE program is that it gives the student a chance to think about a subject and then discuss it in a nonpressured environment. The student can express an opinion to a group of people that really care and really listen. This can be very good for a student's morale, especially for a shy student who has trouble speaking in front of other people. Trust me, many students (and adults, too) have this problem. It's a problem that can be overcome when the listeners are actually listening, not snickering.

It's true that after-school programs can be difficult to set up and keep going. Even if a club is popular at the beginning, students can lose interest and drop out. Also, these programs are sometimes expensive and can add too much to our school budget. These are good reasons to question starting up another after-school club. The DCE program deserves special consideration, though, because it might be very popular. After all, students like to discuss and even argue. They just need a place to go and a little direction to help guide the discussion. And my program would not be very expensive, since we wouldn't travel and the program doesn't need any extra equipment.

This school needs some extracurricular activities that involve social skills, patience, maturity, and intelligence, and we can start with DCE.

By refuting opposing views, Josh strengthens his own position.

Josh's concluding statement is forceful and shows his confidence in his idea.

▶ Critical Viewing
Explain the power of debating skills in law-making bodies such as the United Nations, shown here. [Apply]

Connected Assignment
Persuasive Advertisement

You may not read a persuasive essay every day, but there's one kind of persuasive writing you can hardly avoid—advertisements. Day after day, advertisements flood into our lives, from full-page ads in magazines to 30-second television commercials to posters in bus shelters.

An **advertisement** is a persuasive message in print or broadcast form, sponsored by an individual, a business, or another group to achieve a particular end, such as selling a product or spreading a specific view. Advertisements may include

- the use of visual, musical, or dramatic elements, such as pictures, jingles, and skits.
- a **"concept,"** or central theme. (A commercial for an automobile, for instance, might focus on *luxury* by showing a ride along a beautiful, sunlit country road, or it might focus on *power* by showing a fast ride on a rough mountain track.)
- a **"hook,"** such as a catchy jingle, a memorable slogan, or an attention-grabbing image.
- appeals to people's concern with their image (for example, how beautiful, responsible, or wealthy they appear).
- **charged language**—words that imply a certain view of a product or issue.
- repetition of key elements, such as words or music, to ensure that the advertisement is memorable.

Create your own advertisement, following the strategies outlined here:

Prewriting First, make up a product, service, or a position to advertise.

MODEL

The concept of this anti-violence poster is that being against violence is an exciting, powerful stand. The hook is the slogan "Choose to Defuse," combined with the comic book style drawing.

Once you have chosen something to advertise, select your medium: magazine advertisement or television or radio commercial. Next, invent a "concept" for your campaign. For instance, you might decide that the room-cleaning service you are advertising should appeal to students' laziness.

After creating a concept, sum it up in a hook—such as a slogan, jingle, or photograph. Then, list art, music, images, or special effects you wish to include. To help you gather ideas, use a chart like the one below.

Drafting As you draft, focus on presenting your "concept" clearly by using easily interpreted images (for instance, a cowboy), situations (for example, a fancy party), and phrases.

For a **television commercial,** create a storyboard—drawings laid out comic-strip style to show the sequence of visuals. Follow your storyboard in drafting your script—the dialogue to be spoken by actors. Indicate music and special effects in your script.

For a **print ad,** use heads (words set in larger type) to grab readers. Feature your hook in one or more of these heads. Then, lay out your ad to achieve an eye-catching look, arranging pictures and text and selecting typestyles for the best effect.

Revising and Editing Review your draft to ensure that events or ideas are organized logically. Make sure your "concept" is clearly presented. Cut material that distracts from your message.

Publishing and Presenting Consider recording your broadcast commercial or creating a poster of your print ad and presenting it to the class.

Television Commercial for "Kids on the Go" Room Cleaners

Spotlight on the Humanities

Evaluating Performances

Focus on Music: Giacomo Puccini and Opera

The words in an essay may hold great persuasive power, but perhaps nothing moves an audience as directly as music. In an opera, the persuasive force of music is combined with a story (often tragic) acted out by singers. Though the stories may be hard to believe, many spectators find the emotions portrayed in opera overwhelmingly convincing.

The first operas were written in the 1590's and 1600's in Italy. A chorus would sing parts telling the story, while soloists would sing of their character's feelings. A small orchestra or a harpsichord accompanied the singers.

Italian opera blossomed in the nineteenth century. Composer Giacomo Puccini (1858–1924) brought a new sense of realism (*verisimo*) and theater to opera. His works include *Madama Butterfly* (1904), *Tosca* (1900), and *La Bohème* (1896)—all ending with the tragic death of the heroine!

Literature Connection One of Puccini's most successful interpreters, and one of the most important contributors to the art of opera, was singer Maria Callas (1923–1977). A talented actress as well as a gifted singer, she played tragic parts like Turandot in Puccini's opera of that title. Fortunately, videos and recordings exist of her performances, preserving her art for the future.

Film Connection Music from Puccini's *Gianni Schicchi* (1918) and *La Rondine* (1917) is woven beautifully throughout the film *A Room With a View* (1986). Directed by James Ivory and produced by Ismail Merchant, the film gives evidence of the lasting emotional power of Puccini's music.

Persuasive Writing Activity: Presentation on Opera

Listen to a section of an opera by Puccini. Then, in a brief presentation, persuade classmates of the value of listening to his work.

▲ **Critical Viewing**
What qualities does this portrait of Puccini convey? **[Interpret]**

▶ **Critical Viewing**
What mood does this cover for *Turandot* create? **[Interpret]**

Media and Technology Skills

Analyzing Bias in the Media
Activity: Evaluating Objectivity of News Reports

If someone gets up at a meeting and starts making a speech, you can recognize his or her persuasive purpose right away. Persuasion takes subtler forms as well. When a news report that claims to be objective actually takes a side, that report is said to be **biased**—it has a concealed persuasive purpose. Learn to detect bias in the news.

Think About It Bias in the news may take a few forms:

- **Loaded language** is the use of emotionally charged words to suggest a view of a subject without supporting the view with argument or evidence. For example, a news report on youth curfew laws might use the phrase "rowdy youths" without documenting any rowdy behavior.

- **Hasty generalizations** appear when a general statement is made based on only a few cases. For example, the news report on curfews might state that "Unsupervised teenagers are likely to turn to crime."

- **Inflammatory images** show actions or events that will elicit strong emotions from an audience, such as teenagers causing mischief. If an inflammatory image does not illustrate a specific fact in a news report, if the circumstances in which it was taken are not made clear, or if there are few contrasting images, then its use may reflect bias.

- **One-sided presentations** appear when all or most of the facts and images accompanying a report support a certain response to the story. Objective news reporting generally involves presenting more than one side of any controversial issue.

Evaluate It Fill out a chart like this one for a magazine article, a newspaper article, and a television news segment.

Review your chart and write a brief evaluation of how biased or objective each report was.

Other Forms of Bias

- **Opinions stated as facts** Example: "The best solution is to . . ."
- **Story "angle"** Example: The writer might report on efforts to save an endangered animal, stressing its uniqueness but not mentioning the potential harm it might cause humans.
- **Relative weight given an aspect of a story** Example: A newspaper editor features on the front page the damage done by protesters while "burying" in the back pages reports about new developments in the issue they are protesting.

BIAS DETECTOR

Source: _____ Report on:_____

Loaded Language	Hasty Generalizations	Inflammatory Images	One-sided Presentation: Y/N

Standardized Test Preparation Workshop

Responding to Persuasive Writing Prompts

The writing prompts on standardized tests often measure your ability to write persuasively. Your writing will be evaluated according to your demonstrated ability to:

- use language and arguments appropriate to the purpose and audience named in the prompt.
- use a consistent method of organization suited to the topic, such as pro-and-con organization.
- present effective support of arguments using descriptions, facts, and other details.
- use correct grammar, spelling, and punctuation.

Practice for such tests by responding to the following sample persuasive writing prompt. Use the suggestions on the following page to help you respond. The clocks suggest the portion of your allotted time that you should devote to each stage.

Sample Prompts

For thousands of years, people have wondered about distant stars and planets. Many people believe that the information gained about the universe through space exploration is important enough to justify support of the space program. Others regard space exploration as frivolous, saying that it diverts money from practical needs, such as education and care of the elderly.

Choose between the following writing prompts:

- State your position on public funding for the space program in a letter to a school astronomy club.
- State your position on public funding for the space program in a letter to your legislator.

Prewriting

Allow close to one fourth of your time for prewriting.

Consider Your Audience and Purpose Your purpose is to convince your readers that your position on the space program is the correct one. If you choose to write for members of an astronomy club, you can assume that they support space exploration. If you choose to write to a legislator, you can assume that he or she is interested in balancing various interests against one another. These facts about your audience should shape the kind of support you offer and the tone of your letter. For instance, if you were persuading the astronomy club not to support space exploration, you would probably want to suggest alternative ways to gather astronomical information.

Gather Support Use a T-chart to gather logical arguments, facts, examples, and strong images or phrases on both sides of the issue. Look for ways to refute the strongest arguments against your position. (See p. 131 for more information on using a T-chart.)

Drafting

Allow almost half of your time for drafting.

Introduce and Develop Your Position Begin by writing an interest-grabbing introduction in which you present your position with a strong image or story. Then, develop support for your position in the body of your response. Refer to your T-chart for details as you write. Before the end, introduce opposing arguments and refute them. You might save your strongest argument for the end of your response. In your conclusion, sum up your main points and restate your position.

Elaborate to Add Precise Language and Detail As you draft, make sure you include descriptive details and use precise words to make your writing vivid. Choose illustrations and descriptive words that will appeal to your chosen audience. Astronomy club members might like the sound of *far-sighted.* Legislators might prefer the sound of *responsible.*

Revising, Editing, and Proofreading

Allow almost one fourth of your time to revise. Use the last few minutes to proofread your work.

Evaluate Details and Word Choice Eliminate any details that are distracting or irrelevant. Change language that is inappropriate for your audience. Also, note places in your paper where you have used vague words, such as *good, bad, right,* and *wrong.* Replace them with precise words by answering the question, "Good (or bad) in what way?"

Work Neatly Check your work for errors in grammar, spelling, or punctuation. When making changes, place one line through the text to eliminate and use a caret (^) to indicate insertions.

Exposition
Comparison-and-Contrast Essay

The King of Prospect Park Triptych, 1994 (light), Anders Knutsson, Courtesy of the artist.

The King of Prospect Park Triptych, 1994 (dark), Anders Knutsson, Courtesy of the artist.

Comparison-and-Contrast Writing in Everyday Life

If you move to a new home, you can't help but compare your new neighborhood to your old one. Maybe you miss the corner store, but welcome a new friend across the street. You don't have to move, though, to start comparing. Making decisions means making comparisons. "I'll wear sneakers today," you might decide—comparing them to the sandals you wore the day before.

A comparison-and-contrast essay builds on such everyday comparisons. By creating new comparisons, writers can help us make decisions or see old things in fresh ways.

▲ **Critical Viewing**
This painting may be viewed under ordinary light (top) or in the dark (below). List three similarities and three differences between the two views. [**Compare and Contrast**]

What Is a Comparison-and-Contrast Essay?

A **comparison-and-contrast essay** analyzes the similarities and differences between two or more things. It can help you to decide which bicycle to buy. A good comparison-and-contrast essay can even change your perspective—as when a reviewer compares the latest hit song with an old album, letting you hear the startling similarities. A comparison-and-contrast essay includes

- a topic involving two or more things that are neither nearly identical nor extremely different.
- details illustrating both similarities and differences.
- clear organization that highlights the points of comparison.

To learn the criteria on which your essay may be evaluated, see the Rubric for Self-Assessment on page 166.

Types of Comparison-and-Contrast Essays

In addition to an ordinary comparison-and-contrast essay, some specialized essays also use comparison and contrast:

- **Product comparisons** compare two or more products, providing up-to-date information on each and discussing the advantages and disadvantages of purchasing each one.
- **Plan evaluations** compare two or more alternative plans or decisions, discussing the circumstances and comparing the advantages and disadvantages of each plan.

Writers in
ACTION

In his books and articles, Richard Lederer compares English to other languages and different English words to each other. He knows the value of saying more in fewer words:

". . . writing is hard work, and writing concisely is even more difficult."

PREVIEW
Student Work
IN PROGRESS

To develop your comparison-and-contrast writing skills, follow the work of Dylan Parker of Carr Lane VPA Middle School in St. Louis, Missouri. In this chapter, Dylan uses featured prewriting, drafting, and revising techniques to develop the comparison-and-contrast essay "Skateboards for Success." At the end of the lesson, you can read Dylan's completed essay.

Model From Literature

Laura Allen (1972–) is a former editor of the magazine *Superscience*. In this article, she uses research results from a new "field" of science—sports physics. Physics is the study of the natural laws governing the motion of physical bodies. For a physicist, the world can be described in terms of simple mathematical formulas. For a sports fan, the world is a more colorful—and rougher—place. The physicist watches a fly ball and sees a sphere traveling along a mathematical curve. The sports fan sees a game-clinching homer.

Sports physics combines these two views into one. It is the study of the laws of physics as they apply to the actions of objects and materials in sports. The sports physicist studies how balls travel through the air, how pucks slide across the ice, and how the material of a gym floor affects the bounce of a ball. Sports officials may use the findings of physicists to make decisions about equipment and regulations.

▲ **Critical Viewing**
After reading this essay, which bat would you rather use—the one pictured here, or the one on the next page? Explain. **[Apply]**

Reading ◄►**Writing** **Connection**

Reading Strategy: Identify Main Points
By **identifying an author's main points**—the points he or she wants you to remember—you can better understand the information presented. For instance, in "Bat Attacks?" you might identify one main point as follows: The amount of energy a bat gives a ball determines how fast the ball travels.

Bat Attacks?

Laura Allen

If you play baseball, you may swing an aluminum bat. Metal bats make balls fly faster than wooden bats, and that has some baseball officials worried. They say metal bats just might seriously injure players.

Slugging a ball gives it *kinetic energy*—the energy of motion. The more kinetic energy a ball has, the harder it strikes a player who misses a catch!

The author uses the point-by-point method of organizing a comparison. She compares each feature of the two bats in turn.

If you use a wooden bat, the baseball compresses briefly. (The bat does too, but only slightly.) The compression causes friction in the ball, transforming some kinetic energy into heat. That means less kinetic energy for a fast hit.

But an aluminum bat compresses much more than the baseball does. "That's because metal bats are more *elastic* (springy) than wooden bats," says Yale University baseball physicist Robert Adair. Unlike a solid wooden bat, aluminum bats are hollow inside. The compressed bat bounces back like a trampoline, giving the ball an added thrust forward. That's why pro players don't use aluminum—there'd be too many home runs!

[Both a metal bat and a wooden bat have "sweet spots."] A metal bat[, though,] sports larger sweet spots than wooden bats. That's another reason metal bats slug balls so fast. Sweet spots are areas on a bat that drive the farthest hits.

Any bat vibrates along its length when struck, says Adair. But at the sweet spots, there are no energy-sucking vibrations. That leaves more energy to send the ball sailing.

But a metal bat is stiffer (lengthwise) than a wooden bat. Stiff bats vibrate less *overall*. So aluminum bats may guarantee you a home run, but there's a tradeoff—if the ball hits a player, you've struck him or her out.

Most coaches haven't noticed an increase in injuries. But batter beware!

Writing Application: Help Readers Identify Main Points As you write your own comparison-and-contrast essay, make sure to help readers identify main points. You can do this by using transition words such as *first, second,* and *third,* or phrases such as "in addition," "by contrast," or "at the same time."

LITERATURE

For a different kind of comparison-and-contrast writing, see the poem "Fable" by Ralph Waldo Emerson in *Prentice Hall Literature: Timeless Voices, Timeless Themes,* Bronze.

The writer elaborates on the main idea here by explaining what a "sweet spot" is and why larger sweet spots make a metal bat so powerful.

The writer concludes with a point of high interest—the very power that makes a metal bat a home-run hitter may also make it dangerous to other players.

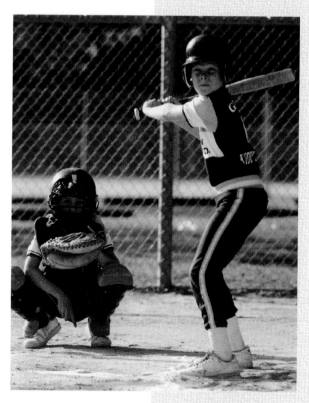

▶ **Critical Viewing** Judging from the essay, is this batter's chance of hitting a home run greater or less than if he were swinging a wooden bat? **[Deduce]**

Choosing Your Topic

Use these strategies to find an interesting comparison-and-contrast topic:

Strategies for Generating a Topic

1. **Quicklist** Fold a piece of paper in thirds lengthwise. In the first column, write a list of recent choices you have made—for instance, products you have bought. In the second column, next to each choice, write a descriptive phrase. In the third column, give an alternative to your choice. Review your list, and choose the most interesting topic.

2. **BUT Chart** Fold a piece of paper in half. Write the word *BUT* down the middle. In the left column, list items with something in common. Write down differences among them in the right column. Choose your topic from this list.

Try it out! Use the interactive BUT Chart in **Section 8.2**, on-line or on CD-ROM.

Student Work
IN PROGRESS

Name: Dylan Parker
Carr Lane VPA Middle School
St. Louis, MO

Using a BUT Chart
Here is how Dylan used a BUT chart to come up with a topic:

Things That Are Similar		Differences Between Them
My skateboard and Jimmy's skateboard: board plus 4 wheels	**B U T**	Jimmy's has a slick deck. My board is just wood. My board has high-quality wheels. Jimmy's board has cheap wheels.
Monday morning and Saturday morning: we wake up, eat breakfast, and leave the house		Mondays, we all grab our own breakfast. Saturdays, we make breakfast for Mom. Mondays, I have to get up at 6:00 (groan!). Saturdays, I sleep until 9:00 AT LEAST.

TOPIC BANK

If you're having trouble finding a topic, consider one of the following suggestions:

1. **The Book or the Movie?** It's fascinating to see how writers make a movie from a book—or a book from a movie. What is stressed? What is left out? What is added? Compare and contrast a book and the movie that was made from it. Explain which you enjoyed more, and why.

2. **Saturday Morning and Monday Morning** You wake up in the same body on the same planet—but a lot of other things may be different between Saturday morning and Monday morning. Write an essay comparing the two mornings.

Responding to Fine Art

3. Jot down similarities and differences between the two objects in this painting and among different parts of the canvas. Explore the reasons the artist might have included apparently dissimilar objects. How is the shape of the flowers similar to that of the skull? How are their meanings different? Write an essay comparing and contrasting the parts of this painting or comparing this painting with another by Georgia O'Keeffe.

Summer Days, 1936, Georgia O'Keeffe, Collection of Whitney Museum of American Art, New York

Responding to Literature

4. Read the Greek myths of Phaëton and Persephone. Compare the characters, the mistakes they make, and their fates. You can find these myths in *Prentice Hall Literature: Timeless Voices, Timeless Themes,* Bronze.

☑ Cooperative Writing Opportunity

5. **Travel Brochure** The mountains and the seashore are both attractive places to visit. With a group, compare and contrast these two vacation destinations. Divide your group into two smaller groups. One subgroup can write about the similarities, the other about the differences. Present your work to the class as an illustrated folder or pamphlet.

Narrowing Your Topic

Once you've chosen a topic, consider whether it is too broad to cover in a brief essay. Use cubing to narrow your topic.

Use Cubing to Narrow a Topic

To "cube" a topic, follow these steps:

1. **Describe it** to someone who is not familiar with it.
2. **Associate it** with someone, something, or some event in your life.
3. **Apply it,** explaining what you can do with it, on it, or to it.
4. **Analyze it** by breaking it into parts.
5. **Compare and contrast it** with things that are similar and different.
6. **Argue for or against it**, explaining good and bad points.

Circle details from your cube to create a focused topic.

Try it out! Use the interactive Cubing activity in **Section 8.2**, on-line or on CD-ROM.

Student Work
IN PROGRESS

Name: Dylan Parker
Carr Lane VPA Middle School
St. Louis, MO

Using Cubing

Here is how Dylan used cubing to narrow his broad topic "Skateboards."
He decided to focus on the best board to buy.

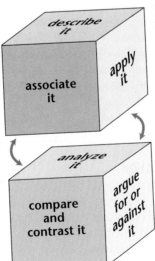

Skateboards

Describe:
Speedy wooden platforms on wheels, with curved noses and tails

Associate:
Kids love skateboards.

Apply:
I won a contest doing a front-side one-eighty.

Analyze:
Four wheels
Trucks
Bearings
Wooden decks

Compare/contrast:
Some skateboards are lighter and thicker than others.
Skateboarding is more fun than bicycling, but it's harder to learn.

Argue for or against it:
The better board to learn on is the cheaper one.

Considering Your Audience and Purpose

Your **audience**—who your readers are—and **purpose**—your reason for writing—should determine your choice of details and writing style. Before you begin writing, consider what details and vocabulary will best suit your audience's level of knowledge. Also, examine your purpose.

Analyze Your Purpose

Answer the following questions before you gather details and draft:

- Am I trying to **persuade** my audience to do or believe something? *If so, emphasize details that prove your case.*
- Will my writing **instruct** my readers, providing them with information? *If so, think of questions that your readers would probably ask, and answer them in your essay.*
- Will I **entertain** my readers—make them laugh or share a personal experience or insight? *If so, use vivid language to convey the humor, beauty, or other qualities of your subject.*

Gathering Details

For a comparison-and-contrast essay, focus on gathering details that show similarities and differences between your subjects.

Use a Venn Diagram

Draw two large circles that overlap in the middle, like the ones below. Fill in details about your two subjects, using the middle for features they have in common.

Technology Tip

If the subject of your topic is not always accessible to you, film it with a video camera to record its details. For example, if you are comparing and contrasting dawn and dusk at a nearby lake, record the sights and sounds there at each time of day. Review the tape to recall concrete details when you begin to write.

VENN DIAGRAM

Everyday Meals   **Holiday Meals**

Everyday Meals	Common	Holiday Meals
any day	cook and eat food	holiday
my family sits in kitchen together	clean up	grandparents, aunts, uncles, cousins
use everyday plates		sit in dining room
wear everyday clothes		use good china and tablecloths
eat good food		dress extra nicely
talk about our days		eat great holiday food
		talk about family news and history

Drafting

Shaping Your Writing

You cannot simply write down all the details you have gathered and call the result an essay. First, you must organize these details logically, so that a reader can assemble them into a clear picture of your subject.

Select an Effective Organization

There are two main ways to organize a comparison: the block method and the point-by-point method.

Block Method

- Present all details about one subject first.
- Next, present all the details about the second subject (then, about the third, fourth, and so on).

EXAMPLE: **Steam Engine vs. Gas Engine**

A. Steam engine
1. fuel
2. operation
3. efficiency

B. Gas engine
1. fuel
2. operation
3. efficiency

▲ **Critical Viewing**
If the people in the photograph are choosing among destinations, what three aspects of their choices are they probably discussing?
[Speculate]

The block method works well if you are writing about more than two things or if your topic is complex.

Point-by-Point Method

- First, discuss one aspect of both subjects.
- Next, discuss another aspect of both subjects, and so on, for each important aspect of the topic.

EXAMPLE: **Snow-Skiing vs. Water-Skiing**

A. Different equipment
1. snow-skiing
2. water-skiing

B. Length of time to learn
1. snow-skiing
2. water-skiing

Choose a method of organization suited to your topic. Then, make an outline arranging details according to this method.

Providing Elaboration

As you draft your essay, incorporate the details you have gathered, following the organization you have chosen. Think of yourself as an artist, adding vivid images, interesting examples, and clear reasons like touches of color on a canvas. Layering is a technique for writing in this careful and colorful way.

Layer Ideas Using SEE

To layer a paragraph, begin by writing out the main idea. Then, elaborate on—give more details about—that idea.

State the main idea of the paragraph in a sentence.

Extend your main idea. You might restate it with a new emphasis, show how it applies in a particular case, or distinguish it from another point.

Elaborate on your main idea in one or more sentences. Give examples, explanations, or other supporting details.

Student Work
IN PROGRESS

Name: *Dylan Parker*
Carr Lane VPA Middle School
St. Louis, MO

Using Layering

Notice how Dylan uses layering to craft a strong paragraph in which each sentence connects with the others.

Statement: These boards have many features in common, so you might think there is no reason to buy one instead of the other.

Extension: However, the boards are different in many ways. **Elaboration:** The "Zigzag" has a thicker but lighter board than the "Pulsion." The trucks and bearings on the two boards are also different. The "Pulsion" has better trucks and bearings. They last longer and give more control. I can do a three-sixty on the "Pulsion" but not on the other board.

Revising

Once you have completed your draft, begin revising your work. Michelangelo, the great Italian artist of the Renaissance, once said that his sculpture was inside the piece of marble before he began to work. He simply chipped away until it revealed itself. There is a good essay hidden in what you have written. Chip away at problems in your draft to reveal it.

Revising Your Overall Structure
Check the Effectiveness of Your Organization

A consistent organization that builds to a point helps readers understand and enjoy a comparison-and-contrast essay. Make sure that you have followed the block or the point-by-point method consistently. Also, make sure that your essay is balanced—that it includes an equal amount of information on both of the subjects you are comparing. Color-code details to make sure your essay is well-organized and balanced.

▶ **REVISION STRATEGY**
Color-Coding Details for Effective Organization and Balance

Highlight in one color the details pertaining to one of the items you are comparing. Use another color to highlight points about the other item.

- If most details in one color are grouped together, review stray details in that color: Do they make sense where they are placed, or should they be joined with the others?

- If one color alternates with another regularly, review longer clumps of a single color: Should these clumps be broken up, with some details moved elsewhere?

If you notice that you have more highlights in one color than in another, add details about the item for which there are fewer highlights.

▶ **Critical Viewing** Read the "Student Work in Progress" on the next page. Which skateboard model is this skateboarder more likely to use, and why? **[Apply]**

Revise Your Introduction and Conclusion

Review your **lead**—your introductory paragraph. If it seems boring to you, consider adding interest with a statement that invites your reader in, such as "You may think all mountain bikes are alike." You could also start off with a strong image or a surprising comparison.

Next, review your conclusion. It should leave your readers with a vivid image or with something to think about. If it does not, consider "tagging high points" to help create such a conclusion.

▶ **REVISION STRATEGY**
Tagging High Points

As you reread your draft, use a sticky note to flag any points of comparison or contrast that stand out as vivid, especially important, or surprising. Consider moving such a point to the end and building up to it.

Writers in
ACTION

Richard Lederer knows the importance of revising for any writer. Like others, he notes that writing only becomes effective after the revision stage:

"Good writing is rewriting. A writer is someone who will work for great lengths of time so that it looks easy."

Student Work
IN PROGRESS

Name: Dylan Parker
Carr Lane VPA Middle School
St. Louis, MO

Tagging High Points

Dylan tagged high points in his draft and moved one for an effective conclusion.

. . . To slide, the skateboarder rides the board in the air while part of it slides along a curb or even the railing on some stairs. I can do more tricks on a "Pulsion," because it has better trucks and wheels. I'm glad I started on a "Zigzag," though, because you can pick up tricks faster on a light, thick board.

I should save this point for the end, because it is an important point. Saving it till the end will be effective in another way, as well. First, readers will learn that the "Pulsion" is a better board, and then they will be surprised that I recommend the "Zigzag" for amateurs.

Conclusion

It sounds like the "Pulsion" is a much better board. Actually, it is not the best board for a beginner. If you are just starting out, you should get the "Zigzag" board. It is made thicker and lighter, and it is more affordable than the "Pulsion." If you learn with a thick but light board, you will be able to do tricks much more easily. This brand was my first board, and now I'm a great skater!

Revising Your Paragraphs
Check Your Paragraph Structure

Most paragraphs in your essay probably contain

- **T:** a **topic** sentence, stating the main idea.
- **R:** a **restatement** of the main idea in the topic sentence.
- **I:** **illustrations** of the main idea (including facts, examples, descriptions, and so on).

EXAMPLE: **T**—Not all brands of cat food are alike.

  R—Some brands are tastier than others.

  I—My cat will eat a quart of Brand X, even if he has eaten an hour earlier. He won't touch Brand Y, though, even if he is starving.

Read the *I* sentences above. On their own, they do not make a good paragraph. In paragraphs that explain main ideas, use at least one sentence of each kind, even if their order varies. Mark paragraph patterns to help strengthen paragraphs.

▶ REVISION STRATEGY
Marking Paragraph Patterns

Mark each of your sentences as a *T*, an *R*, or an *I*. Review your draft. If you find a group of *I*'s, make sure there is a *T* they support. If you find a *T* by itself, add an *I* sentence.

Student Work
IN PROGRESS

Name: Dylan Parker
Carr Lane VPA Middle School
St. Louis, MO

Marking Paragraph Patterns

Dylan marked a paragraph in his draft, adding a needed topic sentence.

The "Pulsion" skateboard and the "Zigzag" skateboard have many things in common. Both have the basic features that every skateboard has.   **T** **R**

Each ~~skateboard~~ has four rubber wheels. The wheels are   **I**

held onto the board by metal trucks, or axles. They both   **I**

have bushings and pads for the trucks. These parts are   **I**

like cushions that help the trucks work smoothly and last

longer. Both skateboards have ball bearings to keep the

wheels rolling fast.   **I**

> Dylan noticed that this paragraph contained only "illustrations," so he added two sentences: a statement of the main idea of the paragraph, along with a restatement of that main idea.

Revising Your Sentences

Combining Sentences
Using Compound Subjects

When you mention a similarity between two things, you can often cover it in one sentence by using a compound subject.

TWO SENTENCES:	Water-skiing is fun. Snow-skiing is fun, too.
COMBINED WITH COMPOUND SUBJECT:	Both **water-skiing and snow-skiing** are fun.

By combining sentences in this way, you can eliminate unnecessary wordiness. Use the following strategy to help.

▶ **REVISION STRATEGY**
Circling Repetitious Sentences

Review your draft, looking for places where you say the same thing about two items, each in its own sentence (see the example above). Circle these sentences. Review them, and see whether you can combine such sentences using a compound subject.

Get instant help! For additional assistance with subject-verb agreement, complete selected practice items in **Section 24.1**, on-line or on CD-ROM.

Grammar in Your Writing
Subject-Verb Agreement: Compound Subjects

A **compound subject** consists of two subjects joined by a conjunction such as *and, or,* or *nor.* When the subjects joined are singular, two simple rules will help you make sure that a compound subject agrees with its verb:

Two or more singular subjects joined by *and* take a plural verb.

EXAMPLE: Swimming *and* tennis **are** both fun sports.

Two or more singular subjects joined by *or* or *nor* take a singular verb.

EXAMPLES: A swimming lesson *or* a tennis lesson **is** good exercise.
Neither a swimming lesson *nor* a tennis lesson **is** a waste of time.

Find It in Your Reading   Read "Bat Attacks?" by Laura Allen on page 152. Identify one compound subject and the verb it takes. Explain what form the verb has—plural or singular—and why.

Find It in Your Writing   Identify any singular subjects joined by *and, or,* or *nor* in your draft. Identify the verb for each. Is the verb plural or singular? Does it agree with the subject? Correct any errors you find.

For more on subject-verb agreement, see Chapter 24.

Revising Your Word Choice

Avoid Unnecessary Repetition

It is important to include everything you want to say in your essay, but you don't have to say it twice! Check your writing for unnecessary repetition. A good way to spot redundancy is to read your work aloud.

▶ **REVISION STRATEGY**
Reading Aloud for Repeated Words

Read your work aloud, underlining any nouns, verbs, or adjectives you use more than once. (You can ignore commonly repeated words such as *the*, *a*, and *of*.) After you have marked your repeated words, evaluate each to determine whether you should replace the word with a synonym.

Peer Review

Summarize

In a small group, read your comparison-and-contrast essay twice, asking group members to listen the first time and to respond the second time. After the second reading, ask your classmates to summarize:

• the main similarities you discuss

• the main differences you discuss.

If your group cannot easily summarize your essay, review your writing again to make sure you have used well-organized paragraphs to develop your topic.

⚙ **Grammar and Style Tip**

One way to avoid repeating the same noun is to use a pronoun in its place. Another is to use a referring term, such as "the former," "the latter," or "the first one." (For more about pronouns, see Chapter 14.)

◀ **Critical Viewing** Would you feel comfortable having this group summarize your essay? Give two details from the photograph to explain your response. **[Relate]**

8.5 Editing and Proofreading

Carefully review your draft for errors in spelling, grammar, punctuation, and usage.

Focusing on Pronouns

Check your draft to make sure that you have used the correct pronoun for each antecedent.

Grammar in Your Writing
Pronoun-Antecedent Agreement

Pronouns are words that take the place of a noun or nouns.

SINGULAR		PLURAL	
Personal	**Possessive**	**Personal**	**Possessive**
I, me	my, mine	we, us	our, ours
you	your, yours	you	your, yours
he, she, it him, her	his, hers, its	they them	their, theirs

A pronoun must agree with its antecedent in both **person** and **number**. A **first-person** pronoun refers to the person speaking; a **second-person** pronoun refers to the person spoken to; and a **third-person** pronoun refers to the person, place, or thing spoken about.

INCORRECT: A *skateboarder* should wear a helmet. You would be a fool not to. (third person/second person)

CORRECT: A *skateboarder* should wear a helmet. He or she would be a fool not to. (third person/third person)

Number indicates whether a pronoun is **singular** (referring to one) or **plural** (referring to more than one).

INCORRECT: A *person* should practice their tricks. (singular/plural)

CORRECT: A *person* should practice his or her tricks. (singular/singular)

Find It in Your Reading Review "Bat Attacks?" by Laura Allen on page 152. Find two examples of pronouns. Identify their antecedents.

Find It in Your Writing Find three pronouns and their antecedents in your draft. For each, determine whether they agree in person and number.

For more on pronouns and their antecedents, see Chapter 24.

8.6 Publishing and Presenting

Building Your Portfolio

Consider these ideas for publishing and presenting your work:

1. **Be a Consumer Watchdog** If your essay contains information useful to consumers, form a Consumer Information Panel with classmates. Read your essays to the class, using visual aids to help convey the facts you've gathered.

2. **Present to Your Family or Friends** If you wrote about something in your own life, arrange to read your essay aloud to family or friends. Ask audience members to share their reactions.

Reflecting on Your Writing

Write down a few notes on your experience with comparing and contrasting, answering the questions below.

- Did the process of comparing and contrasting lead you to new ideas about your topic? Explain.

- What was the most important improvement you made to your essay when revising? Explain.

Internet Tip

To review a comparison-and-contrast essay scored according to this rubric, go on-line: PHSchool.com Enter Web Code: ebk-7001

Rubric for Self-Assessment

Use the following criteria to evaluate your comparison-and-contrast essay:

	Score 4	Score 3	Score 2	Score 1
Audience and Purpose	Clearly attracts audience interest in the comparison-contrast analysis	Adequately attracts audience interest in the comparison-contrast analysis	Provides a reason for the comparison-contrast analysis	Does not provide a reason for a comparison-contrast analysis
Organization	Clearly presents information in a consistent organization best suited to the topic	Presents information using an organization suited to the topic	Chooses an organization not suited to comparison and contrast	Shows a lack of organizational strategy
Elaboration	Elaborates ideas with facts, details, or examples; uses all information for comparison and contrast	Elaborates most ideas with facts, details, or examples; uses most information for comparison and contrast	Does not elaborate all ideas; does not use enough details for comparison and contrast	Does not provide facts or examples to support a comparison and contrast
Use of Language	Demonstrates excellent sentence and vocabulary variety; includes very few mechanical errors	Demonstrates adequate sentence and vocabulary variety; includes few mechanical errors	Demonstrates repetitive use of sentence structure and vocabulary; includes many mechanical errors	Demonstrates poor use of language; generates confusion; includes many mechanical errors

8.7 Student Work
IN PROGRESS

8.7

FINAL DRAFT

Skateboards for Success

Dylan Parker
Carr Lane VPA Middle School
St. Louis, Missouri

Lots of kids are interested in learning to skateboard because they see how much fun skateboarding is. They may not know which is the best skateboard to buy, though. Anyone who is interested in skateboarding needs to compare the different brands of skateboards that are out there. Different features are good for different levels of skaters. I have owned two good models, one called the "Pulsion" and the other called the "Zigzag."

The "Pulsion" skateboard and the "Zigzag" skateboard have many things in common. Both have the basic features that every skateboard has. Each has four rubber wheels. The wheels are held onto the board by metal trucks, or axles. They both have bushings and pads for the trucks. These parts are like cushions that help the trucks work smoothly and last longer. Both skateboards have ball bearings to keep the wheels rolling fast.

The deck is the part of the skateboard that you stand on. Both the "Pulsion" and the "Zigzag" have wooden decks instead of "slick" ones. (A slick deck is also made of wood, but it has plastic along the bottom.) The deck of each has a nose, which is the front curve, and a tail, which is the curve in back. Both models come with grip tape on the boards. A skateboarder needs grip tape to help him or her stay on when doing tricks on the skateboard.

Some skateboard brands do not put a design on the bottom of the deck, but these two do. Both skateboards are represented by a cartoon of an alien on their decks.

▲ **Critical Viewing**
Judging by Dylan's essay, why might this skateboarder prefer the "Pulsion"? **[Apply]**

In his introduction, Dylan draws his audience in by noting a problem his readers may face. He also introduces the two items he is going to compare.

Following a point-by-point organization, Dylan first discusses the features the two boards share with all others. In this next paragraph, he compares other basic features of the two.

Both skateboards go very fast. Both are easy to control. Using either a "Pulsion" or a "Zigzag," I can do many tricks. For instance, I can do an ollie, a "shove it," a kick flip, a heel flip, a front-side one-eighty, and a nose slide. An ollie is the basic skateboarding trick. To ollie, the skateboarder jumps up. As he or she jumps, he or she snaps the tail of the skateboard so that it comes up with the skateboarder. When a skateboarder does a "shove it" or a flip, he or she turns the board around or over while it is in the air. When a skateboarder does a one-eighty, he or she spins his or her body around while in the air. To slide, the skateboarder rides the board in the air while part of it slides along a curb or even the railing on some stairs.

▲ **Critical Viewing**
Compare this use of a skateboard with a more ordinary use.
[Compare and Contrast]

The "Zigzag" and the "Pulsion" are easy to find. They are sold at almost every skateboarding store. The companies have professional representatives and are known by skaters all across the United States of America.

These boards have many features in common, so you might think there is no reason to buy one instead of the other. However, the boards are different in many ways. The "Zigzag" has a thicker but lighter board than the "Pulsion." The trucks and bearings on the two boards are also different. The "Pulsion" has better trucks and bearings. They last longer and give more control. I can do a three-sixty on the "Pulsion" but not on the other board. The grip tape on the two boards is also different. The "Pulsion" has grip tape like sandpaper, and the "Zigzag" grip tape is just like regular paper stuck onto the board.

Here, Dylan turns to the important differences between the two boards. He keeps the point toward which he is building —which board is better to buy?—in the reader's mind.

It sounds like the "Pulsion" is a much better board. Actually, it is not the best board for a beginner. If you are just starting out, you should get the "Zigzag" board. It is made thicker and lighter, and it is more affordable than the "Pulsion." If you learn with a thick but light board, you will be able to do tricks much more easily. This brand was my first board, and now I'm a great skater! When you are a beginner, you should go with an inexpensive board first, and then, once you've gotten more advanced in your skills, you can get a more expensive skateboard. If you choose the right board, you will learn faster and save money!

Dylan presents the high point of his comparison—the better, more expensive board is actually not better for a beginner!

Connected Assignment *Consumer Report*

Need advice on purchasing a product? It's helpful to turn to a **consumer report**—a comparison of the strengths and weaknesses of different products and the advantages of using one over another. Useful consumer reports feature

- a detailed comparison of two or more similar products.
- a rating of the products, backed by facts.

Prewriting To choose a topic, consider these suggestions:

- **A Recent Purchase** Choose an important purchase you or your family has recently made. Write a report evaluating the product and an alternative.
- **Report on Music Magazines** Choose two magazines that cover music. Compare the type of stories they publish, their advertising, and their features. Recommend one to readers.

Once you have chosen a topic, focus on only a few items— for example, if your topic is CD-players, focus on two in the same price range. Then, jot down a description of who will use your report on an index card: What are their needs? How much money do they have to spend? To meet your audience's needs, consult this card as you gather details.

To gather the details you need, read brochures, user guides, and magazine articles. Record details in a Venn diagram like the one shown.

▲ Critical Viewing Describe a time when you felt as the person in this picture appears to. **[Relate]**

Drafting After you've gathered and organized all of the information you need, begin drafting. Write the body of your consumer report first. Then, create an introduction that leads into it and a conclusion in which you make your recommendation.

Revising and Editing After completing a draft, check it against your audience description. Is there information you have not included that your readers need to make a good decision? If so, add these details. Have you included details your readers don't need? If so, consider deleting them.

VENN DIAGRAM

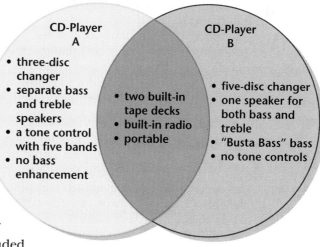

CD-Player A
- three-disc changer
- separate bass and treble speakers
- a tone control with five bands
- no bass enhancement

- two built-in tape decks
- built-in radio
- portable

CD-Player B
- five-disc changer
- one speaker for both bass and treble
- "Busta Bass" bass
- no tone controls

Publishing and Presenting After revising your consumer report, proofread it for errors in spelling, grammar, or punctuation. Consider publishing it on a class consumer Web site.

Spotlight on the Humanities

Evaluating Performances

Focus on Music: Gilbert and Sullivan

Sometimes, one movie may remind you of another. When you compare and contrast the two, you may realize that one movie is making fun of the other!

Two masters of the sneaky art of making fun by making comparisons were British composers William Gilbert (1836–1911) and Arthur Sullivan (1842–1900). In their musical comedies, they spoofed everything from the plays about pirates popular at the time (*The Pirates of Penzance*) to the Victorian craze for Japanese culture (*The Mikado*).

Gilbert and Sullivan's comedies are in a form called operetta—a mix of songs and spoken dialogue. (Musically and in subject matter, operetta is lighter than its cousin, opera.) Their fourteen operettas are still performed today.

Art Connection In *The Mikado,* Gilbert and Sullivan made fun of a fashionable fascination with all things Asian, a trend that was underway in England by 1875. The preoccupation with Japanese art, especially ceramics and pottery, was called **japonisme**. Using Japanese and other elements, mid- to late Victorian decorators favored a lush, cluttered look in interior furnishings.

Film Connection In 1983, a film version of Gilbert and Sullivan's *The Pirates of Penzance* was released starring Kevin Kline and Angela Lansbury. Spawned by the successful New York stage production of the operetta at The New York Shakespeare Festival, the film captures the whimsical Gilbert and Sullivan style.

◀ Critical Viewing What type of person might Gilbert and Sullivan be making fun of with this character? **[Speculate]**

The Little White Girl, James Abbott McNeill Whistler, Tate Gallery, London

▲ Critical Viewing What elements of japonisme can you find in this painting? **[Analyze]**

Comparison-and-Contrast Writing Activity: Compare Two Versions of a Musical

Choose a musical that you've seen both on film and in the theater, or in two different movie versions. Write a comparison and contrast of the two versions, explaining which you prefer.

Media and Technology Skills

Comparing Media

Activity: Comparing Book and Movie Versions

Books don't always stay on the page. Sometimes, a movie maker takes a favorite story and puts it on screen. There are a few ways in which movie makers change stories when they film them.

Learn About It

- **Form** Books unfold in the mind. Anything that can engage the mind—an exciting scene, a poetic description, a scientific explanation—can find a place in one book. A movie, though, holds viewers' attention through images of action. Movie makers do not often include parts of a book that cannot be shown in actions.

- **Time** Movie makers often leave out events that appear in a book. They will also eliminate characters or combine them. The reason is simple: While a reader can read a book over the course of days, putting it down, then picking it up again, most movies are viewed continuously. A movie rarely exceeds two hours in length. To hold to this time, movies include only essential parts of a story.

- **Image and Sound** While a writer shapes your appreciation of a person or event with well-chosen words, movie makers make use of actors' abilities, various camera techniques (close-ups on faces, panoramic views of backgrounds), and the pacing of shots to create drama, mood, and character. A movie maker can also add a piece of lush orchestral music to create romantic longing or a deafening explosion to create excitement.

- **Audience** To help pay for their cost, movies must make a great deal of money during their short "run." For this reason, movie makers try to appeal to current tastes. They may change the period in which a story is set. They may cast the latest star in a role, disregarding the physical appearance of the character in the book.

Evaluate It Watch a movie production of a book you have read. Take notes using a chart like the following. Then, write a brief evaluation of the two versions, explaining which you preferred and why.

Other Differences to Consider

Purpose
Recognize that the purposes of the author and of the movie maker may not be the same—both may wish to entertain, but one might also wish to instruct.

Period
Consider the values and beliefs of people in the period in which the book was written, versus popular values and beliefs at the time the movie was produced. For instance, a book written when women were expected to behave in certain ways might treat a certain incident as shocking. A modern movie might treat the incident as humorous.

Book
Characters: _____
Plot: _____
Setting: _____

Movie
Characters: _____
Plot: _____
Setting: _____

Similarities/ Differences
_____
_____
_____

Standardized Test Preparation Workshop

Responding to Expository Writing Prompts

The writing prompts on standardized tests often measure your ability to write an expository piece, such as a comparison-and-contrast essay. Your writing will be evaluated according to your ability to

- respond directly to the prompt, selecting only details directly connected to the topic.

- organize ideas so they are easy to follow.

- elaborate ideas through the use of appropriate details.

- unify your work through the use of transitions.

- write with few errors in spelling, grammar, usage, or mechanics.

Following is an example of an expository writing prompt. Use the suggestions on the following page to help you respond. The clocks show the suggested percentage of your test-taking time to devote to each stage.

Test Tip

To check the spelling of a word of which you are unsure, write out each possible spelling on scratch paper. Quickly choose the spelling that looks correct.

Sample Writing Situation

> Writers often use contrasting characters in their stories. By placing unlike characters together in a situation, they are able to emphasize the personality traits of each.
>
> In "Rip Van Winkle" by Washington Irving, Dame Van Winkle and her husband Rip have very different personalities. Write an essay in which you compare and contrast the two characters. Use specific incidents from the story to support your analysis of each.

Prewriting

Allow close to one fourth of your time for prewriting.

Use a Venn Diagram Gather information about the two characters using a Venn diagram. (To review an example of a Venn diagram, see page 157.)

Keep a Consistent Purpose As you begin to gather details for your essay, keep in mind your purpose in writing, set by the prompt. The sample prompt does not ask you to retell the story. Instead, it asks you to provide examples from the story that reveal the personalities of the two characters.

Drafting

Allow almost half of your time for drafting.

Organize Details Choose a method of organization. To use the block method, discuss all qualities of one subject first, then all qualities of the next subject. To use the point-by-point method, discuss each aspect of the two subjects in turn. After you choose a method, sketch an outline that fits your chosen method.

Elaborate After organizing details, write an introductory paragraph making a general statement about what the contrast between Irving's characters shows the reader. Then, follow your organization in presenting details that reveal the personality of each character. In your conclusion, sum up your essay by restating the lesson the comparison teaches.

Use Transitions As you draft, use transitional words to indicate the connections between ideas. The following words show comparison-and-contrast relationships: *however, nevertheless, yet, likewise, in the same way, on the contrary, similarly, instead,* and *nonetheless.*

Revising, Editing, and Proofreading

Allow almost one fourth of your time to revise and edit. Use the last few minutes to proofread your work.

Use Precise Language Review your paper for areas where your descriptions are vague. Decide on the best way to phrase each description, and then neatly add the new phrasing to your paper.

Make Corrections Check for errors in spelling, grammar, and punctuation. When making changes, place one line through text that you are eliminating. Use a caret (^) to indicate the places where you are adding words.

Exposition
Cause-and-Effect Essay

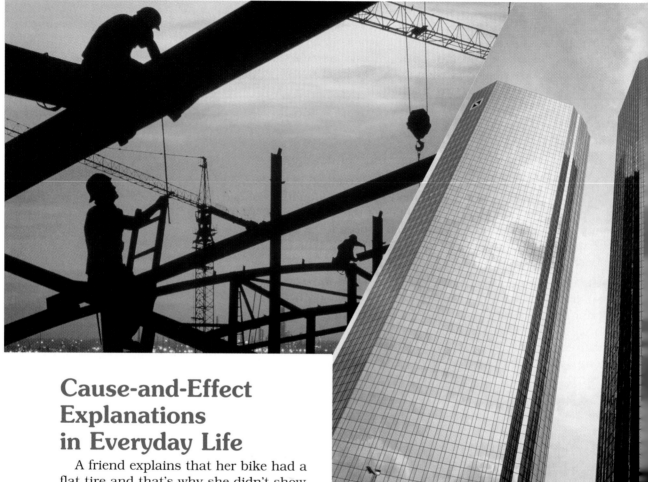

Cause-and-Effect Explanations in Everyday Life

A friend explains that her bike had a flat tire and that's why she didn't show up at the mall. Your brother arrives late for dinner and complains that his soccer game started an hour later than scheduled. These excuses are also **cause-and-effect explanations**—explanations of why something happened.

Without cause-and-effect explanations, there would be no excuses—but neither would there be sciences, plans, or games. Why hit a ball if you don't believe the bat will cause it to fly into the outfield? Why change the batteries if you don't think that electricity causes the flashlight to work? Cause-and-effect explanations help us make sense of our world and discover new possibilities.

▲ **Critical Viewing** Explain briefly what cause-and-effect relationships connect the subjects of these two photographs. **[Interpret; Connect]**

What Is a Cause-and-Effect Essay?

Exposition is writing that informs or explains. A **cause-and-effect essay** is expository writing that explains the reasons why something happened or the results an event or situation will produce. A cause-and-effect essay might focus on causes, as in an explanation of why the days get shorter in the fall, or it might focus on effects, as in an essay on why chemicals are used in farming. In either case, a cause-and-effect essay explains one group of events or facts with another group.

Cause-and-effect essays include

- a well-defined topic that can be covered in a few pages.
- detailed, factual explanations of events or situations and the relationships among them.
- a clear organization with transitions that indicate the relationships among details.

Types of Cause-and-Effect Essays

The following are a few of the types of cause-and-effect essays you might write:

- **Science reports** describe a series of events (including experiments) and explain them according to natural laws.
- **Historical accounts** describe the causes or effects of an event, such as a war or an election.
- **Cause-and-effect investigations** describe the causes or effects of something you have noticed in your own life, such as a new road or a change in weather patterns.

PREVIEW
Student Work
IN PROGRESS

Jake Sommer is a student at Maplewood Middle School in Maplewood, New Jersey. In his essay "Why Trains Are No Longer Popular," Jake looks at why train travel has become less popular than travel by car and plane. In this chapter, you will see how Jake used featured prewriting, drafting, and revising strategies to develop his final draft. At the end of the chapter, you can read Jake's completed essay.

How in the World? *is a collection of brief articles explaining various facts and phenomena—from why you don't fall out of a roller coaster when it turns upside down to how physicists count tiny nuclear particles.*

This form of literature—brief scientific explanations for ordinary readers—has become quite popular. Its popularity shows the importance of science in our lives. It also shows people's need to understand the causes and effects that shape their world.

▲ **Critical Viewing**
What are some cause-and-effect explanations that this photograph brings to mind? **[Analyze]**

Reading Writing Connection

Reading Strategy: Infer Even in a cause-and-effect essay, a writer cannot explain every detail. As a result, when you read you must **make inferences**—use explanations and details that are provided to draw conclusions about details that are left out. You can also use your knowledge and experiences to help you make inferences. As you read this essay, use your knowledge to make inferences about why scientists would attempt to cause rain.

How Do Rainmakers Make It Rain?

from **How in the World?**

. . . In 1946 Vincent Schaefer and Irving Longmuir started their work at the General Electric Research Laboratories in Schenectady, New York, which proved that rain clouds could be artificially encouraged to produce showers.

Clouds are made up of billions of particles of water too small to fall as rain. Only when the droplets grow to a quarter of a millimeter or more will they fall as a fine drizzle. Smaller droplets evaporate before reaching the ground.

One way the droplets grow is by freezing to form particles of ice. In a cloud containing some ice particles and some water droplets, the ice particles grow rapidly as the droplets evaporate and the vapor is transferred to the ice. Since the temperature of clouds is often below freezing it might be expected that the droplets would freeze easily. But the water can be 10 or 20 degrees below freezing (supercooled) without actually freezing.

The reason for this is that the water in clouds is absolutely pure, without any dust or other contaminants which can form the center of an ice crystal. If tiny particles are provided, the droplets freeze, grow quickly until they are large enough to fall, and then melt as the temperature rises, reaching the ground as rain.

Schaefer and Longmuir proved that small particles, usually of silver iodide, added to supercooled clouds could create rapidly growing ice crystals. These particles have been dropped from aircraft, carried by rockets or even released at ground level for air currents to carry them aloft.

In the [former] Soviet Union, 70mm artillery guns have been used to fire silver iodide particles into clouds, exploding at the right height to disperse the chemical.

As long as the clouds are supercooled the technique may work—increasing rainfall by up to a fifth. But since it is impossible to know how much rain would have fallen anyway there are still question marks over the method's economic effectiveness.

The authors present a sequence of causes and effects. First, they describe what needs to happen before rain will fall—water particles must grow in size. Next, they give one cause of this growth.

Here, the authors explain an additional condition needed to cause rain to fall.

By explaining what causes rain to fall naturally, the authors make it possible for readers to understand how scientists have tried to cause it to rain.

◀ Reading ▶ Writing
Connection

Writing Application:
Help Readers Infer

As you write your own cause-and-effect essay, help readers draw inferences by providing thorough evidence for your cause-and-effect explanation.

LITERATURE

To read a humorous example of cause-and-effect writing, see James Thurber's story "The Night the Bed Fell." This story can be found in *Prentice Hall Literature: Timeless Voices, Timeless Themes*, Bronze.

Prewriting

Choosing Your Topic

Perhaps you have always wondered why leaves change color or why hair turns gray as people age. Choose a question that interests you as the topic of your essay. Use the following strategies to help stimulate ideas:

Strategies for Generating a Topic

1. **Brainstorming** In a group, brainstorm for topics by filling in the blanks in two questions: "What Causes X?" and "What Are the Effects of Y?" One member should list ideas on the chalkboard. Select your topic from those listed.

2. **Blueprinting** Draw the plan of a house, apartment, or other place you know, labeling each room or area. For each part of the plan, list connected people, things, words, or activities. Then, reread what you have written. Circle items about which you can ask, "What caused this?" or "What effects does this have?" Choose your topic from these items.

3. **Media Flip-Through** Sometimes you browse through the refrigerator looking for just the right snack. You can browse for writing ideas as well. Scan the newspaper, look through magazine racks, or go to the library. Skim for ideas until you find an interesting topic involving causes and effects.

Student Work
IN PROGRESS

Name: Jake Sommer
Maplewood Middle School
Maplewood, NJ

Media Flip-Through

Jake watched the news, looked at magazines, and poked around his house gathering topic ideas. From his notes, he selected the one that interested him most.

Ideas for Cause-and-Effect Essay

TV news story: Increases in airfares

Landfill article in <u>Newsweek</u> magazine

Radio: Diary from Kosovo

Conversation between Uncle Robert and Dad—

    our team's offensive line

Radio documentary: people who watch and track trains

TOPIC BANK

If you're having trouble finding a topic, consider the following possibilities:

1. **Explanation of a Cycle** Choose a cycle, such as the life cycle of plants, the creation of new toys every year, or television show "repeats." Write an essay explaining what keeps the cycle going.

2. **Causes of Victory or Defeat** Write an explanation of the performance of a favorite team or athlete over a season or in a playoff. Explain how ability and other factors, such as the weather and level of confidence, shaped the outcome.

Responding to Fine Art

3. This painting hints at forces in the sky. Choose an event in the sky, such as the seasonal "movement" of the stars, a thunderstorm, or the Northern Lights, and explain what causes it.

Responding to Literature

4. Read Robert Frost's "Stopping by Woods on a Snowy Evening." Then, write about a time when you stopped in the middle of an activity. Explain what caused you to stop, what the effects of the pause were, and whether you felt as Frost did. You can find Frost's poem in *Prentice Hall Literature: Timeless Voices, Timeless Themes*, Bronze.

Aloha #6, Paul Brach, Courtesy Bernice Steinbaum Gallery, Miami, FL

☑ Cooperative Writing Opportunity

5. **Cause-and-Effect Pamphlet** With a group of classmates, choose a major event in history with many causes and effects, or select a broad topic with many subtopics—weather events, for example. Brainstorm a list of causes and effects. Then, each group member should choose a specific topic or set of causes and effects. Work individually to write cause-and-effect essays on your chosen topics. Then, regroup to revise the essays and assemble them into a pamphlet with a cover and contents page.

Narrowing Your Topic

Consider whether your topic is narrow enough to discuss thoroughly in a brief essay. A topic with many causes and effects, such as the causes of storms, is far too broad. However, the effects of a tornado would be appropriate. The following strategy will help you narrow your topic.

Use Classical Invention to Narrow Your Topic

In ancient Greece, thinkers developed the strategy of Classical Invention to analyze a topic. Here are the steps:

1. Replace the topic in the example below with your own topic, and answer the questions shown.

2. Review your responses, and circle a series of related events that catch your interest.

3. Write a statement summing them up. Use this as your narrowed topic.

Student Work
IN PROGRESS

Name: Jake Sommer
Maplewood Middle School
Maplewood, NJ

Asking Questions to Narrow a Topic
Here's how Jake focused his topic:

General Topic: Trains

- In what category does your topic belong?
  Hobbies (train counting, collecting models); transportation

- How is your topic similar to or different from others in the category?
  Hobbies: train counting is for outdoors; Transportation: trains carry groups of people—not like cars; Transportation: trains are not as popular as cars.

  Narrowed Topic
  Why are trains no longer popular?

- What causes and effects are involved with this topic?
  Causes: invention of steam engine; goods needed to be moved across the country quickly; invention of cars, trucks, and airplanes caused trains to become less popular.
  Effects: The U.S. was able to grow westward.

Considering Your Audience and Purpose

Identify your intended **audience**—your readers—and your **purpose** for writing. Answer these questions to help you choose words and details that fit your audience and purpose:

- How much do my readers know about my topic?

- With what type of language will they be most comfortable? Formal? Informal? A combination?

- In addition to informing my audience, what else do I hope to accomplish? Do I want my audience to accept a point of view or take action?

Gathering Details

Do Research

You may not know all the causes and effects you need to cover. Do research to fill in any gaps in your knowledge. Use library resources, on-line references, and primary sources—for example, interviews with experts or your own observations. Use a T-chart and note cards to help you gather details.

Use a T-Chart Focus your research by asking good questions. Draw a large T on a piece of paper. Write your topic above it. Label each side as shown below. List key causes and effects involved in your topic on either side. Fill in the answers as you do research.

🔲 Research Tip

Encyclopedias on CD-ROM make browsing especially easy. Many allow you to begin by identifying an area of interest, such as Performing Arts, Science, Hobbies, Sports, or Pets. Then, you can scan the alphabetical list until something sparks your interest.

Topic: **How the Sun Heats and Lights the Earth**

What causes _____ ?	What are the effects of _____ ?
1. the sun to rise and set:	**1. the sun rising and setting:**
The Earth spins around on its axis.	Day and night, warmth and light, cold and darkness result.
2. the sun to give heat and light:	**2. the sun giving heat and light:**
Atomic reactions, like a long-lasting explosion, go off inside the sun.	Animals and plants can live on Earth. Plants use sunlight to grow, and animals eat the plants.

9.3 **Drafting**

Shaping Your Writing
Organize Logically

Using the information you've gathered, begin writing your first draft. Start your essay with an introduction that includes a sentence or two summing up the main point you'd like to make about your topic. Then, organize your body paragraphs using these suggestions:

RUBE GOLDBERG™ and © Rube Goldberg Inc. Distributed by United Media

Many Causes/Single Effect If you're writing about a single event with many causes—as illustrated in this diagram—devote one paragraph to each cause and follow these paragraphs with one paragraph about the effect.

▲ **Critical Viewing** Describe two of the processes linking cause and effect in this cartoon. **[Analyze]**

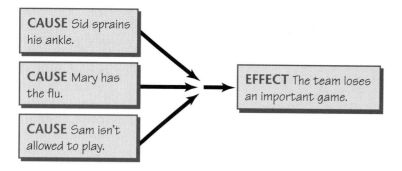

CAUSE Sid sprains his ankle.

CAUSE Mary has the flu.

CAUSE Sam isn't allowed to play.

EFFECT The team loses an important game.

Single Cause/Many Effects If your topic involves a single event or situation that has produced many effects, devote one paragraph to each effect.

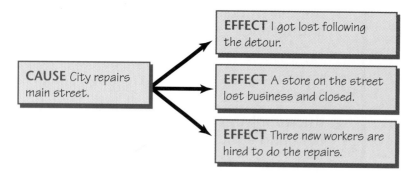

CAUSE City repairs main street.

EFFECT I got lost following the detour.

EFFECT A store on the street lost business and closed.

EFFECT Three new workers are hired to do the repairs.

Series of Causes and Effects If your topic consists of a series of causes and effects, organize your body paragraphs in chronological, or time, order.

Providing Elaboration

Provide detailed explanations of each cause or effect. Make sure that your explanations include enough evidence to enable readers to follow the logic of the connections you're making.

Elaborate Causal Connections

Following are three different types of connections:

- **Natural laws** link some causes to their effects.

CAUSE AND EFFECT: The shape of a steel ship causes it to float.

EXPLAIN THE LOGIC: An object will float if the amount of fluid it pushes aside weighs more than it does. *(Law of Buoyancy)*

- **Physical processes** link some causes to their effects.

CAUSE AND EFFECT: Sunlight causes plants to grow.

EXPLAIN THE LOGIC: Chlorophyll in the plant uses energy from sunlight in a chemical reaction that nourishes the plant. *(Process: Photosynthesis)*

- **Motives and habits** usually explain the way people act.

CAUSE AND EFFECT: Unfair laws caused the colonists to revolt.

EXPLAIN THE LOGIC: The colonists wanted control over the laws by which they were ruled. *(The Desire for Freedom)*

As you draft, explain the logic of each causal connection you describe.

Student Work
IN PROGRESS

Name: *Jake Sommer*
Maplewood Middle School
Maplewood, NJ

Elaborating Causal Connections

As Jake drafted, he explained the logic of some causal connections:

Traveling by train then became the main source of transportation between small towns and from big cities to other cities. One important cause of the growth of the railroad was the convenience of train travel and shipping. By having trains everywhere, the people could travel thousands of miles in only days instead of weeks.

To explain one reason for the growth of trains, Jake wrote a sentence about people's motives: People used trains because they liked the convenience of the railroad.

Revising

Revising Your Overall Structure

Check Logical Structure

Start revising by using this strategy to check that you have presented causes and effects in a logical sequence.

▶ **REVISION STRATEGY**
Connecting the Steps

Following is the procedure for "Connecting the Steps":

1. Highlight each sentence that sums up an event or condition.

2. Number each in the order of occurrence or importance.

3. Draw arrows connecting each step in numbered order.

4. If any arrows point backward, reorganize some of your details so that all of the arrows point forward.

Student Work
IN PROGRESS

Name: Jake Sommer
Maplewood Middle School
Maplewood, NJ

Connecting the Steps

*When Jake saw arrows crisscrossing his draft,
he realized he needed to rearrange sentences.*

By the early 1900s, there were 252,000 miles of track. [3]
The biggest advance in railroads came in 1869 when
the transcontinental railroad was completed. [1] It took seven
years to build the tracks between the east coast and the
west coast. Then came the Golden Age of Railroads. [2] Before
the Civil War there were approximately 31,000 miles of
track. Traveling by train then became the main source of
transportation [4] between small towns and from big cities to
other cities.

Revising Your Paragraphs

State Main Ideas Clearly

Simply by starting a new paragraph, you signal readers that a new idea is coming up. Effective writers state the main idea in each paragraph clearly. Use the following strategy to make sure that each of your paragraphs has a clearly stated main idea:

▶ **REVISION STRATEGY**
Finding the "Tug"

Reread each paragraph to find the main idea that draws your attention—the "tug" of the paragraph. Summarize this "tug" in one or two words in your margin. Then, check whether your paragraph includes a sentence that expresses this idea clearly. If not, craft a "tug" sentence, weaving it into the beginning, middle, or end of the paragraph.

The Earth is attracted to the sun by the force of gravity. This force keeps it from flying off into space. Gravity alone, though, would just pull the Earth straight into the sun. Inertia, the force that keeps the Earth speeding along through space, keeps it from falling into the sun.

Tug: There are two forces that cause the Earth to revolve around the sun.

Show Connections

Once you're confident that each paragraph has a topic sentence, use the following strategy to strengthen the connections among your other sentences:

▶ **REVISION STRATEGY**
Coding Cause-and-Effect Connections

Reread each paragraph. Each time you find a sentence describing a cause next to a sentence describing one of its effects, circle the space between those sentences. Go back and add transitions—such as *because of* and *as a result*—to help readers see cause-and-effect connections.

Revising Your Sentences
Use the Appropriate Verb Tense

Generally, you should use one verb tense (your "dominant tense") consistently throughout your paper. However, to show the order of events, you sometimes need to shift tenses.

EVENTS AT DIFFERENT TIMES: Because my puppy **chewed** [past] my catcher's mitt, I **need to** [present] buy a new one.

EVENTS THAT RECUR: Yesterday, I **bought** [past] a new mitt. Because my puppy **chews** [present] my mitt every day, I **buy** [present] a new one every week.

▶ **REVISION STRATEGY**
Circling Verbs in an Inconsistent Tense

Review your essay to determine the tense of the majority of your verbs. Then, circle any verbs in a different tense. If these verbs do not show events at different times or show a recurring event, consider changing them to your dominant tense.

Student Work
IN PROGRESS

Name: Jake Sommer
Maplewood Middle School
Maplewood, NJ

Circling Verbs in an Inconsistent Tense

Jake's dominant tense was the past. He circled verbs in the present and future. He determined that these shifts in tense were necessary.

So what happened to the trains? By the 1970's, most of the private railroad companies went bankrupt and were sold to the U.S. government. The government created Amtrak to take over passenger operations for long-distance trips. Amtrak's 23,000 miles (go) to just 500 stations. Not many people (make) cross-country trips by train anymore. However, in the future, high-speed trains like they (have) in Europe and Japan (may come) to the U.S. and (spark) a revival of train travel.

Grammar in Your Writing
Verb Tense

Every verb has a few different forms, called tenses. The **tense** of a verb indicates the time when the action it expresses takes place—past, present, or future. (If the verb does not express an action, its tense tells when a fact or condition is the case.)

Forms of Regular Verb Tenses		
Tense	Forms of *Speak*	
Present	I speak you speak he, she, it speaks	we speak you speak they speak
Past	I spoke you spoke he, she, it spoke	we spoke you spoke they spoke
Future	I will speak you will speak he, she, it will speak	we will speak you will speak they will speak

Find It in Your Reading Read "How Do Rainmakers Make It Rain?" on page 176. Find one example each of the use of past, present, and future tenses. In each case, explain why the use of that tense is appropriate.

Find It in Your Writing Circle past events mentioned in your draft in one color, current events in another color, future events in a third, and recurring events in a fourth. Make sure you use a past tense for all past events, present tense for current or recurring events, and future tense for events that have not yet occurred.

To find out more about verb tense, see Chapter 22.

▶ **Critical Viewing** Write a sentence describing events suggested by this photograph. Use verbs in both the present and future tenses. **[Analyze]**

Revising Your Word Choice

Use Precise Verbs

In addition to using verbs in the correct tense, it is important to make your verbs as precise as possible. Notice how the verbs in these examples make the action much more vivid.

GENERAL: Sara **sat** in her chair.

PRECISE: Sara **slouched** in her chair.

GENERAL: Martha **ate** her soup.

PRECISE: Martha **slurped** her soup.

GENERAL: Anthony **swam** across the pool.

PRECISE: Anthony **splashed** across the pool.

Use the following strategy to help you revise key verbs to make them more precise:

▶ **REVISION STRATEGY**
Highlighting Key Events

Highlight five sentences in your draft that focus on key events, and examine the verbs you use in them. Replace general or vague verbs with vivid, precise ones.

Peer Review

After you've finished revising on your own, enlist some of your classmates to help you identify potential problems you may have missed. Follow this strategy:

"Say Back"

Read your essay aloud to a group of classmates. Ask them to write down things that stood out in your essay. Pause for one minute while they write. (Look at the clock; a minute is longer than it feels!) Then, read your essay a second time. Ask reviewers to tell you

- what causes you discuss.
- what effects these causes produce.
- anything about which they would like to know more.

What your reviewers tell you should match what you believe your essay says. If they do not mention an important cause or effect, consider adding more information about it or even reorganizing your draft to make connections between events clear.

▲ Critical Viewing
What is the mood of the peer review session in the photograph? Explain how this mood would affect the productivity of the session. **[Interpret]**

9.5 Editing and Proofreading

Just by changing one word, you can turn "the man in the moon" into "the man on the moon." The first is an imaginary figure. The second might be a real astronaut. A tiny preposition like *in* can make a big difference to readers. Carefully proofread your work. Focus on making certain that the prepositions you use express the relationship you intend.

Focusing on Prepositions

Review a list of common prepositions. Then, check your draft to make sure that, in each case, you have used the preposition that expresses your meaning. Also, make sure you have not used two prepositions where one will do.

Grammar in Your Writing
Prepositions

A **preposition** relates the noun or pronoun following it to another word in the sentence. Prepositions show relationships between things. Review the following examples:

on the table	above the table
under the table	around the table

Do not use two prepositions where one will do.

Avoidable: He fell **off of** the diving board.

Preferred: He fell off the diving board.

Avoidable: Margaret put the desserts **up on** the counter.

Preferred: Margaret put the desserts on the counter.

Find It in Your Reading Find three prepositions in "How Do Rainmakers Make It Rain?" on page 176. For each preposition, cite the two words in the sentence that it most clearly links.

Find It in Your Writing Highlight each preposition in your draft. In each case where you have highlighted two in a row, see whether you can use only one.

For more about prepositions, see Chapter 17.

Publishing and Presenting

Building Your Portfolio

Here are some ideas for presenting your cause-and-effect essay:

1. **Present a Diagram** On posterboard or an overhead slide, create a diagram of the causal chain in your essay. Read your essay aloud, pointing out appropriate parts of the diagram as you go.

2. **Produce a Skit** Prepare a brief skit in which you and several classmates act out the sequence of causes and effects in your essay. While a narrator reads your essay aloud, the actors might enact the events the narrator is describing.

Reflecting on Your Writing

Jot down a few notes on the experience of writing your essay. To get started, answer these questions:

- What did you enjoy about analyzing the cause(s) and effect(s) of your topic? What did you not enjoy?
- What was the most interesting thing you learned?

Internet Tip

To see a cause-and-effect essay scored according to this rubric, go on-line: PHSchool.com
Enter Web Code: ebk-7001

Rubric for Self-Assessment

Use the following criteria to evaluate your cause-and-effect essay:

	Score 4	Score 3	Score 2	Score 1
Audience and Purpose	Consistently targets an audience through word choice and details; clearly identifies purpose in introduction	Targets an audience through most word choices and details; identifies purpose in introduction	Misses a target audience by including a wide range of word choice and details; presents no clear purpose	Addresses no specific audience or purpose
Organization	Presents a clear, consistent organizational strategy to show cause and effect	Presents a clear organizational strategy with occasional inconsistencies to show cause and effect	Presents an inconsistent organizational strategy; creates illogical presentation of causes and effects	Demonstrates a lack of organizational strategy; creates a confusing presentation
Elaboration	Successfully links causes with effects; fully elaborates connections among ideas	Links causes with effects; elaborates connections among most ideas	Links some causes with some effects; elaborates connections among some ideas	Develops and elaborates no links between causes and effects
Use of Language	Chooses clear transitions to convey ideas; presents very few mechanical errors	Chooses transitions to convey ideas; presents few mechanical errors	Misses some opportunities for transitions to convey ideas; presents many mechanical errors	Demonstrates poor use of language; presents many mechanical errors

9.7 Student Work IN PROGRESS

FINAL DRAFT

Why Trains Are No Longer Popular

Jake Sommer
Maplewood Middle School
Maplewood, New Jersey

Passenger trains, commuter trains, freight trains, high-speed trains—I've always liked trains, but I've often wondered whatever happened to them. Why don't more people travel by train? Do they enjoy being cramped up in a car or an airplane for their long trips? Maybe they haven't enjoyed the comfort of a passenger train or the unique hospitality of the crew or the unforgettable sights out the window as the train slowly eases through a mountain pass. So I was thinking about these questions one day and decided to do some research on the rise and fall of trains.

Trains didn't arrive in the United States until almost 1830. At first, some people were afraid of this new form of transportation. They were used to horses and buggies, and they didn't like the

In his first paragraph, Jake introduces the main question that his essay will answer.

He organizes his explanation into a series of causes and effects. First, he looks at the causes of the rise of trains.

steam and sparks coming out of the trains. However, after about ten years, the railroads began to spread quickly across the country. By the time of the Civil War, trains were used to transport troops and supplies.

The biggest advance in railroads came in 1869 when the transcontinental railroad was completed. It took seven years to build the tracks between the east coast and the west coast. Then came the Golden Age of Railroads. Before the Civil War, there were approximately 31,000 miles of track, and by the early 1900's, there were 252,000 miles of track. Traveling by train then became the main source of transportation between small towns and from big cities to other cities.

Jake elaborates on the effects of the success of railroads, using his research to give specific details about the length of track.

One important cause of the growth of the railroad was the convenience of train travel and shipping. By having trains everywhere, people could travel thousands of miles in only days instead of weeks. Also, freight could be shipped from the East and Midwest to shopkeepers in the West.

Henry Ford changed everything by mass-producing the automobile. Because it cost him less to make cars, more people could buy them. By the early 1920's, cars and buses started to make trains less popular. Manufacturers used trucks to ship freight because it was cheaper and more reliable. Railroads might pick up freight only once a week, but trucks could come for pickups and deliveries every day. Railroads began their decline.

▲ **Critical Viewing**
What would you enjoy the most if you were able to travel across the United States by train? **[Speculate]**

The last great era of trains was during World War II when trains were used to transport soldiers, arms, and supplies. By the end of the war, heavy use had damaged the rail system, but government money was being spent on building interstate highways and airports instead of on repairing the railroads.

The effect of having the interstate highways was staggering. Millions of dollars were taken from what would have been spent on railroad tickets and was used to buy cars. Americans chose driving over relaxing, leisurely train trips.

Jake identifies a main cause—the rise of the automobile—and explains its logical connections with the decline of the railroad.

So what happened to the trains? By the 1970's, most of the private railroad companies went bankrupt and were sold to the U.S. government. The government created Amtrak to take over passenger operations for long-distance trips. Amtrak's 23,000 miles go to just 500 stations. Not many people make cross-country trips by train anymore. However, in the future, high-speed trains like they have in Europe and Japan may come to the U.S. and spark a revival of train travel. Then, people will know what it's like to see our beautiful country through the window of a train.

Connected Assignment
Documentary Video Script

You can often find examples of cause-and-effect writing just by flipping through the channels on your television set. Newsmagazine shows often contain video segments that explain the cause-and-effect relationships behind a news story.

A **documentary video script** outlines the words to be used, either those recorded in interviews or those written for a narrator. It also includes directions to the camera operators, the technicians who are providing sound and lighting, and the editor who will put the video together.

Challenge yourself to write a documentary video script. Use the suggestions that follow to guide you.

▲ **Critical Viewing**
Will the final documentary include every word this interviewee says? Explain your answer. **[Hypothesize]**

Prewriting Watch a television newsmagazine show. Note the alternation between narration and interview footage and the use of camera angles and sound. Then, choose a situation that interests you—for example, a current event or a technological advance—as your topic.

Next, conduct an investigation into your topic. Use a variety of sources—if possible, include interviews with experts or eyewitnesses. Take careful notes as you gather information. If possible, use an audio or video recorder to capture interviews.

Drafting Format your script to include the words spoken (interviews or commentary) and instruction for the creation and arrangement of visuals (video clips), including lighting and sound directions.

Organize your script to present facts in the most effective way. A chronological organization will allow you to trace how each cause triggered each effect. You might instead pinpoint a major event (an effect) and then examine the various causes that contributed to it.

Revising and Editing After drafting, read your script aloud and listen to how it sounds. Revise to make the segment flow better and to improve the connections among key ideas.

Publishing and Presenting If you have access to video equipment, produce your segment and show it to the class.

Spotlight on the Humanities

Analyzing Ideas Represented in Various Art Forms

Focus on Drama: A Broadway Fairy Tale

Causes and effects occur in the literary world, as well as in history and science. For example, the creators of *Once Upon a Mattress* were deeply affected by the Hans Christian Andersen fairy tale "The Princess and the Pea"—so much so that they created a successful Broadway play based on it. Opening off-Broadway in 1959, the musical *Once Upon a Mattress* moved to Broadway and was nominated for two Tony Awards. With music by Mary Rodgers and lyrics by Marshall Barer, this musical made a star of the young Carol Burnett and continues to entertain audiences in productions all over the world.

Literature Connection Considered one of Denmark's greatest storytellers, Hans Christian Andersen (1805–1875) is primarily known for his fairy tales. Along with "The Princess and the Pea," Andersen wrote the fairy tales "The Snow Queen," "The Ugly Duckling," and "The Red Shoes," among others. In addition to his fairy tales, Andersen wrote poems and plays.

Art Connection Frenchman Edmund Dulac (1882–1953) illustrated Hans Christian Andersen's "The Princess and the Pea." He was one of the foremost illustrators and artists of the late nineteenth and early twentieth centuries. Dulac began his career as an illustrator just as a new technology for printing color illustrations began. With this process, colors were printed separately, allowing for clearer definition of the shapes on a page.

Cause-and-Effect Writing Activity: Diagraming Cause-and-Effect in Fairy Tales

Select a fairy tale. Create an illustrated diagram of causes and effects in the story. Read the story to the class, pointing out events on your diagram. Conclude with an observation about the importance of cause-and-effect relationships in fairy tales.

Illustration to "The Princess and the Pea" by Hans Christian Andersen, c. 1911, Edmund Dulac, Victoria & Albert Museum, London, UK

▲ **Critical Viewing** Compare the main impression created by the drawing of the princess with that created by the photograph from the play. **[Compare and Contrast]**

Media and Technology Skills

Analyzing Media Images

Activity: Captioning a Photograph

Television, newspapers, and magazines all use photographs to record events. Each image also makes a statement about the person, event, or situation it depicts. Learn more about how an image can cause a certain effect in those who view it.

Learn About It An effective photograph uses

- **a central point of interest**—the actions, objects, or people that the photograph focuses on. In this photograph by Dorothea Lange, the woman's face is the focus.

- **composition**—the placement of objects and the use of space and of light. For instance, in the photograph shown, the woman is centered between her children. She looks outward, while the children huddle inward. The space is full—the people take up most of the image. There is a contrast between the light on the woman's face and the shadows around it. All of these features emphasize how much depends on the mother's strength.

- **emotional impact.** A photograph can inspire fear, anger, pity, and other emotions. The photograph shown might inspire compassion.

- **choice of subject.** Photographs of widely differing scenes can be used to illustrate the same topic. This photo was used to show the plight of displaced farmers in the 1930's. Notice that a grim-faced woman was chosen as the subject. A photograph of men lounging about would make a different statement.

Apply It A caption is a statement describing a photograph and providing additional information. Select two photographs from the media and cover up their captions. Using a chart like the one below, take notes on them. Then, write your own caption for each. Compare yours with the published ones.

Types of Photographs

- **Candid**—shows natural, unposed behavior
- **Documentary**—records an event
- **Portrait**—portrays people
- **Abstract**—evokes mood
- **Landscape**—shows a place

▲ **Critical Viewing**
List three details in this photo that capture your interest.
[Analyze]

	What Is the Central Point of Interest?	Describe Its Composition	What Is Its Emotional Impact?	What Effect Does the Choice of Subject Have?
Photograph 1				
Photograph 2				

Standardized Test Preparation Workshop

Responding to Expository Writing Prompts

Some writing prompts on standardized tests require you to show the relationships between causes and their effects. Your writing will be evaluated on your ability to

- respond directly to the prompt.
- make your writing thoughtful and interesting.
- organize ideas so they are clear and easy to follow.
- develop your ideas thoroughly by using appropriate details and precise language.
- stay focused on your purpose by making sure that each sentence contributes to your composition as a whole.
- use correct spelling, capitalization, punctuation, grammar, usage, and sentence structure.

Following is an example of an expository writing prompt. Use the suggestions on the following page to help you respond. When writing for a timed test, you should plan to devote a specified amount of time to prewriting, drafting, revising, and proofreading. The clocks next to each stage show a suggested percentage of time to devote to each stage.

Sample Writing Situation

> Writer Rudyard Kipling explores the conflict between natural enemies—a mongoose and a cobra— in his famous short story, "Rikki-tikki-tavi."

> What causes the conflict between the mongoose Rikki-tikki-tavi and the cobra Nag in the short story? Use details and information from the story to explain why the two are natural enemies, what specifically causes the conflict in this story, and what causes the story to end as it does.

Prewriting

Allow close to one fourth of your time for prewriting.

Use a Cluster Diagram When gathering details for your cause-and-effect response, use a cluster diagram. Write each cause the prompt asks you to explain on a piece of paper and circle it. Then, write the effects of each cause in new circles. Draw lines linking effects to their causes.

Keep a Consistent Purpose As you gather details, include only those relevant to the prompt. The purpose assigned by the example prompt is to explain the cause-and-effect relationships in the story—not to retell every event that occurs in it.

Drafting

Allow almost half of your time for drafting.

Organizing Details When writing a cause-and-effect response, organize details in chronological order, the sequence in which they occurred. Organizing using this method will enable you to clearly show the relationship between causes and effects.

Use the Story as Support As you write the body of your response, elaborate your ideas using specific details and examples from the story to explain cause-and-effect relationships. Each time you mention an event, look for ways to explain its connection to the events before and after it.

Using Precise Language As you write, elaborate using precise, strong words. For example, if you are describing Nag's personality, use a strong word, such as *nasty*, instead of a weak and vague word, such as *bad*.

Revising, Editing, and Proofreading

Allow almost one fourth of your time to revise and edit. Use the last few minutes to proofread your work.

Make Clear Connections Review your draft. Add transitional words, such as *as a result*, *because of*, *before*, and *after*, where needed to indicate the cause-and-effect relations between events. Neatly cross out any details that do not support your purpose. Replace vague or general modifiers, such as *good*, with precise words, such as *brave*.

Make Corrections Review your response for errors in spelling, grammar, and punctuation. When making changes, draw a line through text that you want eliminated. Use a caret (^) to indicate the place where you would like to add words.

How-to Essays in Everyday Life

You read "how-to's" all the time. The instruction booklet for a computer game, the directions on microwave popcorn, safety warnings, repair instructions, guidelines for caring for your bike or washing your clothes—these are all forms of writing that explain how to do something.

In your own life, you probably do a lot of explaining as well. You might explain to your teacher how you created invitations with your new word-processing program, or you might tell a friend the rules for street hockey before a pickup game. In this chapter, you will learn the process for writing a clear, effective how-to essay.

▲ **Critical Viewing**
What title would you give a how-to essay that might accompany this photo? **[Connect]**

What Is a How-to Essay?

Writing that explains or informs is called expository writing. One of the most common types of expository writing is the how-to essay.

In a **how-to essay,** you explain how to do or make something. You break the process down into a series of logical steps and explain the steps in the order in which the reader should do them.

The following features are characteristics of a useful, effective how-to essay:

- a narrow, focused topic that can be fully explained in the length of an essay
- a list of materials needed
- a series of logical steps explained in chronological order
- details that tell *when, how much, how often,* or *to what extent*
- an essay format with an introduction, a body, and a conclusion.

To learn the criteria on which your how-to essay may be assessed, see the Rubric for Self-Assessment on page 215.

Writers in ACTION

Richard Lederer writes how-to's that make learning fun! His humorous books and articles on the English language have helped many readers learn how to write and speak more effectively. He shares the following thoughts on expository writing:

"Expository writing is taking an idea or cluster of ideas and transferring it from the writer, as clearly as possible, to the reader, so that the reader participates in those ideas."

Types of How-to Essays

Following are some of the types of how-to essays you might write:

- How to do something ("How to Hit a Baseball")
- How to make something ("How to Make Trail Mix")
- How to improve a skill ("How to Improve Your Test Scores")
- How to achieve a desired effect ("How to Organize Your Locker")

PREVIEW
Student Work
IN PROGRESS

Felix Espinoza, a student at Palo Alto Middle School in Killeen, Texas, wrote an essay explaining how to make his favorite cake. In this chapter, you will see his work in progress, including strategies he used to choose a topic, to gather details, to elaborate, and to revise his overall structure and his word choice. At the end of the chapter, you can read the completed essay Felix wrote.

In this how-to essay, science writer Janice VanCleave (1942–   ) lets readers see how erosion moves mountains.

Reading Writing Connection

Reading Strategy: Identify Cause-and-Effect Relationships

In this how-to essay, look for **cause-and-effect relationships**—explanations of *why* something happens or is done.

▲ **Critical Viewing** What kind of force might it take to change the position of a mountain in the Himalayas, such as this one? **[Speculate]**

Moving Mountains

Janice VanCleave

The Himalayas, the highest mountain system in the world, lie just south of the Tibetan Plateau, where the Yangtze River originates. According to Professor Douglas Burbank of the University of Southern California, the normal process of erosion is affecting the Himalayas in two major ways. First, the enormous glaciers on the mountains are grinding down rock into huge amounts of gravel and silt, which are then washed away by streams and rivers. The Himalayas are gradually losing mass.

Second, the loss of mass is affecting the Himalayas' position on Earth's surface. Mountains are part of Earth's *crust*, or rigid outer layer. The crust floats on the *mantle*, a layer of molten rock, in the same way that a boat floats on an ocean.

How does the Himalayas' loss of mass affect its position on Earth's mantle? Try this demonstration to find out.

VanCleave introduces the topic of her how-to essay by giving general background information.

She provides a cause-and-effect explanation to help explain erosion.

What You Need

- a lightweight wooden block measuring 5 centimeters by 10 centimeters by 5 centimeters (roughly 2 inches by 4 inches by 2 inches)
- a black marking pen
- a red marking pen
- masking tape
- sand
- a clear container twice as large as the wooden block
- a pencil and paper
- a tablespoon
- a ruler

Here the writer lists all the materials the reader will need.

What to Do

1. Fill the container about half full with water, and place a piece of masking tape down the outside of the container.
2. Starting at the top of the tape, mark it off in centimeters with the black pen. Mark the level that the water comes to with the red pen.
3. Place a piece of masking tape down one side of the wooden block and mark it off in centimeters with the black pen.
4. Float the wooden block in the container of water, and pour several spoonfuls of sand on top of the block. Using the red pen, record the level that the water comes to on the block and the level that the water now comes to in the container.
5. Use the spoon to scrape some sand from the top of the block into the water. Record the water level on the block and in the container again.
6. Scrape off some more sand and again record the water levels.

MODEL DEMONSTRATION: EROSION'S EFFECTS

What Happens?

After you have completed the experiment, you have the information you need to understand the effect of erosion on the Himalayas. Interpret the experiment by answering these questions:

- What happens to the block as it loses sand to the water?
- How do the objects in this experiment compare to the Himalayas and Earth's mantle?
- What conclusions can you draw about the effect of erosion on the Himalayas?

Writing Application: Help Readers See Cause-and-Effect Relationships As you write your how-to essay, give reasons why following the exact order of steps is important.

The writer presents steps in logical order. She does not put too much information into a step, but instead focuses each step on one action or a group of closely related actions.

LITERATURE

For an example of nonfiction that explains how to do something, read "How to Enjoy Poetry" in *Prentice Hall Literature: Timeless Voices, Timeless Themes,* Bronze.

The writer concludes by guiding the reader in drawing conclusions from the demonstration. This type of conclusion is appropriate for a how-to essay explaining how to conduct an experiment.

Prewriting

Choosing Your Topic

The first step in writing a good how-to essay is to choose an appropriate topic. Choose a topic you know well enough to explain clearly. Also, make sure the topic you choose is simple enough that a reader can easily learn the steps involved by following your explanation. The following strategies will help you find a suitable topic:

Try it out! Use the interactive Listing activity in **Section 10.2**, on-line or on CD-ROM.

Strategies for Generating a Topic

1. **Invisible Ink** Place a piece of carbon paper between two blank sheets of paper. Using a pen that has run out of ink, "write" on the blank top sheet. Begin by writing about any part of your day that you enjoy. After five minutes, look at what has been recorded on the carbon copy. Circle any words or sentences that suggest a topic for your essay. (You can also do this activity by writing on the computer with your monitor turned off. When you are finished, turn your monitor on to see what you have written.)

2. **List** Begin by making a list of people, places, things, and events that you associate with your home or school. Circle words and draw lines to show connections between items on the list. These links may suggest a topic. The model below shows an example of how listing led one student to a topic.

Student Work
IN PROGRESS

Name: _Felix Espinoza_
Palo Alto Middle School
Killeen, TX

Listing to Discover a Topic

Felix listed the people, places, things, and events that he associates with school. He discovered connections by remembering that his classmate Mike helped him make a cake for the class party. This led him to choose "Making a Cake" as his topic.

People	Places	Things	Events
Mike	school	bus	soccer game
Mrs. Flood	classroom	locker	class party
Gary	soccer field	desk	
Maria		cake	
		movie	

TOPIC BANK

If you're having trouble coming up with a topic, think about the following possibilities:

1. **How to Make a Gift** Explain how readers can make a homemade gift, such as a collage, trinket box, picture, or beaded bracelet.

2. **How to Improve a Sports Skill** Explain how readers can improve a specific skill, such as making free throws in basketball, hitting a baseball or softball, or serving in tennis.

Responding to Fine Art

3. Look at the painting on this page. What steps might be involved in the activity portrayed? Write a how-to essay about what you think is happening in this painting or about some other process or activity involving a pet.

Responding to Literature

Man Playing With Dog, Serge Hollerbach, Courtesy of Sanders and Newman Gallery, PA

4. Read "If—" by Rudyard Kipling. Write a how-to essay explaining how readers can achieve one of the goals expressed in the poem. For example, you might write an essay explaining how to respond calmly in a crisis or how to avoid giving in to negative peer pressure. You can find "If—," as well as background on the poem and the poet, in *Prentice Hall Literature: Timeless Voices, Timeless Themes,* Bronze.

☑ Cooperative Writing Opportunity

5. **How to Organize a Game for Young Children** With a group, explain how to organize a game for young children. Some group members can explain the equipment or playing area, others can draw diagrams or illustrations, and others can list and explain rules.

Narrowing Your Topic

Once you have chosen a topic, evaluate whether it can be covered fully in an essay. Some topics are so broad that entire books could be written about them. For example, the topic "How to Get Organized" is too broad for an essay. The topic could be narrowed to focus on how to organize study time or how to organize a locker. If your topic is too broad, focus on a single, manageable aspect of the topic.

Considering Your Audience and Purpose

The topic you choose for your how-to essay reflects your purpose in writing. Your **purpose** is most likely to explain your topic. Considering your **audience**—the people who will be reading your essay—is not as simple, but it is one of the most important parts of writing a good how-to essay. Ask yourself the following questions when you think about your audience:

- **How much does my audience know about this topic?** Do they need a lot of background or just a little? Will they need definitions of any special terms I use?

- **What is the age of my audience?** Should I use simple vocabulary for young children, or can I use vocabulary appropriate for people my age or older?

- **What skills might my audience have?** Do they have the basic skills needed to learn what I am teaching?

Thinking about your audience may even lead you to change or further narrow your topic. For example, readers who are very familiar with cooking will not need to have special cooking terms or the names of utensils defined. If your audience is familiar with your topic, you might narrow the focus of your essay to a subtopic that requires special knowledge or expertise.

▼ **Critical Viewing** Based on what you see in this picture, do you think the man needs much background on cooking? **[Analyze]**

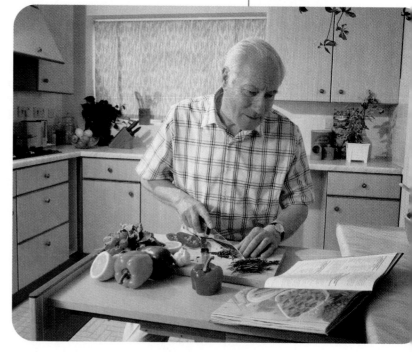

Gathering Details

Once you have identified your audience, you can focus on gathering details. Since your topic is an activity or skill that you know well, most of your details can be gathered from your own knowledge and experience. If you need help getting started, try the itemizing strategy.

Itemize to Gather Details

One way to start gathering details is to itemize. Begin with a simple list, such as materials or steps. Then, itemize each part of the list, generating specific details for each area. If you find your itemized lists are becoming too long or unmanageable, evaluate whether your topic is still too broad or whether you are including more details than your audience needs.

Try it out! Use the interactive Itemizing activity in **Section 10.2**, on-line or on CD-ROM.

Student Work
IN PROGRESS

Name: *Felix Espinoza*
Palo Alto Middle School
Killeen, TX

Itemizing the Details

Felix made a list of steps for making the cake. Then, he itemized the details related to each step. Here, you see Felix's itemized lists for mixing the dry ingredients and preparing the bananas.

Preheat oven.

Mix dry ingredients.

Mix other ingredients.

Prepare bananas.

Ice the cake.

- 2 ½ c. flour
- 1½ c. sugar
- ¾ t. baking soda
- ½ t. baking powder

Bananas should be ripe.

Mash them.

Pour vanilla on them.

Mix them with yogurt.

Drafting

Shaping Your Writing

Once you have gathered your details, you need to put them into some kind of order. Think of the details as a recipe for the ingredients in a cake. Throwing all the ingredients together without a plan just makes a mess. On the other hand, if you put the ingredients together in a logical way, following the recipe, and pour the batter into a pan for baking, you will make a cake that holds together. Drafting is the mixing and baking time in your writing process. It is the time for bringing the details together and making some sense of them.

Organize Details in Chronological Order

The logical organization for most how-to essays is chronological order. Because one step usually affects the following steps, explaining steps in time order will help readers follow the logical sequence. Organize the steps you wish to explain by creating a sticky-note timeline. If you don't have sticky notes, you can use note cards or slips of paper.

Use a Timeline to Organize Details By putting details on individual sticky notes or note cards, you can arrange the steps in order and add steps as needed. Notice how "Get a second bowl" can easily be added because each step is written on a separate note.

STICKY-NOTE TIMELINE

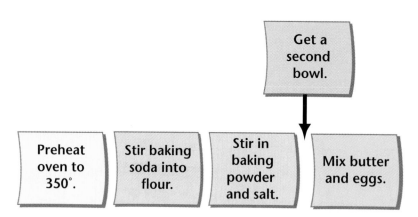

Providing Elaboration

As your writing takes shape, you may find that parts of your explanation need more details. Through elaboration—the adding of details—you can help your readers understand exactly what is required at each step. Look for places where adding details—how much, how long, to what degree—will make your how-to essay more precise.

Add Details by "Exploding the Moment"

Cut out several "bursts" or "explosions" from colored paper. As you write your draft, pause occasionally to look for places where you can "explode a moment" in the directions by adding details that give more specific information. Use words that indicate actions, times, or amounts as clues showing where you may need to add information. Write additional details on the colored paper explosions, and lightly paste them to your draft. The example below shows how Felix added details to his draft by exploding the moment.

Student Work
IN PROGRESS

Name: Felix Espinoza
Palo Alto Middle School
Killeen, TX

Exploding the Moment

Felix pasted explosions on his draft to add details about parts of the process.

First, gather your ingredients. Then, (preheat) **to 350°**
the oven. Mix together the flour, baking soda, and salt. Put ½ cup butter in a second bowl. Add eggs, and (mix them.) Set bowl aside. **beat for five minutes after adding each**
In a third bowl, mash the bananas. Add the vanilla and the yogurt. Combine the butter and eggs with the flour mixture. Put the **until the mixture is smooth** bananas into the bowl. Stir it for a (while.) Then, add the rest.

Revising

Revising Your Overall Structure

Add an Introduction and Conclusion

After writing your first draft, reread your how-to essay, looking for ways to improve and polish it. You will probably recognize that you don't want to jump right in with step one and end abruptly at the last step. Instead, give a general overview of your topic in an introduction. Then, explain the different steps in the body of the essay. Review, summarize, or briefly comment on the procedures in a conclusion.

▶**REVISION STRATEGY**
Writing a Strong Lead

Begin with an image or idea that "leads" your reader into the essay. Look through your prewriting notes to find details that remind you why you enjoy the activity or why you decided to write about your topic. The detail that grabbed your interest may spark your audience's interest as well. Use one of these details to make that first sentence an attention grabber!

Student Work
IN PROGRESS

Name: Felix Espinoza
Palo Alto Middle School
Killeen, TX

Writing a Strong Lead

Felix reviewed his prewriting notes and found that his class party gave him the idea for the topic "How to Make Banana Cake." He used an exaggerated image of hungry students to write an attention-grabbing lead.

Our teacher, Ms. Tallman, knows that it takes more than an ordinary cake to feed twenty ravenous seventh-graders. That's why she always asks Mike or me to make our famous Banana Cake. Making Banana Cake takes a little more time than making a cake from a box, but you will find that every bite of the finished product is worth the time it takes. By following the steps outlined here, you can learn how to make this delicious dessert.

> Felix introduces his topic with details that make it appealing.

Revising Your Paragraphs

Identify Paragraph Purpose

Once you're comfortable with the general structure of your paper, carefully focus on each individual paragraph. The purpose of each paragraph will determine the words or phrases you may need to add to make your meaning clearer.

▶**REVISION STRATEGY**
Using Steps, Stacks, Chains, and Balances

- **Steps** If the paragraph explains a step or several related steps for which time order is important, make sure you have indicated the sequence. Use words such as *first*, *next*, and *finally*.

- **Stacks** If the paragraph explains how one part of a process contributes to another, show the connection between ideas with words such as *and*, *furthermore*, and *for instance*.

- **Chains** If the paragraph explains the cause-and-effect relationship between steps, use words such as *so*, *because*, and *consequently*.

- **Balances** If the paragraph shows choice or contrast, use words such as *but*, *however*, *on the other hand*, and *rather*.

▶ **Critical Viewing** Do you think these boys successfully followed the directions for making a cake? **[Evaluate]**

Revising Your Sentences
Vary Your Sentence Beginnings

Within each paragraph, look even more closely at the individual sentences. You may find that by varying the ways your sentences begin, you can make your meaning clearer and make your essay more interesting to read.

▶ **REVISION STRATEGY**
Using Clues to Sentence Beginnings

Fold a piece of lined loose-leaf paper in half lengthwise, then in half again, to make a long strip. Place the strip on the side of your draft. Write the first word of each sentence on its own line to create a list of first words. Review the list, and circle words that are repeated frequently. Rewrite or combine sentences to eliminate some of the words that appear more than once. Look at the following example to see how Felix revised his sentence beginnings:

Student Work
IN PROGRESS

Name: Felix Espinoza
Palo Alto Middle School
Killeen, TX

Varying Sentence Beginnings

Felix listed the first words of all the sentences in his draft. His list showed that he began more than one sentence with the verbs "put" and "add." He varied his sentence beginnings by using transitional words and prepositional phrases.

| Put |
| Use |
| Add |
| Set |
| Put |
| Add |

Put ½ cup butter in a second bowl.

Then, Use an eggbeater to cream it. Add 2 eggs and beat for five minutes after adding each egg.

Finally, Set this bowl aside, and get out a third bowl.

Put the bananas into the third bowl. Add the vanilla and the yogurt.

Felix revised this sentence to begin with the prepositional phrase.

Felix added transitional words to these sentences to vary sentence beginnings and to make the order of the steps clearer.

Because Felix created variety by revising earlier sentences, he decided these could be left as they were.

Grammar in Your Writing
Adverb Clauses and Adverb Phrases

For many of the steps in your how-to essay, you may add words or groups of words that give more information about a step. **Adverb phrases** and **clauses** can be used to add details that tell *how, where, when, why,* and *under what circumstances* the step is being done. For example, in Felix's revision on the previous page, he uses the phrase "in a second bowl." This phrase acts as an adverb, telling where the reader should put the ingredients.

How: Beat the eggs with an eggbeater.

Where: In a third bowl, prepare the bananas.

When: Before you gather the ingredients, set the oven to preheat.

Why: Preheat the oven so the cake will bake evenly.

Under what circumstances: If the knife is clean, the cakes are finished.

When an adverb phrase or clause comes before the main clause in the sentence, set it off with a comma. When the phrase or clause follows the main clause, do not set it off with a comma.

Phrase follows the main clause:
Beat the eggs with an eggbeater.

Phrase comes before the main clause:
With an eggbeater, beat the eggs.

Adverb clause comes before the main clause:
Before you gather the ingredients, set the oven to preheat.

Adverb clause follows the main clause:
Set the oven to preheat before you gather the ingredients.

Find It in Your Reading Find one adverb phrase and one adverb clause in "Moving Mountains" by Janice VanCleave on page 200. Explain what information is added with each example you find.

Find It in Your Writing Identify three adverb clauses and three adverb phrases that you have used in your how-to essay. Find at least one of each that precedes the main clause. If you can't find three examples, consider whether you have given readers enough information about *how, when, where, why,* and *under what circumstances* they perform the required steps. Identify at least one sentence to which you can add an adverb phrase or clause to give more detail.

To learn more about adverb phrases and clauses, see Chapter 20.

Revising Your Word Choice

Eliminate Repeated Words

Varying your word choice is as important as varying your sentence beginnings. Variety is a quality of sophisticated, mature writing. Go back through your essay and look for overused words. One way to evaluate whether you have overused any words is to highlight repeated words.

▶ **REVISION STRATEGY**
Highlighting Repeated Words

Go through your essay, and use a highlighter to mark any nouns, verbs, or adjectives that you have used more than once. After marking repeated words, evaluate each use to determine whether you should replace the word with a synonym.

Writers in **ACTION**

Good advice on revising your how-to essay comes from Sophocles, a writer of ancient Greece whose works are still read today. He said:

"One learns by doing a thing; for though you think you know it, you have no certainty until you try."

Take Sophocles' advice and try out your how-to essay with some class-mates. Use this technique to be certain that you have included all the necessary steps and information.

Student Work
IN PROGRESS

Name: Felix Espinoza
Palo Alto Middle School
Killeen, TX

Highlighting Repeated Words

Felix went through his essay and highlighted verbs and nouns that he had used more than once. When he looked at the words he had highlighted, he realized that he was overusing the words make, mix, *and* bowl.

Combine
Make a mix of the dry ingredients in the first bowl with the butter and egg mixture, and mix in the
create
second bowl well to make a smooth batter.

> Felix eliminated a few uses of mix, make, and bowl. He realized he didn't need to repeat these words to make his meaning clear.

Peer Review

Getting feedback from your classmates is especially helpful in revising a how-to essay. Because the purpose of a how-to essay is to explain, peer reviewers can give you objective opinions about how clear the explanation is and whether any additional information is needed.

Ask a Group to Try It Out

First, read your essay aloud to a small group of classmates as they listen. Then, read it aloud again, as if you were guiding the group through the activity or procedure you are explaining. Have the group go through the motions of each step, taking notes on where they are confused or unsure. After you have finished reading the essay a second time, ask reviewers to respond to the following questions:

- Which step or steps could have been explained more clearly?
- What was confusing about those steps?
- In which sections did you feel you needed more or less information? What information would you have added or eliminated?
- What other questions or comments do you have about the activity or process I explained?

Use the comments and questions to guide you in making a final revision of your essay.

Get instant help! Use the Language Variety Revision Checker, accessible from the menu bar, on-line or on CD-ROM. The Checker will help you find words that you may have overused. Evaluate which ones you should replace with synonyms.

▼ **Critical Viewing** What procedures or processes do you find it helpful to try with a group of peer reviewers? **[Relate]**

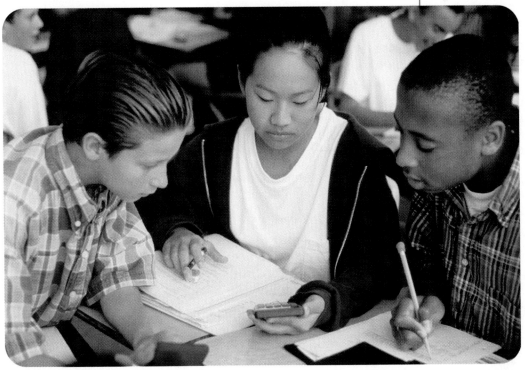

Editing
and Proofreading

Errors in spelling, punctuation, grammar, or usage can create confusion. Proofread your essay to discover and eliminate these errors in your essay. Be especially careful that you have used commas correctly.

Focusing on Commas

As you proofread your how-to-essay, check to make sure that you have used commas where they are needed. As is explained on page 211, you might use commas to set off introductory adverb clauses. You will also need commas to separate items in lists.

Grammar in Your Writing
Using Commas to Separate Items in a Series

Use commas to separate items in a series, or list. Separating the items with commas makes your meaning clear to readers. Look at the following examples:

Commas separate individual items in a series:
Add the sugar, baking soda, baking powder, and salt.

Commas separate groups of words in a series:
Begin by gathering your tools, reviewing the recipe, and preheating the oven.

Note: Most writers use a comma before the *and* that connects the last two items in the series because it prevents misreading. (See the commas following *baking powder* and *recipe* in the examples above.) Some do not use a comma before the final *and* if the meaning is clear without one. Follow your teacher's directions about whether to use the comma before the *and*.

Find It in Your Reading Read "Moving Mountains" by Janice VanCleave on page 200. Find an example of items in a series, and rewrite part of the list using commas.

Find It in Your Writing Review your essay, and circle any lists or series of items. Remember that the series can include either individual words or groups of words. Check that you have correctly used commas to separate the items in each series or list that you find.

To learn more about the correct use of commas, see Chapter 26.

10.6 Publishing and Presenting

Building Your Portfolio

Consider the following possibilities for publishing or presenting your how-to essay:

1. **Give a Demonstration** Distribute copies of your how-to essay as a handout to accompany a demonstration of the activity you will explain. Your audience can follow along as you demonstrate the steps. Then, they can take your explanation with them to follow on their own.

2. **Make a Poster** Make a poster of your topic, with pictures of each step of the activity. Copy your essay, and cut the paragraphs apart so they can be attached in appropriate places on the poster.

Reflecting on Your Writing

Write down a few thoughts about writing a how-to essay. You might start off by answering these questions:

- Did explaining an activity increase or decrease your enjoyment of the activity? Explain.

- After writing your essay, do you think the activity you explained would be difficult or easy to learn? Why?

 Internet Tip

To see model essays scored with this rubric, go on-line: PHSchool.com
Enter Web Code:
ebk-7001

Rubric for Self-Assessment

Use the following criteria to evaluate your how-to essay:

	Score 4	Score 3	Score 2	Score 1
Audience and Purpose	Clearly focuses on procedures leading to a well-defined end	Focuses on procedures leading to a well-defined end	Includes procedures related to an end, but presents some vaguely	Includes only vague descriptions of procedures and results
Organization	Gives instructions in logical order; subdivides complex actions into steps	Gives instructions in logical order; subdivides some complex actions into steps	For the most part, gives instructions in logical order	Gives instructions in a scattered, disorganized manner
Elaboration	Provides appropriate amount of detail; gives needed explanations	Provides appropriate amount of detail; gives some explanations	Provides some detail; gives few explanations	Provides few details; gives few or no explanations
Use of Language	Shows overall clarity and fluency; uses transitions effectively; contains few mechanical errors	Shows some sentence variety; uses some transitions; includes few mechanical errors	Uses awkward or overly simple sentence structures; contains many mechanical errors	Contains incomplete thoughts and confusing mechanical errors

Student Work
IN PROGRESS

FINAL DRAFT

Banana Cake

Felix Espinoza
Palo Alto Middle School
Killeen, Texas

Our teacher, Ms. Tallman, knows that it takes more than an ordinary cake to feed twenty ravenous seventh-graders. That's why she always asks Mike or me to make our famous Banana Cake. Making Banana Cake takes a little more time than making a cake from a box, but you will find that every bite of the finished product is worth the time it takes. By following the steps outlined here, you can learn how to make this delicious dessert.

In the introduction, Felix tells readers why they should make the cake.

2 ¼ cups cake flour	½ cup butter, softened
1 ½ cups sugar	2 eggs
¾ teaspoon baking soda	1 cup mashed ripe bananas
½ teaspoon baking powder	1 teaspoon vanilla
½ teaspoon salt	¼ cup yogurt

Felix puts the ingredients in list form.

Before mixing the ingredients, set the oven to preheat to 350 degrees. (Preheating is important, because the cake will come out lopsided if it is not evenly baked.) Grease and flour two 9-inch round cake pans.

Start by mixing the dry ingredients. First, sift the cake flour into a large bowl. Next, add the sugar, baking soda, baking powder, and salt.

Felix explains steps in chronological order. He uses words like first to make the order clear.

In a second bowl, put ½ cup butter. Use an eggbeater to cream it. Then, add 2 eggs and beat for five minutes after adding each egg. Finally, set this bowl aside, and get out a third bowl. Put the bananas into the third bowl. Add the vanilla and the yogurt.

Because Felix's audience of classmates may not know which utensil to use, he tells them—an eggbeater.

Combine the dry ingredients with the butter and egg mixture, and mix well to create a smooth batter. Then, gradually pour the batter over the mashed banana. Mix the batter as you pour. When the batter is smooth and has no lumps, pour half of the cake mixture into each pan. Bake for one-half hour. Let the cake cool for one-half hour before icing.

After following these directions, you should end up with a treat. Ice the cake if you like. The final step is to cut a slice and enjoy it!

Felix rounds off his essay with an inspiring conclusion.

Connected Assignment
Problem-and-Solution Essay

The purpose of a **problem-and-solution essay** is to describe a problem and offer one or more solutions to it. Like a how-to essay, a problem-and-solution essay describes an organized set of steps to achieve a result. Unlike a how-to essay, it must also explain why these steps will work. An effective problem-and-solution essay will:

Why It's a Problem

Recycling is necessary—we're running out of places to put garbage.

Recycling is necessary—we may run out of some resources if we don't conserve them.

Problem

Many citizens don't take the time to sort out recyclables.

Possible Solution

Have inspectors spot-check people's trash and fine them if the recyclables are not sorted out.

Hold a contest with a prize for the kid who turns in the greatest amount of recyclables to the center.

• clearly explain the problem.

• explain and defend the proposed solution.

Prewriting Choose a topic for your essay by browsing news sources. Choose a problem that grabs your interest.

Use a cluster diagram like the one above to gather details about your problem. Then, do research to find solutions. Gather facts, expert opinions, and other evidence for support.

Drafting After gathering facts, clearly state the problem and the solutions your essay will present. Include this statement in your introduction. At the beginning of your draft, provide any necessary background information. Then, lay out your solutions step-by-step, in a clear, well-organized manner. Support your solutions with evidence.

Revising and Editing Review your first draft. When you find a possible objection to a solution you offer, mention the objection in your draft. Answer it, or show that it is outweighed by other considerations. Finally, proofread your essay to eliminate errors in spelling, grammar, or punctuation.

Publishing and Presenting Consider submitting your completed essay to a school or local newspaper.

Grammar and Style Tip

By combining simple sentences into compound or complex sentences, you can emphasize the connections between problems and solutions. For more on sentence structure, see Chapter 20.

Spotlight on the Humanities

Comparing Media

Focus: Science Fiction in Film

It's easy enough to write a how-to essay on baking a cake—others can tell you how it's done. In 1865, though, no one had ever gone to the moon. It took a genius like Jules Verne (1828–1905), the early science fiction writer, to write a how-to on the subject: a novel called *From the Earth to the Moon*.

Much science fiction is like a how-to for what has never been done before. Using today's science, science fiction writers project future technologies and their effect on people's lives.

In 1902, one of the early masters of silent film, Frenchman Georges Méliès (1861–1938), followed Verne's "recipe" and made the short movie *A Trip to the Moon*. The recipe worked a little differently on screen—Verne's serious science fiction turned into hilarious satire. Méliès proved, though, that however far science fiction stretched the mind, the movies could teach the eye to keep up.

A number of Verne's works, including *A Journey to the Center of the Earth* (1864), were also made into movies. While these movies dealt in adventure, other science fiction movies explored people's fears. In the 1950's, movies such as *The Thing* (1951) explored the terrors science had unleashed—including nuclear war. Later, in 1968, Stanley Kubrick's highly acclaimed *2001: A Space Odyssey* showed a computer run amok, making decisions for the people it was meant to serve.

▼▲ **Critical Viewing** Compare Méliès's film version of a moon rocket with this photograph of a real space launch. **[Compare]**

Music Connection In 1896, German composer Richard Strauss wrote *Also Sprach Zarathustra*, his famous tone poem (short musical piece). Matching the majesty of Kubrick's depictions of outer space, the work appeared as the theme of *2001: A Space Odyssey*.

Literature Connection Twentieth-century writers such as Isaac Asimov (1920–1992) and Ray Bradbury (1920–   ) brought science fiction beyond simple adventure stories, dealing with social issues and creating vivid characters.

Expository Writing Activity: Explanation of Special Effects

Research special effects in films of the silent era. Write a how-to essay explaining the steps by which moviemakers created one of these special effects.

Media and Technology Skills

Using Computer Technology

Activity: Getting Help On-line

Computer programs typically come with built-in "how-to's"—on-line help the user can access while using the program. On-line help lets you learn as you work. It is as though the computer were a teacher and a tool rolled into one! By mastering Help, you can turn problems with computers into opportunities to learn.

Learn About It

Balloon Help Turn Balloon Help on or off through a program's menu bar. With Balloon Help on, a balloon appears whenever you roll your mouse pointer over a button, dialogue box, or other feature. Each balloon contains a brief description identifying the function of the feature on which the pointer is resting.

On-line Manuals To consult the on-line manual for a program, select "Help" from the menu bar. "Contents" lists topics by category. "Index" lists topics alphabetically and often provides a Search feature that allows you to search for a particular subject.

Other Kinds of Help Often, the best troubleshooting tips come from the program's "Read Me" file. You may open a "Read Me" file in a text-editor program. Software also comes with a printed manual, which offers detailed information on operating the program.

Apply It Choose an application, such as a word-processing program, to which you have access. Think of a difficulty you have had using the program or a question you might have about the program's use. Use two or more forms of help to solve the problem or answer the question. Take notes in a graphic organizer such as the one to the right. Then, write a mini-manual explaining how to use these different ways of getting help.

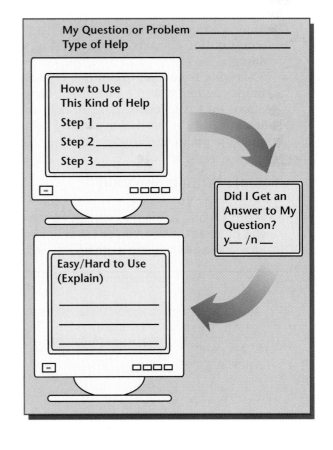

Computer Help

Built-in Help
- Balloon Help
- On-line manuals

Other Kinds of Help
- "Read Me" files
- Printed manuals

My Question or Problem _____
Type of Help _____

How to Use This Kind of Help

Step 1 _____
Step 2 _____
Step 3 _____

Did I Get an Answer to My Question?
y__ /n __

Easy/Hard to Use (Explain)
_____
_____
_____

Standardized Test Preparation Workshop

Responding to Expository Writing Prompts

Some expository writing prompts on standardized tests measure your ability to write a "how-to"—to present clear instructions and explanations in writing. You will be evaluated on your ability to do the following:

- choose a logical, consistent organization
- elaborate with the appropriate amount of detail for your specific audience and purpose
- use complete sentences and follow the rules of grammar
- use correct spelling and punctuation.

The process of writing for a test, or for any other kind of writing, can be divided into stages. Plan to use a specific amount of time for prewriting, drafting, revising, and proofreading.

Following is an example of one type of expository writing prompt you might find on a standardized test. Use the suggestions on the following page to help you respond. The clock icons suggest the portion of the test-taking time that you should spend on each stage.

Test Tip

When writing a how-to for a test, be especially careful to include the appropriate amount of detail for the audience specified in the prompt.

Sample Writing Situation

A friend of yours is about to start going to your school. Unfortunately, you won't be there to show him or her around on the first day. Write a letter to your friend explaining the morning procedures for your class or school.

Prewriting

Allow about one fourth of your time for jotting down the details you want to include.

Think About Your Audience As you jot down your details, keep your audience in mind. Remember that your friend has never been to your school, so include explanations and definitions of terms and place names that will be unfamiliar. For example, if you tell your friend to place his or her backpack next to the entrance, be sure to explain which entrance and where it is. For questions that will help you think about your audience, see page 204.

Drafting

Allow about half of your time for drafting.

Organize Details Use a timeline to organize your explanation in chronological order. Review the example timeline on page 206.

Elaborate Look over the steps you've outlined on your timeline. Add any "in-between" steps or any definitions that will make your explanation clearer. Look for places where you can add details about times and places.

Make Connections Readers find it easier to follow directions when you make connections between steps. Words like *next, then, instead,* or *after* help make these connections. As you draft, use transitional words such as these to help your friend follow your directions.

Revising, Editing, and Proofreading

Allow almost one fourth of your time for revising.

Show Transitions Read over your work, looking for places where you should add a transitional word or more information about a step. You probably won't have time to copy your work over, so make sure you indicate the insertion neatly.

Allow several minutes to give your work one final check for errors in spelling or punctuation.

Be Neat Put a single line through any misspelled word and neatly write the correct spelling above it. Make sure you have begun each sentence with a capital letter and that you have used the correct end punctuation for each sentence.

Le Roman, Rosa Ibarra

Research Reports in Everyday Life

How much does your world hold? You have your home, your school, your town—places you see every day. There are also the places you've never seen but about which you have learned something. They, too, are part of your picture of the world.

Research starts when you ask questions about that picture: "Where is Sri Lanka?" "Who is the leader of Germany?" As soon as you look for answers—in a library book, in an interview with an expert, or on the Internet—you are doing research. Each fact you learn adds to your picture of the world. Learn how to write an effective research report and expand your horizons.

▲ **Critical Viewing** What does this painting suggest about the process of writing a research report? Name one resource you can use to help with this process. **[Analyze]**

What Is a Research Report?

A **research report** presents information gathered from reference books, observations, interviews, or other sources. A good research report does not simply repeat information. It guides readers through a topic, showing them why each fact matters and creating an overall picture of the subject. An effective research report includes

- an overall focus or main idea.
- information gathered from a variety of sources.
- a clear organization and smooth transitions.
- facts and details to support each main point.
- accurate, complete citations identifying sources.

To learn the criteria on which your report may be evaluated, see the Rubric for Self-Assessment on page 240.

Types of Research Reports

Some types of reports you might write include the following:

- **Biographical sketches** report high points in the life of a notable person.
- **Reports of scientific experiments** present the setup and results of experiments.
- **Documented essays** use research to support a point or examine a trend.

Writers in ACTION

Ellie Fries writes "reports"— signs about the animals posted at the Aquarium for Wildlife Conservation in Brooklyn, New York. She focuses on the interests of her audience:

"The elements of the exhibit include, first and foremost, the animal. Well, what is a shark all about? What does it eat? Will it eat me? . . . So we think about what questions the visitors will have. Then we will have to research the answers. . . ."

PREVIEW Student Work IN PROGRESS

Jamie Barraclough, of Los Alamos Middle School in Los Alamos, New Mexico, wrote a research report about whales. In this chapter, you will see Jamie's work in progress, including strategies he used to choose a topic, focus his topic, elaborate, and revise. At the end of the chapter, you can read the final draft of the report Jamie wrote.

This report by nature writer Gillian Standring (1935–) offers a wealth of information about the giant panda.

Reading Strategy: Question To get the most out of reading research reports, **ask questions.** After reading Standring's first paragraph, for example, you might ask, "Why have pandas become so rare?"

Pandas

Gillian Standring

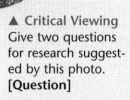

Introducing Pandas The giant panda is one of the best-known animals in the world. It is also one of the rarest. In 1990 there were only about one thousand giant pandas living wild in China, and only fifteen in zoos outside China (Catton 93, 110–111). So if you have seen pandas in a zoo, you are very lucky.

. . . The first living pandas outside China were brought to the United States in 1936 and to Britain in 1938 (Angel 16–24). Ever since, the giant panda has been of great interest to scientists, zookeepers, and all animal lovers. Because it is so popular and so unusual, it was chosen as the symbol of the World Wildlife Fund (WWF), the world's best-known conservation organization.

Life in the Wild Pandas, unlike people, prefer to be cool and damp. Hot, dry weather is bad for them (Dudley 29). High up in the mountains of Sichuan in southwest China, there are thick, misty forests where it is always cool and damp. Pandas spend most of the year in these forests. In winter they come down to the lower slopes to get away from the deep snow and freezing cold (Dudley 30). There are few people living in this part of China.

Pandas are famous for eating bamboo. Their food grows all around them in the bamboo forests, so they never have to hunt

▲ **Critical Viewing** Give two questions for research suggested by this photo. **[Question]**

Standring's introduction sets out her main idea—that the giant panda is a rare, special species.

Standring's report is ordered logically. First, she presents information on the habitat and life of pandas. After providing this necessary background, she discusses the specific reasons pandas are endangered.

for it. However, they like to eat only a few kinds of bamboo, and their digestion is not very good, so they spend almost all the day just eating (Angel 37–38). Pandas also eat grasses, roots, bulbs, and tree bark. Sometimes they catch little cane rats and fish. They often take long drinks from mountain streams and rivers (Dudley 36).

Why Are Pandas So Rare? Giant pandas have probably never been common anywhere. There are several reasons for this. They do not produce many babies (Laidler 133–134). As we have seen, they can live only in cool bamboo forests. Each panda needs a big area of forest to itself, and even large areas of suitable mountain forest have room for only a few pandas (Laidler 109–113).

Pandas also need plenty of their favorite bamboo. This plant has a very unusual way of growing. For perhaps a hundred years, bamboo plants spread by underground branches. Then suddenly, all the bamboo plants over a wide area flower, make seeds, and die. This leaves no food for the pandas until new plants grow from the seeds. Many pandas die of starvation when this happens, as it did in 1975–6 (Schaller 137).

For thousands of years, the giant panda's homeland in southwest China was very hard for people to reach, so it was left undisturbed for pandas and other wildlife. Now the millions of Chinese people need more land for their farms and villages. Modern roads help them to reach even the farthest mountains of Sichuan. As the people cut down the mountain forests, the pandas have fewer unspoiled bamboo groves to live in (Schaller 148–149).

Another reason why pandas are rare is that people have captured them from the wild. . . . The People's Republic of China banned the hunting of pandas in 1962. Now zoos can obtain pandas only as a gift from the Chinese people or from other zoos (Catton 110–111).

However, panda-hunting still goes on in spite of the ban. The pandas are not captured to be taken to zoos but are killed for their skins. Panda fur is too coarse to use for fur coats, but some people like to have a panda skin to decorate their home. In Japan people will pay a great deal (over $200,000) to have a black-and-white panda skin rug on the floor (Catton 110–115).

Of course, this hunting is against the law, and if the hunters are caught they are imprisoned for life or even sentenced to death. However, the hunters still manage to smuggle a few panda skins out of China (Catton 115).

Each paragraph discusses one main idea. Here, it is the panda's diet.

This section explains why pandas are endangered. This paragraph mentions several reasons. Each of the next two paragraphs explores an important reason in more detail.

Notice how Standring varies the structure of her sentences to keep the reader's interest as she presents explanations.

Using the word however, Standring "glues" this paragraph to the previous one.

They take the risk because they are well paid by the people who want the panda skins.

Saving the Panda Although pandas are in danger from hunting, the main threat to them is the loss of their bamboo forests (Dudley 31–33). There is some good news for pandas, however. The Chinese people and international conservation organizations are working hard to protect them.

Now there are [thirteen] special panda reserves in China, where some [800] pandas are living in safety. The reserves were created to protect the pandas and the bamboo forests they need. The cutting down of bamboo and felling of trees by people is strictly controlled. Armed guards patrol the reserves to protect the pandas from hunters and to ensure that local people do not destroy the trees (Schaller 231–233).

Besides protecting the pandas, it is important to tell the local people why these animals are so special. So the people from 5,000 villages in Sichuan are taught about the need to protect pandas and how to care for starving pandas. They are told why they should not cut down trees and bamboo. If a panda causes damage to the local people's farm crops, the people are paid to cover the damage (Laidler 188–189).

The largest reserve, at Wolong, was created in 1975. In 1980, the Chinese government and WWF built a special panda-breeding and research center there (Laidler 177).

The Future for Pandas . . . [T]he giant panda's urgent need for help has brought together conservation workers, vets, scientists, zookeepers, and animal lovers from all over the world. The Chinese people and conservation organizations have managed to protect large areas of bamboo forest and guard the pandas that live in them. We have already found some ways of helping pandas to survive by studying them in the wild and in captivity.

If we can give enough support to the efforts to save pandas, perhaps in the next century there will be more pandas in the world than now. Then the panda on the WWF badge will be the symbol of a success story in wildlife conservation.

The writer uses facts and figures to support her statement that people are working hard to protect pandas.

Standring cites her sources for all specific facts that are not common knowledge. She uses the standard format for internal citations.

Works Cited

Angel, Heather. *Pandas*. Stillwater, MN: Voyageur Press, 1998.

Catton, Chris. *Pandas*. New York: Facts on File, 1990.

Dudley, Karen. *Giant Pandas*. Austin, TX: Raintree Steck-Vaughn, 1997.

Laidler, Keith and Liz. *Pandas: Giants of the Bamboo Forest*. London: BBC Books, 1992.

Schaller, George B. *The Last Panda*. Chicago: University of Chicago Press, 1993.

Reading Writing Connection

Writing Application: Help Readers Answer Questions As you draft your report, think about questions your readers may have. Provide any necessary background and details. Consider providing some information in the forms of charts or graphs to which readers can refer as needed. For example, when Standring writes in her report that pandas have fewer bamboo groves to live in, readers may have questions about how much the habitat has diminished. A map like the one here allows interested readers to find out.

LITERATURE

To read another example of research writing, read "Rattlesnake Hunt" by Marjorie Kinnan Rawlings. You can find the selection in *Prentice Hall Literature: Timeless Voices, Timeless Themes,* Bronze.

CHINA
- Existing Panda Habitat
- Approximate Prehistoric Distribution

CHINA
Beijing

0   500 Miles

0   250   500 Miles
0   250   500 Kilometers

Beijing
Huang Ho (Yellow River)
Wolong Reserve
Xi'an
Qinling Mts.
Qionglai Mts.
Minshan Mts.
Xiangling Mts.
Chengdu
Yangtze River
Liangshan Mts.
Chongqing
Mekong River
Kunming
Xun River

▲ **Critical Viewing** Using the map, estimate the percentage by which panda habitat has shrunk since prehistoric times. **[Analyze]**

11.2 Prewriting

Choosing Your Topic

Use the following strategies to choose a research topic that interests you and on which enough information is available:

Strategies for Generating a Topic

1. **Listing** List ideas in response to one of the following: *animals, famous people,* or *science*. After writing for several minutes, review your list. Circle three ideas, and list words you associate with each. Then, draw lines between related items. Choose a topic from among these items.

2. **Newswatch** Skim recent magazines or newspapers, and listen to the news on radio and television. List people, places, events, or current issues of interest. Review your list, and choose your topic from among current news items.

3. **Self-Interview** Create a chart like the one below, and answer the questions shown. Circle words and draw lines to show connections between items on your list. Choose a topic from among these linked items.

Try it out! Use the interactive Self-Interview in **Section 11.2**, on-line or on CD-ROM.

Name: Jamie Barraclough
Los Alamos Middle School
Los Alamos, NM

Student Work
IN PROGRESS

Conducting a Self-Interview
Jamie chose his topic, whales, from his self-interview answers after connecting his science teacher, Mrs. Mondello, with the film she had shown on ocean life.

People	Places	Things	Events
What interesting people do I know or know about?	What interesting places have I been to or heard about?	What interesting things do I know about or have I seen?	What interesting events have I experienced or heard about?
Mrs. Mondello Gloria Davy Crocket Gilies	Grand Canyon kitchen library ocean	football flag movie clouds whales	class trip to aquarium World Series craft fair

TOPIC BANK

If you're having trouble finding a topic, consider the following possibilities:

1. **Biographical Sketch** Think of a famous person you admire. The person may be someone who is alive today or someone who lived long ago. Research this person's life, and then write a biographical sketch.

2. **Report on a Natural Phenomenon** What are volcanoes? Why do they erupt? Using library and Internet resources, write a report on volcanoes or another natural phenomenon.

Responding to Fine Art

3. Jot down notes describing the painting on this page. From your notes, choose a research topic about Native American life or traditions.

Responding to Literature

4. Read "Rikki-tikki-tavi" by Rudyard Kipling, and then write a report on one of the following topics: mongooses, poisonous snakes of India, or an aspect of everyday life in India today. You can find "Rikki-tikki-tavi" in *Prentice Hall Literature: Timeless Voices, Timeless Themes*, Bronze.

Our Home and Native Land, Danielle Hayes

☑ Cooperative Writing Opportunity

5. **Aquarium Display** As a group, develop the shark exhibit for an aquarium. Each group member should research one type of shark and find a photograph of it. Then, each group member should write an informative caption of two or three paragraphs to accompany the photograph. Work as a group to assemble the photographs and captions into an exhibit in which the "sharks" swim in an "aquarium."

Narrowing Your Topic

After choosing your topic, make sure it is narrow enough to cover in a short report. Use the strategy of "Classical Invention."

Use Classical Invention

Classical Invention is a strategy used by the ancient Greeks to explore a topic. To help you narrow your topic, answer questions about your topic like the ones shown in the Student Model below. Simply replace *whales* with your own topic.

Review your answers to these questions. Circle a series of related ideas that interest you. Sum these ideas up in a sentence. Use this sentence as the focus of your research paper.

Student Work
IN PROGRESS

Name: Jamie Barraclough
Los Alamos Middle School
Los Alamos, NM

Using Classical Invention

Jamie answered the Classical Invention questions for his general topic, whales. Then, for each detail on the list, he itemized more details.

General Topic: Whales

- In what general category does your topic belong?

  Whales are animals. They are mammals, just like dogs and cats. Most (eat sea animals.)

  Some whales eat big squid and fish. Others eat tiny plants and animals called plankton. They have a kind of (strainer in their mouths.)

- How is your topic like, or different from, other topics in this category?

  Unlike most other mammals, whales spend their entire lives in the sea. They do not have legs.

  <u>Narrowed Topic</u>
  What are the different kinds of whales and their different characteristics?

- Into what other topics can your topic be divided?

  There are (different kinds of whales,) like the bowhead, which has a funny head, and the sperm whale with its sharp teeth. Some whales have (baleen instead of teeth.)

  (Baleen) is what some whales use to get food, but these whales only eat plankton. (Sperm whales) don't have baleen, though. They have teeth.

- What cause-and-effect relationships are involved in your topic?

  Hunting and pollution are causing whales to become endangered.

Considering Your Audience and Purpose

Your audience's background on your topic will determine which details you include. If your audience for a report on Indian tigers is a group of young children, you will probably want to explain where India is. For an older audience, you might omit this information but give more details about tigers.

Your purpose will also affect the details you use. For example, if your purpose in a report on recycling is to show its necessity, you might include facts on shrinking landfill areas.

Gathering Details

Use a Variety of Research Sources

Use a variety of sources to ensure that the information you present is accurate and balanced. Cross-check information from the Internet or an interview whenever possible by consulting printed sources. If you find differing versions of the facts, you might simply note the discrepancy in your report.

Take Notes

When you find information related to your topic, use index cards to take detailed notes. Follow these guidelines:

- Write one note on each card.

- Double-check the spelling of names and technical terms.

- Use quotation marks whenever you include exact words from your source in a report.

- On each card, record the title of the book or article and the page number, or write the name of the Web site or your interviewee.

- Create a source card for each book, article, or interviewee. For a source in print, list the author, title, publisher, and place and date of publication. For a Web site, list the title of the main page and the URL address (the address begins with "http://"). For an interviewee, list the person's name, address, and phone number, as well as the date of the interview.

As an alternative to note cards, you can photocopy pages from resources and highlight the information you plan to use. Include information about the source on the photocopy.

🖱 Research Tip

To search the Internet efficiently, use a search engine. Start by using search terms that are as specific as your topic permits. Scan the list of "hits," reading the descriptions of sites and eliminating any not clearly related to your topic. If you have not found any relevant sites by the third page of your search results, try a new search term.

Drafting

Shaping Your Writing

After you have gathered your information for a research report, you must decide how to organize and present it.

Develop a Main Idea or Thesis

Determine the overall focus of your report. For example, in a report about tigers, you could focus on their habitat requirements, or you could emphasize that illegal poaching contributes to their being endangered. Write a single sentence expressing your main idea. This sentence is called a **thesis statement.**

Make an Outline

Choosing a Method of Organization Group your notes by category. For instance, place all cards on tiger habitats in one group and all notes on their hunting strategies in another. Then, choose a method of organization that suits your topic.

- **Chronological Order** You might arrange details according to their sequence in time, as in writing a biographical sketch.

- **Ordering by Type** If your groups of notes are about ideas of equal importance, you might write about each one in turn. For a report on poisonous snakes in India, for example, you might separate your notes for cobras, for kraits, and for vipers into different folders.

Developing an Outline Referring to your chosen method of organization, develop an outline for your report. Use each category of notes as a main point on your outline. Use Roman numerals (I, II, III) to number your most important points. Under each Roman numeral, use capital letters (A, B, C) for the supporting details.

> Title of Your Report
> I. First main point
>   A. First supporting detail
>   B. Second supporting detail
> II. Second main point...

✍ Collaborative Writing Tip

For help providing elaboration, read portions of your draft that you think might need clarification to a group of peers. Ask them if they found anything confusing or surprising in what you read. Use their comments to guide you as you add clarifications to your draft.

◄ **Critical Viewing**
Name two details about tigers that most people already know. Name one type of detail about which readers might need more information. **[Hypothesize]**

Providing Elaboration
Find Points for Clarification

After you write a paragraph, review it, looking for words you did not know before you started your report and for facts that might seem incredible. Consider the following sentence:

Less than a teaspoon of krait venom can kill a person.

Many readers will not know the word *krait*. Some will find it incredible that so little venom can be fatal. Add details to elaborate or clarify such points in your writing.

Student Work
IN PROGRESS

Name: Jamie Barraclough
Los Alamos Middle School
Los Alamos, NM

Finding Points to Clarify

As Jamie drafted, he found a few words, including baleen *and* krill, *that he first learned while doing research on whales. He elaborated on them to help readers.*

Instead of teeth,

~~Baleen~~ whales have a unique physical feature. in their mouths

It is

~~They are~~ called baleen, which grows down from their jaw in

with tiny spaces between them

long, narrow plates. Whales use their baleen to feed by

opening their mouths to let in lots of water. Then, they spit

out the water through the baleen, leaving plankton

, or tiny shrimp,

and krill in their mouths.

Revising

Revising Your Overall Structure

Analyze Organization

During the drafting process, you used your notes to make an outline for your research report. Now that you have completed a first draft, you can analyze your organization to see whether you have achieved the best possible results.

▶ **REVISION STRATEGY**
Matching Your Draft to Your Outline

As you read through your report, stop at the end of each paragraph and refer to your outline. Mark each paragraph with the Roman numeral and capital letter from your outline that designate the subject of the paragraph.

For example, the following might be part of your outline:

> I. Cobras
>   A. front-fanged
>   B. hunting method

In this case, you should mark a paragraph about the fangs of cobras "I.A." If your second paragraph discusses their hunting method, mark it "I.B," and so forth.

When you have finished labeling each paragraph, review your labels. Ask yourself the following questions:

- Are all the paragraphs that are tagged with the same Roman numeral next to each other? Should they be?

- What about the paragraphs with the same Roman numeral-capital letter combination?

- Does the sequence of Roman numerals and capital letters in the report match the sequence on your outline? If not, is the change an improvement? Why or why not?

Reorganize the paragraphs in your draft to achieve the most effective organization.

▼ **Critical Viewing**
Referring to this picture, name a feature of this snake that might appear as a main head on an outline. **[Infer]**

Revising Your Paragraphs

Use Transitions

The space between paragraphs is like a joint in a piece of furniture. The glue you need to hold two paragraphs together —a transition—is a clear indication of their relationship.

Transitions are words, phrases, or whole sentences that clarify the relationships between ideas. For example, transitions like *at first, then, next,* and *finally* show a sequence of events. Transitions like *the reason that, consequently,* and *as a result* show cause and effect.

▶ REVISION STRATEGY
Finding the Glue Between Paragraphs

Read the final sentence of each paragraph. Then, read the opening sentence of the next paragraph. If one or both sentences clearly show the relationship between paragraphs, underline them in blue pencil. If you don't find a transition, draw a squiggly red line in the space between the paragraphs and add a word, phrase, or sentence to "glue" them together.

⚙ Grammar and Style Tip

Transitions make the connections between ideas "visible." If you have difficulty finding a transition to join two paragraphs, your ideas may not be well-connected. Consider rearranging such paragraphs so that you can connect them to others with transitions.

Student Work IN PROGRESS

Name: Jamie Barraclough
Los Alamos Middle School
Los Alamos, NM

Finding the Glue Between Paragraphs

Jamie found a few places where he needed transitions. He added words and phrases there to glue his paragraphs together.

Several of the toothed whales shoot a jet of water at the ocean floor. They use this jet to stir up prey hiding in the sand. These whales include the beluga and the narwhal. These whales also have very flexible necks that help them scan the ocean floor for food.

Other characteristics can help a whale live in a harsh environment.
The bowhead ∧has several interesting physical
,for instance,
features that allow it to live in the Arctic all the time.

Revising Your Sentences

Vary Sentence Length

You can make your writing smoother and more interesting by varying your sentence structure and length.

▶ **REVISION STRATEGY**
Finding the Main Action in a Cluster

Select five paragraphs in your draft. In each, underline sentences in alternating colors (for example, underline the first sentence in green, the second in orange, the third in green, and so on). Then, review your coding. Circle any place where you find clusters of short lines. Reread the sentences in the cluster, and draw a rectangle around the sentence that expresses the main action or point. Then, try combining sentences by substituting a phrase for one sentence and adding it to the sentence expressing the main action.

Text

Get instant help! For more practice varying sentences, complete selected exercises in **Section 21.3**, on-line or on CD-ROM.

Student Work IN PROGRESS

Name: *Jamie Barraclough*
Los Alamos Middle School
Los Alamos, NM

Combining Short Sentences

Jamie used color-coding to find this cluster of short sentences. He drew boxes around two main points in the paragraph. Then, he broke up the cluster by combining short sentences with the sentences expressing main points.

Having teeth allows these whales to eat chewy foods. These foods include squid and octopus. *, such as*
These creatures are abundant in the waters they *, which*
inhabit. Several of the toothed whales shoot a jet *, such as the beluga and the narwhal,*
of water at the ocean floor. They use this jet to stir up prey hiding in the sand. These whales include the beluga and the narwhal.

Grammar in Your Writing
Participial Phrases

A present participle is the *-ing* form of a verb. A past participle is the past form of the verb, often ending in *-ed* or *-d*. A **participial phrase** combines a present or past participle with other words and phrases. Participles and participial phrases act as adjectives: They answer the questions *What kind? Which one? How many?* or *How much?* about something in the sentence.

By using participial phrases, you can combine sentences, as in these examples:

SHORT SENTENCES: The attorney spoke quietly. She summarized the case.

COMBINED: The attorney, speaking quietly, summarized the case.

SHORT SENTENCES: He found the ring. It was hidden in a trunk.

COMBINED: He found the ring hidden in a trunk.

Notice that, as in the first example, a participial phrase can be created by replacing a verb (*spoke*) with its participial form (*speaking*).

Find It in Your Reading Find one participial phrase in the Student Work on page 241. Explain what information the phrase adds to the main action or point of the sentence.

Find It in Your Writing Identify three participial phrases that you have used in your research report. If you can't find three examples, consider whether you could use participial phrases to combine pairs or groups of short, choppy sentences.

To learn more about participial phrases, see Chapter 20.

Revising Your Word Choice
Look Up New Words

In doing research, you may have come across new words, including specialized terms or unfamiliar expressions. If you use these new words in your own report, consider whether they will be familiar to your audience. Code these terms, and consider adding a definition for each.

▶ **REVISION STRATEGY**
Color-Coding Technical Terms

Highlight any technical terms—terms specific to your topic—that you use in your report. Add a definition in parentheses after each highlighted word the first time it appears.

Peer Review

Summarize

Join with a group of four other class-mates. Read your entire report to the group, then pause, and read it a second time. After the second reading, each listener in the group should follow these steps:

1. Determine the main idea of your report.

2. Write the main idea as a single sentence.

3. Choose one word to express the main idea.

4. Think of a synonym for this word.

5. Share the sentences and words with the group and discuss differences among them.

If most listeners have stated a main idea different from the one you had in mind as you drafted, review your draft. Consider these possibilities:

• Your draft fully covers your original main idea. *If so, clarify the statement of your main idea in your introduction and conclusion.*

• Your classmates have discovered a main idea more closely reflected in your draft than the one you had in mind. *If so, revise your introduction and conclusion to include a statement of this main idea.*

Writers in
ACTION

Ellie Fries comments as follows on the importance of peer review:
"Having someone read your work is very important in reassuring you that you are doing the right thing, that your concepts are being developed in the way you want them to be."

▼ **Critical Viewing**
In what way does this picture summarize the game that has just ended? **[Analyze]**

11.5 Editing and Proofreading

Focusing on Citations

In a research report, you must cite the sources for quotations, facts that are not common knowledge, and ideas that are not your own.

Internal Citations A basic form of citation is an internal citation in parentheses. An internal citation directly follows the information that came from the source cited. It includes the author's last name and the page number on which the information appears.

> "I tell my students that the American Indian has a unique investment in the American landscape" (Momaday 33).

Works Cited List Provide full information about the sources in an alphabetical "Works Cited" list at the end of your report. The following is an example of the correct form:

> Momaday, N. Scott. *The Man Made of Words.*
> New York: St. Martin's Press, 1997.

⊙ Technology Tip

To format titles quickly in a word-processing program, check the Help feature to find the keyboard shortcut for italics. Use this shortcut when formatting the titles of long works.

Grammar in Your Writing
Quotation Marks and Underlining With Titles of Works

Underline (or style in italics) the titles of long written works and the titles of periodicals. Also, underline or italicize the titles of movies, television series, and works of music and art.

EXAMPLES: *The Sun Also Rises* (title of a book)
Mona Lisa (title of a painting)

Use quotation marks with the titles of short written works and Internet sites.

EXAMPLES: "Rikki-tikki-tavi" (title of a short story)
"My Home Page" (title of a Web site)

Find It in Your Reading Read the Works Cited list on page 242. Notice how italics and quotation marks are used for the titles of works.

Find It in Your Writing Review your essay to see whether you have used underlining and quotation marks correctly for the titles of works.

To learn more about the form for titles, see Chapters 26 and 27.

Publishing and Presenting

Building Your Portfolio

Consider these suggestions for publishing and presenting:

1. **Create a "Wall of Fame"** In a group, create a bulletin-board display of biographical sketches. Mount each report along with a picture of the subject. Then, label each image with a descriptive title, such as "Famous Inventor."

2. **Design a Web Site** Join with classmates to plan a Web site for your reports. Create illustrations representing each page on the site and a chart showing how each links to the others. The group should find Web links to related Web sites for each report and design icons for each page.

Reflecting on Your Writing

In a brief reflective note, discuss what happened when you wrote your research report. Include this reflection in your portfolio. To get started, use the following questions:

- In the process of writing, what did you learn about the topic you chose?

- Which writing strategies would you recommend to others? Why?

💻 Internet Tip

To see a research report scored according to this rubric, go on-line: PHSchool.com Enter Web Code: ebk-7001

Rubric for Self-Assessment

Use the following criteria to evaluate your research report:

	Score 4	Score 3	Score 2	Score 1
Audience and Purpose	Focuses on a clearly stated thesis, starting from a well-framed question; gives complete citations	Focuses on a clearly stated thesis; gives citations	Focuses mainly on the chosen topic; gives some citations	Presents information without a clear focus; few or no citations
Organization	Presents information in logical order, emphasizing details of central importance	Presents information in logical order	Presents information logically, but organization is poor in places	Presents information in a scattered, disorganized manner
Elaboration	Draws clear conclusions from information gathered from multiple sources	Draws conclusions from information gathered from multiple sources	Explains and interprets some information	Presents information with little or no interpretation or synthesis
Use of Language	Shows overall clarity and fluency; contains few mechanical errors	Shows good sentence variety; contains some errors in spelling, punctuation, or usage	Uses awkward or overly simple sentence structures; contains many mechanical errors	Contains incomplete thoughts and mechanical errors that make the writing confusing

11.7 Student Work
IN PROGRESS

FINAL DRAFT

Built to Survive: Whales

Jamie Barraclough
Los Alamos Middle School
Los Alamos, New Mexico

Whales live in all the oceans of the Earth, both in the shallow and deep waters as well as in Arctic and tropical waters. A whale's physical features help it to survive and meet the challenges of its environment. All whales are aquatic mammals of the Cetacean order. They are separated into two groups: the baleen and the toothed. Whales range in body size from the largest mammal in the world (the blue whale) at over 100 feet long to whales the size of a human—about six feet (Carwardine 14–19).

Instead of teeth, baleen whales have a unique physical feature called *baleen*, which grows down from their jaw in long, narrow plates with tiny spaces between them. Whales use their baleen to

Jamie uses the first paragraph to introduce his research topic. The second sentence states the main idea or thesis of the report—its overall focus.

Jamie's report is organized by type— he discusses each of the main groups of whales in turn.

feed by opening their mouths to let in lots of water. Then, they spit out the water through the baleen, leaving plankton and krill, or tiny shrimp, in their mouths. Using the baleen for feeding allows this kind of whale to eat up to four tons of krill a day. Therefore, it makes sense that baleen whales such as the blue whale, the fin whale, the bowhead whale, the humpback whale, and the sei whale (to name just a few) grow to immense sizes (Carwardine 19–21). The blue whale has grooves running from under its chin to partway along the length of its underbelly. As in some other whales, these grooves expand and allow even more food and water to be taken in (Ellis 18–21).

On the other hand, the toothed whales such as the beluga, the narwhal, the Baird's beaked whale, and the orca are smaller in size. The sperm whale is an exception, growing up to 59 feet long (Whales in Danger). Having teeth allows these whales to eat chewy foods such as squid and octopus, which are abundant in the waters they inhabit (Carwardine 68–69). Several of the toothed whales, such as the beluga and the narwhal, shoot a jet of water at the ocean floor to stir up prey hiding in the sand. These whales also have very flexible necks that help them scan the ocean floor for food (Carwardine 190–191).

Other characteristics can help a whale live in a harsh environment. The bowhead, for instance, has several interesting physical features that allow it to live in the Arctic all the time. The first characteristic is the one from which this species gets its name. The bowhead uses its gigantic head, which is about 40 percent of its total body length, to punch through sheets of ice up to 12 inches thick. Bowheads need to do this to create an airhole in the ice. In addition, their layer of blubber, which is over 2 feet thick, allows them to live in extremely cold water (Whales in Danger).

Sperm whales also have a distinctive physical feature: a cavity in the head called the spermaceti organ, which is a large area full of tubes filled with a kind of yellow wax. This organ is thought to keep sperm whales afloat and to focus their sonar clicks (Whales in Danger).

Whales have many special features that make them well adapted to all of the oceans of the world. They are beautiful, gentle creatures in spite of their enormous size. They are also a critical part of the ocean ecology, living peacefully in their watery world.

Works Cited

Carwardine, Mark, Erich Hoyt, R. Ewan Fordyce, and Peter Gill. *The Nature Company Guides: Whales, Dolphins, & Porpoises*. New York: Time-Life Books, 1998.

Ellis, Richard. *Men and Whales*. New York: Knopf, 1991.

Whales in Danger. "Discovering Whales." http://whales.magna.com.au/DISCOVER

Jamie shows how the physical features of baleen whales help them fit into their environment— a main focus of his report.

The phrases "On the other hand" and "smaller in size" supply transitions, connecting this paragraph to the previous one.

This paragraph discusses a single main point: the unusual features of the bowhead whale.

Throughout his report, Jamie cites his sources for specific facts, using a standard format.

In his final paragraph, Jamie restates the main idea of his report, emphasizing the interest of his topic.

Jamie includes a "Works Cited" list at the end of his report, giving full publication information for each source he cites.

Connected Assignment *I-Search Report*

Even the driest research begins life as a lively question—
"I wonder . . .?" An I-Search report tells the story of that
curiosity. It begins with a topic of immediate concern to
you and provides well-researched information on that
topic. Unlike a research report, an I-Search report tells
the story of your exploration of the topic, using the
pronoun *I*. It gives

- your purpose in learning about the topic.
- the story of how you researched it.
- an account of what you learned.

Prewriting To choose a topic for your report, focus on
subjects in which you have an immediate interest: the best
CD player to buy, how to organize a neighborhood cleanup,
what career to choose. Narrow your topic to a manageable size.
Then, use a K-W-L chart to help you gather details about your
topic. Record the steps you took to learn more about your topic
and the practical lessons you learned.

▲ **Critical Viewing**
Name three specific
topics about which a
person such as the
one in the picture
might be curious.
[Apply]

Know	**W**ant to Know	**L**earned
Graphics programs let you create amazing pictures on the computer.	What are some of the basic programs? What is the difference between bitmapped and vector art?	

Drafting Use an outline to organize your details clearly. In
your outline, consider presenting the story of your interest in
and research on your topic first, followed by a report of the
information you found.

Revising and Editing Review your draft. Circle sentences
that describe your research experience or the practical application of what you have learned. If you find long stretches
without circles, consider adding more details about your
research experience and the importance of information to you.
Add transitions to connect parts of your report that present
information with parts that tell the story of your research.

Publishing and Presenting After revising your I-Search
report, consider posting it on a personal or school Web site to
share your research and experiences with others.

Spotlight on the Humanities

Framing Questions to Direct Research

Focus on Theater: *Oliver!*

To tell even a sentimental story properly, you may need to do research into hard facts. The musical *Oliver!* tells the story of an orphan in nineteenth-century England who runs away from a cruel orphanage to rough-and-tumble London. The plot comes from Charles Dickens's novel *Oliver Twist*, but the costume and scenery designers had to find out about the clothes, buildings, and other details from Dickens's times. The research paid off. *Oliver!* hit the Broadway stage in 1963 and ran for 774 performances. With music and lyrics by Lionel Bart, it won a Tony Award for Best Composer and Lyricist, as well as Best Scenic Design.

Literature Connection British author Charles Dickens (1812–1870) wrote a number of novels that, like *Oliver Twist*, chronicle the sufferings of the poor. Here, Dickens drew on his own experiences. When he was a young child, his family hit financial hard times, and his father went to debtor's prison. Dickens himself, however, was a huge success as a writer. Among his most famous works are *A Christmas Carol*, *David Copperfield*, and *Great Expectations*.

Art Connection Dickens's popularity left its mark on the art of the day. Over four hundred portraits and caricatures of him were created during his lifetime! The illustrations of his works also include caricatures. For example, the drawing from *Oliver Twist* on this page caricatures orphanage officials. Dickens's original illustrators, George Cruikshank (1792–1878), who illustrated *Oliver Twist*, and Hablot K. Browne (1815–1882), who signed his work "Phiz," matched Dickens's distinctive style with their own.

Caricatures have a long history. Some caricatures protest or ridicule their subjects, commenting on character by distorting faces or figures. Others gently exaggerate a colorful personality.

Research Writing Activity: History of Caricatures

Come up with a question about the history of caricatures—for example, "When have caricatures been most popular?" Do research to find an answer, and write up your results in a report.

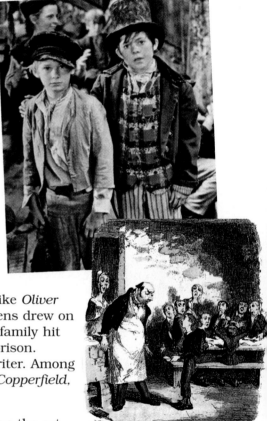

Etching from Charles Dickens's *Oliver Twist*

▲ **Critical Viewing** Compare the orphans in the still from the film version of *Oliver!* with the orphans in Cruikshank's illustration. **[Compare]**

Media and Technology Skills

Using On-line Sources in Research

Activity: Finding and Evaluating On-line Sources

The Internet can be a valuable research tool. Learn how to use it efficiently and critically.

Learn About It

Searching the Web To search for information on the Web, use a search engine. When you arrive at a search engine's home page, type your topic into the appropriate field, hit Enter, and a list of sites related to your topic will come up. If you are not familiar with different search engines, use the Search button on your browser.

Evaluating Sources Before using information from the Internet, evaluate the source from which it comes. Someone's personal home page may not be well researched. A site sponsored by a group with a product to sell or a cause to promote may not always give complete information. Reliable sites include those sponsored by

- the government (address ends in ".gov").
- nonprofit organizations (address ends in ".org").
- educational institutions (address ends in ".edu").
- publishers of educational or reference books, producers of educational television programs, news organizations, and so on.

Evaluate It Choose a topic, and gather information on it using the Internet. Record your search in a chart such as the one below. When you have explored four or more sites, write a brief essay in which you evaluate the credibility of each.

<table>
<tr><td colspan="4">Topic: <u>The Dust Bowl</u></td></tr>
<tr><th>Site Name</th><th>My Search Route</th><th>Site Address</th><th>Evaluation</th></tr>
<tr>
<td>1. Surviving the Dust Bowl

2.
3.</td>
<td>Kid Search site to "Social Studies" link to "History"; I searched for the term "Dust Bowl."</td>
<td>http://www. pbs.org/ wgbh/amex/ dustbowl/</td>
<td>Highly credible source: producer of documentaries and great information</td>
</tr>
</table>

Tips for On-line Research

- Web pages on a particular subject often have links to related sites. Use these links to quickly scout for more information. Use the Back button to return to the page listing the links.
- Use the Bookmark feature of your browser to record the address of any site that seems particularly useful. A bookmark makes returning to the site easy.
- Do not use sites that require personal information or a purchase. There are many free, reliable sources available.

Standardized Test Preparation Workshop

Revising and Editing

One of the most important steps in research is revising the organization of your draft to present information in the clearest way possible. When taking a standardized test, you may be challenged by questions that test your ability to revise and edit a passage. The following sample test item shows one format for such questions.

Test Tip

When answering revising-and-editing questions, place each choice in the context of the passage before choosing an answer.

Sample Test Item

The following is from a report written by Will. As part of a peer conference, you must make suggestions about the report. Read the passage, and answer the question that follows.

1 Benjamin Franklin became clerk
2 of the Pennsylvania Legislature
3 in 1736 and Philadelphia
4 postmaster in 1737. He served in
5 both these positions for over
6 fifteen years. In 1753, he became
7 Deputy Postmaster General in
8 charge of all mail for the northern
9 colonies. Franklin's public
10 duties also led him to travel. In
11 1757, he sailed to England to
12 negotiate between the family of
13 William Penn and the state
14 government in a legal dispute.

1 Which of these sentences would make the **BEST** topic sentence for this paragraph?

A Benjamin Franklin served in the Pennsylvania state government.

B Benjamin Franklin had a genius for negotiating compromises.

C Benjamin Franklin pursued an extensive career in public service.

D Benjamin Franklin made many contributions to the postal system.

Answer and Explanation

The correct answer is C. A concerns Franklin's service in the Pennsylvania government, which is covered in the paragraph, but the paragraph also describes other facets of his career in government. B does not make a good topic sentence for the paragraph because the paragraph says nothing to support the idea that Franklin was a successful negotiator. D does not make a good topic sentence because nothing is said about Franklin's contributions to the postal system, and the paragraph covers other parts of his career as well. C is the best choice because each sentence in the paragraph gives one or more details about Franklin's career in public service.

Practice **Directions:** Read the following passage. Then, answer the questions below, choosing the letter of the best answer.

1 James Madison served as a
2 member of Congress, Secretary of
3 State, and as the fourth president
4 of the United States. He is a great
5 statesman. Madison entered
6 politics in 1774. Later, as an
7 assemblyman, he represented
8 Virginia at the drafting of the
9 Constitution. In Congress,
10 Madison proposed six of the
11 first ten amendments to the
12 Constitution, which are called the
13 Bill of Rights. For his contribution
14 to this important document, he
15 became known as "the father of
16 the Constitution" Columbia
17 Encyclopedia 1193. He was also
18 greatly involved in the war of
19 1812. Enduring defeat by the
20 British and the burning of
21 Washington, D.C., Madison
22 recruited soldiers from earlier
23 battles and trained new soldiers to
24 fight. The war finally ended with
25 victory for Americans with the
26 signing of the Treaty of Ghent in
27 1814.

1 What is the **BEST** change, if any, to make to the sentence in lines 4–5 ("*He . . . statesman*")?
A Change *is* to **are**
B Change *is* to **was**
C Change *he* to **Madison**
D Make no change.

2 Which of the following sentences would **BEST** fit after the sentence in lines 5–6 ("*Madison . . . 1774*")?
F He was very successful in politics.
G His first position was as an elected official to the Committee of Safety in Orange County, Virginia.
H These committees provided local government.
J Madison was born on March 16, 1751.

3 What is the **BEST** change, if any, to make at the beginning of the sentence in line 9 ("*In Congress, . . .*")?
A Change *In Congress,* to **As a member of Congress,**
B Change *In Congress,* to **During Congress,**
C Delete *In Congress,*
D Make no change.

4 Which of these sentences would **BEST** fit the ideas in lines 9–17 ("*In Congress . . . 1193*")?
F The Bill of Rights describes the fundamental rights of the people and forbids government to violate these rights.
G Madison lost an election because of his strong support for the Constitution.
H Madison was a great political thinker.
J Many of the ideas for the constitution were developed in ancient Greece and Rome.

5 Which is the **BEST** change, if any, that should be made to the sentence ("*For his . . . 1193*") in lines 13–17?
A Delete *For his contribution to this important document,*
B Change *Columbia Encyclopedia 1193* to **(Columbia Encyclopedia 1193)**.
C Change *Columbia Encyclopedia 1193* to **(Columbia Encyclopedia, 1193)**.
D Make no change.

6 Which of the following sentences would **BEST** conclude the passage?
F After making great contributions to the development of America, Madison retired in 1817.
G Madison did many great things.
H Now we know why Madison is known as the father of the constitution.
J Madison retired in 1817.

Response to Literature

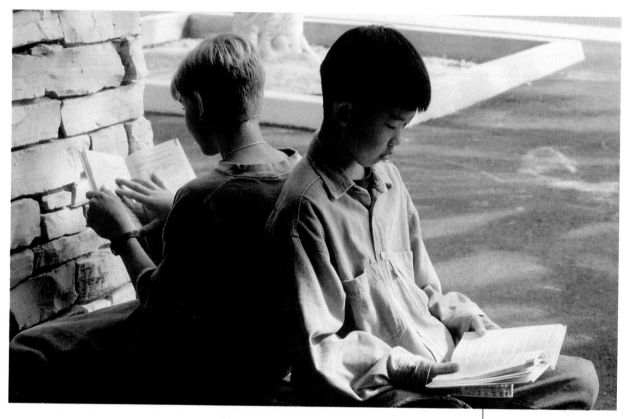

▲ **Critical Viewing**
Explain how these two students might be sharing the same experience, even though they are both absorbed in reading. **[Interpret]**

Responses to Literature in Everyday Life

Reading is usually considered a solitary activity. Picture yourself reading a book in an empty room. Anyone who peeked in would have no way to tell what new adventures were beginning for you. Yet another person, miles away, might share the same images flashing before your mind—just by reading the same book.

When you respond to literature, you can test just how much of your experience of a book you share with others. In a response to literature, you tell readers "what the book was like." You might respond in a quick conversation with a friend or in a review you write for a magazine. Discussing your response brings you closer to other readers and helps show that when we read, we are rarely alone.

What Is a Response to Literature?

A **response to literature** is an essay or other type of writing that discusses what is of value in a book, short story, essay, article, or poem. A response might retell the plot of an exciting story, explain why a poem is beautiful, or show disappointment with a writer's latest play. A response to literature includes

- a strong, interesting focus on an aspect of the work.
- a clear organization that groups related details.
- supporting details for each main idea.
- a summary of important features of the work.
- a judgment about the value of the work.

To preview the criteria on which your response may be assessed, see the Rubric for Self-Assessment on page 265.

Types of Responses to Literature

In addition to a standard literary essay, there are other types of responses to literature:

- **Book reviews** give readers an impression of a book, encouraging them either to read it or to avoid reading it.
- **Letters to an author** let a writer know what a reader found enjoyable or disappointing in a work.
- **Comparisons of works** highlight specific features of two or more works by comparing them.

PREVIEW Student Work IN PROGRESS

Jade Yamamoto, a student at Calvary Lutheran School in Indianapolis, Indiana, wrote a response to two poems by Emily Dickinson. In this chapter, you will follow her work in progress and the strategies she used to choose a topic, to draft, and to revise her work. Her final draft appears at the end of the chapter.

Model From Literature

Zena Sutherland (1915–) has written many works on children's literature. This excerpt is taken from one of them, Children and Books.

Reading Strategy: Identify Evidence
The writer of a response to literature or another piece of nonfiction should provide evidence to support each main point. As you read nonfiction, **identify the evidence** provided for better understanding. For instance, Sutherland claims that Hans Christian Andersen's "heroes and heroines are not stereo-types." You can better understand her claim by identifying her evidence—her descriptions of a few characters.

▲ **Critical Viewing**
Explain how the style of this portrait helps suggest Andersen's dreamy side. **[Analyze]**

Making Fantasy Real

Zena Sutherland

Hans Christian Andersen (1805–1875) was born in Odense, Denmark, of a peasant family. His . . . first book, a travel diary of a walking trip, appeared in 1829, published by himself, and his first volumes of *Fairy Tales, Told for Children* appeared in 1835. . . . Andersen poured himself into his writing; it became the vehicle for expressing his emotions, flashes of humor, commentaries on life, and the follies of humankind. Some of his stories are retellings of folktales: "Little Claus and Big Claus," "The Princess and the Pea," and "The Emperor's New Clothes." In these, Andersen took the traditional story and added to it his own interpretation of character, providing motivation for the action in the tale. The heroes and heroines are not stereotypes; they live and breathe and become individuals, named or not. The princess who can feel a pea under twenty mattresses can never be confused in our thinking with any other princess, sensitive though she may be. Andersen imparted such life to these characters that we feel empathy for the emperor and his courtiers, none of whom naturally wish to admit they are stupid or unfit for office.

But it is in Andersen's own creations, his literary fairy tales, that his genius for characterization is shown. As we read "The

Sutherland introduces her topic—Hans Christian Andersen's characters—in her first paragraph. She also makes clear her opinion of his work.

Sutherland organizes her response logically, moving from the least important to the most important aspects of Andersen's art of characterization. She emphasizes the way Andersen shapes our perceptions, linking each paragraph to her concluding point.

Little Mermaid," we shudder at the pain the mermaid must feel as she puts foot to ground[. A]nd yet, so persuasive is Andersen's art that, in spite of the physical agony, we still agree with her that the prince is worth dying for.

"The Ugly Duckling" is, rightly or wrongly, seen as symbolic of Andersen's own life. The animosity of the neighbors to the "different" one seems so natural that we wonder if we ourselves would have seen the promise implicit in the awkward creature. The conversations in the poultry-yard ring true both to human nature and to the human ear. What mother would not say, "He is my own child and, when you look closely at him, he's quite handsome . . ."? Because of Andersen, every "ugly duckling" promises a swan.

Andersen's ability to draw character does not rest on extensive description. In a few carefully chosen words he establishes important qualities, leaving our imaginations so stimulated that we supply the rest of the picture. Of the hero of "The Steadfast Tin Soldier" Andersen says, "he stood as firm and steadfast on his one leg as the others did on their two." The outward description is not important; what Andersen is emphasizing is the constancy of his character.

Andersen's fantasies do not lack supernatural beings or things, and many of them have otherworldly settings, talking animals, and personifications of inanimate objects. But his main contribution was to make us look more sharply at daily life through the window of his imagination.

Sutherland makes connections to real-life experiences. She also shows again how Andersen's characterization affects our perceptions.

Sutherland builds to her strongest point, showing that Andersen's insight into character helps change the way we see the world.

Writing Application:
Provide Evidence As you draft your own response to literature, provide your readers with evidence for each of your main points.

▶ **Critical Viewing**
What insight of Andersen's does this image represent?
[Interpret]

LITERATURE

For a response to another classic tale, see reviews of Israel Horovitz's dramatic adaptation of *A Christmas Carol.* You can find samples of such reviews in *Prentice Hall Literature: Timeless Voices, Timeless Themes*, Bronze.

12.2 *Prewriting*

Choosing Your Topic

A good response to literature begins with a work to which you react strongly. Use these strategies to choose such a work:

Strategies for Generating a Topic

1. **Interview Yourself** Answer these questions: What is my favorite type of reading? (Give examples.) Which character from my reading would I like to be? Review your answers, and choose as your topic a work you mention.

2. **Browsing** Browse the literature section of a library or bookstore. Choose works you have already read or new short works by familiar authors (avoid works that will take too long to read). Flip through these works, taking notes. Write on the work that most interests you.

Try it out! Use the interactive Browsing activity in **Section 12.2**, online or on CD-ROM.

Student Work
IN PROGRESS

Name: Jade Yamamoto
Calvary Lutheran School
Indianapolis, IN

Browsing
Looking through the poetry at the library, Jade found two poems by Emily Dickinson that seemed to have a common topic.

POEMS BY EMILY DICKINSON	NOTES
"I'm Nobody"	The frog is funny—he tries to get people's attention by croaking all the time.
"Success is counted sweetest"	People really want to succeed.
"He ate and drank the precious words"	Reading takes you places—in your mind.
"How many Flowers fail in Wood"	It's sad that flowers don't know how beautiful they are.

The first and last poems both seem to be about wanting or not wanting people to pay attention to you.

TOPIC BANK

If you're having trouble finding a topic, consider the following possibilities:

1. **Review a Favorite** Choose a favorite—or a disliked—book, short story, essay, or poem. Write a review of it for your classmates. What will they like about the piece? What will they dislike about it? Include details to support your point of view.

2. **Literary Log and Letters** Keep a daily log in which you take notes on the literature you are reading. At the end of a week, review your log. Write one letter to your teacher and one to a friend, in which you discuss what you've read.

Responding to Fine Art

3. Take notes on this painting, focusing on its mood or feeling. Then, decide what literary work you would associate with it. In an essay, compare the mood of the painting with that of the literary work. Use details from the painting and from the literary work to support your points.

Dormer, 1984–1987, Edward Rice, Morris Museum of Art, Augusta, Georgia

Responding to Literature

4. Read O. Henry's story "After Twenty Years." Write an essay describing your response to the ending. Discuss how the ending changes the way you see the beginning. Then, explain how the order in which O. Henry presents information creates these effects. You can find the story in *Prentice Hall Literature: Timeless Voices, Timeless Themes,* Bronze.

☑ Cooperative Writing Opportunity

5. **Panel Talk** Form a group with other students who are writing a response to the same work. Have each member write a paragraph about his or her reaction to the work. List discussion questions based on these statements. Then, hold a talk before the class to respond to these questions and to any others from the audience. Afterward, each member should write a complete response to the work.

Narrowing Your Topic

After you have chosen a work to which to respond, read or review it carefully. Once you have the work "under your skin," use a pentad to select an aspect on which to focus.

Use a Pentad

Draw a large five-pointed star as a graphic organizer. Label each point as follows:

- **Actors** Who did the action?
- **Acts** What was done?
- **Scenes** When or where was it done?
- **Agencies** How was it done?
- **Purposes** Why was it done?

Fill in each point of the star with details matching its label. Then, highlight details that connect in interesting ways. To create a focused topic, sum up your highlighted details in a sentence.

Collaborative Writing Tip

To help fill out your pentad, brainstorm with another student who has read the same work. Try out as many ideas as you can for difficult categories such as "Agencies."

Student Work IN PROGRESS

Name: Jade Yamamoto
Calvary Lutheran School
Indianapolis, IN

Using a Pentad

Jade narrowed her topic by creating a pentad and highlighting interesting details for each of the two poems she had selected. She made the pentad below for "I'm Nobody."

The speaker, the person she is talking to, other people, and the frog.

The speaker finds out the other person is "nobody," too. The other people will banish the two if they find out. The frog croaks all summer long to the bog.

The "nobodies" want to stay private. The other people want to banish them. The frog wants to be admired for his croaking.

Purposes · Actors · Acts · Agencies · Scenes

There isn't one really, except the bog.

Recognition—the speaker just knows the other person is a "nobody." Secrecy—the speaker and the other person don't tell anyone else they are "nobodies." Boasting—the frog croaks all summer long.

Considering Your Audience and Purpose

After focusing your topic, think about your audience and your purpose for writing. Use your answers to the following questions to guide you as you gather details and draft:

- **Are my readers already familiar with this kind of work?** If so, give details showing what is unique about this work or about how it differs from others of its kind.

- **Are my readers unfamiliar with this kind of work?** If so, explain the basic purpose of the work—to tell a suspenseful story, to make music with words, and so on.

- **Are my readers practiced, older readers?** If so, you need not explain every detail. For instance, you might explain a character to these readers as follows: "Jake is a typical adventure-story hero—rugged and able to keep cool under pressure." You might then move on to discuss the plot.

- **Am I writing for less sophisticated readers?** To help these readers picture Jake, you might need to describe him more fully, giving specific examples that reveal his character.

- **Am I trying to persuade readers of something?** If your purpose is to persuade readers that the work is "worth reading" or "not worth reading," concentrate on examples supporting your opinion.

- **Am I trying to enhance readers' appreciation of the work?** If your purpose is to enhance appreciation, point out qualities and patterns in the work that a reader might not see.

◀ **Critical Viewing** What type of literary work might these students enjoy reading? **[Speculate]**

Gathering Details

To give readers a feeling for a work, and to support your judgments about it, you need to present examples. Review the work, taking notes to gather the details you will include in your response.

Use Hexagonal Writing

To gather details about various sides of your topic, use hexagonal writing. Take two different-colored sheets of construction paper. Cut out three triangles of equal size from each sheet. Using alternating colors, arrange the triangles to form a hexagon. Label each triangle as shown in the example below. Then look through the work to find details for each triangle.

Student Work
IN PROGRESS

Name: Jade Yamamoto
Calvary Lutheran School
Indianapolis, IN

Using a Hexagon
Jade gathered details about her topic using a hexagon.

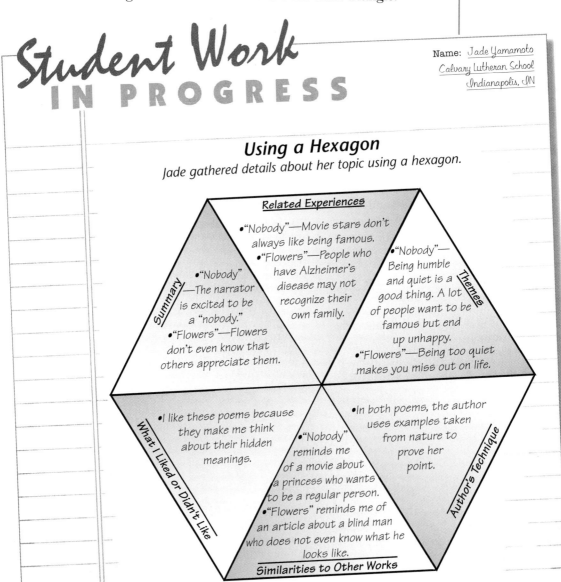

Related Experiences
- "Nobody"—Movie stars don't always like being famous.
- "Flowers"—People who have Alzheimer's disease may not recognize their own family.

Summary
- "Nobody"—The narrator is excited to be a "nobody."
- "Flowers"—Flowers don't even know that others appreciate them.

Themes
- "Nobody"—Being humble and quiet is a good thing. A lot of people want to be famous but end up unhappy.
- "Flowers"—Being too quiet makes you miss out on life.

What I Liked or Didn't Like
- I like these poems because they make me think about their hidden meanings.

Author's Technique
- In both poems, the author uses examples taken from nature to prove her point.

Similarities to Other Works
- "Nobody" reminds me of a movie about a princess who wants to be a regular person.
- "Flowers" reminds me of an article about a blind man who does not even know what he looks like.

What to Look For

As you explore the work you've chosen, look for the following types of details. Jot down notes in the appropriate section of your hexagon.

Summary If you call a book exciting or boring, you need to tell readers about what happens in it. Begin gathering details by exploring the work on a literal level, and then summarize the work:

- Outline the main events, ideas, or images.
- Indicate how these events, ideas, or images are related.
- Briefly describe the characters in the work—the people involved in the story.

Related Experiences Often, a character's experience or a line from a poem reminds you of something in real life. Part of the impact of a work depends on what it shows us about the world. Jot down any experiences or associations from life that you connect with the work.

Themes Many works of literature suggest a question or lesson about life—a **theme.** To discover the theme of a work, look for patterns of events or contrasts between characters. For instance, if one character is greedy while another is generous, you can conclude that generosity is one theme of the work. If the greedy character comes to a bad end, the work may teach a lesson about greed. Write a single sentence that expresses the message or lesson of the work.

Author's Technique Writers create any number of special effects using words. Gather examples of some of these techniques, such as the following:

- A short story writer can create a tragic effect by timing an event just right.
- A poet creates effects using **figurative language**—musical phrases, colorful images, and surprising comparisons.

Similarities to Other Works When different writers address the same subject, the differences in what they write can show you what is special about each writer. Gather specific details about characters, events, or the writer's attitude that show how your chosen work compares with another.

Evaluation and Reaction Responding to a work of literature means telling readers what you thought of it. Find precise words to describe your reactions. Note examples showing exactly what you enjoyed or disliked in the work.

▲ **Critical Viewing** If the man in this picture were a character in a story you had read, what details about him might you include in a response to the story? **[Analyze]**

Drafting

Shaping Your Writing

After gathering details from the work, review your notes to find a focus for your response. Look for connections between details. Find the direction in which many details seem to point or the main idea that most seem to illustrate. Then, organize your writing around this main point, or focus.

Define and Develop Your Focus

A focus statement sums up your reaction to one aspect of the work. For instance, your topic might be a comparison of two characters:

UNFOCUSED RESPONSE:	Cherry has dark hair. Sherri is blonde. Cherry likes adventure. Sherri likes to stay at home.
FOCUSED RESPONSE:	Cherry is easier to like than Sherri. Cherry likes adventure. She always has something sassy to say when people bug her.

To define a focus, review your notes. Then, answer the questions shown here, writing your focus as a single sentence. Include this sentence in your introduction, and elaborate on it in the body of your essay.

QUESTIONS FOR DEFINING A FOCUS

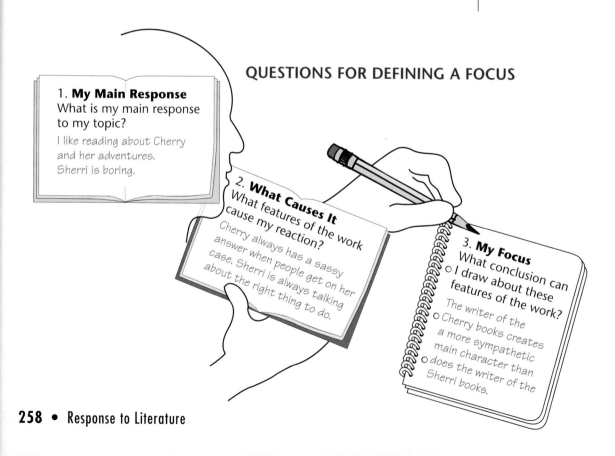

1. My Main Response
What is my main response to my topic?

I like reading about Cherry and her adventures. Sherri is boring.

2. What Causes It
What features of the work cause my reaction?

Cherry always has a sassy answer when people get on her case. Sherri is always talking about the right thing to do.

3. My Focus
What conclusion can I draw about these features of the work?

The writer of the
o Cherry books creates a more sympathetic main character than
o does the writer of the Sherri books.

Providing Elaboration

You've gathered details related to your topic. As you draft, include these details in your response to help readers understand each main point. If necessary, return to the work to gather more support.

Provide Support

As you write, refer to your notes to find support for each main point. Include details such as:

- **Quotations** In a quotation, you take the exact words used in the work and include them in your draft. Use quotation marks to set off these words.

- **Summaries** A summary is a brief retelling of events or ideas.

- **Descriptions** Your own descriptions can help readers picture the setting of a work, its characters, and so on.

- **Comparisons** Writers often create contrasting characters, places, and ideas. By making comparisons between such features, you can better interpret the meaning of a work.

Pause occasionally while drafting, and review what you have written. Add any supporting details you need.

▲ **Critical Viewing**
To which details in this photograph would you refer to show readers that these people are angry? **[Apply]**

Student Work
IN PROGRESS

Name: Jade Yamamoto
Calvary Lutheran School
Indianapolis, IN

Providing Support

After writing one paragraph, Jade reviewed it and added supporting details.

She shows her excitement in the line "Then there's a pair of us!" It's as if the speaker and the reader will make a secret club.

First, Dickinson makes being "nobody" seem fun. The speaker proudly says "'I'm Nobody'" in the very first line. She sounds excited when she discovers the reader also might be "Nobody." Later, she uses the phrases "How dreary" and "How public" to describe being famous. Being famous is not as fun as being "Nobody."

12.4 Revising

Revising Your Overall Structure

A draft is just the first step in creating a response to literature. You have most of your ideas on paper. Now, you need to make sure that they will be clear to your readers. Start by reviewing your organization.

Analyze Your Organization

Your ideas may be good, but if the support for a particular point is scattered throughout your draft, it will be hard for your reader to piece the details together. Use the strategy of color-coding to improve organization.

▶ REVISION STRATEGY
Color-Coding Main Points and Support

As you read over what you have written, circle each main point in a different color. Underline sentences supporting a main point in the same color as that of the main point.

When you have finished color-coding, review your draft:

- If a paragraph is marked in a few different colors, consider reorganizing details so that all of the support for a main point is in the same paragraph.

- Consider eliminating any sentence that is neither circled nor underlined. If such a sentence states a new main idea, consider developing it in a paragraph of its own.

Build to a Point

Readers have a more enjoyable time reading a work when each paragraph carries them closer to a main point. Identify your strongest point, and consider reorganizing your draft to build to this point.

▶ REVISION STRATEGY
Circling the Strongest Point

Review your paper. Circle your strongest point—the one that is most interesting or that summarizes your other main ideas.

Move this point to the end of your piece. Add a transition sentence clearly explaining the relationship of this point to the rest of your ideas. Then, go back and add sentences to other paragraphs in your draft, linking them to this point. (Review "Making Fantasy Real" on page 250. Read the sidenotes that explain how Zena Sutherland links each paragraph to her concluding point.)

▼ **Critical Viewing**
Compare this man's pose with the croaking of the frog described in the Student Work in Progress feature on page 261.
[Compare and Contrast]

Revising Your Paragraphs

Strengthen Support

Use the following strategy to ensure that you are providing enough support.

▶ **REVISION STRATEGY**

Using Points to Illuminate to Add Support

Review your draft, following these steps to illuminate it:

1. Cut out a five-pointed construction paper star for each of your main points. Write your main point in the center and label the points of each star as follows: *quotation, character, event, figure of speech,* and *theme*.
2. Find support in your draft for each main idea. Add a check to each star-point for which you find an example.
3. Use the unchecked points on your stars to assess your support. For example, if none of your stars have "Quotation" checked, consider adding a quotation to your response.

Research Tip

Use library resources to find essays on, or reviews of, the work to which you are responding. You can use quotations from an essay or review, properly cited, as additional support in your own response.

Student Work
IN PROGRESS

Name: Jade Yamamoto
Calvary Lutheran School
Indianapolis, IN

Adding Support With Points to Illuminate

Jade used the strategy of illuminating and discovered that she had no support for the main idea in this paragraph. She decided to add a quotation.

The frog in "I'm Nobody" represents those who brag. Emily Dickinson shows us that those who boast just make ~~, like a frog's croaking. They are like the frog that tells its name "the livelong June/ To an admiring Bog."~~ a lot of noise. Boastful people try to win the compliments of others by making known their every little "amazing" feat.

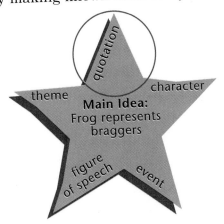

Revising Your Sentences
Combine Sentences to Show Connections

For your writing to flow smoothly, you need to make the connections between ideas as clear as possible. One way to show connections is to combine short sentences into longer ones using connecting words—words that explain the relationships between ideas. (See the Grammar in Your Writing feature on the next page for an example showing how to combine sentences into complex sentences.)

▶ **REVISION STRATEGY**
Highlighting Sentences That Explain Why

Use a colored pencil to highlight points in your writing where you explain *why* something happened or *why* you reached a particular conclusion. At each of these *why* passages, see whether you can combine shorter sentences using one of these connecting words or phrases:

as a result of	for the purpose of
because	for the sake of/in order to
despite	since
due to	so that
even though	

Text

Get instant help! For more practice combining sentences, complete selected exercises in **Section 21.2**, on-line or on CD-ROM.

Student Work
IN PROGRESS

Name: *Jade Yamamoto*
Calvary Lutheran School
Indianapolis, IN

Highlighting Sentences That Explain Why

In this passage, Jade used a connecting phrase to combine a short sentence with another one. The second sentence provides an explanation of the first.

We sometimes assume that being on top is what life is all about. We~~ ~~ ⟨*because we* see famous people, in magazines and on TV, smiling and looking fabulous. "I'm Nobody" makes us think about whether fame is really so important.

Grammar in Your Writing
Combining Ideas in Complex Sentences

To join two ideas, you can create a complex sentence. A **complex sentence** consists of one independent clause and one or more subordinate clauses. An **independent clause** can stand on its own as a sentence. A **subordinate clause** has a subject and a verb, but it cannot stand on its own. One way to form a complex sentence is to use a subordinating conjunction, such as *after, as, because, before, if, since, until, unless, when,* or *while.*

Separate: Emily Dickinson published only a handful of her own poems. It is amazing that she became so widely known.

Combined: Since Emily Dickinson published only a handful of her own poems, it is amazing that she became so widely known.

Find It in Your Reading Find one complex sentence in "Making Fantasy Real" by Zena Sutherland on page 250. Identify the clauses.

Find It in Your Writing Circle two complex sentences in your draft. If you cannot find any, consider combining sentences.

To learn more about complex sentences, see Chapter 20.

Revising Your Word Choice
Choose Precise Words for Evaluation

Use precise words to make your opinion about the work clear. Sharpen your word choice by color-coding value words.

▶ **REVISION STRATEGY**
Color-Coding Value Words

With a colored pencil, draw a box around words that express your opinion, such as *good* or *bad*. Replace general value words with precise ones. Here are some examples:

GENERAL: boring, wonderful
PRECISE: repetitious, plodding, gripping, colorful

Peer Review
Process Share

Read your draft to a small group. The group should ask the following questions and discuss your answers to them:

- What problems did writing pose? How did you solve them?
- What are you planning to do next?

Use the group's suggestions as you prepare your final draft.

Editing and Proofreading

After revising your response, proofread carefully to catch any errors in spelling, punctuation, or grammar. A response to a literary work will probably include a number of quotations from the work. Pay careful attention to the punctuation, indentation, and capitalization of quotations. The following suggestions can help:

Focusing on Quotations

Long quotations (four or more lines) from a literary work should be indented in your writing. Treat shorter quotations just like the dialogue of a story. Be sure that when you quote, you copy the words exactly as they appear in the work.

Grammar in Your Writing
Rules for Punctuating Quotations

The following are two ways to present quotations from a literary work:

Long quotations Introduce the quotation with a colon; indent the entire quotation on both sides.

Max goes through a long debate with himself about the crime he wants to commit:

> He walked the streets, asking himself, "Do I really want to do it? If I steal the plans, I can make a lot of money. Jeanine can have the operation she needs." As he stared out over the city, Max felt desperate. "If I'm caught," he asked himself, "could my family bear the shame?"

Brief quotations Use quotation marks and commas to separate the quotation from the rest of a sentence. Use single quotation marks for a quotation within another quotation:

> The writer portrays Max's feelings clearly when she writes, "Max felt desperate. 'If I'm caught,' he asked himself, 'could my family bear the shame?'"

Find It in Your Reading In "Making Fantasy Real" by Zena Sutherland on page 250, find an example of a quotation and note how it is punctuated.

Find It in Your Writing Read over your response to literature, and check each quotation to be sure it is set off and punctuated correctly.

To learn more about punctuating quotations, see Chapter 26.

12.6 Publishing and Presenting

Building Your Portfolio

Here are a few suggestions for publishing and presenting your response to literature:

1. **Post It at the Library** Arrange to post the responses of the class on a special bulletin board at your local or school library. Attach an eye-catching picture to each response. Students looking for recommendations for reading can browse the board.

2. **Publish It in a Newspaper** Contact the editor of a local paper, and arrange to publish the responses of the class in a weekly "Teen Book Reviews" column.

Reflecting on Your Writing

Jot down a few notes on your experience writing a response to literature. Start off by answering these questions:

- How did writing about the work help me understand it?
- Would I like to write my next response about the same kind of work or about a different kind? Why?

Add your reflection to your portfolio.

 Internet Tip

To see an essay scored according to this rubric, go on-line:
PHSchool.com
Enter Web Code:
ebk-7001

Rubric for Self-Assessment

Evaluate your response to literature using the following criteria.

	Score 4	Score 3	Score 2	Score 1
Audience and Purpose	Presents sufficient background on the work(s); presents the writer's reactions forcefully	Presents background on the work(s); presents the writer's reactions clearly	Presents some background on the work(s); presents the writer's reactions at points	Presents little or no background on the work(s); presents few of the writer's reactions
Organization	Presents points in logical order, smoothly connecting them to the overall focus	Presents points in logical order and connects many to the overall focus	Organizes points poorly in places; connects some points to an overall focus	Presents information in a scattered, disorganized manner
Elaboration	Supports reactions and evaluations with elaborated reasons and well-chosen examples	Supports reactions and evaluations with specific reasons and examples	Supports some reactions and evaluations with reasons and examples	Offers little support for reactions and evaluations
Use of Language	Shows overall clarity and fluency; uses precise, evaluative words; makes few mechanical errors	Shows good sentence variety; uses some precise evaluative terms; makes some mechanical errors	Uses awkward or overly simple sentence structures and vague evaluative terms; makes many mechanical errors	Presents incomplete thoughts; makes mechanical errors that create confusion

Student Work
IN PROGRESS

FINAL DRAFT

◄ **Critical Viewing**
Read Jade's essay. Then, using details from this photograph, explain whether you think Emily Dickinson followed her own advice about how best to live. **[Speculate]**

Frogs vs. Flowers

Jade Yamamoto
Calvary Lutheran School
Indianapolis, Indiana

In the two poems "I'm Nobody" and "How many Flowers fail in Wood," Emily Dickinson describes two paths that people can take to find an identity. She also shows where each leads. I like these poems because they teach important lessons about life.

"I'm Nobody" makes us think about society and our ideals today. This poem helps us to see that we all want to be "somebody." It makes us open our eyes to a major human interest: fame. We sometimes assume that being on top is what life is all about because we see famous people, in magazines and on TV,

Jade introduces the focus of her paper in her first paragraph. She will concentrate on the lessons that two Emily Dickinson poems teach about identity.

I'm Nobody
Emily Dickinson

I'm Nobody! Who are you?
Are you—Nobody—Too?
Then there's a pair of us!

Don't tell! they'd banish us—you know!
5 How dreary—to be—Somebody!
How public—like a Frog—
To tell one's name—the livelong June—
To an admiring Bog!

smiling and looking fabulous. "I'm Nobody" makes us think about whether fame is really so important.

First, Dickinson makes being "nobody" seem fun. The speaker proudly says "I'm Nobody" in the very first line. She sounds excited when she discovers that the reader also might be "Nobody." She shows her excitement in the line "Then there's a pair of us!" It's as if the speaker and the reader will make a secret club. Later, she uses the phrases "How dreary" and "How public" to describe being famous. Being famous is not as much fun as being "Nobody."

This poem is not only about fame. It is also about the boastful. The frog in "I'm Nobody" represents those who brag. Emily Dickinson shows us that those who boast just make a lot of noise, like a frog's croaking. They are like the frog that tells its name "the livelong June/To an admiring Bog." Boastful people try to win the compliments of others by making known their every little "amazing" feat. After a while, they may fall into despair. I like the comparison of boasters to frogs because it is clever. It makes boasters look as ridiculous as a tiny frog who makes a big noise.

"I'm Nobody" praises those who are humble and quiet. I like the poem because it helps us see clearly what we already know: If you are truly friends with someone, it doesn't matter how important you are. The two of you will have a good time just being "nobodies."

Jade tells us what she likes about the poem, using the word clever *and, later, the* phrase *helps us see* clearly *as precise, evaluative terms.*

◀ **Critical Viewing**
Using details from this photograph, explain why a frog is a good image to use for a boastful, self-important person. **[Interpret]**

How many Flowers fail in Wood
Emily Dickinson

How many Flowers fail in Wood—
Or perish from the Hill—
Without the privilege to know
That they are Beautiful—

5   How many cast a nameless Pod
Upon the nearest Breeze—
Unconscious of the Scarlet Freight—
It bear to Other Eyes—

▲ **Critical Viewing**
Using details from this photograph, explain why a flower is a good symbol for a shy, dreamy person. **[Interpret]**

In "How many Flowers fail in Wood," Dickinson describes "nobodies"; but here, it is the bad part of being a "nobody." Dickinson uses a flower to make her point. She wonders how many flowers die "Without the privilege to know/That they are Beautiful." She means that they never realize that others appreciate their beauty. She also says that many flowers may "cast a nameless Pod/Upon the nearest Breeze." This means that they spread their seeds without even thinking. Others may see the beauty of the seeds, but the flowers don't know it. They are "Unconscious." The flowers don't even realize that others see them.

I thought the picture of these flowers was sad. Imagine never hearing anyone praise you. You might not be unhappy, but you would miss out on something enjoyable. Part of the beauty of life lies in interacting with the people around you. If you are too quiet, you end up missing out.

In these two poems, Emily Dickinson compares people's personalities to natural things. These things are a frog and a flower. The frog is a boaster, but the flower is all alone. Although boasting is not a good way to be with others, the opposite extreme, being meek and not calling attention to yourself, is almost just as bad. Instead, you should aim to strike a balance in your life between these two extremes. You should try to be good friends with someone instead of trying to impress people or ignoring them.

Jade's response is clearly organized: First, she discusses one poem, and then she turns to the second poem.

Jade explains why the poem makes her sad by weaving together supporting details with her main points.

Jade concludes with a strong point, summing up the themes of the two poems to draw a lesson about life.

Connected Assignment *Movie Review*

Like a response to literature, a movie review starts with a basic response—did you enjoy the work?—and then explains the reasons for the response. A movie review features

- reactions to and an evaluation of the movie.
- details from the movie used to support your opinions.
- descriptions of and facts about the movie.

Prewriting Choose a movie that has left a lasting impression on you, and view it again. Record your general opinion of the movie in a Topic Web like the one on this page. Then, use the web to begin collecting details to explain your reaction. Include notes about the acting, lighting, pacing, music, use of camera techniques, and special effects, as well as notes on action and dialogue.

Drafting Before drafting, read a few movie reviews in a magazine or newspaper. (Avoid reviews of the movie you are reviewing.) Notice which aspects of a film they focus on, their language, and the support they give to their opinions.

Then, write the introduction to your own piece. Craft it to engage a viewer. Your introduction should include a statement of your general opinion of the film.

In the body of your review, develop your opinion of the movie. Provide examples that explain your reactions and opinions. As you develop your opinions, provide a summary of the movie and identify the actors. Conclude with a recommendation.

▲ **Critical Viewing** Describe the reaction of one of these movie-goers. Then, write the introductory sentence of the review that this person might write of the movie. **[Speculate]**

Revising and Editing Review your draft. If necessary, add information about the plot and the characters to help readers follow your points. Replace vague words, such as *entertaining* or *bad*, with forceful ones, such as *captivating* or *tedious*.

Publishing and Presenting After revising your movie review, submit it to a school or local newspaper.

Compare your review to professionally written reviews of the same movie.

Movie: *Revenge of the Slime Mold*

Main Opinion: Great special effects, but completely unbelievable plot, acting, and dialogue

Special Effect: The slime mold is frightening. It heaves, glistens, ripples, and bubbles as it moves.

Plot: The slime mold is defeated because it is allergic to the hero's brand of chewing gum. Come on!

Acting: Brent Wills thinks that frowning a little shows deep emotion.

Dialogue: "Dr. Quvark, for you that creature is just another science project run amok. For me, it's personal."

Spotlight on the Humanities

Comparing Art With a Written Story

Focus on Art: Henri Matisse

Some people respond to a good story by telling their friends about it. Others respond by creating a new work of art. French painter Henri Matisse (1869–1954) responded to the myth of Icarus by creating the work in paper shown on this page, *Icarus.* Matisse's response to this classic myth is a work famous in its own right.

Considered one of the preeminent painters of the twentieth century, Matisse unleashed bright, untamed colors on his canvasses. His wild use of color earned him the name "King of the Fauves." (*Fauve* means "wild beast," and the Fauves were painters who used violent combinations of color.) After 1941, when he could no longer paint, Matisse continued to create by carving colored paper into various shapes and pasting them together in works like *Icarus.*

In the Greek myth to which Matisse responded, Icarus and his father, the inventor Daedalus, are held prisoner by King Minos of Crete. To escape, Daedalus builds two pairs of wings from wax and feathers. Despite Daedalus' warnings, Icarus flies too close to the sun. The sun melts the wax in his wings, and he falls into the sea. For Matisse and others, this flight and Icarus' end are rich symbols for human ambition and its limits.

Icarus, plate 8 of the 'Jazz' series, 1943, Henri Matisse, Arts Council Collection, Hayward Gallery, London, UK

▲ **Critical Viewing** Explain what Icarus' pose in Matisse's work tells you about his flight: Is he a helpless victim or a daring flyer? **[Interpret]**

Literature Connection The Roman poet Ovid (43 B.C.– A.D. 17) tells the story of Icarus in his greatest work, the *Metamorphoses,* a long poem retelling various Greek myths. Ovid was the first important writer to grow up in the Roman Empire. During the Middle Ages, people studied Ovid's writing for historical information. Many myths came to us through his work.

Response to Literature Writing Activity: Song Lyrics Based on the Myth of Icarus

The portrayal of Icarus in story may be different from Matisse's depiction. Read a version of the myth. Then, compare Matisse's Icarus with the Icarus in the story. (Pay special attention to the pose of Matisse's Icarus.) Write lyrics in which you contrast these two views of Icarus and present your own view.

Media and Technology Skills

Interpreting Literature in a Variety of Media

Activity: Creating a Multimedia Interpretation

Writing an essay or letter is only one way in which to respond to literature. You can also respond to a literary work by presenting it to others—and you can enhance your presentation by using a variety of media. When you create a multimedia presentation, you are actually creating an interpretation of the work—emphasizing the elements you find significant in it.

Learn About It

Learn How to Use Equipment As you plan your presentation, familiarize yourself with the equipment you will use—tape recorders, slide projectors, computer presentation software, and so on. Read the manuals, and ask questions of experienced users.

Use Audio Elements The center of your presentation is your reading of the work. Practice reading your chosen piece slowly and with expression. Incorporate other audio effects into your presentation as well. Choose a piece of music appropriate to the mood of the work. Working with a partner, or using a tape recorder that allows overdubbing, arrange for the right music to come in at the right spots in your reading. Consider adding other sound effects, too. (You may tape your reading along with your "soundtrack," or you may practice synchronizing it with your live reading.)

Use Visual Elements You can add to the words of the work by including visuals in your presentation. You might run a slide show as you read the work. You might videotape others acting out scenes and show the tape as you read. Make sure that the slide show or video is synchronized with your reading.

Apply It Choose a work of literature, and then plan a multimedia presentation of it using a storyboard organizer like this one. Follow your storyboard as you create your presentation.

> **Tips for Creating a Multimedia Interpretation**
> - Choose a piece of literature you enjoy and know well. It is easier to read such a work effectively.
> - If you use background music, make sure that it is not so loud that it drowns out your reading.
> - If you use background visuals, make sure the images do not distract listeners from your reading. If you use complex or provocative images, introduce a few slight pauses in your reading to give listeners time to absorb what they are seeing and hearing.

Effects
Audio
Visual
Text

Scene 1   Scene 2   Scene 3

Standardized Test Preparation Workshop

Responding to Literature-Based Writing Prompts

Some standardized test questions evaluate your ability to respond to literature. Your response to this type of prompt will be evaluated on how well it shows your ability to

- respond directly to a prompt.

- organize ideas in a clear fashion.

- successfully apply concepts such as plot, setting, character, speaker, theme, mood, point of view, and figurative language.

- develop and support ideas thoroughly, using appropriate details and precise language.

- use correct spelling, capitalization, punctuation, and grammar.

The following is one type of literature-based writing prompt found on standardized tests. Although you will need to find in a literature anthology the poems suggested for this prompt, most tests will provide the literature to which you will respond. Respond to the prompt, using the suggestions on the following page. The clocks show the suggested percentage of your test-taking time to devote to each stage of the writing process.

> ### Test Tip
>
> When writing a response to literature, don't simply summarize the piece of literature. Respond specifically to the prompt, giving opinions, examining the author's style, and connecting the work to your life, as the prompt requires.

Sample Writing Situation

Read the poems "Primer Lesson" and "Fog," both by Carl Sandburg. Then, respond to the following prompt:

In a letter to the poet, compare his use of figurative language in the two poems. In what way is the use of figurative language in the poems similar? In what way is it different? Then, explain which poem uses figurative language more effectively. Use details from the poems to support your response.

Prewriting

Allow close to one fourth of your time for prewriting.

Use a Hexagon Read the two Sandburg poems twice. Then, gather details for your response. For each poem, you might sketch a hexagon like the one shown on page 256 and record details in it. Next, review the prompt. Circle items in your notes concerning the literary concept referred to: the author's use of figurative language. (If you cannot find such details, review the poems and take further notes on figurative language.)

Consider Your Audience Your audience, the poet, is named in the response. Because he presumably knows the poems and himself, do not include background information about the poem or its author in your response. Since you are writing to a respected person to whom you have not been introduced, use formal language and avoid slang or clichés.

Drafting

Allow almost half of your time for drafting.

Focus Your Response Review your prewriting notes. Then, write a sentence explaining which poem uses figurative language more effectively. Include this thesis statement in your introduction. To evaluate the poems, consider the following criteria for effective figurative language: It sums up an aspect of life as it creates an easily visualized image or while it catches the ear with the musical use of words.

Organize Details Make an outline listing main points followed by supporting details. Consider using the block method of organization, grouping details about each poem separately.

Elaborate As you draft your response, keep your audience (the poet) clearly in mind. For each point you make, refer to the poem directly, including direct quotations where suitable.

Revising, Editing, and Proofreading

Allow almost one fourth of your time for revising and editing. Use the last few minutes to proofread your work.

Strengthen Support After drafting, review your response. Eliminate details that do not support your focus. Identify points needing more support, and, referring to the poems, add supporting details. Leave a few minutes to proofread your work.

Make Corrections Check for errors in spelling, grammar, and punctuation. When making changes, draw a line through text that you want eliminated. Use a caret (^) to indicate places where you would like to add words.

Writing for
Assessment

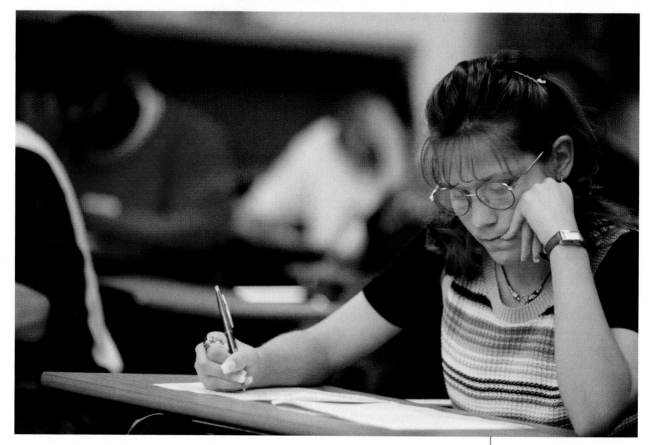

Assessment in School

Writing is not just something you do in English class. Throughout your years in school, you will take essay tests in many subjects, including social studies, science, health, and even math. You may also take standardized writing tests that compare your writing skills with those of students across the state or nation.

The writing you do on these tests is called writing for assessment, and it requires special skills you can learn and practice ahead of time. This chapter will show you how to do your best work when you are writing for assessment.

▲ **Critical Viewing**
What advice might you give this student to help her prepare for writing tests?
[Apply]

What Is Writing for Assessment?

The word *assessment* means "measurement" or "evaluation." **Writing for assessment** is used to measure how much you have learned about a subject or to evaluate the development of your writing skills. Assessment may involve

- specific instructions about what to write, called the *writing prompt.*
- limited time in which to write.
- limited space in which to write.
- no use of textbooks, dictionaries, or other references.

To learn the criteria on which your writing for assessment may be judged, see the Rubric for Self-Assessment on page 284.

Types of Writing for Assessment

Writing prompts may call for the following kinds of writing:

- **Persuasive writing** requires you to support an opinion or position using persuasive language.
- **Expository writing** requires you to give information in a clear and well-organized fashion. It includes

  Comparison-and-contrast writing, which requires you to compare aspects of two or more subjects in an organized way.

  Cause-and-effect writing, which requires you to explain a process or series of events.

▲ **Critical Viewing** This painting suggests that a clock helps us control the power of time, just as a steam engine uses the power of fire. How might keeping track of time during a test help you succeed on it? **[Interpret]**

PREVIEW
Student Work
IN PROGRESS

In this chapter, you'll follow the work of Brittany Wilson, a student at Stuart Middle School in Louisville, Kentucky, as she answers an essay question on a science test. You'll see the featured activities and strategies she uses to gather and organize details and draft her response. You can read her completed essay at the end of the chapter.

Prewriting

It is important to use your time wisely when you are writing for assessment, because your time is often limited. Before you begin, find out how much time you have to complete the test. Plan to spend about one fourth of that time on prewriting. If you have an hour for the test, for example, you can spend 15 minutes reviewing the questions and taking notes.

Choosing Your Topic

When you are taking a standardized test, you don't have to rack your brain to think of a topic: You'll be given a topic in the writing prompt. At most, you may have to choose among a few specific options.

Choosing a Writing Prompt If you do have a choice, carefully consider the topics and the types of writing required for each choice. Eliminate any question about which you do not know enough. Choose the topic that interests you most or about which you know the most.

If the writing prompt tells you who your readers will be, consider whether you feel more comfortable writing for adults or for peers, for people who are already familiar with a topic or for beginners who will need to have everything explained.

To practice writing for assessment, you might ask your teacher for a topic, or you can select from the following writing prompts:

◯ Learn More

To learn more about studying for a test, see Chapter 31.

TOPIC BANK

1. **Explain a Process** Explain a process that you have learned about in science class, such as the circulation of blood in the human body or photosynthesis in plants.

2. **Compare and Contrast Leaders** Choose two important historical leaders. Compare and contrast their abilities and the importance of their respective contributions to history.

3. **Persuade a Historical Figure** Choose an important historical figure. Imagine that you meet this person just before he or she decides to perform one of his or her most memorable actions. Drawing on your knowledge of the person and of history, persuade the person to do or to refrain from doing the action.

Narrowing Your Topic

When you are writing for a test, your possible topics are set for you. You still need to "narrow" the topic you choose by focusing on exactly what the prompt asks you to do.

▲ **Critical Viewing**
If the purpose of your writing is to inform this swimmer about a special swimming stroke, explain what information you would supply. **[Apply]**

Identify the Topic and Purpose

Before you start writing, read the prompt you have chosen carefully and identify each of the following:

- **The topic** is the subject about which you must write. Make sure that you consider all information given about the topic. For instance, an essay explaining why pioneers traveled west is different from an essay explaining what kinds of people became pioneers who traveled west. You may also need to choose among several subtopics. List them, and then choose the one about which you know the most.

- **Your purpose in writing** is identified by key words in the prompt. These words determine what information you should include and how you should organize it.

Key Words	What You Will Do
explain	give a clear, complete account of how something works or why something happened
compare and contrast	provide details about how two or more things are alike and how they are different
argue, convince, persuade	take a position on an issue and present strong reasons to support your side of the issue
summarize	tell the main events, points, or ideas of a topic and briefly describe the relationship between them
classify	organize information into categories based on important similarities and differences

Circle Key Words Study the chart above. Write out the prompt to which you are responding. Circle the key words. Then, find the interpretation of each key word in the chart. Next to the prompt, jot down the kind of information you will need to include in your answer.

You may discover that you were mistaken about the topic or the purpose for writing that was assigned by the prompt. If so, you may wish to choose another prompt.

Gathering Details

Now that you understand your topic and purpose, you can begin gathering details. The way in which you gather details will depend on your purpose in writing.

If a prompt asks you to create a piece of persuasive writing:

• Start by taking a position to defend.

• Then, list reasons that support your view.

If the prompt asks you to create a piece of informative writing:

• Begin by listing the main ideas.

• Then, list supporting details you would like to include.

When gathering details for a piece of informative writing, you might use a Topic Web such as the one below.

Student Work
IN PROGRESS

Name: *Brittany Wilson*
Stuart Middle School
Louisville, KY

Using a Topic Web to Gather Details

Brittany chose the following prompt: "Choose one form of pollution. Describe three of its effects and some possible solutions." She listed different forms of pollution in a Topic Web, chose one, and then gathered details about her topic.

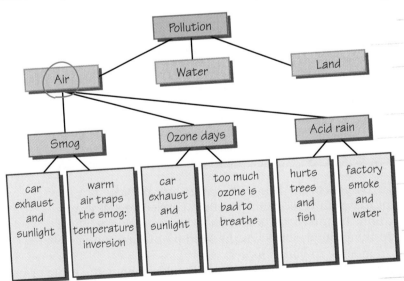

13.2 Drafting

Allow about half of your testing time for drafting. If you have an hour for the test, for example, spend about half an hour writing your draft.

Shaping Your Writing

On a test, it's very important for your writing to have a clear direction and to be logically organized. Once you have gathered details, you're ready to organize your ideas.

Find a Focus

Any effective piece of writing, however short or simple, must have a guiding focus. Review the prompt you have chosen and the details you have gathered. Then, formulate the main idea of your response in a sentence. For instance, the prompt might ask you to support an idea for a school club. Your focus statement might read, "A book club will encourage reading."

Begin your draft with an introduction that includes your focus statement. Use an interesting image or fact to draw your reader in.

Plan Your Organization

Because your time is limited, choose a clear, simple method of organization. Here are some ideas for organizing an essay for assessment, depending on the prompt to which you respond:

- **Persuasive Writing Prompt** If the prompt asks you to persuade people about an issue, use an outline to organize your reasons, or simply number your ideas from least to most important.

- **Cause-and-Effect or How-to Writing Prompt** If the prompt asks you to explain a sequence of steps or events, you should organize your ideas in chronological order. Making a timeline is a quick way to do this.

- **Comparison-and-Contrast Writing Prompt** If the prompt asks you to compare two items, organize your ideas using either the block or the point-by-point method. To use the block method, make an outline grouping all details about one item, followed by all details about the other. To use the point-by-point method, make an outline that groups details about one aspect of both items, followed by details about another aspect, and so on.

▼ **Critical Viewing** Draw a simple timeline charting the series of events suggested by this photo. **[Infer]**

Providing Elaboration

After organizing your ideas, study your timeline or outline. Find places where you can add details to strengthen your writing. Supporting details include the following:

- **Facts** If you are explaining a sequence of events or steps, provide facts showing why or how one event links to another. If you are writing to persuade, prove your points with evidence.

- **Descriptions** If you are comparing things, you need to describe them thoroughly. If you want to persuade, describe situations and ideas in positive or negative ways, in order to help your reader see your point of view.

- **Examples** To help readers grasp your meaning, give examples illustrating any general points you make.

Note supporting details on your outline or timeline in capital letters. As you draft, follow your organizer, and include supporting details.

Student Work
IN PROGRESS

Name: Brittany Wilson
Stuart Middle School
Louisville, KY

Adding Supporting Details to an Outline
Brittany added supporting details about air pollution to her sentence outline, part of which is shown below.

Topic: Air Pollution

What are the major causes?
- Use of fossil fuels
    1. Cars burning gas
    2. Factories burning coal

"FOSSIL FUEL" IS MADE OF THE BODIES OF ANCIENT ANIMALS.

BURNING FOSSIL FUELS MAKES CARBON MONOXIDE.

What are three effects?
- Smog
    1. Cause: sunlight and car exhaust
    2. Warm air traps the smog (temperature inversion)
- Ozone action days
    1. Cause: sunlight and car exhaust
    2. Too much ozone makes it hard to breathe
- Acid rain . . .

OZONE IS A SPECIAL FORM OF OXYGEN.

WE NEED OZONE HIGH IN THE ATMOSPHERE.

13.3 *Revising*

Plan to spend approximately one fourth of your testing time on revising your work. Decide whether you will have time to copy a clean final draft or whether you need to make changes neatly on your first draft. On a school test, you may not have the time or the space to make a clean final draft. Some standardized tests, however, give you blank pages on which to draft and lined pages on which to copy your final work.

Revising Your Overall Structure

The teachers who evaluate your writing on a standardized test will look for a logically organized piece of writing that clearly follows the directions in the writing prompt.

▶ **REVISION STRATEGY**
Checking Your Introduction and Conclusion

Before you begin revising, read the writing prompt again. Then, read the first paragraph of your piece. Your introduction should

- clearly state what your draft explains or argues.
- accurately reflect the instructions in the writing prompt.
- capture interest with a fact, a question, or an example.

Now, look at your final paragraph. Your conclusion should

- restate what you have explained or argued in your draft.
- present a final thought about the subject or a call to action.

▲ Critical Viewing
What facts might you use to persuade someone to take up this hobby? **[Apply]**

Revising Your Paragraphs
Identify Main Ideas and Supporting Details

When evaluating writing, teachers look closely at each paragraph. They expect to find a clear, well-expressed main idea supported by relevant details.

▶ **REVISION STRATEGY**
Checking Support

For each paragraph, identify the main idea, often stated in the topic sentence. If a paragraph does not have a topic sentence, it is best on a test to add one for clarity.

Then, check the details in each paragraph. Neatly cross out sentences that do not support the main idea. Consider replacing them with sentences offering more effective support.

Get instant help! For practice in identifying topic sentences, complete selected exercises in **Section 3.2**, on-line or on CD-ROM.

Revising Your Sentences

On a standardized writing test, teachers evaluate how well your writing hangs together—how easy it is to follow the flow of your ideas. They want to see clear relationships between one sentence and the next.

▶ **REVISION STRATEGY**
Adding Transitions

Reread each paragraph of your draft. Is there a clear, logical relationship between the sentences? If a sentence simply states a new idea without referring to words in the previous sentence, the relationship between the two sentences may not be clear. Consider adding a transitional word or phrase to indicate the relationship. For example, if you want to signal a cause or an effect, add transitions such as *for this reason, therefore,* or *as a result.* If you want to signal chronological order, add transitions such as *then, next, before, after,* or *finally.*

Revising Your Word Choice

Choose Precise and Vivid Words

Teachers will evaluate your writing for assessment to see whether you have a strong command of the English language. Use words that say precisely and vividly what you mean. When writing persuasively, make sure you have chosen words that will influence readers to accept your point of view.

▶ **REVISION STRATEGY**
"Show, Don't Tell"

Reread your draft, looking for sentences with general descriptive words, such as *good, bad, big,* and *small.* Think of the reasons you have used each word. Then, rewrite each of these sentences so that it shows why or how the general word applies.

For instance, you might write "This plan is very bad" because you know the plan will waste a lot of time. To show why the word *bad* applies, rewrite the sentence as follows: "This plan is inefficient." Consider the improvement in the following examples:

TELLING: Our current computer lab is too small. It is very old. The facilities are out of date.

SHOWING: In the computer lab, thirty students are crammed into a tiny classroom, with no space left for lab equipment. Plaster is crumbling off the walls in the hallway. The ancient wiring cannot handle the demands of a high-tech computer lab.

Get instant help!
For more assistance adding transitions, use the interactive Transition Word Bin, accessible from the menu bar, on-line or on CD-ROM.

13.4 Editing and Proofreading

You may have the best ideas in the world, but evaluators can't take them seriously if you don't express yourself in complete, correctly punctuated sentences. Save a few minutes at the end of the test to proofread your work for errors in spelling, mechanics, grammar, and usage. Make sure that you have expressed yourself in complete sentences.

Focusing on Complete Sentences

Look over each sentence in your draft. Read it by itself, starting at the beginning and ending at the period. Ask:

- Does this sentence express a complete thought?
- Does it begin with a capital letter and end with a period?
- Is more than one idea squeezed into the sentence without proper punctuation—for instance, have you used a comma to join two sentences?

Correct any incomplete or run-on sentences you find, crossing out words and punctuation marks neatly with a single line, and marking insertions with a caret (^).

Grammar in Your Writing
Using Complete, Correct Sentences

Every **sentence** must express a complete thought. A fragment is a group of words, punctuated as a sentence, that does not express a complete thought. If you find any sentence fragments in your writing, correct them by adding a subject or a verb. You can also fix a sentence fragment by correctly connecting it to another sentence.

Sentence + Fragment:	We need a computer lab with enough space. And modern, up-to-date equipment, too.
Add Subject and Verb:	We need a computer lab with enough space. We also need modern, up-to-date equipment.
Combine Sentences:	We need a computer lab with enough space and with modern, up-to-date equipment.

Check to make sure that each sentence begins with a capital letter and ends with a period, question mark, or exclamation mark.

To learn more about using complete, correct sentences, see Chapter 19.

Publishing and Presenting

Building Your Portfolio

Consider the following suggestions for publishing and presenting your work:

1. **Prepare for Future Exams** As you get ready to take other writing tests, review your essay. Recall what strategies worked for you when writing under time constraints. If you wrote on a topic covered in a particular class, study your test to refresh your memory about that topic.

2. **Organize a Class Discussion** In a group discussion, compare your responses with those of classmates. Discuss the reasons for the differences in the grades given for each. (Refer to the rubric below for ideas on what teachers look for in an essay written for assessment.)

Reflecting on Your Writing

Jot down your thoughts on writing an essay for assessment. Get started by answering these questions:

- What are your strengths and weaknesses as a test taker?

- Which strategy presented in this chapter might help you complete your next essay test?

 Internet Tip

To view an essay written for assessment that has been scored according to this rubric, go on-line:
PHSchool.com
Enter Web Code:
ebk-7001

Rubric for Self-Assessment

Use the following criteria to evaluate the essay you have written for assessment.

	Score 4	Score 3	Score 2	Score 1
Audience and Purpose	Uses word choices and supporting details appropriate to the specified audience; clearly addresses writing prompt	Mostly uses word choices and supporting details appropriate to the specified audience; adequately addresses prompt	Uses some inappropriate word choices and details; addresses writing prompt	Uses inappropriate word choices and details; does not address writing prompt
Organization	Presents a clear, consistent organizational strategy	Presents a clear organizational strategy with few inconsistencies	Presents an inconsistent organizational strategy	Shows a lack of organizational strategy
Elaboration	Adequately supports the thesis; elaborates each idea; links all details to the thesis	Supports the thesis; elaborates most ideas; links most information to thesis	Partially supports the thesis; does not elaborate some ideas	Provides no thesis; does not elaborate ideas
Use of Language	Uses excellent sentence variety and vocabulary; includes very few mechanical errors	Uses adequate sentence variety and vocabulary; includes few mechanical errors	Uses repetitive sentence structure and vocabulary; includes some mechanical errors	Demonstrates poor use of language; includes many mechanical errors

FINAL DRAFT

Air Pollution

Brittany Wilson
Stuart Middle School
Louisville, Kentucky

▲ **Critical Viewing** Cite details from Brittany's essay to identify the problem this photograph illustrates. **[Interpret]**

> **Writing Prompt** Choose one form of pollution. Describe three of its effects and some possible solutions.

Air pollution is one of the major forms of pollution. By releasing chemicals into the air, we create problems such as smog, ozone action days, and acid rain. As widespread and dangerous as air pollution is, we can take some simple steps to help solve the problem, such as carpooling and controlling the amount of smoke coming from factories.

Much air pollution is caused by the burning of fossil fuels. Fossil fuels include gasoline, coal, and oil. They are called fossil fuels because they come from buried plants and animals that died millions of years ago.

When cars burn gas or when factories burn coal, they release carbon monoxide, hydrocarbons, and other harmful chemicals. These chemicals cause problems such as smog, ozone action days, and acid rain.

Smog is thick brown air that hangs over a city. It is made when the chemicals in car exhaust mix in the sunlight. Smog hurts people's eyes and makes it hard for them to breathe.

Smog would just blow away, except that sometimes there is a temperature inversion. In a temperature inversion, the air in the city is trapped by warmer air above the city. As a result, the air in the city cannot rise up and carry the smog away.

Brittany's introduction clearly identifies her focus: air pollution and three of its effects. This focus addresses the prompt.

Brittany organizes her response logically. First, she discusses a cause of air pollution; then, she discusses three of its effects.

The phrase "as a result" is a transition showing the connection between this sentence and the one before.

◀ Critical Viewing
In addition to help-
ing with the problem
of air pollution, what
other advantages
might carpooling
have, judging from
this picture? [Draw
Conclusions]

Another danger of air pollution is too much ozone. Ozone is a special form of oxygen. It is also caused by car exhaust and sun-light. We need ozone in the top part of the atmosphere. When there is too much of it lower down, it is just as bad to breathe as smog. In addition, you cannot see or smell ozone. Some cities have ozone action days. Scientists tell people when there will be too much ozone in the air.

A third danger caused by air pollution is acid rain. Chemicals in car fumes and factory smoke mix with water in the air. Together, they make burning acid. When the rain falls, it brings the acid down to the trees and ground. It hurts the trees. It can also kill fish in lakes. The acid rain washes into the water and changes the fishes' environment. One problem with acid rain is that it can fall far away from the factory that caused it. The wind can blow clouds with acid rain miles away from the factory before the acid rain falls.

Brittany supports her claim that acid rain is dangerous by explaining how it kills fish.

To solve the problem of air pollution, people can carpool. This will limit the number of cars on the road polluting the air. People can also walk to places. That way, they can get some exercise. For each person walking, there would be one less car on the road. Another way to solve the problem would be to limit the amount of smoke that comes out of stacks at power plants. It is important to find a solution, because air pollution is a real danger to people's health and to nature.

Brittany concludes with a restatement of the importance of her subject.

Connected Assignment *Open-Book Test*

When taking an open-book test, you can refer to a textbook or to class notes. You still need to complete the writing process in a limited time. Your answer should

- include facts, such as specific names, dates, events, or formulas, from your reference materials.
- present your own ideas based on the facts you present.
- sum up your main idea in a thesis statement.
- show a clear and logical organization.

Use these strategies to do your best on open-book tests:

Prewriting Organize your time well. Use a little more than one fourth of your time for prewriting.

Begin by outlining your answer to the question, as in the example on this page. Then, consult your reference materials for each specific point of your outline. If you are referring to a textbook, use the index to locate information quickly. As you gather details about each point, add them to your outline.

Drafting Next, allow half your time for drafting. Include these elements:

- **Thesis statement** Begin with an introduction that includes a thesis statement—a one-sentence statement that sums up your answer and that includes words from the question.

- **Elaboration** In the body of your paper, develop each main point of your outline. Include the specific details you have gathered from your reference materials.

- **Conclusion** In your final paragraph, sum up your answer to the question and your supporting reasons.

Revising and Editing

Allow one fourth of your time for revising.

Reread your essay. Check-mark points that lack sufficient support. Then, review marked paragraphs, and add details from your reference materials.

Publishing and Presenting

Add your graded test to your portfolio.

▲ **Critical Viewing** What advice for taking an open-book test might you give this student? **[Apply]**

	TOPIC: Circulation of Blood
⊙	I. The Heart
	A. The heart pumps blood throughout the body.
	1. made of ? *p. 48 – made of smooth muscle*
	2. four chambers: atria and ventricles
	B. Sends some blood to lungs, some to body
	II. Blood to the lungs
	A. The left atrium sends blood to the lungs.
	1. blood goes through the ? artery *p. 50 – blood goes*
	2. blood needs to go to the lungs, *to lungs through*
	because it is coming back from *pulmonary artery*
⊙	the body and all its oxygen is gone

Spotlight on the Humanities

Comparing and Contrasting Print and Visual Media

Focus on Theater: *Kiss Me Kate*

When one character "assesses" another, putting him or her to a test, it can make for great comedy. In the Broadway musical *Kiss Me Kate*, a sharp-tongued woman puts her husband to the test—and he passes with top grades.

The music for *Kiss Me Kate* was written by the great American composer Cole Porter, who wrote his first song when he was ten years old. This show is considered his best. Bella and Samuel Spewack wrote the book (the words spoken and sung by the characters).

The show opened in New York on December 30, 1948. By the time it closed, *Kiss Me Kate* had passed a popularity test of its own, running on Broadway for 1,077 performances.

Literature Connection In 1594, William Shakespeare wrote his comedy *The Taming of the Shrew*, on which *Kiss Me Kate* is based. The comedic play tells the story of the hot-tempered Katharina and her husband, Petruchio. Elements of *The Taming of the Shrew* are rooted in ancient folk tales.

Film Connection Director Gil Junger and cinematographer Mark Irwin loosely based their 1999 film *10 Things I Hate About You* on *The Taming of the Shrew*. The movie features an ill-tempered older sister and a favored younger one, just as in the play.

Assessment Activity: Proposal

Select a classic story you have read, and write a letter to a producer explaining why a Broadway-show version of the story will be a great success. Compare the show as you envision it to the original story.

▲ **Critical Viewing** Which one of these characters is Kate? Explain how you know. **[Deduce]**

▶ **Critical Viewing** Why might the idea of a woman who nastily rejects all suitors be of interest to playwrights? To what scenes might it lead? **[Hypothesize]**

Media and Technology Skills

Using Technology to Support Learning

Activity: Explore Electronic Tests

These days, you can take all sorts of tests on a computer—academic standardized tests, school entrance exams, even tests for a driver's license. Most of the test-taking skills that apply to print tests also apply to tests taken on a computer. It is important, though, that you be familiar and comfortable with the computer test format before taking a test on-line.

Learn About It

Practice on the Computer If possible, practice beforehand using the computer on which you will be tested. For instance, if the test will be given in the school computer room, visit the room before the test. Start up the computer, use the mouse, and open and close applications. This will reduce stress you might feel during the test because of confusion about using the computer.

Read Instructions Carefully Some computer-based tests will not allow you to change an answer once you have selected it. Make sure that you read all instructions and tips carefully before taking the test. After you read the instructions, decide on the best strategy for answering questions on the test.

Take On-line Practice Tests Practice tests of various kinds are available on CD-ROM and on-line. You may practice with these tests to become comfortable with computer test taking, as well as to familiarize yourself with each particular kind of test. Practice programs also provide you with feedback on your answers to help you learn about the test and the subject matter covered.

Evaluate It With the help of a teacher or school librarian, find print and computer versions of practice tests. Take both tests, and complete the Venn diagram shown here, listing similarities between the two in the area where the two circles cross. Finally, write a summary in which you evaluate which type of test taking you prefer, and why.

> ## Tips on Computer Test Taking
>
> - Read directions carefully—they will explain how to answer a question. Then, move to the next question.
> - Read each question carefully. Questions on a computer test may require you to answer in a different manner from that used on a print test.
> - If you are having trouble with your computer, ask for help immediately. Don't waste time trying to figure out if there is a problem. If something seems wrong, it probably is!

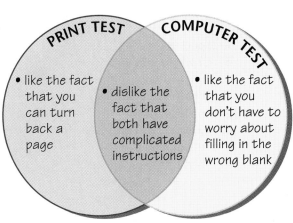

PRINT TEST
- like the fact that you can turn back a page

COMPUTER TEST
- like the fact that you don't have to worry about filling in the wrong blank

- dislike the fact that both have complicated instructions

Standardized Test Preparation Workshop

Proofreading

Standardized test questions often measure your knowledge of basic spelling, punctuation, and capitalization rules. Use the following guidelines when answering these questions:

- When looking for punctuation errors, determine whether a mark is misplaced, missing, or unnecessary.

- To identify capitalization errors, look for errors in titles and proper nouns.

- When identifying spelling errors, look closely at each word.

The following sample test items will help you become familiar with the format of these questions.

Test Tip

Read each sentence from beginning to end before trying to determine what type of error exists in the underlined portion. Just reading the underlined phrase may not provide enough information for you to answer accurately.

Sample Test Items

Answers and Explanations

Sample Test Items	Answers and Explanations

Directions Read the passage, and decide which type of error, if any, appears in each underlined section. Then, choose the letter that identifies the error type.
 	
Almost like a <u>combination of his too most</u> (1)
famous <u>characters Sherlock Holmes</u> and Dr. (2)
Watson, Sir Arthur Conan Doyle was both a
 	
mystery solver and a medical doctor.
 	
1   A   Spelling error
     B   Capitalization error
     C   Punctuation error
     D   No error
	The correct answer for section 1 is *A*. The word *too* should be spelled *two*.

2   F   Spelling error
     G   Capitalization error
     H   Punctuation error
     J   No error
	The correct answer for section 2 is *H*. A comma is needed after *characters* to introduce the appositive phrase *Sherlock Holmes and Dr. Watson*.

Practice **Directions:** Read the passage, and decide which type of error, if any, appears in each underlined section. Then, choose the letter that identifies the error type.

<u>Unlike Sherlock holmes, who catches</u>
(1)
<u>Culverton Smith in *the Dying Detective*</u>
(2)
with a <u>clever trick today's detectives</u> often
(3)
use scientific evidence. <u>They anaylze this</u>
(4)
<u>evidence</u> with the help of forensic experts,

<u>who study the chemical makeup of tiny</u>
(5)
<u>pieces of material—hair, fabric, or soil, for</u>
(6)
<u>example,</u> from a crime scene to link it with

an accused criminal. <u>They may also use:</u>
(7)
<u>fingerprints and shoe impressions to study</u>
(8)
how a crime was commited.

1 **A** Spelling error
  B Capitalization error
  C Punctuation error
  D No error

2 **F** Spelling error
  G Capitalization error
  H Punctuation error
  J No error

3 **A** Spelling error
  B Capitalization error
  C Punctuation error
  D No error

4 **F** Spelling error
  G Capitalization error
  H Punctuation error
  J No error

5 **A** Spelling error
  B Capitalization error
  C Punctuation error
  D No error

6 **F** Spelling error
  G Capitalization error
  H Punctuation error
  J No error

7 **A** Spelling error
  B Capitalization error
  C Punctuation error
  D No error

8 **F** Spelling error
  G Capitalization error
  H Punctuation error
  J No error

2

Grammar, Usage, and Mechanics

Gardeners, 1995, Judy Byford, The Grand Design, Leeds, England

and Pronouns

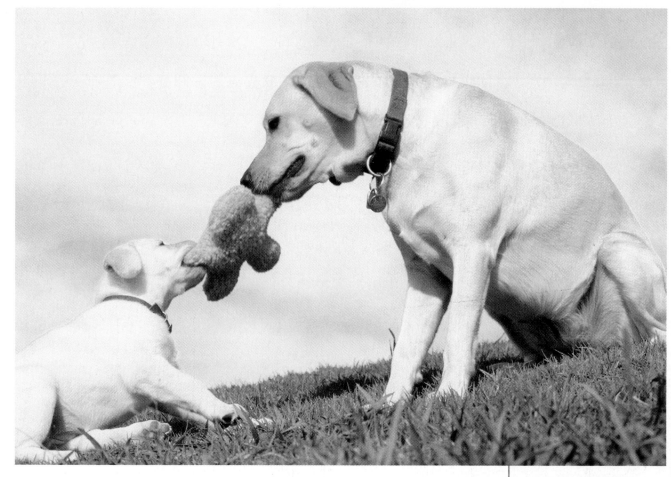

▲ **Critical Viewing**
What nouns can you use to name the things in this picture? **[Relate]**

Nouns are words that name people, places, things, and ideas. Some nouns name things, such as dogs. There are many different kinds of dogs: collies, poodles, terriers, and more. The words that name all the different kinds of dogs and the places where they can be found are nouns. In this chapter, you will learn about different types of nouns, such as common and proper nouns, collective nouns, and compound nouns. You will also learn about **pronouns,** the words that are sometimes used to replace nouns.

Diagnostic Test

Directions: Write all answers on a separate sheet of paper.

Skill Check A. Identify the nouns in each sentence. Explain why each word is a noun by telling whether it is a person, place, or thing.

1. Dogs can be purchased from a breeder.
2. Good pets can also be found at a shelter.
3. Preparations—such as getting food, dishes, toys, a collar, and a bed—need to be made before the arrival of a new puppy.
4. A veterinarian gives the dog shots for rabies and distemper.
5. All dogs must wear licenses, which ensure identification and immunization.

Skill Check B. Identify and label the collective or compound noun in each sentence.

6. The whole family should share in taking care of a pet.
7. Dogs need shelter, such as a doghouse, in which to sleep.
8. Supplies can be purchased at a pet shop.
9. Use caution when introducing the new pet to a large group.
10. Avoid packs of stray dogs when walking your pet.

Skill Check C. Identify each italicized noun as *common* or *proper.*

The (11) *American Kennel Club* was started in 1884. This (12) *organization* is associated with more than 4,000 clubs throughout the (13) *United States.* Frances belongs to a group in her (14) *town.* She goes to shows in (15) *Austin* with her cousin Sarah.

Skill Check D. Identify the pronouns in each sentence. Then, identify each pronoun's antecedent. You may need to refer to previous sentences to find the antecedent.

16. Martin loves dogs, and he has three German shepherds.
17. They are very gentle.
18. His sister, Tanya, helps him care for them.
19. She trained them to sit and stay.
20. The neighbor admires their dogs.

Skill Check E. Identify the italicized pronoun in each sentence as *personal, demonstrative, interrogative,* or *indefinite.*

21. *We* went to the pound to see puppies.
22. My mother asked, "*Which* do you want?"
23. *That* was a difficult decision.
24. Those pups were so cute *I* wanted them all.
25. *Each* had its own special qualities.

Nouns

Nouns are naming words. Words such as *friend, sky, dog, love, courage,* and *Seattle* are nouns. They help people name what they are thinking or talking about.

▶ **KEY CONCEPT** A **noun** names a person, place, thing, or idea. ∎

In English, most nouns fall into four main groups:

People, Places, Things, and Ideas

The nouns in the chart are grouped under four headings. You may know most of the nouns under the first three headings. You may not have realized that all of the words in the fourth group are nouns.

PEOPLE	
veterinarian	Americans
Dr. Robinson	leader
PLACES	
Lake Mead	kennel
classroom	Bunker Hill
THINGS	
bumblebee	motorcycle
collar	notebook
IDEAS	
strength	willingness
honesty	obedience

▶ **Exercise 1** Classifying Nouns Explain why each of the words below can function as a noun.

EXAMPLE: friendship

ANSWER: *Friendship* is a noun because it names a quality, an idea.

1. puppy
2. leash
3. trainer
4. tail
5. family
6. loyalty
7. yard
8. doghouse
9. judge
10. show

▶ **More Practice**

Grammar Exercise Workbook
• pp. 1–4
On-line Exercise Bank
• Section 14.1
  Go on-line:
  PHSchool.com
  Enter Web Code:
  ebk-7002

Complete the exercises on-line! Exercises 1 and 2 are available on-line or on CD-ROM.

Collective Nouns

A few nouns name groups of people or things. A *pack*, for example, is "a group of dogs that travel together." These nouns are called *collective nouns.*

▶ **KEY CONCEPT** A **collective noun** is a noun that names a group of people or things. ■

COLLECTIVE NOUNS		
club	herd	army
troop	orchestra	committee
class	team	group

▶ **Exercise 2** Recognizing Collective Nouns Each of the numbered groups of words below contains one collective noun. Write each collective noun on your paper.

EXAMPLE: bone   pack   collar

ANSWER: pack

1. collar	club	fur
2. team	dish	claw
3. ball	litter	toys
4. snout	group	paw
5. ribbon	brush	class

Compound Nouns

Sometimes two words are used together to form a new word with a different meaning. You know, for example, the two separate words *dog* and *house*. When they are used together, however, as in the sentence "The puppy sleeps in a doghouse," the combined words mean "a house for a dog." Together, the words take on a special meaning. A noun such as *doghouse* is said to be a *compound noun.*

▶ **KEY CONCEPT** A **compound noun** is a noun made up of two or more words. ■

COMPOUND NOUNS		
Separate Words	**Hyphenated Words**	**Combined Words**
post office	bull's-eye	flagship
middle school	daughter-in-law	railroad
Golden Gate Bridge	left-hander	doorknob

⚙ **Grammar and Style Tip**

Use collective nouns to replace the vague word *group* with a more specific one. For example, a *group* of dogs can be called a *pack*.

> **Exercise 3** Identifying Compound Nouns Each of the following sentences has one or more compound nouns. Copy the sentences onto your paper, and underline each compound noun.

EXAMPLE: The dog dragged his blanket into the doghouse.
ANSWER: The dog dragged his blanket into the <u>doghouse</u>.

1. Some purebreds, such as German shepherds, are born with an extra claw on each paw.
2. These extra claws, called dewclaws, are usually removed by a veterinarian.
3. Other dogs, like sheepdogs, have different problems.
4. My sister-in-law has a sheepdog.
5. She found it behind the high school.

> **Exercise 4** Finding the Correct Form of Compound Nouns Use a dictionary to find the correct spelling of each of the compound nouns below. Write the correct form on your paper.

EXAMPLE: dog-catcher   dogcatcher   dog catcher
ANSWER: dogcatcher

1. greyhound   grey hound   grey-hound
2. foxterrier   fox-terrier   fox terrier
3. watch-dog   watch dog   watchdog
4. blood hound   bloodhound   blood-hound
5. dog-eared   dog eared   dogeared

Common and Proper Nouns

All nouns—even if they are collective or compound—can be classified as either *common nouns* or *proper nouns*.

> **KEY CONCEPT** A **common noun** names any one of a class of people, places, or things. A **proper noun** names a specific person, place, or thing. ■

Common nouns are not capitalized unless they begin a sentence or a title. Proper nouns are always capitalized.

Common Nouns	Proper Nouns
writer	Mary Swenson
park	Yellowstone National Park
document	Declaration of Independence

▲ **Critical Viewing** What compound noun names a vehicle in which you might see a Dalmatian? **[Relate; Speculate]**

GRAMMAR IN LITERATURE

from **The Cat Who Thought She Was a Dog and the Dog Who Thought He Was a Cat**

Isaac Bashevis Singer

In this passage, notice that peasant, *a common noun, is often used in place of the proper noun* Jan Skiba. *The proper noun is capitalized, but the common noun is not. Look for other common and proper nouns in this paragraph.*

Once there was a poor *peasant, Jan Skiba* by name. He lived with his wife and three daughters in a one-room hut with a straw roof, far from the village. The house had a bed, a bench bed, and a stove, but no mirror. A mirror was a luxury for a poor *peasant*. And why would a *peasant* need a mirror? Peasants aren't curious about their appearance.

But this *peasant* did have a dog and a cat in his hut. The dog was named Burek and the cat Kot.

LITERATURE

You can read the complete selection "The Cat Who Thought . . ." in *Prentice Hall Literature: Timeless Voices, Timeless Themes,* Bronze.

▶ **Exercise 5** Identifying Common and Proper Nouns Copy each of the following nouns onto your paper. Place a *C* after each common noun and a *P* after each proper noun. Then, for each common noun, write a corresponding proper noun. For each proper noun, write a corresponding common noun.

EXAMPLE: club

ANSWER: club, C   American Kennel Club

EXAMPLE: United States

ANSWER: United States, P   country

1. statue
2. Latin
3. St. Bernard
4. state
5. street
6. Central Park
7. China
8. friend
9. lake
10. town

▶ **More Practice**

Grammar Exercise Workbook
• pp. 5–6
On-line Exercise Bank
• Section 14.1
   Go on-line:
   PHSchool.com
   Enter Web Code:
   ebk-7002

Complete the exercises on-line! Exercises 3, 4, and 5 are available on-line or on CD-ROM.

Section Review

GRAMMAR EXERCISES 6–12

Exercise 6 Identifying Nouns
Identify the nouns in each sentence.

1. Dogs require attention, including proper feeding and medical care.
2. Dogs need regular exercise.
3. Puppies need a combination of solid foods and milk as they grow.
4. Dogs enjoy rawhide strips.
5. A doghouse needs to be comfortable and insulated from heat and cold.

Exercise 7 Identifying Collective and Compound Nouns Copy the paragraph. Underline the collective nouns, and circle the compound nouns.

Several types of dogs are associated with occupations. The courage of the German shepherd is valuable to a police officer. Dalmatians are associated with firefighters and fire engines. Shelties can quickly organize a herd of sheep. A spaniel can point out a flock of birds without even seeing them. Working dogs, as well as their trainers, must have a great deal of self-discipline.

Exercise 8 Distinguishing Between Common and Proper Nouns
Make a list of the common nouns and a separate list of the proper nouns in this paragraph:

Many pieces of literature celebrate the dog. *White Fang,* written by Jack London, is the story of a brave and loyal companion. The story is set in the Yukon, but dogs in suburbs and cities often display similar loyalty. Other writers who have written about the fine qualities of dogs are James Herriot and William Armstrong. Millie, a dog who lived in the White House, is listed as the author of her own book.

Exercise 9 Revision Practice Copy the following paragraph. Replace the italicized words with proper nouns of your choice.

A dog came to *the town.* He walked up *a street* and down *another street. The man,* who lived at the end of *the street,* watched the dog approach.

Exercise 10 Find It in Your Reading Identify two proper nouns, two common nouns, one compound noun, and one collective noun in the following excerpt from "The Cat Who Thought She Was a Dog . . . ":

Burek had to be tied outside, and he howled all day and all night. In their anguish, both the dog and the cat stopped eating.
When Jan Skiba saw the disruption the mirror had created in his household, he decided a mirror wasn't what his family needed.

Exercise 11 Find It in Your Writing Look through your writing portfolio. Find five common nouns, two proper nouns, one collective noun, and one compound noun in your own writing.

Exercise 12 Writing Application
Write about a dog you've known or read about. Use at least two compound nouns, one collective noun, and two proper nouns.

Pronouns

Pronouns are a very useful part of language. They save us from having to say many things twice. Notice the following sentence, for example: *The doctor said that the doctor needed assistance during the surgery.* By replacing the second "the doctor" with the word "he," the sentence becomes much clearer: *The doctor said that he needed assistance during the surgery.* In this section, you will learn how to identify and use different types of pronouns.

▶ **KEY CONCEPT** A **pronoun** is a word that takes the place of a noun or a group of words acting as a noun. ■

Pronouns make it possible to avoid using the same noun over and over. Read the following examples.

WITHOUT PRONOUNS:	The *firefighters* described how the *firefighters* did the *firefighters'* jobs.
WITH PRONOUNS:	The *firefighters* described how *they* did *their* jobs.

The pronouns *they* and *their* stand for the noun *firefighters* at the beginning of the sentence.

A pronoun can also take the place of a noun in an earlier sentence.

EXAMPLE: Finally, the *rescue worker* reappeared. *She* smiled to show the crowd that *she* was unharmed.

The pronoun *she*, used twice in the second sentence, takes the place of the noun *rescue worker* in the first sentence.

Once in a while, a single pronoun takes the place of a whole group of words.

EXAMPLE: *How they rescued Kim* is amazing. *It* is a story that will be told again and again.

In this example, the pronoun *it* in the second sentence takes the place of four words: *How they rescued Kim.*

Theme: Careers in Medicine

In this section, you will learn about pronouns. The examples, sentences, paragraphs, and exercises in this section are about careers in rescue, health, or medicine.

Cross-Curricular Connection: Science and Health

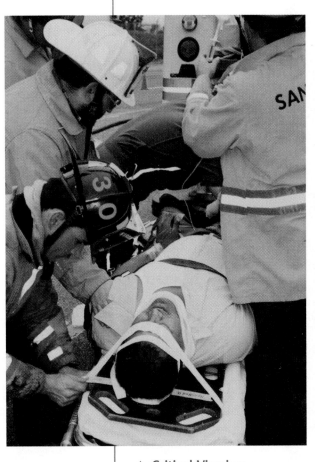

▲ **Critical Viewing** What pronouns would you use to refer to the people in this picture? **[Analyze]**

Antecedents of Pronouns

The word or group of words that a pronoun replaces is called an *antecedent*.

▶ **KEY CONCEPT** An **antecedent** is the noun (or group of words acting as a noun) for which a pronoun stands. ■

ANT.   PRON.   PRON.
The *firefighters* described how they did their jobs.

ANT.   PRON.
Finally, the *rescue worker* reappeared. She appeared to be unharmed.

ANT.   PRON.
How Kim was rescued is amazing. It is a story that will be told often.

Some kinds of pronouns will not have any antecedent.

EXAMPLE: *Everyone* knows what the truth is.

The indefinite pronoun *everyone* does not have a specific antecedent because its meaning is clear without one.

▼ **Critical Viewing** Describe what you think has happened to cause this scene. What pronouns do you use in your description? **[Speculate]**

Exercise 13 Recognizing Antecedents Find the antecedent for each italicized pronoun in the following sentences, and write it on your paper. Some antecedents may appear in other sentences.

EXAMPLE: Martha explained how *she* won the contest.
ANSWER: Martha

1. Pastor Theodor Fliedner began *his* school of nursing in 1836.
2. Florence Nightingale received *her* formal training in nursing at Fliedner's school.
3. This famous reformer of nursing used *her* experience on battlefields during the Crimean War.
4. When *she* returned home, Nightingale established her training program at Saint Thomas's Hospital in London.
5. Any school for nursing can trace *its* pattern for training to Saint Thomas's Hospital in London.
6. In the 1800's, nurses received most of *their* training through apprenticeship programs.
7. An apprentice's training was only as good as the nurse overseeing *it.*
8. A nursing program is responsible for preparing *its* students for the demands of nursing.
9. Nurses have many responsibilities assigned to *them.*
10. *They* need technical knowledge as well as compassion.

More Practice

Grammar Exercise Workbook
• pp. 7–8
On-line Exercise Bank
• Section 14.2
Go on-line:
PHSchool.com
Enter Web Code:
ebk-7002

Get instant feedback! Exercise 13 is available on-line or on CD-ROM.

Personal Pronouns

Personal pronouns are either singular or plural. Depending on to whom or what they refer, they are called *first-person, second-person,* or *third-person pronouns.*

KEY CONCEPT **Personal pronouns** refer to the person speaking (first person), the person spoken to (second person), or the person, place, or thing spoken about (third person). ■

Study the forms in the following chart:

PERSONAL PRONOUNS		
	Singular	Plural
First Person	I, me, my, mine	we, us, our, ours
Second Person	you, your, yours	you, your, yours
Third Person	he, him, his, she, her, hers, it, its	they, them, their, theirs

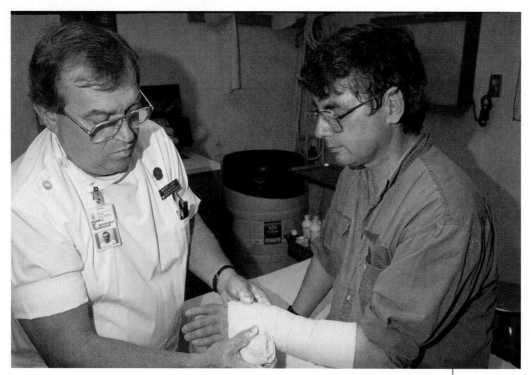

▲ **Critical Viewing** What other people besides a doctor and a physical therapist may have helped this man? What pronouns did you use in your answer? **[Analyze]**

▶ **Exercise 14** **Identifying Personal Pronouns** Copy the italicized pronoun in each of the following sentences onto your paper. Identify the pronoun as *first person*, *second person*, or *third person*.

EXAMPLE: The teacher asked *him* a difficult question.
ANSWER: him (third person)

1. Physical therapy received *its* start in the latter part of the nineteenth century.
2. Physical therapists teach *their* patients different forms of exercise.
3. *You* may be required to take courses in human anatomy.
4. *Your* training will include clinical instruction.
5. *My* physical therapist can offer treatment for different injuries.
6. *It* is used to improve strength, coordination, and endurance.
7. Many people say exercise has helped *them.*
8. A career in physical therapy interests *me.*
9. *Our* aunt will receive a degree in physical therapy after six years of college.
10. *She* looks forward to helping people recover from injuries.

Demonstrative Pronouns

▷ **KEY CONCEPT** A **demonstrative pronoun** points out a specific person, place, or thing. ■

There are two singular and two plural demonstrative pronouns:

DEMONSTRATIVE PRONOUNS			
Singular		**Plural**	
this	that	these	those

A demonstrative pronoun generally appears at the beginning of a sentence, with its antecedent appearing later in the same sentence. However, sometimes the demonstrative pronoun will be placed after its antecedent.

BEFORE: *That* has always been my favorite *subject*.

AFTER: We met an EMT and a doctor. *These* were the most interesting guests.

▷ **Exercise 15** Recognizing Demonstrative Pronouns

Identify five demonstrative pronouns in the following paragraphs:

Science and math are two of my favorite subjects. These are important studies for anyone planning a career in medicine. I hope to become a doctor, specializing in sports medicine. All medical students, no matter what specialty they plan to enter, must do well in all the sciences, as well as math. That is the reason I work hard to get good grades and understand the material. To do well in school, to get into a good pre-med program, and to eventually become "Dr. Sanabria"—those are my goals.

You may think this is too early to plan for college. Some students don't start thinking about their goals until high school. I know there are many careers open to me. I can always change my mind. For now, however, sports medicine is what I hope will be my career. That would be a dream come true.

ⓠ Learn More

The words *this, that, these,* and *those* can also function as adjectives. See Chapter 16 to learn more about pronouns used as adjectives.

▷ **More Practice**

Grammar Exercise Workbook
• pp. 9–10
On-line Exercise Bank
• Section 14.2
  Go on-line:
  PHSchool.com
  Enter Web Code:
  ebk-7002

Complete the exercises on-line! Exercises 14 and 15 are available on-line or on CD-ROM.

Interrogative Pronouns

To *interrogate* means "to ask questions."

KEY CONCEPT An **interrogative pronoun** is used to begin a question. ■

All five interrogative pronouns begin with *w:*

INTERROGATIVE PRONOUNS				
what	which	who	whom	whose

Most interrogative pronouns do not have antecedents.

EXAMPLE: *What* did the doctor say?

Which is the best treatment?

Who wants to be a doctor?

Exercise 16 Recognizing Interrogative Pronouns Identify the interrogative pronoun in each sentence below.

EXAMPLE: What happened to the cookies I baked?
ANSWER: What

1. What does a podiatrist do?
2. Which of these doctors treats foot diseases?
3. Who will be treated by a podiatrist?
4. Whose is the most difficult training?
5. From whom will you receive your podiatry training?

Indefinite Pronouns

KEY CONCEPT An **indefinite pronoun** refers to a person, place, or thing that is not specifically named. ■

EXAMPLES: *Everything* is ready for the field trip.

Everyone wants to see the medical center.

An indefinite pronoun can function either as an adjective or as the subject of a sentence.

ADJECTIVE: *Both* students want to be nurses.
SUBJECT: *Both* want to be nurses.

More Practice

Grammar Exercise Workbook
• pp. 9–12
On-line Exercise Bank
• Section 14.2
   Go on-line:
   PHSchool.com
   Enter Web Code:
   ebk-7002

Get instant feedback! Exercises 16 and 17 are available on-line or on CD-ROM.

INDEFINITE PRONOUNS			
Singular		Plural	Singular or Plural
another	much	both	all
anybody	neither	few	any
anyone	nobody	many	more
anything	no one	others	most
each	nothing	several	none
either	one		some
everybody	other		
everyone	somebody		
everything	someone		
little	something		

▶ **Exercise 17** Recognizing Indefinite Pronouns On your paper, write the indefinite pronoun you find in each sentence.

EXAMPLE: Each wanted to help Susan.

ANSWER: Each

1. One of the doctors is an optometrist.
2. Another is an ophthalmologist.
3. Both treat eye diseases.
4. Each must have a medical degree.
5. Everyone should have regular checkups.

◀ **Critical Viewing** What questions might this person be asking herself about what she sees? What interrogative pronouns might she use? **[Speculate]**

Hands-on Grammar

Nouns and Pronouns Circle Book

1. Cut out two circles of equal size, at least 6 1/2 inches in diameter. Fold each circle into fourths.

2. Label each fourth of the paper as shown.

3. Cut to the center of each circle along the line between sections 3 and 4, and then place the circles back to back, lining up the sections that are shown here in matching colors.

4. Tape the open edge of "Collective Nouns" to the open edge of "Demonstrative Pronouns." This creates a completed circle book.

5. On each section, write the definition of the type of noun or pronoun.

6. Fold your completed circle book, and keep it in your notebook. Add examples of each type of noun or pronoun as you find them.

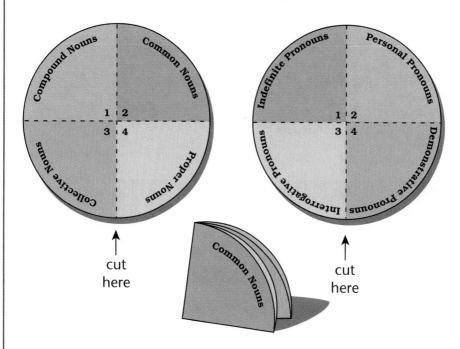

Find It in Your Writing Look through your portfolio to find examples of each kind of noun and each kind of pronoun. Write them down in the appropriate section of your circle book.

Find It in Your Reading Record examples of each type of noun and pronoun as you discover them in your reading. Start by recording examples from the Grammar in Literature example on page 299.

Section 14.2 Section Review

GRAMMAR EXERCISES 18–24

Exercise 18 **Identifying Personal Pronouns** Identify the personal pronoun in each sentence.

1. My brother and sister want to become pharmacists. They must attend a college of pharmacy.
2. After finishing a five-year program, he will graduate.
3. They must complete a one-year internship before becoming pharmacists.
4. She may choose from many schools.
5. All of them offer similar programs.

Exercise 19 **Identifying Antecedents of Personal Pronouns** Fill in the blank with the appropriate personal pronoun. Circle the antecedent of the pronoun you supply.

1. Radiologists must attend medical school. ___?___ spend five years studying radiology.
2. If my brother studies radiology, ___?___ will have to complete a residency program.
3. My aunt is a radiologist. ___?___ has her own practice.
4. After completing ___?___ residency, radiologists may decide to specialize.
5. ___?___ may choose to teach instead.

Exercise 20 **Recognizing Types of Pronouns** Identify each of the pronouns in the sentences below as *personal, demonstrative, interrogative,* or *indefinite.*

1. My brother is in high school. He wants to study forensic medicine.
2. That is the study of medical evidence.
3. It helps police officers solve crimes.
4. You may have seen popular shows about "crime doctors."

5. Who wants to know more?
6. These are copies of fingerprints.
7. Each is unique.
8. Whose is this fingerprint?
9. What can we learn from fingerprints?
10. Few can identify a fingerprint.

Exercise 21 **Revision Practice** Replace each italicized noun in the sentences below with the type of pronoun indicated in brackets. Some sentences may have to be rewritten as questions. Revise punctuation as needed.

1. *Family practitioners* [personal] provide primary medical care.
2. Family doctors know *family doctors'* [personal] patients.
3. *Dedication* [demonstrative] is one reason they enter the field.
4. *Family practitioners* [interrogative] can refer patients to a specialist.
5. *General practitioners* [indefinite] have had many years of medical training.

Exercise 22 **Find It in Your Reading** Identify three personal pronouns in the excerpt from "The Cat Who Thought She Was a Dog . . ." on page 299.

Exercise 23 **Find It in Your Writing** In your own writing, find at least one example of each kind of pronoun.

Exercise 24 **Writing Application** Write a brief description about a person in a job that interests you. Identify the kinds of pronouns you use.

GRAMMAR EXERCISES 25–36

▶ **Exercise 25** Identifying Nouns in Sentences Identify the nouns in each sentence below.

1. The pack of wolves chased the rabbit.
2. The rabbit, filled with fear, ran away.
3. Because of their hunger, the wolves continued to hunt.
4. They found no more prey in the forest.
5. The howls of the hungry animals showed their frustration.

▶ **Exercise 26** Identifying Nouns in Paragraphs Identify the nouns in the paragraph below.

　Wolves are wild animals that look similar to dogs. A wolf has fur that can be white, black, or gray. Wolves travel in packs, using their speed and strength to hunt as a group. They live in most climates, but rarely in deserts or tropical forests.

▶ **Exercise 27** Identifying Common and Proper Nouns Identify the nouns in each sentence below. Then, tell whether each noun is *common* or *proper*.

1. My sister Lucy, my mother, and I took our cat to the animal hospital.
2. The hospital is in Philadelphia.
3. We took the cat on the train.
4. The train passed through cities in New York and New Jersey.
5. Our cat Trudy needed special surgery.
6. Dr. Kim, the veterinarian, was very kind.
7. While we waited, my mother and I read a magazine.
8. We saw a dog that looked like a character from the movie *Benji*.
9. A poodle sat on a chair next to us.
10. Before we returned home, we stopped to see the Liberty Bell.

▶ **Exercise 28** Identifying Collective Nouns Identify the collective noun in each sentence below.

1. My class went on a trip to the animal hospital last week.
2. The team of veterinarians sees many types of patients.
3. Yesterday, they treated a group of monkeys from the zoo.
4. Sometimes, they go to farms to check a herd of cattle.
5. My family brought our cat to this animal hospital.

▶ **Exercise 29** Identifying Compound Nouns Identify the compound noun in each sentence below.

1. My sister-in-law brought a new cat home from the pound.
2. They told her that a police officer had found the cat.
3. It does not get along with the sheepdog in the house.
4. She brought it to the middle school where she teaches.
5. On the way home, they crossed the George Washington Bridge.

▶ **Exercise 30** Identifying Personal Pronouns Identify each personal pronoun below as *first person*, *second person*, or *third person*. Then, tell whether the pronoun is *singular* or *plural*.

1. you
2. she
3. their
4. our
5. them
6. I
7. his
8. yours
9. mine
10. we

Exercise 31 **Identifying Pronouns and Antecedents** Identify the pronoun in each sentence below. Then, identify its antecedent. Remember that the antecedent may be in a previous sentence.

1. The doctor explained that she would order tests.
2. The tests would help her determine what was wrong.
3. She said they are very accurate tests.
4. These are the tests she ordered.
5. This is the medication she prescribed for the cat.

Exercise 32 **Supplying Pronouns** Read the paragraph. Identify the antecedent to which the missing pronoun refers. Then, supply the correct pronoun to fill in the blank.

My friend's father is a veterinarian. ___?___ works at the zoo. Our class took a trip to the zoo. ___?___ learned a lot about animals. We saw a family of monkeys. ___?___ were very funny. Some animals need to be vaccinated. The shots prevent ___?___ from getting sick. At five o'clock, we left the zoo. ___?___ closes to the public at that time.

Exercise 33 **Classifying Pronouns** Identify each underlined pronoun below as *personal, demonstrative, interrogative,* or *indefinite.*

1. What is a veterinarian?
2. This is the doctor who takes care of the animals.
3. Everyone in the office helps care for the animals.
4. All seem concerned and helpful.
5. Whom should we talk to about our cat?
6. These are her medical records.
7. Should we be concerned about her cough?
8. That is one of my biggest concerns.
9. The office staff was reassuring. They told us it's a common ailment.
10. Which is your cat?

Exercise 34 **Using Nouns and Pronouns** Revise the following paragraph. When it will improve the paragraph, replace nouns with pronouns and common nouns with proper nouns.

Last week, my family went to the animal shelter. The director of the shelter, Mr. Miller, said my family could choose a puppy. First, though, my family had to fill out a form. Then, the man took us to the puppy room. In the puppy room, Mr. Miller let my family play with the puppies. My brother liked the little brown mutt. My brother thought the little brown mutt was the cutest. My sister liked the little white poodle. My sister thought the little white poodle was the cutest. The man said my family could come back another day, but my family decided on the spot. My family took both of the puppies!

Exercise 35 **Find It in Your Writing** Look through your portfolio. Identify examples in your own writing of each type of noun and each type of pronoun. Challenge yourself to improve a piece of writing by replacing a vague common noun with a more specific proper noun or compound noun.

Exercise 36 **Writing Application** Write a short paper about an animal that interests you. Use at least one proper noun, one collective noun, and one compound noun. Identify where you have used each type of noun. Remember to use pronouns when they help you avoid awkward repetitions of nouns.

Standardized Test Preparation Workshop

Nouns in Analogies

Many standardized tests contain analogies, items that measure your ability to identify the relationships between words. Analogies are like word-pair puzzles. Two common types of relationships used in analogies are part-to-whole and whole-to-part. For example, fur is to rabbit as feather is to bird. Both pairs of words begin with a noun that names part of the whole thing named by the second noun.

Standardized tests may present a sentence and leave a blank, or they may use two dots to indicate the two related words and a pair of two dots to separate the two pairs of words. The following items will give you practice in responding to analogies. Two different formats are used to show you the two most common ways these items appear on tests.

Sample Test Items	Answers and Explanations
Directions: Complete each item by choosing the word that best completes the sentence. Library is to book as (A) artist is to painting. (B) art is to history. (C) page is to book. (D) museum is to painting.	The correct answer is *D*. The library is the whole that contains the part—book—and the museum is the whole that contains the part—painting.
Directions: Each question below consists of a related pair of words followed by five pairs of words labeled *A* through *E*. Select the pair that best expresses a relationship similar to that expressed in the original pair. SLEEVE : SHIRT :: (A) flag : country (B) tree : branch (C) window : house (D) temperature : fever (E) whale : fish	The correct answer is *C*. A sleeve is part of the whole shirt, so the answer should reflect a part-to-whole relationship. In *A*, the flag is a symbol for the country, not a physical part of it. In *B*, a tree is the whole of which the branch is a part. The relationship is the reverse of part-to-whole. *D* and *E* are incorrect because the word pairs do not express any kind of part-whole relationships.

Practice 1 Each question below consists of a related pair of words, followed by five pairs of words labeled *A* through *E*. Select the pair that best expresses a relationship similar to that expressed in the original pair.

1. METAL : COIN ::

   (A) queen : crown
   (B) wool : sheep
   (C) clay : vase
   (D) liquid : cup
   (E) painting : frame

2. FOOT : INCH ::

   (A) year : summer
   (B) lemonade : lemon
   (C) pound : ounce
   (D) bicycle : wheel
   (E) day : week

3. SAND : DUNE ::

   (A) water : ocean
   (B) thunder : lightning
   (C) stove : kitchen
   (D) flake : snow
   (E) rain : flower

4. WAR : BATTLE ::

   (A) fruit : pit
   (B) concert : song
   (C) soldier : courage
   (D) king : dignity
   (E) ship : sail

5. BOOK : LIBRARY ::

   (A) magazine : page
   (B) desk : school
   (C) money : bank
   (D) head : hat
   (E) disk : computer

Practice 2 Choose the phrase that best completes each sentence below.

1. Handle is to cup as

   (A) wheel is to tire.
   (B) branch is to tree.
   (C) bird is to wing.
   (D) ear is to nose.

2. Point is to score as

   (A) game is to field.
   (B) math is to numbers.
   (C) table is to furniture.
   (D) error is to correction.

3. Sentence is to word as

   (A) pail is to water.
   (B) pile is to leaves.
   (C) hand is to finger.
   (D) melody is to note.

4. Traffic is to car as

   (A) crowd is to person.
   (B) ocean is to boat.
   (C) motor is to gasoline.
   (D) dinner is to food.

5. Bird is to flock as

   (A) fan is to audience.
   (B) runner is to race.
   (C) student is to class.
   (D) letter is to number.

Verbs are words that name an action or describe a state of being. They describe what is happening in the sentence. Every complete sentence needs to include at least one verb.

Some verbs describe specific actions. If you were writing about the migration of people to the United States from foreign countries, you might use verbs for the actions of immigrants. For instance, you might tell what these people did as they left their homelands and traveled to the United States.

In this chapter, you will learn about *action verbs* and *linking verbs* and the ways that these verbs can be used with *helping verbs* in verb phrases.

▲ **Critical Viewing** Identify three verbs that could name actions by immigrants when they first saw the Statue of Liberty. **[Analyze]**

Diagnostic Test

Directions: Write all answers on a separate sheet of paper.

Skill Check A. Write the action verb in each sentence below and label it *transitive* or *intransitive*.

1. Thousands of people entered the United States in the nineteenth century.
2. These immigrants traveled from many different countries all around the world.
3. Many brought customs and traditions from their native lands.
4. They envisioned new opportunities in the United States.
5. Whole families moved from their homeland for numerous reasons.

Skill Check B. Identify the underlined word or words in each of the following sentences as an *action verb* or a *linking verb*.

6. Some <u>left</u> their homeland to look for better jobs.
7. Many people <u>had</u> hopes of owning their own land.
8. The United States <u>was</u> a land of opportunity for countless numbers of people.
9. Many people <u>looked</u> for wealth in a new land.
10. Some <u>hoped</u> for adventure.
11. The immigrants <u>were</u> joyful and hopeful.
12. Some <u>fled</u> their country because of war.
13. Many people <u>moved</u> to the United States for religious freedom.
14. The people <u>walked</u> away from everything familiar to them.
15. Some immigrants quickly <u>felt</u> comfortable in their new land.
16. Some <u>describe</u> the United States as a tapestry of cultures.
17. Ellis Island <u>was</u> the first stopping place for many immigrants.
18. This location <u>became</u> known worldwide as the entry to America.
19. People from all walks of life <u>entered</u> America through Ellis Island.
20. Life in the United States <u>seemed</u> exciting to the new arrivals.

Skill Check C. Identify the helping verbs and the main verbs in the following sentences.

21. The immigrants must have been waiting to see the Statue of Liberty.
22. They had often heard stories about the great wealth in America.
23. They should have been warned about the immigration laws.
24. Everyone was being thoroughly checked for physical ailments.
25. The number of immigrants each year was being limited.

Action Verbs

Verbs such as *walk, sailed, played, migrate, raced, crossed, learn,* and *arrive* all show some kind of action.

▶ **KEY CONCEPT** An **action verb** tells what action someone or something is performing. ■

EXAMPLES: Father *packed* our suitcases.
The ship *chugged* into the harbor.

The verb *packed* explains what Father did to the suitcases. The verb *chugged* tells what the ship did.

Some actions, such as *sailed* or *mingled,* can be seen. Some actions, such as *believe* or *recall,* cannot be seen.

▶ **Exercise 1** Recognizing Action Verbs Copy the following sentences onto your paper. Underline the action verb in each sentence.

EXAMPLE: The ship from Barcelona <u>arrived</u> three hours late.

1. Lines of people walked to the ship for their voyage across the ocean.
2. On board, many passengers wondered about their new homeland.
3. The waves lashed at the ship during storms.
4. Eventually, the immigrants completed the journey.
5. From the decks, children and their parents studied the coastline of their new homeland.
6. Some cried at the sight of the Statue of Liberty.
7. The ships full of passengers docked in New York Harbor.
8. Families adapted to the new culture.
9. Most of the people found jobs in America.
10. Their previous skills helped some of them find jobs.

▶ **KEY CONCEPT** A **transitive verb** is an action verb that directs action from the performer of the action toward the receiver of the action. The "receiver" of the action is a person, place, or thing—that is, a noun or pronoun. An **intransitive verb** expresses action or tells something about the subject of the sentence but does not direct action toward another noun or pronoun. ■

TRANSITIVE: The captain *rang* the bell.
INTRANSITIVE: The bell *rang* for dinner.
TRANSITIVE: The captain *sailed* the ship.
INTRANSITIVE: The ship *sailed* out to sea.

Theme: Immigration

In this section, you will learn about action verbs. The examples and exercises in this section are about immigration.

Cross-Curricular Connection: Social Studies

▶ **More Practice**

Grammar Exercise Workbook
• pp. 13–14
On-line Exercise Bank
• Section 15.1
Go on-line:
PHSchool.com
Enter Web Code:
ebk-7002

Get instant feedback! Exercises 1 and 2 are available on-line or on CD-ROM.

> **Exercise 2** Identifying Transitive and Intransitive Verbs

Write the underlined action verb in each of the sentences below. After each verb, write *transitive* or *intransitive*. If you label a verb *transitive*, identify the noun toward which the action is directed.

EXAMPLE: Marcia picked a bushel of apples from the tree.

ANSWER: picked—transitive; action is directed at bushel

1. Early settlers hoped for new lives in the United States.
2. They explored the new territory.
3. Some colonists sailed back to their homelands.
4. The other immigrants stayed in the U.S. permanently.
5. These people shared a dream of a better life.
6. They dared to cross the ocean.
7. They settled in the new land.
8. All built new lives.
9. Some regretted their decision.
10. Most believed in the promise of America.

⚙ Grammar and **Style Tip**

Use vivid action verbs such as *dash, scurry,* and *rush* to convey the way an action happens.

◄ **Critical Viewing**
Name at least four action verbs that describe what people on this crowded ship are doing. **[Relate]**

Hands-on Grammar

Action Verb Showdown

To increase your understanding of action verbs, create and play an Action Verb Showdown game.

Work with a partner to brainstorm for a list of action verbs. Give each verb a "rating" from 1 to 5, based on the intensity of the action. With your partner, discuss whether some mental actions, such as *ponder,* are more intense than some visible actions, such as *sit.* Come to an agreement with your partner about the rating for each verb.

VISIBLE ACTION		MENTAL ACTION	
sail	swim	remember	decide
rip	migrates	understand	hope
bring	smile	expect	think
traveled	cried	consider	forgot

When you have listed approximately fifty verbs, write each verb and its rating on a separate piece of paper. Fold each piece of paper so that the verbs and ratings cannot be seen. Then, put all the verbs into a container such as a shoebox or coffee can. To play, each partner takes one of the pieces of paper from the container. The partner with the action verb that has the highest action rating gets to keep both verbs if he or she can explain why one verb is rated higher than the other. Otherwise, return both verbs to the box.

Then, each player takes another verb from the container. Continue playing until all verbs are taken from the container.

To score, add up the activity ratings of the verbs that each player has. The player with the highest total wins.

Find It in Your Reading Read the excerpt from "Melting Pot" on page 324. Give a rating to the action verb that is repeated in the passage. Think of a similar or related verb to which you would give a higher rating.

Find It in Your Writing Review a piece of writing from your portfolio. Identify the action verbs you have used. Challenge yourself to replace any verbs that do not express the precise intensity of the action to which you are referring.

Section 15.1 Section Review

GRAMMAR EXERCISES 3–9

Exercise 3 Finding Action Verbs
Identify the action verbs in the sentences that follow. One sentence contains more than one verb.

(1) Teachers in neighborhood schools helped immigrants with their English. (2) Sometimes, they taught groups in the evenings and very early in the mornings. (3) Soon, many immigrants spoke and wrote in English. (4) Some older people stumbled over the strange new language. (5) Many immigrants helped each other with their new language.

Exercise 4 Identifying Action Verbs Copy the headings below. Under *performer*, list who or what is performing the action. Under *action*, list the verb.

EXAMPLE: The captain shouted at the crew.
ANSWER: PERFORMER   ACTION
          captain   shouted

1. The first immigrants arrived from England.
2. The ship approached the harbor.
3. The mayor announced the arrival of the immigrants.
4. The people celebrated their arrival in America.
5. A committee greeted the immigrants.

Exercise 5 Recognizing Transitive and Intransitive Verbs Label each underlined verb *transitive* or *intransitive*.

1. The Statue of Liberty impressed most immigrants.
2. They asked about its meaning.
3. The statue stands as a symbol of liberty.
4. France gave the statue to the United States as a gift.
5. Americans appreciated the gift and built the pedestal for the statue.

Exercise 6 Revision Practice: Verbs
Revise each sentence by replacing the underlined words with a single, precise verb.

1. The ship moved gracefully away from the dock.
2. The family quickly and eagerly accepted the chance to immigrate.
3. We moved quickly toward the refreshment stand.
4. We noisily sipped our sodas.
5. We walked as if we were very tired back to the boat.

Exercise 7 Find It in Your Reading
Identify two action verbs in this passage from "Melting Pot" by Anna Quindlen. Do not include the verb phrases *doesn't carry* and *can buy*.

The greengrocer stocks yellow pepper and fresh rosemary for the gourmands, plum tomatoes and broadleaf parsley for the older Italians, mangoes for the Indians. He doesn't carry plantains, he says, because you can buy them in the bodega.

Exercise 8 Find It in Your Writing
Look through your writing portfolio. Find three examples of transitive verbs and three examples of intransitive verbs.

Exercise 9 Writing Application
Write a paragraph about the people in your neighborhood, including at least two transitive verbs and two intransitive verbs.

Linking Verbs

Some verbs do not show action. Instead, they link two parts of a sentence. These *linking verbs* thus show a relationship between words in a sentence.

KEY CONCEPT A **linking verb** connects a noun or pronoun with a word that identifies or describes it. ■

EXAMPLES: New York *is* a city.

The best swimmers *were* Margie and Pia.

Lucy *seems* unhappy.

Linking verbs act almost as equal signs. *City* identifies *New York; Margie* and *Pia* identify the *swimmers; unhappy* describes *Lucy.*

The Most Common Linking Verb

In English, the most common linking verb is *be.* This verb has many forms.

FORMS OF *BE*		
am	can be	have been
are	could be	has been
is	may be	had been
was	might be	could have been
were	must be	may have been
am being	shall be	might have been
are being	should be	must have been
is being	will be	shall have been
was being	would be	should have been
were being		will have been
		would have been

Exercise 10 Writing Sentences With Linking Verbs Write a sentence using each form of *be* listed below.

1. might have been
2. should have been
3. could be
4. were being
5. will be
6. has been
7. shall be
8. is being
9. would be
10. had been

Theme: Immigration

In this section, you will learn about linking verbs. The examples and exercises in this section are about immigration.

Cross-Curricular Connection: Social Studies

> **Exercise 11** Recognizing Forms of the Linking Verb *Be*
Copy the following sentences onto your paper. Underline the form of *be* in each one. Then, draw an arrow connecting the words that are linked by the verb.

EXAMPLE: The immigrants <u>were</u> happy.

1. Ellis Island was the busiest immigrant processing center in the United States.
2. The Immigration Service determines whether immigrants will be citizens.
3. Citizenship may have been open to people of all origins.
4. However, not all immigrants would be able to receive it.
5. The children may be cranky from waiting in the long lines.
6. An elderly man is sick from the long trip.
7. It had been a difficult voyage.
8. Soon, he will be a citizen of the United States.
9. Most of the people with him are his cousins.
10. The new Americans must have been nervous.

> **More Practice**
Grammar Exercise Workbook
• pp. 15–16
On-line Exercise Bank
• Section 15.2
Go on-line:
PHSchool.com
Enter Web Code:
ebk-7002

▼ **Critical Viewing**
In what ways did Ellis Island serve a linking role for American immigrants? **[Analyze]**

Other Linking Verbs

Be is the most commonly used linking verb, but there are some other important linking verbs you should know.

Internet Tip

To learn more about immigration, use search words such as *Ellis Island, immigration, emigration,* and *Immigration and Naturalization Service.*

OTHER LINKING VERBS		
appear	look	sound
become	remain	stay
feel	seem	taste
grow	smell	turn

Like *be*, these verbs are often used to link two parts of a sentence.

EXAMPLES: She later became a citizen.

The cream tastes sour.

The food stayed fresh and crisp.

▶ **Critical Viewing**
Use linking verbs—such as *are, was, seem,* or *feel*—in sentences that describe the immigrants in a waiting room at Ellis Island. **[Analyze]**

▶ **Exercise 12** Identifying Other Linking Verbs Copy each of the following sentences onto your paper. Underline the linking verb in each one. Then, draw arrows connecting the words that are linked by the verb.

EXAMPLE: During the storm, the road quickly <u>turned</u> muddy.

1. The atmosphere on the ship seemed exciting.
2. Everyone stayed quiet at the very beginning of the voyage.
3. The waves sounded rough and frightening to the passengers.
4. The captain appeared gruff.
5. The voyage became an adventure for the young children.
6. During the long trip, each child grew hungry and tired.
7. At that point, anything tasted delicious to them.
8. Regardless of their condition, the immigrants felt happy to be in the United States.
9. They remained hopeful.
10. Some immigrants looked discouraged because of the long delays.

Action Verb or Linking Verb?

Many of the twelve verbs in the preceding chart can be used as either linking verbs or action verbs.

LINKING: The bread *smelled* stale. (*Smelled* links *bread* and *stale*.)

ACTION: Charles *smelled* the sea air. (Charles is performing an action.)

LINKING: The Dutch bulbs *grow* tall. (*Grow* links *bulbs* and *tall*.)

ACTION: Annemarie *grows* tulips. (Annemarie is performing an action.)

To test whether a verb is a linking verb or an action verb, substitute *am, are,* or *is* for the verb. If the sentence with the new verb still makes sense, then the original verb is a linking verb.

LINKING	ACTION
Tina *felt* weak. (Tina *is* weak?) Yes, it's a linking verb.	Tina *felt* the cloth. (Tina *is* the cloth?) No, it's an action verb.

▶ **More Practice**

Grammar Exercise Workbook
• pp. 17–18
On-line Exercise Bank
• Section 15.2
  Go on-line:
  PHSchool.com
  Enter Web Code:
  ebk-7002

Get instant feedback! Exercise 12 is available on-line or on CD-ROM.

GRAMMAR IN LITERATURE

from **Melting Pot**
Anna Quindlen

Notice the linking verbs printed in blue in the passage and the action verbs printed in red. What words does each linking verb connect?

My children *are* upstairs in the house next door, having dinner with the Ecuadorian family that *lives* on the top floor. The father *speaks* some English, the mother less than that. The two daughters *are* fluent in both their native and their adopted languages, but the youngest child, a son, a close friend of my two boys, *speaks* almost no Spanish.

⚙ Grammar and Style Tip

Avoid using too many linking verbs in your sentences. A balance of action verbs and linking verbs will help your writing sound varied and interesting.

▶ **Exercise 13** **Distinguishing Between Action Verbs and Linking Verbs** On your paper, write the verb(s) from each of the sentences below. After each action verb, write *AV*, and after each linking verb, write *LV*.

EXAMPLE: Suddenly the sun broke through the clouds.
ANSWER: broke—AV

1. The father looked at his family.
2. He felt sad about leaving them.
3. His family looked so tiny from the ship.
4. The rain smelled fresh, like his new start.
5. The crowds on the ship appeared happy.
6. The immigrants became weary after the long journey.
7. Suddenly, the Statue of Liberty appeared through the fog.
8. Many immigrants stayed in New York.
9. They grew comfortable with their new surroundings.
10. Farmers grew vegetables to sell in the city.

▼ **Critical Viewing** Identify four verbs that describe what the people in this picture from 1900 are doing. **[Relate]**

Section 15.2 Section Review

GRAMMAR EXERCISES 14–19

Exercise 14 **Identifying Linking Verbs** Identify the linking verbs in the following sentences, and write them on your paper.

1. Immigrants are people who transfer residence from one country to another.
2. The first immigrants to the United States were western Europeans.
3. Up until 1860, most immigrants had been British, Irish, or German.
4. Many immigrants stayed loyal to their old customs.
5. Between 1890 and 1910, most new immigrants were from southern and eastern Europe.

Exercise 15 **Recognizing Linking Verbs in a Paragraph** Copy the following sentences onto your paper, and underline the linking verb in each one. Then, draw arrows connecting the words that are linked by the verb.

(1) Ellis Island is one of New York's most popular tourist attractions. (2) It seems very small when viewed from the island of Manhattan. (3) Liberty Island and Roosevelt Island are other islands near Manhattan. (4) Liberty Island has become a popular tourist site. (5) This and many more islands remain part of greater New York Harbor.

Exercise 16 **Distinguishing Between Action Verbs and Linking Verbs** Each underlined verb in the following sentences is either a linking verb or an action verb. On your paper, write each underlined verb and label it either *LV* for *linking verb* or *AV* for *action verb*.

1. Some new immigrants <u>felt</u> nervous.
2. Towns <u>grew</u> as more and more people <u>arrived</u> from Europe.
3. Adjusting to the new country <u>felt</u> strange.
4. Some did not <u>stay</u> long.
5. Nonetheless, America <u>remains</u> a nation of immigrants.

Exercise 17 **Find It in Your Reading** Identify the linking verb in each sentence of this passage from "Melting Pot" by Anna Quindlen.

My first apartment in New York was in a gritty warehouse district, the kind of place that makes your parents wince. A lot of old Italians lived around me, which suited me just fine because I was the granddaughter of old Italians.

Exercise 18 **Find It in Your Writing** Select a writing sample from your portfolio that contains sentences with linking verbs. Underline the linking verbs. Then, draw arrows connecting the words that are linked by those verbs.

Exercise 19 **Writing Application** Write a short description about the first place you remember living. Use at least three of the linking verbs from this list.

appeared	seemed
became	smelled
felt	sounded
grew	stayed
looked	tasted
remained	turned

Helping Verbs

Sometimes, a verb in a sentence is just one word. Often, however, a verb will be made up of several words. This type of verb is called a *verb phrase*. A verb phrase can have one, two, or three helping verbs before the main part of the verb.

> **KEY CONCEPT** **Helping verbs** are added before another verb to make a **verb phrase.** ■

The helping verbs in the following examples are italicized. Notice how they help to change the meaning of *put*, the key part of the verb.

EXAMPLES: put
had put
will have put
might have put
should have been put

Recognizing Helping Verbs

The various forms of *be* shown in the chart on page 320 are often used as helping verbs in front of other verbs. In the chart below, a number of different forms of *be* are used as helping verbs. All are italicized.

SOME FORMS OF *BE* USED AS HELPING VERBS	
Helping Verbs	**Main Verbs**
am	growing
has been	warned
was being	told
could have been	reminded
will have been	waiting

Some other common verbs are also used as helping verbs.

OTHER HELPING VERBS				
do	have	would	will	can
does	has	shall	might	could
did	had	should	must	may

Theme: Governments
....
In this section, you will learn about helping verbs. The examples and exercises in this section tell more about immigration.
....

Cross-Curricular Connection: Social Studies

VERB PHRASES	
Helping Verbs	**Main Verbs**
do	remember
has	written
would	hope
can	believe
may	attempt
must have	thought
should have	grown

▶ **Exercise 20** Identifying Helping Verbs On your paper, write the verb phrase in each sentence below. Underline the helping verbs.

EXAMPLE: Immigrants have been arriving in the United States for nearly two centuries.

ANSWER: <u>have been</u> arriving

1. Early arrivals in the United States from northern and western Europe were called old immigrants.
2. Many old immigrants had entered the country in the 1850's.
3. People from southern and eastern Europe would have been known as new immigrants.
4. The Carlucci family may have arrived before 1900.
5. The family members were escaping a terrible famine in their area of Italy.

▼ **Critical Viewing** Looking at the picture, list four verb phrases that answer the question, "What are they doing?" [Analyze]

▶ **Exercise 21** Finding Helping Verbs and Main Verbs Copy the sentences below onto your paper. Draw one line under each helping verb and two lines under each main verb.

(1) The large number of immigrants was considered a threat by some people already living in the United States. (2) New immigration laws were being passed by Congress. (3) Some immigrants were tested to see whether they could read English. (4) Health examinations were given to many others. (5) The immigrants should have been warned about the new requirements.

▶ **More Practice**

Grammar Exercise Workbook
• pp. 19–20
On-line Exercise Bank
• Section 15.3
Go on-line:
PHSchool.com
Enter Web Code:
ebk-7002

Helping Verbs Can Be Separated

Words in a verb phrase can sometimes be separated by other words. Very often, words such as *not, certainly,* and *seldom* come between a helping verb and the key part of the verb. In questions, verbs of two or more words are frequently separated. In the following examples, the parts of each verb phrase are italicized.

WORDS TOGETHER: They *must have been taken* by taxi to the airport.

WORDS SEPARATED: Marie *has* certainly not *contacted* us.
He *had* carefully *kept* all the records.
Can they really *build* their own home?

▶ **Exercise 22**   **Finding Complete Verb Phrases**   On your paper, write the complete verb phrase in each of the following sentences. Include all the helping verbs, but do not include any of the words that may separate the parts of the verb phrase.

EXAMPLE: Have you walked the dogs yet?
ANSWER: Have walked

1. After the Civil War, immigration from China was rapidly increasing.
2. The immigrants were, at first, hoping to work as laborers for the railroad.
3. Congress had, however, passed the Chinese Exclusion Act.
4. Some Chinese laborers were now being prohibited from coming to the United States.
5. Other groups of immigrants were also affected by new laws.
6. A ceiling had actually been established to limit immigration.
7. Government officials would soon establish quotas.
8. Only a limited number of immigrants could now move to the United States from other countries.
9. Some people did not agree with the limits.
10. Others might possibly have been concerned about job competition.

💡 Spelling Tip

The word *immigrate* means to move <u>into</u> a new country. The word *emigrate* means to move <u>out</u> of a country.

▼ **Critical Viewing** List several verb phrases to describe the action in this picture. Then, compare them to the verb phrases you used to describe the action in the picture on the previous page. How do your lists compare? **[Compare and Contrast]**

Section 15.3 Section Review

GRAMMAR EXERCISES 23–27

▶ **Exercise 23** Recognizing Helping Verbs Write the helping verb(s) in each sentence below.

1. As the immigrants arrived in America, they would be taken to Ellis Island.
2. They had been gathered into large groups.
3. Impatient guards were shouting instructions to the nervous crowds.
4. Most of the people could not understand the guards who were directing them.
5. The immigrants had been carrying their bags for hours.
6. They were being led into a large room.
7. There, they were given a choice about their baggage.
8. They could check their bags, or they could carry them into the next room.
9. Numbered tags should have been placed on each bag.
10. Many of the tags were accidentally torn off.

▶ **Exercise 24** Finding Complete Verb Phrases Write the verb phrase in each of the following sentences, and underline the helping verbs. Do not include any of the words that may separate parts of the verb phrase.

1. The medical inspectors had stood on the balcony in the Great Hall.
2. The immigrants were being closely observed by the inspectors.
3. They would eventually be checked by each inspector.
4. Every person would be marked in chalk with a large letter.
5. The letter would designate the person's level of health.
6. The inspectors had been trained to spot illness or disease.

7. Some people with physical disabilities were marked with an "L" for "lame."
8. If they were found coughing, they would have been marked with "TB" for tuberculosis even if they did not have the disease.
9. Immigrants who were breathing heavily might have been unfairly marked with an "H" for heart disease.
10. People could not pass through customs if inspectors suspected they had a dangerous, contagious disease.

▶ **Exercise 25** Find It in Your Reading Identify two verb phrases in this passage from "Melting Pot" by Anna Quindlen. (One of the helping verbs is part of a contraction.)

Drawn in broad strokes, we live in a pressure cooker: oil and water, us and them. But if you come around at exactly the right time, you'll find members of all these groups gathered around complaining about the condition of the streets, on which everyone can agree.

▶ **Exercise 26** Find It in Your Writing Select a writing sample from your portfolio that includes at least three verb phrases composed of a helping verb and a main verb. Circle the verb phrases, and underline the helping verbs.

▶ **Exercise 27** Writing Application Imagine that you have just arrived at Ellis Island. Write a brief description of your feelings and impressions. Underline any verb phrases that you use.

Chapter Review

GRAMMAR EXERCISES 28–37

Exercise 28 Identifying Action Verbs On your paper, write the verb and the performer of the action in each sentence.

EXAMPLE: The women completed the voyage.

ANSWER: <u>PERFORMER</u>   <u>ACTION</u>
           women   completed

1. Officials detained more than twenty percent of the immigrants on Ellis Island.
2. The immigrants first went to a waiting room.
3. Family members often sat in separate places.
4. Men and boys stayed on one side of the room.
5. Women and girls stood on the other side of the room.
6. Usually, families reunited later in the day.
7. A young man cried quietly before his examination.
8. The medical examiners looked at him carefully.
9. At last, he passed the test.
10. The young immigrant smiled.

Exercise 29 Distinguishing Transitive and Intransitive Verbs In each sentence below, the verb is underlined. Label each verb *transitive* or *intransitive*.

1. Immigrants <u>took</u> a test to enter the United States.
2. Most people <u>worried</u> about the test.
3. Interpreters <u>helped</u> the nervous immigrants as much as possible.
4. Sometimes, the guards <u>asked</u> only a few questions of the immigrants.
5. The immigrants <u>answered</u> as well as they could.

Exercise 30 Identifying Linking Verbs Copy the sentences below onto your paper. Underline each linking verb, and draw an arrow connecting the words that are linked by the verb.

1. The food choices on Ellis Island were limited.
2. Some food vendors seemed unkind.
3. In addition, the food often tasted bad.
4. Some ate the food and became sick.
5. Many immigrants grew very angry at the poor treatment and long waits.

Exercise 31 Supplying Linking Verbs and Action Verbs On your paper, write the sentences, filling in the blanks with verbs from the following list. Use each verb only once. Then, indicate whether each verb is an action verb or a linking verb, based on its use in the sentence.

had become   stayed   would be felt
seemed   appeared   remained sounded
knew   could be   were

1. The twelve-year-old boy ___?___ older than he was.
2. He ___?___ with the other children in his family for the physical exam.
3. If he failed the exam, he ___?___ heart-broken.
4. Sadly, the examiner ___?___ he had to order the boy back to his homeland.
5. His grandfather ___?___ ready to return with the boy.
6. It ___?___ tragic to split up the family.
7. The rest of the family ___?___ terrible about the situation.
8. The steamship officials ___?___ as if they would pay for the return trip.
9. The boy and his grandfather ___?___ hopeful about returning to America.
10. For them, Ellis Island ___?___ a sad place.

Exercise 32 Identifying Action Verbs and Linking Verbs Write the verbs you find in the following sentences. Label each verb *LV* for *linking verb* or *AV* for *action verb.*

1. The young immigrant tasted new foods during his first days in America.
2. After he drank a glass of sour lemonade, the boy's face turned green.
3. A peddler's wagon appeared on the street where the boy lived.
4. The roasted meat on the wagon smelled wonderful.
5. Because of the smell, the boy grew hungry.

Exercise 33 Writing Action Verbs and Linking Verbs Write a verb to complete each sentence. Label each verb *LV* for *linking verb* or *AV* for *action verb.*

1. Suddenly, his stomach ___?___ very empty.
2. He ___?___ in his pocket to locate a coin.
3. He ___?___ his one coin over inside his pocket.
4. The boy ___?___ sadly at the peddler.
5. The boy ___?___ hungry.

Exercise 34 Recognizing Verb Phrases Write the verb phrase in each of the following sentences. Underline the helping verbs.

1. Europeans had sometimes waited for years to emigrate to the United States.
2. Some families may have been saving most of their working lives to make such a trip.
3. In some cases, they traveled many miles just to reach the ship that would carry them across the ocean.
4. Many surely must have thought that they should have stayed home.
5. However, most must have overcome their fears, because they eventually did board their ships.

Exercise 35 Identifying the Helping Verb and the Main Verb Write each verb phrase. Circle the helping verb(s), and underline the main verb.

1. The ship was rocking back and forth on the waves in the harbor.
2. The passengers had been told that they could leave the ship soon.
3. The immigrants should have disembarked hours ago.
4. They were hoping that relatives would greet them on the shore.
5. The relatives were huddled behind barricades.

Exercise 36 Writing Application Write a brief paragraph about one of your older relatives. Include sentences that contain action verbs, linking verbs, and verb phrases. Circle each verb you use.

Exercise 37 CUMULATIVE REVIEW Nouns, Pronouns, and Verbs List the nouns, pronouns, and verbs that you find in the sentences below. Label each noun *CN* for *common noun* or *PN* for *proper noun.* For each pronoun, indicate its antecedent. For each verb, indicate whether it is an action verb or a linking verb. Identify the helping verb and the main verb in each verb phrase.

(1) Italians were one group of people who emigrated from Europe. (2) They had suffered from war in their homeland. (3) Sometimes, one person came to the United States ahead of his relatives. (4) My great-grandfather arrived at Ellis Island in 1908. (5) After he had worked for two years, he brought his wife to New York.

Standardized Test Preparation Workshop

Standard Usage for Parts of Speech: Verbs

Some questions on standardized tests are designed to measure your ability to recognize standard English usage within the context of a written passage. Often, these questions are designed as fill-in-the-blanks. When using verbs—words that express actions or states of being—to complete sentences, read through the entire passage to get an idea of the writer's purpose. Then, eliminate those answers that would change the meaning of the sentence. Also, determine the time frame—past, present, future—of the sentence and eliminate verbs that do not indicate the appropriate tense.

The following test item will give you practice with the format used for items testing verb usage.

Test Tip

• When choosing verbs, make sure to read the whole passage that gives the context. There may be two verbs that could fit in the numbered space, but only one will make sense in the context of the passage.

Sample Test Item

Directions: Read the passage, and choose the letter of the word or group of words that belongs in each space.

An erupting volcano ____(1)____ great clouds of ash and gas into the atmosphere. Sometimes rivers of red-hot lava ooze from its opening.
A shoots
B will be shooting
C shot
D has been shooting

Answer and Explanation

The correct answer is *A.* The verb *shoots* is consistent with the time of the passage, which is in the present. (Notice the present-tense verb *ooze* in the second sentence.) *Will be shooting* indicates a future action, and *shot* and *has been shooting* are past-tense forms.

Practice 1

Directions: Read each passage, and choose the letter of the word or group of words that belongs in each space.

Volcanoes ____(1)____ thousands of people, and they have caused great damage to property. Perhaps someday, we ____(2)____ to predict volcanic eruptions.

1 **A** will hurt
 B have been hurting
 C have hurt
 D hurt

2 **F** will learn
 G learn
 H learned
 J are learning

At this time, scientists ____(1)____ special technology to measure activity under the Earth's crust. They ____(2)____ not always entirely accurate.

3 **A** use
 B used
 C will use
 D were using

4 **F** are
 G is
 H were
 J will be

Practice 2

Directions: Read each passage, and choose the letter of the word or group of words that belongs in each space.

More and more people ____(1)____ the outdoors. The choices for enjoyable, healthful activities are endless. Some people ____(2)____ winter sports, such as cross-country skiing or snowboarding. Other people ____(3)____ warm-weather activities, such as baseball, swimming, or tennis. No matter what your seasonal preference is, you ____(4)____ sure there is an activity for you.

1 **A** enjoyed
 B is enjoying
 C are enjoying
 D would enjoy

2 **F** choose
 G chosen
 H would have chosen
 J might have chosen

3 **A** may prefer
 B preferred
 C have preferred
 D preferring

4 **F** will be
 G are
 H might be
 J can be

Adjectives and Adverbs

Adjectives are words that describe. When used properly, they sharpen and polish the meaning of nouns and pronouns.

Adjectives help a writer paint a picture with words. For example, we get a clear picture of Hans Christian Andersen's ugly duckling because of the adjective *ugly*. If the waterfowl in the story had been a mallard duck instead of a swan, the best adjective to describe the duckling might have been *colorful*.

Adverbs, too, play an important part in sentences. Adverbs include words such as *carefully, often, seldom, finally, never, very,* and *soon*. Like adjectives, adverbs are modifiers. Adjectives can modify *two* different parts of speech—nouns and pronouns. Adverbs, on the other hand, can modify *three* different parts of speech—verbs, adjectives, and other adverbs. Using adverbs to modify words can create a more vivid picture in a reader's mind. For example, instead of writing, "Redwood trees grow in California," it would be more descriptive to write, "The giant redwood trees of Northern California tower majestically above the landscape."

In this chapter, you will learn how to use adjectives and adverbs.

▲ **Critical Viewing**
How many adjectives can you think of to describe the flamingo's appearance?
[Analyze]

Diagnostic Test

Directions: Write all answers on a separate sheet of paper.

Skill Check A. Write the adjective(s) in the following sentences. Next to each one, write the noun it modifies.

1. Birds live in all parts of the world.
2. There are about 8,700 kinds of birds.
3. Many birds have gorgeous colors or sing sweet songs.
4. The fastest birds can reach speeds of more than 100 miles per hour.
5. Although every bird has wings, not all birds can fly.

Skill Check B. Write the nouns or pronouns used as adjectives in the following sentences. Next to each, write the noun it modifies.

6. Ducks, gulls, and herons are kinds of water birds.
7. Penguins can also be put into this category.
8. Bird-watchers have a special fascination for penguins.
9. Penguins use their wings as flippers when they swim.
10. A penguin's temperature doesn't change, despite its very cold surroundings.

Skill Check C. Copy the sentences below. Underline any compound adjectives, and circle any proper adjectives.

11. Like mammals, birds are warmblooded animals.
12. Some American water birds nest in seacoast habitats.
13. Birds belonging to the waterfowl family live in freshwater areas.
14. Many sandpipers and other arctic birds visit American and Canadian shores while traveling to winter homes in the tropics.
15. Some North American birds migrate to faraway Chile.

Skill Check D. Write the adverb(s) in each sentence below. Next to each, indicate whether it modifies a verb, an adjective, or another adverb.

16. Native Americans were among the very first people in California.
17. They hunted and fished skillfully for much-needed food.
18. Trappers traded with Native American groups for absolutely essential food.
19. Trappers were almost immediately followed to California by settlers from the East.
20. Many settlers traveled quite slowly by wagon to California.

Skill Check E. Label each underlined word *adverb* or *adjective*.

21. The journey was not an <u>easy</u> one.
22. Settlers worked <u>hard</u>.
23. After they had cleared the land, there was more <u>hard</u> work.
24. Settlers who arrived <u>late</u> in the year faced more difficulties.
25. <u>Gradually</u>, towns grew.

Adjectives

Adjectives are used with nouns and pronouns.

▶ **KEY CONCEPT** An **adjective** is used to describe a noun or a pronoun. ■

Using Adjectives as Modifiers

To *modify* means to "change slightly." Adjectives modify nouns and pronouns by slightly changing their meanings. For example, when you hear the noun *house*, a certain picture of a house may come to mind. However, when you say "a small house," "a large wooden house," or "an old white colonial house," the adjectives change the picture slightly.

Adjectives usually answer one of these four questions about the nouns and pronouns they modify: *What kind? Which one? How many? How much?*

What Kind?	
new car	*striped* tie
Which One?	
this swan	*every* page
How Many?	
one hamburger	*many* geese
How Much?	
no food	*little* rain

When adjectives modify nouns, they usually come directly before the nouns. Occasionally, they may come after.

BEFORE: She saw a bright, smiling face.

AFTER: The room, narrow and dark, frightened us.

Adjectives may also modify pronouns. When they do, they usually come after a linking verb. Occasionally, they may come before.

AFTER: They are happy and talkative.

BEFORE: Quiet and sullen, he sat in a corner.

Theme: Birds
· · · · · · · · · · · · · · · · · · · ·
In this section, you will learn how adjectives are used to modify nouns and pronouns. The examples and exercises in this section are about birds that live on or near water.
· · · · · · · · · · · · · · · · · · · ·
Cross-Curricular Connection: Science

 Grammar and Style Tip

The English language is full of descriptive clichés like *busy as a bee.* If you want to be fresh and original in your writing, try to avoid them and find vivid, precise adjectives instead.

Exercise 1 Recognizing Adjectives and the Words They Modify Copy each of the following sentences onto your paper. Draw an arrow pointing from each underlined adjective to the noun or pronoun it modifies.

EXAMPLE: He has not been <u>well</u> for <u>several</u> months.

1. Ducks, geese, and swans are <u>aquatic</u> birds.
2. <u>All</u> waterfowl swim and float.
3. <u>These</u> birds have <u>webbed</u> feet.
4. Ducks are <u>smaller</u> than <u>other</u> waterfowl.
5. A <u>female</u> duck has <u>dull</u> feathers that blend in with <u>her</u> surroundings.
6. <u>Male</u> ducks, also called drakes, are slightly <u>larger</u> than the females and have more <u>colorful</u> feathers.
7. A mallard drake has <u>many</u> <u>green</u> feathers on its head.
8. <u>These</u> <u>colorful</u> birds are often called greenheads.
9. A mallard duck plucks feathers from <u>her</u> <u>own</u> body to build a <u>soft</u>, <u>warm</u> nest.
10. A <u>baby</u> mallard can already swim and feed itself when it is <u>one</u> day old.

More Practice

Grammar Exercise Workbook
• pp. 21–22
On-line Exercise Bank
• Section 16.1
  Go on-line:
  PHSchool.com
  Enter Web Code:
  ebk-7002

▼ Critical Viewing
Think of several adjectives to describe the color, shape, and size of the mallard drakes in the photo. **[Analyze]**

Using Articles

Three common adjectives—*the, a,* and *an*—are known as *articles.* Unlike other adjectives, which may sometimes come after the nouns they modify, articles always come before nouns. Articles answer the question *Which one?*

The article *the* is called the *definite article.*

▶ **KEY CONCEPT** The **definite article** *the* refers to a specific person, place, or thing. ■

The word *the* notes one particular person, place, or thing.

EXAMPLES: *the* canoe

the trumpeter swan

A and *an,* the other two articles, are called *indefinite articles.* These two articles are not as specific as *the.*

▶ **KEY CONCEPT** *A* and *an,* the other two articles, are called **indefinite articles.** They point out a type of person, place, or thing, but they do not refer to a specific one. ■

EXAMPLES: *a* pond (perhaps one of several)

an old sweater (any one of many)

You should also know when to use *a* and when to use *an.* *A* is used before consonant sounds. *An* is used before vowel sounds. Notice that you choose between *a* and *an* based on sound. The letter *h,* a consonant, may sound like either a consonant or a vowel. The letters *o* and *u* are also problems. They are vowels, but they sometimes sound like consonants.

| USING *A* AND *AN* ||
A With Consonant Sounds	*An* With Vowel Sounds
a *y*ellow hat	an *e*ndangered water bird
a *h*appy time (*h* sound)	an *h*onest person
a *o*netime nesting area	(no *h* sound)
(*w* sound)	an *o*ld map (*o* sound)
a *u*nicorn (*y* sound)	an *u*ncle (*u* sound)

More Practice

Grammar Exercise Workbook
• pp. 23–24
On-line Exercise Bank
• Section 16.1
Go on-line:
PHSchool.com
Enter Web Code:
ebk-7002

💡 **Spelling Tip**

Before a word beginning with a consonant, *the* is pronounced "thə" *(the swan).* Before a vowel, *the* is pronounced "thē" *(the only swan).* However it is pronounced, it is always spelled the same way.

▶ **Exercise 2** Distinguishing Between Definite and Indefinite Articles On your paper, write the articles that will complete each of the following sentences correctly. The word in parentheses tells you which kind of article to use.

EXAMPLE: (Definite) ambulance raced up
             (indefinite) one-way street.
ANSWER: The, a

1. (Indefinite) lake is (indefinite) ideal place for swans to live.
2. (Definite) water must not be too deep.
3. Swans must be able to reach (definite) bottom to find food.
4. (Indefinite) lake with gently sloping sides is (definite) best.
5. This allows (definite) birds to get in and out of (definite) water easily.
6. (Definite) plants growing in and around (indefinite) lake are very important to swans.
7. They provide (indefinite) essential supply of nest material and (indefinite) marvelous place to nest.
8. Some types of swans may spend (indefinite) entire year on (definite) same lake.
9. Other swans, especially those living in (indefinite) cold climate, have to leave before (definite) winter sets in.
10. (Definite) following spring, they return to (definite) same lake.

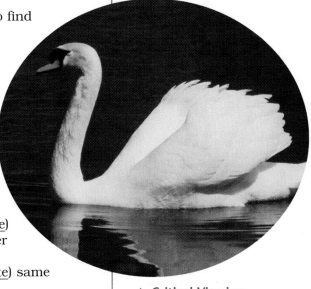

▲ **Critical Viewing** What are some *definite* traits of a swan that make it stand out from other birds? **[Compare and Contrast]**

GRAMMAR IN
LITERATURE

from **The Third Wish**
Joan Aiken

In this excerpt from "The Third Wish," you can see examples of articles (in red) and other adjectives (in blue).

The primroses were just beginning but the trees were still bare, and it was cold; the birds had stopped singing an hour ago.

As Mr. Peters entered a straight, empty stretch of road he seemed to hear a faint crying, and a struggling and thrashing, as if somebody was in trouble far away in the trees.

Adjectives • **339**

Using Nouns as Adjectives

Nouns can sometimes be used as adjectives. A noun used as an adjective usually comes directly before another noun and answers the question *What kind?* or *Which one?*

NOUNS	USED AS ADJECTIVES
shoe	a *shoe* salesperson (*What kind* of salesperson?)
waterfowl	the *waterfowl* refuge (*Which* refuge?)

▶ **Exercise 3** **Identifying Nouns Used as Adjectives** On your paper, write the noun(s) used as an adjective in the following sentences. Next to each adjective, write the noun it modifies.

EXAMPLE: A duck feather floated through the air.
ANSWER: duck (feather)

1. As with other members of the waterfowl family, geese gather in large flocks each autumn.
2. They travel long distances to spend the winter season in warm climates.
3. While migrating, geese often fly in a wedge formation.
4. This V flight pattern helps the birds fly for a greater distance than they could if they traveled alone.
5. It also provides an uplift that helps each flock member more easily overcome any air resistance.
6. When the leader goose tires, it rotates back into the formation and another goose flies to the point position.
7. When the geese honk while flying, they are encouraging the formation leaders to keep up their flight speed.
8. Flocks will return year after year to the same summer home.
9. Wildlife experts have set up refuges in these areas for waterfowl protection.
10. On some refuges, the goose population may increase to half a million birds for short times during migration periods.

▼ **Critical Viewing**
Try to think of at least five phrases in which the word *duck, goose,* or *bird* is used as an adjective—for example, *bird song.* [**Identify**]

Using Proper Adjectives

A *proper adjective* begins with a capital letter. There are two types of proper adjectives:

> **KEY CONCEPT** A **proper adjective** is (1) a proper noun used as an adjective or (2) an adjective formed from a proper noun. ■

A proper noun used as an adjective does *not* change its form. It is merely placed in front of another noun.

PROPER NOUNS	USED AS PROPER ADJECTIVES
Truman	the *Truman* library (*Which* library?)
Florida	*Florida* wetlands (*What kind* of wetlands?)
December	*December* weather (*What kind* of weather?)

When an adjective is formed from a proper noun, the proper noun does change its form.

PROPER NOUNS	PROPER ADJECTIVES FORMED FROM PROPER NOUNS
America	*American* history (*Which kind* of history?)
Victoria	*Victorian* ideas (*What kind* of ideas?)

Text

Get instant feedback! Exercises 3 and 4 are available on-line or on CD-ROM.

> **Exercise 4** Recognizing Proper Adjectives On your paper, write the proper adjective(s) in each of the following sentences. Then, write the noun each proper adjective modifies.

EXAMPLE: An Austrian tourist watched the geese in flight.
ANSWER: Austrian (tourist)

1. Snow geese live in the Arctic region surrounding the North Pole.
2. Some spend winters along the Atlantic coast.
3. The Canada goose is another popular North American bird.
4. It usually lays its eggs during warm March or April days.
5. Some geese gather in winter at California refuges.

> **More Practice**

Grammar Exercise Workbook
• pp. 23–26
On-line Exercise Bank
• Section 16.1
  Go on-line:
  PHSchool.com
  Enter Web Code:
  ebk-7002

Using Compound Adjectives

Adjectives, like nouns, can be compound.

▶ **KEY CONCEPT** A **compound adjective** is made up of more than one word. ■

Most *compound adjectives* are written as hyphenated words. Some are written as combined words, as in "a *runaway* horse." If you are unsure about how to write a compound adjective, look up the word in a dictionary.

HYPHENATED	COMBINED
a *well-known* actress	a *featherweight* boxer
a *full-time* job	a *freshwater* lake

▶ **Exercise 5** Recognizing Compound Adjectives In the following sentences, find the compound adjectives and write them on your paper. Next to each adjective, write the noun it modifies.

EXAMPLE: After the accident, the oil-covered highway slowed traffic for hours.

ANSWER: oil-covered (highway)

1. Ducks, geese, and swans are web-footed birds that come in all sizes, shapes, and colors.
2. The ruddy duck has a broad, fan-shaped tail and a small body.
3. The black-necked swan of South America has a snow-white body.
4. To help in catching fish, merganser ducks have sharp, backward-facing teeth.
5. Pintail ducks are surface-feeding birds, named for their pointed tails and wingtips.
6. The trumpeter swan has a wedge-shaped head and a unique trumpetlike call.
7. The whistling swan has a very high-pitched call.
8. The canvasback duck has high-powered wings, making it among the fastest ducks in North America.
9. During the fall, they migrate from northern lakes and ponds to saltwater marshes and other coastline refuges.
10. Some swans also migrate from freshwater lakes and rivers to seacoast homes.

▶ **More Practice**

Grammar Exercise Workbook
• pp. 25–28
On-line Exercise Bank
• Section 16.1
 Go on-line:
 PHSchool.com
 Enter Web Code:
 ebk-7002

 Text

Get instant feedback! Exercise 5 is available on-line or on CD-ROM.

Using Nouns and Pronouns as Adjectives

▲ Critical Viewing
How do you think
pintail ducks got
their name? [Relate]

KEY CONCEPT A noun or pronoun is used as an adjective if it modifies a noun. ■

EXAMPLES: The <u>duck</u> pond sometimes freezes in winter.
We see the ducklings on <u>this</u> side of the pond.
<u>Which</u> ducks are the males?

In the first example, the noun *duck* functions as an adjective modifying *pond.* In the second example, the demonstrative pronoun *this* modifies *side,* and in the third example, the interrogative pronoun *Which* modifies *ducks.*

Using Possessive Nouns and Pronouns as Adjectives

These personal pronouns are often called *possessive adjectives: my, your, his, her, its, our,* and *their.* They are adjectives because they are used before nouns and answer the question *Which one?* They are pronouns because they have antecedents.

EXAMPLE: The ducks flapped their wings.

Their is an adjective because it modifies *wings.* At the same time, it is a pronoun because it stands for the antecedent *ducks.*
Note About *Possessive Nouns:* Possessive nouns function as adjectives when they modify a noun.

The pond is on Mr. <u>Smith's</u> property.
The <u>duck's</u> feathers are colorful.

Exercise 6 Identifying Possessive Adjectives In each of the following sentences, a possessive adjective is underlined. On your paper, make three columns, as shown in the example. Write the underlined word in the first column. Then, write the noun it modifies in the second column and its antecedent in the third.

EXAMPLE: The puppy was chasing <u>its</u> tail.

ANSWER:

Possessive Adjective	Noun Modified	Antecedent
its	tail	puppy

1. Europeans first spotted hummingbirds during <u>their</u> explorations of the New World.
2. In <u>his</u> diary, Christopher Columbus wrote accounts of hummingbirds.
3. At first, he thought the hummingbird was an insect because of <u>its</u> size.
4. He brought several hummingbirds back to Spain as presents for <u>his</u> patron, Queen Isabella.
5. The queen let them fly free in <u>her</u> garden.
6. My brother and I found an article about hummingbirds in the library in <u>our</u> school.
7. We learned that the hummingbird was hunted because of <u>its</u> colorful skin.
8. Every fashionable European woman wanted to impress <u>her</u> neighbors with objects made of hummingbird skin.
9. To meet the demand, hundreds of thousands of hummingbirds lost <u>their</u> lives.
10. Audubon included several paintings of hummingbirds in <u>his</u> book of art prints.

📺 **Internet Tip**

For interesting Web sites about birds, search using words like *ornithology, avian, birds,* or the names of specific birds in which you are interested. You may also specify regions, such as *birds of Australia.*

▼ **Critical Viewing** What are some special qualities that hummingbirds possess? **[Assess]**

Using Demonstrative Adjectives

This, that, these, and *those*—the four demonstrative pronouns—are often used as demonstrative adjectives.

PRONOUN: We saw *that.*

ADJECTIVE: *That* lake is home to many geese.

PRONOUN: What are *these*?

ADJECTIVE: *These* gulls are searching for food.

Exercise 7 **Recognizing Demonstrative Adjectives** Write the demonstrative pronoun in each of the following sentences. If it is used as a pronoun, write *pronoun.* If it is used as an adjective, write the noun it modifies.

EXAMPLE: I learned that last year.
ANSWER: that (pronoun)

EXAMPLE: I did well on that test.
ANSWER: that (test)

1. Those are yellow-legged gulls gathered on the beach, searching for food.
2. These gulls have dark-yellow legs and a distinctive red spot on their lower jaw.
3. That one is a herring gull.
4. These two types of sea gulls are very similar and are often mistaken for each other.
5. This is how you can tell the difference between the two kinds of gulls.
6. Notice the pinkish-colored legs on these herring gulls and the smaller red spots on their jaws.
7. There are other differences between the two birds besides those.
8. The feathers of this bird are slightly darker than those of the other.
9. These darker feathers belong to the herring gull.
10. Do you think you can remember all of this?

More Practice

Grammar Exercise Workbook
• pp. 29–30
On-line Exercise Bank
• Section 16.1
    Go on-line:
    PHSchool.com
    Enter Web Code:
    ebk-7002

Get instant feedback! Exercises 6 and 7 are available on-line or on CD-ROM.

Using Interrogative Adjectives

Which, what, and *whose*—three of the interrogative pronouns—can be used as *interrogative adjectives.*

PRONOUN: *Which* do you think he will choose?

ADJECTIVE: *Which* parrot do you think he will buy?

PRONOUN: *Whose* can that be?

ADJECTIVE: *Whose* macaw can that be?

▶ **Exercise 8** **Recognizing Interrogative Adjectives** Write the interrogative pronoun in each of the following sentences. If it is used as a pronoun, write *pronoun*. If it is used as an adjective, write the word it modifies.

EXAMPLE: What do you want?
ANSWER: What (pronoun)

EXAMPLE: What words can she speak?
ANSWER: What (words)

1. Which is the most interesting pet to own?
2. What tips should you learn before purchasing a macaw?
3. Which pet shop carries the healthiest macaws?
4. Whose idea was it to come to this pet store?
5. What are we supposed to do to prepare our home for the new parrot?
6. Whose voice does the parrot seem to be imitating?
7. Which are the most unusual sounds that your bird makes?
8. Which brand of food is the most popular?
9. Whose is the best Web site for locating information about macaws?
10. What items did you put inside the parrot's cage?

Learn More

For more practice with pronouns, refer to Chapter 14.

▼ **Critical Viewing**
Which colors can you spot in this macaw's feathers? **[Distinguish]**

Section Review

GRAMMAR EXERCISES 9–15

Exercise 9 Recognizing Adjectives and the Words They Modify Copy each sentence. Draw an arrow from each underlined adjective to the word it modifies.

1. The swan is a graceful water bird.
2. Like geese, swans have a flattened bill.
3. They also have long necks, short tails, and webbed feet.
4. Most swans are larger than ducks.
5. Swans live in mild or cold climates.

Exercise 10 Distinguishing Between Definite and Indefinite Articles Rewrite each sentence, filling in the kind of article indicated in parentheses.

1. Swans nest along (definite) shores of ponds and marshes during summer.
2. Some move to (indefinite) large lake or bay for (definite) winter season.
3. Swans feed mostly on plants that they find under (definite) water.
4. Because of its webbed feet, (indefinite) swan is (indefinite) excellent swimmer.
5. The swan's long neck helps it locate (indefinite) underwater meal.

Exercise 11 Identifying Nouns and Pronouns Used as Adjectives Write the nouns and pronouns used as adjectives and the noun each one modifies.

1. The wings of a duck are small for its body weight.
2. Its rapid wing beat helps a duck to stay airborne.
3. The record speed for a duck is more than 70 miles per hour.
4. What factors affect flight altitude?
5. Weather conditions can affect this altitude.

Exercise 12 Recognizing Proper and Compound Adjectives Write the proper and compound adjectives below and the noun each one modifies.

1. In 1903, the first American wildlife refuge was established.
2. The flamingo once lived in the wild in Florida coastline areas.
3. The flamingos of the Caribbean area have coral-red feathers.
4. South American flamingos have pinkish-white feathers.
5. One group that lives on the African continent has many wingtips.

Exercise 13 Find It in Your Reading Read this sentence from "The Third Wish" by Joan Aiken. List all of the adjectives you find in the sentence.

. . . Then he took her to his house in a remote and lovely valley and showed her all his treasures—the bees in their white hives, the Jersey cows, the hyacinths, the silver candlesticks, the blue cups and the luster bowl for putting primroses in.

Exercise 14 Find It in Your Writing Select a writing sample from your portfolio that contains several different kinds of adjectives. Circle the adjectives, and tell what word each modifies.

Exercise 15 Writing Application Imagine that you live in a house near a shoreline. Write a description of different birds you see when you look out your window. Use several kinds of adjectives in your description. Circle each adjective.

Adverbs

Adverbs can modify three different parts of speech:

▶ **KEY CONCEPT** An **adverb** modifies a verb, an adjective, or another adverb. ■

Although adverbs may modify adjectives and other adverbs, they generally modify verbs.

Using Adverbs That Modify Verbs

An adverb that modifies a verb will answer one of these four questions: *Where? When? In what way? To what extent?*

ADVERBS THAT MODIFY VERBS

Where?	
push *upward* fell *there*	travels *everywhere* go *outside*
When?	
arrived *yesterday* comes *daily*	swims *often* exhibits *yearly*
In What Way?	
works *carefully* speaks *well*	chews *noisily* acted *willingly*
To What Extent?	
hardly ate *really* surprised	*almost* cried *partly* finished

▶ **Exercise 16** Identifying How Adverbs Modify Verbs
Decide which question each underlined adverb answers and write it on your paper: *Where? When? In what way?* or *To what extent?*

1. One of California's main attractions is the coastline, which stretches <u>continuously</u> along the western border of the state.
2. Some people enjoy watching the gray whales as these whales migrate <u>yearly</u> to the California coast.
3. Others <u>intently</u> view the tide pools for hours at a time.
4. The ocean life seems to disappear as the water rushes <u>in</u> and <u>out</u>.
5. The seals <u>calmly</u> sunbathe on some of the rocky cliffs and swim <u>lazily</u> in the ocean waters.

Using Adverbs That Modify Adjectives

An adverb modifying an adjective answers only one question: *To what extent?*

ADVERBS THAT MODIFY ADJECTIVES	
To What Extent?	
very upset	*extremely* tall
definitely wrong	*not* hungry

⚙ **Grammar
and Style Tip**

Adding a descriptive adverb can improve your writing by creating a more vivid picture in the reader's mind.

▷ **Exercise 17** Recognizing Adverbs That Modify Adjectives
On your paper, write the adverb in each of the following sentences. After each adverb, write the adjective it modifies.

EXAMPLE: California is the most productive state for certain crops.

ANSWER: most (productive)

1. California's central valley has soil abundantly rich in nutrients.
2. The state's warm weather allows for an unusually long growing season.
3. Farmers are able to grow many different kinds of fruits and vegetables.
4. The broccoli and spinach that are grown in California are dark green and nutritious.
5. California avocados are tasty, but they have a very high fat content.
6. Grapes and peaches are extremely sweet fruits that many people enjoy.
7. Cantaloupes and honeydew melons are packed in very large containers for shipping to market.
8. Plums and apricots are small fruits, but they have unusually large seeds.
9. The constantly humid weather of southern California is good for growing oranges.
10. California's delicious fruits and vegetables are widely known throughout the world.

▲ Critical Viewing
Use adverbs modifying adjectives to describe how magnificent this coastline is. [Describe]

Using Adverbs
That Modify Other Adverbs

Sometimes, adverbs sharpen the meaning of other adverbs. An adverb modifying another adverb answers one question: *To what extent?* In the following chart, each example contains two adverbs. The first adverb in each modifies the second.

ADVERBS MODIFYING ADVERBS
To What Extent?
moved *very quickly*   *not completely* wrong
climbed *almost over*   *only just* recognizable

▶ **Exercise 18** Recognizing Adverbs That Modify Other Adverbs In each sentence, find the adverb that modifies another adverb by answering the question, *To what extent?* On your paper, write this adverb and the adverb it modifies.

EXAMPLE: The French visitors to California spoke too rapidly for me to understand them.

ANSWER: too (rapidly)

1. Many animals have adapted quite successfully to life in the California desert.
2. The grizzly bear almost entirely disappeared from the state in the 1920's.
3. Cougars and bobcats too greatly populate the foothills and woodlands.
4. They very often prey on herds of deer and other small animals.
5. The mountain lion population has only slightly increased over the past twenty years.
6. Smaller animals—such as marmots, raccoons, and chipmunks—are quite easily spotted in the forest.
7. The golden eagle and bald eagle can be seen soaring extremely high above the trees.
8. Smaller birds can quite frequently be heard chirping their own songs.
9. Reptiles slither rather silently through the underbrush.
10. California most definitely has the largest variety of animals in the United States.

▼ **Critical Viewing** What qualities of the bald eagle earned it the status of national symbol of the United States of America? **[Analyze]**

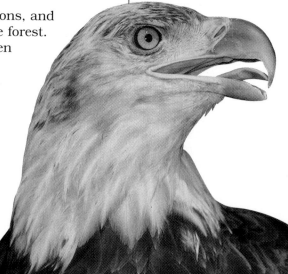

Finding Adverbs in Sentences

The chart below shows examples of possible locations of adverbs. Arrows point to the words that the adverbs modify.

LOCATION OF ADVERBS IN SENTENCES	
Location	**Example**
At the Beginning of a Sentence	*Silently*, she approached the ocean.
At the End of a Sentence	She approached the ocean *silently*.
Before a Verb	She *silently* approached the ocean.
After a Verb	She tiptoed *silently* into the ocean.
Between Parts of a Verb Phrase	She had *silently* entered the ocean.
Before an Adjective	Her father was *always* quiet.
Before Another Adverb	Her father spoke *rather* quietly.

▶ **Exercise 19** Locating Adverbs in Sentences Each of the following sentences contains an adverb. Copy the sentences onto your paper, and underline each adverb. Then, draw arrows pointing from the adverbs to the words they modify.

EXAMPLE: She has <u>never</u> forgotten the tree's

<u>consistently</u> blossoming flowers.

1. Trees have been effectively used for many things.
2. Loggers carefully cut down the necessary trees.
3. Often, the trees are taken to a sawmill.
4. The trees are made into lumber there.
5. This lumber is sometimes used to build homes.

💡 **Spelling Tip**

The adverb *almost* sounds like the two words *all* and *most*. However, when writing it, bring the two words together and drop one of the *l*'s to make the word *almost*.

More Practice

Grammar Exercise Workbook
• pp. 35–36
On-line Exercise Bank
• Section 16.2
Go on-line:
PHSchool.com
Enter Web Code:
ebk-7002

Get instant feedback! Exercises 18 and 19 are available on-line or on CD-ROM.

GRAMMAR IN
LITERATURE

from **The Californian's Tale**
Mark Twain

In the following passage, two adverbs have been highlighted. Although these adverbs end in -ly, it is important to remember that not all adverbs do.

. . . The delight that was in my heart showed in my face, and the man saw it and was pleased; saw it so *plainly* that he answered it as if it had been spoken.

"All her work," he said *caressingly*; "she did it all herself—every bit," and he took the room in with a glance which was full of affectionate worship.

Adverb or Adjective?

Some words can function as adverbs or as adjectives, depending on their use in a sentence. An adjective will modify a noun or pronoun and will answer one of the questions *What kind? Which one? How many?* or *How much?* An adverb will modify a verb, an adjective, or another adverb and will answer one of the questions *Where? When? In what way?* or *To what extent?*

ADVERB MODIFYING VERB: Lumberjacks work *hard.*

ADJECTIVE MODIFYING NOUN: Lumberjacks enjoy *hard* work.

You should know also that while most words ending in *-ly* are adverbs, some are not. Several adjectives also end in *-ly.* These adjectives are formed by adding *-ly* to nouns.

ADJECTIVES WITH -*ly* ENDINGS: A *kingly* feast.
                     A *friendly* person.

> **More Practice**
>
> **Grammar Exercise Workbook**
> • pp. 31–34
> **On-line Exercise Bank**
> • Section 16.2
>   *Go on-line:*
>   PHSchool.com
>   *Enter Web Code:*
>   ebk-7002

> **Exercise 20** Distinguishing Between Adverbs and
Adjectives On your paper, write whether the underlined word
in each sentence is an adverb or an adjective.
> 1. Some fruit trees bloom <u>earlier</u> than others.
> 2. Usually, the blossoms don't last <u>long</u>.
> 3. Sharing the fruit from one's trees is a <u>neighborly</u> gesture.
> 4. In autumn, it seems that the leaves of our oak tree fall
<u>last</u>.
> 5. Squirrels act <u>fast</u> to collect and
store the acorns.
> 6. The Japanese maple is <u>slow</u> to
shed its leaves.
> 7. Its branches spread <u>wide</u>, shad-
ing a large area.
> 8. Another tree with <u>wide</u> branch-
es is the elm.
> 9. The long branches of the willow
tree dip <u>close</u> to the water.
> 10. The seeds of many trees are
carried <u>far</u> away by winds.

▼ Critical Viewing
Use adjectives and
adverbs to describe
the feeling you get
from these trees.
[Relate]

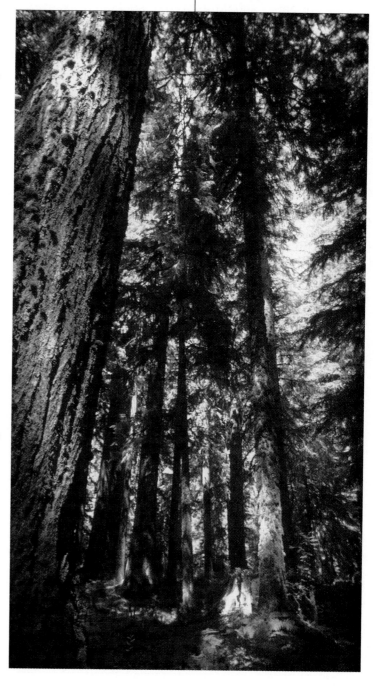

> **Exercise 21** Writing Sentences
With Adjectives and Adverbs Use
each of the following words in two
sentences, first as an adjective
and then as an adverb.
> 1. daily
> 2. hard
> 3. fast
> 4. early
> 5. wide

> **Exercise 22** Revising Sentences
by Adding Adverbs and Adjectives
Revise each sentence about the
photograph by adding adjectives
and adverbs.
> 1. The trees reach into the sky.
> 2. The angle of the photograph
reinforces the size of the trees.
> 3. The trunks are like poles.
> 4. Not much light reaches the
ground.
> 5. The sunlight filters through
the branches.

Hands-on Grammar

Adjective or Adverb?

Create a window frame for sliding word strips, as shown in the model below. Then, create three word strips that are narrow enough to fit through the slots in the frame. One strip of paper should list nouns, such as *avocado, highway, gold,* and *surfer.* The second strip of paper should list verbs, such as *drive, run, eat, speak.* The third strip of paper should list words that you want to test for function. These should be adjectives, adverbs, and modifiers that can function as both adjectives and adverbs, such as *hard, wide, fast, daily.*

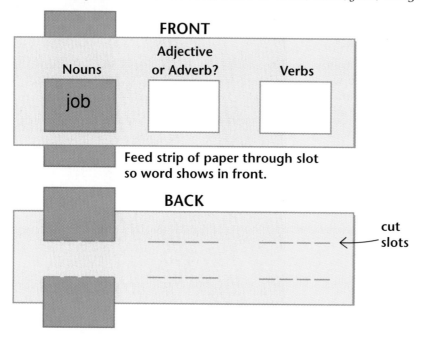

Feed the strips into the slots, as shown in the illustration. Slide each strip to reveal different words. For each combination, decide whether the word in the center window can modify the noun in the left window, the verb in the right window, or both. Tell whether the word functions as an adjective, an adverb, or both. Note that not all word combinations will make sense.

Find It in Your Reading In your reading, find examples of words that can function both as adverbs and as adjectives. Create strips to challenge a partner to identify how these words function when they modify different parts of speech.

Find It in Your Writing Review a piece of writing from your portfolio and identify sentences that could be made more descriptive by adding adjectives and adverbs. Challenge yourself to use colorful, precise words, rather than vague words such as *big* or *very.*

Section Review

GRAMMAR EXERCISES 23–28

> **Exercise 23** Identifying Adverbs
On your paper, write the adverb in each sentence.

1. Lakes and rivers in California frequently attract many tourists.
2. The Sacramento River flows south from Mount Shasta.
3. The San Joaquin and Sacramento rivers have tributaries that mainly drain into the central valley.
4. Dams have been used successfully to create small lakes.
5. These lakes continuously provide recreation such as fishing and boating.

> **Exercise 24** Recognizing Adverbs and the Words They Modify For each of the following sentences, write the adverbs and the part of speech modified.

1. California has extremely varied climates and geographical features.
2. The very active San Andreas Fault runs through northern California.
3. Often, people travel north to see the redwoods.
4. In the northwestern part of the state is the remarkably rugged Sierra Nevada mountain range.
5. To appreciate the best view of the Sierra Nevada, you must get up early.
6. Do you think you will ever visit central California?
7. There, you can sample delicious fruits.
8. Oranges, however, are very widely grown.
9. In southern California, there is too little rainfall to support many crops.
10. We had good weather almost every day.

> **Exercise 25** Distinguishing Between Adverbs and Adjectives On your paper, write whether the underlined word is an adjective or an adverb.

1. We took a long hike through the pine forest.
2. We walked straight down the path.
3. The early morning is the best time to take photographs here.
4. The rangers patrol the area daily.
5. They prepare daily reports on what they find.

> **Exercise 26** Find It in Your Reading Identify at least five adverbs in this excerpt from "The Californian's Tale" by Mark Twain.

Thirty-five years ago I was out prospecting on the Stanislaus, tramping all day long with pick and pan and horn, and washing a hatful of dirt here and there, always expecting to make a rich strike, and never doing it.

> **Exercise 27** Find It in Your Writing Review several pieces of work from your portfolio. Identify the adverbs you have used. Challenge yourself to increase the detail in one piece by adding adverbs.

> **Exercise 28** Writing Application Write a postcard message to someone who lives in another state. Share details about the interests and attractions a tourist in your state might visit. Use adverbs to add details about *when, where, in what way,* and *to what extent.*

Chapter Review

GRAMMAR EXERCISES 29–37

Exercise 29 Recognizing Adjectives and the Words They Modify
On your paper, write the adjective(s) (excluding articles) in each sentence. Then, write the word each one modifies. If the adjective is a proper or compound adjective, label it that way on your paper.

1. A play is a live performance before a real-life audience.
2. The script is the written text that the actors memorize.
3. The director of a Broadway play has a difficult job.
4. The first task of the director is to select the actors for each part.
5. Some roles require an actor to sing and dance.
6. Makeup technique is important in establishing the complete costume of an actor.
7. For many roles, the appearance of the performer is not changed dramatically.
8. In character makeup, however, an actor looks very different.
9. Many United States high schools have some kind of dramatic arts program.
10. A huge hometown crowd turns out for the heartfelt performance.

Exercise 30 Distinguishing Between Definite and Indefinite Articles Write the article(s) that will correctly complete each of the following sentences. The word in parentheses tells you which kind of article to use.

1. Have you purchased (indefinite) ticket for the play yet?
2. (Definite) box office opens again tomorrow at 10:00 A.M.
3. Let's try to sit close to (definite) stage.
4. (Definite) critic gave (definite) play (indefinite) excellent review.
5. She said (definite) acting was superb.

Exercise 31 Writing Sentences With Proper and Compound Adjectives
Write a sentence about each topic below.

1. a Mississippi river town
2. a Broadway play
3. a heartbreaking story
4. a bluish-green dress
5. a hometown picnic
6. European visitors
7. an absent-minded relative
8. snow-covered roads
9. an April rain
10. a Shakespearean comedy

Exercise 32 Identifying Pronouns Used as Adjectives On your paper, write the underlined word in each sentence. If the word functions as a pronoun, label it *PN*. If the word functions as an adjective, label it *ADJ*, and write the word it modifies.

1. My favorite class this semester was drama.
2. It helped me decide to focus my studies on the dramatic arts.
3. Colleges and universities offer many courses in dramatic literature and its history.
4. There are many career options available to those who are interested.
5. What kind of career in the theater sounds most interesting to you?

Exercise 33 Identifying Adverbs and the Words They Modify On your paper, write the adverb in each of the following sentences. After each adverb, write the word it modifies.

1. Local theaters often depend on their own members to do set construction.
2. Sets are frequently constructed from large frames covered with painted canvas.
3. Lighting also helps to create an illusion.
4. Usually, the director, the set designer, and the lighting designer will meet.
5. It is vitally important that the designers and the director understand one another.
6. If many people help, a set can be built very quickly.
7. Painting and sanding are not difficult jobs.
8. Carpentry and electrical wiring of the set are more complicated tasks.
9. Some jobs require highly specialized knowledge.
10. The process of set building is definitely rewarding.

Exercise 34 Distinguishing Between Adjectives and Adverbs On your paper, write whether the underlined word in each sentence functions as an adjective or an adverb.

1. Set building is <u>hard</u> work.
2. We arrive <u>early</u> to begin construction.
3. Everyone is <u>friendly</u>.
4. Everyone works <u>hard</u>, but nobody complains.
5. We do not take a <u>long</u> lunch break.
6. Mary arrived too <u>late</u> for lunch.
7. The <u>early</u> shift is working now.
8. She was sorry to arrive <u>last</u>.
9. She hoped the others had not been waiting <u>long</u>.
10. Usually, Mary is not <u>late</u>.

Exercise 35 Revising Sentences With Adjectives and Adverbs Revise each sentence by adding at least one adjective and one adverb.

1. We were sad about the end of summer.
2. Many people think snails are delicious.
3. The rowboat drifted.
4. I will finish the dishes.
5. The leaves fell.
6. The play had an ending.
7. The trip will be dangerous.
8. My friend has moved.
9. He climbed trees.
10. They brought a list to the market.

Exercise 36 Writing Application Write about a performance you've seen. Use adverbs and adjectives to add details to your writing. Identify the question that each modifier answers. Challenge yourself to add modifiers that answer any remaining questions.

Exercise 37 CUMULATIVE REVIEW Parts of Speech On your paper, write each underlined word. Label each word *noun, pronoun, linking verb,* or *action verb.*

(1) A <u>set designer</u> (2) <u>studies</u> the (3) <u>play</u> before deciding on a set design.(4) <u>Music</u>, doorbells, whistles, and telephones (5) <u>are</u> just a few of the effects for which the sound designer is responsible. The director (6) <u>meets</u> with (7) <u>his</u> or <u>her</u> production team. Then, team members (8) <u>present</u> their ideas to the <u>group</u>. (9) <u>This</u> is an important part of the process, because it allows (10) <u>everyone</u> to share his or her thoughts.

Standardized Test Preparation Workshop

Standard English Usage: Adjectives and Adverbs

Knowing when to use an adverb or adjective is one of the skills measured on standardized tests. When answering a question that tests these skills, read the entire passage first. Then, ask yourself what type of description is needed for a word in the sentence—an adjective will tell *what kind*, *how much*, and *how many*, and an adverb will tell *when*, *where*, or *how*. Then, choose the modifier that will add that information.

The following test item will give you practice with questions that test your ability to choose the correct modifier.

Test Tip

Read through the answer choices and eliminate modifiers that would change the meaning of the sentence.

Sample Test Item

Answers and Explanations

Sample Test Item	Answers and Explanations
Directions Read the passage, and choose the letter of the word or group of words that belongs in each space. When examining the details of some paintings, there is no doubt that the artist's hand moved _____ and deliberately over the canvas, taking time and great care to create a masterpiece.	The correct answer is *B* because the modifier needs to tell how the hand moved. It had to be a modifier that described an action—the adverb *slowly*. Since the movement is described as deliberate, it could not have been done quickly.

1 A slow
   B slowly
   C quick
   D quickly	

▶ **Practice 1** **Directions:** Read the passage, and choose the letter of the word or group of words that belongs in each space.

Artist Mary Cassatt painted __(1)__ renderings of mother and child. Her impressionistic techniques create a __(2)__ soft image that is natural and captures the relationship between mother and child. She studied and worked in France when it was __(3)__ for her to achieve status as a woman artist in America. Her work *The Banjo Lesson* shows a woman playing the banjo with a __(4)__ girl watching __(5)__ over her shoulder.

1 **A** beautiful
　B beautifully
　C artistically
　D beauteously

2 **F** real
　G really
　H perfect
　J reality

3 **A** hardly
　B perfect
　C difficult
　D serious

4 **F** young
　G beautifully
　H youthfully
　J some

5 **A** daily
　B interested
　C intense
　D intently

▶ **Practice 2** **Directions:** Read the passage, and choose the letter of the word or group of words that belongs in each space.

Diana Ong is a pioneer in the __(1)__ field of using computer graphics programs as a medium for fine art. Because painting on a computer __(2)__ translates hand movements on a pressure-sensitive pad into images that seem to appear __(3)__ on screen, Ong says she feels like her ideas travel __(4)__ from her brain to her hand to her computer. She is one of the first __(5)__ artists in this field.

1 **A** artistically
　B back
　C technical
　D technically

2 **F** usually
　G never
　H usual
　J hardly

3 **A** magic
　B magical
　C never
　D magically

4 **F** direction
　G directly
　H really
　J very

5 **A** really
　B major
　C minor
　D male

When you look at the night sky, the moon is *above* your head, *in* the sky. If there is no moonlight, darkness may be all *around* you.

Words like *above, in,* and *around* are called prepositions. Prepositions show relationships between words in a sentence. This chapter will introduce prepositions and show how they are used to relate words to each other.

▲ **Critical Viewing**
Describe the position of the moon in relationship to Earth in this picture. What preposition did you use?
[Describe]

Diagnostic Test

Directions: Write all answers on a separate sheet of paper.

Skill Check A. Identify the preposition(s) in each sentence.
1. The moon and Earth are held together by gravitational pull.
2. The moon moves in an orbit around Earth.
3. From Earth, we see different phases of the moon.
4. These phases occur as the moon moves into Earth's shadow.
5. When the moon moves around Earth, the sun lights the part we see, while Earth shades the part we don't see.

Skill Check B. Identify a compound preposition in each sentence.
6. Out of all the celestial bodies in our solar system, Earth is the only one that has water in three forms: solid, liquid, and gas.
7. Water covers 70 percent of the land on top of Earth's crust.
8. Plants and animals living on Earth recycle water by means of respiration.
9. In addition to the water vapor exhaled through respiration, all the water in living things returns to Earth when the living things die.
10. Rain occurs because of water evaporation and condensation.

Skill Check C. Identify the prepositional phrase(s) in each sentence.
11. The moon has a strong influence on Earth.
12. Tides occur as a result of the moon's effect on Earth.
13. The gravity of the moon pulls Earth's water toward it.
14. The rising of water underneath the moon is called high tide.
15. During high tide, the water level on beaches rises.
16. When Earth rotates on its axis, the waters affected by the moon also change.
17. Any water directly under the moon will be at high tide.
18. However, the moon also creates a high tide on the opposite side of Earth.
19. Water withdraws from spots between the two tidal bulges, creating low tides.
20. There are two high tides and two low tides along the shore every day.

Skill Check D. Write *prep* if the underlined word in each sentence is used as a preposition. Write *adv* if it is being used as an adverb.
21. Have you ever gazed at the moon as you walked <u>about</u> at night?
22. Scientists have different theories <u>about</u> the moon.
23. Some scientists think that the moon once orbited the sun, and Earth attracted the moon when it came <u>near</u>.
24. Others say that the moon and Earth were formed at the same time <u>by</u> the same dust.
25. One thing we do know is that the moon above is the same age as the Earth <u>beneath</u> our feet.

Recognizing Prepositions

Prepositions function as connectors, relating one word to another within a sentence. They allow a speaker or writer to express the link between separate items, such as their relative location or direction.

> **KEY CONCEPT** A **preposition** relates the noun or pronoun following it to another word in the sentence. ■

FIFTY COMMON PREPOSITIONS				
about	behind	during	off	to
above	below	except	on	toward
across	beneath	for	onto	under
after	beside	from	opposite	underneath
against	besides	in	out	until
along	between	inside	outside	up
among	beyond	into	over	upon
around	but	like	past	with
at	by	near	since	within
before	down	of	through	without

Prepositions consisting of more than one word are called *compound prepositions*.

COMPOUND PREPOSITIONS		
according to	by means of	instead of
ahead of	in addition to	next to
aside from	in back of	on account of
as of	in front of	on top of
because of	in place of	out of

Because prepositions have different meanings, using a particular preposition will affect the way other words in a sentence relate to one another. In the following sentence, for example, notice how each preposition changes the relationship between *passed* and *City Hall.*

EXAMPLE: The parade *passed* { near / by / in front of / behind / opposite } *City Hall.*

Theme: Space

In this section, you will learn about prepositions. All the examples and exercises are about space.

Cross-Curricular Connection: Science

▶ **Exercise 1** Identifying Prepositions in Sentences
Identify the preposition(s) in each of the following sentences. Then, rewrite each sentence using a different preposition.

EXAMPLE: The scientist walked around the globe.

ANSWER: around; The scientist walked <u>behind</u> the globe.

1. NASA sent its first satellite beyond Earth's atmosphere.
2. It moved in an orbit around Earth.
3. Scientists gathered measurements of the satellite's orbit.
4. From these measurements, they found that Earth is slightly pear-shaped.
5. The satellite transmitted messages for six years.
6. During that time, it used solar power.
7. Missions to the moon were soon planned.
8. One year later, a Russian probe landed on the moon.
9. *Luna 3* was launched soon afterward, and it took many pictures of the moon.
10. Someday, astronauts may drill into the moon's interior to test its composition.

▲ **Critical Viewing** Which prepositions could be used to talk about the relationship of the clouds to Earth? **[Connect]**

▶ **More Practice**

Grammar Exercise Workbook
• pp. 37–38
On-line Exercise Bank
• Section 17.1
Go on-line:
PHSchool.com
Enter Web Code:
ebk-7002

Complete the exercise on-line! Exercise 1 is available on-line or on CD-ROM.

GRAMMAR IN
LITERATURE

from **All Summer in a Day**
Ray Bradbury

Notice how the highlighted prepositions show the relationships between words in the sentences. Prepositions often show relationships of time or space.

It had been raining *for* seven years; thousands upon thousands *of* days compounded and filled *from* one end *to* the other *with* rain, *with* the drum and gush *of* water, *with* the sweet crystal fall *of* showers and the concussion *of* storms so heavy they were tidal waves come *over* the islands. A thousand forests had been crushed *under* the rain and grown up a thousand times to be crushed again. And this was the way life was forever *on* the planet Venus. . . .

► **Exercise 2** Identifying and Using Compound Prepositions
Identify the compound preposition in each sentence below.
Then, rewrite the sentence using a different compound preposition or a one-word preposition.

EXAMPLE: A cloud passed in front of the moon.

ANSWER: in front of; A cloud passed <u>before</u> the moon.

1. In our solar system, one planet next to Earth is Venus.
2. According to old theories, Venus was much like Earth.
3. However, by means of new technology, we now know that Venus is very different from Earth.
4. For example, on Venus the sun rises in the west instead of in the east.
5. The air is so thick at the surface that humans would need scuba gear in order to breathe.
6. The air pressure next to the surface is twenty-one times greater than that on Earth.
7. In addition to the conditions at the surface, Venus also has three layers of clouds in its atmosphere.
8. These clouds are composed of sulfuric acid instead of water vapor and could quickly destroy a space probe.
9. The clouds at the top of the atmosphere are thin and hazy, and the wind always blows from east to west.
10. Because of the clouds surrounding Venus, its surface can't be seen clearly from space.

► **More Practice**

Grammar Exercise Workbook
• pp. 37–38
On-line Exercise Bank
• Section 17.1
  Go on-line:
  PHSchool.com
  Enter Web Code:
  ebk-7002

ⓘ**Text**

Complete the exercise on-line! Exercise 2 is available on-line or on CD-ROM.

Venus

◄ **Critical Viewing**
Create a sentence about Venus beginning with "In addition to its bright orange color, . . ."
[Relate]

Section 17.1

Section Review

GRAMMAR EXERCISES 3–8

Exercise 3 Identifying Prepositions

Identify the preposition(s) in each sentence below.

1. Neil Armstrong, Michael Collins, and Edwin Aldrin, Jr., rocketed outside Earth's atmosphere on July 16, 1969.
2. They landed on the moon that same week.
3. On July 20, Neil Armstrong stepped out the door of *Apollo 11*.
4. He was the first person in history to walk on the moon.
5. The astronauts collected rocks from the moon.
6. On July 24, they returned to Earth.
7. Since that time, five other ships have carried people to the moon.
8. These flights ended in 1972 with *Apollo 17*.
9. With the information we have collected from the moon, we have answered many questions.
10. We now know that the moon has no life forms of any kind.

Exercise 4 Identifying Compound Prepositions Identify only the compound prepositions in the following sentences.

1. Aside from Jupiter, Saturn is the largest planet.
2. On a solar system chart, it appears in back of Jupiter.
3. It is in front of Uranus.
4. Saturn is easily recognized through a telescope because of its wide rings.
5. In addition to its rings, Saturn also has many moons that orbit it.

Exercise 5 Classifying Prepositions

Copy the following paragraph. Underline the prepositions. Double-underline the compound prepositions.

From Earth, Saturn's rings look like smooth ice. However, according to information gathered by *Pioneer 11*, Saturn's rings include pieces of frozen rock. Instead of solid stationary objects, Saturn's rings are actually millions of tiny orbiting objects. When *Pioneer 11* was above the rings, the radiation readings were high. When it passed through the rings, the radiation readings under the rings were lower than those during takeoff from Earth.

Exercise 6 Find It in Your Reading

Write the prepositions you find in the following excerpt from "All Summer in a Day."

A few cold drops fell on their noses and their cheeks and their mouths. The sun faded behind a stir of mist. A wind blew cool around them. They turned and started to walk back toward the underground house, their hands at their sides, their smiles vanishing away.

Exercise 7 Find It in Your Writing

Look through a sample of your own writing. Identify the prepositions you have used.

Exercise 8 Writing Application

Write a brief description of the scene outside your classroom window. Use prepositions to tell where things are in relation to one another.

Prepositions Used in Sentences

A preposition is never used by itself in a sentence. Instead, it appears as part of a phrase containing one or more other words.

▶ **KEY CONCEPT** A **preposition** in a sentence always introduces a prepositional phrase. ■

Prepositional Phrases

A *prepositional phrase* is a group of words that begins with a preposition and ends with a noun or pronoun. The noun or pronoun following the preposition is the *object of the preposition*.

Some prepositional phrases contain just two words—the preposition and its object. Others are longer because they contain modifiers.

EXAMPLES: from the solar system
            in place of the old, broken antenna

▶ **Exercise 9** Identifying Prepositional Phrases Write the prepositional phrase(s) appearing in each of the following sentences. Underline the preposition. Circle the object of the preposition.

EXAMPLE: The telescope is on the roof.
ANSWER: on the (roof)

1. Mars is the fourth planet from the sun.
2. For 687 Earth days Mars revolves around this giant star.
3. Two moons revolve around the planet.
4. Deimos orbits Mars once in thirty hours, while Phobos orbits in only eight hours.
5. The surface of Mars is red and rusty.
6. Huge dust storms blow across the rocky ground.
7. The dust mixed with the wind makes the air pink.
8. Sometimes the storms can last for several months!
9. The atmosphere on Mars is thin, so asteroids can easily crash into its surface.
10. Because of these crashes, Mars is scarred by craters.

Theme: Space

In this section, you will learn about prepositional phrases. All the examples and exercises tell more about space.

Cross-Curricular Connection: Science

▼ Critical Viewing Which preposition would you use to introduce a phrase about the action of this solar flare? **[Speculate]**

A Solar Flare

Preposition or Adverb?

Some words can be used either as prepositions or as adverbs. When a word is used as a preposition, it begins a prepositional phrase and is followed by the object of the preposition. If the word has no object, it is probably being used as an adverb.

PREPOSITION: The broken panel was *outside* the spacecraft.

ADVERB: The astronauts slowly stepped *outside*.

PREPOSITION: An asteroid belt appears *before* Jupiter.

ADVERB: I had not realized that *before*.

> **Exercise 10** **Distinguishing Between Prepositions and Adverbs** In each of the following pairs of sentences, one sentence contains a word used as a preposition and the other contains the same word used as an adverb. Find the word that appears in both sentences. If the word acts as a preposition, write the prepositional phrase on your paper and underline the preposition. If the word acts as an adverb, write it down and label it *adverb*.

EXAMPLE: The planetarium is down the road.

ANSWER: <u>down</u> the road

EXAMPLE: She examined the rock and then put it down.

ANSWER: down (adverb)

1. Pieces of asteroids that pass through Earth's atmosphere are called meteors.
   They are called meteors only while they are passing through.
2. Once they land on the ground they are called meteorites.
   Eager to examine the meteorite, the scientist switched the electron microscope on.
3. Meteors rain down every day somewhere on Earth.
   Sometimes, people climb down the craters that were created by meteorites.
4. However, most meteorites are so small that a person might walk right by without noticing one.
   Micrometeorites are space-dust particles that have been captured by Earth's magnetic field.
5. Meteor showers are tiny particles a comet leaves behind.
   We watched a recent shower from the field behind our home.

▲ **Critical Viewing**
Create two sentences about this picture. In the first, use *up* as an adverb. In the second, use *up* as a preposition. How are the sentences different? **[Contrast]**

Hands-on Grammar

Preposition Pop-up

Fold a piece of stiff, colored cardboard or paper in half lengthwise. Cut into the fold, about halfway across the folded paper. Unfold the paper, and pop up the cut-out by reversing the fold. This pop-up should create a "shelf" of paper when you leave the paper partly folded. Use a paper fastener to attach a piece of string to the corner of the paper. To the end of the string, attach a paper shape, such as a star. Then, move the star to show the meaning of various prepositions. For example, put the star through the opening, under the shelf, or on the shelf. Record on the paper all the prepositions you can demonstrate with your pop-up.

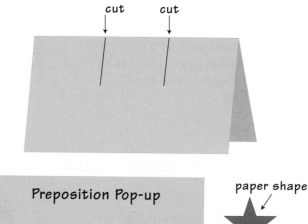

Find It in Your Reading Find examples of prepositions in a short story, novel, or textbook. Challenge yourself to find a way to use pop-ups to illustrate these prepositions.

Find It in Your Writing Look through your portfolio to find at least one use of each of the prepositions you have recorded on your pop-up. For any that you cannot find in your own writing, challenge yourself to add a sentence to your writing, using the preposition. Discuss with a partner what detail was added when you added the prepositional phrase.

Section 17.2

Section Review

GRAMMAR EXERCISES 11–15

Exercise 11 Identifying Prepositional Phrases Identify the prepositional phrase(s) in each sentence.

1. Quasars are the brightest objects in the universe.
2. They occur when two galaxies collide with each other.
3. The collision, however, does not send pieces flying through the universe.
4. Because of the huge amount of empty space in the universe, galaxies can pass through each other.
5. Millions of stars form a galaxy, and between any two stars there are light years of space.
6. When galaxies move near each other, gravity pulls them out of shape.
7. The great arms of the galaxies become twisted.
8. Sometimes, they don't separate from each other.
9. In the center of some large galaxies exists a massive black hole.
10. When one galaxy's gas and dust pass on top of another galaxy's black hole, the matter is sucked into a whirlpool.

Exercise 12 Distinguishing Between Prepositions and Adverbs Label the underlined item a *preposition* or an *adverb*. If it is a preposition, write its object.

1. Black holes are created <u>from</u> giant exploding stars.
2. The matter <u>inside</u> the core is so heavy that it collapses in on itself.
3. Matter that comes close to the hole gets swallowed <u>up</u>.
4. Once it is sucked <u>in</u>, it cannot leave.
5. The black hole closest to us is more than 4,800 light years <u>beyond</u> Earth.

Exercise 13 Find It in Your Reading Identify the prepositions in the following excerpt from "All Summer in a Day." Which word, used as an adverb, could function as a preposition? Which words used as prepositions could also function as adverbs? Explain and give examples.

They walked slowly down the hall in the sound of cold rain. They turned through the doorway to the room in the sound of the storm and thunder. . . . They walked over to the closet door slowly and stood by it.

Behind the closet door was only silence.

They unlocked the door, even more slowly, and let Margot out.

Exercise 14 Find It in Your Writing Review a piece of writing from your portfolio. Underline each prepositional phrase you have used. Circle the preposition. Look for at least two places you can use a prepositional phrase to add detail to your writing.

Exercise 15 Writing Application Write a brief description of the night sky. Underline the prepositional phrases you use in your sentences. Circle the prepositions. Use at least five of the following prepositions in your description.

above	along
beyond	beside
near	opposite
next to	over
between	with

GRAMMAR EXERCISES 16–22

▶ **Exercise 16** **Identifying Prepositions** Find the preposition(s), including compound prepositions, in each sentence.

1. A star can burn for billions of years.
2. Small stars are cooler in the middle, so they burn very slowly.
3. Average-size stars are hotter at the core due to their greater gravity.
4. Some massive stars are so hot they emit light with a bluish color.
5. Their fusion is so intense that giant stars live for only a few million years.
6. According to historians, before 1781, scientists believed there were six planets in our solar system.
7. Then, on March 13, 1781, by means of his telescope, William Herschel saw an unusual star.
8. It moved in a circular orbit next to Saturn.
9. Because of strong evidence gathered by scientists, Uranus was declared a planet.
10. In addition to several moons, the atmosphere of Uranus includes a group of thin black rings.

▶ **Exercise 17** **Identifying Prepositional Phrases** Write the prepositional phrase(s) in each sentence. Underline the preposition and circle the object(s).

1. A comet is a ball of ice and minerals that orbits the sun.
2. When it gets near the sun, some of the comet melts away.
3. When it melts, it leaves gases and dust particles behind it.
4. To us, the particles look like a tail.
5. Because of this activity, comets get smaller each time they go around Earth.

6. Eventually, they melt to the core.
7. Each comet is in a different orbit around Earth.
8. With scientific calculations, we can predict when a comet will come closest to us.
9. In the past, comets were sometimes considered warnings of doom.
10. Some people thought a comet was the soul of a hero on its way to heaven.

▶ **Exercise 18** **Distinguishing Between Prepositions and Adverbs** Label the underlined word a *preposition* or an *adverb*.

1. Except for the sun, Jupiter is the largest celestial body <u>in</u> our solar system.
2. It was named <u>by</u> ancient people after the king of the Roman gods.
3. Jupiter has a faint ring that circles the planet <u>around</u> its equator.
4. Its clouds are so thick they can't be seen <u>through</u>.
5. Storms that do not blow <u>over</u> quickly rage on the planet.
6. One storm, the Great Red Spot, has been blowing <u>on</u> Jupiter for 300 years!
7. <u>Within</u> the thick layer of clouds, temperatures are low, but they are significantly greater near Jupiter's core.
8. Io, a moon of Jupiter, orbits <u>within</u> a magnetic field that surrounds the planet.
9. Io moves <u>through</u> the magnetic current and creates an electrical field that a spaceship could not penetrate.
10. The electrical current is 5 million amperes, while the current <u>inside</u> a 100-watt light bulb is one ampere.

Exercise 19 Classifying Prepositions and Adverbs Label each underlined item a *preposition, compound preposition, prepositional phrase,* or *adverb.*

1. <u>According to</u> scientific measurements, Ganymede is Jupiter's biggest moon.
2. Its craters make it look much <u>like</u> our moon.
3. However, it also has great plates of ice above and a core of molten iron <u>below the surface</u>.
4. The second biggest moon, Callisto, has rings that were raised <u>by shock waves</u>.
5. A large asteroid smashed <u>into</u> the moon and formed a crater.
6. <u>Because of</u> the force of the crash, clouds of steam and water erupted.
7. Europa is almost as large as Earth's moon, and <u>as a result of</u> its moving plates, it has few crater marks.
8. Scientists think that <u>underneath the icy surface</u> there is an ocean of liquid water.
9. They believe there is an active core <u>of rock-metal</u>.
10. The moon Io is approximately the size <u>of our moon</u>.
11. However, <u>instead of</u> a quiet, peaceful surface like our moon, Io has at least ten active volcanoes.
12. Volcanoes blast <u>out</u> enough matter to cover the entire moon every million years.
13. The surface is eroded by radiation from Jupiter, and it is always being struck <u>by lightning arcs</u>.
14. Until a probe passed <u>by</u>, it was believed that Jupiter had only twelve moons.
15. Every year, scientists learn more <u>about the moons</u> of Jupiter.

Exercise 20 Supplying Prepositional Phrases Supply a prepositional phrase to complete each sentence.

1. The moon travels ___?___.
2. Gravity holds the moon ___?___.
3. Life ___?___ would be impossible without the warmth of the sun.
4. Scientists are searching for new galaxies ___?___.
5. Advancements ___?___ have given scientists the ability to search farther than ever before.

Exercise 21 Writing Application Write ten original sentences that include the following items. Underline the required items in each sentence.

1. prepositional phrase starting with the word *over*
2. the word *near* used as an adverb
3. two prepositional phrases, one starting with *in* and the other starting with *out*
4. any compound preposition
5. the compound preposition *because of*
6. two prepositional phrases—one starting with a compound preposition and the other starting with *outside*
7. the word *around* used both as an adverb and as a preposition
8. two prepositional phrases—one starting with *on* and the other with *under*
9. the word *near* used as a preposition and *Saturn* used as the object of the preposition
10. two compound prepositions

Exercise 22 CUMULATIVE REVIEW Nouns, Verbs, Adjectives, and Adverbs Write a sentence using each word as the part of speech indicated in parentheses.

1. test (noun)
2. space (noun)
3. space (adjective)
4. hard (adverb)
5. test (verb)

Standardized Test Preparation Workshop

Using Prepositions

Standardized test questions measure your ability to choose the best way to combine ideas or rewrite sentences. Often, your knowledge of prepositions will help you respond successfully to these items. Before you answer this type of question, first read the entire passage. Then, choose the answer choice that best uses prepositional phrases to connect similar ideas and eliminate unnecessary words.

The following test item will give you practice with questions that measure your ability to use prepositional phrases.

Sample Test Item

Directions Read the passage, and choose the letter of the best way to write the under-lined sentences.

(1) A typewriter has keys. The keys were originally arranged in alphabetical order. Christopher Sholes found that in this arrangement the letters used most kept jamming; he devised a system, still used today, where the letters were arranged according to how often they were used.

1 **A** A typewriter has keys of the alphabet that were originally arranged in alphabetical order.

  B The keys of a typewriter were originally arranged in alphabetical order.

  C The typewriter has keys that are arranged in alphabetical order.

  D A typewriter has keys, and the keys of the typewriter were originally arranged in alphabetical order.

Answer and Explanation

The best answer is *B*. Since both sentences are about typewriter keys, it is logical to combine the repeated information with the prepositional phrase *of a typewriter.*

Practice 1 **Directions:** Read the passage, and choose the letter of the best way to write the underlined sentences.

(1) The 1890s marked the invention of the zipper. Whitcomb Judson thought he had found a winner when he invented the zipper, but he waited nearly thirty years for it to catch on. (2) In 1917, a contract for 10,000 zippers for uniforms helped them gain popularity. The U. S. Navy held the contract.

1 A In the 1890's, the zipper was invented. Whitcomb Judson thought he had found a winner when he invented the zipper, but he waited nearly thirty years for it to catch on.

B In the 1890's, Whitcomb Judson thought he had found a winner when he invented the zipper, but he waited nearly thirty years for it to catch on.

C Whitcomb Judson thought he had found a winner when he invented the zipper, but he waited nearly thirty years in the 1890's for it to catch on.

D Whitcomb Judson thought he had found a winner when he invented the zipper, but he waited nearly thirty years for it to catch on in the 1890's.

2 F In 1917, a contract for 10,000 zippers for uniforms helped them gain popularity with the U. S. Navy.

G With the U.S. Navy, in 1917, a contract for 10,000 zippers for uniforms helped them gain popularity.

H In 1917, a contract for 10,000 zippers for uniforms helped zippers gain popularity. The U. S. Navy held the contract for the 10,000 zippers.

J In 1917, a contract with the U.S. Navy for 10,000 zippers for uniforms helped zippers gain popularity.

Practice 2 **Directions:** Read the passage, and choose the letter of the best way to write the underlined sentences.

The southeast is Brazil's economic heartland. It is home to forty percent of the population. (1) The region has a mostly humid subtropical climate and fertile soil. Farmers can easily grow great quantities of cash crops. The most important crop is coffee. (2) Thousands of people migrated to the southeast region of Brazil. They migrated during the 1800's.

1 A Farmers can easily grow great quantities of cash crops in the region with a humid subtropical climate and fertile soil.

B Because of the region's mostly humid subtropical climate and fertile soil, farmers can easily grow great quantities of cash crops.

C The region has a mostly a humid subtropical climate and fertile soil; according to farmers, they easily grow great quantities of cash crops.

D In the region is mostly a humid subtropical climate and fertile soil. Farmers can easily grow great quantities of cash crops.

2 F By thousands of people migrating to the southeast region of Brazil, they migrated during the 1800's.

G In thousands, people migrated to the southeast region of Brazil. They migrated during the 1800's.

H During the 1800's, thousands of people migrated to the southeast region of Brazil.

J Thousands of people migrated to the southeast region of Brazil, and they did so during the 1800's.

Chapter
18 *Conjunctions* and *Interjections*

A small piece of evidence can aid detectives in making connections that will help them solve a crime. In grammar, small
words called **conjunctions** can aid you in connecting ideas.
Conjunctions can connect individual words and groups of
words, as well as combine sentences.

Interjections are another small part of speech that can add
a special meaning to a sentence. An **interjection** is a part of
speech that expresses feeling or emotion.

▲ **Critical Viewing**
What words might
the detective use to
express surprise,
interest, or shock?
[Analyze]

Diagnostic Test

Directions: Write all answers on a separate sheet of paper.

Skill Check A. Identify the coordinating conjunction in each sentence. Then, tell which words or groups of words each conjunction joins.

1. Police and scientific researchers cooperate to solve mysteries.
2. Fingerprints are gathered at the scene of the crime, and then they must be matched to a suspect.
3. When a suspect is arrested, his or her fingerprints are taken.
4. People have long been aware of the ridges in fingerprints, but fingerprints were not used to solve crimes until the 1880's.
5. Fingerprints are invisible to the naked eye, so detectives dust a surface with a fine powder to make the prints visible.
6. Fingerprints are kept on file, for they might be needed later.
7. There are three basic fingerprint patterns, but these are further broken down into smaller categories.
8. Fingerprinting is fun, yet it can be very messy.
9. You will need a piece of paper and an ink pad to ink your finger.
10. Ink each finger, and press it firmly on the paper.

Skill Check B. Identify the correlative conjunction in each sentence. Then, tell which words or groups of words are connected.

11. Detectives both gather and study fingerprints as clues.
12. Fingerprints are not only different from person to person, but also from finger to finger on the same person.
13. Fingerprints can be removed from either rough surfaces, such as paper, or hard surfaces, such as metal.
14. Both skin oils and dirt on the fingertips make fingerprints.
15. Whether in court or at the crime scene, experts will collect needed evidence.
16. Both the police and the lab scientist must have positive proof before the case goes to court.
17. The test results will either prove or disprove their hypothesis.
18. Neither the prosecution nor the defense will know the decision of the jury until the jury returns to the courtroom.
19. The jury will either acquit or convict the accused, depending on the evidence.
20. The lawyer will try to build a strong case, whether with testimony or with physical evidence.

Skill Check C. Identify the interjections below. Then, tell what emotion is expressed.

21. Huh! There are only three basic fingerprint patterns!
22. Wow! Fingerprinting is exciting.
23. Oops! We didn't think my fingerprints would be seen.
24. Well, when they use a special powder, they can see them.
25. Ugh! How do I get all this fingerprinting ink off my fingers?

Conjunctions

Conjunctions are like links in a chain; they help you join words and ideas. The conjunction you use often indicates the relationship between the words or groups of words connected.

> **KEY CONCEPT** A **conjunction** connects words or groups of words. ∎

Coordinating Conjunctions

A **coordinating conjunction** connects similar words or groups of words. ∎

COORDINATING CONJUNCTIONS						
but	and	nor	for	so	or	yet

The coordinating conjunctions are circled in these examples:

CONNECTING WORDS:
The *pen* (and) *paper* contained fingerprints.
We will *win* (or) *lose* the case.

CONNECTING PREPOSITIONAL PHRASES:
The forensic specialist sprinkled powder *on the doorknob* (and) *along the windowsill.*

CONNECTING TWO CLAUSES:
The expert examined the evidence, (but) *she could not confirm the identity of the burglar.*

> **Exercise 1** Recognizing Coordinating Conjunctions
Identify the coordinating conjunction in each sentence below. Then, tell which words or groups of words are joined by it.

EXAMPLE: He wants a career in medicine or forensic science.

ANSWER: *or* connects *medicine* and *forensic science.*

1. Detectives analyze clues and solve crimes.
2. They gather evidence at the crime scene, but they take it back to the police laboratory for examination.
3. It is a fascinating yet difficult procedure.
4. The analysis must be precise, for if it's not, wrong conclusions could be drawn.
5. The detective must gather evidence carefully, so every clue remains intact.

Theme: Forensics

In this section, you will learn about conjunctions. All the examples, sentences, and questions are about forensics—the use of science to gather and evaluate evidence in a criminal investigation.

Cross-Curricular Connection: Science

> **More Practice**

Grammar Exercise Workbook
• pp. 41–42
On-line Exercise Bank
• Section 18.1
Go on-line:
PHSchool.com
Enter Web Code:
ebk-7002

Get instant feedback! Exercise 1 is available on-line or on CD-ROM.

Correlative Conjunctions

Correlative conjunctions are *pairs* of words that connect similar kinds of words or groups of words.

CORRELATIVE CONJUNCTIONS		
both . . . and	neither . . . nor	whether . . . or
either . . . or	not only . . . but also	

The correlative conjunctions are circled in these examples:

CONNECTING NOUNS: (Either) the small *van* (or) the *bus* will pick us up.

CONNECTING PRONOUNS: (Neither) *he* (nor) *she* is to be blamed.

CONNECTING VERBS: Every morning she (both) *runs* (and) *swims*.

CONNECTING PREPOSITIONAL PHRASES: She'll come—(whether) *by train* (or) *by plane*, I can't say.

CONNECTING TWO CLAUSES: (Not only) *can they sing,* (but) *they can* (also) *tap-dance.*

▼ Critical Viewing
How important are small details that can be seen with this microscope? How important are small words in sentences? **[Connect]**

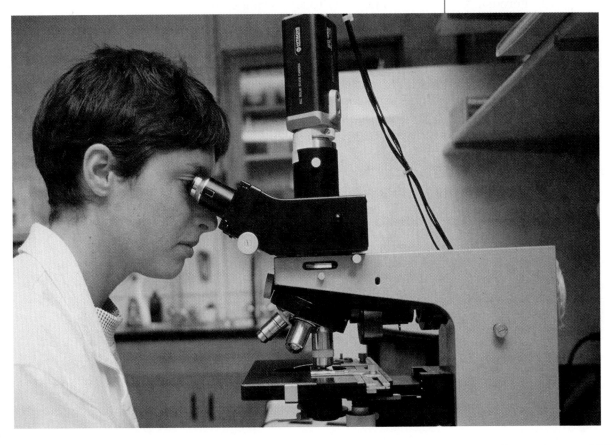

GRAMMAR IN LITERATURE

from **The Dying Detective**
from a story by Sir Arthur Conan Doyle
Michael and Mollie Hardwick

Notice how the author uses one coordinating and *one pair of correlative conjunctions in the passage. The conjunctions are shown in blue italics.*

WATSON. . . . You go along, Mrs. Hudson, *and* leave this to me. *Whether* he likes it *or* not, I shall ensure that everything possible is done.

▶ **Exercise 2** Identifying Correlative Conjunctions Identify the correlative conjunctions in each sentence below. Then, tell which words or groups of words are joined.
1. Forensic science solves not only today's crimes but also past crimes.
2. Old bones can give clues to death by either disease or poison.
3. Whether analyzing an ancient skeleton or studying a more recent one, scientists use the same techniques.
4. Both a comparison microscope and a polarized-light microscope are used to compare evidence.
5. A comparison microscope not only magnifies an object but also gives a side-by-side view.

▶ **Exercise 3** Supplying Correlative Conjunctions Supply the second half of the correlative conjunction in each sentence.
1. The polarized light microscope can show both the shape ___?___ the thickness of a fiber.
2. Often, ___?___ a comparison microscope nor a polarized light microscope gives the whole story.
3. ___?___ in a crime lab or at an archaeological site, a forensic scientist should use the best tools.
4. Working ___?___ together or alone, scientists investigate the evidence.
5. Not only scientists ___?___ detectives work to uncover the facts.

💡 Spelling Tip

When confronted with difficult words, look for smaller words inside larger ones, such as *junction* inside of *conjunction*.

▶ **More Practice**

Grammar Exercise Workbook
• pp. 41–42
On-line Exercise Bank
• Section 18.1
Go on-line:
PHSchool.com
Enter Web Code:
ebk-7002

🛈 Text

Get instant feedback! Exercises 2, 3, and 4 are available on-line or on CD-ROM.

▶ **Exercise 4** Combining Sentences Using Conjunctions

Combine each pair of sentences below using either a coordinating or a correlative conjunction.

EXAMPLE: Mary wanted to be a detective.
Mary wanted to be a doctor.

ANSWER: Mary wanted to be *either* a detective *or* a doctor.

1. Kim had not been to a police lab before. Lashonda had not been to a police lab before.
2. They saw the detectives at work. They saw evidence being examined.
3. They were interested in the work. They did not want to be detectives.
4. The class enjoyed the visit. They wrote a thank-you note.
5. Kim wrote a report about the visit. Lashonda wrote a report about the visit.
6. They didn't just write reports. They gave an oral presentation.
7. Kim wasn't sure that she would give the presentation. She wasn't sure that she would not give the presentation.
8. Kim got a good grade on the presentation. Lashonda got a good grade on the presentation.
9. Lashonda wants to be a veterinarian. She might be a teacher instead.
10. She likes animals. She enjoys working with children.

▲ Critical Viewing
Using a single sentence, describe what two people in this picture are doing. What conjunction did you use? **[Connect]**

Section Review

GRAMMAR EXERCISES 5–10

Exercise 5 Recognizing Conjunctions Copy each sentence onto your paper. Circle the conjunction, and underline the words or groups of words that are joined by it.

1. Neither the judge nor the jury had ever heard of fingerprints before.
2. The lawyer asked the jury whether they believed the finger smudges or the witnesses.
3. Either all the witnesses were lying or this new science of matching fingerprints was pure nonsense.
4. The prosecutor had fifteen people press their index fingers to drinking glasses, and then one of them also pressed a finger on the judge's desk.
5. The prosecutor matched a fingerprint from one of the glasses to the one on the desk, so people were convinced.

Exercise 6 Identifying Types of Conjunctions In each of the following sentences, find the conjunction and label it *coordinating* or *correlative*. If a sentence does not contain a conjunction, write *NC* for "no conjunction."

1. After detectives have evidence and a suspect, the case goes to trial.
2. A trial is the process by which the accused is found guilty or not guilty.
3. The evidence is shown not only to the judge, but also to the jury.
4. The prosecution must prove the case, for the defendant is presumed innocent until proven guilty.
5. The accused's lawyer can question witnesses after the prosecutor presents the evidence to the jury.
6. Whether by argument or by evidence, the lawyer must build a strong case.
7. In one case, witnesses swore that a defendant was at the theater, yet fingerprints at the crime scene were his.
8. Neither his wife nor the other witnesses would change their stories.
9. Either the suspect was lying or the fingerprints were not his.
10. Whether or not he knew it, his fingerprints betrayed him.

Exercise 7 Revision Practice: Sentence Combining Where appropriate, use conjunctions to combine sentences in this paragraph.

An expert was brought in to match the single print on the judge's desk to one of the fifteen on the glasses. The expert matched the one fingerprint to the correct person. He did it in only four minutes. The judge was surprised at this new kind of evidence. The jury was surprised at this new kind of evidence.

Exercise 8 Find It in Your Reading In a chapter in your social studies book, find examples of at least two of the different conjunctions that connect similar words or groups of words.

Exercise 9 Find It in Your Writing Look through examples of your own writing to find conjunctions. Challenge yourself to use conjunctions to combine at least two sentences in one piece of writing.

Exercise 10 Writing Application Write a description of a person you know well. Use conjunctions to combine ideas as you describe his or her personality and qualities. Circle the conjunctions you use.

Interjections

The *interjection* is the part of speech that is used least often.

KEY CONCEPT An **interjection** is an exclamation that expresses feeling or emotion. ∎

In the examples below, the interjections are circled. Notice that interjections are set off by either one or two commas or an exclamation point. Generally, use commas to set off interjections expressing mild emotion, and exclamation points to set off those expressing strong emotion.

SURPRISE: Oh, we did not expect you today.
JOY: Goodness! How good it is to see you!
PAIN: Ouch! He stubbed his toe!
HESITATION: I can't explain, uh, exactly how it happened.
IMPATIENCE: Tsk! I think we've waited long enough.

The following chart lists some common interjections.

INTERJECTIONS			
Wow	Whew	Uh . . .	Well
Hey	Aaack	Er . . .	Huh
Oh	Ugh	Say	Hmmm

Grammar and Style Tip

Interjections are used to express both strong and mild feelings. Use them to help written dialogue sound like real speech.

◀ Critical Viewing
What interjections might someone use when he or she looks through a microscope? **[Speculate]**

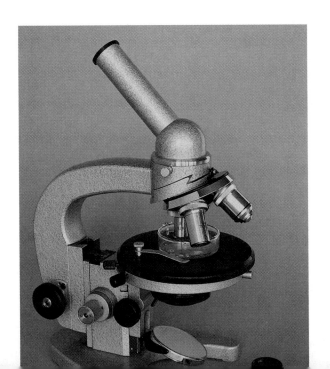

GRAMMAR IN
LITERATURE

from **The Dying Detective**
from a story by Sir Arthur Conan Doyle
Michael and Mollie Hardwick

Sir Arthur Conan Doyle uses an interjection to make his characters' speech sound believable. The interjections are highlighted in blue italics.

WATSON. Holmes? It's I—Watson.

HOLMES. *[Sighs] Ahh*! *Well*, Watson? We . . . we seem to have fallen on evil days.

WATSON. *My dear fellow*!
[*He moves to reach for* HOLMES's pulse.]

HOLMES. *[Urgently] No, no*! Keep back!

WATSON. *Eh*?

▶ **Exercise 11** **Recognizing Interjections** Rewrite each of the following sentences using an appropriate interjection in place of the feeling shown in parentheses. Punctuate each interjection according to the feeling expressed.

EXAMPLE: (Disappointment) we lost again.
ANSWER: Aw, we lost again.

1. (Surprise) I can't believe Lafarge committed the crime!
2. (Hesitation) I know that sounds hard to believe.
3. (Impatience) how did they prove it?
4. (Hesitation) they used toxicology, the science that studies poisons.
5. (Amazement) Marie had no chance of not being convicted!
6. (Interest) do you know a lot about forensics?
7. (Disgust) I think it's a very unpleasant topic.
8. (Surprise) I didn't know you felt that way!
9. (Embarrassment) I'm afraid I'm a little squeamish.
10. (Reassurance) don't be upset. It's nothing to worry about.

▶ **Exercise 12** **Writing Dialogue With Interjections** Recall a memorable conversation you had in the last several days. Capture the conversation in a written dialogue like the one by Conan Doyle. Use at least four interjections.

▶ **More Practice**

Grammar Exercise Workbook
• pp. 43–44
On-line Exercise Bank
• Section 18.2
   Go on-line:
   PHSchool.com
   Enter Web Code:
   ebk-7002

Complete the exercises on-line! Exercises 11 and 12 are available on-line or on CD-ROM.

Hands-on Grammar

Interjections Wheel

Cut two circles from stiff paper or cardboard, approximately four inches in diameter. On one of the circles, write emotions or feelings such as *surprise* or *joy*. Do not limit yourself to the examples shown on this wheel. On the other circle, write interjections that express the emotions you have written on the first circle.

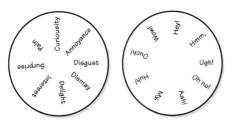

Next, cut two windows in a piece of 6 $\frac{1}{2}$-by-8 $\frac{1}{2}$ inch cardboard. The windows should be large enough so that the words you have written on the circles can fit into them. Label the paper as shown.

Front

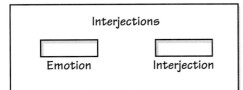

Use paper fasteners to attach the circles to the back of the window sheet. Adjust so that the words show through the windows.

Back

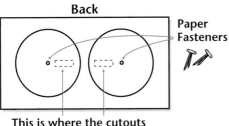

This is where the cutouts are under the circles.

Spin the first wheel to choose an emotion. Spin the other wheel to find the corresponding interjection. Make up a sentence that appropriately uses the interjection to show the emotion. Write the sentence on loose-leaf paper or tell it to a partner. Continue spinning until you have tried all the combinations that make sense.

Front

Find It in Your Reading Find examples of interjections in a story or novel you have recently read.

Find It in Your Writing Find examples of interjections in a narrative you have written. If you cannot find any, challenge yourself to add one or two to the dialogue in the narrative.

Section Review

GRAMMAR EXERCISES 13–18

▶ **Exercise 13** Identifying
Interjections Identify the interjection in each numbered item.

1. Wow! Did you know that there's a machine that can tell whether you are lying?
2. Uh, no, what is it called?
3. Well, it's called a polygraph.
4. Hey, do you want to see one?
5. Gee! I think that would be exciting!
6. Goodness! Do you think they will show us how it works?
7. I can't say. It depends, uh, on how busy they are.
8. Oh, I think it would be interesting to see someone being tested.
9. Um, they won't let you watch.
10. Well, we won't know for certain if we don't ask, so let's go.

▶ **Exercise 14** Supplying
Interjections For each emotion, suggest an interjection that could be used to express that emotion.

1. shock
2. anxiety
3. pride
4. hesitation
5. curiosity
6. joy
7. relief
8. excitement
9. disgust
10. interest

▶ **Exercise 15** Writing With
Interjections Add an interjection to each sentence in the following dialogue. Be sure to use the correct punctuation.

1. ___?___ I just finished *The Dying Detective!*
2. ___?___ did you enjoy it?
3. ___?___ it was one of the best mysteries I've ever read.
4. ___?___ I'm not a mystery fan!

5. ___?___ then you probably wouldn't enjoy it.

▶ **Exercise 16** Find It in Your
Reading Identify examples of interjections in the following dialogue from *The Dying Detective.*

MRS. HUDSON. Well, you know what he is for coming in at all hours. I was just taking my lamp to go to my bed on Wednesday night when I heard a faint knocking at the street door. I . . . I found Mr. Holmes there. He could hardly stand. Just muttered to me to help him up to his bed here, and he's barely spoken since.
WATSON. Dear me!
MRS. HUDSON. Won't take food or drink . . .
WATSON. But, goodness gracious, Mrs. Hudson, why did you not send for another doctor in my absence?
MRS. HUDSON. Oh, I told him straightaway I was going to do that, sir . . .

▶ **Exercise 17** Find It in Your
Writing Revise a piece of dialogue from your own writing by adding interjections.

▶ **Exercise 18** Writing Application
Write ten sentences using the following interjections. Make sure that you capitalize and punctuate correctly.

1. my
2. well
3. oh
4. oops
5. wow
6. whew
7. goodness
8. hurray
9. tsk
10. amazing

Chapter Review

GRAMMAR EXERCISES 19–26

▶ **Exercise 19** Recognizing
Coordinating Conjunctions Identify the
coordinating conjunctions in the following
sentences. Some sentences may contain
more than one.

1. Francisco and Michael had to write a
   report on forensic science, so they
   decided to visit a police lab.
2. They asked the lab assistant to
   explain forensic science and the
   vocabulary that it uses.
3. He told them that a hypothesis is a
   theory based on observed facts and
   that it is used to explain evidence.
4. A hypothesis must be proved or dis-
   proved through laboratory testing.
5. Evidence is gathered at the crime
   scene, but it is examined in the lab.
6. Evidence is anything that can prove
   the guilt or innocence of a suspect.
7. A pathologist is a doctor who special-
   izes in determining the cause of death
   or disease.
8. Toxicology is the science that studies
   poisons and their effects.
9. A polygraph is an instrument that
   measures changes in a person's blood
   pressure, breathing, heartbeat, and
   perspiration while being questioned.
10. Many defendants take a polygraph
    test, yet the results cannot be used as
    evidence in court.

▶ **Exercise 20** Using Coordinating
Conjunctions Identify the coordinating
conjunctions in each sentence. Then, tell
which words or groups of words are joined
by the conjunction.

1. The boys were eager to learn, so they
   asked many questions.
2. They learned about magnifying glasses
   but were more interested in microscopes.
3. They learned that a microscopic look

at cut fibers or other materials can
reveal how the cuts were made.
4. Scientists had known about fingerprints for some time, but it wasn't
   until the late 1800's that police used
   them to solve crimes.
5. There are three basic fingerprint patterns: loop, arch, and whorl.
6. An eyewitness is a person who actually sees a crime happening and can
   give a report of it.
7. It was time for the lab assistant to
   leave, but the boys didn't want to leave.
8. They had learned many new and fascinating things during their visit.
9. The boys asked if they could come
   back, for they wanted to learn more.
10. Francisco wants to study forensic sci-
    ence, yet he knows it will require work.

▶ **Exercise 21** Recognizing
Correlative Conjunctions Write down
the correlative conjunctions and the words
or groups of words they join in each sentence below. Then, circle the conjunctions.

1. Students in Mr. Smith's science class
   were not only assigned to collect samples, but they were also asked to make
   presentations of their experiences.
2. Class members wondered whether they
   would find samples or be disappointed.
3. Their presentations could be either
   oral or written.
4. Both Carlos and Ricardo decided to go
   camping by the lake to gather samples
   for their project.
5. The teacher told them to look not only
   for fossils, but also for arrowheads.
6. They could collect them either separately or as a team.
7. Neither Carlos nor Ricardo had done
   anything like this before.
8. The boys enjoyed not only the camping
   but also the challenge. *(continued)*

Chapter Review Exercises cont'd.

9. Both Margaret and Juanita wanted to go to the mountains for their project.
10. They decided not only to sketch footprints, but also to collect fur samples.

▶ **Exercise 22** Classifying Conjunctions Identify the conjunctions you find in the paragraph. Then, tell whether each conjunction is *coordinating* or *correlative*.

[1] We can learn about past civilizations from studying their burial sites and dwellings. [2] Archaeologists study the remains of ancient human life and collect various samples as well. [3] They specialize not only in finding clues but also in putting the clues together. [4] Using the clues available, archaeologists determine how people lived, whether by hunting or by farming. [5] A stone ax or an arrowhead can provide valuable information. [6] Artifacts—such as a basket full of seeds, a wooden post, or the bones of animals—help the scientists learn something about the physical environment. [7] Both archaeologists and historians work together to create a picture of the past. [8] Historians study writings, and archaeologists study physical remains. [9] Around 1770, Thomas Jefferson uncovered an Indian burial mound and carefully wrote down what was contained in the mound. [10] Not only did he list the items he took from the mound, but he also noted the order in which they were found.

▶ **Exercise 23** Identifying Conjunctions and Interjections Identify the conjunctions and interjections in the following excerpt from *The Dying Detective*.

WATSON. . . . You're sick and as helpless as a child. Whether you like it or not, I'm going to examine you and treat you.
HOLMES. *[Sneering]* If I'm to be forced to

have a doctor, let him at least be someone I've some confidence in.
WATSON. Oh! You . . . After all these years, Holmes, you haven't . . . confidence in me?

▶ **Exercise 24** Supplying Interjections Supply an interjection to complete each sentence.

1. ___?___, forensic science is interesting!
2. ___?___! Did you see that fiber under the microscope?
3. ___?___, it really looks strange.
4. ___?___, my eyes are getting tired from looking through the microscope.
5. ___?___! How do scientists do this hour after hour every day?

▶ **Exercise 25** Using Conjunctions and Interjections Supply a conjunction or an interjection to complete each sentence.

1. Juanita wanted to know ___?___ she should make the plaster casts or collect the fur samples.
2. Their teacher told them to collect their samples ___?___ in the early morning or in the late evening.
3. ___?___ This is an interesting project.
4. ___?___ I think I hear a snake!
5. ___?___ did their class learn from this experience, but they also had fun.

▶ **Exercise 26** Writing Application Write a comparison of two things. Circle the conjunctions you used to connect words and ideas.

Standardized Test Preparation Workshop

Standard English Usage: Conjunctions

Some standardized test questions are designed to measure your mastery of the conventions of English, including the proper use of conjunctions.

The following test item will give you practice in answering these types of questions.

Sample Test Item

Directions Read the passage, and choose the letter of the best word or words to complete the sentence.

Sculptor Henry Moore was inspired not only by unusual pebbles, _____ by unusual shells.
  A and also
  B but also
  C and
  D yet

Answer and Explanation

The best answer is *B*. The words *but also* complete the correlative conjunction begun with *not only*.

▶ **Practice** **Directions** Read the passage, and choose the letter of the best word or words to complete the sentence.

1 Moore was a great sketch artist _____ he is best known for his sculptures.
  A so
  B and
  C yet
  D but also

2 His sculptures _____ drawings can be seen in museums.
  F yet
  G so
  H and
  J but also

3 He enjoyed nature,_____ he spent much of his time outside.
  A or
  B so
  C whether
  D but also

4 He is known not only for his sketches _____ for his sculpture.
  F yet
  G so
  H and
  J but also

Cumulative Review

PARTS OF SPEECH

▶ **Exercise A** Classifying Nouns
Identify the underlined nouns in the following sentences as *collective, compound, common* or *proper,* and *singular or plural.*

1. The Milky Way is one of several hundred million galaxies.
2. The sun, the closest star to the Earth, is a typical star.
3. Supergiants are the largest known stars.
4. A committee of astronomers gave numbers to some stars.
5. In the second century A.D., Ptolemy compiled the first catalog of stars.

▶ **Exercise B** Classifying Pronouns
Label the underlined pronouns in the following sentences *personal, demonstrative, interrogative, indefinite,* and *singular or plural.*

1. Who designated stars by Greek letters?
2. Johann Bayer listed them in a star atlas in 1603; it included many that Ptolemy had not cataloged.
3. John Flamsteed listed these stars according to their constellations.
4. Most of our modern catalogs are not like those used earlier; instead, they use copies of photographs.
5. Which of the charts includes the southern sky?

▶ **Exercise C** Recognizing and Classifying Verbs Write the verbs in the following sentences. Label each *action* or *linking.* Include and identify all helping verbs. Classify action verbs as *transitive* or *intransitive.*

1. Many stars vary their brightness when they expand and contract.
2. They can become very brilliant and then fade within days.
3. Some stars' cycles will last for years.
4. Most variations in brightness may be invisible to the human eye.
5. Scientists say that even the sun has a cycle of brightness.

▶ **Exercise D** Recognizing Adjectives and Adverbs Label the underlined words in the following sentences *adjectives* or *adverbs.* Then, write the word each modifies.

1. The star called Rigel in the constellation Orion has a bluish-white tint.
2. Orion is located almost squarely on the celestial equator.
3. The stars form a picture of Orion, a hunter from Greek mythology.
4. He is standing with an uplifted club.
5. Three bright stars accurately represent his belt.
6. To the south, three fainter stars form his sword.
7. Another constellation, Pleiades, is a loose group of almost 3,000 stars.
8. The cluster was initially named by the Greeks after the mythological "Seven Sisters."
9. Observers can sometimes see up to twelve of the stars without a telescope.
10. Pleiades lies 375 light-years from our solar system.

▶ **Exercise E** Recognizing Prepositions Write the prepositions in the following sentences, and then write the object of the preposition.

1. Tycho Brahe, a Danish astronomer, made measurements of the solar system.

2. This data was the most reliable until the invention of the telescope in the seventeenth century.
3. Brahe studied law and philosophy at universities in Copenhagen and Leipzig.
4. At night, he was busy with his observations of the stars.
5. Johannes Kepler, his assistant until 1601, used Brahe's data to formulate his three laws of planetary motion.

▶ **Exercise F** Identifying Conjunctions Write the conjunctions in the following sentences and label them *coordinating* or *correlative.*

1. Both North Star and Pole Star are names for the star that roughly marks the direction of the North Pole.
2. Pole Star has been used by sailors, for they needed to find their direction when sailing at night.
3. It is used today for determining latitudes and other measurements.
4. Not only is Polaris the current North Star, but it also is part of the Little Dipper constellation.
5. Polaris is very accurate, but in the future, other stars will point more accurately to the North Pole.

▶ **Exercise G** Recognizing Interjections Write an interjection that replaces the feeling shown in parentheses in the following sentences.

1. __(surprise)__! Did you see that meteor shower last night?
2. __(hesitation)__, I wasn't sure what that was.
3. __(disappointment)__, did that happen while I was sleeping?
4. __(amazement)__! I couldn't believe my eyes.
5. __(agreement)__, it is a natural event.

▶ **Exercise H** Identifying All the Parts of Speech Write the part of speech of the underlined words in the following paragraph. Be as specific as possible.

These large comets <u>were</u> first <u>explained</u> by Tycho Brahe. Sir Isaac Newton and <u>Edmund Halley</u> made important observations about comets. The <u>American</u> astronomer Fred Whipple first described comets as a "dirty <u>snowball</u>," a combination of ice and dust. <u>Gee,</u> that doesn't sound very scientific, <u>but</u> it is true. <u>Many</u> of the different comets pass by the Earth. Some are <u>easily</u> visible to the human eye.

▶ **Exercise I** Revising Sentences Revise each sentence according to the directions in parentheses.

1. Halley's Comet is a famous comet. (Add an adverb that modifies *famous.*)
2. Halley's Comet was discovered by Edmond Halley. (Replace *Halley's Comet* with a pronoun.)
3. Before he made his discovery, people believed that comets traveled at random, with no set path. (Replace *he* with a proper noun.)
4. Halley believed, however, that comets traveled regular patterns. (Add a preposition before *regular.*)
5. Halley's Comet takes a time—approximately seventy-seven years—to travel its orbit. (Add an adjective to modify *time* and another adjective to modify *orbit.*)

▶ **Exercise J** Writing Application Write a short narrative about a trip into outer space. Underline at least one noun, pronoun, verb, adjective, adverb, preposition, conjunction, and interjection. Then, label the part of speech of each as specifically as possible.

Basic Sentence Parts

The eight parts of speech are the building blocks of language. Whenever you speak and write, you use these basic units to express ideas. Patterns of words that communicate ideas are called *sentences.*

Not every pattern of words is a sentence. For example, the pattern "Fed Jana cat her" is not a sentence because it does not communicate an idea. The same words in a different pattern can form a sentence when you say, "Jana fed her cat."

This chapter will introduce you to the basic sentence parts and describe how nouns, pronouns, verbs, and adjectives play key roles in sentences.

▲ **Critical Viewing**
In two complete sentences, describe the shape of the cat's eyes and the feel of its fur. **[Analyze]**

Diagnostic Test

Directions: Write all answers on a separate sheet of paper.

Skill Check A. Copy each of the following sentences onto your paper. Underline the subject once and the verb twice. Then, draw a vertical line between the complete subject and the complete predicate.

1. Cats make excellent pets.
2. Responsible owners train their cats methodically.
3. The manx is an interesting breed.
4. My sister and I enjoy going to cat shows.
5. The wide variety of cats intrigues and entertains us.

Skill Check B. On your paper, write *sentence* for each group of words below that is a sentence. Write *incomplete* for each group of words below that is not a sentence.

6. Running along the shelf.
7. Although my cat is playful.
8. Since we spend so much time with her and enjoy her company.
9. She plays.
10. Her many playful qualities are charming.

Skill Check C. Each of the following sentences contains a compound subject, a compound verb, or both. On your paper, write the compound subjects and the compound verbs. Label each one a *compound subject* or a *compound verb*.

11. Dogs and cats sometimes fight.
12. Playful cats chase any small moving object and trap it.
13. Adult cats and kittens play together and wrestle with old socks.
14. Hungry cats stand in the kitchen and meow.
15. The gray kitten and its striped mother licked their paws and cleaned their faces.

Skill Check D. Copy each of the following sentences onto your paper. Label the direct objects *DO*, the indirect objects *IO*, the adverbs *ADV*, the prepositions *PREP*, and the objects of prepositions *OP*.

16. Scientists study the leopards, lions, and cheetahs of Africa.
17. These powerful predators fascinate them.
18. Which cats will you study during the next six months?
19. Send me a pamphlet about cats soon.
20. I will also access information about them on the Internet.

Skill Check E. In the following sentences, label the predicate nouns *PN*, the predicate pronouns *PP*, and the predicate adjectives *PA*.

21. The cougar is dangerous.
22. Purring leopards may seem gentle to zoo visitors.
23. Mrs. Gunderson is one of the zoo's animal handlers.
24. It is she who teaches many of the classes.
25. The facility is highly respected and a model for other zoos and wildlife centers.

The Basic Sentence

In order to be considered complete sentences, all sentences must have two things: a subject and a verb.

The Two Basic Parts of a Sentence

Every sentence, regardless of its length, must have a subject and a verb.

▶ **KEY CONCEPT** A **sentence** contains a subject and a verb and expresses a complete thought. ■

The Subject A sentence must have a *subject*. Subjects are usually found at or near the beginning of a sentence. Most subjects are nouns or pronouns.

▶ **KEY CONCEPT** The **subject** of a sentence is the word or group of words that names the person, place, or thing that performs the action or is described. ■

In the following examples, each subject is underlined.

EXAMPLES: The <u>cat</u> is hungry.
<u>Mrs. Meow</u> broke her dish.
<u>She</u> knows several tricks.

The noun *cat* is the subject in the first sentence. It tells *what* is hungry. In the next sentence, *Mrs. Meow* tells *who* broke her dish. The pronoun *she* in the third sentence also tells *who: Who* knows several tricks? *She* knows.

The Verb As one of the basic parts of a sentence, the verb tells something about a subject.

▶ **KEY CONCEPT** The **verb** in a sentence tells what the subject does, what is done to the subject, or what the condition of the subject is. ■

In the following examples, the verbs are underlined twice.

EXAMPLES: My cat <u>won</u> a ribbon.
The award <u>was given</u> in a big ceremony.
He <u>seems</u> tired now.

Won tells what *my cat* did. *Was given* explains what was done with *award. Seems,* a linking verb, tells something about the condition of *he* by linking the subject to *tired.*

Theme: Cats

In this section, you will learn about subjects and verbs and how sentences form complete thoughts. The examples and exercises in this section are about domestic and wild cats.

Cross-Curricular Connection: Science

▶ **Exercise 1** Identifying Subjects and Verbs Copy each of the following sentences onto your paper. Underline the subject once and the verb twice.

EXAMPLE: The tiny <u>kitten</u> <u>cries</u> for its mother.

1. Cat associations sponsor cat shows.
2. These events attract many cat lovers.
3. Many owners exhibit their cats.
4. Hundreds of cats compete for a small number of prizes.
5. Many expert judges are at the show.
6. Each judge works independently.
7. Each association has its own set of rules.
8. Awards are given to ten winners in each category.
9. The event lasts all day.
10. Winners receive large ribbons.

Using Subjects and Verbs to Express Complete Thoughts

Every basic sentence must express a complete thought.

▶ **KEY CONCEPT** A group of words with a subject and a verb expresses a complete thought if it can stand by itself and still make sense. ■

COMPLETE THOUGHT: The <u>kitten</u> <u>sleeps</u> in the basket.

This example is a complete sentence because it expresses a *complete thought*.

INCOMPLETE THOUGHT: In the basket in the hall.

This incomplete thought contains two prepositional phrases. In this case, the phrases can become a sentence only after *both* a subject and a verb are added to them.

COMPLETE THOUGHT: The kittens are in the basket in the hall.

With a subject and a verb, this group of words makes sense. It can stand by itself as a sentence.

In grammar, incomplete thoughts are often called *fragments*.

More Practice

Grammar Exercise Workbook
• pp. 45–46
On-line Exercise Bank
• Section 19.1
 Go on-line:
 PHSchool.com
 Enter Web Code:
 ebk-7002

Get instant feedback! Exercise 1 is available on-line or on CD-ROM.

▼ Critical Viewing
What is the subject of this picture? What verb could you use with that subject to express a complete thought about the picture? [**Analyze**]

The Basic Sentence • **393**

▶ **Exercise 2** Correcting Incomplete Thoughts None of the following groups of words expresses a complete thought. On your paper, correct each one by adding the punctuation and words needed to make a basic sentence. Each group of words may come at the beginning, middle, or end of the sentence.

EXAMPLE: the sailors on the ship
ANSWER: The sailors on the ship found a stowaway cat.

1. a pride of lions
2. called a litter
3. playfully pouncing on each other
4. a large, beautiful mane
5. run very fast
6. no longer kept in cages
7. enjoy natural habitats
8. monorails through some large animal parks
9. lions basking in the sun
10. photographing the animals

▶ **Exercise 3** Recognizing Sentences Some of the numbered items below are sentences; the others are incomplete thoughts. If a group of words is a sentence, write *sentence* on your paper. If a group of words expresses an incomplete thought, add the words needed to make a sentence. Underline the subject once and the verb twice in each new sentence.

EXAMPLE: The kittens in the woodpile.
ANSWER: The kittens hid in the woodpile.

1. Cats have soft paws and sharp claws.
2. The cat's long whiskers.
3. The body of a cat is more flexible than a dog's.
4. Grooms its fur.
5. Cats purr.
6. Remarkable night vision.
7. Popular household pets.
8. A litter of kittens.
9. Chases a ball.
10. Finding warm places, cats sleep.

More Practice
Grammar Exercise Workbook
• pp. 45–46
On-line Exercise Bank
• Section 19.1
Go on-line:
PHSchool.com
Enter Web Code:
ebk-7002

Text

Complete the exercises on-line! Exercises 2 and 3 are available on-line or on CD-ROM.

Section Review

GRAMMAR EXERCISES 4–9

Exercise 4 Recognizing Subjects and Verbs Copy each of the following sentences onto your paper. Underline the subject once and the verb twice.

1. The lion has a most distinctive face.
2. One can distinguish the male lion from the female lion by the male's mane.
3. The mane makes the male lion appear more threatening.
4. Only mature males develop manes.
5. The lion's frightening roar adds to its fierce presence.
6. Lions are highly social animals.
7. They live in groups known as prides.
8. Unlike most other cats, lions hunt their prey in groups.
9. Many other animals try to run from lions.
10. Lions are counted among the animal kingdom's mightiest hunters.

Exercise 5 Correcting Incomplete Thoughts Rewrite the numbered items below, adding any words needed to make each fragment a complete sentence.

1. bring companionship to their owners
2. all young cats that like to play
3. live for ten to twenty years
4. although indoor cats may be healthy
5. spend much time hunting for food

Exercise 6 Proofreading for Complete Sentences If a group of words in the following list is a sentence, write *sentence* on your paper. If a group of words expresses an incomplete thought, add the words needed to make a sentence. Underline the subject once and the verb twice.

1. Cats depend on their highly developed senses.

2. Excellent sense of smell.
3 They see well.
4. Can see better at night.
5. Their padded paws make it possible to surprise their quarry.
6. Rely on their acute hearing.
7. Detects high-pitched sounds.
8. Its funnellike outer ears.
9. Their ears aid cats' survival.
10. Hearing loss could put a cat at risk.

Exercise 7 Find It in Your Reading Tell whether each underlined section of this excerpt from "Cat on the Go" expresses a complete thought.

(1) The upturned face had an anxious look. (2) I went down the long flights of steps two at a time (3) and when I arrived slightly breathless on the ground floor (4) Tristan beckoned me through (5) to the consulting room at the back of the house.

Exercise 8 Find It in Your Writing Choose a piece from your writing portfolio. Underline each subject once and each verb twice in the sentences of the first paragraph. Note that some sentences may have more than one subject and verb.

Exercise 9 Writing Application Write a description of an animal. When you are finished, underline the subject once and the verb twice in each sentence. Proofread your paper to eliminate any fragments by adding words to the sentence or connecting the group of words to another sentence. Some of your sentences may have more than one subject and verb.

Complete Subjects and Predicates

Have you ever seen tiles laid on a floor? First, a line is drawn down the center of the room. One tile is placed to the left of the line, and another is placed to the right. Then, more tiles are added in the same way: one to the left, and one to the right.

Imagine that the first tile on the left is a subject and the first tile on the right is a verb. You would then have a subject and a verb separated by a vertical line, as shown in the example:

EXAMPLE: <u>Fur</u> | <u>flew</u>.

Now, in the same way that you would add a few more tiles if you were tiling a floor, add a few more words:

EXAMPLE: <u>Ginger fur</u> | <u>flew through the air.</u>

At this point, you could add still more words:

EXAMPLE: <u>Oscar's ginger fur</u> | <u>flew through the air.</u>

The center line is important in laying tiles. It is just as important in dividing a sentence into two parts. All the words to the left of the line in the preceding examples are part of the *complete subject.* (The main noun in the complete subject, *fur,* is often called the *simple subject.*)

▶ **KEY CONCEPT** The **complete subject** of a sentence consists of the subject and any words related to it. ■

As the examples above show, the complete subject may be just one word—*fur*—or several words—*Oscar's ginger fur.*

All the words to the right of the line in the preceding examples are part of the *complete predicate.* (The verb *flew,* or a verb phrase such as *had flown,* on the other hand, is often called the *simple predicate.*)

▶ **KEY CONCEPT** The **complete predicate** of a sentence consists of the verb and any words related to it. ■

As the examples show, a complete predicate may be just the verb itself or the verb and several other words.

Theme: Cats

In this section, you will learn about complete subjects and predicates. The examples and exercises in this section are about cats in different parts of the world.

Cross-Curricular Connection: Science

(?) **Learn More**

To review verbs, see Chapter 15.

GRAMMAR IN LITERATURE

from **Cat on the Go**
James Herriot

In the following excerpt from James Herriot's "Cat on the Go," the complete subjects are underlined once, the complete predicates twice. The simple subjects are shown in blue; the verbs are shown in red.

He walked over and opened the door and our Oscar strode in with all his old grace and majesty. He took one look at Helen and leaped onto her lap. With a cry of delight she put down her cup and stroked the beautiful fur.

> **More Practice**

Grammar Exercise Workbook
• pp. 47–48
On-line Exercise Bank
• Section 19.2
   Go on-line:
   PHSchool.com
   Enter Web Code:
   ebk-7002

Text

Get instant feedback! Exercise 10 is available on-line or on CD-ROM.

> **Exercise 10** Recognizing Complete Subjects and Complete Predicates Copy each of the following sentences onto your paper. Underline the simple subject once and the verb twice. Then, draw a vertical line between the complete subject and the complete predicate.

EXAMPLE: The cat with the blue eyes | is a Siamese.

1. Cats have become very popular house pets over the years.
2. Leonardo da Vinci included cats in his work.
3. Several popular comic strips feature feline characters.
4. The first domestic cats in North America arrived with the colonists.
5. At one time, some people in Thailand and China worshiped cats as deities.
6. *Alice's Adventures in Wonderland* introduced the Cheshire cat.
7. Cat lovers of all ages collect cats of all kinds.
8. Phoenician sailors traded cats for other treasures.
9. The Renaissance was the golden age of cats.
10. Images of cats appeared on many Greek coins in the fifth century.

▼ Critical Viewing *Kitten waits.* Add details to this simple subject and verb to form a sentence about *why* or *for what* the kitten waits. **[Draw Conclusions]**

Hands-on Grammar

Sentence Part Flip Book

To explore the way subjects and predicates function, create a sentence parts flip book. Alone or with a partner, create two sets of index cards. On the first set, write the part of a sentence that tells the person, place, or thing that does the action, including all the adjectives, adverbs, phrases, and clauses that rename or describe the noun.

EXAMPLE: The cat with the orange stripe on its head

On the second set of cards, write actions or conditions.

EXAMPLE: wants us to feed it.

After you have created six or seven cards for each set, label a long, narrow strip of posterboard as shown.

Use a hole punch to put a hole in the top center of each card. Use a paper fastener to attach each set to the appropriate end of the posterboard strip. Attach the cards loosely enough so that you can swivel each card away to reveal the card beneath. Experiment with different combinations of cards to create different sentences with different complete subjects and complete predicates. If you used a wide variety of nouns, verbs, and modifiers, some of your sentences should be very humorous. No matter how silly the sentence, the subject indicates the doer of the action. The complete subject can contain a verb, as long as the verb is not the main action being performed by the subject in the sentence.

Find It in Your Reading Choose several sentences from a short story, and add them to your flip book. You may need to reorder some words to get all the words of the complete predicate on one card.

Find It in Your Writing Review your portfolio, and choose several sentences to add to the flip book. If necessary, reorder the words to get all the words of the complete predicate on one card.

Section 19.2 **Section Review**

GRAMMAR EXERCISES 11–15

Exercise 11 Identifying Complete Subjects and Predicates Copy each of the following sentences onto your paper. Underline the subject once and the verb twice. Then, draw a vertical line between the complete subject and the complete predicate.

1. Leopards are members of the family of big cats.
2. The Latin name for the cat family is *Felidae.*
3. *Panthera pardus* is the Latin name for the leopard.
4. Leopards are good tree climbers.
5. They may be found in Africa and Asia.
6. The habitat of the Amur leopard is found in Korea.
7. The leopard's body is specifically designed to survive cold winters.
8. Its pale or yellowish-brown coat features widely spaced dark brown spots.
9. Its fur changes from a deep reddish yellow in the summer to a lighter shade in the winter.
10. An average adult female weighs from 62 to 132 pounds.

Exercise 12 Writing Sentences With Complete Subjects and Predicates Develop each item into a complete subject and predicate by adding details to the subject and verb. The first word of each of the following pairs is a noun that can be used as a subject. The second word is a verb.

	NOUN	VERB
1.	leopard	raced
2.	cougar	climbed
3.	cat	grooms
4.	antelope	escaped
5.	speed	helped

Exercise 13 Find It in Your Reading Rewrite each underlined section of this excerpt from James Herriot's "Cat on the Go." Then, draw a vertical line between the complete subject and the complete predicate. Finally, underline the simple subject once and the simple verb twice.

In this passage, the veterinarian Herriot and one of his partners struggle to save a cat's life.

Even now, when we are both around the sixty mark, <u>he often talks to me about the cat</u> he has had for many years. It is a typical relationship—<u>they tease each other unmercifully</u>—but it is based on real affection.

"It's no good, Triss," I said gently. "It's got to be done." I reached for the syringe but <u>something in me rebelled against plunging a needle into that mutilated body</u>. Instead I pulled a fold of the blanket over the cat's head.

Exercise 14 Find It in Your Writing Review a piece of writing from your portfolio. Choose several sentences, and identify the simple subject and the simple predicate in each. You may find that some sentences have more than one part, each containing a simple subject and a simple predicate.

Exercise 15 Writing Application Describe an animal that would make a good pet for your area. Identify the simple subject and simple predicate in each of your sentences. You may find that some sentences have more than one part, each containing a simple subject and a simple predicate.

Compound Subjects and Compound Verbs

Some sentences have more than one subject. Some have more than one verb.

Recognizing Compound Subjects

A sentence containing more than one subject is said to have a *compound subject*.

▶ **KEY CONCEPT** A **compound subject** is two or more subjects that have the same verb and are joined by a conjunction such as *and* or *or*. ■

In the examples in the chart, the parts of the compound subject are underlined once. The verbs are underlined twice.

SENTENCES WITH COMPOUND SUBJECTS
<u>Cats</u> and <u>kittens</u> <u>are</u> popular as pets.
<u>She</u> and <u>I</u> <u>will feed</u> the cat.
<u>Cats</u>, <u>dogs</u> and <u>other pets</u> <u>can learn</u> to live together.

⚙ **Grammar and Style Tip**

When using a compound subject, make sure the verb agrees in number with the subject. For instance, *My cat <u>likes</u> tuna* has a single subject: *cat.* Here's the same sentence with a plural subject: *My cat and my dog <u>like</u> tuna.*

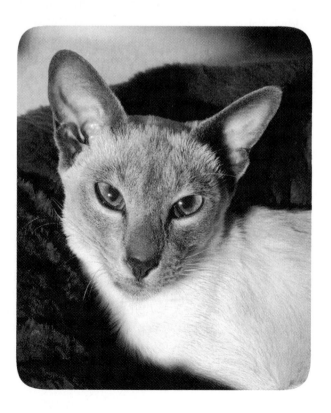

◀ Critical Viewing
Use a compound subject in a sentence describing the unusual features of this cat. [Describe]

▶ **Exercise 16** Recognizing Compound Subjects Each of the following sentences contains a compound subject. Copy the sentences onto your paper, and underline the simple subjects that make up each compound subject.

EXAMPLE: <u>Manx</u> and <u>Siamese</u> are two domestic cat breeds.

1. Indoor cats and outdoor cats require lots of attention.
2. A cat and her kittens should be fed a high-quality commercial cat food daily.
3. Food and water should always be put in the same place.
4. A litter box or pet door should be accessible to the cat.
5. People food and chemicals should be kept out of a cat's reach.
6. Fleas and mites can cause irritation to cats.
7. Dogs and small children can harm a cat.
8. Loose fur and dirt should be removed every week with a brush.
9. Toys, treats, and a scratching post help keep cats happy.
10. Cats and humans can be great friends.

More Practice

Grammar Exercise Workbook
• pp. 49–50
On-line Exercise Bank
• Section 19.3
  Go on-line:
  PHSchool.com
  Enter Web Code:
  ebk-7002

Get instant feedback! Exercise 16 is available on-line or on CD-ROM.

GRAMMAR IN LITERATURE

from **Cat on the Go**
James Herriot

Notice how the author has used compound subjects (in blue) and compound verbs (in red) in this passage to name people and show actions.

"Well, I reckon I'd better leave 'im with you. You'll be going to put him out of his misery. There's nothing anybody can do about . . . about that?"

I *shrugged* and *shook* my head. The girl's eyes filled with tears; she *stretched* out a hand and *touched* the emaciated animal, then *turned* and *walked* quickly to the door.

"Thanks again, Marjorie," I called after the retreating back. "And don't worry—we'll look after him."

In the silence that followed, *Tristan* and *I* looked down at the shattered animal. . . .

Recognizing Compound Verbs

Just as sentences can have compound subjects, they can have compound verbs. Compound verbs are also joined by conjunctions.

KEY CONCEPT A **compound verb** is two or more verbs that have the same subject and are joined by a conjunction such as *and* or *or.* ∎

In the following chart, the parts of the compound verbs are underlined twice. The subjects are underlined once.

SENTENCES WITH COMPOUND VERBS
Kittens sleep, eat, and play.
I have to feed the cat and walk the dog.
The cat yawned, settled into the blanket, and fell asleep.

Sometimes a sentence will have both a compound subject and a compound verb.

EXAMPLE: The house and the garden face the lake and are protected by hedges.

Exercise 17 Recognizing Compound Verbs Each of the following sentences contains a compound verb. Copy the sentences onto your paper, and draw two lines under the verbs that make up each compound verb.

EXAMPLE: The kitten crawled out of the box and explored the garage.

1. The cat bites and shreds with its teeth rather than chewing, as humans do.
2. The cat uses its senses and depends on them to survive in the environment.
3. The cat tests obstacles and senses changes in the environment through its whiskers.
4. The cat tears meat from bones, laps liquids, and grooms itself with its tongue.
5. The cat can hear a wide range of sounds and focus on them.

More Practice

Grammar Exercise Workbook
• pp. 49–50
On-line Exercise Bank
• Section 19.3
  Go on-line:
  PHSchool.com
  Enter Web Code:
  ebk-7002

Get instant feedback! Exercises 17, 18, and 19 are available on-line or on CD-ROM.

Exercise 18 Recognizing Compound Subjects and
Compound Verbs Each of the following sentences contains a
compound subject, a compound verb, or both. On your paper,
write the compound subjects and the compound verbs. Then,
label each one *compound subject* or *compound verb*.

1. For each domestic breed, a set of rules describes the ideal
   cat and mentions its faults.
2. The Manx, Russian blue, and Siamese began as naturally
   occurring varieties of domestic cats.
3. Curly-coated Rex breeds and the tailless Manx were developed and perfected by selective breeding.
4. Proper grooming and quality care are mandatory for all
   breeds of cats.
5. Bookstores and local humane societies sell or give away
   educational materials about proper cat care.
6. Fatal feline diseases and parasites are found frequently in
   the stray cat population.
7. Individuals and organizations work to reduce the stray cat
   population.
8. Declawed cats and kittens should not go outside unless
   confined to a covered enclosure.
9. Sometimes, outdoor cats have been struck by a car, poi-
   soned by common pesticides, or injured by other animals.
10. However, outside cats hunt small animals, interact with
    other cats, and get plenty of exercise.

▼ Critical Viewing
What two things
would you have to do
in order to photo-
graph a cat in such a
stance? Explain in a
sentence with a com-
pound verb. **[Relate]**

Exercise 19 Combining Sentences With
Compound Subjects and Compound Verbs
Combine each set of sentences by using a
compound subject or a compound verb.

1. A cat's coat protects its skin. The coat
   also provides insulation.
2. The outercoat is one part of the cat's coat.
   The undercoat is the other part of the
   cat's coat.
3. The color of the coat varies among cats.
   The length of the coat also varies. The
   texture of the coat varies, too.
4. A cat's whiskers help it feel its way in the
   dark. A cat's whiskers can help it detect
   changes in wind direction.
5. The sense of smell is better in cats than
   in humans. The sense of hearing is better
   in cats than in humans.

Compound Subjects and Compound Verbs • 403

Section Review

GRAMMAR EXERCISES 20–24

Exercise 20 Identifying **Compound Subjects and Compound Verbs** Copy the following sentences onto your paper. Underline the subject(s) once and the verb(s) twice. Draw a vertical line between the complete subject and the complete predicate. Then, tell which sentences have compound subjects and/or compound verbs, and which have neither.

1. Cats are efficient hunters.
2. Their speed and keen eyesight make them a match for any other animal.
3. Most cats hunt at dusk or at night.
4. They have powerful legs and a muscular neck to help them catch prey.
5. Most cats survive on what they catch.
6. An adult lioness needs twelve pounds of meat per day.
7. Hunting and eating take a considerable amount of time.
8. All felines, including domestic cats, attack and react with lightning speed.
9. Lions are the only type of cat that hunts in a group.
10. Most mother cats and their young hunt and eat together.

Exercise 21 Revision Practice: **Combining Sentences With Compound Subjects and Compound Verbs** Revise the following passage by combining sentences as appropriate, using compound subjects or compound verbs.

Scientists are researching the habits of leopards. Zookeepers, too, research the habits of leopards. Leopards see very well. They also hear very well. These are solitary cats. They hunt alone. They eat alone. They do not travel in groups as lions do. Leopards are similar to other big cats, however, because they sleep during the day. Leopards usually hunt at night. A leopard's diet includes wild boar. Leopards may also eat deer.

A leopard's physical abilities are amazing. A leopard can run at thirty-seven miles per hour. It can leap twenty feet horizontally. Great strength makes the leopard a feared predator. Its nocturnal habits also make it a feared predator.

Exercise 22 Find It in Your **Reading** Read the following passage from James Herriot's "Cat on the Go." Identify the sentence that has a compound subject, as well as the two parts of that compound subject.

Three nights later he was missing again. This time Helen and I didn't bother to search. We just waited. He was back earlier than usual. I heard the doorbell at nine o'clock. It was the elderly Mrs. Simpson peering through the glass. And she wasn't holding Oscar—he was prowling on the mat waiting to come in.

Exercise 23 Find It in Your **Writing** Review a piece of writing from your portfolio. Identify a sentence with a compound subject or a compound verb. If you can't find one, challenge yourself to add one to your writing.

Exercise 24 Writing Application Describe the habits of a species of wildlife. Use at least three sentences with a compound subject or verb.

Special Problems With Subjects

In most sentences in English, the subject comes before the verb. This pattern is called *normal word order.* As long as the subject comes before the verb, the sentence is in normal word order, regardless of whether the subject and verb come near the beginning of the sentence, in the middle, or near the end.

NORMAL WORD ORDER: A <u>cheetah</u> <u>raced</u> across the plain.
On the nature program, <u>we</u> <u>saw</u> a cheetah.
As part of their daily routine, <u>cheetahs</u> <u>roam</u> their territory.

Not all sentences are in normal word order. In some, the verb comes before the subject. In others, such as questions, the subject can appear between parts of a verb phrase. In still others, the subject may seem to be missing altogether.

Finding subjects in sentences that are not in normal word order can be a problem. This section will give you practice in finding these difficult subjects.

Theme: Cats

In this section, you will learn about changes in word order in questions and in sentences beginning with *there* and *here.* The examples and exercises in this section are about wild cats.

Cross-Curricular Connection: Science

▼ **Critical Viewing**
Describe this cheetah in sentences beginning with "Wide is . . . ," "Spotted is . . . ," and "Sharp are. . . ." **[Analyze]**

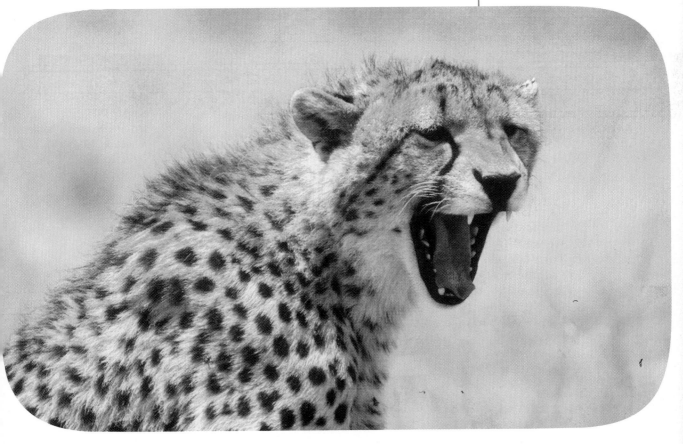

Recognizing Subjects in Orders and Directions

Stop! Finish your homework now. These sentences and others that give orders or directions seem not to have subjects. In fact, the subject in such cases is not stated, but understood.

▶ **KEY CONCEPT** In sentences that give orders or directions, the subject is understood to be *you*. ■

The following chart lists examples of sentences that give orders or directions. The verbs are underlined twice. To the right, the same sentences are repeated with the understood subject in parentheses.

Orders or Directions	With Understood *You* Added
Look at the lion.	(You) Look at the lion.
After reading the background, watch the video.	After reading the background, (you) watch the video.
Leonard, tell us what lions eat.	Leonard, (you) tell us what lions eat.

▶ **Exercise 25** Recognizing Subjects That Give Orders or Directions On your paper, write the subject of each of the sentences that follow. Six of the ten sentences give orders or directions. The other four are ordinary sentences in normal word order.

EXAMPLE: Tom, help plan the field trip.

ANSWER: (you)

1. Jamie, watch the zookeeper feed the Siberian tigers.
2. She had better be careful!
3. We want to see the big cat exhibit.
4. Turn left just past the monkeys.
5. Call the Species Survival Plan to find out more about tiger facilities.
6. Find the cheetah area last.
7. I don't want to miss the ocelots.
8. Don't the lions get fed at 2:00?
9. Don't be late.
10. Anna, find the shortcut through the bird sanctuary.

▶ **More Practice**

Grammar Exercise Workbook
• pp. 51–52
On-line Exercise Bank
• Section 19.4
  Go on-line:
  PHSchool.com
  Enter Web Code:
  ebk-7002

 Text

Get instant feedback! Exercises 25 and 26 are available on-line or on CD-ROM.

Finding Subjects in Questions

When the subject comes after the verb, a sentence is said to be in *inverted word order.* Inverted word order is found most often in questions.

▶ **KEY CONCEPT** In questions, the subject often follows the verb. ■

Some questions in inverted word order begin with the words *what, which, whom, whose, when, where, why,* and *how.* Others begin with the verb itself or with a helping verb. In the sentences below, both the subject and the verb are underlined.

EXAMPLES: How <u>are</u> the <u>kittens</u> today?
<u>Did</u> <u>you</u> <u>feed</u> them in the morning?

If you ever have trouble finding the subject in a question, use this trick: Change the question into a statement. The subject will then appear in normal word order, before the verb.

Questions	Reworded as Statements
How <u>are</u> the <u>pups</u> today?	The <u>pups</u> <u>are</u> how today.
What <u>did</u> the <u>doctor</u> <u>say</u>?	The <u>doctor</u> <u>did</u> <u>say</u> what.
<u>Were</u> the <u>labels</u> ready?	The <u>labels</u> <u>were</u> ready.
<u>Did</u> <u>she</u> <u>bring</u> her camera with her?	She <u>did bring</u> her camera with her.

Not every question is in inverted word order. Some are in normal word order, with the subject before the verb.

EXAMPLES: <u>Who</u> <u>has</u> the camera?
<u>Whose story</u> <u>won</u> the writing contest?

▶ **Exercise 26** Finding the Subjects in Questions Copy the following sentences onto your paper. Underline the subject in each. Note that two of the sentences are in normal word order.

EXAMPLE: How did <u>you</u> get interested in leopards?

1. Where do leopards live?
2. A leopard can run at what speed?
3. What method do conservationists use to count leopard populations?
4. How are a cheetah's spots different from a leopard's?
5. Which scientists study the behavior of these big cats?

▼ Critical Viewing
Inverting normal sentence word order, ask a question about the differences between this leopard and other big cats. [Contrast]

Finding Subjects in Sentences Beginning With *There* or *Here*

A sentence beginning with *there* or *here* is usually in inverted word order.

▶ **KEY CONCEPT** *There* or *here* is never the subject of a sentence. ■

There has two uses in a sentence. First, it can be used simply as a sentence starter. *There* can also be used as an adverb at the beginning of a sentence. *Here* can be used in the same way. As adverbs, *there* and *here* point out *where*.

EXAMPLES:

There <u>are</u> three <u>birds</u> in that cage.

There <u>goes</u> the football <u>team</u>.

Here <u>is</u> the <u>recipe</u> for enchiladas.

If you have trouble finding the subject of a sentence beginning with *here* or *there*, reorder the sentence. The subject will then appear near the beginning.

Sentences Beginning With *There* and *Here*
There <u>are</u> two <u>lions</u> in that enclosure.
Here <u>is</u> the <u>exhibit</u>.
Reworded With Subjects Before Verbs
Two <u>lions</u> <u>are</u> in that enclosure.
The <u>exhibit</u> <u>is</u> here.

▶ **Exercise 27** Finding the Subjects in Sentences Beginning With *There* or *Here* Copy the following sentences onto your paper. Underline the subject in each.

1. Here are answers to your questions about the big cats.
2. There are leopards, lions, and cheetahs in this area.
3. There is a large variety of wildlife living on the savannah.
4. Here is a picture of a cheetah.
5. There was a program about the big cats on television last night.

💡 Spelling Tip

Writers often confuse the spelling of *their* and *there*. Remember that *their* is a pronoun that shows possession (e.g., Children love *their* pet cats). *There* denotes place or the fact of something's existence (e.g., The cougar's cage is over *there*, or *There* is a rare species of cat in the zoo).

Get instant feedback! Exercise 27 is available on-line or on CD-ROM.

▶ **More Practice**

Grammar Exercise Workbook
• pp. 53–54
On-line Exercise Bank
• Section 19.4
  Go on-line:
  PHSchool.com
  Enter Web Code:
  ebk-7002

Section 19.4 Section Review

GRAMMAR EXERCISES 28–33

▶ **Exercise 28** Finding Subjects in Orders, Questions, and Directions
On your paper, write the subject of each sentence.

1. How heavy does a tiger get?
2. That tiger weighs up to 675 pounds.
3. Go to southeastern Asia or central India to see a Bengal tiger.
4. What do Bengal tigers eat?
5. Does the Bengal tiger inhabit grassy or swampy areas?
6. Where do Bengal tigers live?
7. Be cautious when observing tigers in their natural habitat.
8. Which tiger is not dangerous to man?
9. What is the Bengal tiger's classification?
10. Why are Bengal tigers protected?

▶ **Exercise 29** Finding Subjects in Sentences Beginning With *There* or *Here*
Copy the following sentences. Underline the subject in each.

1. There were several types of saber-toothed tigers.
2. There are fascinating exhibits about them.
3. Here, it is the most common mammal fossil found.
4. Here are saber-toothed tiger skeletons.
5. There are tar pits containing tiger skeletons at Rancho La Brea in California.

▶ **Exercise 30** Revising Sentences
Revise each of the following sentences to begin with the subject. Make any other minor changes that are necessary.

1. There is a large cat found on the grassy plains of Africa.
2. Although there are many fast cats, there are none as fast as the cheetah.

3. Seventy miles an hour a cheetah can run.
4. There are usually two to four cubs in a cheetah litter.
5. There are many predators—including hyenas, leopards, and lions—that pose a threat to young cheetahs.
6. There were once cheetahs throughout Africa, central Asia, and India.
7. Today, there are fewer cheetahs than in the past.
8. Declining are their numbers.
9. There are several reasons, such as predators and loss of habitat, that contribute to the problem.
10. Here is a picture of a cheetah.

▶ **Exercise 31** Find It in Your Reading Read the following excerpt from "Cat on the Go." Identify the subject and the verb of each underlined part. If necessary, reorder the sentence to find the subject.

<u>Tell me</u>," I said. "This cat you lost. <u>What did he look like</u>?

▶ **Exercise 32** Find It in Your Writing Revise several sentences from your own writing to begin with *There* or *Here*. If you find a sentence already beginning with "There is . . ." or There are . . . ," try revising it to eliminate those words.

▶ **Exercise 33** Writing Application
Write a letter to a zoo or wildlife center, asking for information on big cats. Include three specific questions. Identify the subject and verb in each of your questions.

Complements

In Section 19.1, a *complete thought* was defined as a group of words that contains a subject and a verb and that can stand by itself and still make sense. Sometimes, just a subject and a verb by themselves will express a complete thought. The following sentences, for example, do express complete thoughts.

EXAMPLES:
$\overset{S}{\text{Snakes}}$ $\overset{V}{\text{slither.}}$ $\overset{S}{\text{Lizards}}$ $\overset{V}{\text{scurry.}}$

Sometimes, however, a subject and verb alone will not express a complete thought.

EXAMPLES:
$\overset{S}{\text{Tracy}}$ $\overset{V}{\text{fed.}}$ $\overset{S}{\text{That}}$ $\overset{V}{\text{is.}}$ $\overset{S}{\text{It}}$ $\overset{V}{\text{seems.}}$

These sentences need other words to complete the thoughts begun by the subjects and verbs. The words needed are complements.

▶ **KEY CONCEPT** A **complement** is a word or group of words that completes the meaning of a subject and a verb. ∎

Complements usually appear right after the verb or very close to it. Most complements are nouns, pronouns, or adjectives. In the examples below, the complements are labeled and boxed.

EXAMPLES:
Tracy fed the COMPLEMENT [lizard.]

That is a COMPLEMENT [problem.]

COMPLEMENT
It seems [sick.]

▶ **Exercise 34** Adding Complements On your paper, write one word to complete each sentence.
1. The snake looks ___?___.
2. It feels ___?___.
3. The lizard seems ___?___.
4. Its skin is ___?___.
5. We like ___?___.

The next three parts of this section describe three types of complements: *direct objects, indirect objects,* and *subject complements.* The first part focuses on direct objects.

Theme: Reptiles

In this section, you will learn about direct and indirect objects and predicate nouns and adjectives. The examples and exercises in this section are about reptiles.

Cross-Curricular Connection: Science

Complete the exercise on-line! Exercise 34 is available on-line or on CD-ROM.

▶ **More Practice**

Grammar Exercise Workbook
• pp. 55–60, 65–66
On-line Exercise Bank
• Section 19.5
   Go on-line:
   PHSchool.com
   Enter Web Code:
   ebk-7002

Recognizing Direct Objects

Direct objects follow action verbs.

KEY CONCEPT A **direct object** is a noun or pronoun that receives the action of a verb. ■

You can find a direct object by asking *What?* or *Whom?* after an action verb.

EXAMPLES:

My older brother found a [grass snake.] [DO]

Found *what?* Answer: a grass snake.

I told [Ricky] not to take it home. [DO]

Told *whom?* Answer: Ricky

Grass snake and *Ricky* are the direct objects of the verbs in the examples. In the first sentence, *grass snake* answers the question *Found what? Ricky*, in the second sentence, answers the question *Told whom?*

Like subjects and verbs, direct objects can be compound. That is, one verb can have two or more direct objects.

EXAMPLES:

The lizard eats [crickets] and other [bugs.] [DO] [DO]

Eats *what?* Answer: crickets, bugs

The committee chose [Mrs. Franks], [Mr. Lynch], [DO] [DO]

and [Ms. Rossi] to organize the reptile show. [DO]

Chose *whom?* Answer: Mrs. Franks, Mr. Lynch, and Ms. Rossi.

◀ **Critical Viewing**
What do you notice, like, or dislike about this snake? Answer with a sentence containing a compound direct object. **[Evaluate]**

▶ **Exercise 35** Recognizing Direct Objects Each of the following sentences contains either a simple or a compound direct object. Copy the sentences onto your paper, and underline each direct object.

EXAMPLE: Snakes often scare <u>people</u>.

1. Scales cover a snake's body.
2. Snakes do not have legs or arms.
3. Snakes lose their fangs periodically.
4. Some species also shed their skin.
5. Snakes eat rats, mice, and frogs.

▶ **Exercise 36** Combining Sentences With Compound Direct Objects Combine each pair or group of sentences by using a compound direct object. You may make other minor changes as necessary.

EXAMPLE: We saw alligators at the zoo. We saw crocodiles, too.
ANSWER: We saw alligators and crocodiles at the zoo.

1. The crocodile family includes crocodiles. It also includes alligators. Caimans are also part of the crocodile family.
2. Crocodiles inhabit Asia. They are also found in Africa. Crocodiles also live in some areas of North America.
3. The hardy crocodile can survive droughts. It can also survive cool weather.
4. Crocodiles eat birds. They also eat mammals.
5. For nesting sites, a crocodile might choose a sandy beach. It might choose a muddy bank instead.

◀ Critical Viewing
If you were suddenly the direct object of a hungry alligator, what might its actions be? [Evaluate]

Finding Direct Objects in Questions

In normal word order, a direct object follows a verb. In questions, which are often in inverted word order, the position of a direct object often changes as well.

KEY CONCEPT A direct object in a question will sometimes be found before the verb. ■

In the chart below, questions are paired with sentences reworded in normal word order. Compare the positions of the direct objects in each.

Questions	Sentences With Normal Word Order
DO What <u>does</u> a <u>snake</u> <u>eat</u>?	DO A <u>snake</u> <u>does</u> <u>eat</u> what.
DO Which T-shirt <u>do</u> <u>you</u> <u>like</u>?	DO You <u>do</u> <u>like</u> which T-shirt.
DO Whom <u>did</u> <u>you</u> <u>meet</u> in the cafeteria?	DO You <u>did</u> <u>meet</u> whom in the cafeteria.

In each of the three questions, the direct object appears before, rather than after, the verb. To locate the direct object in a question, put the sentence into normal word order. Then, the direct object will be found in its usual position after the verb.

Exercise 37 Finding Direct Objects in Questions Copy each of the sentences below, and underline the direct object.

EXAMPLE: <u>What</u> should we take with us to Reptile Park?

1. Whom did you invite to come with us?
2. What will you do with those interesting photographs?
3. Which reptile do you like?
4. Which species of reptile shall we visit first?
5. What should we see next?
6. Which reptiles can you touch?
7. Whom have they chosen to talk to us?
8. Whose questions will the guide answer?
9. What effect does the weather have on reptiles?
10. What reptile book shall I buy?

Speaking and Listening Tip

With a partner, take turns reading the questions in Exercise 37 aloud. First, read each one as it is written, and then read it again as a statement with normal word order. Pay attention to the changing position of the direct objects.

Text

Get instant feedback! Exercises 35, 36, and 37 are available on-line or on CD-ROM.

More Practice

Grammar Exercise Workbook
• pp. 55–60
On-line Exercise Bank
• Section 19.5
Go on-line:
PHSchool.com
Enter Web Code:
ebk-7002

Recognizing Indirect Objects

Sentences with direct objects may also have another kind of complement, called an *indirect object*. An indirect object is found only in a sentence that has a direct object.

> **KEY CONCEPT** An **indirect object** is a noun or pronoun that comes after an action verb and before a direct object. It names the person or thing that something is given to or done for. ■

Always look for the direct object first in a sentence. Then, look for an indirect object before it. An indirect object answers the question *To or for whom?* or *To or for what?* after the action verb.

EXAMPLES:

               IO   DO
Lucy told him the news.
Told to *whom?* Answer: him

               IO   DO
I gave each paper a number.
Gave to *what?* Answer: paper

Most sentences with indirect objects will follow the same pattern: Subject + Action Verb + Indirect Object + Direct Object. An indirect object will almost always come between the verb and the direct object.

Like direct objects, indirect objects can be compound. The verb can be followed by two or more indirect objects.

EXAMPLE:

               IO   IO   DO
He gave his lizard and turtle their food.
Gave to *what?* Answer: lizard, turtle

Learn More

To review nouns and pronouns, see Chapter 14.

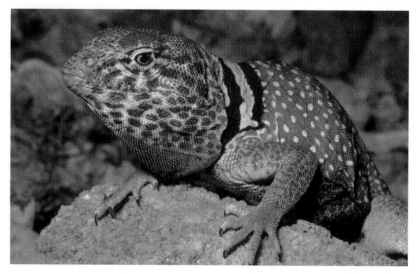

◄ Critical Viewing Use an indirect object and a direct object in a sentence describing the kind of look this Gila monster seems to be giving you. **[Connect]**

Exercise 38 Recognizing Indirect Objects Each of the following sentences contains a direct object and an indirect object. Some indirect objects are compound. Copy the sentences onto your paper, and underline each indirect object.

EXAMPLE: We gave <u>John</u> a surprise for his birthday.

1. Yesterday, I gave John a pet lizard.
2. He will give his pet special treats.
3. We gave his lizard the name Lizzy.
4. John told his brother and sister details about Lizzy.
5. We made Lizzy a new home.
6. I showed my teacher and classmates the new habitat.
7. It gives her some space to grow.
8. John feeds Lizzy bugs.
9. We gave Mary a picture.
10. John gave me a picture of Lizzy, too.
11. We built her an outdoor enclosure for the warm days.
12. Everyone asks John and his family questions about her.
13. They tell them facts about lizards.
14. With Lizzy, they give them demonstrations.
15. Sometimes, when Lizzy is with them, people give them frightened looks.

Exercise 39 Combining Sentences With Compound Indirect Objects Combine each pair or group of sentences by using compound indirect objects. You may make other minor changes as needed.

EXAMPLE: Have you shown your teacher the snake article?
             Have you shown your classmates the article?

ANSWER: Have you shown your teacher and your classmates the snake article?

1. Mr. Benson assigned Steve a report on snakes. He assigned me a report on snakes as well.
2. We gave Mary a book with facts on crocodiles. We also gave a book to Keisha.
3. We asked Mr. Benson some questions. We asked Tom some questions, too.
4. Mr. Benson showed Lucy several Internet sources. He also showed me the sources.
5. I will read the class my report. I might read my family the report instead.

More Practice

Grammar Exercise Workbook
• pp. 61–62
On-line Exercise Bank
• Section 19.5
  Go on-line:
  PHSchool.com
  Enter Web Code:
  ebk-7002

Get instant feedback! Exercises 38 and 39 are available on-line or on CD-ROM.

Recognizing Subject Complements

Action verbs can be followed by direct objects and indirect objects. Linking verbs can be followed by another kind of complement, called a *subject complement*.

▶ **KEY CONCEPT** A **subject complement** is a noun, a pronoun, or an adjective that follows a linking verb and tells something about the subject. ■

Predicate Nouns and Pronouns

Nouns and pronouns used as subject complements follow linking verbs.

▶ **KEY CONCEPT** A **predicate noun** or **predicate pronoun** follows a linking verb and renames or identifies the subject. ■

PREDICATE NOUNS AND PRONOUNS	
Sentences	**Relationships**
PN A lizard is a reptile.	lizard = reptile
PP The leader will be he.	leader = he

A predicate noun or predicate pronoun is never the object of a preposition. In the following sentence, *superstars* is not a predicate noun. It is the object of the preposition *of*.

		PP		OBJ OF PREP
EXAMPLE:	Steve Young was one of football's superstars.			

▶ **Exercise 40** Recognizing Predicate Nouns and Pronouns
Copy the following sentences onto your paper, and underline each predicate noun or predicate pronoun.
1. The largest lizard is the Komodo dragon.
2. Komodo dragons are huge monsters.
3. The dragon's home is the Indonesian island of Komodo.
4. The Komodo dragon is really one type of lizard—the monitor.
5. The second largest monitor lizard is Australia's giant perentie.

📖 Journal Tip

This section focuses on several types of reptiles. In your journal, note some facts about the reptiles that especially interest you, along with your impressions of these creatures. You can review your notes later to find a possible topic for a report.

Text

Get instant feedback! Exercises 40 and 41 are available on-line or on CD-ROM.

▶ **More Practice**

Grammar Exercise Workbook
• pp. 65–66
On-line Exercise Bank
• Section 19.5
  Go on-line:
  PHSchool.com
  Enter Web Code:
  ebk-7002

Predicate Adjectives

A linking verb may also be followed by a predicate adjective.

> **KEY CONCEPT** A **predicate adjective** follows a linking verb and describes the subject of the sentence. ■

Because a predicate adjective comes after a linking verb, it is considered part of the complete predicate of a sentence. In spite of this, a predicate adjective does *not* modify the words in the predicate. Instead, the predicate adjective describes the subject of the sentence.

PREDICATE ADJECTIVES	
Sentences	**Relationships**
PA Her <u>story</u> <u>seems</u> strange to us.	strange story
PA Komodo dragons <u>are</u> huge.	huge Komodo dragons

> **Exercise 41** **Recognizing Predicate Adjectives** Copy each sentence and underline the predicate adjectives.

1. The long, thin cobra is olive brown.
2. It is unbelievably scary.
3. This snake's bite can be lethal.
4. It is extremely poisonous.
5. Cobras are useful to a snake charmer.
6. The music of the snake charmer is enchanting.
7. However, snakes are deaf.
8. The motion of the snake charmer, though, is fascinating to the snake.
9. The charmer must remain calm as the cobra flares its hood menacingly.
10. Snake charmers may be brave, but I think they are extremely foolish.

◀ Critical Viewing Use several vivid predicate adjectives to fill in the blank: This Komodo dragon is/seems/might become _____. **[Infer]**

Compound Subject Complements

Like other sentence parts, subject complements can be compound. That is, a linking verb may be followed by two or more predicate nouns, pronouns, or adjectives.

EXAMPLES:

PN   PN
The snake's <u>owners</u> <u>are</u> Nancy and Melissa.

PN   PP
The report <u>writers</u> <u>were</u> Maureen and he.

PA   PA
The <u>rattlesnake</u> <u>looks</u> mean and dangerous.

Exercise 42 Recognizing Compound Subject Complements Write the parts of each subject complement in the following sentences. The complements may be predicate nouns (PN) or predicate adjectives (PA). Label them correctly.

EXAMPLE: The assignment is a report or project.
ANSWER: report (PN), project (PN)

1. The diamondback rattlesnake is large and dangerous.
2. Rattlesnakes grow long and heavy.
3. They appear both beautiful and frightening.
4. Rattlesnakes are poisonous and carnivorous.
5. A rattlesnake's prey can be rabbits, mice, or gophers.
6. Their home is either the desert or the forest.
7. The snake's skin is smooth but scaly.
8. A rattlesnake's skeleton is bone and cartilage.
9. The rattlesnake's most important senses are taste and smell.
10. The sound of their rattles may be loud or soft.

Exercise 43 Writing Sentences With Subject Complements Write sentences with subject complements, following the directions below.

1. Use a predicate adjective in a sentence describing a turtle.
2. Use a predicate noun in a sentence about a pet.
3. Write a sentence with compound predicate adjectives, describing how you would feel if you came upon a Komodo dragon in the wild.
4. Use compound predicate nouns in a sentence about three favorite animals.
5. Use compound predicate pronouns in a sentence about yourself and a friend.

More Practice

Grammar Exercise Workbook
• pp. 67–68
On-line Exercise Bank
• Section 19.5
Go on-line:
PHSchool.com
Enter Web Code:
ebk-7002

Get instant feedback! Exercises 42 and 43 are available on-line or on CD-ROM.

Section 19.5 Section Review

GRAMMAR EXERCISES 44–49

▶ **Exercise 44** Recognizing Direct Objects and Compound Direct Objects On your paper, write only the nouns or pronouns that make up each direct object or compound direct object.

1. Rattlesnakes frighten people.
2. The sun warms their skin and their blood.
3. Whose opinion do you value on the care and feeding of snakes?
4. Their rattles warn people and other intruders of their presence.
5. They use rocks and trees to conceal themselves.
6. Their tongues sense temperature changes and people.
7. I will take you to find more information on snakes.
8. Before eating prey, poisonous snakes paralyze it.
9. If undisturbed, rattlesnakes won't attack us.
10. Large birds of prey eat snakes and other small reptiles.

▶ **Exercise 45** Recognizing Compound Subject Complements Write the subject complements in the following sentences. Label predicate nouns *PN*, predicate pronouns *PP*, and predicate adjectives *PA*.

1. My friend is knowledgeable and concerned about hawksbill turtles.
2. It was he and I who wrote a report on them.
3. The hawksbill is passive and graceful.
4. Its natural habitat is warm seas.
5. This species is neither quick nor powerful.

▶ **Exercise 46** Revision Practice: Sentence Combining Combine sentences in the following paragraph by using compound complements.

The sea turtle is an excellent swimmer. It is also a good diver. It eats mollusks. It also eats shellfish. One type of sea turtle is the hawksbill. Another interesting type of sea turtle is the green turtle. Hawksbill turtles are beautiful. They are rare.

▶ **Exercise 47** Find It in Your Reading Read an article about reptiles in an encyclopedia, on a Web page, or in a science textbook. Identify at least three examples of subject complements that are used in the article.

▶ **Exercise 48** Find It in Your Writing Review some of the finished work in your writing portfolio. Identify any places where you have used subject complements. Challenge yourself to add two more sentences—one containing compound predicate adjectives and the other containing compound predicate nouns.

▶ **Exercise 49** Writing Application Write a short description of a reptile. Circle the complements in each sentence, and identify direct and indirect objects, as well as predicate nouns, pronouns, or adjectives.

Chapter Review

GRAMMAR EXERCISES 50–59

Exercise 50 Identifying Complete Subjects and Complete Predicates
Copy each of the sentences below onto your paper. Underline the subject once and the verb twice. Then, draw a vertical line between the complete subject and the complete predicate.

1. Tennis is a great personal sport.
2. The only equipment needed is a racquet and a ball.
3. The players must learn how to score.
4. Two or four people can play the game.
5. A special court is necessary to play tennis.

Exercise 51 Recognizing Complete Thoughts On your paper, copy each group of words below. Label complete thoughts *sentence*. Label incomplete thoughts *fragment*.

1. The Frisbee hit the market in 1957.
2. Sailed through the air.
3. Frisbees have been manufactured by many companies.
4. Taken anywhere, with a leash.
5. Many dogs, but mostly my dog.

Exercise 52 Completing Sentences With Compound Subjects and Compound Verbs Each of the following sentences contains a single subject and verb and one or two blanks. On your paper, rewrite the sentences, filling in each blank with another noun or verb that would create a logical compound.

1. Skateboards and ___?___ are very popular.

2. Many stores and ___?___ buy and ___?___ inline skates.
3. Beach boardwalks and ___?___ are common places to use inline skates.
4. Helmets and ___?___ are important safety equipment for this sport.
5. Serious inline skaters practice and ___?___ tricks on specially constructed ramps.

Exercise 53 Locating Hard-to-Find Subjects On your paper, write the subject of each sentence. If the subject is understood, write it in parentheses.

1. Stay off the grass!
2. Wear the proper equipment for all sports.
3. On which field will you be playing?
4. There was another game played this afternoon.
5. Here are the tickets for tonight's football game.

Exercise 54 Identifying All Kinds of Complements Each of the following sentences contains one or more complements. Copy the sentences onto your paper. Underline each complement, and tell whether it is a direct object, an indirect object, a predicate noun, or a predicate adjective.

1. Serious runners often run marathons.
2. Marathon runners are dedicated.
3. They are outstanding athletes.
4. Spectators at a marathon give the runners encouragement.
5. Their cheers add excitement to the race.
6. A runner usually feels tired but proud at the end of a marathon.

7. In a way, each participant is a winner.
8. Big marathons make news throughout the world.
9. Many marathons raise money for charities.
10. The organizers of these marathons are busy people.

▶ **Exercise 55** Recognizing Parts of Sentences Write the following sentences, and label the direct objects *DO*, the predicate nouns *PN*, and the predicate adjectives *PA*.

1. Water-skiing is both fun and exciting.
2. The best water-skiers on the trip were Mindy and Tanya.
3. This morning, the lake was calm and smooth.
4. We like Lake Shasta and Lake Powell for water-skiing.
5. Water-skiers must be strong and steady to stay up on their skis.

▶ **Exercise 56** Completing Sentences With Complements Complete each sentence by adding a complement. You may add other words as needed to make sense. Tell whether the complement you add is a direct object, a predicate noun, or a predicate adjective.

1. We watched ___?___.
2. It was ___?___.
3. Which runner was ___?___?
4. That runner seems ___?___.
5. She won ___?___.
6. They played ___?___.
7. Someone asked ___?___.
8. They made ___?___.
9. We are ___?___.
10. He felt ___?___.

▶ **Exercise 57** Revision Practice: Sentence Combining Combine some sentences in the following paragraph by using compound complements. You may make other minor changes as necessary.

Of all the backyard games, badminton is my favorite. The equipment is not expensive. It isn't hard to set up, either. You need a net. You also need some racquets. You need a "birdie," too. Two or four people play the game. Badminton resembles tennis. Badminton and tennis are played with a net. They are both played with racquets as well. However, tennis is played with a tennis ball that can bounce on the ground during play. Badminton is played with a "birdie" that must not touch the ground during play. Last week, my brother and I played badminton. The game was fast. It was also exciting.

▶ **Exercise 58** Writing Application Write an explanation of an activity you enjoy. Identify the simple subject and simple predicate of each sentence.

▶ **Exercise 59** CUMULATIVE REVIEW Parts of Speech Read the following paragraph. Then, on your paper, write the part of speech of each underlined word.

(1) Buzz, an irritable, <u>ugly</u> old tortoise, moved into a pond in our back yard. (2) The big pond was just the right size <u>for</u> him. (3) He built a nest and chased all the ducks and geese <u>away</u>. (4) Then, he befriended <u>our</u> dog, Spike. (5) He <u>and</u> Spike became inseparable. (6) Soon, Buzz seemed <u>different</u>. (7) He <u>appeared</u> happy. (8) Spike gave <u>him</u> affection. (9) It seemed that Buzz had wanted <u>affection</u> and a friend all along. (10) <u>Who</u> frightened the ducks and geese?

Standardized Test Preparation Workshop

Recognizing Appropriate Sentence Construction

Knowing how to use the basic parts of a sentence correctly is the foundation for building good writing. Standardized tests measure your ability to identify a complete sentence. Every sentence must contain a subject (the *who* or *what* that performs the action) and a verb (the action the subject is performing) and express a complete thought. If one of these parts is missing, you have an incomplete sentence, or a fragment. When answering these test questions, check each group of words for a subject and a verb, and then determine whether it expresses a complete thought. Finally, choose the group of words that contains all of the elements of a complete sentence to replace any sentence fragments.

The following question will give you practice with the format used for testing your knowledge of basic sentence parts.

Sample Test Item

Choose the letter of the best way to write each underlined section. If the underlined section needs no change, choose "Correct as is."

If inventors weren't able to pursue their ideas. We would still have to get up and walk to the television to change the channel.

A If inventors weren't able to pursue their ideas. We would still have to get up, and walk to the television to change the channel.

B If inventors weren't able to pursue their ideas, we would still have to get up and walk to the television. To change the channel.

C If inventors weren't able to pursue their ideas, we would still have to get up and walk to the television to change the channel.

D Correct as is

Answer and Explanation

The correct answer is C. The sentence fragment "If inventors weren't able to pursue their ideas" contains a subject—*inventors*—and a verb—*pursue*—but it does not express a complete idea. Answer C combines the fragment with the complete sentence that follows by making the fragment an introductory clause.

Practice 1 **Directions:** Choose the letter of the best way to write the underlined section. If the underlined section needs no change, choose "Correct as is."

King Camp Gillette was a traveling
(1)
hardware salesman, from Fond du Lac

Wisconsin. Invented the first razor with

disposable blades. While shaving with the
(2)
long, single-edged razor used at the time. He

realized only a small part—the blade—of it

was really needed.

1 **A** King Camp Gillette was a traveling hardware salesman from Fond du Lac, Wisconsin, who invented the first razor with disposable blades.

B King Camp Gillette was a traveling hardware salesman. From Fond du Lac, Wisconsin, invented the first razor with disposable blades

C King Camp Gillette was a traveling hardware salesman and inventor from Fond du Lac, Wisconsin. The first razor with disposable blades.

D Correct as is

2 **F** While shaving with the long, single-edged razor used at the time, he realized only a small part of it—the blade—was really needed.

G While shaving with the long, single-edged razor. Used at the time, he realized only a small part of it—the blade—was really needed.

H While shaving with the long, single-edged razor used at the time, he realized, only a small part of it. The blade was really necessary.

J Correct as is

Practice 2 **Directions:** Choose the letter of the best way to write the underlined section. If the underlined section needs no change, choose "Correct as is."

By creating a razor with disposable blades.
(1)
Gillette created a smaller, safer razor.

Safety razors were not an instant success. In
(2)
1903, only 51 razors and 168 blades were

sold. However, two years later, sales of
(3)
90,000 razors and 12,400,000 blades.

1 **A** Gillette created a smaller, safer razor, and by creating a razor with disposable blades.

B Gillette created a smaller, safer razor. When creating a razor with disposable blades.

C By creating a razor with disposable blades, Gillette created a smaller, safer razor.

D Correct as is

2 **F** Safety razors were not an instant success, in 1903, only 51 razors and 168 blades were sold.

G In 1903, sold only 51 razors and 168 blades. Not an instant success.

H Safety razors, not an instant success in 1903. Only 51 razors and 168 blades were sold.

J Correct as is

3 **A** Two years later, sales of 90,000 razors and 12,400,000 blades.

B However, two years later, sales climbed to 90,000 razors and 12,400,000 blades.

C However, climbed to 90,000 razors and 12,400,000 blades.

D Correct as is

Phrases *and Clauses*

▲ **Critical Viewing**
What groups of words would you use to describe the storm in this photograph? **[Describe]**

A **phrase** is a group of words that functions in a sentence as a single part of speech. Phrases do not contain a subject and a verb. For example, in the sentence "I just started reading an excellent book about tornadoes," *about tornadoes* acts as a prepositional phrase. In this chapter, you will learn about prepositional phrases, verbal phrases, and appositive phrases. Each type of phrase has a different use in a sentence.

Just as the development of a tornado depends on a variety of factors, such as temperature and wind, sentences depend on individual clauses to make complete thoughts. A **clause** is a group of words with its own subject and verb. Unlike a phrase, a clause is sometimes, but not always, a complete sentence. In this chapter, you will learn the difference between independent and dependent clauses, as well as how to recognize adjective and adverb clauses.

Diagnostic Test

Directions: Write all answers on a separate piece of paper.

Skill Check A. Copy the prepositional phrase in each sentence below, labeling each one *adjective phrase* or *adverb phrase*.

1. The study of weather is called meteorology.
2. Meteorologists make predictions about the weather.
3. Their forecasts are broadcast on television and radio.
4. People listen with a mixture of trust and disbelief.
5. With the help of new technology, accuracy is improving.

Skill Check B. Identify the verbal phrases in the following sentences as *participial* or *infinitive*. Indicate how each phrase is used and the word(s) it modifies.

6. Feared wherever they occur, tornadoes are the most violent storms.
7. A tornado consists of winds swirling in the shape of a funnel.
8. Blowing at speeds up to 200 miles per hour, tornado winds can tear up just about anything in the path of the storm.
9. These devastating storms may travel at up to 60 miles per hour.
10. People build storm cellars in which to shelter during tornadoes.

Skill Check C. In each sentence, identify the appositive phrase.

11. Hurricanes, another kind of storm, may spread out over 200 miles.
12. Hurricanes are caused by areas of low pressure in the trade winds, strong ocean winds that blow towards the equator.
13. Winds in a hurricane swirl around the eye, its calm center.
14. Wall clouds, the clouds surrounding the eye, produce heavy rains.
15. Hurricane Gilbert, the most violent hurricane on record for the Western Hemisphere, struck the West Indies and Mexico in 1988.

Skill Check D. Copy the sentences below, underlining every adjective or adverb clause. Label each one *adjective* or *adverb*.

16. A harmonica, which produces a sound when you blow into it, is an example of a wind instrument.
17. Whenever air is forced through the harmonica, it vibrates the individual reeds.
18. Because the reeds are vibrating, the air around them vibrates.
19. Anyone who plays the harmonica will find that all the holes on the front are of different sizes.
20. Different sounds are created when air passes through the holes.

Skill Check E. Identify each sentence below as *simple, compound,* or *complex.*

21. The National Federation of Music Clubs is the largest charitable music group in the world.
22. It publishes *Music Clubs* magazine and supports music causes.
23. The federation offers scholarships to young musicians, who each receive $5,000 awards.
24. Sponsoring National Music Week is another of its activities.
25. The group was founded in 1898; it is located in Indianapolis.

Phrases

There are many types of phrases, but they all have one thing in common: The words that make up a phrase work together as one.

> **KEY CONCEPT** A **phrase** is a group of words that functions in a sentence as a single part of speech. Phrases do *not* contain a subject and a verb. ■

Recognizing Prepositional Phrases

By itself, a *prepositional phrase* has at least two parts: a preposition and a noun or pronoun that is the object of the preposition.

EXAMPLE:
    PREP OBJ
    near airports

The object of the preposition may be modified by one or more adjectives.

EXAMPLE:
    PREP ADJ   ADJ   OBJ
    near busy urban airports

The object may also be compound.

EXAMPLE:
    PREP   OBJ   OBJ
    near busy urban highways and airports

No matter how long a prepositional phrase is or how many different parts of speech it contains, a prepositional phrase in a sentence always acts as if it were a one-word adjective or adverb.

Phrases That Act as Adjectives

A prepositional phrase that acts as an adjective in a sentence is called an *adjective phrase.*

> **KEY CONCEPT** An **adjective phrase** is a prepositional phrase that modifies a noun or pronoun by telling *what kind* or *which one.* ■

One-word adjectives modify nouns or pronouns. Adjective phrases also modify nouns and pronouns. However, instead of coming before the noun or pronoun, an adjective phrase usually comes after it.

Theme: Severe Weather

In this section, you will learn about different types of phrases. The examples and exercises in this section are about severe weather events such as hurricanes, tornadoes, and thunderstorms.

Cross-Curricular Connection: Science

💡 Spelling Tip

Although the preposition *through* is pronounced the same way as the verb *threw,* they are spelled differently.

⚙ Grammar and Style Tip

Because prepositional phrases act as adjectives and adverbs, you can use them in your sentences to add description and to clarify action.

Adjectives	Adjective Phrases
The *asphalt* roadway began there.	The roadway *with two lanes* began there.
The *angry* rancher stopped us.	The rancher *with the angry face* stopped us.

Adjective phrases answer the same questions as one-word adjectives do. *What kind* of highway began there? *Which* rancher stopped us?

An adjective phrase can modify almost any noun or pronoun in a sentence.

MODIFYING
SUBJECT: The sound *of the wind* scared us.

MODIFYING
A DIRECT OBJECT: It rattled windows *in the room.*

When two adjective phrases appear in a row, the second phrase may modify the object of the preposition in the first phrase or both phrases may modify the same word.

MODIFYING
THE OBJECT   The weather vane *on the roof of the barn*
OF A PREPOSITION: spun wildly.

MODIFYING
THE SAME WORD: There was a smell *of rain in the air.*

▶ **Exercise 1** Identifying Adjective Phrases Copy the sentences below onto your paper. Then, underline each prepositional phrase used as an adjective, and draw an arrow from it to the word it modifies.
1. Changes in air pressure can cause wind movement.
2. An anemometer measures the speed of the wind.
3. Cups on the anemometer catch the wind.
4. Rushes of air spin the cups.
5. A speedometer on the axle of the anemometer indicates the wind speed.

▼ **Critical Viewing**
Write two sentences about this photograph. Include one phrase beginning with *below* and another beginning with *near.* **[Analyze]**

Get instant feedback! Exercise 1 is available on-line or on CD-ROM.

▶ **More Practice**

Grammar Exercise Workbook
• pp. 69–70
On-line Exercise Bank
• Section 20.1
Go on-line:
PHSchool.com
Enter Web Code:
ebk-7002

Phrases That Act as Adverbs

A prepositional phrase that acts as an adverb modifies the same parts of speech as a one-word adverb does.

KEY CONCEPT An **adverb phrase** is a prepositional phrase that modifies a verb, an adjective, or an adverb. Adverb phrases point out *where, when, in what way,* or *to what extent.* ■

Adverb phrases are used in the same way as one-word adverbs, but they sometimes provide more precise details.

Adverbs	Adverb Phrases
Bring your saddle *here.*	Bring your saddle *to the barn.*
The parade began *early.*	The parade began *at exactly eleven o'clock.*

Adverb phrases can modify verbs, adjectives, and adverbs.

MODIFYING A VERB:	Raindrops fell *in heavy torrents.* (Fell *in what way?*)
MODIFYING AN ADJECTIVE:	The day was warm *for December.* (Warm *in what way?*)
MODIFYING AN ADVERB:	The tornado struck suddenly, *within minutes of the warning.* (Suddenly *to what extent?*)

Adverb phrases, unlike adjective phrases, are not always located near the words they modify in a sentence.

EXAMPLE: *During the storm,* ranchers chased the herd.

Two or more adverb phrases can also be located in different parts of the sentence and still modify the same word.

EXAMPLE: *In an instant,* a tornado tore *through our house.*

Exercise 2 Identifying Adverb Phrases Each of the sentences below contains at least one prepositional phrase used as an adverb. Copy the sentences onto your paper. Then, underline each adverb phrase, and draw an arrow from it to the word it modifies.

EXAMPLE: Thunderstorms are heavy rainstorms

            accompanied by thunder and lightning.

1. Thunderstorms form within large cumulonimbus clouds.
2. Cumulonimbus clouds form when warm air collides with a cold front.
3. Warm, humid air is forced upward into the sky.
4. At the higher altitude, the warm air cools.
5. In a short time, the cooling air creates dense thunderheads.
6. Heavy rain falls and is sometimes accompanied by hail.
7. Inside the clouds, thunderstorms produce strong upward and downward drafts.
8. When a downdraft strikes the ground, the air spreads in all directions.
9. In some instances, the spreading air produces wind bursts called "wind shear."
10. Wind shear has caused airplane accidents during takeoff and landing.

Exercise 3 Revising With Adverb Phrases Complete each of the sentences below with an adverb phrase that answers the question in parentheses.

EXAMPLE: The fog thickened (to what extent?).

ANSWER: The fog thickened through the night.

1. The weather balloon floated north (when?).
2. Take your umbrella (where?).
3. He ran (in what way?) to get out of the storm.
4. Flowing quickly down the mountain, the runoff from the rain spilled (to what extent?).
5. The clouds gathered and darkened (to what extent?).

More Practice

Grammar Exercise Workbook
• pp. 71–72
On-line Exercise Bank
• Section 20.1
Go on-line:
PHSchool.com
Enter Web Code:
ebk-7002

▼ Critical Viewing Describe what you imagine happened in the scene pictured below. Be sure to include the ideas *where, when, in what way,* and *to what extent.* [Infer]

Recognizing Verbal Phrases

To understand the next two kinds of phrases, you must learn about *verbals*. A *verbal* is any verb that is used in a sentence not as a verb, but as another part of speech. The verbals discussed in the next two sections are *participles* and *infinitives*. Participles are used as adjectives. Infinitives are used as nouns, adjectives, or adverbs.

Although they are used as nouns, adjectives, or adverbs, verbals keep certain characteristics of verbs. They can be modified by an adverb or adverb phrase. They can also be followed by a complement, such as a direct object. A verbal used with a modifier or a complement is called a *verbal phrase.*

Participles

Participles are verb forms with two basic uses. When they are used with helping verbs, they are verbs. When they are used alone to modify nouns or pronouns, they become adjectives.

> **KEY CONCEPT** A **participle** is a form of a verb that is often used as an adjective. ■

There are two kinds of participles: *present participles* and *past participles.* Each kind can be recognized by its ending. All present participles end in *-ing.*

EXAMPLES: talking   doing   eating   wanting

Most past participles, however, end either in *-ed* or in *-d.*

EXAMPLES: opened   jumped   played   moved

Other past participles end in *-n, -t, -en,* or another irregular ending.

EXAMPLES: grown   felt   bought   eaten   held

In the following chart, both present and past participles are used in sentences as adjectives.

Present Participles	Past Participles
A *walking* tour was arranged.	The *cooked* food won't spoil.
Playing, she grabbed his hand.	He was by then, of course, a *grown* man.

Participles, like other adjectives, tell *what kind* or *which one.*

Participial Phrases

A participle can be expanded into a *participial phrase* by adding a complement or modifier.

KEY CONCEPT A **participial phrase** is a present or past participle and its modifiers. The participle can be modified by an adverb or adverb phrase or a complement. The entire phrase acts as an adjective in a sentence. ∎

Participles can be expanded in many different ways.

PARTICIPIAL PHRASES
The instructor, *speaking slowly*, explained the use of skis.
The skier, *choosing her slope*, looked at its features carefully.
The esteemed poet, *honored by the award*, expressed his thanks.

The first participial phrase is formed by adding the adverb *slowly* to the participle *speaking*. The second is formed by adding the direct object *her slope* to the participle *choosing*. The third is formed by adding the adverb phrase *by the award* to the participle *honored*.

In the chart, each participial phrase is located after the noun it modifies. It could also go at the beginning of the sentence.

EXAMPLE: *Honored by the award*, the esteemed poet expressed his thanks.

Exercise 4 Recognizing Participial Phrases Copy the sentences below onto your paper. Then, underline each participial phrase and draw an arrow pointing from it to the word it modifies.

EXAMPLE: On the table, I saw several packages <u>wrapped in gold paper</u>.

1. Known for its cold weather, Minnesota has an abundance of snow.
2. My neighbor needed help shoveling his sidewalk.
3. Gripping the shovel, I went to work.
4. The driveway, covered in ice, seemed huge.
5. Finishing up, we went inside to warm our hands.

Text

Get instant feedback! Exercise 4 is available on-line or on CD-ROM.

More Practice

Grammar Exercise Workbook
• pp. 75–78
On-line Exercise Bank
• Section 20.1
Go on-line:
PHSchool.com
Enter Web Code:
ebk-7002

Infinitives and Infinitive Phrases

Infinitives are verb forms that are used as nouns, adjectives, and adverbs. Like participles, they can be combined with other words to form phrases.

KEY CONCEPT An **infinitive** is a verb form that can be used as a noun, an adjective, or an adverb. The word *to* usually appears before the infinitive. ■

EXAMPLES: It is important *to listen*.
He is the one *to ask*.

KEY CONCEPT An **infinitive phrase** is an infinitive with modifiers or a complement, all acting together as a single part of speech. ■

EXAMPLES: It is important *to listen carefully*.
It is not polite *to listen through the keyhole*.
I want *to hear the news*.
They want *to give you a present*.

▼ **Critical Viewing**
Write a short paragraph comparing this nature scene with your favorite natural scenery. Use infinitives and infinitive phrases in your comparison. **[Compare and Contrast]**

Using Infinitive Phrases

An infinitive phrase can be used in a sentence as a noun, an adjective, or an adverb. As a noun, an infinitive phrase can function as a subject, an object, or an appositive.

USED AS A SUBJECT: *To listen carefully* is important.

USED AS AN OBJECT: She wanted *to listen carefully.*

USED AS AN ADJECTIVE: You can rely on me *to listen carefully.*

USED AS AN ADVERB: They waited *to listen carefully* to her.

USED AS AN APPOSITIVE: His suggestion, *to listen carefully*, was appreciated.

▶ **Exercise 5** Identifying Infinitive Phrases and Their Functions Copy the infinitive phrase(s) in each of the following sentences onto your paper, and then write how each phrase functions in the sentence.

EXAMPLE: To reach the top was her goal.
ANSWER: To reach the top (subject)

1. We wanted to get home as soon as possible.
2. To drive up the hill was impossible.
3. Our decision, to stop and get a cup of coffee, proved to be the wrong one.
4. The snow seemed to pile up more quickly than before.
5. We had no choice except to drive on.
6. To understand the problem required us to listen.
7. The boys were about to jump when their mother arrived.
8. The soldier tried to follow orders.
9. My dream, to fly an airplane, was finally coming true.
10. No one seemed to know he was there.

▶ **Exercise 6** Writing Sentences With Infinitive Phrases
Write sentences using each of the following infinitive phrases according to the function indicated in parentheses.
1. to become a doctor (object)
2. to travel to Russia (subject)
3. to roast the chestnuts (direct object)
4. to study harder (appositive)
5. to wait until summer (object of preposition)
6. to bake a cake (appositive)
7. to see them again (predicate noun)
8. to go camping (object of preposition)
9. to learn about art (subject)
10. to visit grandmother's house (direct object)

▶ **More Practice**

On-line Exercise Bank
• Section 20.1
  Go on-line:
  PHSchool.com
  Enter Web Code:
  ebk-7002

Get instant feedback! Exercises 5 and 6 are available on-line or on CD-ROM.

Recognizing Appositive Phrases

Appositives are nouns or pronouns placed directly after other nouns or pronouns to give additional information about these words. Appositives are often set off from the rest of the sentence by commas or dashes.

> **KEY CONCEPT** An **appositive** is a noun or pronoun placed after another noun or pronoun to identify, rename, or explain the preceding word. ∎

Note the way appositives are used in the chart below:

APPOSITIVES
The painter *Pablo Picasso* lived in Spain.
I want to visit Spain's famous museum, *The Prado.*
His painting *Guernica* impressed my father.

> **KEY CONCEPT** An **appositive phrase** is a noun or pronoun with modifiers. It stands next to a noun or pronoun and adds information or details. ∎

The modifiers in the phrase are usually adjectives or adjective phrases.

APPOSITIVE PHRASES
Willa Cather, *an American novelist,* wrote *My Ántonia.*
Lisbon, *a thriving port in Portugal,* has often been the scene of espionage.
The shopping center—*a network of cars, shops, and people*—provides many jobs.

Appositives and appositive phrases can be compound.

EXAMPLE: The two settings, *a city in England* and *a city in Russia,* are contrasted in the book.

Grammar and Style Tip

Using appositives can add important details to the nouns in your sentences, which can make your writing more clear and more interesting.

▶ **Exercise 7** Identifying Appositives and Appositive Phrases
Underline the appositive or appositive phrase in the sentences below. Then, draw an arrow to the word each one modifies.

1. Kublai Khan, the Mongol emperor of China, sent a fleet of ships carrying a huge army to attack Japan.
2. A typhoon, a powerful Pacific Ocean hurricane, struck the fleet.
3. The ships were buffeted by hurricane-force winds, some measuring more than 119 kilometers per hour.
4. The typhoon actually saved the Japanese from their enemies, the Chinese.
5. The Japanese gave the storm a special name, *kamikaze*, which means "divine wind."

▶ **Exercise 8** Combining Sentences Using Appositives and Appositive Phrases Combine each pair of sentences to form a single sentence containing an appositive or appositive phrase.

EXAMPLE: Pilgrims were also known as Separatists. The Pilgrims decided to establish a colony in the New World.

ANSWER: The Pilgrims, a group also known as Separatists, decided to establish a colony in the New World.

1. In 1620, a group of English Pilgrims set sail for North America. They were colonists seeking religious freedom.
2. Their ship was thrown off course by rough seas and storms. Their ship was named the *Mayflower*.
3. Instead of landing near the Hudson River, the *Mayflower* was blown to the Cape Cod peninsula. The Cape Cod peninsula is a spot farther east.
4. John Winthrop was one of the leaders of the Pilgrims. Winthrop thought the landing spot was a good place for their colony.
5. The newest settlement could thank a storm for its beginnings. The settlement was named Plymouth Colony.

More Practice

Grammar Exercise Workbook
• pp. 73–74
On-line Exercise Bank
• Section 20.1
  Go on-line:
  PHSchool.com
  Enter Web Code:
  ebk-7002

Text

Get instant feedback! Exercises 7 and 8 are available on-line or on CD-ROM.

◀ **Critical Viewing** Imagine that you are below the clouds, in the midst of this storm. Write two sentences that include appositive phrases to describe the storm. **[Describe]**

Section Review

GRAMMAR EXERCISES 9–18

Exercise 9 Writing Sentences Using Adjective and Adverb Phrases
Write ten sentences, each using a preposi-tional phrase according to the instructions in parentheses.

1. with little warning (as an adverb phrase)
2. from out of nowhere (as an adverb phrase)
3. in a raincoat and boots (as an adjec-tive phrase)
4. in the eye of the storm (as an adjective phrase)
5. in spite of the weather report (as an adverb phrase)
6. above the clouds (as an adjective phrase)
7. of mud and rain (as an adjective phrase)
8. by gusting winds (as an adverb phrase)
9. as fast as she could (as an adverb phrase)
10. on the radar screen (as an adjective phrase)

Exercise 10 Identifying Participles and Infinitives On your paper, identify the participle or infinitive in the following sentences.

1. Snow is frozen precipitation.
2. Ski resorts are fun to visit when there is a lot of snow.
3. Between 1971 and 1972, Mt. Rainier had an amazing 1,122 inches of snow.
4. It might be hard to believe, but Syracuse, New York, is the snowiest large city.
5. Nearly every area in the United States receives snow-producing storms.

Exercise 11 Identifying Verbal Phrases On your paper, write the par-ticipial phrase or the infinitive phrase in the following sentences.

1. The day, interrupted by a blizzard, seemed very long.
2. That afternoon, the snow began to fall less rapidly.
3. Continuing for several hours, the bliz-zard covered the highway with snow.
4. The snow plows could not clear the snow-clogged roads.
5. He attempted to drive home, but was forced to turn back.
6. Newly frozen ice lay beneath the snow.
7. Skidding on the ice, two trucks nearly collided.
8. The snow, changing to sleet as it got warmer, made the roads dangerous.
9. To be safe, several roads were closed.
10. The storm was predicted to last two days.

Exercise 12 Writing Sentences With Verbal Phrases On your paper, write ten sentences using the verbal phras-es below. Underline each phrase and draw an arrow pointing from it to the word it modifies.

1. growing without roots
2. to improve the soil
3. blooming only in the summer
4. dropping to -30°F in the winter
5. to avoid weeds
6. to prepare for planting
7. caught in the direct sun
8. to dig rapidly
9. to write about gardening
10. nourished by the sun and rain

▶ **Exercise 13** Adding Verbal
Phrases to Sentences On your paper,
complete each sentence below by filling in
the blank according to the instructions in
parentheses.

1. Living near the Arctic Circle, the Inuit
   have learned ___?___ . (infinitive
   phrase)
2. The Inuit, ___?___ , are isolated. (participial phrase)
3. ___?___ , they catch fish and hunt
   whales and seals. (infinitive phrase)
4. Clothing, ___?___ , varies from area to
   area. (participial phrase)
5. Caribou skin, ___?___ , is lightweight
   and warm. (participial phrase)

▶ **Exercise 14** Identifying
Appositive Phrases On your paper,
write the appositive phrase found in each
sentence in the following paragraph.

(1) Satellites and weather balloons, two
important weather-prediction tools, have
been greatly improved in recent years. (2)
Short-range forecasts, predictions for up
to five days, are now fairly reliable. (3)
Weather balloons carry instruments into
the troposphere, the lowest layer of
Earth's atmosphere. (4) The instruments
gauge three important measurements,
temperature, air pressure, and humidity.
(5) The first weather satellite was
launched in 1960, the year before my
father was born.

▶ **Exercise 15** Identifying
**Appositives and the Nouns They
Modify** On a separate sheet of paper,
write the appositives and appositive phrases in the following sentences, and indicate
the noun each one renames.

1. A barometer, an instrument that
   measures changes in air pressure,
   helps in forecasting weather.

2. There are two kinds of barometers—
   mercury barometers and aneroid
   barometers.
3. A mercury barometer consists of a
   glass tube that is open at the bottom
   and partially filled with mercury, a
   metallic element.
4. The space in the tube above the mercury is almost a vacuum, an airless
   area.
5. Increases in air pressure will cause
   the column of mercury in the tube
   to rise above its normal level,
   76 centimeters.

▶ **Exercise 16** Find It in Your
Reading List the prepositional and participial phrases you find in these sentences from "The Chase" by Annie Dillard.

He chased us silently over picket
fences, through thorny hedges,
between houses, around garbage
cans, and across streets. Every time
I glanced back, choking for breath,
I expected he would have quit.

▶ **Exercise 17** Find It in Your
Writing Look through your writing
portfolio. Find examples of sentences that
contain prepositional phrases, participial
phrases, or infinitive phrases. Underline
any phrases you find, and tell how they
are used. If your writing does not contain
any of these types of phrases, then revise
your writing to include them.

▶ **Exercise 18** Writing Application
Write a brief description of a rainstorm
or snowstorm. Include sentences that contain prepositional phrases, participial
phrases, infinitive phrases, and appositive
phrases in your description.

Clauses

There are two basic kinds of clauses: *independent clauses* and *subordinate clauses.*

KEY CONCEPT An **independent clause** has a subject and a verb and can stand by itself as a complete sentence. ■

INDEPENDENT
CLAUSES:

      S   V
The air vibrated.

          S   V
In the morning, he began to play the cello.

KEY CONCEPT A **subordinate clause**, also known as a dependent clause, has a subject and a verb but cannot stand by itself as a complete sentence. It is only part of a sentence. ■

SUBORDINATE
CLAUSES:

   S V
after she performed her solo

     S   V
while the band practiced in the garage

Why is the thought in a subordinate clause *not* complete? Part of the answer is found in the first word of each clause. Such words as *after* and *while* will often make a clause *dependent* on another clause. To make a complete thought from a subordinate clause, it is necessary to add an independent clause.

In the following example, the subordinate clause is italicized; the independent clause is not.

EXAMPLE:

       S   V   S   V
After she performed, Debbie felt relieved.

Exercise 19 Identifying and Classifying Clauses Copy the following sentences, underlining the independent clauses once and the subordinate clauses twice. Some sentences have no subordinate clause.

1. The singer was terrific.
2. Before she came out on stage, the band played several instrumental numbers.
3. The guitar player, who was especially good, played one solo with his teeth.
4. The music was extremely loud.
5. The audience cheered wildly when she began singing the first song.
6. The lights focused on her as she sang and danced.
7. In the middle of the concert, the band took a break.
8. My favorite song was called "In the Midnight Hour."
9. Everyone sang along as they performed the last song.
10. When the curtain closed and the lights came on, we knew the show was over.

Theme: Music

In this section, you will learn about the different types of clauses and how to classify sentences by structure. The examples and exercises in this section are about music and musicians.

Cross-Curricular Connection: Music

More Practice

On-line Exercise Bank
• Section 20.2
  Go on-line:
  PHSchool.com
  Enter Web Code:
  ebk-7002

Get instant feedback! Exercise 19 is available on-line or on CD-ROM.

Adjective Clauses

A subordinate clause will sometimes act as an adjective in a sentence.

▷ **KEY CONCEPT** An **adjective clause** is a subordinate clause that modifies a noun or a pronoun. ■

Like one-word adjectives and adjective phrases, an *adjective clause* answers w*hat kind* or *which one.*

Recognizing Adjective Clauses Most adjective clauses begin with the words *that, which, who, whom,* and *whose.* Sometimes, an adjective clause begins with an adverb, such as *since, where,* or *when.*

The adjective clauses in the following chart are italicized. The arrow in each sentence points from the adjective clause to the word in the independent clause that the adjective clause modifies. Notice that the adjective clauses come right after the words they modify.

ADJECTIVE CLAUSES
The student *whom I asked for help* turned pages of music for me. (*Which* student?)
By pushing the pedal *that is connected to the drum,* you will make sound. (*Which* pedal?)
The harp, *which was played in ancient Egypt,* was forbidden for women to play. (*Which* harp?)
In the centuries *since that time,* other instruments with strings have been invented. (*Which* centuries?)
The piano, *whose strings are hit by hammers to produce sound,* can be made louder or softer by foot pedals. (*What kind* of piano?)
At the moment *when the pedal is pushed,* the damper inside the piano changes the tone. (*Which* moment?)
People *who make stringed instruments* have to keep in mind the size, shape, material, and string tension of the instrument in order to create the perfect sound. (*What kind* of people?)

▲ **Critical Viewing** In a short paragraph, use independent and subordinate clauses to compare this cello with other stringed instruments. How are they similar? How are they different? **[Distinguish]**

Clauses • **439**

More Practice

Grammar Exercise
Workbook
• pp. 79–80
On-line Exercise Bank
• Section 20.2
Go on-line:
PHSchool.com
Enter Web Code:
ebk-7002

Exercise 20 Identifying Adjective Clauses Copy the following sentences, and underline the adjective clause in each.

1. A person who is willing to devote much time and effort to it may find a career in music satisfying.
2. For a future in music, start taking lessons from a teacher who has excellent credentials.
3. After high school, you can enroll in a conservatory, which is a specialized music school.
4. Students who are inquisitive can find many ways to use their interest in music.
5. Many musicians who study in conservatories plan to become professional composers or performers.

Exercise 21 Writing Sentences With Adjective Clauses
Use each of the adjective clauses below to write a complete sentence.

EXAMPLE: that the band featured

ANSWER: The instrument *that the band featured* was an electronic keyboard.

1. whose talent is exceptional
2. where the newest bands play
3. which has a beautiful sound
4. who are in professional orchestras
5. that you can find in the music field
6. which is played the loudest
7. where I buy printed music
8. that plays the lowest notes
9. who enjoy classical music
10. whom I wanted to hear

▶ Critical Viewing Use adjective clauses to describe the qualities that these brass instruments share. [**Classify**]

Adverb Clauses

Subordinate clauses can also be used as adverbs.

> **KEY CONCEPT** An **adverb clause** is a subordinate clause that modifies a verb, an adjective, or an adverb. ■

Adverb clauses can answer any of the following questions about the words they modify: *Where? When? In what way? To what extent? Under what conditions?* or *Why?* Adverb clauses begin with *subordinating conjunctions.* The following chart lists a number of common subordinating conjunctions:

COMMON SUBORDINATING CONJUNCTIONS	
after	so that
although	than
as	though
as if	unless
as long as	until
because	when
before	whenever
even though	where
if	wherever
in order that	while
since	

A subordinating conjunction always introduces the adverb clause. In a sentence, the conjunction will usually appear in one of two places—either at the beginning, when an adverb clause begins the sentence, or in the middle, connecting the independent clause to the subordinate clause.

EXAMPLES:

ADVERB CLAUSE | IND CLAUSE
Since you expect to be late, I will prepare dinner.

ADVERB CLAUSE | IND CLAUSE
Whenever you are late, I expect you to call.

IND CLAUSE | ADVERB CLAUSE
I will prepare dinner *since* you expect to be late.

IND CLAUSE | ADVERB CLAUSE
I expect you to call *whenever* you are late.

> **KEY CONCEPT** A **subordinating conjunction** introduces an adverb clause. ■

💡 Spelling Tip

Be careful when writing the word *although.* You may be tempted to write *all though,* but the subordinating conjunction *although* is one word with only one *l.*

In the chart below, the adverb clauses are italicized. The arrows point to the words the clauses modify. Notice that each clause answers *Where? When? In what way? To what extent? Under what conditions?* or *Why?* about the word it modifies.

ADVERB CLAUSES

Modifying Verbs	Put the package *wherever you find room.* (Put *where?*)
	The concert will begin *when the conductor enters.* (Will begin *when?*)
	Leo spoke *as if he were frightened.* (Spoke *in what manner?*)
	I will have some lemonade *if you do too.* (Will have *under what conditions?*)
Modifying an Adjective	I am tired *because I have been chopping wood all day.* (Tired *why?*)
Modifying an Adverb	She knows more *than the other engineers do.* (More *to what extent?*)

▶ **Exercise 22** Writing Sentences With Adverb Clauses Use each of the adverb clauses below to write a complete sentence.

EXAMPLE: before we performed

ANSWER: *Before we performed*, we practiced daily.

1. when a composer writes some music
2. until the music develops the proper sound and rhythm
3. unless someone plays the music
4. until the music is played perfectly
5. when the two musicians get together
6. whenever the music begins
7. if the music catches on with the public
8. so that their songs are played on the radio
9. since music influences our emotions
10. after a composer sets poetry to music

▶ **More Practice**

Grammar Exercise Workbook
• pp. 81–82
On-line Exercise Bank
• Section 20.2
  Go on-line:
  PHSchool.com
  Enter Web Code:
  ebk-7002

Complete the exercise on-line! Exercise 22 is available on-line or on CD-ROM.

Classifying Sentences by Structure

All sentences can be classified according to the number and kinds of clauses they contain.

The Simple Sentence The *simple sentence* is the most common type of sentence structure.

▶ **KEY CONCEPT** A **simple sentence** consists of a single independent clause. ■

Simple sentences vary in length. Some are quite short; others can be several lines long. All simple sentences, however, contain just one subject and one verb. They may also contain adjectives, adverbs, complements, and phrases in different combinations.

Simple sentences can also have various compound parts. They can have a compound subject, a compound verb, or both. Sometimes, they will also have other compound elements, such as a compound direct object or a compound phrase.

All of the following sentences are simple sentences. The subjects are underlined once, and the verbs are underlined twice.

ONE SUBJECT AND VERB:	The <u>monsoon</u> <u>came</u>.
COMPOUND SUBJECT:	<u>Landslides</u> and <u>avalanches</u> <u>are</u> common.
COMPOUND VERB:	The <u>door</u> <u>squeaked</u> and <u>rattled</u>.
COMPOUND SUBJECT AND VERB:	My <u>mother</u> and <u>father</u> <u>said</u> goodbye and <u>left</u> on vacation.
COMPOUND DIRECT OBJECT:	He <u>opened</u> the letter and the box. DO DO
COMPOUND PREPOSITIONAL PHRASE:	It <u>can rain</u> from the east or PREP PHRASE from the west.

What does a simple sentence *not* have? First, a simple sentence never has a subordinate clause. Second, it never has more than one independent clause.

Exercise 23 Recognizing Simple Sentences Copy each simple sentence below onto your paper, and underline the subject once and the verb twice. Notice that some of the subjects and verbs are compound.

EXAMPLE: <u>Miles Davis</u> <u><u>played</u></u> the trumpet and <u><u>made</u></u> more than fifty jazz recordings.

1. In the late 1940's, a new style of jazz emerged, known as cool jazz.
2. Miles Davis and other young musicians were influened by and adopted this new style.
3. Their approach to cool jazz blended strong rhythms with flowing melodies.
4. The musicians used softer tones, syncopation, and a more even beat than other jazz players.
5. Cool-jazz players also created complex harmonies and experimented on new instruments.
6. For the first time, cellos, flutes, and tubas were featured in jazz performances.
7. Throughout the 1950's, many jazz groups became identi- fied with this new sound.
8. Some music critics objected to the new style and wrote negative reviews.
9. The new sound became popular with college students and intellectuals.
10. Jazz concerts became more popular than ever before.

The Compound Sentence A *compound sentence* is made up of more than one simple sentence.

KEY CONCEPT A **compound sentence** consists of two or more independent clauses. ∎

In most compound sentences, the independent clauses are joined by a comma and a coordinating conjunction (*and, but, for, nor, or, so,* or *yet*). They may also be connected with a semicolon (;) or a colon (:).

EXAMPLES: Jamal manned a two-day music festi- val, <u>and</u> eight bands agreed to play.

All the bands performed on the first day<u>;</u> two were missing the second day.

Notice in both of the preceding examples that there are two separate and complete independent clauses, each with its own subject and verb. Like simple sen- tences, compound sentences never contain subordi- nate clauses.

More Practice

Grammar Exercise Workbook
• pp. 83–86
On-line Exercise Bank
• Section 20.2

Go on-line:
PHSchool.com
Enter Web Code:
ebk-7002

Get instant feedback! Exercises 23 and 24 are available on-line or on CD-ROM.

▼ **Critical Viewing** Use simple sentences to identify your favorite musical instrument and explain why you prefer it. **[Support]**

► **Exercise 24** **Recognizing Compound Sentences** The sentences below are compound sentences. Copy each onto your paper. Then, underline the subject once and the verb twice in each independent clause.

EXAMPLES: Country <u>music</u> <u>has become</u> very popular today, and several <u>radio stations</u> <u>feature</u> country artists.

1. Country music is played all over the country, but its roots are in the Appalachian region.
2. Actually, the history of country music goes back to Europe; settlers brought folk ballads with them to their new homeland.
3. Appalachian musicians used different instruments to play the folk ballads, and they tried different singing styles.
4. Radio played an important role in spreading country music, for people in remote areas were able to hear it.
5. Singers in the Southwest added a western swing style, so they called their blend country western music.

The Complex Sentence *Complex sentences* contain subordinate clauses, which can be either adjective clauses or adverb clauses.

► **KEY CONCEPT** A **complex sentence** consists of one independent clause and one or more subordinate clauses. ■

In a complex sentence, the independent clause is often called the *main clause.* The main clause has its own subject and verb, as does each subordinate clause.

MAIN CLAUSE   SUBORD. CLAUSE
EXAMPLES: January 26, 1947, <u>is</u> the day that <u>India</u> <u>won</u> its independence.

SUBORD. CLAUSE   MAIN CLAUSE
Because the <u>day</u> <u>is</u> so important, many of the <u>festivities</u> <u>are</u> official.

In the next example, the complex sentence is more complicated because the main clause is split by an adjective clause.

┌──────── MAIN CLAUSE ────────┐
          ┌─SUBORD. CLAUSE─┐
EXAMPLE: <u>Schoolchildren</u>, <u>who</u> <u>have</u> the day off, <u>participate</u> in an exciting parade.

The two parts of the independent clause form one main clause: *Schoolchildren participate in an exciting parade.*

⊙ Technology Tip

When typing on a computer, make sure to put only one space after every comma or period.

20.2

> **Exercise 25** Recognizing Complex Sentences The follow-
ing are complex sentences. Copy each onto your paper.
Underline the subject once and the verb twice in each clause.
Then, put parentheses around each subordinate clause.

EXAMPLE: (Since many teenagers love to dance), they enjoy
rock-and-roll music.

1. Rock-and-roll melodies are simple, which makes them
   easy to play and sing.
2. When singers perform on stage, people in the audience
   sing along with them.
3. The electric guitars that some musicians play add exciting
   sounds to the songs.
4. Teenage girls in the audience often screamed while Elvis
   Presley performed on stage.
5. Though Presley was very popular, several other singers
   sold just as many records.

> **Exercise 26** Identifying the Structure of Sentences On
your paper, identify the structure of each of the following sentences as *simple, compound,* or *complex.*

EXAMPLE: When the Beatles arrived in New York in 1964,
they began a "British invasion" of American
music.
ANSWER: complex

1. The Beatles consisted of four musicians in their twenties.
2. Because they were quite poor, they struggled at first.
3. They could not afford music lessons, so they taught themselves to play and sing.
4. They had been playing together for several years before
   they had their first hit record.
5. They listened to many American recordings, and then they
   added new ideas to their music.
6. Because the group's voices blended so well, many of their
   songs feature strong harmonies.
7. The Beatles had long hair, but they wore suits on stage.
8. Others, such as the Rolling Stones, had a different image.
9. They wore casual clothes and sang more raucous songs.
10. Whereas the Beatles sang a lot of love songs, the Rolling
    Stones focused on blues.

More Practice

Grammar Exercise
Workbook
• pp. 83–86
On-line Exercise Bank
• Section 20.2
Go on-line:
PHSchool.com
Enter Web Code:
ebk-7002

Get instant feedback!
Exercises 25, 26 and
27 are available on-
line or on CD-ROM.

Grammar and Style Tip

A complex sentence is
a good way to effec-
tively combine two
simple sentences.

GRAMMAR IN LITERATURE

from **The Treasure of Lemon Brown**

Walter Dean Myers

In the following passage, the writer has used simple, compound, and complex sentences.

The person who called himself Lemon Brown peered forward, and Greg could see him clearly. He was an old man. His black, heavily wrinkled face was surrounded by a halo of crinkly white hair and whiskers that seemed to separate his head from the layers of dirty coats piled on his smallish frame. His pants were bagged to the knee, where they were met with rags that went down to the old shoes. The rags were held on with strings, and there was a rope around his middle. Greg relaxed. He had seen the man before, picking through the trash on the corner and pulling clothes out of a Salvation Army box.

▶ **Exercise 27** Revising the Structure of Sentences On your paper, rewrite the following sentences according to the directions in parentheses.

EXAMPLE: Bob Dylan influenced many musicians during the 1960's. He is credited with inventing folk rock. (combine to make one compound sentence)

ANSWER: Bob Dylan influenced many musicians during the 1960's, and he is credited with inventing folk rock.

1. Dylan made an important contribution to rock, but he was originally a folk singer. (Break into two simple sentences.)
2. He began his career in New York City. He recorded in Nashville. (Combine into a complex sentence.)
3. His early songs contained a strong social message, but later Dylan's music became more personal. (Change from a compound to a complex sentence.)
4. Later, Dylan played his songs on electric instruments. He used a strong rock beat. This style became known as folk rock. (Combine to make one complex sentence.)
5. Many of Dylan's original fans did not like his electrified music. They even booed at many of his performances. (Combine to make one compound sentence.)

Hands-on Grammar

Silly Sentence Structures

Explore compound and complex sentences by building silly sentence structures. First, create a set of coordinating conjunctions. On individual cards, write *and, but, for, so,* and *yet.* Write a comma in front of each word.

Next, create a set of subordinating conjunctions—connecting words used in complex sentences. Use the following words: *after, although, because, before, since, unless,* and *where.* Do not use commas in front of these words. Mix the two sets of cards together and place them face down so that the words cannot be seen.

Work with a partner to create two clauses. Decide who will write the clause that begins the sentence and who will write the clause that ends the sentence. Capitalize and use end punctuation accordingly. Write your clauses on separate strips of paper. Lay the two strips with the finished clauses next to each other. Draw one of the face-down connecting cards and place it between the two strips. Read the resulting sentence, and decide whether it is a compound or a complex sentence.

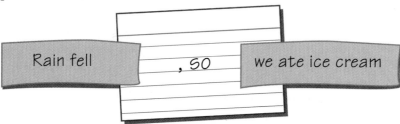

Continue joining clauses until you have used each of the cards at least once. Remember, you are creating these silly sentences to explore sentence structure. In your own writing, you should join only related ideas.

Find It in Your Reading In a short story or a textbook, find examples of compound and complex sentences using the coordinating and subordinating conjunctions on your cards. Write each sentence you find on the back of the appropriate card.

Find It in Your Writing Look through a piece of your writing to find examples of compound and complex sentences. If you cannot find at least three examples of each, challenge yourself to combine sentences, if possible.

Section 20.2 Section Review

GRAMMAR EXERCISES 28–34

Exercise 28 Writing Sentences Using Dependent and Independent Clauses Identify each of the following clauses as independent or dependent.

1. Tuareg, which is a tribe in Africa
2. music is the heart of a Tuareg party
3. the singer plays an instrument with only one string
4. when the men pass around a bowl
5. musicians sing in a high voice

Exercise 29 Writing Sentences Using Adjective Clauses Write sentences using each of the following adjective clauses correctly.

1. that a composer wants to convey
2. when we are sad
3. who inspires us to dance
4. who find music relaxing
5. which is enjoyed by all
6. who leads the group
7. that it became a fan favorite
8. which the dancers ignored
9. whose name we shall never forget
10. where the fans gathered to celebrate

Exercise 30 Writing Sentences Using Adverb Clauses Write sentences using each of the following adverb clauses correctly.

1. when you write music
2. if a song is difficult to sing
3. because it sounds strange
4. as the group performed
5. although they played well
6. before we arrived at the concert
7. even though they danced for hours
8. unless the guitar was too loud
9. while we were watching
10. until the recording was complete

Exercise 31 Identifying Sentence Structure Identify each sentence in the following paragraph as *simple, compound,* or *complex.*

(1) Asian musicians use different instruments from those used by Western musicians, so their music sounds different. (2) While most Western music has harmony, traditional Chinese music has no harmony. (3) Two Chinese stringed instruments, the quin and the pipa, are very popular. (4) Bamboo grows extensively in Japan, and many Japanese instruments are made from bamboo. (5) One bamboo flute, which is called the *shakuhachi,* can be found in every Japanese orchestra.

Exercise 32 Find It in Your Reading Look back at the passage from "The Treasure of Lemon Brown" on page 447. Write down three adjective clauses you identify in the selection. Write three original sentences using the adjective clauses you have identified.

Exercise 33 Find It in Your Writing Look through your writing portfolio and choose a piece of writing in which you have used simple, compound, and complex sentences. Identify at least one example of each.

Exercise 34 Writing Application Imagine that you have attended a concert of your favorite musical group. Write a brief review of the performance using a variety of sentence structures.

Chapter Review

GRAMMAR EXERCISES 35–44

> **Exercise 35** Identifying
Prepositional Phrases On your paper,
write the prepositional phrase(s) in the
sentences below, and identify whether
each acts as an *adjective* or an *adverb*.

1. A tornado is a display of power.
2. The winds in a tornado are incredibly
   turbulent.
3. Tornado winds are the most violent
   winds that occur on Earth.
4. A funnel descends from a dark cloud.
5. It whirls over the ground in a narrow
   path.
6. Tornadoes occur during violent
   thunderstorms.
7. Spring and summer are the typical
   seasons for tornadoes.
8. Tornadoes can cause millions of dollars in damage.
9. Strong tornadoes can lift cars, homes,
   and animals into the air.
10. The National Weather Service continu-
    ally looks for tornadoes.

> **Exercise 36** Revising Sentences
Using Appositives and Appositive
Phrases Combine each of the following
sentence pairs by using appositives or
appositive phrases.

1. In 1989, Hurricane Hugo struck. That
   was a year of devastating weather.
2. Charleston is a city in South Carolina.
   Hugo killed eighteen people in
   Charleston.
3. Guadeloupe is a French-owned island.
   Guadeloupe was also hit by Hugo.
4. Hugo was a hurricane of only medium
   strength. Hurricane Hugo was one of
   the most costly storms in history.
5. The worst-hit areas were the
   Caribbean and the southern United
   States. These areas were declared dis-
   aster areas.

> **Exercise 37** Revising Sentences
Using Participial Phrases Use participial
phrases to combine each of the following
sentence pairs.

1. Acid rain contains sulfuric and nitric
   acids. The polluted rain falls to Earth.
2. Water mixes with air containing sulfur
   dioxide and nitrogen oxides. The combination creates acid rain.
3. These chemicals are caused by auto-
   mobiles, factories, and other sources.
   The sources burn fossil fuels.
4. Acid rain has polluted thousands of
   lakes and streams. This pollution kills
   fish and other aquatic life.
5. The Clean Air Act was amended in
   1990. The act tightened emissions
   standards.

> **Exercise 38** Classifying Different
Kinds of Phrases Label each of the
underlined phrases below a *prepositional
phrase*, a *participial phrase*, or an *appositive phrase*.

(1) Meteorologists study hurricanes, a
type of tropical storm. (2) Any tropical
storm with winds over 39 miles per hour
receives a name. (3) The eye-wall, the
area around the eye of the storm, can
produce 2 inches of rain hourly. (4)
Flooding is a threat in low-lying areas.
(5) Meteorologists using satellite data are
able to track hurricanes. (6) The Saffir-
Simpson scale designates five levels of
hurricanes. (7) Beginning over warm
waters, a hurricane picks up moisture.
(8) Hurricanes, the most destructive of
natural disasters, cause devastation. (9)
The center of a hurricane is calm. (10)
Typhoons, a type of hurricane, occur in
the western Pacific.

▶ **Exercise 39** Classifying and Writing Sentences With Phrases and Clauses Classify each numbered item below as a *phrase*, an *independent clause*, or a *dependent clause*. Then, write a sentence using each.

1. who play in the orchestra
2. a gentle, flowing melody
3. most musicians played off-key
4. when the conductor raised the baton
5. drums beat out a steady rhythm

▶ **Exercise 40** Identifying Adjective and Adverb Clauses Copy the following sentences. Underline and identify the adjective and adverb clauses. Draw an arrow to the word each clause modifies.

1. The arts, which differ greatly in each Indian state, have been highly developed in India for thousands of years.
2. Indian music is based on a different scale from the one Western culture uses.
3. Its harmonies, which have different sounds as a base, are distinctive.
4. Even though the music is different, the instruments are similar to those of the Western world.
5. In India, some stringed instruments look like long guitars, although they have many more strings.

▶ **Exercise 41** Identifying Sentence Structures Identify the sentences below as *simple*, *compound*, or *complex*.

(1) Johann Sebastian Bach came from a musical family, and several of his sons also became composers. (2) He lived in Germany and served as a violinist, organist, and choir director. (3) Bach wrote hundreds of compositions, but he did not gain fame during his lifetime. (4) Most of Bach's compositions were ignored until long after he died. (5) When they are played today, Bach's compositions please audiences.

▶ **Exercise 42** Revising to Vary Sentence Structure On a separate sheet of paper, revise the following paragraph. Combine some of the simple sentences into compound and complex sentences.

In India, you can see ancient architecture in monasteries and shrines. These structures were built by Buddhist monks. On the walls, you can see beautiful frescoes. The frescoes are paintings on fresh plaster. Hindu temples offer another kind of architecture. Hindu temples feature tall towers. They have curving sides and taper at the top. In southern India, there are rectangular pyramids. The steps are carved to tell stories.

▶ **Exercise 43** CUMULATIVE REVIEW Sentence Parts On your paper, label the underlined word(s) in each sentence *subject, verb, direct object, indirect object, predicate noun,* or *predicate adjective.*

(1) Wolfgang Amadeus Mozart was <u>a child prodigy</u>. (2) He first <u>composed and performed</u> music at the age of five. (3) There have been few <u>people</u> as talented as Mozart. (4) His father gave <u>him</u> piano lessons. (5) Soon, Mozart surpassed his <u>father</u> in musical ability. (6) Mozart's father was <u>willing to give up his own career to manage his son's</u>. (7) Mozart's music is still <u>popular</u> today. (8) It <u>is</u> featured in concerts around the world. (9) Have <u>you</u> ever listened to a composition by Mozart? (10) I have several <u>CDs</u> in my collection.

▶ **Exercise 44** Writing Application Write a paragraph about a song or musician that you enjoy. Use adjective and adverb phrases in your paragraph, and include simple, compound, and complex sentences.

Standardized Test Preparation Workshop

Revising and Editing

Knowledge of grammar is tested on standardized tests. Questions that measure your ability to use phrases and clauses reveal your understanding of basic sentence construction and style. Remember that a phrase is a group of words without a subject and a verb that acts as a single part of speech, and a clause is a group of words that contains a subject and a verb. Use the following strategies when answering questions that test your knowledge of phrases and clauses:

- First, read the entire passage to get an idea of the author's purpose.
- Focus on the underlined words, and note any similarities between underlined sentences. Can they be combined by using a phrase or clause without changing meaning?
- Choose the answer that best uses a phrase or clause to combine similar ideas without changing the meaning.

The following will give you practice with the format of questions that test rules of standard grammar.

Test Tip

Although an answer choice may make sense, it may not be the best way to rewrite the original. Read every choice carefully before deciding on your answer.

Sample Test Item

Choose the letter of the best way to write the underlined section. If the underlined section needs no change, choose "Correct as is."

Many cultures have folk tales. These folk
(1)
tales communicate important values and

ideas.

A   Many cultures have folk tales that communicate important values and ideas.

B   Many cultures have folk tales, and these folk tales communicate important values and ideas.

C   Folk tales, which communicate important values and ideas, belong to few cultures.

D   Correct as is.

Answer and Explanation

The correct answer is A. This is the best rewrite of the two sentences because it combines related ideas without changing the meaning. Changing the second sentence into a clause eliminates the repetition of the words *folk tales*.

▶ **Practice 1** **Directions:** Choose the letter of the best way to write each underlined section. If the underlined section needs no change, choose "Correct as is."

One popular folk tale is the story of Cin-
(1)
derella. The story is known and loved

around the world. It is the story of a poor,
(2)
hard-working girl. She suffers under an

evil stepmother. There are more than 900
(3)
versions of Cinderella. The oldest is

more than a thousand years old. Most
(4)
Americans are familiar with the story writ-

ten in the 1600's. It is the only one with a

fairy godmother and a midnight time limit.

There are many differences between the
(5)
stories. The poor girl always escapes her

stepmother, marries the prince, and lives

happily ever after.

1 A One popular folk tale is the story of Cinderella, and the story is known and loved around the world.

  B One popular folk tale, known and loved around the world, is the story of Cinderella.

  C Known and loved around the world is one popular folk tale. This is the story of Cinderella.

  D Correct as is.

2 F It is the story of a poor, hard-working girl; she suffers under an evil stepmother.

  G Suffering under an evil stepmother is the poor, hard-working girl.

  H It is the story of a poor, hard-working girl who suffers under an evil stepmother.

  J Correct as is.

3 A There are more than 900 versions of this Cinderella, the oldest is more than a thousand years old.

  B There are more than 900 versions; the oldest is more than a thousand years old.

  C The oldest of the versions is more than a thousand years old.

  D Correct as is.

4 F Most Americans are familiar with the story written in the 1600's. Although it is the only one with a fairy god-mother and a midnight time limit.

  G Most Americans are familiar with the story written in the 1600's, the only one with a fairy godmother and a midnight time limit.

  H Written in the 1600's, most Americans are familiar with the story, the only one with a fairy god-mother and a midnight time limit.

  J Correct as is.

5 A The poor girl always escapes her stepmother, marries the prince, and lives happily ever after.

  B There are many differences between the stories, and the poor girl always escapes her stepmother, marries the prince, and lives happily ever after.

  C Although there are many differences between the stories, the poor girl always escapes her stepmother, marries the prince, and lives happily ever after.

  D Correct as is.

▲ **Critical Viewing**
What are some problems that can block sentences from achieving their goal? **[Evaluate]**

The sentence is a basic unit of communication. You use sentences every day—to ask questions, give directions, make statements, express emotion, or share information. Some of your sentences may be short and direct, and others may be long and complicated. In either case, you will need to follow certain rules and suggestions to make sure your sentences are correct, interesting, and meaningful. Putting words together in effective sentences is the first step in making sure that you are communicating clearly.

In this chapter, you will learn about the different functions of sentences. You will also learn how to combine ideas in sentences and how to vary the style of your sentences. Finally, you will learn how to avoid some of the problems that writers often confront when they are writing sentences.

Diagnostic Test

Directions: Write all answers on a separate sheet of paper.

Skill Check A. Identify each sentence as *declarative, interrogative, imperative,* or *exclamatory,* and indicate which end mark to use.

1. Look at this article about Jim Thorpe
2. Didn't he win two Olympic gold medals in track and field events
3. He was also one of the first professional football stars
4. What an amazing athlete he was
5. Isn't there a town in Pennsylvania named after Jim Thorpe

Skill Check B. Combine each pair of sentences into one compound or complex sentence.

6. Soccer is the most popular sport in most of the world. Soccer has not always been a popular sport in the United States.
7. Today, many American children play soccer at school. They play soccer in organized leagues on weekends.
8. Sports are good for children. Sports teach children cooperation.
9. The net seems large. Scoring a goal is difficult.
10. A goal is scored. Everyone cheers.

Skill Check C. Rearrange each sentence to begin with the part of speech indicated in parentheses.

11. Pele joined Brazil's top soccer league at age sixteen. (preposition)
12. He became a star player quickly. (adverb)
13. Brazil relied on his skills to win three World Cup titles. (infinitive)
14. One trick was kicking a ball backwards over his head. (participle)
15. Pele remarkably scored 1,282 goals in 1,363 matches. (adverb)

Skill Check D. On your paper, write *F* if the numbered item below is a fragment, *RO* if it is a run-on, *MM* if it contains a misplaced modifier, and *DN* if it contains a double negative.

16. Two sports were invented in Massachusetts in the 1890's, one was basketball and the other was volleyball.
17. The net suspended between seven and eight feet above the ground.
18. Standing at the back, the ball is sent over the net by a server.
19. The other team can't hit the ball no more than three times.
20. They must return the ball, if not, the other team gets a point.

Skill Check E. Choose the word that best completes the sentence.

21. I am a good player (accept, except) for my strength.
22. Once, I hit the ball hard, with an unexpected (affect, effect).
23. The ball sailed over the other team and landed in (their, there, they're) bleachers.
24. The reason I hit the ball so hard was (because, that) I was thinking of the upcoming math test.
25. I will try not to hit the ball (to, too, two) hard in the future.

Classifying the Four Functions of a Sentence

Sentences can be classified according to what they do. Some sentences present facts or information in a direct way; others pose questions to the reader or listener; still others present orders or directions. A fourth type of sentence expresses strong emotion. These four types of sentences are called *declarative, interrogative, imperative,* and *exclamatory.* Each type of sentence has a different purpose and is constructed in a different way.

The type of sentence you are writing determines the punctuation mark you use to end the sentence. The three end marks are the period (.), the question mark (?), and the exclamation mark (!).

Declarative sentences are the most common type. They are used to state or "declare" facts.

▶ **KEY CONCEPT** A **declarative sentence** states, or declares, an idea and ends with a period. ■

DECLARATIVE: Soccer is a team sport.
Golf is a sport that can be played throughout a lifetime.
Although most schools fund team sports, many students choose to participate in individual sports.

Interrogative means "asking." An *interrogative sentence* is a question. What end mark do you think you would use after an interrogative sentence?

▶ **KEY CONCEPT** An **interrogative sentence** asks a question and ends with a question mark. ■

INTERROGATIVE: What is your best time in the one-mile run?
Where is the county track meet being held this year?
Who is the fastest runner on the school track team?

The word *imperative* is related to the word *emperor,* a person who gives commands. *Imperative sentences* are like emperors: They give commands.

Theme: Sports and Games

In this section, you will learn about the four functions sentences can perform. The examples and exercises in this section are about sports and games.

Cross-Curricular Connection: Physical Education

GRAMMAR IN LITERATURE

from **Tiger: A Biography of Tiger Woods**
John Strege

In the following passage, the last sentence is an imperative sentence. The other sentences Earl [Tiger Woods's father] speaks are declarative. Since many imperative sentences leave the you *understood, the final sentence might also have been spoken as "Do what you want to do."*

"Tiger," Earl said, "you're not out there playing for me. You're out there playing for yourself. On the golf course you're the boss. You do what you want to do."

▶ **KEY CONCEPT** An **imperative sentence** gives an order or a direction and ends with either a period or an exclamation mark. ■

Most imperative sentences start with a verb. In this type of imperative sentence, the subject is understood to be *you*.

IMPERATIVE: Follow my instructions carefully.
              Run as hard as you can!

Notice the punctuation at the end of these examples. In the first sentence, the period suggests that a mild command is being given in an ordinary tone of voice. The exclamation mark at the end of the last sentence suggests a strong command, one given in a loud voice.

▶ **Critical Viewing** Describe the question you might ask about the result of this shot, as well as the end mark you would use. **[Question]**

Tiger Woods tees off during a golf tournament.

▶ **KEY CONCEPT** An **exclamatory sentence** conveys strong emotion and ends with an exclamation mark. ■

EXCLAMATORY: She's going to crash into that hurdle!
                  What an outstanding runner she is!

To *exclaim* means to "shout out." *Exclamatory sentences* are used to "shout out" emotions such as happiness, fear, delight, or anger.

▶ **Exercise 1** Identifying the Four Types of Sentences Read each of the following sentences carefully, and identify it as *declarative, interrogative, imperative,* or *exclamatory.* After each answer, write the appropriate punctuation mark to end that sentence.

EXAMPLE: Do you plan to run in the relay
ANSWER: interrogative (?)

1. The World Cup is the most famous international soccer competition
2. Isn't it held every year
3. Grab the soccer ball, and throw it to me
4. Do you know which country's team won the first World Cup trophy
5. I want to know right now
6. Look up Uruguay in the encyclopedia
7. Does it say that Uruguay's team won the first World Cup in 1930
8. Pele was a Brazilian soccer star
9. Did I read that he played in the United States for several seasons
10. That was the most exciting game I have ever seen
11. Can you dribble the ball with your feet
12. What an amazing header she took
13. She scored the winning goal in the last minute of the over-time period
14. When France won the World Cup, fans in Paris cheered all night long
15. No night was as exciting as that one

▶ **More Practice**

Grammar Exercise Workbook
• pp. 87–88
On-line Exercise Bank
• Section 21.1
  Go on-line:
  PHSchool.com
  Enter Web Code:
  ebk-7002

Text

Complete the exercise on-line! Exercise 1 is available on-line or on CD-ROM.

Section Review

GRAMMAR EXERCISES 2–7

Exercise 2 Identifying the Four Types of Sentences Read each sentence carefully, and identify it as *declarative, interrogative, imperative,* or *exclamatory.*

1. Horseshoes is an easy game to play.
2. The iron stakes are set 40 feet apart.
3. Pound the stakes into the ground carefully.
4. The stakes should stick out of the ground 15 inches.
5. How do you score the game?
6. A ringer is a throw in which the shoe hooks the stake.
7. Show me how to throw.
8. I love to play horseshoes!
9. How many people can play at one time?
10. I won the game!

Exercise 3 Supplying the Correct Punctuation Mark Copy each sentence below onto your paper. Add the appropriate end mark, and identify the sentence type.

1. There are many fun and simple yard games
2. Get the neighborhood together, and have some fun
3. My favorite games are games of tag
4. Do you know any new forms of tag
5. You're it
6. Try to reach home base before I touch you
7. How will the game end
8. Count slowly by fives to one hundred
9. I am going to duck behind the big azalea bush
10. Stay out of the street
11. You never touched me
12. When do you have to go home
13. I am wearing my new sneakers
14. No, you cannot borrow them
15. Can you come over tomorrow, so we can play again

Exercise 4 Revising to Write the Four Types of Sentences Rewrite each sentence below to fit the function indicated in parentheses. Add the appropriate end mark.

1. Are the world's greatest badminton players from Indonesia (declarative)
2. A badminton smash can go over 200 miles per hour (exclamatory)
3. More than one million Americans play badminton regularly (interrogative)
4. You can get more information by writing to the U.S. Badminton Association (imperative)
5. They have a team (interrogative)

Exercise 5 Find It in Your Reading
Read this declarative sentence from *Tiger: A Biography of Tiger Woods.* Write an *imperative* sentence, an *interrogative* sentence, and an *exclamatory* sentence that might have been part of Earl Woods's lecture to his son.

Earl's lecture, delivered at decibels with which Tiger was unfamiliar, centered on the theme that golf owes no one anything, least of all success, and that quitting is a flagrant foul, intolerable.

Exercise 6 Find It in Your Writing
Look through your portfolio for examples of all four types of sentences. If you can't find examples of each, challenge yourself to revise a piece of writing to vary your sentence types.

Exercise 7 Writing Application
Write a short explanation of how to play your favorite sport. Include each of the four types of sentences.

Sentence Combining

Books written for very young readers present information in short, direct sentences. While these short sentences make the book easy to read, they don't make the book enjoyable or interesting to older readers. Writing for mature readers should include sentences of varying lengths and complexity to create a flow of ideas. One way to achieve sentence variety is to combine sentences—to express two or more related ideas or pieces of information in a single sentence. Look at the first two examples below. Then, look at how the two ideas are combined in different ways in the last three sentences.

EXAMPLES: We went to the zoo.
                 We saw monkeys.

COMBINED: We went to the zoo and saw monkeys.
                 We saw monkeys at the zoo.
                 We saw monkeys when we went to the zoo.

Combining Sentence Parts

In the examples and exercises below, you will learn several different ways to combine sentences in order to write in a more mature and interesting way.

▶ **KEY CONCEPT** Sentences can be combined by using a compound subject, a compound verb, or a compound object. ■

EXAMPLE: Moira enjoyed watching the monkeys.
              Tom enjoyed watching the monkeys.

COMPOUND   Moira and Tom enjoyed watching the
SUBJECT: monkeys.

EXAMPLE: Lisa played the game.
              Lisa won a stuffed animal.

COMPOUND   Lisa played the game and won a stuffed
VERB: animal.

EXAMPLE: Scott rode the roller coaster.
              Scott rode the Ferris wheel.

COMPOUND   Scott rode the roller coaster and the
OBJECT: Ferris wheel.

Theme: Fun Places

In this section, you will learn different ways to combine sentences to make your writing more interesting. The examples and exercises in this section are about fun places to visit.

Cross-Curricular Connection: Social Studies

▶ **Exercise 8** Combining Sentences Combine each pair of sentences in the way that makes the most sense. Identify what parts of the two sentences you made compound as you combined them.

1. My class went to the amusement park. We also went to the zoo.
2. At the amusement park, the carousel played music. It also rang bells.
3. Jen rode the carousel. Todd rode the carousel, too.
4. The carousel was too mild for Glenn. The Ferris wheel was too mild for Glenn.
5. He preferred the log flume. He rode it three times in a row.
6. At lunch, we ate sandwiches. We ate apples for lunch. We also ate raisins.
7. I enjoyed the roller coaster. I enjoyed the carousel. I enjoyed the Ferris wheel.
8. No one wanted to end our day at the amusement park. No one wanted to go home.
9. The class trip to the amusement park was fun. It was exciting.
10. Everyone thanked our chaperones. Everyone asked them to come back next year.

More Practice

Grammar Exercise Workbook
• pp. 89–92
On-line Exercise Bank
• Section 21.2
Go on-line:
PHSchool.com
Enter Web Code:
ebk-7002

Text

Complete the exercise on-line! Exercise 8 is available on-line or on CD-ROM.

◀ **Critical Viewing** Use a compound verb to describe the ways in which this carousel pony might combine fun and fear for a young rider. [**Draw Conclusions**]

Joining Clauses

Use a compound sentence when combining related ideas of equal weight. To create a compound sentence, join the two independent clauses with a comma and a coordinating conjunction. Common conjunctions include *and, but, nor, for, so, or,* and *yet.* You can also link the two sentences with a semicolon (;) if they are closely related.

> **KEY CONCEPT** Sentences can be combined by joining two independent clauses to create a compound sentence. ■

EXAMPLE:	The wind whipped against our faces. The screams of other riders excited us.
COMPOUND SENTENCE:	The wind whipped against our faces, and the screams of other riders excited us.
EXAMPLE:	The ride lasted just a few minutes. My stomach continued to rumble for several hours.
COMPOUND SENTENCE:	The ride lasted just a few minutes, but my stomach continued to rumble for several hours.
EXAMPLE:	The roller coaster is such fun. It's very popular.
COMPOUND SENTENCE:	The roller coaster is such fun; it's very popular.

> **Exercise 9** Combining Sentences

Combine each pair of sentences by joining the clauses, following the instructions in parentheses.

1. The roller coaster had six loops. It was the wildest one Mark had ever ridden. (comma and conjunction)
2. He wanted to ride it several times. The lines were too long. (comma and conjunction)
3. Lynette was determined to ride it again. She waited in line. (comma and conjunction)
4. The amusement park had a wide variety of rides. All of us found something we liked. (semicolon)
5. This is my favorite amusement park. The rides are all really exciting. (semicolon)

▼ **Critical Viewing** After coming out of the big twist, how do you think these riders feel? What sounds are they making? Answer with a compound sentence. **[Infer]**

> **KEY CONCEPT** Sentences can be combined by changing one of them into a subordinate clause. ■

Combine sentences into a complex sentence to emphasize the relationship between two ideas, one of which depends on the other. A subordinating conjunction will help readers understand the relationship. Common subordinating conjunctions are *after, although, because, before, since,* and *unless.*

EXAMPLE:	We were frightened. The ride went so fast.
COMBINED WITH A SUBORDINATE CLAUSE:	We were frightened because the ride went so fast.

> **Exercise 10** Combining Sentences With Subordinating Conjunctions Combine each pair of sentences with a subordinating conjunction.
> 1. We rode the carousel. We rode the Ferris wheel.
> 2. Jamie rode the log flume to cool off. The day was so hot.
> 3. Brendan tried the roller coaster. He doesn't like loops.
> 4. Arthur promised to ride the monster coaster. It was closed.
> 5. We went home. The sun went down.

> **KEY CONCEPT** Sentences can be combined by changing one of them into a phrase. ■

When combining sentences in which one of the sentences simply adds details, change one of the sentences into a phrase.

EXAMPLE:	My team plays tomorrow. We play the Cougars.
COMBINED:	My team plays against the Cougars tomorrow.
EXAMPLE:	My team will play against the Cougars. It is the only undefeated team in the league.
COMBINED:	My team will play against the Cougars, the only undefeated team in the league.

> **Exercise 11** Using Phrases to Combine Sentences Combine the following pairs of sentences by rewriting information from one sentence as a phrase and adding it to the other.
> 1. Our class went to the amusement park. We went there for the entire day.
> 2. The whole class went. We traveled by bus.
> 3. The roller coaster thrilled us. The roller coaster has six loops.
> 4. This roller coaster is not for everyone. This roller coaster is the fastest in the area.
> 5. The trip to the amusement park was fun. It was on Tuesday.

Learn More

For a more complete list of subordinating conjunctions, turn to Chapter 20.

> **More Practice**
>
> Grammar Exercise Workbook
> • pp. 89–92
> **On-line Exercise Bank**
> • Section 21.2
>   *Go on-line:*
>   PHSchool.com
>   *Enter Web Code:*
>   ebk-7002

iText

Complete the exercises on-line! Exercises 9, 10, and 11 are available on-line or on CD-ROM.

Section Review

GRAMMAR EXERCISES 12–17

▶ **Exercise 12** Combining Sentence Parts Combine each pair of sentences by creating a compound subject, verb, or object.

1. Ferris wheels can be found in almost every amusement park. Roller coasters can be found in almost every amusement park.
2. Most amusement parks have games. Most also have food stands.
3. You can enjoy the rides at an amusement park. You can spend time with your friends at an amusement park.
4. Some amusement parks offer special discounts. Some amusement parks offer two-for-one tickets.
5. When we go to the amusement park, we arrive early. We also stay late.

▶ **Exercise 13** Combining Clauses Combine each pair of sentences into a single compound or complex sentence.

1. Amusement parks have permanent rides. Traveling carnivals have rides that can be disassembled and moved.
2. We went to the state fair last year. We wanted to see the 4-H judging.
3. We left before dawn. The parking area was already crowded when we arrived.
4. We left right after lunch. It rained.
5. Next month, we might go to a theme park. We haven't decided which one.
6. I want to go to one with lots of rides. My parents want to go to one nearby.
7. The drive might be long. I think it's worth the time.
8. There are many reasons to go to a theme park. The main one is to have fun.
9. People in costumes greet guests. The greeting makes everyone feel festive.
10. There is so much to see. You probably can't see it all in one day.

▶ **Exercise 14** Using Phrases to Combine Sentences Combine each pair of sentences by changing one of them into a phrase.

1. We planned a family outing. It was a trip to the zoo.
2. We saw monkeys there. The monkeys were in a large habitat.
3. We rode the monorail. It went around the park.
4. The monorail is comfortable and convenient. It is the best way to see the whole park quickly.
5. We saw hundreds of animals. The animals were below the monorail.

▶ **Exercise 15** Find It in Your Reading Read the following sentences from "Zoo" by Edward D. Hoch. Identify the ideas that have been combined, and state each idea as a separate sentence.

All day long it went like that, until ten thousand people had filed by the barred cages [that were] set into the side of the spaceship. Then, as the six-hour limit ran out, Professor Hugo once more took the microphone in hand.

▶ **Exercise 16** Find It in Your Writing Look through your portfolio for a paragraph that contains several short sentences. Combine two of the short sentences to form one longer sentence.

▶ **Exercise 17** Writing Application Write a paragraph about a fun place you have visited with your family or friends. Combine ideas, using one of the ways suggested in this section.

Section 21.3 *Varying Sentences*

Varying the length and form of the sentences you write can help create a rhythm, achieve an effect, or emphasize the connections between ideas. There are several ways you can introduce variety in the sentences you write.

Varying Sentence Length

Reading too many long sentences in a row is as uninteresting as reading too many short sentences. When you want to emphasize a point or surprise a reader, insert a short, direct sentence to interrupt the flow of several long sentences.

Some longer sentences contain only one main idea and should not be broken into separate sentences. Other sentences contain two or more ideas and might be shortened by breaking up the ideas.

LONGER SENTENCE: You may have learned that many animals in many parts of the world fear snakes, but the mongoose does not.

TWO SENTENCES: You may have learned that many animals in many parts of the world fear snakes. The mongoose does not.

> ### Theme: Real and Fictional Animals
>
> In this section, you will learn how to make your writing more interesting by varying your sentences. The examples and exercises in this section are about real and fictional animals.
>
> **Cross-Curricular Connection: Science**

GRAMMAR IN LITERATURE

from **Rikki-tikki-tavi**
Rudyard Kipling

In the following passage, the last sentence is emphasized because it is shorter and simpler than the preceding sentences.

. . . When a snake misses its stroke, it never says anything or gives any sign of what it means to do next. Rikki-tikki did not care to follow them, for he did not feel sure that he could manage two snakes at once. So he trotted off to the gravel path near the house, and sat down to think. It was a serious matter for him.

▶ **Exercise 18** Forming Short Sentences On a separate sheet of paper, rewrite the following sentences by breaking each into two sentences or forming a simpler, more direct sentence.

EXAMPLE: The mongoose is an animal that can fight with snakes because it is quick and agile. (Rewrite as a more direct sentence.)

ANSWER: The quick and agile mongoose is able to fight snakes.

1. The mongoose views the snake as a dangerous enemy, and the snake reacts to the mongoose in the same way. (Break into two sentences.)
2. The mongoose can be found in India, and it can be found in Jamaica. (Rewrite as a more direct sentence.)
3. The mongoose in Rudyard Kipling's story seems quite friendly with people, but his behavior does not truly reflect the behavior of a wild mongoose. (Break into two sentences.)
4. The snake in the story is devious and clever, and he is constantly trying to catch Rikki-tikki-tavi. (Rewrite as a more direct sentence.)
5. In the end, the family is very grateful to the little mongoose, and it has good reason to be thankful. (Break into two sentences.)

Spelling Tip

Remember that in words such as *grateful* and *thankful,* the suffix *-ful* is spelled with only one *l.*

Varying Sentence Beginnings

Another way to vary your sentences is to start your sentences in different ways. For instance, you can start sentences with different parts of speech.

Start with a noun (or an article and a noun).	Birdhouses, surprisingly, are not difficult to make.
Start with an adverb.	Surprisingly, birdhouses are not difficult to make.
Start with an infinitive.	To make birdhouses is, surprisingly, not difficult.
Start with a gerund.	Making birdhouses is, surprisingly, not difficult.

▶ **Exercise 19** Varying Sentence Beginnings Rearrange each sentence to begin with the part of speech indicated in parentheses.

1. The snake silently slithered through the grass. (adverb)
2. The mongoose was hiding in the tall weeds. (participle)
3. The snake would have to be quick to catch the mongoose. (infinitive)
4. Cautiously, the mongoose peeked around the corner. (article and noun)
5. The mongoose cleverly waited until the snake had gone away. (adverb)

You can also vary sentence beginnings by reversing the traditional subject-verb order.

Subject-Verb Order	Verb-Subject Order
The snake is waiting.	Waiting is the snake.
The boy watched cautiously.	Cautiously watched the boy.

▶ **Exercise 20** Inverting Subject-Verb Order Rewrite each of the following sentences by inverting the subject-verb order to verb-subject order. Rearrange the rest of the words in the sentence as needed.

1. The land is full of wildlife.
2. In the air the humming of insects vibrates.
3. Some type of living thing exists under every rock.
4. Numerous animal species appear at the water's edge.
5. The sun dawns on a new day.

▶ **More Practice**

Grammar Exercise Workbook
• pp. 91–92
On-line Exercise Bank
• Section 21.3
  Go on-line:
  PHSchool.com
  Enter Web Code:
  ebk-7002

Get instant feedback! Exercises 18, 19, and 20 are available on-line or on CD-ROM.

◀ Critical Viewing In two or three sentences, tell what this pair of mongooses might be watching. Use a different beginning for each sentence. [Speculate]

Section Review

GRAMMAR EXERCISES 21–26

Exercise 21 Revising Long
Sentences Rewrite the following sentences by breaking each into two sentences or forming a simpler, more direct sentence.

1. Artists and writers have often used lions as symbols of courage, and lions have been portrayed in many paintings, statues, stories, and movies. (Rewrite as a more direct sentence.)
2. The lion is a universal symbol in literature and art, and it is featured in works from China, Greece, and Rome. (Break into two sentences.)
3. A popular fable by Aesop is about a lion, and the fable teaches a good lesson. (Rewrite as a more direct sentence.)
4. The Sphinx is a character from Greek and Egyptian mythology, and it has the head of a human, and it also has the body of a lion. (Rewrite as a more direct sentence.)
5. Even today, the lion is a popular subject, and it has been featured in movies such as *The Lion King*. (Break into two sentences.)

Exercise 22 Varying Sentence
Beginnings Rearrange each sentence below to begin with the part of speech indicated in parentheses.

1. Aesop used the fable "The Fox and the Crow" to teach a lesson. (infinitive)
2. A crow is sitting in a tree with a piece of cheese in her beak. (participle)
3. A fox nearby spies on the crow. (adverb)
4. To trick the crow is the fox's plan. (article and noun)
5. His goal is to get her cheese. (gerund)
6. The fox flatters her to distract the crow's attention. (infinitive)

7. He asks her slyly to sing just one song. (adverb)
8. The crow drops the cheese on opening her mouth to sing. (participle)
9. The fox snaps up the cheese in a flash. (preposition)
10. Aesop adds a moral to end the fable. (infinitive)

Exercise 23 Inverting Subject-
Verb Order Invert the subject-verb order in the following sentences.

1. A leopard is hunting in the dark.
2. Its senses are alert to any movement.
3. Its prey is caught by surprise.
4. Two lions are gaining on the giraffe.
5. The chase ends not long after.

Exercise 24 Find It in Your
Reading Notice the use of long and short sentences in this passage from "The Fox and the Crow." Which parts of the long sentence are independent clauses?

The Crow lifted up her head and began to caw her best, but the moment she opened her mouth the piece of cheese fell to the ground, only to be snapped up by Master Fox. "That will do," said he. "That was all I wanted."

Exercise 25 Find It in Your
Writing Find examples of long sentences in compositions in your portfolio. Rewrite them, forming shorter, more direct sentences.

Exercise 26 Writing Application
Write a paragraph about your favorite fictional animal. Use both short and long sentences in your paragraph.

Section 21.4

Avoiding Sentence Problems

Correcting Sentence Fragments

Some groups of words, even though they have a capital at the beginning and a period at the end, are not complete sentences. They are *fragments*.

▶ **KEY CONCEPT** A **fragment** is a group of words that does not express a complete thought. ■

A sentence expresses a complete thought; a fragment does not. A fragment can be a group of words with no subject; a group of words that includes a possible subject but no verb; a group of words with a possible subject and only part of a possible verb; or even a subordinate clause standing alone.

FRAGMENTS	COMPLETED SENTENCES
In the early evening.	The flight arrived *in the early evening.*
Felt happy and relaxed.	I *felt happy and relaxed.*
The sign in the corridor.	*The sign in the corridor* is surprising.
The train coming around the bend.	*The train* was *coming around the bend.*
When she first smiled.	*When she first smiled*, the whole world seemed to light up.

▶ **Exercise 27** Recognizing Sentence Fragments Each of the following is either a sentence or a fragment. Write *F* if it is a fragment and *S* if it is a complete sentence.

EXAMPLE: Tourists climbing pyramids.
ANSWER: F

1. The parched sands of the desert.
2. The streets of Cairo are narrow and winding.
3. We shopped.
4. Bought a souvenir in the open bazaar.
5. Since there is very little rain in the area.

Theme: Ancient and Modern Egypt

In this section, you will learn how to avoid problems that make your sentences incorrect or hard to understand. The examples and exercises in this section are about ancient and modern Egypt.

Cross-Curricular Connection: Social Studies

▼ **Critical Viewing** Use complete sentences to describe the environmental conditions that may cause fragments to fall from this ancient statue. **[Speculate]**

The Sphinx rises majestically in the Egyptian desert.

Correcting Phrase Fragments

A phrase by itself is a fragment. It cannot stand alone because it does not have a subject and a verb.

> **KEY CONCEPT** A phrase should not be capitalized and punctuated as if it were a sentence. ■

A *phrase fragment* can be corrected by adding it to a nearby sentence. The example below shows a prepositional phrase following a complete sentence.

FRAGMENT:	The travelers rode camels. *On the morning of March 4.*
ADDED TO NEARBY SENTENCE:	The travelers rode camels *on the morning of March 4.*

You can also correct a phrase fragment by adding to the phrase whatever is needed to make it a complete sentence. This method often requires adding a subject and a verb.

CHANGING PHRASE FRAGMENTS INTO SENTENCES

Phrase Fragment	Complete Sentence
In the ancient tomb	The treasure was found *in the ancient tomb.*
Touching his hand	*Touching his hand,* she asked for her father's advice.
To observe Ramadan	Sam learned *to observe Ramadan.*

> **Exercise 28** Changing Phrase Fragments Into Sentences
> Use each of the following phrase fragments in a sentence. You may use the phrase at the beginning, at the end, or in any other position in the sentence. Check to see that each of your sentences contains a subject and a verb.

EXAMPLE:	In the morning after breakfast.
EXPANDED:	Sheri visited the mosque in the morning after breakfast.

1. To grow crops.
2. Waiting for rain.
3. In the Nile River.
4. Lost in the desert.
5. In Egypt.

> **More Practice**
>
> Grammar Exercise Workbook
> • pp. 95–98
> On-line Exercise Bank
> • Section 21.4
> *Go on-line:*
> PHSchool.com
> *Enter Web Code:*
> ebk-7002

Text

Complete the exercise on-line! Exercise 28 is available on-line or on CD-ROM.

Correcting Clause Fragments

All clauses have subjects and verbs, but some cannot stand alone as sentences.

▶ **KEY CONCEPT** A subordinate clause should not be capitalized and punctuated as if it were a sentence. ■

Subordinate clauses do not express complete thoughts. Although a subordinate adjective or adverb clause has a subject and a verb, it cannot stand by itself as a sentence. (See Chapter 20 for more information about subordinate clauses and the words that begin them.)

Like phrase fragments, *clause fragments* can usually be corrected in either of two ways: (1) by attaching the fragment to a nearby sentence, or (2) by adding whatever words are needed to turn the fragment into a sentence.

Notice how the following clause fragments are corrected using the first method.

FRAGMENT:	The class enjoyed the poem. *That I recited to them as part of my oral report on Egypt.*
ADDED TO NEARBY SENTENCE:	The class enjoyed the poem *that I recited to them as part of my oral report on Egypt.*
FRAGMENT:	I'll give my report today. *As long as you give yours, too.*
ADDED TO NEARBY SENTENCE:	I'll give my report today *as long as you give yours, too.*

To change a clause fragment into a sentence by the second method, you must add an independent clause to the fragment.

CHANGING CLAUSE FRAGMENTS INTO SENTENCES

Clause Fragment	Complete Sentence
That you described.	I found the necklace *that you described.*
	The necklace *that you described* has been found.
When he knocked.	I opened the door *when he knocked.*
	When he knocked, I opened the door.

Learn More

For more information about sentences and fragments, turn to Chapter 19.

21.4

More Practice

Grammar Exercise Workbook
• pp. 95–98
On-line Exercise Bank
• Section 21.4
Go on-line:
PHSchool.com
Enter Web Code:
ebk-7002

▶ **Exercise 29** **Changing Clause Fragments Into Sentences**
Use each of the clause fragments below in a sentence. Make sure that each sentence contains an independent clause.

EXAMPLE: That she wanted to use.
EXPANDED: I lent her the camera *that she wanted to use.*

1. If you send me a postcard from Cairo.
2. Which has an average temperature between 55 degrees and 70 degrees in the cool season.
3. That she taught us about the Nile River.
4. Who we thought were friendly and polite.
5. When the Nile River flooded the valley.

▶ **Exercise 30** **Changing Fragments Into Sentences** Decide what is missing in each fragment, and then rewrite it as a complete sentence.

EXAMPLE: In the fall of each year.
EXPANDED: *In the fall of each year,* the Nile River floods.

1. Countries in Africa.
2. Where there are deserts, mountains, and rivers.
3. The third pyramid that we visited.
4. Saving money for a trip to Egypt.
5. In the morning.
6. Frightened by the mummy.
7. To listen to the music in the marketplace.
8. Whom you met in Sinai.
9. Four blankets in Egypt.
10. While they crossed the Suez Canal.

Complete the exercises on-line! Exercises 29, 30, and 31 are available on-line or on CD-ROM.

▼ **Critical Viewing** Explain the impression these pyramids make on you, and tell why. **[Connect]**

Exercise 31 Revising to Correct Fragments in a
Paragraph There are five fragments in the following paragraph. Rewrite the entire paragraph, correcting each fragment.
You may correct a fragment by attaching it to a nearby sentence or by adding words to it to form a new sentence.

EXAMPLE: Needed a translator.
EXPANDED: Because we could not speak Arabic, *we needed a
             translator.*

(1) Before written records existed. (2) Egypt was established.
(3) In the northeastern part of Africa. (4) Today, Egypt's capital
is Cairo. (5) The most populated city in Africa. (6) Cairo is the
center of government, industry, and business. (7) Important
for commerce, transportation, and education. (8) The Nile
River is a major resource for Cairo. (9) It is a waterway for
transportation. (10) Water for irrigation.

Journal Tip

In your journal, take
notes on some of
the facts about
Egypt that interest
you. Then, review
them later to find a
topic for a report.

Correcting Run-ons

A fragment is an incomplete sentence. A *run-on*, on the
other hand, crowds together complete ideas without using the
punctuation needed to see their relationship.

KEY CONCEPT A **run-on** is two or more complete sentences that are not properly joined or separated. ■

Run-ons are usually the result of haste. Learn to check
your sentences carefully to see where one sentence ends and
the next one begins.

Two Kinds of Run-ons There are two kinds of run-ons.
The first one is made up of two sentences that are run together without any punctuation between them. The second type of
run-on consists of two or more sentences separated only by a
comma.

WITH NO   I use our library often the reference section is
PUNCTUATION: my favorite part.

WITH ONLY   The library contains a wealth of information
A COMMA: about Egypt, it is located on the second floor.

A good way to distinguish between a run-on and a sentence
is to read the words aloud. Your ear will tell you whether you
have one or two complete thoughts and whether you need to
make a complete break between the thoughts.

> **Exercise 32** Recognizing Run-ons On your paper, write *S* if the item is a sentence and *RO* if the item is a run-on.

EXAMPLE: At nine, Tutankhamen became king of Egypt, at eighteen he died.

ANSWER: RO

1. After Narmer unified the northern and southern kingdoms of Egypt, he became Egypt's first king.
2. The kings of ancient Egypt were known as pharaohs, they were believed to have been chosen and favored by the gods.
3. Egyptians worshiped the pharaohs as though they were gods, some people even said that the pharaohs were the sons of the gods.
4. Cheops is one of the better-known pharaohs of Egypt, and his tomb is visited by millions of people every year.
5. The Egyptians constructed one pyramid in a twenty-year time period it is not surprising that it took so long to cut, move, and assemble the two million stone blocks, which weigh more than two tons each.

▲ **Critical Viewing** What elements of this image reflect the status of the individual? Answer in complete sentences. [Analyze]

Three Ways to Correct Run-ons

There are three easy ways to correct a run-on sentence.

Using End Marks **End marks** are periods, question marks, and exclamation marks.

> **KEY CONCEPT** Use an end mark to separate a run-on into two sentences. ■

Properly used, an end mark splits a run-on into two shorter but complete sentences.

RUN-ON: The ancient Egyptians left remarkable monuments to their civilization, their huge temples and pyramid tombs still stand along the Nile today.

CORRECTED SENTENCES: The ancient Egyptians left remarkable monuments to their civilization. Their huge temples and pyramid tombs still stand along the Nile today.

🌀 **Learn More**

For help in identifying conjunctions, see Chapter 18.

Using Commas and Coordinating Conjunctions

Sometimes the two parts of a run-on are related and should be combined into a compound sentence.

> **KEY CONCEPT** Use a comma and a coordinating conjunction to combine two independent clauses into a compound sentence. ∎

The most common coordinating conjunctions are *and, but, or, for,* and *nor.* To separate the clauses properly, use both a comma and a conjunction.

RUN-ON: I want to go on a Nile cruise, I need more money.
CORRECTED I want to go on a Nile cruise, but I need more
SENTENCE: money.

Using Semicolons
You can sometimes use a semicolon to connect the two parts of a run-on.

> **KEY CONCEPT** Use a semicolon to connect two closely related ideas. ∎

Do not overuse the semicolon. Use a semicolon only when the ideas in both parts of the sentence are closely related.

RUN-ON: The first train to Luxor leaves at 6:05, the
           express doesn't leave until an hour later.

CORRECTED The first train to Luxor leaves at 6:05; the
SENTENCE: express doesn't leave until an hour later.

> **Exercise 33** Revising to Correct Run-ons Correct the following run-ons, using one of the methods you have learned.
> 1. There are three pyramids at Giza, a sphinx is also there.
> 2. A sphinx is a monster it has a human head and a lion's body.
> 3. The Great Sphinx is in Giza, it is called the Father of Terror because of its size and location.
> 4. Imagine standing next to the Great Sphinx, it is 66 feet tall.
> 5. If you could put the statue on a football field, it would cover almost the entire field, it is 242 feet long.
> 6. The Great Sphinx faces the Nile River, which is toward the east, its back faces the three great pyramids.
> 7. The age of the creature is unknown, evidence shows that it may be older than the pyramids.
> 8. There are many chambers in the Great Sphinx, an ancient passageway leads to one in the center of the statue.
> 9. Engraved in the body are several drawings, they are known as hieroglyphics.
> 10. Hieroglyphics are pictures that are symbols for sounds and words they were used as a writing system.

Grammar and Style Tip

Words such as *however, therefore, thus,* and *consequently* are effective words to start a sentence that may have originally been part of a run-on. These words connect the ideas in the sentences and clarify their meaning.

> **More Practice**
>
> Grammar Exercise Workbook
> • pp. 99–102
> On-line Exercise Bank
> • Section 21.4
>   *Go on-line:*
>   PHSchool.com
>   *Enter Web Code:*
>   ebk-7002

Complete the exercises on-line! Exercises 32 and 33 are available on-line or on CD-ROM.

Correcting Misplaced Modifiers

If a phrase or clause acting as an adjective or adverb is not placed near the word it modifies, the meaning of the sentence may be unclear.

> **KEY CONCEPT** A *modifier* should be placed as close as possible to the word it modifies. ■

A modifier placed too far away from the word it modifies is called a *misplaced modifier.*

MISPLACED MODIFIER: We rented a boat at the lake with an outboard motor.

The misplaced phrase *with an outboard motor* makes it seem as though the lake has an outboard motor.

CORRECTED SENTENCE: At the lake, we rented a boat with an outboard motor.

Below is a somewhat different type of misplaced modifier.

MISPLACED MODIFIER: *Walking to the pyramid,* the sand felt hot under our feet.

In this sentence, *walking to the pyramid* should modify a person. Instead, it incorrectly modifies sand.

CORRECTED SENTENCE: *Walking to the pyramid,* we felt the hot sand under our feet.

> **Exercise 34** Recognizing Misplaced Modifiers Check the placement of the modifier in each sentence. If it is correct, write *C* on your paper. If it is misplaced, write *MM.*

EXAMPLE: My brother Richard bought a loaf of bread at the open bazaar that was warm and crusty.

ANSWER: MM

1. Originally, tools and weapons were used by the people that were made of stone and organic materials.
2. Later, people made tools of copper and other metals.
3. People who were richer or more influential were buried in graves that were larger and more ornate.
4. Early civilizations built ships for trade along the Nile River that were large and efficient.
5. Two domains emerged in Egypt that became known as the northern and the southern kingdoms.

 Spelling Tip

Remember that the sound *us* at the end of an adjective is often spelled *-ious;* for example, *cautious, ambitious.*

> **More Practice**

Grammar Exercise Workbook
• pp. 103–106
On-line Exercise Bank
• Section 21.4
  Go on-line:
  PHSchool.com
  Enter Web Code:
  ebk-7002

 Text

Get instant feedback! Exercises 34 and 35 are available on-line or on CD-ROM.

Exercise 35 Revising to Correct Misplaced Modifiers On your paper, rewrite the following sentences to correct problems caused by misplaced modifiers. In each rewritten sentence, underline the modifier that was misplaced in the original. Then, draw an arrow from the modifier to the word it modifies.

EXAMPLE: My brother Richard bought a loaf of bread at the open bazaar that was warm and crusty.

ANSWER: At the open bazaar, my brother Richard bought a loaf of bread that was warm and crusty.

▼ Critical Viewing
How does this sculpture convey that the subject is a queen? In your answer, use a sentence with an adjective or adverb clause. [Evaluate]

1. In the dynastic period, King Narmer of ancient Egypt who was later called "the founder" unified the northern and southern kingdoms.
2. Built of stone, kings were buried in pyramids during the early dynastic period of Egypt.
3. Pyramids were the burial chambers of kings that increased in complexity and size as time passed.
4. Egyptians built temples, buildings, and statues to honor the kings next to the pyramids.
5. During the fifth dynasty, temples were built that were dedicated to the sun god.
6. The king demanded labor to build the pyramids and temples by many people.
7. Mastabas covered the graves of the royal family and government officials, which are large stone structures with many rooms.
8. In this time period, Egyptian paintings were done mostly on mastabas of food, drink, and objects to benefit the dead.
9. Using military power, other countries felt the expanding influence of Egypt.
10. The pharaohs eventually reduced the power of officials in provinces of Egypt who threatened the control of the king.

This bust of Queen Nefertiti is thousands of years old.

Avoiding Double Negatives

Negative words, such as *nothing* and *not*, are used to deny or to say *no*. Some people mistakenly use *double negatives*—two negative words—when only one is needed.

> **KEY CONCEPT** Avoid writing sentences that contain double negatives. ■

The sentences on the left in the following chart contain double negatives. Notice on the right how each can be corrected in either of two ways.

Double Negatives	Corrected Sentences
The lightning didn't damage nothing.	The lightning did*n't* damage *anything*. The lightning damaged *nothing*.
I haven't no time now.	I have*n't* any time now. I have *no* time now.
She never told us nothing about the thunderstorm.	She *never* told us anything about the thunderstorm. She told us *nothing* about the thunderstorm.

> **Exercise 36** **Revising to Correct Double Negatives** The following sentences contain double negatives, which are underlined. Correct each sentence in two ways.

EXAMPLE: We did<u>n't</u> want to miss <u>no</u> sites along the Nile.

ANSWER: We didn't want to miss any sites along the Nile.
            We wanted to miss no sites along the Nile.

1. The tour guide would<u>n't</u> let <u>nobody</u> explore alone.
2. She said she did<u>n't</u> want <u>no one</u> to get lost.
3. Because of the bright sun outside, we could<u>n't</u> see <u>nothing</u> when we first entered the underground tomb.
4. We had<u>n't</u> read <u>no</u> descriptions of the Temple of Luxor before we visited it.
5. The Temple of Luxor is <u>not</u> like <u>no</u> other Egyptian temple.
6. There were<u>n't</u> <u>no</u> words that could adequately express our feelings about the temple.
7. We could<u>n't</u> <u>hardly</u> believe our eyes at the treasures inside.
8. For thousands of years, the temple was buried under sand, and <u>no one</u> knew <u>nothing</u> about it.
9. Was<u>n't</u> there <u>nothing</u> written about the temple by biographers of Alexander the Great?
10. After visiting Egypt, we would<u>n't</u> want to go <u>nowhere</u> else.

⚡ Spelling Tip

As you can see in the chart on this page, *thunderstorm* is a compound word and should not be written as *thunder storm* unless interrupted by the word *lightning*—for example, "They traveled through many thunder and lightning storms."

More Practice

Grammar Exercise Workbook
• pp. 107–108
On-line Exercise Bank
• Section 21.4
  Go on-line:
  PHSchool.com
  Enter Web Code:
  ebk-7002

Avoiding Common Usage Problems

This section contains fifteen common usage problems in alphabetical order. Some of the problems are expressions that you should avoid in both your speaking and your writing. Others are words that are often confused because of similar spellings or meanings.

(1) accept, except Do not confuse the spelling of these words. *Accept*, a verb, means "to take what is offered" or "to agree to." *Except*, a preposition, means "leaving out" or "other than."

VERB: She *accepted* responsibility for the others.
PREPOSITION: Everyone *except* him wanted to ride a camel.

(2) advice, advise Do not confuse the spelling of these related words. *Advice*, a noun, means "an opinion." *Advise*, a verb, means "to give an opinion."

NOUN: My friend gave me *advice* about hotels in Cairo.
VERB: My friend *advised* me to find a good guide.

(3) affect, effect *Affect*, a verb, means "to influence" or "to cause a change in." *Effect*, usually a noun, means "result."

VERB: The sandstorm *affected* the caravan.
NOUN: What is the *effect* of getting sand in your ears?

(4) at Do not use *at* after *where*.

INCORRECT: Do you know *where* we're *at*?
CORRECT: Do you know *where* we are?

(5) because Do not use *because* after *the reason*. Eliminate one or the other.

INCORRECT: *The reason* I am sad is *because* our trip was canceled.
CORRECT: I am sad *because* our trip was canceled.
The reason I'm sad is *that* our trip was canceled.

Get instant feedback! Exercises 36 and 37 are available on-line or on CD-ROM.

> **More Practice**
>
> **Grammar Exercise Workbook**
> • pp. 109–110
> **On-line Exercise Bank**
> • Section 21.4
>   *Go on-line:*
>   PHSchool.com
>   *Enter Web Code:*
>   ebk-7002

Exercise 37 Avoiding Common Usage Problems Choose the correct word in parentheses, and write it on your paper.
1. Everyone (accept, except) James took pictures in the tomb.
2. The reason James didn't take pictures was (because, that) the batteries for his flash had run down.
3. We all gave him (advice, advise) about buying new batteries.
4. The hotel where we (were, were at) had a gift shop.
5. Our suggestions had no (affect, effect) on James's actions.

(6) beside, besides These two prepositions have different meanings and cannot be interchanged. *Beside* means "at the side of" or "close to." *Besides* means "in addition to."

EXAMPLES: We picnicked *beside* the Nile.
No one *besides* us had blankets on which to sit.

(7) different from, different than *Different from* is preferred over *different than.*

EXAMPLE: The pyramids were *different from* what I expected.

(8) farther, further *Farther* is used to refer to distance. *Further* means "additional" or "to a greater degree or extent."

EXAMPLES: We walked much *farther* than he. After he raised his voice, I listened no *further.*

(9) in, into *In* refers to position. *Into* suggests motion.

POSITION: The tourists are *in* the tomb.
MOTION: They walked *into* a hall before a pharaoh's shrine.

(10) kind of, sort of Do not use *kind of* or *sort of* to mean "rather" or "somewhat."

INCORRECT: This CD of Egyptian music is *sort of* new.
CORRECT: This CD of Egyptian music is *rather* new.

(11) like *Like,* a preposition, means "similar to" or "in the same way as." It should be followed by an object. Do not use *like* before a subject and a verb. Use *as* or *that* instead.

PREPOSITION: The pyramids looked *like* giant triangles.
INCORRECT: This stew doesn't taste *like* it should.
CORRECT: This stew doesn't taste *as* it should.

(12) that, which, who *That* and *which* refer to things. *Who* refers only to people.

THINGS: The photograph *that* I took won first prize.
PEOPLE: The dancer *who* performed is my cousin.

▲ **Critical Viewing**
Contrast the image of the man in this painting with the one on page 474. Use the word *different* in your response. **[Contrast]**

💿 **Technology Tip**

Most word processors have a grammar-check feature. Practice some of these special problems on the computer. Observe to see whether the word processor catches usage errors or double negatives.

(13) their, there, they're Do not confuse the spelling of these three words. *Their,* a possessive adjective, always modifies a noun. *There* is usually used either as a sentence starter or as an adverb. *They're* is a contraction of *they are.*

POSSESSIVE ADJECTIVE: The tourists boarded *their* bus.
SENTENCE STARTER: *There* are many tours available.

ADVERB: The tour guide is standing over *there.*
CONTRACTION: *They're* trying to board the bus now.

(14) to, too, two Do not confuse the spelling of these words. *To* plus a noun is a prepositional phrase. *To* plus a verb is an infinitive. *Too,* with two *o*'s, is an adverb and modifies adjectives and other adverbs. *Two* is a number.

PREPOSITION: *to* the house   *to* Egypt
INFINITIVE: *to* meet   *to* hide

ADVERB: *too* sad   *too* quickly
NUMBER: *two* clouds   *two* camels

(15) when, where, why Do not use *when, where,* or *why* directly after a linking verb such as *is.* Reword the sentence.

INCORRECT: To see the Sphinx is *why* we came to Egypt.
CORRECT: We came to Egypt to see the Sphinx.

Exercise 38 Avoiding Common Usage Problems On your paper, write the correct form from the choices in parentheses.
1. (Beside, Besides) seeing the Temple of Luxor, we visited the pyramids at Giza.
2. Luxor is (the place where, where) the pharaohs lived around 2000 B.C.
3. I climbed (farther, further) up the steps of the Great Pyramid than did either of my brothers.
4. The true story of how the Great Pyramid was built is (different from, different than) what I had heard before.
5. The myth that he made slaves build the pyramid earned Pharaoh Khufu a (kind of, somewhat) negative reputation.
6. Instead, Khufu employed farmers (which, who) were out of work because (there, their) land was flooded by the Nile.
7. Each huge limestone block used in the Great Pyramid seems almost (to, too) heavy to have been lifted into place.
8. Only the high priests were permitted to walk (in, into) the burial chamber of some of the pyramids.
9. We entered the ancient burial chamber (as, like) the high priests might have done thousands of years ago.
10. The camels (who, that) carried us across the desert are standing (beside, besides) the palm tree over (their, there).

More Practice

Grammar Exercise Workbook
• pp. 109–110
On-line Exercise Bank
• Section 21.4
Go on-line:
PHSchool.com
Enter Web Code:
ebk-7002

Get instant feedback! Exercise 38 is available on-line or on CD-ROM.

Hands-on Grammar

Sentence Breakup and Makeup

Practice correcting run-ons and fragments by doing this *Sentence Breakup and Makeup* activity.

First, form an even number of groups of four or five students each. Designate half the groups *Run-ons*, and half *Fragments*. Each group should cut eight to ten strips of colored paper—one color for run-ons and another for fragments. Next, each group of *Run-ons* students should brainstorm for **fragments**, and write one on each strip of paper; *Fragments* students should do the same, but with **run-on sentences**. You should end up with two fragments or run-on sentences for each member of the group. When finished, fold each strip two or three times, and place all of them in an envelope labeled either "Run-ons" or "Fragments." See the example below.

Then, each *Run-ons* group should pair up with a *Fragments* group, and exchange envelopes. Each group member draws two strips from the envelope. It is then the job of *Run-ons* group members to "break up" the run-on sentences, writing the corrections on the back of the strip of paper. It is the job of each *Fragments* group member to "make up"—or complete—the sentences by adding whatever is necessary to the fragments. After finishing, the two groups should exchange strips and check the corrections.

Find It in Your Reading Run-on sentences and fragments don't usually occur in formal writing. However, fragments often do appear in the dialogue of a story. Look through a story you have read, and identify one or two fragments in the dialogue. Challenge yourself to turn them into sentences.

Find It in Your Writing Review an essay in your portfolio, and note any run-on sentences or fragments. Then, correct them, using the methods presented in this section.

Section 21.4 Section Review

GRAMMAR EXERCISES 39–44

▶ **Exercise 39** Revising to Correct Fragments Correct the fragments in the following paragraph by adding them to a nearby sentence or by adding words to them to form new sentences.

Some records of early people have survived. Especially pictures on stone. From southern Africa to the Sahara, archaeologists have studied paintings on rock cliffs and cave walls. The paintings, which show the tools, weapons, and food-gathering methods of early people. The rock art of the Sahara lets us look at the lives of people. Who once lived there. Figures moving in graceful patterns. The paintings also reveal that herds of animals once roamed the Sahara.

▶ **Exercise 40** Revising to Correct Run-ons Rewrite each of these run-ons correctly.

1. Egyptians had many gods, they represented nature and ideas.
2. There were gods of the sun and moon, there were gods of the sky and earth.
3. The Nile flooded its valley every year, there was even a god of the Nile flood.
4. The Egyptians had many gods, there were gods of truth, learning, and craftsmanship.
5. When a relative died, Egyptians would turn to the god Osiris this god gave them hope for life after death.

▶ **Exercise 41** Revising to Correct Misplaced Modifiers Rewrite these sentences to correct any misplaced modifiers.

1. To serve as burial places, pharaohs built large and elaborate tombs.
2. Archaeologists found treasures in the tomb of King Tutankhamen made of wood, gold, and precious stones.
3. Imagine a crown on the mummy of pure gold and precious stone.
4. Looking through the treasures, six chariots made of wood, rope, and leather were discovered by archaeologists.
5. A beautiful collar was found on the mummified body of King Tut in the shape of a vulture and a cobra.

▶ **Exercise 42** Revising to Correct Double Negatives and Usage Errors Rewrite these sentences, correcting any double negatives or usage errors.

1. Accept for a small strip of fertile land along the Nile, most of Egypt is desert.
2. Farmers can't grow no crops in the desert area because it is to dry.
3. The reason the Nile valley is kind of overcrowded is because most of Egypt's population lives their.
4. Dams built along the Nile have had both a positive and a negative affect.
5. No one wants to see none of the ancient sites washed away by redirected river water.

▶ **Exercise 43** Find It in Your Writing Look through your portfolio to see whether you have used fragments, run-ons, or misplaced modifiers in any of your compositions. Rewrite the incorrect sentences, and explain how you have corrected the errors.

▶ **Exercise 44** Writing Application Write a description of an interesting place you have visited. Use a variety of short and long sentences, but make sure you have not included any fragments or run-ons. Check for other errors that might make your sentences less effective.

Section Review • 483

GRAMMAR EXERCISES 45–52

▶ **Exercise 45** Writing the Four Types of Sentences Rewrite each sentence to fit the function indicated in parentheses. Add the appropriate end mark.

1. The tax system in ancient Egypt was how unusual? (exclamatory)
2. Could you pay taxes by doing work for the government? (declarative)
3. Some people joined the army as a way to pay their taxes. (interrogative)
4. You can look at this picture of the pyramids. (imperative)
5. Did many people work on the pyramids to pay their taxes? (declarative)

▶ **Exercise 46** Combining Sentences and Varying Sentence Length Rewrite this paragraph, combining some short sentences and leaving others short for emphasis.

(1) Ancient Egyptians had a writing system. (2) It consisted of several hundred picture signs. (3) These signs were called hieroglyphics. (4) Some of the signs represented sounds. (5) Other signs represented ideas. (6) A word could be written using only sound signs. (7) A word could be written using only idea signs. (8) Most words were a combination. (9) Egyptians used hieroglyphics for writing down ideas. (10) They used hieroglyphics for decoration.

▶ **Exercise 47** Revising to Correct Fragments, Run-ons, and Misplaced Modifiers Identify each numbered item in the following paragraph as a *fragment, run-on,* or *misplaced modifier.* Then, rewrite the paragraph, correcting the errors.

(1) The ambition of Alexander the Great was to conquer the world, he also wanted to spread Greek culture. (2) To establish a capital for his kingdom in Egypt, Alexandria was founded in 332 B.C. by Alexander the Great. (3) Located on the northern Mediterranean coast of Egypt. (4) Ideal site because of its natural resources. (5) There was sufficient water from Lake Maryut, the Nile River provided a transportation waterway and irrigation, the island of Pharos made a good site for anchoring ships to deliver their goods.

▶ **Exercise 48** Revising to Correct Fragments, Run-ons, and Misplaced Modifiers Rewrite this paragraph, correcting all sentence errors. Some sentences may be correct.

(1) Originally, Egyptians buried their dead kings, queens, and nobles in the dry deserts that bordered the Nile River, the dry soil preserved the bodies in their graves. (2) However, these graves could be dug up easily by animals or robbers. (3) Decided to build tombs. (4) There was not sufficient heat from the sun inside the tomb to dry a body. (5) In order to preserve the bodies. (6) Egyptians used a process known as mummification. (7) First, they removed the brain and all other large organs from the body. (8) Packing it in salt, they dried the body. (9) Linen rags were then put into the body cavity soaked with scented resins. (10) The bodies were finally wrapped in bandages, they were placed in elaborate wooden coffins. (11) Took seventy days to complete the process. (12) Jewels and magic charms were placed between layers of bandage. (13) To protect the mummy's spirit. (14) Intricately engraved, some pharaohs' mummies were covered with gold masks. (15) Over the centuries, these valuable mummies attracted robbers they pillaged many of the tombs.

▶ **Exercise 49** Revising to Correct Double Negatives On your paper, write *C* for each sentence that is correct, and *DN* for each sentence that contains a double negative. Then, correct the double negatives.

1. Most people don't know nothing about camels.
2. You won't find no animals as well suited for desert life as a camel.
3. Because a camel has short hair, its body doesn't hold no heat for very long.
4. Because a camel sweats very little, it doesn't lose water it needs to survive.
5. Sand doesn't never get into a camel's eyes because of its long lashes.
6. A camel's large feet help it to walk on sand without sinking into it.
7. Camels can shut their nostrils so no sand doesn't get into them.
8. Did you know that camels don't store no water in their humps?
9. The hump contains stored fat that nourishes the camel so it won't starve, even during a long journey.
10. In cool weather, a camel can go six months without drinking no water.

▶ **Exercise 50** Identifying and Correcting Usage Problems The following sentences contain underlined words or phrases. On your paper, write *yes* if the underlined word or phrase contains a usage problem and *no* if it does not. Correct each problem.

1. Anwar Sadat was <u>different from</u> many modern Egyptian leaders.
2. Sadat was a man <u>which</u> was very concerned about peace in the Middle East.
3. When he was a young man, Sadat was only <u>sort of</u> interested in peace.
4. At the time, he was very angry that his country was forced to <u>except</u> being ruled by Great Britain.
5. Then, Sadat received valuable <u>advice</u> from Indian leader Mohandas Gandhi.
6. Gandhi's teachings about nonviolent revolt had a big <u>affect</u> on Sadat.
7. When he became Egypt's president, Sadat fought <u>to</u> wars against Israel.
8. The reason he decided to try a peaceful settlement was <u>because</u> the wars were draining Egypt's economy.
9. In 1979, Sadat stood <u>besides</u> Israeli leader Menachem Begin as they signed a historic peace treaty.
10. Sadat went <u>farther</u> toward establishing peaceful relations with Israel than some Egyptians wanted him to go, and he was later assassinated.

▶ **Exercise 51** Revision Practice Rewrite the following paragraph, combining or revising sentences and correcting errors in sentence structure or usage.

(1) Cairo is a modern city. (2) Cairo is an ancient city, to. (3) The capital of Egypt and largest city in Africa. (4) Bustling with traffic and pedestrians. (5) You can find many bargains there. (6) You are willing to haggle with vendors in different shops and bazaars. (7) Most of Cairo's sixteen million residents are religious the city contains hundreds of mosques and several churches, and their is even one synagogue that dates back to the fourth century A.D. (8) You don't have to drive no further than a few miles west of downtown Cairo to reach the pyramids. (9) The only one of the Seven Wonders of the World that is still standing. (10) A sound and light show is held their most nights the combination of the ancient structures and modern technology has an affect on anyone which attends the show.

▶ **Exercise 52** Writing Application Explain what you find most intriguing or interesting about Egypt. Vary the length and form of the sentences you use. Proofread your writing to correct any errors, especially those discussed in this chapter.

Standardized Test Preparation Workshop

Effective Sentences

Whether you are writing an e-mail or an essay for a test, using sentences correctly and effectively is critical to achieving logical, clear communication. Because this skill is so important, standardized tests often evaluate your ability to write effectively. When choosing the most effective sentence, use the following strategies:

- Avoid choosing **run-on** sentences in which two or more complete sentences are written as if they were a single sentence.

- Identify **sentence fragments** in your choices. **Fragments** are missing either a subject or a verb or in some other way do not complete a thought.

- Do not choose sentences with **misplaced modifiers** that confuse the reader and change the meaning of the passage.

- Choose a sentence that will add variety by using a different type of sentence beginning.

- Avoid choosing a sentence that will repeat the same format as the others and create a sequence of choppy sentences.

Test Tip

Place each answer choice in the passage, and see how it fits. Then, choose the sentence that fits the passage best.

Sample Test Item

Directions: Read the passage, and answer the questions that follow.

The artist painted with black, gray, and dark green on hulking canvasses. (1) At the chic gallery downtown.

1 Which of the following revisions best corrects part 1?

  A She displayed her works at the chic downtown gallery.
  B The artist in the chic gallery downtown.
  C Displayed at the chic gallery downtown.
  D Correct as is.

Answer and Explanation

The correct answer is A. The original item and the other answer choices are sentence fragments. Choice A is a complete sentence.

▶ **Practice 1** **Directions:** Carefully read the following passage. Choose the letter of the best revision for each sentence.

(1) It was only two days into the grueling Iditarod race. (2) A cold wind raged across Alaskan snow, it blew into great drifts. (3) Like sand dunes in an Arabian desert. (4) The lone musher's whip sang out over the heads of the exhausted dogs. (5) His eyes ached from the cold. (6) He looked across the barren expanse. (7) He saw no sign of the next checkpoint he should have been there long ago. (8) Even his breath was beginning to freeze on the fleecy scarf his daughter had given him, leaving for the dangerous journey into the Alaskan wilderness.

1 Which of the following is the best revision for part 2?

A A cold wind raged, blowing Alaskan snow into great drifts.

B Wind blew the snow into great drifts.

C A cold wind raged and, it blew into great drifts.

D Correct as is

2 Which of the following is the best revision for part 3?

F The drifts were like sand dunes in an Arabian desert.

G Like sand dunes in an Arabian desert blew the snow.

H Like sand dunes were the drifts in an Arabian desert.

J Correct as is

3 Which of the following is the best revision for part 4?

A The lone musher's whip. Sang out over the heads of the exhausted dogs.

B The lone musher's whip sang out over the exhausted heads of the dogs.

C The lone musher's whip; sang out over the exhausted heads of the dogs.

D Correct as is

4 Which of the following is the best way to rewrite parts 5, 6, and 7?

F His eyes ached from the cold; he looked across the barren expanse, he saw no sign of the next checkpoint, he should have been there long ago.

G Eyes aching from the cold, he looked across the barren expanse. He saw no sign of the next checkpoint, where he should have been long ago.

H His eyes ached from the cold, and he looked across the barren expanse. He saw no sign of the next checkpoint. He should have been there long ago.

J Correct as is

5 Which of the following is the best way to rewrite part 8?

A His breath was beginning to freeze on the fleecy scarf his daughter had given him before he made the dangerous journey into the Alaskan wilderness.

B His daughter had given him before leaving on the dangerous journey into the Alaskan wilderness the fleecy scarf on which his breath was beginning to freeze.

C His breath was beginning to freeze on the fleecy scarf. His daughter had given him before leaving for the dangerous journey into the Alaskan wilderness.

D Correct as is

Cumulative Review

PHRASES, CLAUSES, AND SENTENCES

Exercise A Recognizing Subjects, Predicates, and Sentence Types Copy these sentences, underlining each simple subject once, and each simple predicate twice. Then, identify each sentence as *declarative*, *interrogative*, *imperative*, or *exclamatory*.

1. Look at this globe. Here is Australia down in the Southern Hemisphere.
2. Wow! What a surprise that is!
3. Aborigines first migrated there and remained undisturbed until the seventeenth century.
4. Didn't the first European settlers arrive at Botany Bay in 1788?
5. Were they British convicts? Please answer the question.

Exercise B Identifying Complements Write the complements in the following sentences, and label each *direct object*, *indirect object*, *predicate noun*, or *predicate adjective*.

1. Australia's mountains are not high.
2. In fact, Australia is almost the world's flattest landmass.
3. Australians gave the interior the name *Outback*.
4. The Central-Eastern Lowlands is an area extending from the Great Dividing Range to the Great Western Plain.
5. The Nullarbor Plain seems strange with its caverns and tunnels.

Exercise C Recognizing Phrases Identify the underlined phrases as *prepositional*, *appositive*, or *participial*.

1. The climate of Australia varies <u>from region</u> to region.
2. The southern states—<u>warm, temperate regions</u>—have four seasons.
3. <u>Located in the Southern Hemisphere</u>, Australia has seasons opposite those in the Northern Hemisphere.
4. Queensland, <u>on the north coast</u>, experiences a great deal of rain.
5. However, <u>in the drier grasslands</u>, unpredictable rainfall must be supplemented <u>by irrigation</u>.
6. The deserts, <u>making up most of central and western Australia</u>, receive even less rainfall.
7. <u>Applying many modern irrigation techniques</u>, Australia has increased its agricultural production.
8. The Australian Alps, <u>a mountain range in New South Wales</u>, receives heavy snowfall.
9. <u>Lying in the temperate zone</u>, Tasmania has heavy rainfall and frequent winter storms.
10. Hot and dry winds are common <u>in the southern states</u>.

Exercise D Recognizing Clauses Identify the underlined clauses as *independent* or *subordinate*. Identify the subordinate clauses as *adjective* or *adverb*.

1. The platypus is an aquatic mammal of the Monotreme order <u>that has a bill like a duck</u>.
2. The spiny anteater is also categorized as a Monotreme <u>because it is an egg-laying mammal</u>.
3. While the kangaroo is a marsupial, <u>it is still a type of mammal</u>.
4. Possums and koalas are marsupials <u>that live in trees</u>.
5. Marsupials are animals that give birth to live young <u>even though the young are then nourished in an external pouch</u>.

▶ **Exercise E** Recognizing Sentence Structure Label each sentence *simple*, *compound*, or *complex*.

1. Kangaroos' powerful hind legs are used for hopping, and their thick, long tails are used for balancing.
2. The large red or gray kangaroo may stand as tall as seven feet.
3. Wallabies and kangaroo rats are smaller animals that are also members of the kangaroo family.
4. Although it does not bark, the dingo is a dog-like animal.
5. Rabbits, foxes, and cats were introduced into Australia by Europeans.

▶ **Exercise F** Varying Sentences
Rewrite the following sentences according to the instructions in parentheses.

1. Australia has two species of crocodiles. (Start with "Actually.")
2. The larger crocodile lives in the northern coastal swamps and can grow to be twenty feet long. (Revise the sentence so that it begins with "Living in the northern coastal swamp.")
3. Smaller species of crocodiles can be found living contentedly in inland fresh water. (Revise sentence to begin with "In inland fresh waters.")
4. More than 370 species of lizards are living in Australia. (Invert the subject-verb order.)
5. About 100 species of venomous snakes live in Australia. (Start with "Australia" as the subject, and change the verb as necessary.)

▶ **Exercise G** Combining Sentences
Rewrite the following sentences according to the instructions in parentheses.

1. Australian waters contain hundreds of sharks. Some are a danger to humans. (Combine into a compound sentence.)
2. Edible shellfish are abundant. Oysters, abalone, and crayfish have been exploited. (Combine by turning one sentence into a subordinate clause.)
3. Seals live around the southern coast. They also inhabit the surrounding islands. (Combine by making a compound verb.)
4. The waters around Australia support many fish. There are also many aquatic mammals. (Combine sentences by creating a compound direct object.)
5. The Queensland lungfish breathes with a single lung. It does this instead of using gills. (Combine by changing one sentence into a phrase.)

▶ **Exercise H** Identifying and Revising Sentence Problems Label the error in each sentence *fragment, run-on, double negative, misplaced modifier,* or *common usage problem.* Then, correct the errors.

1. Believe the Aborigines were always in Australia.
2. By taking advantage of low sea levels that allowed land travel, researchers think the Aborigines migrated to Australia.
3. Tasmania was once part of Australia, a rise in sea level made Tasmania an island.
4. The Aborigines didn't have no domesticated animals other than the dingo.
5. There most recent history features the use of tools.

▶ **Exercise I** Writing Application
Write a short description of a place you have visited. Vary the length and structure of your sentences. Circle at least three phrases and three clauses. Try to avoid fragments, run-ons, double negatives, misplaced modifiers, and the common usage problems you have studied.

Using Verbs

Usage refers to the way a word or expression is used in a sentence. Verb usage is an area that can cause many problems. Since verbs have many forms and uses, you may find yourself occasionally using them incorrectly in your writing.

If you were writing a report on exotic birds, for instance, you would want to choose the correct forms of verbs, you would want to write in the correct verb tenses, and you would want to avoid certain mistakes that people often make in using verbs.

This chapter will help you learn to use verbs correctly in your speaking and in your writing.

▲ **Critical Viewing**
Think of three verbs that describe what these flamingos are doing. **[Analyze]**

Diagnostic Test

Directions: Write all answers on a separate sheet of paper.

Skill Check A. Identify the principal part used to form each underlined verb (*present, present participle, past,* or *past participle*). Label the verb *regular* or *irregular.*

1. Storks <u>possess</u> long legs, webbed toes, and strong, straight bills.
2. Artists <u>have</u> often <u>drawn</u> pictures of them.
3. One species, the white stork, <u>migrated</u> from its native Asia.
4. We saw that the head, neck, and body of the stork <u>were shimmering</u> in the sunlight.
5. Spreading its wings, it <u>displayed</u> partly black tips.
6. Its long legs <u>extended</u> from a white body.
7. Its neck <u>arched</u> gracefully.
8. Storks <u>have fed</u> on eels and other fish, amphibians, reptiles, young birds, and small mammals.
9. We noticed that one <u>was flying</u> over a marsh, looking for food.
10. A guide told us that the white stork <u>makes</u> a nest of sticks and reeds.

Skill Check B. Copy each of the following verbs onto your paper, supplying the tense indicated in parentheses.

11. The stork (surprise—future) you as you learn more about it.
12. It never (make—present perfect) a sound as far as we know.
13. That is to say, the stork (have—present) no voice.
14. The visitors (see—past) one fly powerfully through the air.
15. They learned that it (reach—future perfect) a very high altitude soon after liftoff.
16. Another type of stork, the black stork, (live—present perfect progressive) in Europe and Asia.
17. This stork (inhabit—future perfect progressive) Africa, as well.
18. People (confuse—present perfect) the white stork with a similar stork, the maguari.
19. The maguari (frequent—past perfect progressive) marshes and savannas in search of food.
20. However, the maguari stork (make—present perfect progressive) its home in South America rather than Europe and Asia.

Skill Check C. Choose the correct word from the pair in parentheses, and write it on your paper.

21. We could (of, have) seen the albatross if we had looked closely.
22. Some bird-watchers (saw, seen) them wandering great distances over the ocean.
23. They (lie, lay) on the ocean surface when they sleep, rocking with the waves.
24. The ocean (isn't, ain't) just temporary lodgings for the albatross; it's home.
25. The only time it (sets, sits) its webbed foot on land is at breeding time.

The Four Principal Parts of Verbs

Theme: Exotic Birds

In this section, you will learn about the principal parts of verbs. The examples and exercises in this section are about exotic birds.

Cross-Curricular Connection: Science

Verbs have different forms to express time. The form of the verb *walk* in the sentence "They *walk* very fast" expresses action in the present. In "They *walked* too far from home," the form of the verb shows that the action happened in the past. In "They *will walk* home from school," the verb expresses action in the future. These forms of verbs are known as *tenses.* To use the tenses of a verb correctly, you must know the *principal parts* of the verb.

KEY CONCEPT A verb has four **principal parts:** the *present*, the *present participle,* the *past*, and the *past participle.* ■

Here, for example, are the four principal parts of the verb *walk.*

THE FOUR PRINCIPAL PARTS OF *WALK*			
Present	Present Participle	Past	Past Participle
walk	(am) walking	walked	(have) walked

The first principal part, called the present, is the form of the verb that is listed in a dictionary. Notice also the helping verbs in parentheses before the second and fourth principal parts. These two principal parts must be combined with helping verbs before they can be used as verbs in sentences. The result will always be a verb phrase.

Here are four sentences, each using one of the principal parts of the verb *walk.*

EXAMPLES: He *walks* toward us in a hurry.
June *was walking* behind us a minute ago.
They *walked* to the park.
We *have walked* three miles in search of our friends.

The way the past and past participle of a verb are formed shows whether the verb is *regular* or *irregular.*

Using Regular Verbs

Most verbs are *regular*, which means that their past and past participle forms follow a standard, predictable pattern.

> **KEY CONCEPT** The past and past participle of a **regular verb** are formed by adding *-ed* or *-d* to the present form. ■

To form the past and past participle of a regular verb such as *chirp* or *hover*, you simply add *-ed* to the present. With regular verbs that already end in e—verbs such as *move* and *charge*—you simply add *-d* to the present.

PRINCIPAL PARTS OF REGULAR VERBS			
Present	**Present Participle**	**Past**	**Past Participle**
chirp	(am) chirping	chirped	(have) chirped
hover	(am) hovering	hovered	(have) hovered
move	(am) moving	moved	(have) moved
charge	(am) charging	charged	(have) charged

> **Exercise 1** Recognizing the Principal Parts of Regular Verbs The verb or verb phrase in each of the following sentences is underlined. Identify the principal part used to form each verb.

EXAMPLE: Ginny is <u>watching</u> a hummingbird in flight.

ANSWER: present participle

1. Hummingbirds <u>have consumed</u> tiny insects and nectar from our flowers for years.
2. They <u>hover</u> in front of these flowers to get the food.
3. They <u>gather</u> nectar from each blossom.
4. When they <u>have finished</u>, they move on.
5. A hummingbird's heart <u>beats</u> up to 1,200 times a minute.
6. <u>Have</u> you ever <u>noticed</u> a hummingbird flying backward?
7. This skill <u>enables</u> hummingbirds to move away from a flower easily.
8. Some <u>are living</u> in mountain areas over 15,000 feet high.
9. Their small wings <u>are beating</u> constantly.
10. We <u>learned</u> that a hummingbird breathes over 250 times a minute.

> **More Practice**

Grammar Exercise Workbook
• pp. 111–112
On-line Exercise Bank
• Section 22.1
  Go on-line:
  PHSchool.com
  Enter Web Code:
  ebk-7002

Get instant feedback! Exercise 1 is available on-line or on CD-ROM.

▲ Critical
Viewing
Use the present
participles of
hover and *flutter*
to explain the
actions of this
hummingbird.
[Analyze]

▶ **Exercise 2** Using the Principal Parts of Regular Verbs
Copy each of the following sentences onto your paper, writing
the principal part of the verb indicated in parentheses.

EXAMPLE: They have (look—past participle) everywhere for
            a hummingbird nest.

ANSWER: They have *looked* everywhere for a hummingbird
            nest.

1. Every season, hummingbirds (create—present) small cup-
    shaped nests for their young.
2. Some have (use—past participle) spider webs and pieces of
    bark in their nests.
3. The hermit hummingbirds (design—present) their nests
    differently, however.
4. They have been (view—past participle) as unique among
    hummingbirds.
5. They (structure—present) their nests long and hanging.
6. They have (fasten—past participle) these long nests to
    large leaves.
7. The female hummingbirds (stay—past) in the nest once
    eggs were laid.
8. The females (incubate—present) the two white eggs alone.
9. Those visitors are (look—present participle) at a humming-
    bird's nest.
10. I am (wonder—present participle) if the birds will migrate.

▶ **More Practice**

Grammar Exercise
Workbook
• pp. 111–112
On-line Exercise Bank
• Section 22.1
  Go on-line:
  PHSchool.com
  Enter Web Code:
  ebk-7002

Using Irregular Verbs

While most verbs are regular, many very common verbs are *irregular*—their past and past participle forms do not follow a predictable pattern. These are the verbs that cause the most problems.

▶ **KEY CONCEPT** The past and past participle of an **irregular verb** are not formed by adding *-ed* or *-d* to the present form. ■

IRREGULAR VERBS WITH THE SAME PAST AND PAST PARTICIPLE			
Present	**Present Participle**	**Past**	**Past Participle**
bring	(am) bringing	brought	(have) brought
build	(am) building	built	(have) built
buy	(am) buying	bought	(have) bought
catch	(am) catching	caught	(have) caught
fight	(am) fighting	fought	(have) fought
find	(am) finding	found	(have) found
get	(am) getting	got	(have) got *or* (have) gotten
hold	(am) holding	held	(have) held
lay	(am) laying	laid	(have) laid
lead	(am) leading	led	(have) led
lose	(am) losing	lost	(have) lost
pay	(am) paying	paid	(have) paid
say	(am) saying	said	(have) said
sit	(am) sitting	sat	(have) sat
spin	(am) spinning	spun	(have) spun
stick	(am) sticking	stuck	(have) stuck
swing	(am) swinging	swung	(have) swung
teach	(am) teaching	taught	(have) taught

Check a dictionary whenever you are in doubt about the correct form of an irregular verb.

IRREGULAR VERBS WITH THE SAME PRESENT, PAST, AND PAST PARTICIPLE			
Present	**Present Participle**	**Past**	**Past Participle**
bid	(am) bidding	bid	(have) bid
burst	(am) bursting	burst	(have) burst
cost	(am) costing	cost	(have) cost
hurt	(am) hurting	hurt	(have) hurt
put	(am) putting	put	(have) put
set	(am) setting	set	(have) set

IRREGULAR VERBS THAT CHANGE IN OTHER WAYS

Present	Present Participle	Past	Past Participle
arise	(am) arising	arose	(have) arisen
be	(am) being	was	(have) been
begin	(am) beginning	began	(have) begun
blow	(am) blowing	blew	(have) blown
break	(am) breaking	broke	(have) broken
choose	(am) choosing	chose	(have) chosen
come	(am) coming	came	(have) come
do	(am) doing	did	(have) done
draw	(am) drawing	drew	(have) drawn
drink	(am) drinking	drank	(have) drunk
drive	(am) driving	drove	(have) driven
eat	(am) eating	ate	(have) eaten
fall	(am) falling	fell	(have) fallen
fly	(am) flying	flew	(have) flown
freeze	(am) freezing	froze	(have) frozen
give	(am) giving	gave	(have) given
go	(am) going	went	(have) gone
grow	(am) growing	grew	(have) grown
know	(am) knowing	knew	(have) known
lie	(am) lying	lay	(have) lain
ride	(am) riding	rode	(have) ridden
ring	(am) ringing	rang	(have) rung
rise	(am) rising	rose	(have) risen
run	(am) running	ran	(have) run
see	(am) seeing	saw	(have) seen
shake	(am) shaking	shook	(have) shaken
sing	(am) singing	sang	(have) sung
sink	(am) sinking	sank	(have) sunk
speak	(am) speaking	spoke	(have) spoken
spring	(am) springing	sprang	(have) sprung
swear	(am) swearing	swore	(have) sworn
swim	(am) swimming	swam	(have) swum
take	(am) taking	took	(have) taken
tear	(am) tearing	tore	(have) torn
throw	(am) throwing	threw	(have) thrown
wear	(am) wearing	wore	(have) worn
write	(am) writing	wrote	(have) written

> **Exercise 3** Completing the Principal Parts of Irregular Verbs On your paper, make four columns with the principal parts of verbs as the heads. Then, write the missing parts of the following irregular verbs. See how many you can fill in without looking back at the charts.

EXAMPLE:	*Present*	*Present Participle*	*Past*	*Past Participle*
	_____	_____	began	_____
ANSWER:	begin	beginning	began	begun

	Present	*Present Participle*	*Past*	*Past Participle*
1.	put	_____	_____	put
2.	_____	swinging	swung	_____
3.	choose	_____	chose	chosen
4.	rise	rising	_____	_____
5.	drink	_____	drank	_____
6.	hurt	hurting	_____	hurt
7.	_____	going	went	_____
8.	_____	_____	came	_____
9.	set	setting	_____	_____
10.	eat	_____	ate	_____

> **Exercise 4** Using the Principal Parts of Irregular Verbs For each of the following sentences, identify the irregular verb(s) and the principal part(s) used.

EXAMPLE: I found a Web site devoted to ostriches.

ANSWER: found (past)

1. The ostrich never flies.
2. Those ostriches are running.
3. As that one has matured, its legs have grown very powerful.
4. We have drawn pictures of ostriches.
5. We begin our study of a new animal this week.

More Practice

Grammar Exercise Workbook
• pp. 113–114
On-line Exercise Bank
• Section 22.1
Go on-line:
PHSchool.com
Enter Web Code:
ebk-7002

▼ Critical Viewing What qualities of an ostrich make it seem "irregular" compared to most other birds? Use two or three irregular verbs in your answer. **[Compare and Contrast]**

▶ **Exercise 5** Using the Past Participle of Irregular Verbs

For each of the following sentences, write the past participle of the verb in parentheses.

EXAMPLE: Charlayne has (choose) the parakeet.

ANSWER: chosen

1. Have you ever (see) a great spotted kiwi?
2. They have been (find) only in New Zealand and on nearby islands.
3. Like the large ostrich, kiwis have never (fly) through the air.
4. We had not (know) that kiwis hide themselves beneath their thick plumage.
5. Often, we see that kiwis have (come) to forage for food such as worms, seeds, and berries.

▶ **Exercise 6** Supplying the Correct Principal Part of Irregular Verbs For each of the following sentences, write the principal part of the verb given in parentheses.

EXAMPLE: You should have (bring—past participle) binocu-
            lars with you.

ANSWER: You should have *brought* binoculars with you.

1. Researchers have (study—past participle) the Chilean flamingo.
2. It has been (find—past participle) in the Andes Mountains.
3. The flamingo (feed—present) by dipping its head under water.
4. I am (watch—present participle) one trap food in its bill.
5. The same one (catch—past) a lot of food earlier today.
6. The flamingo's upper jaw (fit—present) over its lower jaw like the lid of a box.
7. We are (learn—present participle) that the food source (affect—present) the color of the flamingo's feathers.
8. Yesterday, we (see—past) the greater flamingo, which is larger than other flamingos.
9. It had (build—past participle) a nest on a cone-shaped mound in the water.
10. Then, it (take—past) good care of its young for seventy-five days.

▶ **More Practice**

Grammar Exercise Workbook
• pp. 113–114
On-line Exercise Bank
• Section 22.1
  Go on-line:
  PHSchool.com
  Enter Web Code:
  ebk-7002

Get instant feedback! Exercises 5 and 6 are available on-line or on CD-ROM.

Section 22.1

Section Review

GRAMMAR EXERCISES 7–13

Exercise 7 Identifying Regular and Irregular Verbs Label the following verbs *regular* or *irregular*.

1. fly
2. hover
3. run
4. eat
5. hurt
6. sing
7. chirp
8. move
9. begin
10. catch

Exercise 8 Identifying Principal Parts of Regular Verbs Identify the principal part used to form each underlined regular verb in the sentences below.

1. The cattle egret, a species of heron, once <u>inhabited</u> only Africa.
2. By the 1870's, it <u>had crossed</u> the Atlantic to South America.
3. It <u>reached</u> Florida in 1942.
4. It now <u>frequents</u> areas across both North and South America.
5. It is <u>living</u> in almost all of the United States.

Exercise 9 Recognizing Principal Parts and Regular or Irregular Verbs Identify the principal part used to form each underlined verb in the following sentences. Then, specify whether the verb is *regular* or *irregular*.

1. Scientists <u>have given</u> the common name of *ibis* to about thirty different species, including the sacred ibis.
2. These long-necked, long-legged birds <u>are living</u> throughout the world.
3. They <u>inhabit</u> areas of Africa, Turkey, and North and South America.
4. Historians studying ancient Egyptians <u>have written</u> about the sacred ibis.
5. It <u>became</u> a religious symbol in Egypt.

Exercise 10 Supplying the Correct Principal Part Copy the following sentences onto your paper. Supply the correct principal part. If there is no helping verb in the sentence, do not add one.

1. Some bird-watchers have (mistake) the ibis for the heron.
2. My biology teacher (speak) about a major difference between these birds.
3. The heron has always (fly) with its head back and its neck bent into an S-curve.
4. Flying ibises can be (see) with their necks straight and heads held forward.
5. We have (learn) that cranes, like ibises, fly with their necks straight.

Exercise 11 Find It in Your Reading Identify the principal part used to form each underlined word in these sentences from "The Hummingbird That Lived Through Winter" by William Saroyan.

The new life of the little bird <u>was</u> magnificent. It <u>spun</u> about in the little kitchen, <u>going</u> to the window, coming back to the heat, <u>suspending</u>, circling as if it were summertime and it <u>had</u> never <u>felt</u> better in its whole life.

Exercise 12 Find It in Your Writing Look through your writing portfolio. Find several examples of regular and irregular verbs. Identify the principal part of each verb you find.

Exercise 13 Writing Application Describe the habits of a bird or other animal in your area. Identify the four principal parts of the verbs you use.

The Tenses and Forms of Verbs

Theme: Historic New York

In this section, you will learn about the six tenses of verbs in their basic and progressive forms. The examples and exercises in this section are about the history of New York State.

Cross-Curricular Connection: Social Studies

In English, verbs have six *tenses*. Each of the six tenses has a *basic* form and a *progressive* form. This section will explain first the basic forms and then the progressive forms.

> **KEY CONCEPT** A **tense** is a form of a verb that shows when something happens or when something exists. ■

The Basic Forms of the Six Tenses

The chart below shows the *basic* forms of the six tenses, using *begin* as an example. The first column gives the name of each tense. The third column gives the principal part needed to form each tense. Only three of the four principal parts are used in the basic forms: the present, the past, and the past participle.

BASIC FORMS OF THE SIX TENSES OF *BEGIN*		
Tense	**Basic Form**	**Principal Part Used**
Present	I begin	Present
Past	I began	Past
Future	I will begin	Present
Present Perfect	I have begun	Past Participle
Past Perfect	I had begun	Past Participle
Future Perfect	I will have begun	Past Participle

Study the chart carefully. First, learn the names of the tenses. Then, learn the principal parts needed to form them. Notice also that only the last four tenses need helping verbs.

> **Exercise 14** Supplying Verb Tenses Complete each sentence below with the verb and tense indicated in parentheses.

EXAMPLE: Rip Van Winkle __?__ (fall—past) asleep in the Catskill Mountains.

ANSWER: fell

1. Hiking in the Catskills, we __?__ (lose—past) our compass.
2. Before we __?__ (go—past perfect) far, we found an arrowhead.
3. We __?__ (find—present perfect) several during our hikes.
4. By the end of the day, we __?__ (hike—future perfect) about ten miles.
5. Next time, we __?__ (keep—future) an eye on our compass.

⚙ **Grammar and Style Tip**

Whenever it makes sense in your writing, use different tenses to make your ideas more precise. For instance, when you write in the present tense, you might also use the present perfect to clarify some ideas.

▶ **Exercise 15** Identifying the Basic Forms of Verbs Identify the tense of each underlined verb in the following sentences.

EXAMPLE: We <u>have completed</u> our study of the early settlement of New York.

ANSWER: present perfect

1. I often <u>had wondered</u> about the history of New York.
2. "If I ask my mom," I thought, "she <u>will tell</u> me it is rich in history."
3. She <u>will say</u>, "It extends back to the settlement of the area by Native Americans."
4. They first <u>occupied</u> New York's shores and river valleys.
5. Archaeological sites <u>exist</u> all the way from downstate Staten Island to upstate Lake Champlain.
6. Archaeologists <u>have found</u> evidence of ancient sites.
7. Some of these sites <u>had been</u> home to Cayuga and Seneca Native Americans.
8. For food, members of the ancient culture <u>had relied</u> on hunting and gathering.
9. A later culture <u>substituted</u> agriculture for hunting and gathering.
10. After more research, I <u>will have learned</u> other interesting facts about New York history.

▶ **More Practice**

Grammar Exercise Workbook
• pp. 115–116
On-line Exercise Bank
• Section 22.2
  Go on-line:
  PHSchool.com
  Enter Web Code:
  ebk-7002

 Text

Get instant feedback! Exercises 14 and 15 are available on-line or on CD-ROM.

▼ **Critical Viewing** Use future and future perfect verb tenses to tell what you think will become of this forest. **[Assess]**

The Tenses and Forms of Verbs • **501**

Conjugating the Basic Forms of Verbs

Conjugating verbs can help you become familiar with the many forms of verbs.

KEY CONCEPT A **conjugation** is a list of the singular and plural forms of a verb in a particular tense. ■

Each tense in a conjugation has six forms that fit with first-, second-, and third-person forms of the personal pronouns.

To conjugate any verb, begin by listing its principal parts. For example, the principal parts of the verb *hide* are *hide*, *hiding*, *hid*, and *hidden*. The following conjugation of *hide* shows all of the basic forms of this verb in the six tenses.

CONJUGATION OF THE BASIC FORMS OF *HIDE*		
	Singular	**Plural**
Present	I hide you hide he, she, it hides	we hide you hide they hide
Past	I hid you hid he, she, it hid	we hid you hid they hid
Future	I will hide you will hide he, she, it will hide	we will hide you will hide they will hide
Present Perfect	I have hidden you have hidden he, she, it has hidden	we have hidden you have hidden they have hidden
Past Perfect	I had hidden you had hidden he, she, it had hidden	we had hidden you had hidden they had hidden
Future Perfect	I will have hidden you will have hidden he, she, it will have hidden	we will have hidden you will have hidden they will have hidden

▲ **Critical Viewing**
In this painting, do you think the artist's vision was idealized or realistic? Use past tense forms in your answer. **[Relate]**

> **Exercise 16** Conjugating the Basic Forms of Verbs The following sentences are written in the present tense. Rewrite each sentence in each of the other five tenses.

1. It exists.
2. You move.
3. We bring.
4. They begin.
5. I go.

> **Exercise 17** Supplying the Correct Tense Copy each of the following sentences onto your paper, supplying the basic form of the verb indicated in parentheses.

EXAMPLE: Diane (buy—past) a book on New York history.

ANSWER: Diane *bought* a book on New York history.

1. Two major Native American language groups (emerge— past) in northeastern North America after A.D. 1000.
2. Archaeologists (identify—present perfect) these groups as the Algonquian and the Iroquoian.
3. The group that (speak—past perfect) Algonquian soon spread the language.
4. These Algonquian tribes (include—present) the Mahican, the Delaware, and the Wappinger.
5. This knowledge (bring—future) new understanding of the area's history.

> **More Practice**

Grammar Exercise Workbook
• pp. 115–116
On-line Exercise Bank
• Section 22.2
  Go on-line:
  PHSchool.com
  Enter Web Code:
  ebk-7002

Get instant feedback! Exercises 16 and 17 are available on-line or on CD-ROM.

The Six Progressive Forms of Verbs

Each of the six tenses introduced in this section also has a progressive form, which indicates continuing action. The present participle and a form of the verb *be* are used to make all six progressive forms.

The following chart, using *sing* as an example, shows the progressive forms of the six tenses.

PROGRESSIVE FORMS OF THE SIX TENSES OF *SING*

Tense	Progressive Form	Principal Part
Present	I am singing	
Past	I was singing	
Future	I will be singing	
Present Perfect	I have been singing	Present Participle
Past Perfect	I had been singing	
Future Perfect	I will have been singing	

▶ **Exercise 18** Identifying the Progressive Forms of Verbs Study the preceding chart. Then, identify the tense of each of the following verbs.

EXAMPLE: will have been waiting

ANSWER: future perfect progressive

1. has been going
2. is progressing
3. will be eating
4. had been exploring
5. was explaining
6. have been staying
7. had been building
8. had been thinking
9. will have been having
10. have been giving

▶ **Exercise 19** Supplying Helping Verbs for Progressive Forms For each sentence below, supply the helping verbs necessary to form the progressive tense indicated in parentheses.

EXAMPLE: We (present perfect) hoping to visit the *Half Moon* exhibit.

ANSWER: We *have been* hoping to visit the *Half Moon* exhibit.

1. In 1609, aboard his ship *Half Moon*, Henry Hudson (past) searching for a Northwest passage to Asia.
2. He (past perfect) sailing for six months when he discovered the wide river that would bear his name.
3. Now, the New Netherland Museum in New York (present) exhibiting a replica of the *Half Moon*.
4. It (future) sailing around as an example of living history.
5. By 2005, the *Half Moon* replica (future perfect) giving visitors a taste of the era of exploration for almost fifteen years.

✎ Spelling Tip

When forming the progressive form of verbs, be careful with verbs that end in *c*, such as *picnic*. To avoid having the *c* join with the *i* to make an *s* sound, add a *k* after the *c* to form *picnicking*.

GRAMMAR IN LITERATURE

from **Rip Van Winkle**
Washington Irving

The legend of "Rip Van Winkle" is set in the Dutch colony of New Netherland. In this passage from the story, notice the use of past tense and past progressive forms of both regular and irregular verbs.

On waking, he *found* himself on the green knoll whence he had first seen the old man of the glen. He *rubbed* his eyes—it *was* a bright sunny morning. The birds *were hopping* and *twittering* among the bushes, and the eagle *was wheeling* aloft, and *breasting* the pure mountain breeze. "Surely," *thought* Rip, "I have not slept here all night."

▶ **Exercise 20** Supplying the Correct Form of Progressive Verbs On your paper, rewrite each sentence, supplying the indicated progressive form of the verb in parentheses.

EXAMPLE: The threat of fire (worry—past progressive) leaders of Albany.

ANSWER: The threat of fire *was worrying* leaders of Albany.

1. A new law passed in 1670 (prohibit—future progressive) thatched roofs.
2. Other laws (require—present perfect progressive) that streets be kept clear of flammable materials.
3. The mayor (appoint—past perfect progressive) wardens to report fire hazards.
4. The wardens (fine—present progressive) violators of fire laws.
5. By 1732, the city (purchase—past progressive) its first fire engine.

▶ **More Practice**

Grammar Exercise Workbook
• pp. 117–118
On-line Exercise Bank
• Section 22.2
  Go on-line:
  PHSchool.com
  Enter Web Code:
  ebk-7002

Get instant feedback! Exercises 18, 19, and 20 are available on-line or on CD-ROM.

Hands-on Grammar

Verb Fortune Teller

Practice verb tenses and forms with a "fortune teller." Take a 6 1/2-inch-square sheet of paper, and fold in the corners so they meet in the middle. Turn the paper over, and again fold in the corners. Then, crease the paper by folding it in half, and in half again. You will have a small square. Unfold only the small square, and lay the paper flat so that four square sections are facing upward. Write a different verb on each of the four squares. (See example A.)

A

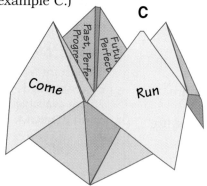

Next, turn the paper over, and on each of the eight triangular sections, write a different verb tense or form—for example, *present perfect, future progressive, past perfect, future, past, past perfect progressive.* (See example B.) Then, lift up each triangle, and write underneath it the corresponding forms of the verb on the back of the square. Each verb will have two forms.

B

Finally, refold the square so that the verbs are on the outside. Place your thumbs and index fingers in each of the four slots formed by the small squares, and pinch them together. You should be able to open and close the square in two directions, exposing different verb tenses each time. (See example C.)

C

With a partner, take turns choosing a verb from the other's "fortune teller." After opening and closing the square in different directions four or five times, each person must give the form of the verb indicated on the triangle. Check your answers by lifting up the triangle.

Find It in Your Reading Read two or three paragraphs of a story or article, and see how many different verb tenses and forms you recognize.

Find It in Your Writing Review the verbs in a piece of your writing, and make sure you used and formed the tenses correctly.

Section Review

GRAMMAR EXERCISES 21–27

Exercise 21 Identifying Basic and Progressive Tenses Identify the tense of the underlined verb in the following sentences.

1. The Iroquois are fascinating to study.
2. For years, historians have been disagreeing on where the Iroquois first lived.
3. The debate will probably continue until more evidence is found.
4. Perhaps you will be learning about the famous Iroquois Confederacy.
5. Five Iroquois tribes had united in 1570.
6. They formed the Iroquois Confederacy.
7. This group has sometimes been called the Five Nations.
8. It includes the Mohawk, Onandaga, Cayuga, Oneida, and Seneca tribes.
9. In the 1600's, the Iroquois had been extending the area where they lived.
10. The confederacy added a sixth tribe, the Tuscarora, in the early 1700's.

Exercise 22 Forming Progressive Tenses of Verbs Write the tense indicated for each verb below.

1. present perfect progressive of *resist*
2. future progressive of *rename*
3. past perfect progressive of *grow*
4. present progressive of *become*
5. past progressive of *help*

Exercise 23 Revising Verb Forms Revise the following sentences by writing the correct form of the underlined verb. If the verb is used correctly, write *correct*.

(1) New York State has have a full and rich history. (2) The state receive its name from the Duke of York in the 1660's. (3) Before that, its name be New Netherland, since it had begin as a Dutch settlement. (4) Dutch leaders run the colony for years. (5) In fact, many places still bear Dutch names.

Exercise 24 Supplying the Correct Progressive Form Copy each of the following sentences onto your paper, supplying the progressive form of the verb indicated in parentheses.

(1) In 1665, Governor Nicolls called a meeting of settlers who (live—past perfect progressive) around Long Island. (2) He told them he (refuse—past progressive) their request for an assembly. (3) "However," he said, "I (give—present progressive) you a small degree of self-government." (4) "From this time on, you (elect—future progressive) your own town boards and constables." (5) By the Tricentennial of the United States, citizens (enjoy—future perfect progressive) freedom for more than 400 years.

Exercise 25 Find It in Your Reading Look back through the passage from "Rip Van Winkle" on page 505. Locate one verb in present perfect tense and one in past perfect tense.

Exercise 26 Find It in Your Writing Look through your writing portfolio. Find examples of sentences with verbs in different basic and progressive tenses. Identify the tense of each verb.

Exercise 27 Writing Application Write several sentences about the history of a place that you have visited or read about. Try to use different tenses in your sentences. Make sure you can identify the tense you use in each sentence.

Troublesome Verbs

Many people have problems with the verbs listed in this section. Some of the problems arise when the wrong principal part is used. Other problems are caused when the meanings of certain pairs of verbs are confused. As you read through the list, concentrate on those verbs that have caused you difficulty in the past. Then, use the exercises to test your understanding. When you are writing and revising your compositions, refer to this section for help in checking your work.

ain't *Ain't* is not correct English. Avoid using it in speaking and in writing.

INCORRECT: This *ain't* the Statue of Liberty.

CORRECT: This *isn't* the Statue of Liberty.

did, done *Done* is a past participle and can be used as a verb only with a helping verb such as *have* or *has*. If you find you are using *done* without a helping verb, try using *did* instead. Otherwise, add the helping verb before *done*.

INCORRECT: I *done* all my studying of New York.

CORRECT: I *did* all my studying of New York.
     I *have done* all my studying of New York.

gone, went *Gone* is the past participle of *go* and can be used as a verb only with a helping verb such as *have* or *has*. *Went* is the past of *go* and is never used with a helping verb.

INCORRECT: The Martins *gone* on vacation to New York.
     Niva *has went* along with them.

CORRECT: The Martins *have gone* on vacation to New York.
     The Martins *went* on vacation to New York.
     Niva *has gone* along with them.
     Niva *went* along with them.

have, of In conversation, the words *have* and *of* sound very much alike. Be careful not to write *of* when you really mean the helping verb *have* or its contraction *'ve*.

INCORRECT: He *should of* apologized.

CORRECT: He *should have* apologized.
     He *should've* apologized.

Theme: Historic New York

In this section, you will learn about several different verbs that often give writers and speakers trouble. The examples and exercises in this section will tell you more about the history of New York State.

Cross-Curricular Connection: Social Studies

Exercise 28 Avoiding Problems With Troublesome Verbs
For each of the following sentences, choose the correct verb from the pair in parentheses, and write it on your paper.

EXAMPLE: (Ain't, Aren't) you ready to leave yet?
ANSWER: Aren't

1. In 1682, Thomas Dongan (did, done) become governor of the New York colony.
2. Students of American politics should (of, have) heard of him.
3. However, he (isn't, ain't) as well known as he should be.
4. The Charter of Liberties he proposed for New York (did, done) a lot to promote democracy there.
5. His actions have (gone, went) down in history as early examples of American democratic principles at work.

lay, lie These verbs cause many problems because some of their forms are alike and have similar meanings. The first step in learning to distinguish between *lay* and *lie* is to memorize their principal parts.

PRINCIPAL PARTS: lay   laying   laid   laid
                      lie   lying   lay   lain

Next, compare the meaning and use of the two verbs.

Lay usually means "to put (something) down" or "to place (something)." This verb is almost always followed by a direct object. In the examples below, the direct objects are labeled.

EXAMPLES: The captain *lays* his map on the galley table.
            The colonists *have laid* cobblestones to pave the new road.

Lie usually means "to rest in a reclining position." It can also mean "to be situated." *Lie* is never followed by a direct object.

EXAMPLES: My father usually *lies* down after dinner.
            The food *had lain* in the sun all afternoon.

When using *lay* and *lie*, pay special attention to one particular area of confusion: *Lay* is the present tense of *lay*. *Lay* is also the past tense of *lie*.

PRESENT TENSE
OF *LAY:*   The settlers always *lay* their clothes out in the sun to dry.

PAST TENSE
OF *LIE:*   Because she was tired, my mother *lay* down for a nap after dinner.

More Practice

Grammar Exercise Workbook
• pp. 119–120
On-line Exercise Bank
• Section 22.3
    Go on-line:
    PHSchool.com
    Enter Web Code:
    ebk-7002

Get instant feedback! Exercise 28 is available on-line or on CD-ROM.

raise, rise *Raise* has several common meanings: "to lift (something) upward," "to build (something)," "to grow (something)," or "to increase (something)." Its principal parts are *raise, raising, raised,* and *raised*. *Raise* is usually followed by a direct object.

EXAMPLES:
$$\overset{\text{DO}}{}$$
Raise the colonial flag higher.

Colonists in New Netherland *raised* their children
$$\overset{\text{DO}}{}$$
to speak Dutch.

Rise, on the other hand, is usually not followed by a direct object. Rise means "to get up," "to go up," or "to be increased." Its principal parts are *rise, rising, rose,* and *risen*. *Rise* is usually followed by an adverb or a prepositional phrase.

EXAMPLES:
The moon will *rise* at 8:00 P.M.
The sailors *have been rising* before 5:00 A.M. each day.
The waves *have risen* steadily, and the colonists' boat has been unable to land.

▼ Critical Viewing Use the verbs *raise* and *rise* correctly to describe the man at the rear of the canoe-like boat and suggest the purpose of his gesture. **[Speculate]**

saw, seen *Seen* is a past participle and can be used as a verb only with a helping verb such as *have* or *has.* If you find you are using *seen* without a helping verb, try using *saw* instead. Otherwise, make sure to add a helping verb before *seen.*

INCORRECT: We *seen* important changes in colonial rule.
The governor *seen* how the colonists responded.

CORRECT: We *saw* important changes in colonial rule.
We *have seen* important changes in colonial rule.
The governor *saw* how the colonists responded.
The governor *had seen* how the colonists responded.

set, sit These verbs are often confused. The first step in learning to distinguish between *set* and *sit* is to learn their principal parts.

PRINCIPAL PARTS:
set	setting	set	set
sit	sitting	sat	sat

Set commonly means "to put (something) in a certain place." It is usually followed by a direct object.

EXAMPLES:
DO
Set the candle on top of the mantle.
DO
He *is setting* maps of New York in the rack.
DO
Felix *set* the clock back an hour.
DO
The king *has set* a new governor over the colony.

Sit usually means "to be seated" or "to rest." In its usual meanings, *sit* is never followed by a direct object. In the following examples, the words following the verbs are adverbs and prepositional phrases.

EXAMPLES: The duke's castle *sits* high up on that mountain.

The governor's council *has been sitting* in a private session for several hours.

Queen Mary *sat* for a portrait.

A book on New York history *has sat* on that library shelf for two weeks.

📖 Journal Tip

This chapter contains information on the history of New York State. In your journal, take notes on some of the facts and topics that interest you. Then, you can review them later to find a subject for a report.

▶ **Exercise 29** Avoiding Problems With Troublesome Verbs
For each of the sentences below, choose the correct verb from
the pair in parentheses, and write it on your paper.

EXAMPLE: The governor (sat, set) the idea before the
             Colonial Assembly.
ANSWER: set

1. The idea for the Charter of Liberties came to Governor
   Dongan one night as he (lay, laid) in his bed.
2. According to the charter, a group of colonial legislators
   would (sit, set) together to discuss and pass new laws.
3. They would also decide how high the tax rate must (rise,
   raise) to meet the colony's needs.
4. The charter also (saw, seen) to it that citizens would be
   guaranteed trial by jury and freedom of worship.
5. According to the charter, many important decisions would
   (lie, lay) with the people themselves instead of with the
   governor.

▶ **Exercise 30** Revising to Correct Misused Verbs Rewrite
each sentence below on your paper, correcting any misused
verbs. If a verb is used correctly, write *correct*.
1. Sadly, the groundwork for liberty laid by Governor Dongan
   was torn up before it could be put into effect.
2. The charters he passed could of done a lot for New York
   before the Revolutionary War.
3. The newly crowned King James II, former Duke of York,
   seen a different course for New York, however.
4. He set New York within the boundaries of New England.
5. Now, both New York and New England laid within the new
   colony's boundaries.
6. A royal governor was to set and watch closely over the
   colony.
7. King James should have saw how unhappy New Yorkers
   were about being linked with New England.
8. Their anger raised even more when the king dismissed
   Governor Dongan.
9. They raised protests when they were placed under Sir
   Edmund Andros, the New England governor.
10. After that, several New Yorkers had went to meet with
    Governor Andros in his Boston offices.

▶ **More Practice**

Grammar Exercise
Workbook
• pp. 119–120
On-line Exercise Bank
• Section 22.3
  Go on-line:
  PHSchool.com
  Enter Web Code:
  ebk-7002

Get instant feedback!
Exercises 29 and 30
are available on-line
or on CD-ROM.

Section 22.3 Section Review

GRAMMAR EXERCISES 31–36

Exercise 31 Recognizing Verbs That Use Direct Objects Write each verb on your paper. Write *yes* next to each verb that usually takes a direct object and *no* next to each one that does not.

1. raised
2. laid
3. lie
4. rise
5. sat
6. set
7. lay (past tense)
8. rose
9. sit
10. lay (present tense)

Exercise 32 Revising to Correct Misused Verbs On your paper, rewrite each incorrect sentence, and correct the misused verb. Write *correct* if the verb is used correctly.

1. She laid down for a nap.
2. The council will raise the issue.
3. They should've acted more quickly.
4. The king should of left the colony alone.
5. The matters have went before the king.
6. James done a terrible job of ruling.
7. The level of unhappiness has raised.
8. We seen to it that our views were noted.
9. The governor sat the plans for the city before the colonists.
10. They saw the plans and protested.

Exercise 33 Revising to Correct Usage of Troublesome Verbs Rewrite the following sentences, correcting the misused verbs. If the verb is used correctly, write *correct*.

1. Tensions raised between the English and the French in the 1680's.
2. It ain't hard to see why: They both wanted American colonies.
3. New York lay between the opposing forces.

4. Each nation would of liked to control New York's lakes.
5. They both seen the importance of controlling the Mohawk and Hudson rivers, along with the lakes.
6. The Iroquois, who held a strategic position near the waterways, did remain neutral at first.
7. However, in the French and Indian War, they had went into battle.
8. Some Iroquois were persuaded to raise up in arms to help the British.
9. Other Iroquois sat an alliance with the French.
10. In 1763, the British, with Iroquois help, won the war and seen to it that the French left New York for good.

Exercise 34 Find It in Your Reading Look through magazines and newspapers to find sentences in which troublesome verbs are used correctly.

Exercise 35 Find It in Your Writing Look through your writing portfolio. Find examples of sentences in which you have used some of the troublesome verbs discussed in this section. Make certain that you have used them correctly.

Exercise 36 Writing Application Imagine that you are upset at the dismissal of Governor Dongan by King James II (see Exercise 30). Write a brief letter to the king, raising some issues about what you think he should have done. Try to use some of the troublesome verbs discussed in this section.

Chapter Review

GRAMMAR EXERCISES 37–46

Exercise 37 Identifying Principal Parts and Regular and Irregular Verbs
Identify the principal part used to form each of the following verbs. Then, label the verb *regular* or *irregular*.

1. fetching
2. practiced
3. have found
4. type
5. have listed
6. has put
7. fell
8. laid
9. raising
10. have lain

Exercise 38 Using and Identifying Regular and Irregular Verbs
Write a sentence for each verb below—five should be in the past tense, and five in the present perfect tense. Then, label each verb *regular* or *irregular*.

1. find
2. wish
3. leave
4. stay
5. tie
6. give
7. belong
8. present
9. do
10. see

Exercise 39 Recognizing Principal Parts Used to Form Tenses
Identify the principal part used to form each underlined verb.

1. In July 1776, the New York Congress <u>ratified</u> the Declaration of Independence.
2. Then, it <u>changed</u> its own name to the Convention of Representatives of the State of New York.
3. New York <u>drafts</u> its first state constitution the next year.
4. They <u>had decided</u> to set up a legislature.
5. Consequently, the first legislature <u>met</u> in Kingston later that same year.
6. The citizens of New York <u>were holding</u> their first election as a state in 1777.

7. Soon, they <u>had chosen</u> George Clinton as their first governor.
8. He also <u>serves</u> as a delegate to the Second Continental Congress.
9. New constitutions and elections <u>were appearing</u> all over New England.
10. The revolutionary spirit <u>had caught</u> fire there.

Exercise 40 Identifying and Using Verb Tenses
Identify the tense of each of the following verbs, indicating whether it is in basic or progressive form. Then, write a sentence using each one.

1. have been washing
2. have extended
3. will name
4. am knowing
5. had been noticing
6. will have been entering
7. had patterned
8. have worked
9. was writing
10. will have fainted

Exercise 41 Identifying the Tenses of Verbs
Write the tense of the underlined verb in each sentence below.

1. The American Revolution <u>had lasted</u> eight years when it ended in 1783.
2. Almost one third of the battles <u>had been fought</u> in New York State.
3. Americans <u>were capturing</u> key forts on Lake Champlain during early fighting.
4. By September 1776, the British <u>are occupying</u> New York City.
5. They <u>hold</u> it until the end of the war.
6. The Americans <u>will be experiencing</u> a victory at Saratoga in October 1777.

7. This victory <u>will become</u> a turning point of the war.
8. The British <u>planned</u> to occupy Albany.
9. From Albany, they <u>were going</u> to control the Hudson River.
10. By controlling the Hudson, they think they <u>will have cut</u> New England off from the other colonies.

Exercise 42 Revising Usage of Troublesome Verbs Rewrite the following sentences, correcting the verbs. If a verb is used correctly, write *correct*.

1. When the Iroquois seen the Revolution break out, they didn't know which side to support.
2. They couldn't decide if they should have went with the Americans or not.
3. They thought perhaps they should just set quietly and wait.
4. They also couldn't agree if they should lie low and remain neutral.
5. Some individual Iroquois tribes laid plans to join with the British.
6. That is just what the Mohawks done.
7. In the summer of 1779, an American army was risen to fight the Mohawks.
8. The ending to this story ain't pleasant.
9. The American army went on to a decisive victory.
10. The Mohawks realized that they should of sided with the Americans.

Exercise 43 Using Verb Tenses On your paper, write logical sentences, using the verbs and tenses given below.

1. Use the present tense of *like* in a sentence about a friend.
2. Use the past tense of *want* in a sentence about your lunch.
3. Use the future tense of *go* in a sentence about next weekend.
4. Use the present perfect tense of *finish* in a sentence about your homework.
5. Ask a question using the present progressive tense of *think*.

Exercise 44 Supplying the Correct Tense On your paper, supply the form of the verb indicated in parentheses.

(1) After the Revolution ended, many New Yorkers (oppose—past perfect) a strong national government. (2) They (prefer—past progressive) to retain a weaker structure that (place—past) more power with the states. (3) When delegates (draw—past) up the U.S. Constitution in 1787, Alexander Hamilton was the only New Yorker to sign the final draft. (4) He (hope—past perfect progressive) that more New Yorkers would join him. (5) New York finally (ratify—past) the Constitution.

Exercise 45 Revision Practice Rewrite the paragraph below, correcting all errors in verb usage.

(1) In the 1750's, Samuel Stringer become one of Albany's leading citizens. (2) He had came to Albany in the 1750's while he holded a position as a surgeon with the British army. (3) Soon, Stringer had took in his new city. (4) He builded up a successful medical practice in Albany, and his income steadily raised. (5) Many people thunk that Stringer would of supported the British during the Revolution. (6) However, he done just the opposite. (7) He seen that his loyalty was with the revolutionary movement. (8) In 1775, he was chose for the post of chief physician of all the hospitals in the North. (9) He begun work on a new hospital to train American army doctors. (10) Following the war, Stringer starts the first medical library in Albany.

Exercise 46 Writing Application Write a paragraph about an important person in your city or town. Use at least three different verb tenses in your paragraph. Try to use both progressive and basic forms.

Standardized Test Preparation Workshop

Using Verbs

Your knowledge of verb usage is frequently measured on standardized tests. Your ability to determine the correct tense of a verb—present, present perfect, past, past perfect, future, and future perfect and their progressive forms—is tested when you must choose a verb or verb phrase to complete a sentence. When choosing a verb, first read the sentence aloud and determine when the action is taking place. Then, choose a verb that indicates the same point in time or tense as the sentence.

The following test items will give you practice with the format of questions that test verb usage.

Sample Test Items

Read the passage, and choose the letter of the word or group of words that belongs in each space.

Yesterday, I ___(1)___ my bike when I ___(2)___ my mother call me. Then I rode home.

1 A riding
   B will have been riding
   C had ridden
   D was riding

2 F heard
   G had heard
   H had been hearing
   J was hearing

Answers and Explanations

The correct answer is *D.* The passage hints at a continuing action that took place at the time of another past event. Therefore, the past progressive form *was riding* is the correct choice for completing the sentence.

The correct answer is *F.* The passage indicates an action that occurred in the past. The *had* in *G* and *H* implies that the action happened before the bike riding, while *was hearing* implies a continuing action, which doesn't make sense. Therefore, the past tense verb *heard* is the correct choice for completing the sentence.

▶ **Practice 1** **Directions:** Read the passage, and choose the letter of the word or group of words that belongs in each space.

Often, a bicycle __(1)__ by those who __(2)__ the age of sixteen or do not have access to mass transit. However, whatever your size or shape, you __(3)__ the benefits of bike riding. Just hop on, and you __(4)__ on your way. No doubt you __(5)__ that, although bikes __(6)__ easy to use, they __(7)__ a danger if not used properly. Soon, in most areas, wearing a helmet __(8)__ the law. Also, use of hand signals __(9)__ required. By following the rules, you __(10)__ a safer environment for yourself and others on the road.

1 **A** rode
  B has been riding
  C is riding
  D is ridden

2 **F** don't reach
  G have not reached
  H are not reaching
  J have not been reaching

3 **A** enjoy
  B will have enjoyed
  C enjoyed
  D had enjoyed

4 **F** have been
  G will be
  H will have been
  J were

5 **A** have learned
  B were learning
  C learn
  D had learned

6 **F** are being
  G were being
  H are
  J have been

7 **A** present
  B did present
  C were presenting
  D have presented

8 **F** become
  G have become
  H became
  J will have become

9 **A** was
  B will have been
  C will be
  D have been

10 **F** create
   G have been creating
   H will have created
   J had created

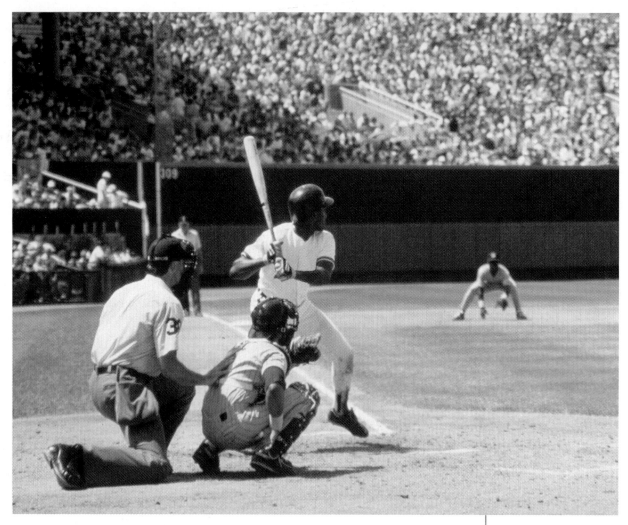

There are three different kinds, or cases, of personal pronouns: nominative, objective, and possessive. Pronouns are used to give writing variety. For example, when reading or writing about the history of baseball, it would be monotonous to repeat the noun *Brooklyn Dodgers* every time a reference to this team is made. Using a pronoun such as *they* allows the writing to flow more smoothly.

▲ **Critical Viewing**
What is about to happen in this photograph? Use the personal pronouns *he* and *his* in your answer. **[Infer]**

Diagnostic Test

Directions: Write all answers on a separate sheet of paper.

Skill Check A. List the personal pronouns in the sentences below. Label each pronoun *nominative, objective,* or *possessive.*

1. Our team is the wild-card team, and it will be included in the playoffs.
2. It was the Cougars who won in their division, and they will now be in the playoffs as well.
3. They are an excellent team, and we will probably see them in the county championship series.
4. The league also has All-Star Games, but it holds those in the summer.
5. The All-Star Game matches the best players in each league, so you should try to see one someday!

Skill Check B. Write each underlined pronoun in the nominative case. Then, label the pronoun subject *(S)* or predicate pronoun *(PP).*

6. Jenny and I started our careers in T-ball with my father's help.
7. It was he who coached our first team.
8. Jenny knows that no one hits as well as she can.
9. It was she who led our team to victory this season.
10. Next year, we are going to play without the T-ball stand.

Skill Check C. Identify how each underlined pronoun in the objective case is used.

11. Baseball uses equipment such as balls, bats, gloves, cleats, helmets, and pads; all players use one or more of them.
12. The gloves and cleats were used by her.
13. The coach showed us the cork center of the baseball.
14. Knowing the equipment well helps us in the game.
15. He is the catcher, so the larger, more padded glove belongs to him.

Skill Check D. Write the correct possessive pronoun from the pair in parentheses.

16. The manager is responsible for giving the team (its, it's) strategy.
17. It is (his', his) choice who plays first base.
18. Umpires have complete authority over the game; therefore, the responsibility of enforcing rules is (their's, theirs).
19. That manager is (ours, our's).
20. (My, Mine) dad is an umpire, and he removed the pitcher from the game.

Many pronouns change form according to usage. *Case* is the relationship between a pronoun's form and its use. This chapter will explain the three cases and show you how to use the various forms of pronouns correctly.

The personal pronouns listed in Section 14.2 are presented in three groups: those that refer to the person speaking; those that refer to the person spoken to; and those that refer to the person, place, or thing spoken about. Pronouns can also be grouped according to three cases.

▶ **KEY CONCEPT** Pronouns have three cases: *nominative, objective,* and *possessive.* ■

Identifying the Three Cases of Personal Pronouns

The personal pronouns are grouped in the following chart according to the three cases.

THE USES OF PERSONAL PRONOUNS BY CASE	
Nominative Case	**Use in Sentence**
I, we you he, she, it, they	Subject of a Verb Predicate Pronoun
Objective Case	**Use in Sentence**
me, us you him, her, it, them	Direct Object Indirect Object Object of a Preposition
Possessive Case	**Use in Sentence**
my, mine, our, ours your, yours his, her, hers, its, their, theirs	To Show Ownership

SUBJECT OF A VERB: <u>We</u> badly wanted to see the game.

PREDICATE NOMINATIVE: It was <u>they</u> who got the tickets.

DIRECT OBJECT: Please give me <u>them</u>.

INDIRECT OBJECT: Please give <u>me</u> the tickets.

OBJECT OF A PREPOSITION: Please give the tickets to <u>me</u>.

TO SHOW OWNERSHIP: They are <u>our</u> tickets, not theirs.

Theme: Baseball

In this chapter, you will learn about using pronouns. The examples and exercises are about baseball.

Cross-Curricular Connection: Physical Education

🔵 **Learn More**

Pronouns are used to replace nouns. For more information on nouns, refer to Chapter 14.

▶ **Exercise 1** Identifying Case Identify the case of the personal pronouns that are underlined in the following sentences.

EXAMPLE: Didn't Richard give <u>her</u> the directions?
ANSWER: objective

1. Baseball got <u>its</u> start from other stickball games.
2. <u>It</u> is similar to a game called rounders.
3. During the Civil War, the game was introduced to <u>us</u> by traveling soldiers.
4. <u>They</u> played and provided free entertainment, while owners of the ball fields made profits.
5. The players became professional in 1869, when owners of the ball fields first began to pay <u>them</u>.

Using the Nominative Case

Personal pronouns in the nominative case have two uses in sentences:

▶ **KEY CONCEPT** Use the nominative case for the subject of a verb. ■

SUBJECTS: *I* collect baseballs.
             She wrote a letter to the President.

▶ **KEY CONCEPT** Use the nominative case when a pronoun is used as a predicate nominative. ■

A predicate nominative renames the subject. Pronouns used as predicate nominatives always follow a form of the verb *be* or a verb phrase ending in *be* or *been*.

PREDICATE   It is *she*.
NOMINATIVE: It might have been *they*.

To make sure you are using the correct case of a personal pronoun in a compound subject, use just the pronoun with the verb in the sentence. In the following examples, "Me collect" clearly sounds wrong. The nominative case *I* is correct and should be used.

INCORRECT: Gina and *me* collect stamps.
              Me and Gina collect stamps.
CORRECT: Gina and *I* collect stamps.

More Practice

Grammar Exercise Workbook
• pp. 121–122
On-line Exercise Bank
• Chapter 23
  Go on-line:
  PHSchool.com
  Enter Web Code:
  ebk-7002

Get instant feedback! Exercise 1 is available on-line or on CD-ROM.

▶ **Speaking and Listening Tip**

Accustom yourself to using nominative pronouns correctly. With one or two classmates, take turns reading aloud the correct examples on this page and Exercises 2 and 3 on the next page.

▶ **Exercise 2** Identifying the Use of Personal Pronouns in the Nominative Case Write each nominative pronoun in the following sentences, and indicate how each one is used.

EXAMPLE: She memorized the rules of the game.

ANSWER: She (subject)

1. Josh Gibson hit approximately 800 home runs in the 17 years he played baseball.
2. Many of his statistics are undocumented, but they are known to be outstanding.
3. It is known that Gibson had a lifetime batting average of .347.
4. Some people were opposed to integrating professional baseball; it was they who opposed the signing of African American players.
5. Josh Gibson died the year that Jackie Robinson signed with the Dodgers. Soon, we saw the integration of professional major league baseball.

▶ **Exercise 3** Using Personal Pronouns in the Nominative Case Complete each of the following sentences by writing an appropriate nominative pronoun. Then, indicate how each pronoun is used in the sentence.

EXAMPLE: ___?___ think that this photograph is best.

ANSWER: We (subject)

1. ___?___ were excited when he won Rookie of the Year in 1947.
2. ___?___ was an exciting and controversial time in baseball.
3. The person who made the Dodgers the first multiracial team was ___?___ .
4. The biggest fans of Jackie Robinson were Jenny, Sarah, and ___?___ .
5. ___?___ read every baseball biography.

▲ **Critical Viewing** Use the nominative pronouns it and he in a sentence describing one of Jackie Robinson's achievements in baseball. **[Relate]**

Using the Objective Case

Personal pronouns in the objective case have three uses:

▶ **KEY CONCEPT** Use the objective case (1) for a direct object, (2) for an indirect object, and (3) for the object of a preposition. ■

DIRECT OBJECTS:	Kate invited *me* to the game.
	The dog chased *us* across the lawn.
INDIRECT OBJECTS:	Diego wrote *her* a letter.
	I told *them* the story.
OBJECTS	Were they talking to *me*?
OF PREPOSITIONS:	Give this message to *them*.

Mistakes with pronouns in the objective case usually occur only when the object is compound.

INCORRECT: Kate invited Ron and *I* to the game.
Diego wrote his mother and *she* a letter.
Were they talking about Lois and *I*?

Again, to check whether the case of the personal pronoun is correct, use the pronoun by itself after the verb or preposition. In the preceding examples, "Kate invited I," "Diego wrote she," and "Were they talking about I?" all sound wrong. Objective pronouns are needed.

CORRECT: Kate invited Ron and *me* to the game.
Diego wrote his mother and *her* a letter.
Were they talking about Lois and *me*?

▶ **Exercise 4** Identifying the Use of Personal Pronouns in the Objective Case Write the objective pronouns in the sentences below, and indicate how each one is used.

EXAMPLE: Baseball has given us many exciting moments.
ANSWER: us (indirect object)

1. Baseball teams have undergone many changes over the years; World War II caused them to lose many players.
2. When a player had to go to war, there was no one to play for him.
3. Latin American players played for us at that time.
4. If a woman was interested in baseball, the All-American Girl's Baseball League gave her a chance to play.
5. From 1943 to 1954, the league helped promote women athletes and made them into celebrities.

▶ **More Practice**

Grammar Exercise Workbook
• pp. 123–124
On-line Exercise Bank
• Chapter 23
  Go on-line:
  PHSchool.com
  Enter Web Code:
  ebk-7002

Get instant feedback! Exercises 2, 3, and 4 are available on-line or on CD-ROM.

▶ **Exercise 5** Using Personal Pronouns in the Objective Case
Complete each of the following sentences by writing an appropriate objective pronoun. Then, indicate how each pronoun is used in the sentence.

EXAMPLE: Why didn't Edwin invite ___?___ to the game?
ANSWER: me (direct object)

1. If we hadn't recruited women and players from other countries, there would have been no one to play for ___?___ .
2. When a player returned after the war, the coach would give ___?___ his position back.
3. Foreign players continued to play for ___?___ even after the return of the veterans.
4. The girl's league lasted only a few years because people didn't follow ___?___ after the regular players returned.
5. Baseball still gives ___?___ many issues to consider.

◀ **Critical Viewing**
Why do you think these women are so happy? Answer using the objective-case pronouns *her* and *them*. **[Draw Conclusions]**

Complete the exercises on-line! Exercises 5 and 6 are available on-line or on CD-ROM.

▶ **Exercise 6** Writing Sentences With Objective Pronouns
Write five sentences about an event or activity that has caught your interest. Use objective pronouns as indicated. Of course, you may use other pronouns in your sentences as necessary.
1. *me* or *us* as an indirect object
2. *it* or *them* as a direct object
3. *me, us,* or *them* as the object of a preposition
4. *him* or *her* as a direct object
5. *them* or *it* as the object of a preposition

More Practice

Grammar Exercise
Workbook
• pp. 123–124
On-line Exercise Bank
• Chapter 23
  Go on-line:
  PHSchool.com
  Enter Web Code:
  ebk-7002

Using the Possessive Case

Personal pronouns in the possessive case show ownership.

> **KEY CONCEPT** Use the possessive case of personal pronouns to show possession before nouns. Also, use certain personal pronouns by themselves to show possession. ■

BEFORE NOUNS:	The bat found *its* target.
	Have you seen *their* gloves?
BY THEMSELVES:	Is this hat *yours* or *his?*

Notice that personal pronouns ending in -*s* are never written with an apostrophe.

INCORRECT:	*Our's* is the last seat in the row.
	That lemonade is *his',* not *her's.*
CORRECT:	*Ours* is the last seat in the row.
	That lemonade is *his,* not *hers.*

The possessive form of *it* is *its*. *It's* is a contraction for *it is*.

CONTRACTION:	*It's* time to start the game.
POSSESSIVE PRONOUN:	A team is only as good as *its* players.

🗸 Spelling Tip

The possessive pronoun *their* does not follow the "i before e except after c" rule.

GRAMMAR IN LITERATURE

---

from **Was Tarzan a Three-Bandage Man?**

Bill Cosby

In this passage, the nominative pronouns are blue, the objective pronouns are red, and the possessive pronouns are green. What noun does each pronoun replace?

"Why *you* walkin' like that?" said *my* mother one day.

"This is Jackie *Robinson's* walk," *I* proudly replied.

"There's somethin' wrong with *his* shoes?"

"*He's* the fastest man in baseball."

"*He'd* be faster if *he* didn't walk like that. *His* mother should make *him* walk right."

▶ **Exercise 7** Using Personal Pronouns in the Possessive
Case For each of the following sentences, write the correct
personal pronoun from the choices in parentheses.

EXAMPLE: Now that Kim has gone away to school, this
            room is all (your's, yours).

ANSWER: yours

1. The team plays (it's, its) best at home.
2. The first baseman took (his', his) place near
   the base.
3. The field is (their's, theirs) to play on until
   they get three outs.
4. That designated hitter is (our's, ours), but
   he doesn't play on the field.
5. Center field is (his', his) responsibility.
6. The shortstop position is (your's, yours), so
   stand between second and third base.
7. (It's, Its) the infielders who throw players
   out at bases.
8. I play catcher, and the pitching position is
   (his', his).
9. I always forget which position is (your's,
   yours).
10. The fastball is (his', his) best pitch.

▶ **Exercise 8** Checking the Case of Personal Pronouns
Write the underlined pronouns in the following sentences
that are incorrect. Then, write the form of the pronoun that
should be used in formal writing. For sentences with no errors,
write *correct*.

EXAMPLE: Is this uniform your's?
ANSWER: your's—yours

1. The three players to strike out were Alex, Willy, and <u>me</u>.
2. <u>His'</u> hit was a high fly ball.
3. When <u>our</u> favorite team came to town, we went to the game.
4. When deciding who should hit first, the coach couldn't
   decide between her and <u>I</u>.
5. <u>You</u> will be happy to hear that the right-field position is
   now <u>your's</u>.
6. The coach showed Jose and <u>I</u> the batting order.
7. <u>It's</u> the second out of the inning.
8. It was <u>him</u> who took <u>my</u> glove.
9. The pitcher could not believe that <u>his'</u> was the winning team.
10. Kevin, Larry, and <u>me</u> are playing on the same team.

▲ **Critical Viewing**
Imagine that one of
these baseballs has
been autographed
by a favorite or
famous player. Use
possessive pronouns
to briefly describe
the ball, the player,
or a particular play.
[Relate]

▶ **More Practice**

Grammar Exercise
Workbook
• pp. 125–126
On-line Exercise Bank
• Chapter 23
  Go on-line:
  PHSchool.com
  Enter Web Code:
  ebk-7002

Hands-on Grammar

Pronoun Case Checker

Errors in pronoun case often occur when the first-person singular pronoun is used as part of a compound. Many people have the tendency to use the nominative case *I* in all situations. In many cases, however, the objective case is correct. Use a pronoun case checker to illustrate that the correct case of a pronoun can often be determined by eliminating the rest of the compound.

On a strip of paper, write the following sentence, in which the object of the preposition is compound.

Fold the paper so that the first-person singular pronouns fold over the other words in the compound. By eliminating the other words, you can more easily recognize that the objective case is correct in this situation.

Complete strips for each of the following sentences. Fold each one so that only the first-person pronoun shows. Determine which case is correct.

Find It in Your Reading Look through a short story you are reading, and find sentences with compound objects that contain a first-person pronoun. Complete a sentence strip to check that the case is correct.

Find It in Your Writing Use a pronoun case checker to check the case of any compound pronouns in your own writing.

Chapter Review

GRAMMAR EXERCISES 9–16

▶ **Exercise 9** Identifying Personal Pronouns List the personal pronouns used in the sentences below.

1. Baseball players field the ball with their gloves.
2. They wear uniforms to differentiate between teams.
3. Spectators watch them play from the stands.
4. Professional players are not allowed to wear their hats backwards.
5. Baseball camps can teach you basic skills.
6. A high earned run average made her very valuable.
7. After the winning run, the players threw their hats in the air.
8. Over the left-field wall is where he hit the ball.
9. His batting average is the highest on the team.
10. It was he who struck him out.
11. Throwing curve balls is what she does best.
12. The coach asked her to pinch-hit.
13. Caring for the balls and bats is his responsibility.
14. The mascot entertains us between innings.
15. He hit the ball that the pitcher threw.

▶ **Exercise 10** Distinguishing Case List the pronouns from the sentences below. Label each pronoun *nominative*, *objective*, or *possessive*.

1. Ballplayers entertain us with winning runs and fast throws.
2. The team bus will take them to the games.
3. We played against my brother's team.
4. The outfielder threw us a ball.
5. He hit a grand slam.

6. His uniform number is six.
7. José was her biggest fan.
8. They played in the rain.
9. The foul ball was hit by him.
10. The catcher's glove was his.
11. The balls and bats are ours.
12. The pitcher struck us both out.
13. The umpire gave him the mask.
14. She hoped they would make the playoffs.
15. They sometimes missed games because of the weather.

▶ **Exercise 11** Identifying the Use of Personal Pronouns in the Nominative Case Identify whether the underlined pronoun in the nominative case is used as the subject of a verb or as a predicate nominative.

1. <u>She</u> hit the ball over third base.
2. Eventually, <u>he</u> caught the fly ball.
3. The player with the best record is <u>he</u>.
4. <u>We</u> have tickets to the series.
5. The best hitters are Tom, Joe, and <u>he</u>.
6. <u>I</u> caught the foul ball.
7. It was <u>he</u> who walked.
8. <u>He</u> struck out all three hitters.
9. <u>I</u> had great seats at the last game.
10. It was <u>we</u> who enjoyed the mascot's antics.

▶ **Exercise 12** Determining the Use of Personal Pronouns in the Objective Case Identify how each underlined pronoun in the objective case is used.

1. Who will pitch for <u>them</u> in the next game?
2. The coach showed <u>him</u> the playbook.
3. This season has prepared <u>her</u> for the championship game.
4. When you find the uniform, bring <u>it</u> to the game.

5. The manager made a mistake and told <u>them</u> the team's strategy.
6. The umpire called Judy and <u>her</u> out.
7. The play was a secret between Jane and <u>me</u>.
8. As the season progressed, the coach had greater expectations of <u>us</u>.
9. The manager presented <u>him</u> with the MVP award.
10. The pitcher caught the ball and then threw <u>it</u> home.

Exercise 13 Supplying Personal Pronouns in the Possessive Case Write an appropriate possessive pronoun to complete each sentence below.

1. The coach told the team about ___?___ new plays for the championship game.
2. The bats are ___?___, but we can use them.
3. How many of the fans are ___?___, and how many are ___?___?
4. He told me it's now ___?___ turn at bat.
5. I think this equipment is ___?___.

Exercise 14 Revising to Eliminate Problems in the Case of Personal Pronouns For each sentence, replace any incorrect underlined pronoun with a correct one. If the pronoun is not wrong, write *correct*.

1. The players at bat will be Patti, Maxine, and <u>me</u>.
2. <u>Her</u> and <u>I</u> have practiced hard, and <u>our</u> playing ability has improved.
3. When the players arrived, the manager let <u>them</u> onto the field.
4. The coach couldn't decide between her and <u>I</u>.
5. You will be happy to know that the position is now <u>your's</u>.
6. The team needs to change <u>its</u> habits.
7. The trainer asked Tom and <u>he</u> to stretch.
8. The victory is <u>theirs</u>.

9. Steve, Jerry, and <u>me</u> will celebrate after the game.
10. The team had <u>it's</u> best season ever.

Exercise 15 Writing Application Write an article about a sports event. Use three nominative pronouns, three objective pronouns, and four possessive pronouns.

Exercise 16 CUMULATIVE REVIEW Problems With Sentences, Usage, Shifts in Verb Tense, and Pronouns Revise the following paragraph, correcting sentence errors, usage problems, unnecessary shifts in verb tense, and misused pronouns.

(1) The team members told I that they were not frozen in terror on opening night. (2) They will know that they rose above being nervous. (3) First, too team members busted (4) there legs in a skiing accident. (5) Then, the manager caught a cold. (6) Two days before the first game, the uniform rental agency admitted that the uniforms were still on a field in a neighboring state! (7) Nevertheless, it became clear that the affect of all these difficulties (8) was to draw the team together. (9) The manager gave his' best wishes to the team, (10) and they will perform with confidence. (11) The players hoped to play a good game they were nervous but knew they were ready. (12) Any game you see on that field is good. (13) Their always ready to perform (14) in spite of any obstacles that you face. They always play a good game. (15) Even when its difficult.

Standardized Test Preparation Workshop

Using Pronouns

Standardized tests measure your knowledge of the rules of standard grammar, such as correct pronoun usage. Questions test your ability to use the three cases of personal pronouns correctly. When answering these questions, determine what type of pronoun is needed in the sentence—nominative case pronouns are used as subjects or predicate pronouns; objective case pronouns are used as direct objects, indirect objects, or objects of prepositions; and possessive case pronouns are used to show ownership.

The following test item will give you practice with the format of questions that test your knowledge of pronoun usage.

Test Tip

When an object or subject is compound, check to see if the case is correct by using only the pronoun in the compound construction—for example, *She invited Kate and I/me.* Correct: *She invited me.* Incorrect: *She invited I.*

Sample Test Items	Answers and Explanations
Read the passage, and choose the letter of the word or group of words that belongs in each space.	The correct answer is *B.* Since the sentence calls for a subject, a pronoun in the nominative case is the only choice. Therefore, the nominative pronoun *I* best completes the sentence.
Last night, Brooke and ____(1)____ watched a program on President Kennedy. Although ____(2)____ presidency was brief, he is one of the presidents most remembered.	
1 A me **B** I **C** them **D** us	
2 F he **G** him **H** his **J** my	The correct answer is *H.* Since the sentence calls for a word that shows ownership, a pronoun in the possessive case is the only choice. *My* is possessive, but doesn't make sense in context. Therefore, the possessive pronoun *his* best completes the sentence.

Practice 1 **Directions:** Read the passage, and choose the letter of the word or group of words that belongs in each space.

____(1)____ group was assigned a presentation on President John F. Kennedy. Finding information on ____(2)____, especially ____(3)____ years as president, has not been too difficult for ____(4)____. Each member has a specific job to fulfill. I am in charge of assigning and collecting research, but Brooke is the group leader. It is ____(5)____ who makes the final decisions. ____(6)____ help her keep group members on task, but ____(7)____ don't always appreciate when Brooke or ____(8)____ remind ____(9)____ of ____(10)____ jobs.

1 **A** He
   B Him
   C Our
   D Its

2 **F** it
   G he
   H him
   J her

3 **A** his
   B him
   C our
   D her

4 **F** we
   G us
   H him
   J its

5 **A** her
   B she
   C him
   D his

6 **F** Me
   G I
   H Him
   J Her

7 **A** them
   B they
   C him
   D her

8 **F** me
   G I
   H him
   J her

9 **A** them
   B they
   C him
   D her

10 **F** her
   G their
   H our
   J us

Making Words Agree

▲ Critical Viewing
Describe what is happening in this photograph in a sentence that begins "Bursts of color . . . ." Be sure your verb agrees with this subject.
[Analyze]

Have you ever seen people dressed in green on St. Patrick's Day? Have you watched fireworks on the Fourth of July?

Just as special events can "fit" with certain celebrations, subjects and verbs must fit together in sentences. For example, you would never say, "*I are* the winner!" or "*Is they* your best friends?" You would hear that something is wrong with these sentences. The problem is that the subjects and verbs do not *agree*.

In most of the sentences you speak and write, the subjects and verbs agree almost automatically. You would probably say, "*I am* the winner!" or "*Are they* your best friends?" In some sentences, however, you might be tempted to make a verb agree with a word that is not the subject. In such a case, check to find the real subject and make sure that it agrees with its verb. Pronouns and the words they stand for must also agree. This chapter will explain the rules of agreement and how to make parts of sentences work together correctly.

Diagnostic Test

Directions: Write all answers on a separate sheet of paper.

Skill Check A. For the following sentences, choose the correct word from each pair in parentheses.

1. Celebrations (is, are) ways in which we remember important events.
2. Some celebrations (comes, come) in the form of holidays, others as feasts or festivals.
3. Customs and traditions (plays, play) important roles in the way we celebrate.
4. For many people, traditions (has, have) been passed from generation to generation.
5. Each person (celebrates, celebrate) an event in his or her own way.
6. Mary (cheers, cheer) when she gets an *A* on an exam.
7. I hope either Joey or Nate (has, have) a large party after (his, their) graduation.
8. The students at school (holds, hold) a victory dance after winning a big game.
9. Almost everyone (enjoys, enjoy) a celebration.
10. What events (does, do) you like to celebrate?

Skill Check B. In some of the sentences below, subjects and verbs do not agree in number. If a sentence is correct, write *correct* on your paper. If it is incorrect, rewrite the sentence correctly.

11. Several holidays throughout the year has big celebrations.
12. Many children dresses up in costumes for parties.
13. Leslie and her family stays up until midnight on New Year's Eve.
14. Both Ed and Neil spend Thanksgiving at their grandmother's house.
15. Michael likes St. Patrick's Day parades because people usually wear green.
16. Neither Kit nor Stewart want to miss the fireworks on July fourth.
17. Danny said that Christmas are his favorite holiday.
18. His family have many long-standing Christmas traditions.
19. Jason and Tom prefers birthday celebrations.
20. There are always a big party with all of his friends.

Skill Check C. All of the following sentences are in the present tense. On your paper, write a verb or pronoun to complete each sentence, making sure to maintain agreement.

21. She follows holiday customs from ___?___ native land.
22. The holidays of some countries differ from ___?___ .
23. In Mexico, Carlos and ___?___ family celebrate Cinco de Mayo.
24. After a successful harvest, people in some cultures have a feast to celebrate ___?___ good fortune.
25. Anybody who celebrates that holiday must be following the ways of ___?___ ancestors.

Agreement Between Subjects and Verbs

Subject-verb agreement has one main rule:

▶ **KEY CONCEPT** A verb must agree with its subject in number. ■

The number of a word can be either singular or plural. Singular words indicate *one*. Plural words indicate *more than one*. Only nouns, pronouns, and verbs have number.

Recognizing the Number of Nouns and Pronouns

Most of the time, it is easy to tell whether a noun or pronoun is singular or plural. Compare, for example, the singular and plural forms of the nouns in the following chart:

NOUNS	
Singular	**Plural**
custom	customs
box	boxes
knife	knives
mouse	mice

Most nouns are made plural by adding *-s* or *-es* to the singular form (friend*s* and box*es*). Some nouns become plural in other ways (kni*ves* and m*ice*). Pronouns have different forms to indicate singular and plural. For example, *I, he, she, it,* and *this* are singular. *We, they,* and *these* are plural. *You, who,* and *some* are either singular or plural.

▶ **Exercise 1** Recognizing the Number of Nouns and Pronouns On your paper, indicate whether each of the following words is *singular* or *plural*.

EXAMPLE: children—plural

1. turkey
2. geese
3. Thanksgiving
4. they
5. it
6. I
7. veteran
8. festivals
9. shamrocks
10. we
11. fireworks
12. women
13. street fair
14. flag
15. feasts

Theme: Holidays and Celebrations

In this section, you will learn about the singular and plural forms of nouns and verbs. The examples and exercises are about holidays and celebrations.

Cross-Curricular Connection: Social Studies

Text

Get instant feedback! Exercises 1 and 2 are available on-line or on CD-ROM.

▶ **More Practice**

Grammar Exercise Workbook
• pp. 127–128
On-line Exercise Bank
• Section 24.1
Go on-line:
PHSchool.com
Enter Web Code:
ebk-7002

Recognizing the Number of Verbs

Like nouns, verbs have singular and plural forms. Problems involving the number of verbs normally involve the third-person forms in the present tense (*she wants, they want*) and certain forms of the verb *be* (*I am; he is* or *was; we are* or *were*).

Spelling Tip

If a noun ends in *fe* (such as *knife*), its plural is usually formed by changing *fe* to *ve* and adding *s* (*knives*).

SINGULAR AND PLURAL VERBS IN THE PRESENT TENSE	
Singular	**Plural**
The girl *runs*.	The girls *run*.
The boy *plays*.	The boys *play*.
I *am* happy.	We *are* happy.
This *was* great!	Those *were* great!

Exercise 2 Recognizing the Number of Verbs On your paper, write the verb from the choices in parentheses that agrees in number with the pronoun. After each answer, write whether the verb is *singular* or *plural*.

EXAMPLE: they (meets, meet)
ANSWER: meet (plural)

1. this (is, are)
2. he (votes, vote)
3. I (is, am)
4. she (gives, give)
5. we (is, are)
6. it (bark, barks)
7. they (was, were)
8. we (has, have)
9. those (has been, have been)
10. they (counts, count)

▶ **Critical Viewing** Write a sentence describing this dog. Then, identify the number of the verb(s) you have used. **[Apply]**

Making Verbs Agree With Singular and Plural Subjects

To check for agreement between a subject and a verb, begin by determining the number of the subject. Then, make sure the verb has the same number.

KEY CONCEPT A singular subject must have a singular verb. A plural subject must have a plural verb. ■

In the following examples, the subjects are underlined once and the verbs are underlined twice.

SINGULAR SUBJECT AND VERB:	Jeff always <u>has</u> a good time at the beach. She <u>was</u> here earlier today. A picnic <u>is being planned</u> for Independence Day.
PLURAL SUBJECT AND VERB:	The <u>surfers</u> always <u>have</u> a good time at the beach. They <u>were</u> here earlier today. <u>Picnics</u> <u>are being planned</u> for Independence Day.

All the subjects in the preceding examples stand next to or near their verbs. Often, however, a subject is separated from its verb by a prepositional phrase. In these cases, it is important to remember that the object of a preposition is never the subject of a sentence.

KEY CONCEPT A prepositional phrase that comes between a subject and its verb does *not* affect subject-verb agreement. ■

In the first example below, the subject is *arrival*, not *firemen*, which is the object of the preposition *of*. Because *arrival* is singular, the plural verb *have caused* cannot agree with it. In the second example, the subject is the plural *cheers*, not *crowd*; therefore, it takes the plural verb *were heard*.

INCORRECT:	The <u>arrival</u> of the firemen <u>have caused</u> much excitement at the picnic.
CORRECT:	The <u>arrival</u> of the firemen <u>has caused</u> much excitement at the picnic.
INCORRECT:	The <u>cheers</u> of the crowd <u>was heard</u> several blocks away.
CORRECT:	The <u>cheers</u> of the crowd <u>were heard</u> several blocks away.

▶ **Exercise 3** Making Verbs Agree With Singular and Plural Subjects For each of the following sentences, choose the correct verb from the pair in parentheses, and write it on your paper.

EXAMPLE: People often (gathers, gather) on holidays.

ANSWER: gather

1. Independence Day (commemorates, commemorate) the beginning of our freedom from English rule.
2. The Declaration of Independence (was, were) signed by many leading statesmen.
3. More than two hundred years (has, have) passed since this great event.
4. This holiday (occurs, occur) every Fourth of July.
5. Many cities around the nation (has, have) parades and other special celebrations.
6. Marching bands in a parade often (wears, wear) red, white, and blue uniforms.
7. Some people in the parade (likes, like) to dress up as American colonists.
8. The decorations seen around town (uses, use) the colors of the flag.
9. A picnic with hot dogs and apple pie (seems, seem) like a good summertime meal.
10. A bright display of fireworks (is, are) often the grand finale of this day of fun and pride.

▶ **More Practice**

Grammar Exercise Workbook
• pp. 129–130
On-line Exercise Bank
• Section 24.1
Go on-line:
PHSchool.com
Enter Web Code:
ebk-7002

Text

Get instant feedback! Exercise 3 is available on-line or on CD-ROM.

◀ **Critical Viewing** What sounds do fireworks make? Answer this question in a sentence using two colorful plural verbs. **[Analyze]**

Making Verbs Agree With Compound Subjects

A compound subject is made up of two or more subjects joined by a conjunction such as *or*, *nor*, or *and*.

KEY CONCEPT Two or more singular subjects joined by *or* or *nor* must have a singular verb. Two or more plural subjects joined by *or* or *nor* must have a plural verb. ■

INCORRECT: Either the <u>turkey</u> or the <u>stuffing</u> <u>are cooking</u>.
CORRECT: Either the <u>turkey</u> or the <u>stuffing</u> <u>is cooking</u>.
CORRECT: Neither the <u>potatoes</u> nor the <u>peas</u> <u>are</u> done.

KEY CONCEPT When singular and plural subjects are joined by *or* or *nor*, the verb must agree with the closer subject. ■

SINGULAR SUBJECT CLOSER: Neither the <u>lights</u> nor the <u>wreath</u> <u>is</u> in the box.
PLURAL SUBJECT CLOSER: Neither the <u>wreath</u> nor the <u>lights</u> <u>are</u> in the box.

Exercise 4 Making Verbs Agree With Compound Subjects Joined by *or* or *nor* For each of the sentences listed below, choose the correct verb from the pair in parentheses, and write it on your paper.

EXAMPLE: Neither the twins nor their dog (has, have) remained long at the parade.
ANSWER: has

1. Either historical occasions or distinguished persons (is, are) commemorated on secular holidays.
2. Neither Father's Day nor Mother's Day (is, are) celebrated in many foreign countries.
3. Usually, Bob or Liz (makes, make) a gift for Mother.
4. Either Anne or her sister (buys, buy) her mother a card.
5. Concert tickets or a fancy dinner (is, are) a great gift.
6. Often, either Chinese or Italian food (tastes, taste) good.
7. Sunday or Monday (is, are) the day for holidays.
8. Either flowers or balloons (is, are) delivered to the house.
9. Neither Mom nor Dad (works, work) on a holiday.
10. Neither Groundhog Day nor Valentine's Day (is, are) a national holiday.

More Practice

Grammar Exercise Workbook
• pp. 131–132
On-line Exercise Bank
• Section 24.1
  Go on-line:
  PHSchool.com
  Enter Web Code:
  ebk-7002

Text

Get instant feedback! Exercise 4 is available on-line or on CD-ROM.

▲ **Critical Viewing**
In a sentence using *neither . . . nor,* explain how the marchers at each end of the row differ from those in the middle. **[Connect]**

▶ **KEY CONCEPT** A compound subject joined by *and* is usually plural and must have a plural verb. ■

And usually acts as a plus sign. Whether the parts of the compound subject are all singular, all plural, or mixed in number, they usually add up to a subject that takes a plural verb.

EXAMPLES: The boy and girl are waiting for the parade.
The boys and girls are waiting for the parade.
The boys and the girl are waiting for the parade.

This rule has two exceptions. First, if the parts of the compound subject taken together are thought of as a single unit, then the compound subject is considered singular and must have a singular verb.

SINGULAR COMPOUND
SUBJECT: Bacon and eggs is a very popular breakfast. (Bacon + eggs = one breakfast)

The second exception involves the words *every* and *each.* Either of these words before a compound subject indicates the need for a singular verb.

SINGULAR COMPOUND
SUBJECT: Every town and village celebrates.

▶ **Exercise 5** Making Verbs Agree With Compound Subjects **Joined by** *and* Choose the correct verb from the pair in parentheses, and write it on your paper.

1. Memorial Day and Veterans Day (is, are) national holidays.
2. Soldiers and sailors (has been, have been) remembered on these days for many years.
3. Each boy and girl in school (learns, learn) that General John Alexander Logan originated Memorial Day.
4. Nearly every city and town (pays, pay) tribute to those killed in battle.
5. Parades and speeches (marks, mark) this day's importance.
6. In some towns, the tombstone or grave marker of every deceased service person (is, are) decorated with an American flag.
7. My family and I (visits, visit) Arlington National Cemetery every year on this important holiday.
8. Both Veterans Day and Memorial Day (honors, honor) those who served in America's armed forces.
9. While both Memorial Day and Veterans Day (commemorates, commemorate) all those who served, Veterans Day is dedicated to those who survived the fighting.
10. World War II and the Vietnam War (is, are) two wars that people think of on Memorial Day.

▶ **Exercise 6** Avoiding Errors in Subject-Verb Agreement

On your paper, write the correct verb from the pair in parentheses.

1. Veterans Day and Armistice Day (is, are) different names for the same holiday.
2. The Allied countries that fought in World War I (observes, observe) this holiday.
3. Each country (remembers, remember) those who served in this war.
4. Americans (calls, call) the holiday Veterans Day.
5. This day (honors, honor) veterans of all wars.
6. The President always (delivers, deliver) a speech on Veterans Day to pay tribute to those who served.
7. Great Britain and Canada (has, have) different names for this holiday.
8. Both countries (celebrates, celebrate) the day on November 11.
9. France and Italy also (honors, honor) the soldiers who fought in World War I on this day.
10. Neither Bolivia nor Kenya (celebrates, celebrate) this holiday.

▶ **Speaking** and **Listening Tip**

After choosing the correct verb, read each sentence aloud to a partner. As you read, stress the conjunction that connects the two parts of the compound subject.

▶ **More Practice**

Grammar Exercise Workbook
• pp. 131–132
On-line Exercise Bank
• Section 24.1
  Go on-line:
  PHSchool.com
  Enter Web Code:
  ebk-7002

Get instant feedback! Exercises 5, 6, and 7 are available on-line or on CD-ROM.

▶ **Exercise 7** Correcting Errors in Subject-Verb Agreement

In some of the sentences below, subjects and verbs do not agree in number. If a sentence is correct, write *correct*. If it is incorrect, rewrite the sentence correctly.

EXAMPLE: Neither the moon nor the stars is visible tonight.

ANSWER: Neither the moon nor the stars are visible
             tonight.

1. Neither Valentine's Day nor Memorial Day are celebrated in September.
2. However, a law in the United States declare that the first Monday in September is Labor Day.
3. Most people in the business world are given a holiday from work on Labor Day.
4. Many in my class, including Joe, is looking forward to Valentine's Day this year.
5. Kara or Sue plan to send him a card.

◀ Critical Viewing
Tell about gift-giving
on Valentine's Day in
a sentence that
begins "Roses or
chocolate . . . ."
[Evaluate]

Checking Agreement in Sentences With Unusual Word Order

In most sentences, the subject comes before the verb. In some sentences, however, this normal word order is turned around, or inverted. In other sentences, the helping verb comes before the subject even though the main verb follows the subject.

KEY CONCEPT When a subject comes after the verb, the subject and verb still must agree with each other in number. ■

Sentences beginning with *there* or *here* are almost always in inverted word order. In the following sentences, the subjects are underlined once and the verbs are underlined twice.

EXAMPLES: There <u>were</u> several <u>books</u> about holidays.
             Here <u>is</u> a <u>book</u> about the holiday.

The contractions *there's* and *here's* both contain the singular verb *is*: *there is* and *here is*. Do not use these contractions with plural subjects.

INCORRECT: Here's the <u>keys</u> to the house.
CORRECT: Here <u>are</u> the <u>keys</u> to the house.

Many questions are also in inverted word order.

EXAMPLE: Where <u>are</u> the <u>keys</u> to the house?

Exercise 8 Checking Agreement in Sentences With Inverted Word Order On your paper, write the subject in each of the following sentences. Choose the correct verb from the pair in parentheses, and write it next to the subject.

EXAMPLE: There (is, are) a few new rules in this pamphlet.
ANSWER: rules—are

1. There (is, are) many different customs associated with holidays in December.
2. Where (is, are) the gifts?
3. Which customs (does, do) you know?
4. Here (is, are) a big box of decorations.
5. There (is, are) some holidays very close together.
6. Which day (has, have) they chosen?
7. When (was, were) the bells rung?
8. Where (has, have) the children been?
9. There (was, were) a string of lights decorating the house.
10. Why (is, are) he waiting?

⚙ Grammar and Style Tip

You can make your writing more interesting by varying the style of your sentences. Inverting the subject-verb order of some sentences helps to create variety.

More Practice

Grammar Exercise Workbook
• pp. 133–134
On-line Exercise Bank
• Section 24.1
  Go on-line:
  PHSchool.com
  Enter Web Code:
  ebk-7002

Get instant feedback! Exercise 8 is available on-line or on CD-ROM.

Checking Agreement
With Indefinite Pronouns

Indefinite pronouns used as subjects can also cause agreement problems.

Some pronouns are always singular: *anyone, everyone, someone, anybody, everybody, somebody, each,* and *either.*

ALWAYS
SINGULAR:
Each of the banners is blue.
Everyone in the first five rows was delighted
by the play.
Either of those hats is warm.

Some pronouns are always plural: *both, few, many, others,* and *several.*

ALWAYS
PLURAL:
Few have chosen a gift yet.
Many are waiting until they finish reading
the book.
Several have not started reading the book.

► **KEY CONCEPT** Many indefinite pronouns can take either a singular or a plural verb. The choice depends upon the meaning given to the pronoun. ■

The following indefinite pronouns can be singular or plural: *all, any, more, most, none,* and *some.*

SINGULAR: Some of the milk is frozen.

PLURAL: Some of the cookies are frozen, too.

With an indefinite pronoun that can be either singular or plural, the antecedent of the pronoun determines its number.
In the example above, *some* is singular when it refers to *milk,* plural when it refers to *cookies.*

► **Critical Viewing**
Describe what these
two students are doing,
first in a sentence that
begins *Each of . . .* , and
then in a sentence that
begins with *Both of . . . .*
[Compare]

▶ **Exercise 9** Checking Agreement With Indefinite Pronouns
For each of the following sentences, choose the correct verb
from the pair in parentheses, and write it on your paper.

EXAMPLE: Most of the story (was, were) written from a
             child's point of view.

ANSWER: was

1. Many of the children in school (was, were) performing in
   the program.
2. Several (has been, have been) helping with the props.
3. (Does, Do) anyone know if there is a large audience?
4. All of the children (has, have) costumes.
5. Some of the people (has, have) not arrived yet.
6. All of the children (was, were) given scripts.
7. Each of the songs (was, were) practiced.
8. Every boy and girl in the program
   (tells, tell) about a holiday.
9. Both Jeff and Patty (wants, want)
   to do well.
10. Everyone (enjoys, enjoy) hearing
    the children laugh with delight.

◀ **Critical Viewing**
These girls are
expressing very
different attitudes.
How do you think
others might react
to this large wooden
soldier? Begin your
answer with *Anyone
who* . . . . [**Draw
Conclusions**]

GRAMMAR IN LITERATURE

from A Christmas Carol: Scrooge and Marley

dramatized by Israel Horovitz

In the following lines, the subjects are highlighted in red, the verbs in blue. In both examples, plural subjects take plural verbs. All is an indefinite pronoun that is plural in this case.

SCROOGE sits near the tiny low-flamed fire, sipping his gruel. There *are* various *pictures* on the walls: *all* of them now *show* likenesses of MARLEY. SCROOGE blinks his eyes.

▶ **Exercise 10** Supplying Verbs Rewrite the following sentences, supplying a verb that completes each one logically. Make sure the verbs you use agree with their subjects.

EXAMPLE: Most of the children ___?___ parts in the holiday pageant.

ANSWER: Most of the children have parts in the holiday pageant.

1. There ___?___ many reasons to celebrate.
2. Each of the children ___?___ about a holiday tradition.
3. Here ___?___ the children now.
4. Most ___?___ their parts.
5. Everyone ___?___ to do well.
6. Where ___?___ the sign for the beginning of the show?
7. ___?___ they made popcorn for the guests?
8. There ___?___ several other programs like this one.
9. All ___?___ wonderful.
10. Each ___?___ special.
11. Anyone who ___?___ the show will come away smiling.
12. Amy and Matt ___?___ looking forward to attending.
13. Neither of them ___?___ ever ___?___ the holiday pageant.
14. Before this year, there ___?___ no live music.
15. However, this year there ___?___ a pianist and a cellist.

▶ **More Practice**

Grammar Exercise Workbook
• pp. 133–134
On-line Exercise Bank
• Section 24.1
  Go on-line:
  PHSchool.com
  Enter Web Code:
  ebk-7002

Text

Complete the exercises on-line! Exercises 9 and 10 are available on-line or on CD-ROM.

Hands-on Grammar

Agreement Flip Book

Make an Agreement Flip Book to see how subjects and verbs must "match up" in order to agree. On lined index cards, write the following nouns and verbs, and underline them in green: *boy, girl, man, woman, child, dog, cat, plays, eats, thinks, waits, goes, runs, walks.* Write the following nouns and verbs, and underline them in orange: *boys, girls, men, women, children, dogs, cats, play, eat, think, wait, go, run, walk.* Use the lines on the index cards as guides to ensure that each word and its underlining are the same distance from the bottom of each card.

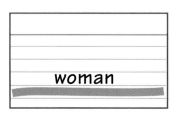

Punch a hole in the top center of each index card. Use a paper fastener to fasten the cards to a cardboard strip. Make sure all the nouns are on the left and all the verbs are on the right, but do not worry about keeping each side in a particular order.

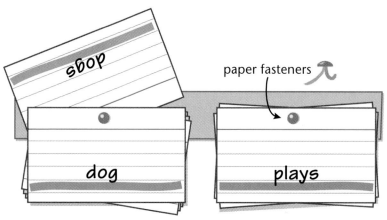

paper fasteners

Create different combinations of nouns and verbs by rotating the top cards up. When the colors of the underlining match, the verb form agrees with the noun. Use the word pair in a sentence. Create another flip book, using nouns and verbs related to a topic of interest to you, such as sports, music, or computers.

Find It in Your Reading Create a flip book with five nouns and verbs from a short story in your literature book. Use the singular and plural forms of each word you choose.

Find It in Your Writing Choose a piece of writing from your portfolio. Underline singular subjects and verbs in red. Underline plural subjects and verbs in blue. If the colors in a sentence do not match, check the subject-verb agreement. (Ask your teacher for help in evaluating sentences that have more than one verb.)

Section 24.1 Section Review

GRAMMAR EXERCISES 11–16

Exercise 11 Recognizing the Number of Nouns, Pronouns, and Verbs On your paper, write whether the noun-verb or pronoun-verb pair in each sentence is singular or plural.

1. You are welcome.
2. The children on stage sing beautifully.
3. The light gleams in the window.
4. People cheer at the celebration.
5. Music plays during the ceremony.
6. The teachers clap for the students.
7. Banners decorate the stage.
8. Balloons add a festive air.
9. The final song is sung.
10. Everyone leaves the auditorium.

Exercise 12 Making Verbs Agree With Their Subjects In some of the sentences below, subjects and verbs do not agree in number. If a sentence is correct, write *correct* on your paper. If it is incorrect, rewrite the sentence correctly.

1. Either Joe or his twin brothers graduate from high school this year.
2. English and math is required for graduation.
3. Cap and gown have become standard attire at graduations.
4. Neither Mike nor Amy want to speak at the ceremony.
5. Dances and parties are common celebrations of graduation.
6. Each graduating boy and girl receive a diploma.
7. Here is a group of teachers and the principal.
8. There are the students.
9. Do either Mikael or Tomas have a speech prepared?
10. Most students are happy when the ceremonies begin.

Exercise 13 Revising for Subject-Verb Agreement Copy the following paragraph into your notebook. Correct any errors in subject-verb agreement.

(1) There's many different ways to celebrate holidays. (2) Some families has special traditions and customs. (3) A few of these has been passed from generation to generation. (4) Often a custom or holiday come from other countries. (5) How does people in another country celebrate?

Exercise 14 Find It in Your Reading Read the following excerpt from *A Christmas Carol.* Identify which of the underlined subjects and verbs are singular, and which are plural. Explain why the verb agrees with any compound subjects you find.

SCROOGE. They owe me money and I will collect. I will have them jailed, if I have to. . . . [MARLEY *moves towards* SCROOGE; *two steps. The spotlight stays with him.*] **MARLEY.** [*Disgusted*] He and I were partners for I don't know how many years.

Exercise 15 Find It in Your Writing Choose an early draft of a piece of writing from your portfolio. Check the subject-verb agreement in all sentences. Explain any corrections you make.

Exercise 16 Writing Application Write an explanation of how you celebrate a special occasion. In each sentence, underline the subject once and the verb twice. Indicate whether the subject is plural or singular.

Agreement Between Pronouns and Antecedents

An **antecedent** is the word or words for which a pronoun stands. A pronoun's antecedent may be a noun, a group of words acting as a noun, or even another pronoun. This section will explain the ways in which pronouns must agree with their antecedents. If you are not sure that you can quickly recognize pronouns and antecedents, review Section 14.2 before continuing with this section.

Making Personal Pronouns and Antecedents Agree

Personal pronouns should agree with their antecedents in three important ways:

▶ **KEY CONCEPT** A personal pronoun must agree with its antecedent in person, number, and gender. ■

Person tells whether a pronoun refers to the person speaking (first person), the person spoken to (second person), or the person, place, or thing spoken about (third person). *Number* tells whether the pronoun is singular (referring to one) or plural (referring to more than one). *Gender* tells whether a third-person-singular antecedent is masculine or feminine.

EXAMPLE: I told *David* to bring a bathing suit with *him*.

In the example above, the pronoun *him* is third person and singular. It agrees with its masculine antecedent, *David*, which is also third person (the person spoken about) and singular.

Avoiding Shifts in Person Shifts in person usually involve the careless use of *you* (the second-person pronoun) to refer to a noun in the third person.

INCORRECT: *Stephanie* has learned French. This is the language *you* need to know when *you* go to Paris.

CORRECT: *Stephanie* has learned French. This is the language *she* needs to know when *she* goes to Paris.

Whenever you use the word *you*, make sure it refers to the person to whom you are speaking or writing and not to any other person.

Theme: Urban and Rural Contrasts

In this section, you will learn about pronoun and antecedent agreement. The examples and exercises are about the similarities and differences between life in big cities and life in small towns.

Cross-Curricular Connection: Social Studies

▲ **Critical Viewing** What parts of this picture could you refer to using a plural pronoun? **[Analyze]**

Avoiding Problems With Number and Gender

Making pronouns and antecedents agree in number and gender may sometimes be a little more difficult. Problems may arise, for example, when the antecedent is a compound joined by *or* or *nor*, or when the gender of the antecedent is not known.

More Practice

Grammar Exercise Workbook
• pp. 135–136
On-line Exercise Bank
• Section 24.2
  Go on-line:
  PHSchool.com
  Enter Web Code:
  ebk-7002

KEY CONCEPT Use a singular personal pronoun to refer to two or more singular antecedents joined by *or* or *nor*. ■

Two or more singular subjects joined by *or* or *nor* must have a singular verb. In the same way, two or more singular antecedents joined by *or* or *nor* must have a singular pronoun.

INCORRECT: Either *Becca* or *Megan* will take *their* backpack.

CORRECT: Either *Becca* or *Megan* will take *her* backpack.

If a compound antecedent is joined by *and*, however, the pronoun should be plural.

EXAMPLE: *Becca* and *Megan* will take *their* backpacks.

KEY CONCEPT When the gender of a third-person-singular antecedent is not known, you may make the pronoun agree in one of these three ways: (1) Use *he or she*, *him or her*, *his or hers*. (2) Rewrite the sentence so that the antecedent and pronoun are plural. (3) Rewrite the sentence to eliminate the pronoun. ■

Exercise 17 Making Pronouns and Antecedents Agree
Rewrite each of the following sentences, filling in the blank with an appropriate pronoun.

EXAMPLE: My parents had left ___?___ travel brochures all over the living room.

ANSWER: My parents had left their travel brochures all over the living room.

1. Jack was excited about ___?___ visit to New York City.
2. He and his family planned ___?___ trip well.
3. They learned that a tourist must watch ___?___ luggage carefully.
4. Each boy selected the places ___?___ wanted to visit.
5. The family members will have ___?___ picture taken at the Statue of Liberty.

Exercise 18 Revising Sentences to Eliminate Pronoun
Shift Each sentence below contains one error in pronoun-
antecedent agreement. Rewrite each sentence correctly, underlining the pronoun that you have changed and its antecedent.

EXAMPLE: A member of the girls' tour spends much of their
time sightseeing.

ANSWER: A <u>member</u> of the girls' tour spends much of <u>her</u>
time sightseeing.

1. Mary knows that you could get lost in a big city.
2. Either Curtis or Tim will bring their city map today.
3. It is the statue or that tall tree that is casting their shadow
   over the sidewalk.
4. The drivers should know that you can only turn left on
   that one-way street.
5. The taxicab and the delivery truck made its way through
   the busy traffic.
6. Tourists know that you have many cultural activities from
   which to choose in a big city.
7. Elsa is planning to go shopping in the big city, where you
   have a large selection of stores from which to choose.
8. Either Sandra or Audrey will spend their vacation visiting
   relatives in a big city.
9. Al likes to visit Manhattan, where you can do a lot of
   sightseeing without a car.
10. Joe and Marc know that you could spend a whole day in
    Central Park.

More Practice

Grammar Exercise
Workbook
• pp. 135–136
On-line Exercise Bank
• Section 24.2
  Go on-line:
  PHSchool.com
  Enter Web Code:
  ebk-7002

▼ **Critical Viewing**
Using at least two
pronouns, write a
sentence describing
a scene that could
take place in a park
like this one. Make
sure your pronouns
agree in number.
[Describe]

Making Personal Pronouns and Indefinite Pronouns Agree

Indefinite pronouns (listed in Chapter 14, p. 307) are words such as *each, everybody, either,* and *one.* Pay special attention to the number of a personal pronoun when the antecedent is a singular indefinite pronoun.

▶ **KEY CONCEPT** Use a singular personal pronoun when its antecedent is a singular indefinite pronoun. ■

Do not be misled by a prepositional phrase that follows an indefinite pronoun. The personal pronoun agrees with the indefinite pronoun, not with the object of the preposition.

Incorrect	Correct
One of the cats has lost *their* collar.	*One* of the cats has lost *its* collar.
Everyone in the two groups expressed *their* opinion.	*Everyone* in the two groups expressed *his or her* opinion.

▶ **Exercise 19** Making Personal Pronouns and Indefinite Pronouns Agree For each of the following sentences, choose the correct personal pronoun from the choices given in parentheses, and write it on your paper.

EXAMPLE: One of these houses has a weather vane on (its, their) roof.

ANSWER: its

1. Every one of the towns has a city hall at (its, their) center.
2. Some of the homes have fences around (its, their) yards.
3. Each street has trees shading (its, their) sidewalk.
4. Neither of the towns has (its, their) own television station.
5. Every child rides the bus to (his or her, their) school.
6. Both of those towns are famous for (its, their) history.
7. Each of the towns has (its, their) own mayor.
8. Many in this town grow (its, their) own vegetables.
9. Everyone in that town keeps (its, his or her) lawn neat.
10. Each town's news is published in (its, their) local paper.

 Spelling Tip

Make sure that you are using *their, there,* and *they're* correctly in your writing. If you're unsure which is appropriate, check the definitions of these three words in a dictionary.

▶ **Exercise 20** Revising Sentences to Eliminate Errors in Pronoun-Antecedent Agreement Most of the following sentences contain errors in pronoun-antecedent agreement. Find the sentences with errors, and rewrite them on your paper. Write *correct* for those sentences without errors.

EXAMPLE: Each of the brochures has a map printed on their cover.

ANSWER: Each of the brochures has a map printed on its cover.

1. Most large cities offer its residents a choice of sports teams to follow.
2. Jess believes that you can attend many sporting events in a large city.
3. Neither Judy nor Carol has their tickets to the basketball game.
4. Not one of the available seats was as close as it looked in the diagram.
5. Several of the fans were attending his first professional sporting event.
6. Each of the players has their own fan club.
7. All of the teams wear its colors proudly.
8. Some of the teams play their games out of town.
9. Each of the fans must provide his or her own transportation to the game.
10. Patsy forgot her bus schedule, which you really needed to get around in a big city.

▶ **More Practice**

Grammar Exercise Workbook
• pp. 135–136
On-line Exercise Bank
• Section 24.2
  Go on-line:
  PHSchool.com
  Enter Web Code:
  ebk-7002

Complete the exercise on-line! Exercise 20 is available on-line or on CD-ROM.

◀ **Critical Viewing** What features do the buildings in this photograph have in common? Use the words *its* and *their* in your answer, and make sure they agree with their antecedents. **[Analyze]**

Section 24.2 *Section Review*

GRAMMAR EXERCISES 21–26

▶ **Exercise 21** Making Personal Pronouns Agree For each of the following sentences, choose the correct personal pronoun from the pair in parentheses, and write it on your paper.

1. A city is a community where thousands, or even millions, of people make (its, their) homes.
2. According to the United Nations, any place that has more than 20,000 people living within (its, their) boundaries is considered a city.
3. Over forty percent of the people in the world make (its, their) homes in cities.
4. Some people don't like living far from (his, their) neighbors.
5. Neither Jim nor Larry moved (his, their) family from a farm town to the city.

▶ **Exercise 22** Making Pronouns and Antecedents Agree Supply a personal pronoun to complete each sentence.

1. John lives with ___?___ parents in a small town.
2. Neither John nor Wally has ___?___ own car.
3. Both of them ride the bus to ___?___ school.
4. Wally says ___?___ can walk to school in about thirty minutes.
5. Each student has ___?___ own locker.

▶ **Exercise 23** Revising Sentences to Eliminate Errors in Pronoun-Antecedent Agreement The following sentences contain errors in pronoun-antecedent agreement. Rewrite them on your paper, correcting the errors.

1. Every day, Bob and Jane walk together to a city college in her neighborhood.
2. Monica said that you have many classes from which to choose.
3. Everyone at the college selects their own class schedule.
4. Mr. Roberts hosts his or her drama class on Friday evenings at a local theater.
5. Each student in the class purchases their own ticket to the theater.

▶ **Exercise 24** Find It in Your Reading Read the following excerpt from "The Monsters Are Due on Maple Street." Identify the number of each pronoun, as well as its antecedent.

> MRS. GOODMAN *comes through her porch door, glass of milk in hand. The entry hall, with table and lit candle, can be seen behind her.*
>
> *Outside, the camera slowly pans down the sidewalk, taking in little knots of people who stand around talking in low voices. At the end of each conversation they look toward* LES GOODMAN'S *house. . . .*

▶ **Exercise 25** Find It in Your Writing Review a piece of writing from your portfolio. Check pronoun-antecedent agreement—especially agreement between personal pronouns and indefinite pronouns.

▶ **Exercise 26** Writing Application Write a description of your town, village, or city. Underline all the pronouns you use. Make sure that each agrees with its antecedent.

GRAMMAR EXERCISES 27–34

▶ **Exercise 27** Identifying Subjects and Checking for Agreement On your paper, write the subject of each of the following sentences. Choose the correct verb from the pair in parentheses, and write it next to the subject.

1. The slower pace of life (is, are) one reason many people choose to live in a small town.
2. The amount of traffic (makes, make) it is easy to get around.
3. Some towns (has, have) only one stoplight.
4. Quite often, everyone in a small town (knows, know) everyone else.
5. Most of the townspeople (is, are) very friendly.
6. The grocery and the department stores (is, are) located down the street.
7. Each of the stores (has, have) an awning over the front door.
8. The barber next door still (cuts, cut) hair for one dollar.
9. Several of the children (attends, attend) school in another town.
10. How many people (lives, live) in your town?

▶ **Exercise 28** Supplying Appropriate Verbs Rewrite each of the following sentences, supplying an appropriate verb in the present tense.

1. When Stan ___?___ home, Vinnie ___?___ with him for a visit.
2. Vinnie ___?___ to ride the horses at Stan's house.
3. All of the horses ___?___ very gentle.
4. Each of the boys ___?___ an excellent rider.
5. Many hours ___?___ spent riding over the foothills nearby.

6. Both Stan and Vinnie ___?___ to ride their horses fast.
7. The boys ___?___ to swim and fish in a pond near the house.
8. Stan ___?___ the record for the largest fish caught in the pond.
9. There ___?___ many outdoor activities to enjoy in the country.
10. When the week is over, Vinnie ___?___ sad to go back to the city.

▶ **Exercise 29** Checking for Agreement Between Pronouns and Antecedents For each of the following sentences, choose the correct word from the pair given in parentheses, and write it on your paper. Note that the antecedent for a pronoun may appear in a previous sentence.

1. Every city offers (its, their) residents opportunities for work and play.
2. Jack studied large cities in (his, their) social studies class.
3. A typical city, (he, they) told me, covers many square miles.
4. Everyone living in a city has choices as to how (he or she, they) will travel to work.
5. Many people work in the city, but it's the suburbs where (he or she, they) live.
6. Everyone living in the suburbs can choose (his or her, their) means of travel to work.
7. Some choose buses or trains, while others use (his, their) cars.
8. Jack would like to visit a large city because (you, he) will see interesting, different neighborhoods.
9. Almost any city dweller can be found living in close proximity to (his or her, their) neighbors.
10. Neither Jim nor his brother could decide which city (he, they) would like most to visit.

Exercise 30 **Using All the Rules of Agreement** For each of the following sentences, choose the correct word from the pair given in parentheses.

1. Lil and her family (has, have) an apartment in a big city.
2. There (is, are) an amusement park in the big city.
3. Most of the rides at the park (has, have) very long lines.
4. Neither Mary nor Lil (minds, mind) waiting for the rides.
5. Both of the girls (has, have) decided that Italian food is (her, their) favorite.

Exercise 31 **Revising Sentences to Eliminate Problems in Agreement** Rewrite the sentences below, eliminating any errors in agreement and making any other minor changes needed.

1. There's many reasons people like to live in either a small town or a big city.
2. Each type of city has their own attractions and problems.
3. Neither a small town nor a large city are apt to satisfy everyone.
4. My brother thinks that small towns is too boring.
5. He likes big cities because you can do so much.

Exercise 32 **Revising a Paragraph to Eliminate Problems in Agreement** Rewrite the paragraph below, correcting all errors in agreement.

(1) Holidays is celebrated in both small towns and big cities. (2) However, each of the holidays are celebrated differently. (3) There's more big parades in a big city. (4) Each small-town storekeeper is likely to close their store for a holiday. (5) Both big cities and small towns usually celebrate its founders' days. (6) Almost everyone say they like a fireworks display. (7) Either a picnic or a dance are also great ways to celebrate. (8) Civic leaders likes to give speeches at these events. (9) Cultural traditions of the community is featured at many celebrations. (10) Almost everybody have a good time.

Exercise 33 **Writing Sentences With Correct Agreement** Write five sentences, using combinations of the words listed below. Be sure subjects and verbs, and pronouns and antecedents, agree.

she	travel	fly	packs	they
suitcase	taxi	them	friend	Ellen
tourist	her	hers	theirs	map

Exercise 34 **Writing Application** Write five sentences about how a favorite holiday is celebrated in your city or town. In each sentence, underline the subject once and the verb twice. Write in the present tense, and make sure the subject and verb agree in every sentence.

Exercise 35 **CUMULATIVE REVIEW Problems With Verbs, Pronouns, and Agreement** Revise the following paragraph, correcting errors in verb and pronoun usage and agreement.

(1) John and his family has a special way of celebrating New Year's Eve. (2) To prepare, they have spent the evening making food. (3) Each of them have their own specialty. (4) John's specialty will be apple pie. (5) After they have finished in the kitchen, the family will watch their favorite movie again. (6) They had seen it so many times, everyone know the dialogue by heart. (7) While the family watches, one member serves they. (8) This year, John says, it is him who must serve. (9) Neither John nor his brothers has to go to bed early on that night. (10) All of them, even his youngest brother, stays up until midnight.

Standardized Test Preparation Workshop

Recognizing Appropriate Sentence Construction

Standardized tests frequently test your knowledge of the rules of subject-verb agreement. When checking a sentence for errors, first identify the subject. Next, identify the type of subject: singular, plural, or compound. Then, apply the rules of agreement to make sure that the verb in the sentence agrees with the subject.

The following questions will give you practice with different formats used for items that test knowledge of subject-verb agreement.

Test Tip

If you are having trouble with a sentence revision, eliminate any answer choices in which the subject and verb clearly do not agree.

Sample Test Items

Directions: Identify the underlined word or phrase that contains an error in the following sentence.

Neither Carolyn nor her visitors hears the
   (A)   (B)   (C)

car approaching. No error.
   (D)   (E)

Directions: Choose the revised version of the following sentence that eliminates all errors in grammar, usage, and mechanics.

Neither Carolyn nor her visitors hears the car approaching.

A Either Carolyn or her visitors hear the car approaching.

B Neither Carolyn nor her visitors hear the car approaching.

C Carolyn, and her visitors, hears the car approaching.

D The car approaching are not heard by Carolyn or her visitors.

Answers and Explanations

The correct answer is *C*. The compound subject of the sentence is *Neither Carolyn nor her visitors*. When a singular and a plural subject are joined by *or* or *nor*, the verb must agree with the subject closest to it. In this case, the subject *visitors* is plural, so the plural verb *hear* should be used in the sentence.

The correct answer is *B*. The compound subject of the sentence is *Neither Carolyn nor her visitors*. When a singular and a plural subject are joined by *or* or *nor*, the verb must agree with the subject closest to it. In this case, the subject *visitors* is plural, so the plural verb *hear* should be used in the sentence. Answers *A* and *C* change the meaning of the sentence. Answer *D* contains an error in agreement.

> **Practice 1** **Directions:** Identify the underlined word or phrase that contains an error in each of the following sentences.

1 The president and vice president
    (A)
wave as they move through the crowd.
    (B)   (C)   (D)
No error.
    (E)

2 Each one wears pins made for them
        (A)   (B)
by the children of Cedar Grove.
    (C)   (D)
No error.
    (E)

3 My sister and I is attending their
        (A)   (B)
address to the community. No error.
    (C)   (D)   (E)

4 Here is the doors to get
    (A)   (B)   (C)
into the community center. No error.
            (D)   (E)

5 Either my sister or I hope to ask them
            (A)   (B)
questions about environmental concerns.
        (C)   (D)
No error.
    (E)

> **Practice 2** **Directions:** Choose the revised version of each numbered sentence that eliminates all errors in grammar, usage, and mechanics.

1 The study of American presidents often reveal that they was once simply average citizens.

A The study of American presidents often reveal that they were once simply average citizens.

B The study of American presidents often reveals that they was once simply average citizens.

C The study of American presidents often reveals that they were once simply average citizens.

D The study of American presidents which reveal that they was once simply average citizens.

2 Perhaps our greatest president, Abraham Lincoln came from very humble beginnings, but neither poverty nor lack of formal education hold a man of Lincoln's brilliance and integrity back.

F Perhaps our greatest president, Abraham Lincoln came from very humble beginnings, but neither poverty nor lack of formal education holds a man of Lincoln's brilliance and integrity back.

G Perhaps our greatest president, Abraham Lincoln come from very humble beginnings. However, neither poverty nor lack of formal education holds a man of Lincoln's brilliance and integrity back.

H Perhaps our greatest president, Abraham Lincoln comes from very humble beginnings, but neither poverty nor lack of formal education hold a man of Lincoln's brilliance and integrity back.

J Perhaps our greatest president, Abraham Lincoln come from very humble beginnings, but neither poverty nor lack of formal education holds a man of Lincoln's brilliance and integrity back.

Chapter 25 Using Modifiers

Adjectives and adverbs can be used in comparing people, places, or things. The form of an adjective or adverb depends on the kind of comparison that is being made.

The following example shows how adjectives change form: "Ben Attow is a *high* mountain in Scotland (1,032 meters). It is *higher* than Ben Hope (927 meters). Ben Nevis is the *highest* mountain in Scotland (1,343 meters)." Adverbs also change form, as shown in these sentences: "Ian plays the bagpipes *well.* Mary plays the bagpipes *better* than Ian does, but Angus plays the bagpipes *best* of all." These different forms of adjectives and adverbs are known as *degrees of comparison.*

▲ Critical Viewing
Use adjectives and adverbs to compare these two bagpipe players. Which one is wearing a *brighter* color? Which one appears to be *more interested* in playing music? **[Analyze]**

Diagnostic Test

Directions: Write all answers on a separate sheet of paper.

Skill Check A. Write the comparative and superlative degrees of the following modifiers. Whenever possible, use the *-er* and *-est* forms.

1. nervous
2. quick
3. painful
4. short
5. quiet

Skill Check B. Write the comparative and superlative degrees of the following modifiers.

6. generous
7. attractive
8. suddenly
9. capable
10. powerfully

Skill Check C. Indicate the degree of the underlined word in each of the following sentences.

11. Judy and Mark enjoyed the Highland games in Scotland <u>more</u> than the rest of the trip.
12. Judy thought the <u>best</u> part of the Highland games was the Scottish dancing.
13. Mark thought the shot-put event was <u>better</u> than the dancing.
14. The tallest athlete threw the shot the <u>farthest</u>.
15. Judy also thought the musicians played <u>well</u>.

Skill Check D. Revise the following sentences, correcting all errors in degree. If the sentence contains no errors, write *correct*.

16. Mark realized more sooner than Judy that the Scottish castles were just ahead.
17. They wondered which of the two castles had the highest tower.
18. Judy grew more fonder of the castles as she explored them.
19. Balmoral Castle is the most famous of the two castles.
20. Mark liked the other castle better.

Skill Check E. Revise the sentences below that contain errors in degree or usage. If a sentence contains no errors, write *correct*.

21. The kilt looked badly after the dance.
22. There were fewer dancers in the Highland fling than in the sword dance.
23. Mark just reached his seat one minute before the dance began.
24. Judy thought the dancer performed good.
25. There only were seven dancers (not eight) for the Scottish reel.

Comparison of Adjectives and Adverbs

You may recall from Chapter 16 that adjectives and adverbs are modifiers. Adjectives can modify nouns or pronouns. Adverbs can modify verbs, adjectives, or other adverbs. These two parts of speech can be either *regular* or *irregular.* Luckily, most adjectives and adverbs in English are regular—that is, their comparative and superlative degrees are formed in predictable ways. How these degrees are formed depends on the number of syllables in the positive form.

KEY CONCEPT Most adjectives and adverbs have three degrees of comparison: the *positive*, the *comparative*, and the *superlative.* ■

The *positive* degree is used when no comparison is being made. This is the form listed in a dictionary. The *comparative* degree is used when two things are being compared. The *superlative* degree is used when three or more things are being compared.

Regular Modifiers With One or Two Syllables

The comparative and superlative degrees of most adjectives and adverbs of one or two syllables can be formed in either of two ways:

KEY CONCEPT Use *-er* or *more* to form the comparative degree and *-est* or *most* to form the superlative degree of most one- and two-syllable modifiers. ■

Adding *-er* for the comparative degree and *-est* for the superlative degree are the most common ways to form these degrees.

COMPARATIVE AND SUPERLATIVE DEGREES FORMED WITH *-ER* AND *-EST*		
Positive	Comparative	Superlative
fast	faster	fastest
tall	taller	tallest
narrow	narrower	narrowest
sunny	sunnier	sunniest

Theme: Scotland

In this section, you will learn about degrees of comparison. The examples and exercises are about Scotland.

Cross-Curricular Connection: Social Studies

Learn More

To learn more about adjectives and adverbs, refer to Chapter 16.

More and *most* can also be used to form the comparative and superlative degrees of most one- and two-syllable modifiers. These words should not be used when the result sounds awkward, as in "A greyhound is *more fast* than a beagle."

Notice in the following chart that two of the examples from the preceding chart—*narrow* and *sunny*—can be used with *more* and *most*. *More* and *most* are also used to form the comparative and superlative degrees of most adverbs ending in *-ly* and of one- and two-syllable modifiers that would sound awkward with *-er* and *-est*.

COMPARATIVE AND SUPERLATIVE DEGREES FORMED WITH *MORE* AND *MOST*		
Positive	**Comparative**	**Superlative**
narrow	more narrow	most narrow
sunny	more sunny	most sunny
quickly	more quickly	most quickly
just	more just	most just

Use *-er* and *-est* with the last two examples above. Notice how awkward they sound. If you are not sure which form to use, say the words aloud and it will become clear.

Exercise 1 Forming the Comparative and Superlative Degrees of One- and Two-Syllable Modifiers Write the comparative and superlative degrees of the following modifiers. If the degrees can be formed in either way, write the *-er* and *-est* forms.

1. high
2. smart
3. mean
4. pretty
5. clear
6. brightly
7. tall
8. late
9. young
10. slowly

Exercise 2 Supplying Modifiers Copy the following sentences, supplying the form of the modifier indicated in parentheses.

1. Scotland is (small—comparative) than the United States.
2. The Highlands is the (rugged—superlative) area.
3. The River Clyde is Scotland's (important—superlative) river.
4. The Tay, the (long—superlative) river, is 120 miles long.
5. Before engineers widened the Clyde River in the 1700's, it was (narrow—comparative) and (shallow—comparative) than it is now.

Spelling Tip

When adjectives and adverbs end with a consonant plus *-y*, drop the *-y* and add *-ier* or *-iest*. Words ending with the suffix *-ly* are an exception to this rule.

More Practice

Grammar Exercise Workbook
• pp. 137–138
On-line Exercise Bank
• Section 25.1
Go on-line:
PHSchool.com
Enter Web Code:
ebk-7002

Text

Get instant feedback! Exercises 1 and 2 are available on-line or on CD-ROM.

Regular Modifiers With Three or More Syllables

When an adjective or adverb has three or more syllables, its comparative and superlative degrees are easy to form.

KEY CONCEPT Use *more* and *most* to form the comparative and superlative degrees of all modifiers of three or more syllables. ■

Never use *-er* or *-est* with modifiers of more than two syllables.

DEGREES OF MODIFIERS WITH THREE OR MORE SYLLABLES		
Positive	Comparative	Superlative
popular	more popular	most popular
affectionate	more affectionate	most affectionate
intelligently	more intelligently	most intelligently

Exercise 3 Forming the Comparative and Superlative Degrees of Modifiers With More Than Two Syllables On your paper, write the comparative and superlative degrees of the following modifiers.

EXAMPLE: beautiful

ANSWER: more beautiful, most beautiful

1. envious
2. talented
3. secretly
4. comfortable
5. delicate
6. friendly
7. original
8. recently
9. natural
10. emotionally

▼ Critical Viewing What modifiers would you use to compare this scene to the area where you live? [Compare]

Irregular Adjectives and Adverbs

A few adjectives and adverbs are *irregular*. Their comparative and superlative degrees must be memorized.

> **KEY CONCEPT** Memorize the irregular comparative and superlative forms of certain adjectives and adverbs. ■

The following chart lists the most common irregular modifiers.

DEGREES OF IRREGULAR ADJECTIVES AND ADVERBS		
Positive	**Comparative**	**Superlative**
bad	worse	worst
badly	worse	worst
far (distance)	farther	farthest
far (extent)	further	furthest
good	better	best
well	better	best
many	more	most
much	more	most

> **Exercise 4** Recognizing the Degree of Irregular Modifiers
On your paper, indicate the degree of the underlined word in each of the following sentences.

EXAMPLE: We could see <u>farther</u> as the fog lifted.

ANSWER: comparative

1. The head of a clan was called the chief, and the clan members served him <u>well</u>.
2. <u>Most</u> clan members were both the chief's tenants and his relatives.
3. Out of the three clans, the Clan Stewart had the <u>most</u> members.
4. The Clan Campbell had <u>more</u> members than the Clan MacDonald.
5. The Clan Fergusson can be traced the <u>furthest</u> back in history.
6. The clans in the Highlands of Scotland fought <u>many</u> battles long ago.
7. The Scottish Clan MacDonald fought even <u>more</u> battles against the Clan Campbell.
8. The warriors looked <u>bad</u> after a long battle.
9. The clans became <u>more</u> tired as they fought.
10. The <u>most</u> impressive characteristic of a Scottish clan is the loyalty of its members.

Grammar and Style Tip

When you write, try not to overuse the various forms of *good* and *bad*. Be as precise as possible when writing descriptions.

> **More Practice**

Grammar Exercise Workbook
• pp. 139–140
On-line Exercise Bank
• Section 25.1
 Go on-line:
 PHSchool.com
 Enter Web Code:
 ebk-7002

Text

Get instant feedback! Exercises 3 and 4 are available on-line or on CD-ROM.

▶ **Exercise 5** Using the Comparative and Superlative Degrees of Irregular Modifiers Copy the following sentences, supplying the form of the modifier indicated in parentheses.

EXAMPLE: The fog seems (bad—comparative) this morning.
ANSWER: The fog seems worse this morning.

1. Judy and Mark hiked (much—comparative) in the Highlands than in the Border Country.
2. The (good—superlative) part of the hike was the beautiful scenery.
3. The weather was the (bad—superlative) on the first day of the trip.
4. The weather turned (good—comparative) after that.
5. That was the (far—superlative) trip they had ever taken.

▶ **Exercise 6** Revising a Passage to Eliminate Errors With Modifiers In your notebook, revise the following passage. Correct any errors in the way modifiers are used.

Some of the violentest struggles in Scottish history occurred during the late 900's. Each king from 900 to 1005 gained control by killing his predecessor. Each one was badder than the one before. One of my teacher's most favorite plays, *Macbeth,* is based on this period in history. Even though the play itself is violent, the actual events were probably more bloodier than the play.

GRAMMAR IN LITERATURE

from **Lochinvar**
Sir Walter Scott

In the following excerpt, the positive and superlative forms of the irregular adjective good *are italicized in* blue.

O, young Lochinvar is come out of the West,
Through all the wide Border his steed was the *best,*
And save his *good* broadsword he weapons had none;
He rode all unarmed, and he rode all alone.

More Practice

Grammar Exercise Workbook
• pp. 141–142
On-line Exercise Bank
• Section 25.1
  Go on-line:
  PHSchool.com
  Enter Web Code:
  ebk-7002

Get instant feedback! Exercises 5, 6, and 7 are available on-line or on CD-ROM.

💻 **Internet Tip**

Adjectives generally do not help to narrow your searches on the Internet. Avoid including adjectives as key words because they will link to topics unrelated to your search.

Comparative and Superlative Degrees

Remember the following rules when you use the comparative and superlative degrees:

> **KEY CONCEPT** Use the **comparative** degree to compare *two* people, places, things, or occurrences. Use the **superlative** degree to compare *three or more* people, places, things, or occurrences. ■

COMPARE TWO:	These bagpipes sound *better* than those. The bagpipes sound *better* now. (present compared to past)
COMPARE MORE THAN TWO:	Cameron is the *best* bagpipe player in town. (Cameron compared to all others.)

Do not combine the use of *-er* and *more* to form the comparative degree or *-est* and *most* to form the superlative degree.

INCORRECT:	This assignment is *more easier* than I thought. Edinburgh is the *most beautifulest* city in Scotland.
CORRECT:	This assignment is *easier* than I thought. Edinburgh is the *most beautiful* city in Scotland.

▲ **Critical Viewing** Use at least one comparative and one superlative modifier to describe the place pictured here. **[Apply]**

> **Exercise 7** Correcting Errors in Degree On your paper, revise the sentences that contain errors in degree. Write *correct* if the sentence contains no errors.

EXAMPLE:	This mountain is the *highest* of the two.
ANSWER:	This mountain is the *higher* of the two.

1. The sword dance is more harder than the Scottish reel.
2. Bagpipe music is played most softly for dances than for parades.
3. The bagpipes are played most loud during a parade.
4. Bagpipe bands have been formed in more areas of the world where large numbers of Scots have settled.
5. Bagpipe music is a more bigger part of the Highland games than tossing the caber is.

 Learn More

To practice using modifiers in a standardized test format, see the Standardized Test Preparation Workshop on pages 574–575.

Section Review

GRAMMAR EXERCISES 8–14

▶ **Exercise 8** Identifying the **Comparative and Superlative Degrees** On your paper, label the following modifiers *comparative* or *superlative*.

1. more compact
2. coolest
3. greasier
4. rounder
5. moldiest

▶ **Exercise 9** Recognizing the **Degree of Irregular Modifiers** On your paper, indicate the degree of the underlined word in each of the following sentences.

1. Mark and Judy had a <u>bad</u> scare on their way to the Border Country.
2. They had an even <u>worse</u> time getting to the Lowlands.
3. Judy thought the kilt the mannequin was wearing looked <u>good</u>.
4. Mark looked <u>better</u> in the kilt than the mannequin did.
5. The store owner looked <u>best</u> in the kilt.

▶ **Exercise 10** Forming the **Comparative and Superlative Degrees** On your paper, write the comparative and superlative degrees of the modifiers below.

1. fresh
2. clammy
3. carefully
4. correctly
5. confident

▶ **Exercise 11** Using the **Comparative and Superlative Degrees of Irregular Modifiers** Copy each of the following sentences onto your paper, supplying the form of the modifier requested in parentheses.

1. Scotland has (many—comparative) mountains in the Highlands than in the Lowlands.

2. The Border Country is the (good—superlative) place to see castles.
3. The Tay River flows (far—comparative) than the Tweed River.
4. Loch Ness is the (much—superlative) famous lake in Scotland.
5. The (bad—superlative) part of visiting Scotland was leaving.

▶ **Exercise 12** Find It in Your **Reading** Identify the comparative and superlative degrees of the underlined modifiers in the following excerpt from "Lochinvar."

So <u>faithful</u> in love, and so dauntless in war,/There never was knight like the <u>young</u> Lochinvar. . . ./But, ere he alighted at Netherby gate,/The bride had consented, the gallant came <u>late</u>. . . ./"There are maidens in Scotland more <u>lovely</u> by far/That would <u>gladly</u> be bride to the young Lochinvar."

▶ **Exercise 13** Find It in Your **Writing** In a draft from your portfolio, find examples of modifiers in the comparative or superlative degree. Challenge yourself to add two modifiers that will add detail to your writing.

▶ **Exercise 14** Writing Application Write a letter to a travel agent requesting information about Scotland. Use modifiers of different degrees to indicate the level of interest you have in different features of the country.

Troublesome Adjectives and Adverbs

The common adjectives and adverbs listed below often cause problems in both speaking and writing.

(1) bad, badly *Bad* is an adjective. Use it after linking verbs, such as *are, appear, feel, look,* and *sound. Badly* is an adverb. Use it after action verbs, such as *act, behave, do,* and *perform*.

                      LV

INCORRECT: Jan looked *badly* after the trip.

                      LV

CORRECT: Jan looked *bad* after the trip.

                  AV

INCORRECT: I did *bad* on the test.

                  AV

CORRECT: I did *badly* on the test.

(2) fewer, less Use the adjective *fewer* to answer the question "How many?" Use the adjective *less* to answer the question "How much?"

HOW MANY: *fewer* calories   *fewer* chores
HOW MUCH: *less* food   *less* work

(3) good, well *Good* is an adjective. *Well* can be either an adjective or an adverb, depending on its meaning. A common mistake is the use of *good* after an action verb. Use the adverb *well* instead.

                              AV

INCORRECT: The children have behaved *good* all day.

                              AV

CORRECT: The children have behaved *well* all day.

As adjectives, *good* and *well* have slightly different meanings, which are often confused. *Well* usually refers simply to a person's or an animal's health.

EXAMPLES: Janet felt *good* after the hike.
                   The fresh bread smells *good*.
                   That puppy is not *well*.

(4) just When used as an adverb, *just* often means "no more than." When *just* has this meaning, place it right before the word it logically modifies.

Theme: Scotland

In this section, you will learn about degrees of comparison. The examples and exercises tell more about Scotland.

Cross-Curricular Connection: Social Studies

▼ **Critical Viewing** How can using language carefully help to improve communication, both at home and abroad? **[Evaluate]**

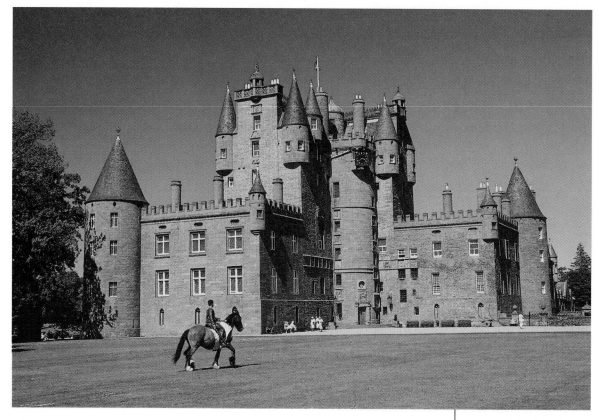

▲ Critical Viewing
Based on the picture,
what can you guess
about the lives of the
people who lived in
this castle? [Make a
Judgment]

INCORRECT:	Do you *just* want one baked potato with your steak?
CORRECT:	Do you want *just* one baked potato with your steak?

(5) only The position of *only* in a sentence sometimes affects the sentence's entire meaning. Consider the meaning of these sentences:

EXAMPLES: *Only* she answered that question. (Nobody else answered that question.)
She *only* answered that question. (She did nothing else with the question.)
She answered *only* that question. (She answered that question and no other question.)

Mistakes involving *only* usually occur when its placement in a sentence makes the meaning unclear.

UNCLEAR: *Only* take advice from me.
BETTER: Take advice *only* from me.

Whenever you use *only* in a sentence, make sure it indicates your exact meaning.

Exercise 15 Correcting Errors Caused by Troublesome Modifiers In the sentences that follow, each underlined modifier is used incorrectly. On your paper, revise each sentence, correcting the misused modifier.

EXAMPLE: The team played <u>bad</u> yesterday.
ANSWER: The team played badly yesterday.

1. Scotland <u>only</u> is attached to England; it is not part of England.
2. The people from Scotland are called Scots or Scottish, but they will react <u>bad</u> to being called English.
3. The Scots and the English have lived in peace for <u>less</u> centuries than they have lived at war with each other.
4. It is <u>fewer</u> time than you might imagine since the Scots' last battle with the English.
5. The clans in the Highlands of Scotland fought <u>good</u> in their battles with the English.

Exercise 16 Identifying and Correcting Errors Caused by Troublesome Adjectives and Adverbs Rewrite the sentences below that contain errors in the use of modifiers. If a sentence contains no errors, write *correct*.

EXAMPLE: There are less flowers in the garden now.
ANSWER: There are fewer flowers in the garden now.

1. When they weren't fighting against England, few clans got along good.
2. Before the English tried to break up the clans, the people of Scotland spoke Gaelic, but only about 2 percent of Scots speak it today.
3. After England tried to break up the clans, many Scots were recruited into Highland regiments and fought for the royalty that had treated them so bad.
4. The Clan MacDonald marched to war very good.
5. The Highland troops looked badly after the war.
6. The Highland warriors didn't feel good after the battle.
7. The internal rivalry for chieftainship in the fifteenth century left some in the Clan Campbell feeling badly.
8. The English fought good, but the Scots won the battle.
9. The Scots fought especially good in the last battle at Culloden.
10. Castles were not built only by kings: Many noble families also had strongholds from which they could defend themselves against their enemies.

▶ **More Practice**

Grammar Exercise Workbook
• pp. 143–144
On-line Exercise Bank
• Section 25.2
  Go on-line:
  PHSchool.com
  Enter Web Code:
  ebk-7002

Get instant feedback! Exercises 15 and 16 are available on-line or on CD-ROM.

Hands-on Grammar

Troublesome Modifiers Fold-Up

Create a fold-up booklet to keep in your folder as a handy reference for using troublesome modifiers such as *bad, badly* and *good, well.* Cut a strip of colored paper approximately three inches wide. Fan-fold the strip into sections approximately 1 inch deep. (The number of folds you make will depend on the length of the strip you've created.)

On one side of the strip, write ADJ for *adjective.* In each section, write a linking verb followed by the adjective. The example below shows several linking verbs followed by *bad,* the adjective.

On the reverse side of the same strip, write ADV for *adverb* in the top section. Then, in each section, write an action verb followed by the adverb. In the example, the adverb *badly* is used.

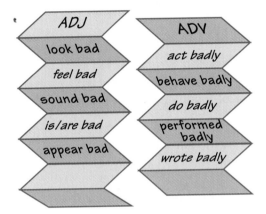

Keep your fold-up in your notebook or folder. Tape additional fan-folded strips to the end as you find more examples of words with which you would use the adjective and the adverb. Create a separate strip for *good* and *well.*

Find It in Your Reading Look through a short story or novel to find uses of these adjectives and adverbs that do not already appear on your fold-up. Add to the list.

Find It in Your Writing Use your fold-ups when you proofread your writing.

Section 25.2 Section Review

GRAMMAR EXERCISES 17–21

Exercise 17 Correcting Errors in Adjective and Adverb Usage Rewrite the following paragraph, correcting all errors in adjective and adverb usage.

Judy and Mark are excited to visit Scotland. (1) However, only they can travel for a few days. (2) They are planning on using their time good. Judy wants to be sure they go on a hike in the Highlands and see some castles. (3) She has also heard that the dancers and bagpipe music at the Highland games are really well. (4) She wants to see the dancers bad. (5) Mark wants just to be sure to visit the Highland games. (6) He's heard the tossing-the-caber event is especially well. (7) They are planning on spending fewer time in the Border Country and more time focusing on the tourist attractions. (8) The trip is going to be for less days than they would like. (9) However, they are going to make the best of it and not feel badly. (10) Whatever happens, the trip is going to be a well one.

Exercise 18 Correcting Errors Caused by Troublesome Adjectives and Adverbs Rewrite the sentences below that contain errors in the use of modifiers. If a sentence contains no errors, write *correct*.

1. Mark, Judy, Natalie, and Sam can only visit Scotland for three days.
2. They were just given eight bus tickets to last the whole vacation.
3. They will have to only ride the bus when they are traveling long distances.
4. Mark and Sam want to see the Highland games badly.
5. Luckily, the friends just reached their seats one minute before the bus left for the games.
6. Natalie only had made four reservations for the Highland games.

7. When they arrived, they were very surprised to see fewer than one hundred spectators in attendance.
8. They would sit only in the front seats; otherwise, it would be hard to see the Highland athletes.
9. Only after the last event were they ready to leave.
10. They all felt well and decided to go on a hike in the Highlands.

Exercise 19 Find It in Your Reading In the following passage from "Lochinvar," identify one word that could be replaced by *only* or *just*. Replace the word, and then explain why the replacement is possible.

"And now I am come, with this lost love of mine,

To lead but one measure, drink one cup of wine. . . ."

Exercise 20 Find It in Your Writing Review a piece of writing in your portfolio to check your usage of troublesome adjectives and adverbs.

Exercise 21 Writing Application Write a brief description of a place you have visited or would like to visit. Use the comparative and superlative forms of modifiers to compare this place to another. Review your work to make sure you have avoided any problems with modifiers.

GRAMMAR EXERCISES 22–30

Exercise 22 Forming the
Comparative and Superlative Degrees
of Modifiers On your paper, write the
comparative and superlative degrees of the
following modifiers.

1. bright
2. intelligent
3. cute
4. natural
5. lazy
6. difficult
7. ordinary
8. clean
9. skinny
10. gorgeous
11. muddy
12. dangerous
13. much
14. elaborate
15. bad

Exercise 23 Recognizing the
Degree of Irregular Modifiers On your
paper, indicate the degree of each underlined word in the following sentences.

1. The Isles are <u>more</u> north than the
Highlands.
2. The Border Country is <u>farther</u> south
than the Highlands.
3. Out of all the regions of Scotland, the
Isles are the <u>farthest</u> north.
4. <u>Most</u> of the people in the Isles earn
their living by fishing.
5. The weather there is not always <u>good</u>.

Exercise 24 Using the
Comparative and Superlative Degrees
of Irregular Modifiers Copy each of the
following sentences onto your paper, supplying the form of the modifier requested
in parentheses.

1. The Scottish reel dancer felt (good—
comparative) after drinking a tall glass
of water.
2. The bagpipe player knows the music to
(many—comparative) Scottish dances
than the dancer does.

3. Which dance did you like the (good—
superlative)?
4. The Highland dancer was not nervous
before the performance, but she felt
(bad—comparative) after she tripped
on stage.
5. (Many—superlative) Highland dancers
wear kilts when they perform.

Exercise 25 Supplying Modifiers
Copy the following sentences, supplying
a modifier for each blank space. Identify
the form you have used. Then, write the
other two forms.

1. "Lochinvar" is the __?__ poem we've
read this semester.
2. The author must have been __?__.
3. The poem we read last week was not
as __?__.
4. Usually, I enjoy reading fiction __?__
than I like reading poems.
5. The __?__ part of this poem was the
ending.

Exercise 26 Correcting Errors in
Degree Revise the sentences below
that contain errors in degree. If the sentence contains no errors, write *correct*.

1. On the Island of Lewis, there is a great
circle of standing stones, together with
a group of cairns, which is one of the
more important relics of the Bronze
Age in the whole of Britain.
2. Writings about Scotland by the Roman
historian Tacitus date farther back in
history.
3. Most modern Scots are descended
from the Celtic tribes that inhabited
the region before the Romans came to
Britain.
4. Before the nineteenth century, the

Scots were a most warlikest people than they are today.
5. The worse battle with the English was the battle of Culloden Moor.

> **Exercise 27** Revising to Eliminate Errors in Adjective and Adverb Usage
Revise the following paragraph, correcting all errors in adjective and adverb usage.

(1) Scotland is the more northern part of Great Britain. (2) It just extends 274 miles north from its border with England. Topographically, Scotland can be divided into three main regions: (3) The Highlands make up the northern two thirds, where Scotland's higher mountain, Ben Nevis, is found. (4) Central Scotland is called the Lowlands and has much isolated hills. (5) It is the more densely populated area. The third region is called the Border Country, as it is located on the English border. (6) Scotland has had a better national system of education for several centuries. (7) Now, fewer than 1 percent of the population is unable to read. (8) Of Scotland's twelve universities, the older is Saint Andrews, established in 1411. (9) Although Scotland has a large percentage of literate people, there are less jobs available for them. (10) More Scots leave Scotland to seek employment elsewhere.

> **Exercise 28** Choosing the Correct Modifier Choose the correct word to complete each sentence.

1. I felt (bad, badly) that I missed the slide show on Scotland.
2. They didn't feel (bad, badly) about killing another king.
3. There were (fewer, less) people willing to support a weak king.
4. If a king ruled (good, well), people would continue to support him.
5. If a battle went (good, well), a king could keep his throne.

6. Thank goodness there is (fewer, less) violence now than there was in ancient times.
7. Do you think you did (good, well) on the test about Scottish history?
8. I hope I didn't do too (bad, badly).
9. I wish there had been (fewer, less) questions about Duncan and Macbeth.
10. Although I think I told the story (good, well), I couldn't remember all the dates.

> **Exercise 29** Revising to Eliminate Errors Caused by Troublesome Adjectives and Adverbs Revise the sentences below that contain errors in the use of modifiers. If a sentence contains no errors, write *correct.*

1. Although kilts are the traditional men's clothing of Scotland, less Scots wear them today than in days of old.
2. Originally, the kilt just was a large piece of cloth Scots wrapped around their waists and put over their shoulders.
3. Wearing a kilt as clothing was not its only use; a kilt also doubled as a blanket.
4. A traditional kilt was made of thick material and would endure good.
5. Most Scots just had one kilt and wore it every day.

> **Exercise 30** Writing Application
Make a travel brochure for a country that interests you. Use modifiers in sentences that highlight the unique features of the country. For example, "Scotland has more lakes than you could visit in a year." Then, meet with a partner to check for any errors in your usage of modifiers and to discuss whether the modifiers you chose are the most effective for your purpose.

Standardized Test Preparation Workshop

Standard English Usage: Forms of Comparison

Standardized test questions often measure your ability to use modifiers correctly. One way this is done is by testing your ability to choose the correct form of comparison to complete a sentence. Use the following strategies to help you determine which form to use in a sentence:

- If no comparison is being made, use the positive form of the modifier.

- If one thing or action is compared to another thing or action, use the comparative degree of the modifier—the form ending in *-er* or preceded by *more*.

- If one thing or action is being compared to more than one other thing or action, use the superlative degree of the modifier—the form ending in *-est* or preceded by *most*.

- Be aware that some modifiers have special forms, such as *good, bad, much*, and *many*.

The following sample items will give you practice in answering these types of standardized test questions.

Test Tip

Be careful not to choose a double comparison, such as *more easier,* to complete a sentence. The correct form is *easier.*

Sample Test Items	Answers and Explanations
Choose the letter of the modifier that best completes each sentence. There were __(1)__ soldiers in the Texas army than in the Mexican army. Although the odds were not in their favor, the people of Texas believed that fighting for their independence was __(2)__ .	

1 A little
  B least
  C fewer
  D most little
	The correct answer for item 1 is *C, fewer.* The comparison is being made between the two armies, so the comparative form should be used.

2 F important
  G importantest
  H more important
  J most important
	The correct answer for item 2 is *F, important.* The fight for independence is not being compared to anything else, so the positive form is used.

▶ **Practice** **Directions:** Choose the letter of the modifier that best completes each sentence.

One of the __(1)__ battles in American history happened at the Alamo. Many historians even believe that the Battle of the Alamo was the __(2)__ massacre ever to take place on American soil. At an __(3)__ time, the Alamo had been a chapel attached to the Spanish mission, San Antonio de Valero. At the time of the battle, the Alamo had become a fort, protecting a small band of Texans against __(4)__ than 2,000 Mexican troops. Davy Crockett, one of the __(5)__ Americans at the time, fought the Mexicans under the command of Colonel William Barret Travis. When the smoke finally cleared at the Alamo, __(6)__ was left of the band of Texans who had resisted. __(7)__ than twenty women and children survived the battle and all the men defending the Alamo were killed. The battle of the Alamo gave Sam Houston __(8)__ time to gather troops to save the independence movement. He retreated __(9)__ east while being pursued by Santa Anna. Houston then turned on the army and a day __(10)__ captured Santa Anna and made him sign a peace treaty.

1 A bloody
   B bloodier
   C bloodiest
   D more bloody

2 F bad
   G worse
   H most bad
   J worst

3 A early
   B earlier
   C earliest
   D more early

4 F many more
   G most
   H more
   J many

5 A most famous
   B more famous
   C famouser
   D famousest

6 F less
   G little
   H least
   J littler

7 A Most few
   B Fewer
   C Fewest
   D Few

8 F more
   G most
   H much
   J many

9 A most farther
   B farthest
   C far
   D farther

10 F latest
   G more later
   H later
   J late

Cumulative Review

USAGE

Exercise A Recognizing the **Principal Parts of Verbs** Identify the principal part used to form the underlined verbs in the following sentences as *present, present participle, past,* or *past participle.*

1. Steve <u>is buying</u> my birthday presents at the local shopping center.
2. He <u>has found</u> some of the lowest prices at one of the stores.
3. Last year, I think I <u>paid</u> too much for his gift.
4. First, I put it in layaway, and I <u>went</u> back to get it a week later.
5. This year, I hope to enter the stores only once because I <u>am going</u> to make a list.

Exercise B Recognizing Verb Tense Identify the tense of each underlined verb or verb phrase in the following sentences. Then, write the principal part used to form the tense.

1. For our vacation, I <u>have been making</u> a list of things that I think I will need.
2. It seems as though summer <u>has taken</u> a long time to arrive.
3. I <u>am looking</u> forward to a shopping trip with my mom and my best friend.
4. I <u>had been hoping</u> we would go this weekend, and we are!
5. We <u>will go</u> to the outlet center that has opened several miles away.
6. Before the outlets opened, the location <u>had been</u> mainly farmland.
7. We were sorry to see the farms go, but we <u>are</u> happy now to buy some of our favorite brands at discounted prices.
8. By the time we finish, we <u>will have shopped</u> for hours.
9. Nowadays, you <u>will find</u> outlet centers just off interstate highways all across the country.

10. Discount stores <u>have found</u> success in Canada and Western Europe, as well.

Exercise C Identifying Pronoun **Case** Identify the case of each personal pronoun in the following sentences as *nominative, objective,* or *possessive.*

1. Most of us shop at our local supermarkets.
2. I remember my great-grandmother telling me that she grew up in a town without a supermarket.
3. Her times were very different from ours.
4. Before the Great Depression of the 1930's, most people bought their food and household items in many different shops.
5. For example, a person would buy his or her meat at a butcher shop, bread at a bakery, and milk and cheese at a dairy.
6. When supermarkets arrived on the scene, combining self-service with lower prices, they experienced immediate growth.
7. In addition, the spread of the automobile meant that shoppers could drive to a store and fill their cars with packaged groceries.
8. Now, in one place, we can buy all our food, cleaning products, greeting cards, batteries, and much, much more.
9. You can see how the supermarket got its name!
10. The theory of supermarkets has spread to other types of stores; it is called "low-cost mass distribution."

▶ **Exercise D** Revising to Eliminate Errors in Agreement Revise the following sentences, eliminating errors in agreement. If a sentence has no errors, write *correct.*

1 A common sight in stores is the "sale" sign.
2. There is chains in many types of businesses.
3. Each town and city has their own branches of certain fast-food restaurants, banks, movie theaters, gas stations, and supermarkets.
4. The products or services of each branch of a particular chain is almost always the same.
5. The chicken burrito that a person buys for their lunch at one fast-food restaurant will be just like the chicken burrito sold at another branch of the same chain.
6. Each of us probably has our own favorites.
7. Developers of the first chain stores were not sure that they would be successful.
8. However, the lower prices and convenience has made chains very popular.
9. Usually in charge of a chain store is managers rather than an individual owner.
10 Managers make the day-to-day decisions concerning their particular stores.

▶ **Exercise E** Writing Sentences With Modifiers Write sentences according to the instructions. Be careful to use the correct forms of modifiers, and make sure your comparisons are complete and logical.

1. Using the comparative form of *expensive*, write a sentence about a shoe store.
2. Using the superlative form of *comfortable*, write a sentence about a new pair of shoes.
3. Using the superlative form of *friendly*, write a sentence about the salesperson.
4. Using the comparative form of *few*, write a sentence about job opportunities at this shoe store.
5. Using the comparative form of *far*, write a sentence about the distance of the store from your home.
6. Using the positive form of *good*, write a sentence about transportation into town.
7. Using the comparative form of *bad*, write about the service in another shoe store.
8. Using the superlative form of *much* as an adverb, describe the variety of styles in the shoe store.
9. Using the comparative form of *quickly*, write about a decision about a pair of shoes.
10. Using the superlative form of *good*, describe a purchase.

▶ **Exercise F** Revising to Eliminate Various Usage Errors Rewrite the following paragraph, correcting errors in agreement and in the usage of verbs, pronouns, and modifiers.

As usual, my parents, brothers, sister, and me had different ideas about where we should go this summer. Each of my two brothers has their own favorite place for fishing, while my sister was insisting on the beach. My parents and me have different ideas. My father thinks that us should see someplace new; he wanted to camp and fish at the shore. His idea is not the most popularest since the rest of us want to be closer to stores, movies, and other conveniences. My mother wants to visit a city because you can do so much there. I think we should of drawn straws instead of arguing for so long.

▶ **Exercise G** Writing Application Describe a store in which you like to shop. Use a consistent verb tense, and check carefully for problems in agreement or in the usage of verbs, pronouns, and modifiers.

▲ **Critical Viewing**
What are some reasons these girls might pause or stop during their walk? **[Speculate]**

All languages have symbols that help people make sense of the words they speak and write. For example, periods let a reader know where a thought ends and a new thought begins. In the English language, symbols such as these are called punctuation marks.

Punctuation marks tell readers to pause, to stop, or to read in a questioning, commanding, or surprised tone. Punctuation marks also connect certain ideas with other ideas or set ideas apart.

In this chapter, you will learn the correct use of punctuation marks.

Diagnostic Test

Directions: Write all answers on a separate sheet of paper.

Skill Check A. Rewrite the following sentences, adding end marks.

1. There are two types of pandas: giant pandas and red pandas
2. What is the difference between the two
3. Giant pandas weigh twenty-five times more than red pandas do
4. The United States received two giant pandas in 1972 from the Chinese government
5. A baby panda weighs only five ounces How amazing

Skill Check B. Rewrite these sentences, adding needed commas.

6. China the most populated country in the world is located in the eastern portion of Asia.
7. To the north it borders Russia Mongolia and North Korea.
8. China covers about 3695000 square miles and it includes hundreds of islands off its coastline.
9. China and its people I think would be fascinating to study.
10. On September 23 1999 my aunt and uncle flew from San Francisco California to Beijing China to visit.

Skill Check C. Rewrite the following sentences, adding semicolons and colons where necessary.

11. So much of China's early art was encouraged by its emperors in fact, artists were employed by their government.
12. Some of these dynasties produced important art the Shang dynasty, the Zhou dynasty, and the Han dynasty.
13. The Shang dynasty produced artifacts of several types ceramics, bronze containers, and jade.
14. The Zhou dynasty followed the Shang it produced rich treasures.
15. Our letter to the Chinese embassy began, "Dear Sir or Madam Please send me travel brochures about your beautiful country."

Skill Check D. Add quotation marks and underlining where needed in the following sentences.

16. What have you learned this year about China? my grandmother asked me.
17. Oh, a great deal! I replied. My favorite topic is Chinese art.
18. Did you read the article about China in the Los Angeles Times? she asked.
19. The Good Earth by Pearl S. Buck is about a girl's life in China.
20. Why did you say, I read that book already?

Skill Check E. Add hyphens and apostrophes where needed below.

21. During the 1800's, China and England fought over trade.
22. The all powerful British army fought against the Chinese.
23. Chinese commanders couldnt defend themselves completely.
24. The Chinese emperor agreed to pay twenty one million dollars.
25. Finally, Chinas major cities were opened for trade.

End Marks

Punctuation is an accepted set of symbols used to give specific directions to the reader. These are the most common punctuation marks:

COMMON PUNCTUATION MARKS					
period	.	comma	,	quotation marks	" "
question mark	?	semicolon	;	hyphen	-
exclamation mark	!	colon	:	apostrophe	'

Sentences, words, and phrases may all be concluded with one of the three *end marks* in the first column of the chart.

▶ **KEY CONCEPT** There are three end marks: the *period (.)*, the *question mark (?)*, and the *exclamation mark (!)*. They usually indicate the end of a sentence. ■

Using the Period

The end mark used most often is the period.

▶ **KEY CONCEPT** Use a period to end a declarative sentence—that is, to end a statement of fact or opinion. ■

DECLARATIVE
SENTENCE: China is a country in Asia.

▶ **KEY CONCEPT** Use a period to end an imperative sentence—that is, to end a direction or command. ■

IMPERATIVE   Use a calligraphy pen to draw the characters.
SENTENCES: Listen carefully to the tour guide.

▶ **KEY CONCEPT** Use a period after initials and most abbreviations. ■

INITIALS: R. F. Nordstrom
TITLES: Mr.   Mrs.   Dr.   Sgt.   Jr.

Note that when an abbreviation is located at the very end of a sentence, only one period is required.

EXAMPLE: Be sure to include Jack Jenkins, Jr.

Theme: China

In this section, you will learn how end marks are used to conclude sentences, end abbreviations, and indicate strong emotion. The examples and exercises in this section are about China's history and culture.

**Cross-Curricular Connection:
Social Studies**

▶ **More Practice**

Grammar Exercise Workbook
• pp. 145–148
On-line Exercise Bank
• Section 26.1
Go on-line:
PHSchool.com
Enter Web Code:
ebk-7002

▶ **Exercise 1** **Using the Period** Copy each of the sentences below onto your paper, adding the missing periods.

EXAMPLE: Mrs M L Richards organized the China tour

ANSWER: Mrs. M. L. Richards organized the China tour.

1. Mr Marco Polo traveled to China in the 1200's
2. He described his travels upon returning to Italy in AD 1295
3. Tell us about your adventures in China, Marco
4. The Chinese had developed a pony express system that traveled as far as Ping Avenue
5. In the 1700's, American ships sailed to China from Salem, Massachusetts
6. One ship was under the command of Capt Cyrus Lincoln from Richmond, Virginia
7. Take us to see the Great Wall of China
8. Sgt E Snow reported on Mao Zedong's regime for US newspapers
9. In 1972, Mao invited President Richard M Nixon to tour China
10. The President was accompanied by Mrs Nixon and an advisor, Dr Elliot Sanderson, Jr

▼ **Critical Viewing** How do you know this picture was taken during a modern period of history? **[Infer; Support]**

Using the Question Mark

The *question mark* is most commonly used to end an interrogative sentence, one that asks a question requiring an answer.

▶ **KEY CONCEPT** Use a question mark to end an interrogative sentence—that is, to end a direct question. ■

The following are direct questions requiring answers:

INTERROGATIVE
SENTENCES: Who turned in a paper with no name on it?

How much money will the trip cost?

Sometimes, a single word or a phrase is used to ask a question. In this situation, the word or phrase is punctuated with a question mark just as a complete sentence would be.

▶ **KEY CONCEPT** Use a question mark to end an incomplete question in which the rest of the question is understood. ■

EXAMPLES: You said that the airplane landed. Where?

She wants to join our tour group. But how?

> **Exercise 2** Using the Question Mark Copy each item below, adding the missing question marks.

EXAMPLE: Which desk is yours

ANSWER: Which desk is yours?

1. Where did the Taiping Rebellion take place
2. Who started the rebellion   Why
3. How many people fought during the rebellion
4. Did the natural disasters have anything to do with the start of the rebellion
5. Hong Xiuguah, leader of the rebels, crowned himself king. But how

Using the Exclamation Mark

Exclamation marks are used to punctuate sentences that show strong feelings.

> **KEY CONCEPT** Use an exclamation mark to end an exclamatory sentence—that is, to end a statement showing strong emotion. ■

EXAMPLE: You surprised me!

> **KEY CONCEPT** Use an exclamation mark after an imperative sentence if the command is urgent and forceful. ■

EXAMPLE: Move away from the fire!

> **KEY CONCEPT** Use an exclamation mark after an interjection expressing strong emotion. ■

EXAMPLE: Goodness! I forgot to bring my homework.

Too many exclamation marks can make your writing too emotional, however. Be sure to use them sparingly.

▶ Critical Viewing What strong emotions does this Chinese lion sculpture make you feel? **[Respond]**

▶ **Exercise 3** Using the Exclamation Mark Copy each item below, adding the missing exclamation marks and periods.

EXAMPLE: Stop Don't forget your money

ANSWER: Stop! Don't forget your money.

1. Hooray The Taiping Rebellion has ended
2. Thirty million people were affected
3. The Taiping rebels fought to abolish torture and to increase personal freedom How brave
4. The Qing regime needs our support
5. Thank goodness The British and French came to the assistance of the Qing regime.
6. It was the largest rebellion of modern China Amazing
7. You can't overestimate the impact of the Taiping Rebellion
8. Imagine The leader was just a country teacher
9. What an amazing act of courage to fight the oppressors
10. They truly risked their lives

▶ **Exercise 4** Revising to Correct the Use of End Marks Revise the following sentences, correcting the use of punctuation marks as necessary. If a sentence is punctuated correctly, write *correct*.

EXAMPLE: China's cities are on the move. How!

ANSWER: China's cities are on the move. How?

1. Daily life in China's major cities has really changed in recent years? In what ways?
2. In 1980, Dr Jay Arena and his family visited several cities in China!
3. What do you think they found on their travels?
4. They saw many small, cramped one-story houses and people riding bicycles everywhere.
5. There must have been 2 million bikes racing by them at once. Amazing.
6. If Dr Arena went to China now, would he see big differences!
7. Today, he would stare up at high-rise apartment and office buildings on Chonwenmen Wai St in Beijing.
8. Would he be surprised to see thousands of cars and buses racing by him! Absolutely!
9. These changes are not all good, however. Why?
10. Today, air pollution has become a major problem in cities both in China and in the United States!

▶ **More Practice**

Grammar Exercise Workbook
• pp. 145–148
On-line Exercise Bank
• Section 26.1
   Go on-line:
   PHSchool.com
   Enter Web Code:
   ebk-7002

Get instant feedback! Exercises 2, 3, and 4 are available on-line or on CD-ROM.

Section Review

GRAMMAR EXERCISES 5–11

Exercise 5 Using a Period with Abbreviations On your paper, add a period to each abbreviation.

1. Mon
2. Dr Smith
3. PT Barnum
4. Sgt Cally
5. John Jones, Jr

Exercise 6 Using End Marks Add a period, exclamation point, or question mark to each sentence below. (In some cases, you may need two end marks.)

1. Rice is the main food in China
2. In fact, the Chinese word *fan* means both rice and meal
3. Believe it or not, there are 7,000 ways to make rice
4. Sometimes Chinese people say they "can't eat rice"
5. What does that expression mean
6. "Cannot eat rice" means that one is ill
7. What do you think the expression "broken the rice bowl" indicates
8. It means that someone has lost a job
9. My how interesting these expressions are
10. Do other foods have symbolic meanings

Exercise 7 Identifying Declarative, Imperative, Interrogative, or Exclamatory Statements Identify each sentence as *declarative*, *imperative*, *interrogative*, or *exclamatory*, and then add the appropriate punctuation mark.

1. Good manners in China are different from American manners
2. Oh, all right you can slurp soup
3. Don't point chopsticks at people
4. Wait It is rude to eat before everyone is at the table
5. Why are you moving the food around

Exercise 8 Revising to Correct End Marks Revise these sentences, correcting the use of end marks as necessary.

1. How impolite?
2. Rapping on the table three times shows gratitude for a full cup of tea?
3. What is usually eaten first in China!
4. Plain rice is the first food tasted!
5. Wow. Some Chinese foods are unusual!
6. Imagine eating bear paws, frog legs, iguanas, snakes, or camel hooves.
7. Those exotic meals are eaten in China!
8. Are you willing to taste them.
9. How do the Chinese remedy bad breath.
10. Just chew tea leaves!

Exercise 9 Find It in Your Reading Read this paragraph from "Yeh-Shen: A Cinderella Story From China." Why has the writer used three different end marks?

That day Yeh-Shen turned many a head as she appeared at the feast. All around her people whispered, "Look at that beautiful girl! Who can she be?"

Exercise 10 Find It in Your Writing Look through your portfolio to find examples of sentences with each type of end mark. Explain why you used each mark. Then, rewrite each sentence so that it calls for a different end mark.

Exercise 11 Writing Application Imagine that you are dining at a Chinese restaurant. Write a dialogue between the waiter and yourself. Include declarative sentences, questions, and exclamations in your dialogue.

Commas

Using Commas to Separate Basic Elements

While an end mark signals a full stop, a comma signals a brief pause. It may be used to separate basic elements in a sentence or to set off elements added to a sentence.

Many people use more commas than are necessary, while others use fewer than they should. To avoid the overuse or underuse of commas, include a comma in your writing only when you know that a specific rule applies.

This section presents the rules that you need to know to use commas correctly.

Commas With Compound Sentences A compound sentence consists of two or more independent clauses joined by one of the coordinating conjunctions (*and, but, for, nor, or, so,* and *yet*).

▶ **KEY CONCEPT** Use a comma before the conjunction to separate two independent clauses in a compound sentence. ■

Notice that each of the following sentences is compound because it is made up of more than one complete thought. In the first sentence, a comma and the conjunction *and* separate the independent clauses. In the second, a comma and the conjunction *but* separate the independent clauses.

| COMPOUND SENTENCES: | Marco Polo was fascinated with China, *and* he took home many souvenirs. |
| | He told Italian friends about China, *but* they did not believe his stories. |

Remember to use a comma before a conjunction only when there are complete thoughts on both sides of the conjunction. Do not use a comma when there is just a word, phrase, or subordinate clause on either side of the conjunction.

WORDS:	Polo visited *cities* and *farming areas.*
PHRASES:	The Chinese established systems *for delivering mail* and *for carrying goods.*
SUBORDINATE CLAUSES:	Kublai Khan was a man *who ruled strictly* but *who could also be kind.*

In some compound sentences, the independent clauses are very brief, and the meaning is clear. When this occurs, the comma before the conjunction may be omitted.

| EXAMPLE: | Jonathan listened carefully but he heard nothing. |

Theme: China

In this section, you will learn how commas are used to separate or set off elements in sentences. The examples and exercises in this section will tell you more about China's history and culture.

Cross-Curricular Connection: Social Studies

Exercise 12 Using Commas With Compound Sentences

Read each sentence below, and decide where a comma is needed. On your paper, write the word before the comma, the comma, and the conjunction following the comma.

1. The Shang dynasty has been dated from 1700 to 1027 B.C. and Shang rulers helped to shape Chinese civilization.
2. Shang bronze workers used their skills to improve farming equipment so farmers were able to produce more food.
3. Shang rulers divided their kingdom into separate states but they also set up a single capital city.
4. The rulers wore silk cloth and they learned to read from books made of bamboo and wood.
5. Under Shang rule, the Chinese developed a writing system yet most of the written records have disappeared.

Exercise 13 Revising Sentences to Correct Comma Usage

Revise each sentence, correcting any misuses of commas.

1. The kingdom was a well-developed society but over time, the government became weaker.
2. The tombs of Shang kings could be very large for the kings were buried with their servants, and belongings.
3. The king held tremendous power for he headed state matters, and was also the leader of the religion.
4. The Shang believed that dead ancestors watched, and guided their descendants so the Shang revered their dead ancestors.
5. Ancestors might die yet they were still, considered part of the living family.

More Practice

Grammar Exercise Workbook
• pp. 149–152
On-line Exercise Bank
• Section 26.2
  Go on-line:
  PHSchool.com
  Enter Web Code:
  ebk-7002

Complete the exercises on-line! Exercises 12, 13, 14, and 15 are available on-line or on CD-ROM.

▼ Critical Viewing What different elements are joined together in this photo? [Identify; Support]

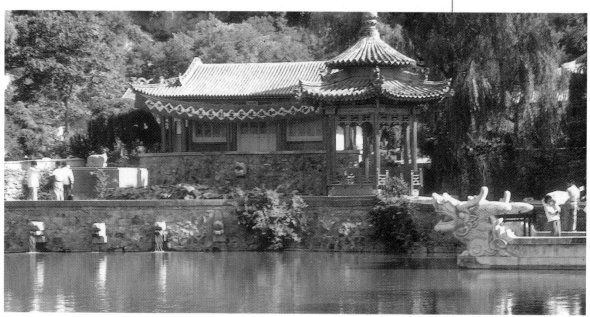

Commas Between Items in a Series When three or more similar items appear in a series, commas are needed to separate them.

KEY CONCEPT Use commas to separate three or more words, phrases, or clauses in a series. ■

Notice in the following examples that the number of items in the series is one more than the number of commas needed. For example, in the first sentence, there are three items in the series that are separated by two commas.

SERIES OF WORDS:	The beverages included *fruit juice, ginger ale,* and *jasmine tea.*
SERIES OF PHRASES:	Ceramic vases were placed *on the table, on the mantel,* and *on the windowsill.*
SERIES OF CLAUSES:	We needed to know *where we would catch the plane, when it would leave,* and *how much baggage we were allowed.*

One exception to the rule for using commas in a series occurs when each item is separated from the others by a conjunction.

EXAMPLE: My sister collects stamps and coins and pottery.

Exercise 14 Using Commas Between Items in a Series
Copy these sentences, adding commas where they are needed.
1. Many historical sites are found in Beijing, such as the Old Palace Museum the Wall of Nine Dragons and the Museum of Chinese Art.
2. Beijing is a city that connects the past present and future.
3. The emperors of ancient Beijing could be found governing China from the Forbidden City enjoying recreation at the Summer Palace or praying at the Temple of Heaven.
4. The four Buddhist temples housed in Beijing are the Yunju Temple the Dazhong Temple the Fahai Temple and the Yonghegong Temple.
5. Beijing has beautiful scenery as the Great Wall surrounds it the Yan Shan Mountains overlook it and the Grand Canal runs by it.

Exercise 15 Writing Sentences With Commas Write five sentences in which you convey what you know about China. Three of the sentences should be compound sentences containing commas, and two should use commas to separate items in a series.

Grammar and Style Tip

Some writers view the comma preceding the conjunction as optional; most professional writers, however, add the last comma to avoid confusion.

Commas Between Adjectives Sometimes adjectives need to be separated by commas.

> **KEY CONCEPT** Use commas to separate adjectives of equal rank. ■

Two methods can be used to help decide whether two or more adjectives are of equal rank. First, if the word *and* can be placed between the adjectives without changing the meaning of the sentence, then the adjectives are of equal rank. Second, if the order of the adjectives can be changed, then they are equal.

Study the following examples. Then, try both methods for deciding whether the adjectives are of equal rank.

EXAMPLES: You have made a *simple, polite* request.
Flavorful, spicy, nutritious soups are common in Chinese cuisine.

If you tried both methods on these examples, you learned that the adjectives are of equal rank. Therefore, commas are needed to separate them. In other sentences, however, placing an *and* between the adjectives or changing their order would alter the meaning of the sentence.

> **KEY CONCEPT** Do not use commas to separate adjectives that must stay in a specific order. ■

Apply the two methods for determining whether the adjectives are of equal rank to the following examples.

EXAMPLES: I read descriptions of *several ancient* temples in my guidebook.
Some colorful birds perched on the temple roof.

As you can see, the italicized adjectives in the examples cannot be separated by *and*, and their order cannot be changed without destroying the meaning of the sentences. Therefore, no commas should be added.

Note About *Commas With Adjectives:* A comma should never be used to separate the last adjective in a series from the noun it modifies.

INCORRECT: An efficient, helpful, interesting, guide led our party.

CORRECT: An efficient, helpful, interesting guide led our party.

▶ **Critical Viewing**
In what ways does the poster show that men and women have equal rank? **[Infer; Support]**

Exercise 16 Using Commas Between Adjectives Copy the underlined adjectives onto your paper, adding commas only in those places where they are needed.

1. Traditionally, Chinese families wished for <u>strong</u> <u>sturdy</u> sons.
2. Sons often carried on <u>their</u> <u>family's</u> traditions.
3. The birth of a daughter was not always accompanied by a <u>warm</u> <u>joyous</u> celebration.
4. Marriages were arranged in <u>traditional</u> <u>Chinese</u> families.
5. Sons were expected to remain in their <u>old</u> <u>family</u> home even after they married,

Exercise 17 Revising Sentences to Correct the Use of Commas Between Adjectives Revise the following sentences, adding or removing commas as appropriate.

1. When a woman married, she had to leave her home to join a new unfamiliar family.
2. Every, young bride was expected to obey her husband's mother.
3. Some mothers-in-law treated the new, family member in a harsh cruel manner.
4. It wasn't until the early, twentieth century that efforts were made to change women's social, status in China.
5. An early custom of foot binding, which produced sore mangled deformed feet, has been mostly discontinued.

⊘ Learn More

To review adjectives, refer to Section 16.1: Adjectives.

Using Commas to Set Off Added Elements

Commas are used not only to separate similar kinds of words and groups of words but also to set off—that is, set apart—certain parts of a sentence from the rest.

As you read the rules for commas used to set off added elements, remember that commas should be used in your writing only when a specific rule applies.

Commas After Introductory Material Sometimes, a sentence begins with introductory material. Generally, the extra word or words are set off from the rest of the sentence by a comma.

▶ **KEY CONCEPT** Use a comma after an introductory word, phrase, or clause. ■

The following examples illustrate three types of introductory material:

KINDS OF INTRODUCTORY MATERIAL	
Introductory Words	*Well*, I need a minute to decide. *Tom*, where are you? *Please*, put some clams in the chowder.
Introductory Phrases	*In the vibrant city of Hong Kong,* trade is booming. *Located on the coast of China,* Hong Kong is an important port. *To visit Hong Kong,* you need a passport.
Introductory Clauses	*If the British had not relented,* they might still rule Hong Kong. *Where there is bustling trade,* there you will find a colorful night life as well.

When a prepositional phrase of only two words begins a sentence, a comma is not absolutely necessary.

EXAMPLES: *At night* we heard the crickets.
    For hours we nervously remained awake.

GRAMMAR IN LITERATURE

from Yeh-Shen: A Cinderella Story From China

Retold by Ai-Ling Louie

Notice how the writer has used commas to separate items in a series and to set off added elements. Do the commas make it easier to read the story?

. . . This time the big fish saw Yeh-Shen's familiar jacket and heaved itself onto the bank, expecting to be fed. But the stepmother, having hidden a dagger in her sleeve, stabbed the fish, wrapped it in her garments, and took it home to cook for dinner.

▶ **Exercise 18** Using Commas With Introductory Material
For each of the following sentences, write the introductory material, the missing comma, and the word following the comma.
1. Oh I'm so excited to fly to Hong Kong!
2. Located on China's southern coast Hong Kong consists of the Kowloon Peninsula and several islands.
3. Though Hong Kong covers only 400 square miles over six million people live there.
4. As you can tell when you visit Hong Kong it is one of the most crowded places in the world.
5. Please will you tell me more about Hong Kong?

▶ **Exercise 19** Revising the Use of Commas With Introductory Material Revise the paragraph below, adding or deleting commas where necessary.
(1) During the twentieth century Hong Kong became an economic power in Asia. (2) An important manufacturing center it contains factories specializing in textiles, clothing, and electronic equipment. (3) While Hong Kong workers produce many, goods nearly all of their products are exported to other countries. (4) Up until recent, times the colony belonged to the British. (5) Determined the Chinese government demanded, that Hong Kong be returned to Chinese control.

More Practice

Grammar Exercise Workbook
• pp. 153–154
On-line Exercise Bank
• Section 26.2
  Go on-line:
  PHSchool.com
  Enter Web Code:
  ebk-7002

Get instant feedback! Exercises 18 and 19 are available on-line or on CD-ROM.

Commas With Parenthetical Expressions A *parenthetical expression* is a word or phrase that is not essential to the rest of the sentence. These words or phrases generally add extra information to the basic sentence.

KEY CONCEPT Use commas to set off parenthetical expressions. ■

Parenthetical expressions are sometimes written at the beginning of a sentence as introductory material. They may also be written in the middle or at the end of a sentence. A parenthetical expression in the middle of a sentence needs a comma before it and a comma after it to set it off. If it is written at the end of the sentence, only one comma is needed.

Examples of parenthetical expressions are shown below:

KINDS OF PARENTHETICAL EXPRESSIONS	
Names of People Being Addressed	Watch, *Frank*, while I show you another early Chinese invention. Stop whispering, *Pamela and Dan*.
Certain Adverbs	You are, *therefore*, the person I would choose. Your answer is incorrect, *however*.
Common Expressions	One Chinese invention, *on the other hand*, helped sailors all over the world. They are not given enough credit, *I believe*.

Exercise 20 Using Commas With Parenthetical Expressions Copy each of the following sentences, adding commas to set off the parenthetical expressions.

EXAMPLE: Their garden however survived the storm.
ANSWER: Their garden, however, survived the storm.

1. The Chinese I think do not get enough credit for their many technological advances.
2. Nevertheless some Chinese inventions deserve recognition.
3. Did you know for example that Chinese naval captains were the first to use magnetic compasses?
4. Sailors all over the world therefore can thank the Chinese for helping them find their way.
5. Helene can you think of any other tools that were invented in China?

More Practice

Grammar Exercise Workbook
• pp. 155–156
On-line Exercise Bank
• Section 26.2
Go on-line:
PHSchool.com
Enter Web Code:
ebk-7002

Get instant feedback! Exercises 20 and 21 are available on-line or on CD-ROM.

Commas With Nonessential Expressions Sometimes, it is difficult to decide when to set off material with commas. Knowing whether a word, phrase, or clause is essential or nonessential to the meaning of a sentence helps.

▷**KEY CONCEPT** Use commas to set off nonessential expressions. Do not set off essential material with commas. ■

Notice that each nonessential expression in the chart below can be left out without changing the meaning of the sentence.

APPOSITIVES AND APPOSITIVE PHRASES	
Essential	The Chinese thinker *Confucius* taught the importance of tradition.
Nonessential	Confucius, *a Chinese thinker*, taught the importance of tradition. The importance of tradition was taught by Confucius, *a Chinese thinker*.
PARTICIPIAL PHRASES	
Essential	The man *leading a European expedition to China* was Marco Polo.
Nonessential	Marco Polo, *leading a European expedition to China*, arrived there in 1275. Marco Polo arrived in 1275, *leading a European expedition*.
ADJECTIVE CLAUSES	
Essential	The invaders *who swept into China in the 1200's* ruled with an iron hand.
Nonessential	The Mongols, *who swept into China in the 1200's*, ruled with an iron hand. The country was ruled by the Mongols, *who swept into China in the 1200's*.

▷**Exercise 21** Using Commas With Nonessential Expressions If the underlined material in a sentence below is nonessential, add a comma or commas as needed. Otherwise, write *E*.

EXAMPLE: The patient had typhoid <u>a contagious disease</u>.
ANSWER: The patient had typhoid, a contagious disease.

1. <u>As early as A.D. 100</u> the Chinese had set up medical schools.
2. The doctors <u>who were trained in these schools</u> learned many advanced techniques.
3. They timed a person's pulse <u>or heart rate</u> to diagnose illness.
4. Anesthetics <u>which render patients unconscious during operations</u> were first used in China.
5. Acupuncture <u>another Chinese invention</u> was used to ease pain.

Using Commas in Special Situations

Commas are also used to set off dates, geographical names, and other special material.

Commas With Dates and Geographical Names

Commas are used to separate the different parts of some dates and geographical names. The following rule applies to dates consisting of several parts:

KEY CONCEPT When a date is made up of two or more parts, use a comma after each item except in the case of a month followed by a day. ■

Notice in the following examples that commas are not used to set off a month followed by a numeral standing for a day. Commas are used, however, when the month and date are used as an appositive to rename a day of the week.

EXAMPLES: On July 12, 1979, Aunt Mai arrived in this country with just a few possessions.

Tuesday, March 18, was carefully circled on his calendar.

When a date contains only a month and a year, commas are unnecessary.

EXAMPLE: I will graduate in June 2004.

KEY CONCEPT When a geographical name is made up of two or more parts, use a comma after each item. ■

EXAMPLES: They lived in Marietta, Georgia, for several years and then moved to Sarasota, Florida.

My friend Pedro was born in El Salto, Durango, Mexico.

Exercise 22 Using Commas With Dates and Geographical Names Add commas where necessary.
1. On January 1 2000 lion and dragon dances were performed in Hangzhou to greet the new year.
2. February 10 was the date of the Spring Flower Fair in Guangzhou China.
3. A carnival in Beijing China on June 17 2000 featured an opera and an acrobatic performance.
4. Our flight left from Seoul South Korea on Thursday June 10 and landed in Seattle Washington seven hours later.
5. We planned a showing of our China slides in Tacoma Washington on Tuesday July 6 2000.

Text

Get instant feedback! Exercises 22 and 23 are available on-line or on CD-ROM.

More Practice

Grammar Exercise Workbook
• pp. 157–158
On-line Exercise Bank
• Section 26.2
Go on-line:
PHSchool.com
Enter Web Code:
ebk-7002

▶ Critical Viewing
How did the Great Wall set apart China from its enemies? **[Speculate]**

Exercise 23 Writing a Letter Using Commas to Separate Dates and Geographical Names Imagine that you have had the opportunity to travel to China. Write a letter or a postcard to a friend describing your experiences. Use the photographs and the information in this section for material. In your letter or postcard, include at least four place names and two dates separated by commas. For a challenge, include a sentence using a comma for each of the other purposes you have learned in this chapter.

Commas in Addresses, Letters, Numbers, and Quotations

Commas are also used in other situations; these include addresses, letter salutations and closings, numbers, and quotations. The following rule governs the use of commas in addresses:

KEY CONCEPT Use a comma after each item in an address that is made up of two or more parts. ■

In the following example, commas are needed after the name, street, and city. Notice, however, that no comma separates the state from the ZIP Code.

EXAMPLE: She is corresponding with her friend Arlene Blackwell, 32 Birdsong Avenue, Falmouth, Massachusetts 02540.

Notice, however, that when the same address is written in three lines—name, street, town, and state—on an envelope, most of the commas are not necessary.

EXAMPLE: Arlene Blackwell
32 Birdsong Avenue
Falmouth, MA 02540

The next rule covers the use of commas in salutations and closings in letters.

> **KEY CONCEPT** Use a comma after the salutation in a personal letter and after the closing in all letters. ■

SALUTATIONS: Dear Kaori,   My dear Ann,
CLOSINGS: With affection,   Sincerely,

Using commas according to the following rule makes it easier to read large numbers:

> **KEY CONCEPT** With numbers of more than three digits, add a comma before every third digit, counting from the right. ■

EXAMPLES: 2,532 bricks
             a population of 1,860,421
             82,471,908 grains of sand

Note About *Commas With Numbers:* No commas should be used with ZIP Codes, telephone numbers, page numbers, or serial numbers.

ZIP CODE: 14878
TELEPHONE NUMBER: (607) 555-1328
PAGE NUMBER: on page 1817
SERIAL NUMBER: 402 36 4113

A final use of the comma is to show where a direct quotation begins and ends.

> **KEY CONCEPT** Use commas to set off a direct quotation from the rest of a sentence. ■

The placement of the commas depends upon the "he said/she said" part of the sentence. As you study the following examples, notice the correct placement of the commas. (See Section 26.4 for more information about punctuating quotations.)

EXAMPLES: Gordon murmured with a yawn, "This is a dull movie."

             "I thought," Lydia said, "that you liked martial arts movies."

             "It's the third time I've seen this one," Gordon replied.

More Practice

Grammar Exercise Workbook
• pp. 157–158
On-line Exercise Bank
• Section 26.2
  Go on-line:
  PHSchool.com
  Enter Web Code:
  ebk-7002

▶ **Exercise 24** **Using Commas in Other Situations** Copy each item below onto your paper, adding commas where they are needed.

EXAMPLE: "My sister is studying Chinese literature" he said.
ANSWER: "My sister is studying Chinese literature," he said.

1. The Chinese philosopher Confucius once said "He who learns but does not think is lost; he who thinks but does not learn is in danger."
2. "By nature" said Confucius "people are pretty much alike; it is learning and practice that set them apart."
3. Dear Amy   Sincerely   Jenny Ling
4. On page 1341 of the atlas, I read that the population of Shanghai is approximately 14329600.
5. The atlas was published by Jayson Books 1437 Langston Blvd. Savannah Georgia 31406.
6. Jayson Books
   1437 Langston Blvd.
   Savannah GA 31406
7. Go to the Temple of the Jade Buddha 170 Anyuan Lu Putuo Shanghai China to see two of China's most famous jade Buddhas.
8. Our tour leader said "Each Buddha is carved from a single piece of white jade."
9. The Yuyuan Garden in Shanghai was planted before the year 1600 and contains more than 1100 different flowers and trees.
10. Standing majestically above Shanghai's harbor is a 1535-foot-high television tower.

▶ **Critical Viewing** How does a ballerina signal the end of her performance? **[Relate]**

Hands-on Grammar

Punctuation Circles

1. Choose a passage from a short story in your literature book. Ideally, it should be a passage that includes dialogue.

2. Input the passage using a word-processing program. Use a large font size—14 or 16 points. Omit all of the punctuation as you input. Print out your completed passage.

3. Obtain packets of differently colored sticky dots at an office supply store.

4. Read the selection aloud. Following the chart below, place the appropriate colored sticky dots in places where you feel punctuation is needed, based on the sound of your reading.

5. Compare the pattern of circles in your version of the passage with the original passage. What did you punctuate differently? Why? What did you punctuate the same? Why?

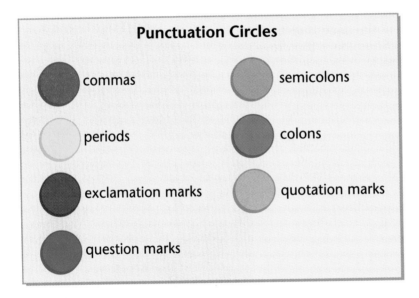

Punctuation Circles

- commas
- periods
- exclamation marks
- question marks
- semicolons
- colons
- quotation marks

Find It in Your Writing Try the above activity with a piece of your own writing. Choose a piece of writing from your portfolio. Eliminate the punctuation, and complete the steps above. How does your color-coded version compare with your original?

Find It in Your Reading Select an article from a newsmagazine. Choose a passage that especially interests you. Then, follow the steps outlined above.

Section 26.2 Section Review

GRAMMAR EXERCISES 25–30

Exercise 25 Revising the Use of Commas in Compound Sentences, Between Adjectives, and Between Items in a Series Revise the following sentences, adding or deleting commas as needed.

1. For Chinese children, school begins at the age of seven but many children participate in day care earlier, in life.
2. A fast-paced active time opens their days at school.
3. Children have the opportunity to play sports such as Ping-Pong swimming, or basketball.
4. They participate in many exciting challenging festivals such as the Lantern Festival the Qing Ming Festival and Liberation Day.
5. Children enjoy listening to a talented animated, storyteller and, they are encouraged to make up stories of their own.

Exercise 26 Revising the Use of Commas to Set Off Added Elements Rewrite the following sentences, adding commas to set off introductory, parenthetical, or nonessential material.

1. Much of China's ancient art contains jade a very valuable gem.
2. Because jade is very durable it can be used for detailed carving without breaking.
3. Nephrite which is one of the minerals that jade comes from is difficult to find.
4. Jade's rarity of course increases its value.
5. Did you know Stephen that if a jade piece is made from dark green stone it is more prized by collectors of Chinese art?

Exercise 27 Using Commas in Other Situations Copy each sentence, adding commas where they are needed.

1. I wrote to the Chinese National Tourist Office 333 West Broadway Suite 201 Glendale California 91204.
2. On Thursday October 14 2000 I received a response to my letter.
3. Enclosed was a videotape about Tianjin China's third-largest city which has a population of 12000000.
4. An announcer said "Tianjin's history dates back over 4000 years."
5. "Even though it is a very large city" the announcer added "Tianjin has a small-town feel about it."

Exercise 28 Find It in Your Reading Read this passage from "Yeh-Shen: A Cinderella Story From China," and explain the purpose of each comma.

. . . She hurried down to the pond, but she was unable to see the fish, for Yeh-Shen's pet wisely hid itself. The step-mother, however, was a crafty woman, and she soon thought of a plan. She walked home and called out, "Yeh-Shen, go and collect some firewood."

Exercise 29 Find It in Your Writing Look through your portfolio to find a paragraph with four or more commas. Explain the purpose of each comma.

Exercise 30 Writing Application Write a brief description of an interesting place you have visited. Include at least two commas in each sentence of your description.

Semicolons and Colons

The *semicolon* looks like a period over a comma (;). The semicolon signals a less final pause than a period but a stronger separation than a comma.

Semicolons are used to join complete ideas within sentences and to avoid confusion in sentences already containing several commas.

The *colon* looks like two periods, one above the other (:). Colons can be used to introduce lists of items and in certain other special situations.

Using Semicolons to Join Independent Clauses

The following rule governs the use of semicolons with independent clauses:

▶ **KEY CONCEPT** Use a semicolon to join independent clauses that are not already joined by the conjunctions *and, but, for, not, or, so,* or *yet.* ■

The following examples show independent clauses joined by a comma and a conjunction.

CLAUSES WITH COMMA:	The Wright brothers read books about flying, and they dreamed of building a flying machine.
	Their first flight lasted just 12 seconds, for the plane traveled only 120 feet.

Notice, however, that when the comma and conjunction are omitted from the sentence, a semicolon must replace them.

CLAUSES WITH SEMICOLON:	The Wright brothers read books about flying; they dreamed of building a flying machine.
	Their first flight lasted just 12 seconds; the plane traveled only 120 feet.

A semicolon should be used only when there is a close relationship between the two independent clauses. If the clauses are not very closely related, they should be written as separate sentences with a period or other end mark to separate them.

INCORRECT:	The Wright brothers' first flight lasted just 12 seconds; the plane had a 40-foot wing span.
CORRECT:	The Wright brothers' first flight lasted just 12 seconds. The plane had a 40-foot wing span.

Theme: The History of Flight

In this section, you will learn how semicolons and colons are used in sentences. The examples and exercises in this section are about flying machines and the history of flight.

Cross-Curricular Connection: Social Studies

▶ **More Practice**

Grammar Exercise Workbook
• pp. 159–160
On-line Exercise Bank
• Section 26.3
Go on-line:
PHSchool.com
Enter Web Code:
ebk-7002

▲ Critical Viewing
How might you describe these astronauts in a single sentence containing two independent clauses joined by a semicolon? [Describe]

▶ **Exercise 31** **Using Semicolons to Join Independent Clauses**
Read each sentence below, and decide where a semicolon is required. On your paper, write the word before each semicolon, the semicolon, and the word that follows it.

EXAMPLE: The first astronauts faced many uncertainties however, the flights were completed successfully.

ANSWER: uncertainties; however

1. American plans to send a man into space required careful planning therefore, the process took several years.
2. Precautions were taken in case of a failure for example, an ejection seat was designed.
3. Parachutes were included to cushion the Mercury capsule's fall into the ocean the water was also expected to help break the impact.
4. Ham, a chimpanzee, went on a trial run into space his flight lasted 18 minutes.
5. Alan Shepard was the first man from the United States launched into space however, his mission did not reach the speed and altitude required to orbit Earth.

Using Semicolons to Avoid Confusion

Sometimes, to avoid confusion, semicolons are used to separate items in a series.

> **KEY CONCEPT** Consider the use of semicolons to avoid confusion when items in a series already contain commas. ■

When the items in a series already contain several commas, semicolons can be used to make a sentence easier to read. Semicolons are placed at the end of all but the last complete item in the series.

EXAMPLE: The fans, cheering loudly; the band, playing a rousing march; and the cheerleaders, turning cartwheels, helped inspire the team to play well.

> **Exercise 32** Using Semicolons to Avoid Confusion Copy each sentence below, adding semicolons where they are needed.
> 1. NASA has many facilities, including the John F. Kennedy Space Center, Merritt Island, Florida the Lyndon B. Johnson Space Flight Center, Houston, Texas and the George C. Marshall Space Flight Center, Huntsville, Alabama.
> 2. The types of orbits are the circular, in which the spacecraft maintains a constant distance from Earth the elliptical, in which the spacecraft travels faster closer to Earth the inclined, which forms an angle with the equator and the polar, which carries the spacecraft over both poles.
> 3. The conveniences of space shuttles have been improved with collections of books, tapes, and computer games nutritious, appetizing foods and permanent shower stalls.
> 4. The first crew to land on the moon consisted of Neil Armstrong, the first person to walk on the moon Edwin Aldrin, who accompanied Armstrong to the moon and Michael Collins, who piloted the *Columbia.*
> 5. Microgravity, or weightlessness, affects the fuel, which must be pumped with high-pressure gas air currents, which must be circulated by fans and the astronauts' vestibular system, the inner-ear organs, which control balance and directional signals.

> **Exercise 33** Writing Sentences Using Semicolons Write five sentences of your own about airplane travel. Each sentence should include a semicolon.

> **More Practice**
>
> **Grammar Exercise Workbook**
> • pp. 159–160
> **On-line Exercise Bank**
> • Section 26.3
>   *Go on-line:*
>   PHSchool.com
>   *Enter Web Code:*
>   ebk-7002

Get instant feedback! Exercises 32, 33, and 34 are available on-line or on CD-ROM.

Using Colons as Introductory Devices

KEY CONCEPT Use a colon before a list of items following an independent clause. ■

In the following example, the colon directs the reader's attention to the list directly following it. The words before the colon make up an independent clause that expresses a complete idea.

EXAMPLE: Sandor's model airplane collection included many different items: a Piper Cub, a P-51 Mustang, a Heinkel Salamander, and a Spitfire.

Notice that a colon should never be used directly after a verb or a preposition.

INCORRECT: The magazine included: an article on model planes, a column about radio controls, and a ballooning poster.
Features in the magazine were on: model planes, radio controls, and ballooning.

CORRECT: Some features in the magazine were the following: an article on model planes, a column about radio controls, and a poster on ballooning.

Exercise 34 Using Colons to Introduce Lists of Items
Read each sentence below, and decide where a colon is needed. On your paper, write the word before the colon, the colon, and the word following the colon.

EXAMPLE: Balloon festivals were held in three cities Chicago, Denver, and San Francisco.
ANSWER: cities: Chicago

1. Hot-air balloons were used for many things racing, exploration, weather forecasting, and recreation.
2. The first passengers of a hot-air balloon were the following animals a duck, a rooster, and a sheep.
3. People tried many methods to control the direction of hot-air balloons rudders, feathered oars, and steam engines.
4. Many types of fuel were used to keep the balloon elevated smoke, hydrogen, helium, and propane.
5. The nylon or Dacron balloon fabric comes in a variety of patterns climbing swirls, herringbone slashes, checkerboards, and stripes.

Internet Tip

Colons are used in Internet addresses but should be omitted from Internet searches.

▼ Critical Viewing
What list of items might you come up with to describe this photograph? [Connect]

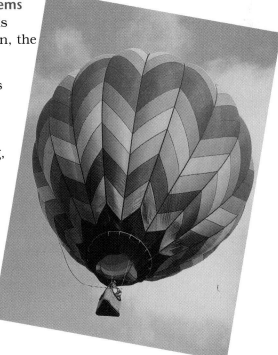

Using Colons in Special Situations

Use a colon in a number of special writing situations to show time with numerals, to end salutations in business letters, and to signal important ideas.

The chart shows the uses of the colon in these special situations:

SPECIAL USES OF THE COLON	
Numbers Giving the Time	12:25 P.M. 3:00 A.M.
Salutations in Business Letters	Gentlemen: Dear Ms. Brown:
Labels Used to Signal Important Ideas	**Caution:** High voltage **Warning:** Trespassers will be prosecuted.

Exercise 35 Using Colons in Special Situations Copy the sentences, adding the colon missing from each.

1. The plane will arrive at 630 P.M.
2. Caution Rocket Launch Area
3. Dear Dr. Von Braun
4. To Whom It May Concern
5. Warning Earplugs Required in Hangars
6. The 930 P.M. plane isn't expected to land until 1215 A.M.
7. Dear Sir or Madam
8. Note All passengers must report for the flight before 715 A.M.
9. Dear Mr. Wright
10. Since the plane is scheduled at 950 A.M., we should arrive at the airport by 830.

Exercise 36 Writing an E-mail With Colons and Semicolons Imagine that you have just visited NASA as part of a school trip. Write an e-mail to a classmate who did not take part in the trip. In your e-mail, use at least four semicolons and three colons. Use semicolons and colons for each of the functions that you have learned in this section.

More Practice

Grammar Exercise Workbook
• pp. 161–162
On-line Exercise Bank
• Section 26.3
  Go on-line:
  PHSchool.com
  Enter Web Code:
  ebk-7002

Get instant feedback! Exercises 35 and 36 are available on-line or on CD-ROM.

Section 26.3 Section Review

GRAMMAR EXERCISES 37–42

Exercise 37 Revising the Use of Semicolons in Independent Clauses
Rewrite each sentence below, adding or deleting semicolons where necessary.

1. Paul MacCready wasn't satisfied with airplane models in a box as a result, he designed his own.
2. Some of them had wings three feet long however, they weighed only 1/15 of an ounce.
3. Paul's models crashed often however, they were easily repaired.
4. At age fifteen, Paul was an expert model builder he won the National Junior Model Airplane Championship.
5. When he was older, Paul built gliders one of his inventions set a world record; for human-powered flight.

Exercise 38 Revising the Use of Semicolons to Avoid Confusion Rewrite this passage, replacing commas with semicolons where necessary to avoid confusion.

Prior to *Apollo 11* came *Apollo 8*, launched in December 1968, *Apollo 9*, launched in March 1969, and *Apollo 10*, launched in May 1969. A series of satellites had also been sent up to take pictures of the moon. The satellites included the Ranger probes, which took pictures and then crashed, the Surveyor probes, and the Luna probes, which were sent up by the Soviets.

The three parts of *Apollo 11* were the command module, which Collins piloted, the lunar module, which Armstrong and Aldrin landed on the moon, and the Saturn V rocket booster, which powered the craft out of orbit.

Exercise 39 Using Colons Correctly Colons are needed below. On your paper, write the word before the colon, the colon, and the word that follows it.

1. Do you know who set each of these flight records flying across the Atlantic, flying around the world, and flying around the world without refueling?
2. The *Voyager* had three designers Dick Rutan, Burt Rutan, and Jeana Yeager.
3. Jeana Yeager brought two key assets to the project team her knowledge of rocketry and her organizational skills.
4. During tests, the team found three major problems leakage, engine malfunctions, and stalls in rainstorms.
5. There were several emergency personnel at Mission Control a doctor, a weather expert, and a radio operator.

Exercise 40 Find It in Your Reading Explain why the author used a colon in this passage from "Icarus and Daedalus" by Josephine Preston Peabody.

. . . He forgot Crete and the other islands that he had passed over: he saw but vaguely that wingèd thing in the distance before him that was his father Daedalus.

Exercise 41 Find It in Your Writing Look through your portfolio for passages containing compound sentences or lists of items. Rewrite five passages, using semicolons or colons correctly.

Exercise 42 Writing Application Write a paragraph describing an unusual flight or car trip you have taken. Include several sentences in which you use semicolons or colons correctly.

Quotation Marks and Underlining

Using Quotation Marks With Direct Quotations

When you write research papers or essays, you may sometimes wish to use the exact words from a book to support your own ideas. When you write fiction, you may sometimes want your characters to speak in their own words to make the story more vivid and interesting. *Quotation marks* identify the exact spoken or written words of others that you are including in your writing. These punctuation marks are used in all kinds of writing situations.

Study this section carefully. It should help you use quotation marks with greater confidence in your own writing.

Direct and Indirect Quotations Before you can use quotation marks correctly, you must first be able to tell the difference between *direct* and *indirect quotations.*

> **KEY CONCEPT** A **direct quotation** represents a person's exact speech or thoughts and is enclosed in quotation marks (" "). ■

EXAMPLES:　　Janine said, "Tomorrow we are going hiking."
"I hope we don't see any wild animals,"
thought Martin.

Indirect quotations do not repeat the exact words a person said or thought. Instead, an indirect quotation paraphrases, or explains, what someone said or thought.

> **KEY CONCEPT** An **indirect quotation** reports only the general meaning of what a person said or thought and does not require quotation marks. ■

EXAMPLES:　　Janine said that we would go hiking tomorrow.

Martin hoped they wouldn't see any wild animals.

Theme: Carnivorous Mammals

In this section, you will learn how quotation marks are used with direct quotations and how quotation marks and underlining are used with titles. The examples and exercises in this section are about meat-eating mammals.

Cross-Curricular Connection: Science

▼ **Critical Viewing** What would you say if you encountered this African lion directly? **[Speculate]**

▶ **Exercise 43** Distinguishing Between Direct and Indirect
Quotations Identify each of the following as a *direct quotation*
or an *indirect quotation*. Then, add proper punctuation to the
direct quotations.

1. Carnivorous mammals help to regulate the balance of
   nature, explained the ranger.
2. Carla wondered what kind of animals were carnivores.
3. Cats, dogs, weasels, bears, and foxes are all carnivores, said
   Jamal.
4. The ranger added, Carnivores have well-developed canine
   teeth.
5. Kent realized that his puppy was an example of a carnivorous mammal.
6. Did you know that carnivores live in all parts of the world
   except Antarctica? asked Kari.
7. My teacher told me that most live on land, but some
   spend time in water.
8. Spencer wondered when the tour would begin.
9. I can't wait to see the bear cub, declared Theresa.
10. Here comes the wildlife tour bus, yelled the ranger.

▶ **Exercise 44** Revising Indirect Quotations as Direct
Quotations Rewrite each of the indirect quotations from the
previous exercise to make them direct quotations, adding the
appropriate punctuation.

Direct Quotations With Introductory, Concluding, and Interrupting Expressions

Quotations are generally
accompanied by expressions such as *he said* or *she replied*.
Expressions of this kind can introduce, conclude, or interrupt
the quoted material. The following rules describe how to punctuate quotations with expressions that come before the direct
quotation, after the direct quotation, or in the middle of the
direct quotation.

▶ **KEY CONCEPT** When an introductory expression precedes
a direct quotation, place a comma after the introductory
expression and write the quotation as a full sentence. ■

EXAMPLES: Timothy told his friend, "I had a great time at
              camp."
              Ginnie added, "We went on trips to the zoo
              and to a wildlife park."

More Practice

Grammar Exercise
Workbook
• pp. 163–164
On-line Exercise Bank
• Section 26.4
  Go on-line:
  PHSchool.com
  Enter Web Code:
  ebk-7002

Get instant feedback!
Exercises 43 and 44
are available on-line
or on CD-ROM.

▶ **KEY CONCEPT** When a concluding expression follows a direct quotation, write the quotation as a full sentence ending with a comma, question mark, or exclamation mark inside the closing quotation mark. Then, write the concluding expression. ■

Notice the kinds of punctuation placed before the final quotation marks in the examples below. In the first example, a comma signals a pause rather than a full stop. The final end mark is not used until the end of the concluding expression. In the last two examples, however, end marks are necessary before the final quotation mark.

EXAMPLES: "I think you would have fun at our camp," Timothy said.

                      "What activities does the camp offer?" inquired Kamilla.

                      "It's everything anyone could want!" exclaimed Ginnie enthusiastically.

Because concluding expressions are not complete sentences, they do not begin with capital letters. Notice also that the closing quotation marks are always placed outside the punctuation at the end of the direct quotations.

Interrupting expressions are governed by their own punctuation rule.

▶ **KEY CONCEPT** When a one-sentence direct quotation is separated by an interrupting expression, end the first part of the direct quotation with a comma and a quotation mark. Place a comma after the interrupting expression. Then, use a new set of quotation marks to enclose the rest of the quotation. ■

Notice the following details in the examples below: (1) the comma inside the quotation mark at the end of the first part of the quotation; (2) the small letter at the beginning of the interrupting expression; (3) the comma inserted after the interrupting expression; (4) the small letter at the beginning of the second part of the quotation; and (5) the end mark inside the last quotation mark.

EXAMPLES: "Since the camp is located on a lake," explained Ginnie, "we can go swimming and boating and water-skiing."

                      "Do you think," interrupted Kamilla, "that I could learn to water-ski?"

Sometimes, a quotation is made up of two sentences, with a complete sentence on each side of the interrupting expression. A final rule is needed for this situation.

▲ **Critical Viewing**
What conversation
might you have with
your friends if you saw
this grizzly bear in its
natural habitat? How
would you capture the
conversation in writing?
[Speculate]

▶ **KEY CONCEPT** When two complete sentences in a direct
quotation are separated by an interrupting expression, end
the first quoted sentence with a comma, question mark, or
exclamation mark and a quotation mark. Next, place a period
after the interrupter. Then, write the second quoted sentence
as a full quotation. ■

Read the examples below carefully and notice the following
details: (1) the different kinds of punctuation at the end of the
first quoted sentence; (2) the small letter at the beginning of
the interrupting expression; (3) the period following the interrupting expression; (4) the capital at the beginning of the second quoted sentence; and (5) the end mark inside the last
quotation mark.

EXAMPLES: "We practically came face to face with a grizzly
             bear on one of our hikes in Alaska," said Juan.
             "It was exciting and scary at the same time."

             "That's amazing!" exclaimed Jenna. "How close
             did you get?"

             "I'd say we were about fifty feet away," re-
             sponded Juan. "We were so close we could see
             its teeth."

Quotation Marks and Underlining • 609

> **Exercise 45** Writing Direct Quotations With Introductory, Concluding, and Interrupting Expressions Copy each of the sentences below onto your paper, correcting punctuation and capitalization as needed.

EXAMPLE: Do wolves live in these woods he asked.

ANSWER: "Do wolves live in these woods?" he asked.

1. Wolf pups learn to hunt by playing with each other explained Virginia.
2. Did you know that wolves hunt caribou and elk asked Kunal they must be quick and clever.
3. When wolves gather to hunt said Saba they howl to warn other wolves to stay out of their territory.
4. Wolves added Joseph are careful that they are downwind from their prey.
5. Wait exclaimed Anna don't wolves hunt in packs?
6. Mica smiled and answered They hunt in a single line until the chase starts.
7. Often the prey gets away said Stephen Wolves chase many more animals than they catch.
8. The objective stated Lorelei is to chase the animal until it becomes weak.
9. Viora commented The hunt can take many hours.
10. Sometimes the wolves give up because the prey is too fast concluded Doug.

> **Exercise 46** Writing an Original Dialogue Imagine that you are on a wilderness trip and that you have just seen the coyote in this picture. Write a dialogue in which you describe what you have seen to your friends. Check to see that you have used correct punctuation.

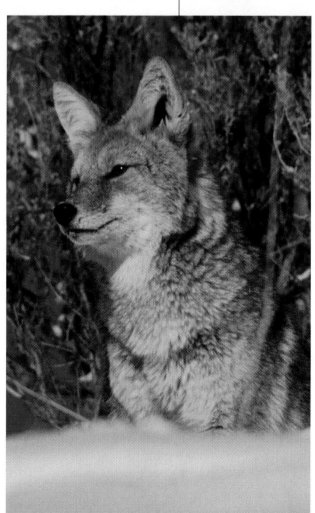

▶ **Critical Viewing** What could a coyote say to you about living in the wild and hunting food? Write your answer in dialogue form. **[Hypothesize]**

Quotation Marks With Other Punctuation Marks

You may sometimes find it hard to decide whether another punctuation mark should go inside or outside the quotation marks. If you study the three rules and the examples that follow, you should be able to make these decisions correctly.

> **KEY CONCEPT** Always place a comma or a period *inside* the final quotation mark. ■

EXAMPLES: "We saw a puma today," Uncle Joe said.
               He added, "It was standing on a high rock."

> **KEY CONCEPT** Place a question mark or an exclamation mark *inside* the final quotation mark if the end mark is part of the quotation. ■

In the following examples, notice that the sentences themselves are declarative. In the first example, however, the quoted material asks a question. In the second, the quoted material shows strong emotion. In these cases, the end marks are placed with the quotations, inside the quotation marks.

EXAMPLES: Jane asked, "Have you seen the fox anywhere?"
               Her sister exclaimed, "No, and I don't want to!"

Remember that it is not necessary to use two end marks. In the following examples, the quoted material requires a question mark and the entire sentence appears to need a period. Because two final punctuation marks are never used, the period is dropped.

INCORRECT: George thought, "Where are we going?".
CORRECT: George thought, "Where are we going?"

In some situations, the entire sentence requires a question mark or an exclamation mark. In these cases, the placement of the final punctuation changes.

> **KEY CONCEPT** Place a question mark or an exclamation mark *outside* the final quotation mark if the end mark is part of the entire sentence and not part of the quotation. ■

Both quotations in the following examples are declarative. The first sentence is a question; the second sentence is an exclamation.

EXAMPLES: Why did you say, "I prefer cats to dogs"?
               Don't ever say "I can't"!

More Practice

Grammar Exercise Workbook
• pp. 165–166
On-line Exercise Bank
• Section 26.4
Go on-line:
PHSchool.com
Enter Web Code:
ebk-7002

GRAMMAR IN LITERATURE

from **The Lion and the Statue**
Aesop

Notice how the writer has used quotation marks with other punctuation marks in the direct quotes in this passage.

. . . The Man contended that he and his fellows were stronger than lions by reason of their greater intelligence. "Come now with me," he cried, "and I will soon prove that I am right." So he took him into the public gardens and showed him a statue of Hercules overcoming the Lion and tearing his mouth in two.

"That is all very well," said the Lion, "but proves nothing, for it was a man who made the statue."

Exercise 47 Using End Marks With Direct Quotations
Read each sentence below, and decide whether the missing end marks go inside or outside the quotation marks. Copy each sentence onto your paper, adding the missing punctuation.

EXAMPLE: He asked the lifeguard, "When can we swim"
ANSWER: He asked the lifeguard, "When can we swim?"

1. Dana commented, "There are seven species of bears"
2. Shay asked the zookeeper, "What do bears eat"
3. Didn't you hear him say, "They eat rodents, fish, berries, and grubs"
4. Chad yelled across the room, "Bears like honey, too"
5. Nathaniel questioned, "Don't the bees sting the bears"
6. Eric answered, "The bear's thick fur protects it from the bee stings"
7. Did the park attendant say, "Bears sometimes raid garbage cans for a snack"
8. Sarah said, "One bear's hunting ground ranges from ten to twelve square miles"
9. Did I hear the ranger say, "Bears are peaceful animals"
10. The ranger exclaimed, "Bears attack only when they or their cubs are threatened"

Quotation Marks for Dialogue A conversation between two or more people is called a *dialogue*.

> **KEY CONCEPT** When writing dialogue, begin a new paragraph with each change of speaker. ■

In the following example of dialogue, capitalization and punctuation are used as they would be for any quotations. Remember, however, to indent whenever a new speaker talks.

EXAMPLE: "Why don't we go to San Diego for a vacation?" Grandfather asked.
       Surprised, Danielle replied, "Why do you want to go to San Diego? Let's go somewhere else. I'd like to visit an interesting zoo or wildlife park."
       "You can't be serious!" exclaimed Grandfather. "San Diego has one of the most famous zoos in the world, or we could visit Sea World and see Shamu, the trained killer whale."
       "In that case," said Danielle, "maybe I should reconsider."

> **Exercise 48** Revising to Punctuate Dialogue Correctly
The example of dialogue below is missing some punctuation marks and indentations. Read the selection carefully, and decide where punctuation marks and indentations are required. Then, copy the paragraphs onto your paper, making the necessary changes. You should have seven paragraphs when you finish.

(1) What exclaimed Darlene, pointing at a strange-looking animal in the cage, is that? (2) Don't you know? asked Mitch. (3) That's a short-tailed weasel. (4) I've never seen a weasel before. (5) What do they do? wondered Darlene. (6) They chase squirrels, mice, and other rodents replied Mitch. (7) The weasel eats earthworms, snakes, lizards, frogs, and small birds. (8) How does it catch its prey? Darlene asked (9) It sneaks its thin body into burrows and narrow crevices to capture its food noted Mitch. (10) I wouldn't want one to sneak up on me! Darlene exclaimed.

> **More Practice**

Grammar Exercise Workbook
• pp. 165–166
On-line Exercise Bank
• Section 26.4
Go on-line:
PHSchool.com
Enter Web Code:
ebk-7002

Complete the exercises on-line! Exercises 47 and 48 are available on-line or on CD-ROM.

Underlining and Other Uses of Quotation Marks

. Certain titles and names should be underlined in your writing. Other titles should be enclosed in quotation marks. Quotation marks are used in all types of writing and printing. Underlining, however, is used only for handwritten or typed materials. Printed materials use italics instead of underlining.

UNDERLINING: The Hobbit

ITALICS: *The Hobbit*

Underlining Long written works that are made up of several parts should be underlined whenever they are written or typed. For example, the title of a book should be underlined.

▶**KEY CONCEPT** Underline titles of long written works and titles of publications that are published as a single work. ■

The following chart shows some of the titles that are covered by this rule:

WRITTEN WORK TITLES THAT ARE UNDERLINED	
Title of a Book	Black Beauty
Title of a Play	What Price Glory?
Title of a Long Poem	The Wasteland
Title of a Magazine	Popular Mechanics
Title of a Newspaper	the Miami Herald
	the Chicago Tribune

The titles of other kinds of major works should also be underlined.

▶**KEY CONCEPT** Underline the titles of movies, television and radio series, and works of art and music. ■

ARTISTIC WORK TITLES THAT ARE UNDERLINED	
Title of a Movie	Revenge of the Pink Panther
Title of a Television Series	Little House on the Prairie
Title of a Long Musical Work	The Magic Flute
Title of a Record Album	Long Distance Voyager
Title of a Painting	The Passage of the Delaware
Title of a Sculpture	Bird in Space

✹ Grammar and Style Tip

Be sure to underline titles of performance artists' cassettes, videos, compact discs, and other performances.

> **KEY CONCEPT** Underline the names of individual air, sea, space, and land craft. ■

AIR: the <u>Hindenburg</u> (zeppelin)
SEA: the <u>Leonardo da Vinci</u> (ship)
SPACE: <u>Voyager 2</u> (spaceship)
LAND: the <u>Southwest Limited</u> (train)

> **Exercise 49** Underlining Titles and Names On your paper, write the items in the following sentences that require underlining and then underline them.

EXAMPLE: Enid Bagnold's novel National Velvet has been a classic for years.

ANSWER: <u>National Velvet</u>

1. Cherie Mason, a naturalist, wrote about nursing an injured fox back to health in her book Wild Fox.
2. The book was reviewed in both Zoo Times magazine and the Los Angeles Times.
3. In Once a Wolf, author Stephen Swinburne explores why people fear wolves and sometimes mistreat them.
4. Our science teacher showed the film Tigers in the Snow to her third-period class.
5. The television series Call of the Wild is based on the famous book by Jack London.
6. If you want to learn why wolves howl, read Mary Ling's book Amazing Wolves, Dogs, and Foxes.
7. Eyewitness: Bear will be shown on the Public Broadcasting System station later this week.
8. Peter and the Wolf is one of my favorite musical pieces.
9. Two articles in the Detroit Free Press focused on Zoo Story, a new sculpture on display at the Fine Arts Museum.
10. Laika, the first dog in space, flew aboard the Soviet craft Sputnik 2 but did not survive the trip.

> **Exercise 50** Writing Dialogue With Titles and Names
Write an imaginary dialogue with friends in which you discuss books and magazines you have read and movies you have seen. Check your use of quotation marks and underlining.

> **More Practice**

Grammar Exercise Workbook
• pp. 167–168
On-line Exercise Bank
• Section 26.4
  Go on-line:
  PHSchool.com
  Enter Web Code:
  ebk-7002

Get instant feedback! Exercises 49 and 50 are available on-line or on CD-ROM.

Quotation Marks The titles of short written works and works that are part of longer works are generally enclosed in quotation marks.

▶ **KEY CONCEPT** Use quotation marks around the titles of short written works. ■

WRITTEN WORK TITLES THAT TAKE QUOTATION MARKS	
Title of a Short Story Chapter From a Book	"The Richer, the Poorer" "Hazel's Decision" from <u>Watership Down</u>
Title of a Short Poem Title of an Article	"The Concord Hymn" "Windmills: Alternative Energy Sources"

▶ **KEY CONCEPT** Use quotation marks around the titles of episodes in a series, songs, and parts of a long musical composition. ■

ARTISTIC WORK TITLES THAT TAKE QUOTATION MARKS	
Title of an Episode Title of a Song Title of a Part of a Long Musical Work	"The Nile" from <u>Cousteau Odyssey</u> "The Best Things in Life Are Free" "The Storm" from the <u>William Tell Overture</u>

▶ **Exercise 51** Using Quotation Marks With Titles Copy the titles in the sentences below onto your paper, adding quotation marks or underlining as needed.

EXAMPLE: How Much Is That Doggy in the Window? was a hit record in the 1950's.

ANSWER: "How Much Is That Doggy in the Window?"

1. Thurber's The Tiger Who Would Be King is a modern fable.
2. Zoo by Edward Hoch is included in Super SciFi Tales.
3. The Grizzly Bear is the first episode in the new PBS series, Our World of Animals.
4. You should read The Lion and the Bulls in Aesop's Fables.
5. This month's National Geographic contains a great article, The Wonders of Wolves.

More Practice

Grammar Exercise Workbook
• pp. 167–168
On-line Exercise Bank
• Section 26.4
  Go on-line:
  PHSchool.com
  Enter Web Code:
  ebk-7002

Get instant feedback! Exercise 51 is available on-line or on CD-ROM.

Section 26.4 **Section Review**

GRAMMAR EXERCISES 52–57

Exercise 52 Revising Direct Quotations With Introductory, Concluding, and Interrupting Expressions Rewrite each quotation below, adding needed quotation marks and other punctuation marks.

1. I thought I heard something howling during the night, I said.
2. It was probably just coyotes singing to each other my mom said Howling is their trademark.
3. The farmer down the road commented Those coyotes are my enemies because they snatch my chickens and my ducks.
4. They are also my friends he added because they prey on mice and rabbits that eat my crops
5. Unlike humans the farmer said coyote babies are ready to be on their own when they're less than a year old That's pretty amazing

Exercise 53 Revising the Use of End Marks in Direct Quotations Revise the following items, correcting capitalization and the use of punctuation where necessary.

1. Abby stated, "The tiger is the largest member of the cat family".
2. Katie asked, "Just how big does a grown tiger get"?
3. Didn't you hear the zookeeper say, "a male tiger can grow to weigh 420 pounds and can be 9 feet long, including his tail."
4. Ariel exclaimed, "No wonder deer, antelope, and wild pigs avoid tigers"!
5. Were you surprised when the zookeeper said, "Tigers especially enjoy dining on porcupines?"

Exercise 54 Punctuating Titles Copy the titles in the sentences below onto your paper, either enclosing them in quotation marks or underlining them.

1. My favorite episode of Wild Kingdom was entitled Cats on the Run.
2. Its host, Marlin Perkins, was featured in an article in the New York Daily News entitled TV's Cat Man.
3. Camille Saint-Saens takes listeners to a pretend zoo with his composition The Carnival of the Animals.
4. The sculpture Three Cougars is on the cover of this month's Zoology Today.
5. Ogden Nash's poem The Hippopotamus is very clever.

Exercise 55 Find It in Your Reading Look back at the passage from "The Lion and the Statue" on page 612. Explain why the passage needs to be divided into two paragraphs.

Exercise 56 Find It in Your Writing Review a story or a report from your portfolio, and either add three direct quotations or rewrite three indirect quotations to make them direct quotations. Use correct punctuation.

Exercise 57 Writing Application Use a reference book or the Internet to find information about a carnivorous mammal that interests you. Write a dialogue in which you explain facts about the animal to one of your classmates. Be sure to start a new paragraph for each new speaker.

Hyphens and Apostrophes

The *hyphen* (-) is used to combine some numbers and some word parts and to show a connection between the syllables of words that are broken at the ends of lines.

The *apostrophe* (') is used mainly in two situations: (1) to show possession in nouns and pronouns or (2) to indicate missing letters in contractions.

Using Hyphens for Numbers

Some compound numbers and fractions require the use of the hyphen.

> **KEY CONCEPT** Use a hyphen when writing out compound numbers from *twenty-one* through *ninety-nine*. ■

EXAMPLES: Before she fell asleep, Tracy counted to *fifty-three*.
             We bought *seventy-seven* tickets for the game.

> **KEY CONCEPT** Use a hyphen when writing fractions that are used as adjectives. ■

EXAMPLE: A *two-thirds* vote of approval was necessary.

When a fraction is used as a noun, do not use a hyphen.

EXAMPLE: *Two thirds* of the players come from California.

> **Exercise 58** Using Hyphens With Numbers Read the following sentences carefully to decide where hyphens are needed. If words in a sentence need a hyphen, rewrite the words correctly on your paper. If a sentence does not have any missing hyphens, write *correct*.

EXAMPLE: Three fourths of the students attended the game.
ANSWER: correct

1. Cynthia Cooper was named the WNBA's first Most Valuable Player when she was thirty four years old.
2. The eight original WNBA teams had ninety six players.
3. Over one tenth of the players were of international origin.
4. The Charlotte Sting was made up of one fourth North Carolina State alumni.
5. Zheng Haixia of the Los Angeles Sparks averaged twenty six points for China during the 1994 World Championship.

Using Hyphens for Word Parts and Compound Words

Hyphens are also used to separate certain prefixes (which begin words) and suffixes (which end words). The next two rules govern the use of hyphens with prefixes and suffixes.

KEY CONCEPT Use a hyphen after a prefix that is followed by a proper noun or adjective. ■

EXAMPLES: The softball tournament takes place in mid-July.
The pro-Atlanta fans sat together in the stands.

Three other prefixes and one suffix always require the use of hyphens.

KEY CONCEPT Use a hyphen in words with the prefixes *all-*, *ex-*, and *self-*, and in words with the suffix *-elect*. ■

EXAMPLES: all-powerful   self-employed
ex-football player   president-elect

In many instances, compound words also require the use of hyphens.

KEY CONCEPT In many cases, a hyphen is used to connect two or more nouns that are used as one compound word. ■

Compound nouns are written in several ways. Some are written as one word. Others are written as separate words. Still others require hyphens. Unless you are sure how a compound word is spelled, consult a dictionary.

ONE WORD:	ballplayer
	shortstop
	footstep
	earthquake
SEPARATE WORDS:	seat belt
	sweet potato
	waiting room
	time limit
WITH HYPHENS:	son-in-law
	secretary-treasurer
	great-grandmother
	six-year-olds

► **More Practice**

Grammar Exercise Workbook
• pp. 169–170
On-line Exercise Bank
• Section 26.5

Go on-line:
PHSchool.com
Enter Web Code:
ebk-7002

▼ **Critical Viewing**
What compound words would you use to describe the girl in this picture? **[Describe]**

Compound modifiers follow a different rule.

> **KEY CONCEPT** Use a hyphen to connect a compound modifier that comes before a noun. ■

In a compound modifier, the hyphen shows that the first modifier describes the second modifier, not the noun.

EXAMPLES: The team used a *full-court* press to slow down the opposing players.
The seven *well-fed* puppies curled up together for a nap.

Sometimes, a compound modifier comes after a noun. Generally, no hyphen is needed in this situation.

BEFORE: The *never-ending* sound of cheering thrilled the players.

AFTER: The sound of cheering was *never ending*.

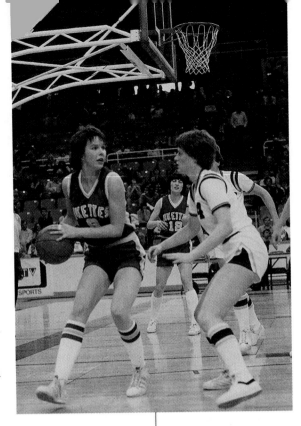

▲ **Critical Viewing** What compound modifiers might you use to describe the action pictured here? **[Describe]**

It is wise, however, to consult a dictionary when you use compound modifiers after nouns.

EXAMPLES: The *happy-go-lucky* goalie rarely worries.
The goalie is *happy-go-lucky*.

You should also remember a final rule when you write compound modifiers:

> **KEY CONCEPT** Do not use a hyphen with a compound modifier that includes a word ending in -*ly*, or in a compound proper adjective or a compound proper noun acting as an adjective. ■

INCORRECT: poorly-written letter South-American tourist
CORRECT: poorly written letter South American tourist

▶ **Exercise 59** Using Hyphens With Word Parts and Compound Words Decide whether hyphens are needed in the phrases below. If a phrase is correct as it is, write *correct*. If a phrase needs hyphenation, rewrite it correctly.

EXAMPLE: an old fashioned story

ANSWER: an old-fashioned story

1. a first round draft pick
2. during the mid season playoffs
3. a mass-produced product
4. a two time champion
5. the all star team
6. a sports oriented family
7. the ten week season of games
8. an All American choice
9. the off-season games
10. WNBA licensed merchandise

Rules for Dividing Words at the End of a Line

Hyphens serve a useful purpose when they are used to divide words at the ends of lines. They should not, however, be used more often than is necessary. Following are several rules that determine how to divide a word at the end of a line.

The first rule for dividing words at the end of a line is the most important rule for you to remember and use whenever you divide words:

▶ **KEY CONCEPT** If a word must be divided, always divide it between syllables. ■

EXAMPLE: The coach's pep talks, usually quite inspir-
             ing, are often characterized by wild hand ges-
             tures and frequent shouts.

In addition to the preceding rule, other details also affect word division. As the following example indicates, a hyphen used to divide a word should never be placed at the beginning of the second line. It must be placed at the end of the first line.

INCORRECT: To make one large room, knock down this par
             -tition.

CORRECT: To make one large room, knock down this par-
             tition.

More Practice

Grammar Exercise Workbook
• pp. 169–170
On-line Exercise Bank
• Section 26.5
  Go on-line:
  PHSchool.com
  Enter Web Code:
  ebk-7002

Get instant feedback! Exercise 59 is available on-line or on CD-ROM.

▶ **KEY CONCEPT** One-syllable words should never be divided, even if they seem long or look like two-syllable words. ■

INCORRECT: fif-th   brow-se   stra-ight
CORRECT: fifth   browse   straight

When a one-syllable word does not fit at the end of a line, just leave the space and write the word, without a hyphen, on the next line.

If you are uncertain about the division of syllables in a specific word, consult a dictionary.

▶ **KEY CONCEPT** Avoid dividing a word so that a single letter stands alone. ■

The following words are correctly broken into syllables. They should usually not, however, be divided at the end of a line.

SYLLABLES: i-dle   a-lone   ink-y

▶ **KEY CONCEPT** Avoid dividing proper nouns or proper adjectives. ■

POOR: Eliza-beth   Ger-man
BETTER: Elizabeth   German

▶ **KEY CONCEPT** Divide a hyphenated word only immediately following the existing hyphen. ■

INCORRECT: It was a post-sea-
              son soccer game.
CORRECT: It was a post-
              season soccer game.

▶ Critical Viewing How is the defender trying to divide the striker's attention? [Analyze]

▶ **Exercise 60** Using Hyphens to Divide Words If a word in the list below can be divided, write the part of the word that would appear at the end of a line. If a word should not be divided, write the complete word.

EXAMPLE: exhaust

ANSWER: ex-

1. backboard
2. net
3. mass-produced
4. scrimmage
5. game

6. defense
7. uniform
8. winning
9. teammate
10. Comets

More Practice

Grammar Exercise
Workbook
• pp. 169–70
On-line Exercise Bank
• Section 26.5
  Go on-line:
  PHSchool.com
  Enter Web Code:
  ebk-7002

Get instant feedback!
Exercise 60 is available
on-line or on CD-ROM.

Using Apostrophes to Form Possessives of Nouns

Use apostrophes with nouns to show ownership.

▶ **KEY CONCEPT** Add an apostrophe and *s* to show the possessive case of most singular nouns. ∎

EXAMPLES: The bat *of the player* becomes the *player's* bat.
              The idea *of Coach Long* becomes *Coach Long's* idea.

Even when a singular noun already ends in *s*, an apostrophe and *s* should usually be added to show possession.

EXAMPLES: The shape *of the lens* becomes the *lens's* shape.
              The fastball *of Jen Wells* becomes *Jen Wells's* fastball.
              The impact *of loss* becomes the *loss's* impact.

▶ **KEY CONCEPT** Add just an apostrophe to show the possessive case of plural nouns ending in *s* or *es*. ∎

EXAMPLES: The flavor *of the strawberries* becomes the *strawberries'* flavor.
              The buzzing *of the bees* becomes the *bees'* buzzing.

Forming the possessive of plural nouns that do not already end in *s* requires a different rule.

KEY CONCEPT Add an apostrophe and *s* to show the possessive case of plural nouns that do not end in *s* or *es.* ∎

EXAMPLES: The tournament *of women* becomes the *women's* tournament.

The game *of the children* becomes the *children's* game.

The following two steps can help you decide where to place the apostrophe and whether an *s* is needed when you form possessives. First, determine the owner of the quality or object involved. Ask yourself, "To whom does it belong?" Second, if the answer to this question is a singular noun, follow the rule for forming singular possessives. If the answer is a plural noun, follow the rules for forming plural possessives.

If you wish to use the phrase *the mountains beauty*, ask yourself, "To what does the beauty belong?" If the answer is "the mountain," then the possessive is singular: *the mountain's beauty.* If the answer is "the mountains," then the possessive is plural: *the mountains' beauty.*

▼ Critical Viewing What possessive nouns might you use to describe a volleyball team? **[Describe]**

Exercise 61 Using Apostrophes to Form Possessives of Nouns The first ten of the following nouns are singular. The last ten are plural. Make two columns on your paper, labeled as in the example. Then, write the correct possessive form for each word in the appropriate column.

EXAMPLE: volleyball player

ANSWER: <u>Singular</u>   <u>Plural</u>
volleyball player's

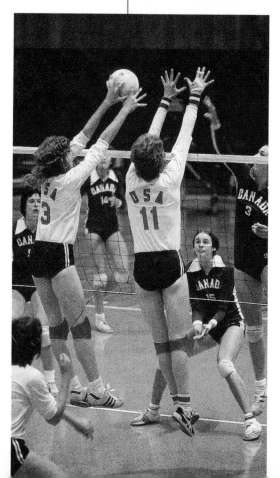

1. trainer
2. team
3. racket
4. swimmer
5. muscle
6. toss
7. track
8. champion
9. game
10. skate

11. gymnasts
12. softballs
13. athletes
14. feet
15. goals
16. trophies
17. coaches
18. skis
19. teeth
20. races

Using Apostrophes With Pronouns

Both indefinite pronouns and personal pronouns can indicate possession. Here are two rules to follow to show possession:

▶ **KEY CONCEPT** Use an apostrophe and *s* with indefinite pronouns to show possession. ■

EXAMPLES: everyone's plan   each one's decision
somebody's book   one another's ideas

▶ **KEY CONCEPT** Do *not* use an apostrophe with possessive personal pronouns. ■

The following personal pronouns show possession: *my, mine, your, yours, his, her, hers, its, our, ours, their,* and *theirs.* Some of these pronouns are generally used as adjectives.

EXAMPLES: *Your* batting stance is unusual.
Carrie broke *her* glasses.

Others can be used as subjects, direct objects, and subject complements.

EXAMPLES: *Yours* is a good idea.
Give me *mine.*
This jacket is *his.*

Whatever the use, a possessive personal pronoun should never include an apostrophe.

▶ **Exercise 62** Using Apostrophes With Pronouns Rewrite each of the following sentences, replacing the blank(s) with the possessive forms of appropriate indefinite pronouns or personal pronouns.

EXAMPLE: They borrowed ___?___ jackets.
ANSWER: They borrowed each other's jackets.

1. When she was eight, Olympic champion Dorothy Hamill received the first pair of ice skates that were really ___?___ .
2. ___?___ father saw how much ___?___ little girl enjoyed skating, so he decided she could take lessons.
3. Soon Dorothy and ___?___ mom were adjusting ___?___ schedules to include daily practice at the ice rink.
4. Dorothy learned quickly, and soon ___?___ skating skills were as good as ___?___ .
5. In ___?___ estimation, she was bound for success.

▶ **More Practice**

Grammar Exercise Workbook
• pp. 171–172
On-line Exercise Bank
• Section 26.5
Go on-line:
PHSchool.com
Enter Web Code:
ebk-7002

Get instant feedback! Exercises 61 and 62 are available on-line or on CD-ROM.

Using Apostrophes
With Contractions

Contractions are shortened forms of words or phrases.

▶ **KEY CONCEPT** Use an apostrophe in a contraction to indicate the position of a missing letter or letters. ■

Contractions are often used in informal speaking and writing. For example, instead of saying, "I am ready," most people would probably say, "I'm ready."

The following chart shows some of the many contractions formed with verbs:

COMMON CONTRACTIONS WITH VERBS		
Verb + *not*	are not (aren't) is not (isn't) was not (wasn't) were not (weren't) cannot (can't)	could not (couldn't) did not (didn't) do not (don't) should not (shouldn't) would not (wouldn't)
Pronoun + the Verb *will*	I will (I'll) you will (you'll) he will (he'll) she will (she'll)	we will (we'll) they will (they'll) who will (who'll)
Pronoun or Noun + the Verb *be*	I am (I'm) you are (you're) he is (he's) she is (she's) it is (it's)	we are (we're) they are (they're) who is (who's) where is (where's) Andy is (Andy's)
Pronoun or Noun + the Verb *would*	I would (I'd) you would (you'd) he would (he'd) she would (she'd)	we would (we'd) they would (they'd) who would (who'd) Penny would (Penny'd)

In a contraction, the exact position of the missing letter or letters is indicated by the apostrophe.

INCORRECT: did'nt   th'eyd
CORRECT: didn't   they'd

Remember that you should avoid using contractions in formal speaking or writing.

INFORMAL WRITING: *What's* the solution?
FORMAL WRITING: *What is* the solution?

GRAMMAR IN
LITERATURE

from **Golden Girls: The 1998 U.S. Women's Hockey Team**
Johnette Howard

Notice the contractions the writer has used in this passage. What word group does each contraction represent?

Sportswriters walked into the final grousing about having to cover it and walked out gushing that it was the best thing *they'd* ever seen. A felicitous line by *Washington Post* columnist Michael Wilbon, who called Mleczko "the first leftwinger *I've* ever had a crush on," was typical.

▶ **Exercise 63** **Using Apostrophes With Contractions** On your paper, write each of the underlined word groups as a contraction.

EXAMPLE: <u>They are</u> leaving at five.

ANSWER: They're

1. <u>Who would</u> have imagined that after only four years on skates, Dorothy Hamill would win the Novice Division at the National Championships?
2. I <u>was not</u> aware that Dorothy trained in Toronto, Canada, for one summer.
3. I <u>cannot</u> believe that the following January, Dorothy won the Eastern Championship in the Junior Division.
4. At Nationals the next month, Dorothy <u>could not</u> believe it when they announced <u>she had</u> won the school figures.
5. She knew <u>she would</u> do well on her freestyle program because she loved doing it the most.
6. She <u>did not</u> place first overall but took second place at the age of thirteen.
7. Dorothy <u>would not</u> be competing as a Junior again since <u>she had</u> passed the test qualifying her as a Senior Lady.
8. People <u>were not</u> too surprised when Dorothy took fifth place at the 1971 Nationals as a Senior Lady.
9. Dorothy, <u>who is</u> remembered most for her 1976 gold medal performance in Innsbruck, won many more competitions.
10. <u>She will</u> always be remembered for her classy skating, her bright smile, and her famous hairdo.

▶ **More Practice**

Grammar Exercise Workbook
• pp. 173–174
On-line Exercise Bank
• Section 26.5
  Go on-line:
  PHSchool.com
  Enter Web Code:
  ebk-7002

Get instant feedback! Exercise 63 is available on-line or on CD-ROM.

> **Exercise 64** Writing Sentences Using Apostrophes
Correctly Write a sentence in which you use the possessive
form of each of the following nouns. Check to see that you
have used apostrophes correctly in each sentence.

1. goalie	11. swimmers
2. golf club	12. softballs
3. tennis star	13. athletes
4. winner	14. professional athlete
5. team	15. competition
6. stadium	16. skiers
7. track	17. coaches
8. champions	18. racket
9. contest	19. bobsledders
10. skates	20. races

> **Exercise 65** Revising to Use Apostrophes Correctly
Rewrite the paragraph below, adding apostrophes where they
are needed.

(1) Gymnastics became the most important thing in the life
of Romanias Nadia Comaneci. (2) Gymnastics was part of
everyones curriculum at her school. (3) Nadias parents knew
shed like gymnastics because she was always running and
jumping. (4) Soon, her skills were better than everyone elses in
her class. (5) Her teachers often heard classmates complaints.
(6) They would say, "Its not fair. Nadia always beats us." (7)
When she entered the National Championship of Romania at
the age of eight, Nadia was the tournaments youngest com-
petitor. (8) Nadia placed thirteenth that year, but she wasnt
happy with her performance. (9) By the next year, shed
improved greatly and the championship medal was hers.
(10) Nadia wouldnt lose in a Romanian competition again.
(11) Nadias trophy case began to fill with medals from international competitions. (12) By early 1976, shed become the best
gymnast in the world. (13) At the 1976 Olympics in Montreal,
Canada, Nadias name was on every fans lips. (14) The tiny
fourteen-year-old carefully followed her coachs advice.
(15) She did so well that she was first on all of the judges
cards.

> **More Practice**

Grammar Exercise Workbook
• pp. 173–174
On-line Exercise Bank
• Section 26.5
  Go on-line:
  PHSchool.com
  Enter Web Code:
  ebk-7002

Get instant feedback!
Exercises 64 and 65
are available on-line
or on CD-ROM.

Section Review

GRAMMAR EXERCISES 66–73

Exercise 66 Using Hyphens in Numbers Write out each number, adding hyphens where needed.

1. 21   2. 17   3. 64   4. 300   5. 33

Exercise 67 Using Hyphens With Word Parts and Compound Words If a phrase below needs hyphenation, rewrite it correctly. If a phrase is correct as it is, write *correct* on your paper.

1. third leading scorer
2. story that was basketball related
3. up to the minute scores
4. poorly thrown pass
5. world class players

Exercise 68 Using Hyphens to Divide Words If a word below can be divided, write the part that would appear at the end of a line. If the word cannot be divided, write the complete word.

1. playing
2. spectators
3. award-winning
4. mini-rounds
5. professional
6. award
7. Monarchs
8. scoring
9. coach
10. rebound

Exercise 69 Using Apostrophes to Form Possessives of Nouns Write the possessive form of each noun below.

1. crowd
2. judges
3. women
4. gymnasts
5. apparatus
6. competitors
7. fan
8. goalie
9. winners
10. James

Exercise 70 Revising to Add Apostrophes and Hyphens Rewrite the paragraph below, adding apostrophes and hyphens where they are needed.

(1) Tara Lipinskis figure skating career started at age three. (2) It didnt begin on blades, however. (3) She was a roller skating champ before shed ever thought about ice skating. (4) At age six, Tara tried skating on ice and wasnt successful at first. (5) She ignored her friends laughter as she flopped on the ice. (6) Within 45 minutes, Taras natural ability took over. (7) Soon, to everyones amazement, she was skating forward and backward. (8) She quickly got her parents permission to take lessons. (9) Tara proved there wasnt any jump she couldn't do. (10) In 1998, she won the Womens Figure Skating gold medal.

Exercise 71 Find It in Your Reading Explain why hyphens and apostrophes are used in this passage from Johnette Howard's "Golden Girls."

In winning the six-team inaugural women's Olympic tournament with a 6–0 record, the U.S. team eclipsed Picabo Street as America's feel-good story of the Winter Games.

Exercise 72 Find It in Your Writing Review your work to find five examples of possessive nouns. Check to see that you've punctuated them correctly, and make any necessary corrections.

Exercise 73 Writing Application Find out about a famous female athlete. Write a biography that includes possessive nouns and contractions.

Chapter Review

GRAMMAR EXERCISES 74–83

▶ **Exercise 74** Revising the Use of **End Marks** Revise these sentences, correcting end marks where necessary.

1. Why did Philip Wrigley establish strict rules for players in the All-American Girls Professional Baseball League.
2. He wanted to show the public that women could be athletic and charming!
3. Wow. The players had so many rules!
4. They received a beauty kit as well as a handbook to reinforce good grace?
5. That's unbelievable?

▶ **Exercise 75** Revising the Use of **Commas** Revise the following, adding or deleting commas where necessary.

1. Originally softball was an indoor sport but in 1895, outdoor games began.
2. Pitcher shortstop, and center fielder are all, positions in softball.
3. The inside of a softball is made with a rubbery stretchy material.
4. The Amateur, Softball Association sets rules so umpires join the association.
5. Some guidelines for slow-pitch softball, include ten players a 12-inch ball and no base stealing.

▶ **Exercise 76** Revising the Use of **Commas** Revise the following, adding or deleting commas where necessary.

1. In gymnastics four, main events are judged I believe.
2. Sue did you know that on the uneven, bars gymnasts must stay in motion?
3. If gymnasts use the whole length of the balance beam their scores go up.
4. Rhythmic gymnastics which involves

holding an object and dancing isn't as popular as traditional gymnastics.
5. The balance beam the best-known apparatus is only four inches wide.

▶ **Exercise 77** Using Commas in **Dates and Places** Write the dates and places in each sentence, adding needed commas.

1. On December 8 1941 the United States entered World War II, and many male baseball players went to war.
2. Philip Wrigley turned to women and formed the All-American Girls Baseball League on February 17 1943.
3. Tryouts were held at Wrigley Field Chicago Illinois.
4. Players came from places such as Red Hill Pennsylvania and Popular Point Manitoba Canada.
5. The Racine Belles from Racine Wisconsin won the 1946 championship on Monday September 16 by just one run.

▶ **Exercise 78** Using Semicolons Replace the comma and conjunction with a semicolon in the sentences below.

1. Bela Karolyi was excited, for he wanted to coach Svetlana Boginskaya.
2. Svetlana was only twenty-three, but she was one of the oldest competitors.
3. When she was little, Svetlana hated following rules, and her parents wanted her to learn a disciplined sport.
4. As Svetlana grew, the skills became more difficult, and practicing also seemed monotonous and routine.
5. Svetlana stuck with gymnastics longer than many other young women, and she became a world champion.

▶ **Exercise 79** Using Colons Add colons where appropriate.

1. There are four events in women's gymnastics balance beam, floor exercise, vault, and uneven bars.
2. **Warning** Beware of Slippery Bars
3. Dominique Moceanu's success involves many things her discipline, her genes, her tenacity, and her positive attitude.
4. Dominique trained in many states Illinois, Florida, California, and Texas.
5. Dear Ms. Moceanu

▶ **Exercise 80** Revising to Apply All Punctuation Rules Revise the following passage, adding, deleting, and correcting punctuation marks where necessary. Also, begin new paragraphs wherever necessary.

(1) During the documentary the commentator said of Olga Korbut; Besides the difficult stunts she had an expression of joy, as she performed! (2) He added before Olga you couldn't sell a thousand tickets to a gymnastics event? (3) Nadia Comaneci scored even, higher than Olga he continued but she did not have as much impact on the sport. (4) Generations of gymnasts were inspired by Olga pointed out one of those interviewed during the one hour special; (5) Those gymnasts included Mary Lou Retton the gold medal champion in the womens all-around in 1984. (6) Mary Lou Retton had the same coach as Nadia Comaneci, Bela Karolyi the announcer informed the audience (7) Can you imagine having two such, accomplished students! (8) After the announcer made this remark the program traced Retton's career and her connection to Karolyi. (9) The program concluded with a tribute to the womens team of 1996? (10) I found the program so interesting; that I taped it and watched it, again.

▶ **Exercise 81** Adding Quotation Marks and Underlining Write the titles below on your paper, adding quotation marks or underlining them.

1. A book called The Development and Decline of the All-American Girls Professional Baseball League, 1943–1954 is a great source of statistics and rules.
2. In the chapter Life in the League, readers get a glimpse into how the players lived their lives on and off the field.
3. Magazines such as Life and Esquire wrote articles about the AAGPBL.
4. Phil Stack mocked the hard-working female baseball players through his short poem All-American Babe.
5. A TV documentary entitled When Diamonds Were a Girl's Best Friend aired in 1987.

▶ **Exercise 82** Using Hyphens and Apostrophes Rewrite these sentences, adding needed hyphens or apostrophes.

1. One fourth of the AAGPBL championships were won by Fort Waynes Daisies.
2. Jean Faut, one of the leagues best players, was twenty one years old when she began playing.
3. While they were poorly paid professional athletes, AAGPBL players salaries were increased if they made the all star team.
4. Angie Pottholf of the Lynx basketball team is involved in D.A.R.E., an anti drug educational program for children.
5. Her coach believes shes a terrific role model because she isnt selfish.

▶ **Exercise 83** Writing Application Write a dialogue that you might have if you could interview a famous woman athlete. Proofread your work carefully for correct punctuation of dialogue.

Standardized Test Preparation Workshop

Punctuation

Some standardized tests include items that test your knowledge of punctuation rules. Most often, this testing involves identifying errors in punctuation. Remember these basic rules to help you identify such errors:

- End marks denote the end of a sentence and will identify the type of sentence. Use a period to end a declarative or imperative sentence, a question mark to end an interrogative sentence, and an exclamation mark to end an exclamatory sentence.

- Use commas to separate items in a series; after introductory words, phrases, or clauses at the beginning of a sentence; and to set off nonessential elements from the rest of the sentence.

- Quotation marks enclose direct quotations—a person's exact speech or thoughts.

- Abbreviations and titles of people end with a period.

Test Tip

Remember this exception: Postal abbreviations for states always have two capital letters and use no punctuation.

Sample Test Items	Answers and Explanations

Directions: Identify which, if any, part of each sentence contains a punctuation error.
 	
1 A The rain, the cold,
  B and the fog,
  C made this winter bitter and dreary.
  D (No mistake)
	The correct answer for item 1 is *B.* There should be no comma between the last item in the series and the verb.

Directions: Read this passage, and decide which type of error, if any, appears in the underlined section.
 	
The <u>rush hour</u> traffic in New York City <u>prevented him</u> from making it to his meeting in Boston.
 	
2 A Spelling error
  B Capitalization error
  C Punctuation error
  D No error
	The correct answer for item 2 is *C.* There should be a hyphen between *rush* and *hour* because the two words are being used together as a compound adjective.

> **Practice 1** **Directions:** Read this passage, and decide which type of error, if any, appears in the underlined section.

My father Dr, Esteban, was ecstatic to
 (1)

read that Tiger Woods had once again been

named Athlete of the Year. I knew he was
 (2)

great! dad exclaimed as he rushed into our
(3)

house with the newspaper.
 (4)

He excitedly, told us that Woods would
 (5)

now be in a prestigious group of two time-

winners, including Michael Jordan, Sandy
 (6)

Koufax, and Carl Lewis. He then sped back

across our street, Mitchell Rd., to alert the

neighborhood!
 (7)

1 A Spelling error
B Capitalization error
C Punctuation error
D No error

2 F Spelling error
G Capitalization error
H Punctuation error
J No error

3 A Spelling error
B Capitalization error
C Punctuation error
D No error

4 F Spelling error
G Capitalization error
H Punctuation error
J No error

5 A Spelling error
B Capitalization error
C Punctuation error
D No error

6 F Spelling error
G Capitalization error
H Punctuation error
J No error

7 A Spelling error
B Capitalization error
C Punctuation error
D No error

> **Practice 2** **Directions:** Identify which, if any, part of each sentence contains a punctuation error.

1 A That was one of the most
B gripping, nail biting
C games I have ever attended.
D (No mistake)

2 F When I left the game
G it was tied;
H I discovered who won when I got home.
J (No mistake)

3 A The game lasted for four hours,
B and by the time it ended,
C it was past midnight.
D (No mistake)

4 What punctuation rule explains the use of commas in this sentence: He then sped back across our street, Mitchell Rd., to alert the neighborhood!
F use commas to separate items in a series
G use commas to set apart parts of an address
H use commas to set apart nonessential elements in a clause
J None–they are incorrectly used in this sentence.

Capital letters are used to indicate important words. A beginning of a sentence or quotation, the word *I*, proper nouns and adjectives, a person's name, and titles are examples of words that are capitalized.

EXAMPLE: In my history class, I am learning about Queen Victoria of England.

In fact, a sentence without capitals can be somewhat confusing.

EXAMPLE: The slaterville art festival will show paintings by picasso from ann wilke's private collection.

When capitals are added, the sentence is easier to understand.

EXAMPLE: The Slaterville Art Festival will show paintings by Picasso from Ann Wilke's private collection.

▲ **Critical Viewing** Elizabeth II was born Elizabeth Alexandra Mary Windsor. By what title is she best known? How would you capitalize it? [**Connect**]

Diagnostic Test

Directions: Write all answers on a separate sheet of paper.

Skill Check A. Each of the following sentences contains one or more words that should be capitalized. On your paper, rewrite the words, adding the missing capitals.

1. Studying british royalty can be confusing, i think.
2. in history I, a few of the rulers we studied were henry VIII, william the conqueror, elizabeth I, and queen victoria.
3. michael and i decided to study william I, while my brother chose to study george III.
4. i learned that william I was crowned on christmas day, 1066.
5. land was given to the normans, the french, and the flemish allies in exchange for their military duties.
6. william used bishop lanfranc, archbishop of canterbury, to administer his government when he was in france.
7. the treaty of abernethy in 1072 marked a truce between scotland's king malcolm iii and william.
8. the church of england was reorganized by lanfranc.
9. churches such as canterbury and durham cathedrals were built during this time.
10. landowners pledged their allegiance to william in the oath of salisbury.

Skill Check B. Rewrite each of the following titles, adding the missing capitals.

11. the story of britain   book
12. "down by the salley gardens"   short poem
13. the market cart   painting
14. the daily mirror   newspaper
15. paradise lost   long poem

Skill Check C. Rewrite the following sentences, correcting all errors in capitalization. If the sentence contains no capitalization errors, write *correct*.

16. aunt Dolly and uncle Pete went to england last month.
17. mom and dad decided to go with them.
18. During their visit, they saw the duke of Edinburgh.
19. He was riding in a parade with the queen mother.
20. My aunt and uncle, along with my mom and dad, spent the day at Trafalgar Square.
21. At three o'clock the next day, they met professor Nevis, who took them on a tour of the houses of parliament.
22. Lord and Lady Seymour sponsored a coronation ball.
23. The first dance was led by a prince.
24. A princess and judge Williams soon joined in.
25. Their postcard began, "dear gary, We wish you were here."

Using Capitals for Sentences and the Word *I*

Every sentence must begin with a capital letter. The word *I* must also be capitalized every time you use it.

Sentences The first word in a sentence must begin with a capital.

▶ **KEY CONCEPT** Capitalize the first word in declarative, interrogative, imperative, and exclamatory sentences. ■

DECLARATIVE: Several members of the royal family were impatiently waiting for the ceremony to begin.

INTERROGATIVE: Isn't anyone going to start?

IMPERATIVE: Bow deeply when introduced to the Queen.

EXCLAMATORY: What an unusual day this is!

There are also situations, especially in informal writing, in which only a part of a sentence is written out. A capital letter is still required for the first word in each partial sentence.

EXAMPLES: Where?   For how much?   Never!

▶ **Exercise 1** Using Capitals to Begin Sentences Copy the following items onto your paper, adding the missing capitals.

EXAMPLE: what do you know about the kings of England?
ANSWER: What do you know about the kings of England?

1. do you know who the first king of England was?
2. no, who was it?
3. after defeating the Mercians at the Battle of Ellandun, Egbert of Wessex became king in A.D. 825.
4. alfred the Great ruled all of England that wasn't occupied by the Danes in A.D. 886.
5. athelstan, the grandson of Alfred, was the first monarch to have his likeness officially reproduced on coins.
6. he was very much entitled to his reputation as a great warrior.
7. he defeated a combined force of Scots, Welsh, and Vikings in one battle.
8. collecting jewelry, art, and relics was how Athelstan liked to spend his social time.
9. the period from A.D. 959 to A.D. 975 was referred to as the reign of Edgar the Peaceable.
10. edgar's great-grandfather was Alfred the Great.

Theme: Great Britain

In this chapter, you will learn the rules of capitalization. The examples and exercises are about the history of Great Britain.

Cross-Curricular Connection: Social Studies

↻ Learn More

For additional information about capitalizing sentences, see Chapter 19: Basic Sentence Parts.

The Word *I* The word *I* must be capitalized wherever it appears.

KEY CONCEPT Always capitalize the word *I*. ■

EXAMPLE: *I* watched the clock while *I* waited for you.

Exercise 2 Capitalizing the Word *I* Copy the following sentences, adding the missing capitals.

EXAMPLE: she and i have always been friends.
ANSWER: She and I have always been friends.

1. kelly and i are doing a report on Queen Victoria.
2. i didn't know she ruled for more than sixty-three years.
3. The Queen was rather stern, i think.
4. i learned that she was only eighteen years old when she became queen.
5. kelly asked if i could find more information on her nine children.

Using Capitals for Proper Nouns

An important use of capitals is to show that a word is a proper noun. It names a specific person, place, or thing.

KEY CONCEPT Capitalize all proper nouns. ■

Names of People The name of a specific person is perhaps the most common kind of proper noun.

KEY CONCEPT Capitalize each part of a person's full name, including initials. ■

EXAMPLES: Margaret Rose Windsor
              L. T. Cornwall

More Practice

Grammar Exercise Workbook
• pp. 175–176
On-line Exercise Bank
• Chapter 27
  Go on-line:
  PHSchool.com
  Enter Web Code:
  ebk-7002

iText

Get instant feedback! Exercises 1 and 2 are available on-line or on CD-ROM.

▶ Critical Viewing As a young woman, before she was crowned Queen of England, what was most likely Victoria's title? How would you capitalize it? **[Speculate]**

Geographical Places The names of geographical places are also proper nouns.

▶ **KEY CONCEPT** Capitalize geographical names. ■

According to this rule, any place that can be found on a map should be capitalized. The following chart includes examples of different kinds of geographical names that need to be capitalized.

GEOGRAPHICAL NAMES	
Streets	Avenue of the Americas, Wildflower Drive
Towns and Cities	Freeville, Youngstown, Cairo
Counties	Dade County, Cook County
States and Provinces	Nebraska, Alberta
Nations	India, Spain, United States of America
Continents	North America, Antarctica, Asia
Valleys and Deserts	Death Valley, Kalahari Desert
Mountains	Cascade Range, Pike's Peak, Mount Everest
Sections of a Country	Gulf Coastal Plain, Northeast, South
Islands	Corsica, Balearic Islands
Scenic Spots	Grand Canyon, Riviera
Rivers and Falls	Danube, Colorado River, Victoria Falls
Lakes and Bays	Lake Champlain, Bay of Biscay
Seas and Oceans	Red Sea, Arctic Ocean

A compass point, such as south or northeast, is capitalized only when it names a specific geographical location. When a compass point refers to a direction, it is not capitalized.

EXAMPLES: The South is experiencing a serious drought.
Drive south for three miles, and you will arrive at the castle.

Technology Tip

Many towns and cities have Web sites that give information about the location's history, cultural events, and tourist attractions. Use the name of a place in a keyword search to get information about the place.

Other Proper Nouns Names of specific events and time periods also need to be capitalized.

▶ **KEY CONCEPT** Capitalize the names of specific events and periods of time. ■

The following chart contains examples of events and periods of time that require capitalization.

SPECIFIC EVENTS AND TIMES	
Historical Periods	Age of Enlightenment, Mesozoic Era, Middle Ages
Historical Events	World War II, Boston Tea Party
Documents	Declaration of Independence, Treaty of Paris
Days	Wednesday, Saturday
Months	December, October
Holidays	Washington's Birthday, Thanksgiving Day, Labor Day
Religious Days	Christmas, Passover, Ramadan
Special Events	Fiddlers' Convention, Boston Marathon

The names of seasons are an exception to the rule. Seasons of the year, despite the fact that they name a specific time of year, are not capitalized unless they are part of a title such as an event.

EXAMPLES: The most popular color this fall is rust.
This book is about a girl who travels in the summer.
Winter Carnival, Fall Fun Fair

Other proper nouns that need capitals are those that name specific groups.

▶ **KEY CONCEPT** Capitalize the names of various organizations, government bodies, political parties, and nationalities, as well as the languages spoken by different groups. ■

EXAMPLES: The ambassador attended the first session of the Austrian Parliament.
She delivered a brief address in German and received warm applause.

Learn More

For additional information about proper nouns, see Chapter 14.

SPECIFIC GROUPS	
Clubs Organizations Institutions Businesses	Kiwanis Club National Governor's Association Massachusetts Institute of Technology Chemstrand Corporation
Government Bodies Political Parties	Congress, Supreme Court Democrats, Republican Party
Nationalities	Chinese, German, Nigerian, Iranian
Languages Spoken by Different Groups	English, Spanish, Italian, Swahili, Dutch

The proper nouns shown in the preceding chart are groups with which many people are familiar. All specific groups, however, must be capitalized, even if they are not well known.

In order to show respect, you should also use capitals for the names of the religions of the world and other related words.

▶ **KEY CONCEPT** Capitalize references to religions, deities, and religious scriptures. ■

The following chart presents a list of five of the world's major religions. Next to each religion are examples of some of the related religious words that you must be sure to capitalize in your writing.

RELIGIOUS REFERENCES	
Christianity	God, Lord, Father, Son, Holy Spirit, Bible, books of the Bible (Genesis, Deuteronomy, Psalms, and so on)
Judaism	God, Lord, Father, Prophets, Torah, Talmud, Midrash
Islam	Allah, Prophet, Mohammed, Koran
Hinduism	Brahma, Bhagavad Gita, Vedas
Buddhism	Buddha, Mahayana, Hinayana

Note in the following examples, however, that the words *god* and *goddess* in references to ancient mythology are not capitalized.

EXAMPLES: the god Jupiter
             the goddess Juno

▶ **KEY CONCEPT** Capitalize the names of specific places and items. ■

This final rule applies to proper nouns such as monuments, memorials, buildings, celestial bodies, awards, the names of specific vehicles, and trademarks.

The following chart gives examples of some of these special places and items that you should capitalize in your writing.

OTHER SPECIAL PLACES AND ITEMS	
Monuments	Statue of Liberty
Memorials	Winston Churchill Memorial
Buildings	Houston Museum of Fine Arts, Empire State Building
Celestial Bodies *(except the moon and sun)*	Earth, Milky Way, Jupiter, Aries
Awards	Newbery Award, Nobel Peace Prize
Air, Sea, Space, and Land Craft	*Spirit of St. Louis, Monitor, Voyager 2*
Trademarks	Krazy Korn, Zenox

▶ **Exercise 3** Capitalizing Proper Nouns Each of the following sentences contains one or more names that need to be capitalized. On your paper, rewrite the names, adding the missing capitals.

EXAMPLE: chris, have you studied the life of King richard I?
ANSWER: Chris, Richard

1. Our class is studying richard the Lion-Hearted.
2. thomas told the class that richard I spent only seven months of his ten-year reign in england.
3. The class invited william r. taras to come and give a lecture on the king of england.
4. k. c. miller and marie lopez wondered where richard spent his years as king.
5. mr. taras told us that besides spending a year on the Crusades, richard had been taken prisoner by the duke of Austria.

▶ **More Practice**

Grammar Exercise Workbook
• pp. 177–180
On-line Exercise Bank
• Chapter 27
Go on-line:
PHSchool.com
Enter Web Code:
ebk-7002

Get instant feedback! Exercise 3 is available on-line or on CD-ROM.

▶ **KEY CONCEPT** Capitalize the names of awards. ∎

Notice in the following examples that *the* is not capitalized.

EXAMPLES: the Academy Awards, the Fulbright Scholarship, the Pulitzer Prize, Eagle Scout

▶ **Exercise 4** **Capitalizing Other Proper Names** Each of the following sentences contains one or more proper nouns that need to be capitalized. On your paper, rewrite the proper nouns, adding the missing capitals.

EXAMPLE: Jane Addams won the nobel peace prize in 1931.

ANSWER: Nobel Peace Prize

1. During our trip to England, we learned a great deal about the country's history, and we even visited the tower of london.
2. We also visited buckingham palace and learned that it had been bombed on september 12, 1940, during world war II.
3. We also visited the house of commons and the house of lords, where Britain's political officers meet.
4. The two major political parties in the early nineteenth century were called whigs and tories.
5. By the second half of the century, the party names were changed to labor and conservative.

▶ **Exercise 5** **Using Capitals for Geographical Names** Rewrite each geographical name, adding the missing capitals.

EXAMPLE: The capital of england is london.

ANSWER: England, London

1. Richard I set off to recapture the holy city jerusalem from the Muslim leader Saladin.
2. He demolished Saladin's forces at acre, in palestine.
3. He also defeated Saladin at arsouf, near jaffa.
4. On his way home through europe, the duke of Austria captured Richard.
5. John, who became king after Richard was killed, was constantly at war with france, scotland, and his own people.

▼ **Critical Viewing** What word or words would you capitalize in a sentence about the country King Richard ruled? **[Relate]**

Using Capitals for Proper Adjectives

When a proper noun or a form of a proper noun is used to describe another noun, it is a proper adjective. As a proper adjective, it will generally need a capital letter.

▶ **KEY CONCEPT** Capitalize most proper adjectives. ■

EXAMPLES: Arabian stallion   Spanish rice
            Olympic champion   British monarch

Many proper adjectives are formed from the brand names of products.

▶ **KEY CONCEPT** Capitalize brand names used as adjectives. ■

EXAMPLES: Clearbright paint   Quickgrow grass seed

▶ **Exercise 6** Supplying Proper Adjectives On your paper, write a meaningful proper adjective to complete each of the following phrases. Be sure to capitalize the phrases correctly.

EXAMPLE: fashions
ANSWER: French fashions

1. ___?___ shampoo
2. ___?___ meatballs
3. ___?___ imports
4. ___?___ designer
5. ___?___ bread
6. ___?___ margarine
7. ___?___ music
8. ___?___ television
9. ___?___ potatoes
10. ___?___ cameras

▶ **Exercise 7** Capitalizing Proper Adjectives Capitalize the proper adjectives in the following sentences.
1. English artists were influenced by the italian artists of the fourteenth century.
2. Many works of art are on display at the tate Gallery in London.
3. We met french-, german-, and spanish-speaking visitors at the museum.
4. The elizabethan age brought about many changes in architecture.
5. The influences of european artists and architects can be seen in american art, as well.

▶ **More Practice**

Grammar Exercise Workbook
• pp. 181–182
On-line Exercise Bank
• Chapter 27
  Go on-line:
  PHSchool.com
  Enter Web Code:
  ebk-7002

 Text

Get instant feedback! Exercises 4, 5, 6, and 7 are available on-line or on CD-ROM.

Using Capitals for Titles of People

Two major rules govern capitals in people's titles.

Social and Processional Titles One rule covers titles used before names and in direct address.

> ▶ **KEY CONCEPT** Capitalize the title of a person when the title is followed by the person's name, when it is used in place of a person's name, or when it is used as an appositive. ■

The following chart shows several common titles.

TITLES OF PEOPLE	
Social	Mister, Madam or Madame, Miss, Sir
Business	Doctor, Professor, Superintendent
Religious	Reverend, Father, Rabbi, Bishop, Sister
Military	Private, Ensign, Captain, General, Admiral
Government	President, Secretary of State, Ambassador, Senator, Representative, Governor, Mayor

The following examples show four titles in use.

BEFORE A NAME: Detective O'Toole, Major Faulks, and Doctor Perkins have arrived.

IN DIRECT ADDRESS: Look, Sergeant, the fingerprints match!

AS AN APPOSITIVE: Charles, Prince of Wales, has arrived.

GRAMMAR IN LITERATURE

from King Arthur: The Marvel of the Sword
Mary MacLeod

Notice how capital letters are used with proper nouns that name people, places, and things in this passage.

When several years had passed, Merlin went to the Archbishop of Canterbury and counseled him to send for all the lords of the realm, and all the gentlemen of arms, that they should come to London at Christmas, and for this cause—that a miracle would show who should be rightly king of the realm.

✅ **Spelling Tip**

When writing names with numerals, such as King George I or John Smith III, always use Roman numerals, not Arabic numerals.

▶ **Exercise 8** Using Capitals for Social and Professional Titles Each of the following sentences contains a title before a name, in direct address, or as an appositive. Rewrite each title, adding the missing capital.

EXAMPLE: A monarch I recently studied was queen Elizabeth.
ANSWER: Queen

1. One day I said to my teacher, "Tell me, professor Holmes, who in the royal family interests you most?"
2. She told me about prince Charles.
3. Even when king George VI ruled, prime minister Winston Churchill was a government leader.
4. It was sir Winston Churchill who was prime minister during World War II.
5. One of the famous military leaders of England during World War II was general Montgomery.
6. During talks at Yalta, president Roosevelt, prime minister Churchill, and premier Joseph Stalin of Russia discussed ways to end the war.
7. Today, queen Elizabeth dedicates many hours to charitable organizations.
8. In 1996, her daughter, princess Anne, had no fewer than 609 public engagements for charitable events.
9. Queen Elizabeth's son Charles, prince of wales, also champions a number of national and world causes.
10. Charles's older son, prince William, was christened by the archbishop of Canterbury.

Titles for Family Relationships Another rule applies to titles for family relationships.

▶ **KEY CONCEPT** Capitalize titles showing family relationships when the title is used with the person's name or as the person's name. The title may also be capitalized in other situations when it refers to a specific person, except when the title comes after a possessive noun or pronoun. ■

BEFORE A NAME: We respect Uncle Frank's opinion.
IN PLACE OF A NAME: We haven't seen Grandmother in almost a year.
AFTER POSSESSIVES: Alan's father is the team's captain. No one knew my sister better.

Notice that the titles used in the last two examples are not capitalized because they are used after the possessive words *Alan's* and *my*.

More Practice

Grammar Exercise Workbook
• pp. 183–184
On-line Exercise Bank
• Chapter 27
Go on-line:
PHSchool.com
Enter Web Code:
ebk-7002

▲ **Critical Viewing** By what title might average English people address this woman? How would she be addressed by Princess Anne or by Prince William? **[Compare]**

Exercise 9 Using Capitals for Family Titles If a title in a sentence lacks a capital or if a title has been incorrectly capitalized, rewrite the title on your paper, correcting the error. If the sentence contains no error, write *correct*.

EXAMPLE: My sister and I are interested in British royalty.

ANSWER: correct

1. Do you like studying British royalty, mom?
2. No, but aunt Margaret enjoys it.
3. Her grandfather came from England.
4. Naturally, she and uncle Harold studied British history.
5. Their Mother met Lady Seymour.
6. Mother Stewart met her at a charity dinner.
7. Was your cousin Charles also at that dinner?
8. Did your Brother ever meet any royalty?
9. No, but his Sister-in-Law saw Prince William at a soccer tournament.
10. Sarah, my Grandmother, has this all written down in her personal journal.

▼ Critical Viewing
What family and professional titles might some of the people in this picture have? How would you capitalize the titles?
[Speculate]

Using Capitals for Titles of Things

Titles of certain things require capitals also.

Written Works and Works of Art The titles of different kinds of written works and works of art must always be capitalized.

KEY CONCEPT Capitalize the first word and all other important words in the titles of books, periodicals, poems, stories, plays, paintings, and other works of art. ■

Each word in a title of this kind should begin with a capital except for the articles (*a, an, the*). Articles and short prepositions or conjunctions should be capitalized only when they are used as the first or last word in a title.

EXAMPLES:
A Separate Peace
Press and Sun-Bulletin
Young Woman With a Water Jug
"The Man That Corrupted Hadleyburg"

Exercise 10 **Using Capitals for Written Works and Works of Art** Rewrite each of the following titles, adding the missing capitals.

EXAMPLE: "of missing persons"
ANSWER: "Of Missing Persons"

1. first knight   (movie)
2. "the wanderer"   (poem)
3. you come too   (book)
4. oliver twist   (book/movie)
5. effect of the sun on the water   (painting)
6. kidnapped   (book)
7. "pomp and circumstance"   (musical work)
8. the shrimp girl   (painting)
9. "the cat who thought she was a dog and the dog who thought he was a cat"   (short story)
10. the adventures of ulysses   (book)

School Courses The titles of certain courses must also be capitalized.

KEY CONCEPT Capitalize the title of a course when the course is a language or when the course is followed by a number. ■

EXAMPLES: French   History 3A   Math 203

Learn More

To practice responding to capitalization items in a standardized test format, use the Standardized Test Preparation Workshop on pages 652–653.

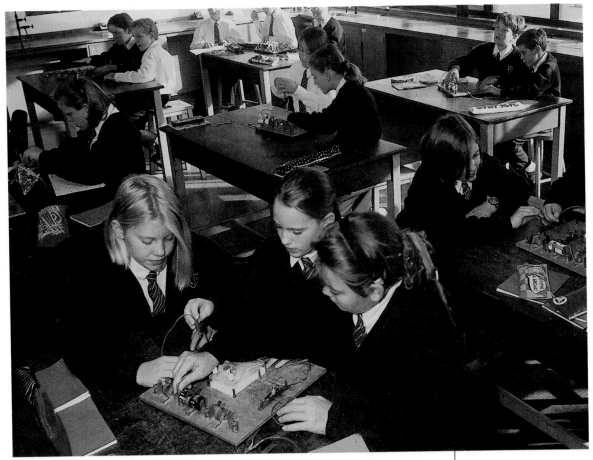

▲ **Critical Viewing** What subject is being studied by the students in this picture? Give an example of a sentence in which the name of the subject would be capitalized. **[Apply]**

▶ **Exercise 11** **Using Capitals for Courses** In each of the following sentences, choose the correctly written course title from the choices in parentheses and write it on your paper.

EXAMPLE: Lisa is a student in my (algebra, Algebra) class.
ANSWER: algebra

1. While studying (history I, History I), I became interested in English royalty.
2. Most royal children were required to learn (french, French), as well as other foreign languages.
3. Prince Charles studied (calculus, Calculus) at the Naval Academy.
4. Shakespeare's plays are studied today in (drama I, Drama I) classes.
5. The study of (Latin, latin) is beneficial for students studying biology and other sciences.

More Practice

Grammar Exercise Workbook
• pp. 185–186
On-line Exercise Bank
• Chapter 27
Go on-line:
PHSchool.com
Enter Web Code:
ebk-7002

Get instant feedback! Exercise 11 is available on-line or on CD-ROM.

Hands-on Grammar

Capitals Card Catalog

Help yourself remember the categories of words that are capitalized by creating a Capitals Card Catalog based on the word *capitals*.

For each letter in C A P I T A L S, cut out several large squares. Use paper of a different color for each letter, or use markers to draw a different colored border for each letter. Next, print one letter of CAPITALS in the middle of each of eight squares. Then, on a square matching the color for each letter, write the categories shown on the examples below. Finally, write several examples of capitalized words beneath each category.

Continue making cards for the remaining letters, using these categories: **I**—The pronoun *I*, Institutions; **T**—Titles, Trademarks, Times of the year (months, days, holidays); **A**—Abbreviations, Adjectives (proper); **L**—Languages; **S**—States, Specific groups, Sentence beginnings. If you think of other categories for a letter, make additional cards.

Find It in Your Reading   Look through a story or piece of non-fiction in your literature book, and see how many capitalized words you can find that fit into the categories in your Capitals Card Catalog. Add several of the words to your cards.

Find It in Your Writing   Review an essay in your portfolio, and note where you used capital letters. Are they used correctly? Into which categories do they fit? Add several of the words to your Capitals Card Catalog.

Chapter Review

GRAMMAR EXERCISES 12–19

> **Exercise 12** Using Capitals to
> **Begin Sentences** Copy any items onto
your paper that require capital letters. Add
the missing capitals.

1. the Queen Mother was born August 4, 1900.
2. the honorable Elizabeth Angela Marguerite Bowes-Lyon spent her childhood in Hertfordshire.
3. lady Elizabeth could speak fluent French by the age of ten.
4. world War I broke out on her fourteenth birthday.
5. her family's home was used as a hospital.
6. elizabeth and her older sisters were childhood friends of George V's children.
7. in January of 1923, she became engaged to Albert, Duke of York, second son of the king and queen.
8. she was married in Westminster Abbey on April 26, 1923.
9. in 1936, Albert ascended to the throne as George VI, and Elizabeth became queen.
10. after George VI died in 1952, his daughter Elizabeth became queen.

> **Exercise 13** Capitalizing
> **Geographical Names** Each of the following sentences contains one or more geographical names that need to be capitalized. On your paper, rewrite the names, adding the missing capitals.

1. Last summer, after we visited france, we decided to cross the north sea and visit great britain.
2. As we traveled up the thames river, we saw our first glimpse of the city of london.
3. We would be in london for only two

days before we traveled north to stratford-on-avon.
4. Also on the list of places to visit were canterbury, gloucester, and other cathedral towns.
5. The pennines, a mountain range in northern and central england, is the industrial center of the country.

> **Exercise 14** Capitalizing Other
> **Proper Nouns and Adjectives** Correct
the proper nouns and proper adjectives in
the following sentences. If a sentence has
no errors, write *correct*.

1. A civil war was fought to decide who should rule england.
2. Charles I and parliament could not agree about how money should be raised for the church of england.
3. Charles failed to get parliament's consent, and so many townspeople supported parliament.
4. At first, charles had better soldiers and leaders than parliament did.
5. Oliver cromwell, a huntingdon gentleman, reorganized the parliament's forces and defeated the King at marston moor and naseby.

> **Exercise 15** Using Capitals for
> **Titles of People, Works, and Things**
Capitalize and lowercase titles as needed
in the following sentences.

1. On October 10, 1951, princess Elizabeth visited Canada.
2. Her visit was reported in all the major newspapers, including *the toronto star.*
3. Her husband, the duke of Edinburgh, made the trip with her.
4. Although the public train service, run by rail canada, is extensive, the duke

and princess traveled by private car.
5. The princess and duke made their television debut while there.
6. Windsor's mayor Cabot appeared with them.
7. Among the welcoming party was the mayor of Detroit.
8. Two songs that were often played during the Royal Visit were "o canada" and "hail, britannia."
9. Canada is home to many fine writers, including author Margaret Atwood.
10. Atwood's novel *The Robber Bride* is set in Toronto.

Exercise 16 Proofreading Sentences to Eliminate Errors in Capitalization Rewrite the sentences, adding or changing capitals as needed. If the sentence has no errors, write *correct*.

1. Last month, i read a book about Prince Charles.
2. I learned that he was born November 14, 1948.
3. he became heir apparent and the duke of Cornwall when his mother became Queen.
4. My sister, Kiera, asked if i knew where he went to school.
5. I told her he went to Cheam and Gordonstoun.
6. she wondered if he also went to school in australia.
7. in my reading, i learned that he had gone to school in melbourne.
8. this was the first time a Royal Family member had attended an overseas school.
9. cambridge university was where charles studied Archaeology.
10. He graduated from Cambridge in 1970.

Exercise 17 Proofreading a Paragraph to Eliminate Capitalization Errors Find the capitalization errors in the following paragraph, and write them on your paper, capitalizing correctly.

(1) in History class, i learned that princess Anne was the second child of queen Elizabeth. (2) she was born august 15, 1950, at clarence house in london. (3) at the age of twelve, she went to france to live for one year. (4) the Professor told my friend and me about her engagement to captain mark phillips. (5) he was a member of the dragoon guards. (6) on november 14, 1973, they were married. (7) i told the professor i had some pictures of their wedding. (8) princess Anne and captain Phillips had two children. (9) while doing this research, i found information about her charity work. (10) she spends long hours raising money for many charities.

Exercise 18 Writing Application Write a short narrative story about your favorite vacation. Be sure to capitalize all the place names correctly.

Exercise 19 Writing Application Write an ad for a grocery store, advertising five different products that are on sale. Be sure to use brand names and to capitalize brand names correctly.

Standardized Test Preparation Workshop

Proofreading for Spelling, Capitalization, and Punctuation Errors

Many standardized tests measure your ability to recognize errors within the context of a written passage. Often, a written passage is provided for you to proofread. Then, you will be asked to identify the type of error, if any. The following sample items will give you practice in responding to these types of test items

Sample Test Items	Answers and Explanations

Directions Read the passage, and decide which type of error, if any, appears in each underlined section.
 	
Sharon <u>glanced at her Aunt. Together,</u>
          (1)
they had planned <u>this surprise</u> birthday party,
 	
and now it was time! As they waited for
 	
Uncle Bob to open the door, <u>they heard only</u>
 	
<u>the shufling feet of a few guests.</u>
          (2)
 	
1 A Spelling error
    B Capitalization error
    C Punctuation error
    D No error
	The correct answer is *B. Aunt* should not be capitalized because it is preceded by a possessive. Words designating family members are capitalized only when they are used in direct address (Are you ready, *Aunt*?), with the person's name (Is *Uncle Louis* ready?), or when used alone (Is *Mother* ready?).

2 F Spelling error
    G Capitalization error
    H Punctuation error
    J No error
	The correct answer is *F.* There should be two *f*s in *shuffling*.

Practice 1 **Directions:** Read the passage and decide which type of error, if any, appears in each underlined section.

When *The Saturday Evening Post* a
                    (1)
popular magazine was purchased by Cyrus

Curtis in 1897, it contained only sixteen

unnillustrated pages and had a circula-
                    (2)
tion of just 2,000. Over the years, the

Magazine shifted its focus from business
                    (3)
to articles of general interest. Lively cover

illustrations were created by noteworthy

artists; including Norman Rockwell.
                    (4)

1 **A** Spelling error
   B Capitalization error
   C Punctuation error
   D No error

2 **F** Spelling error
   G Capitalization error
   H Punctuation error
   J No error

3 **A** Spelling error
   B Capitalization error
   C Punctuation error
   D No error

4 **F** Spelling error
   G Capitalization error
   H Punctuation error
   J No error

Practice 2 **Directions:** Read the passage and decide which type of error, if any, appears in each underlined section.

The city of Tenochtitlán began on an
                    (1)
island in the middle of a swampy lake.

There, the aztecs built their first temple.
                    (2)
The city began to grow impressively after
                    (3)
1385, when Acamapichtli was the King.

The European Bernal Díaz wrote "These

towns and buildings rising from the water
                    (4)
seemed like an enchanted vision."

1 **A** Spelling error
   B Capitalization error
   C Punctuation error
   D No error

2 **F** Spelling error
   G Capitalization error
   H Punctuation error
   J No error

3 **A** Spelling error
   B Capitalization error
   C Punctuation error
   D No error

4 **F** Spelling error
   G Capitalization error
   H Punctuation error
   J No error

Cumulative Review

MECHANICS

▶ **Exercise 1** Proofreading Sentences to Correct Errors in End Marks, Commas, Semicolons, and Colons
Proofread the following sentences, inserting end marks, commas, semicolons, and colons where necessary. Eliminate unnecessary punctuation. Some items are questions.

1. There is an old palace located in the heart of Venice Italy
2. Called the Doges' Palace it was the residence of the elected rulers
3. The waterfront portion was built in 1340 the great balcony was added in 1404
4. Whose paintings cover the inner waiting room the Hall of the Cabinet, and the Hall of the Senate
5. Many rooms and ceilings were decorated by these Italian painters Tintoretto Bellini and Tiepolo
6. The palace contained offices meeting rooms and law courts
7. It also served as a prison: and it even held the famous Casanova
8. Wow You mean the notorious Italian adventurer
9. The Doges' Palace is connected to the New Prisons by a small stone bridge the Bridge of Sighs
10. Do you know the origin of the bridge's name

▶ **Exercise 2** Proofreading Sentences for All the Rules of Punctuation
Proofread the following sentences. Correct all punctuation errors. In the first sentence, the guide's words are directly quoted. Some items are questions.

1. Did you hear the guide say Windsor Castle is the primary residence of British kings and queens
2. Begun in 1474 Saint Georges Chapel

was completed by King Henry VIII in 1528
3. Tradition says that the Round Tower is built on the site where King Arthurs Knights of the Round Table met
4. Valuable paintings statues and decorations are found in these state apartments Saint George's Hall the Waterloo Chamber and the Throne Room
5. Old Windsor was home to the Anglo Saxon kings in fact William the Conqueror built a castle nearby
6. Is that where Edward III met with the Knights of the Garter
7. Leading from Home Park to Great Park the tree lined road is more than three miles long
8. Did you know there was a very destructive fire there in 1992
9. What I cant believe it
10. An article in the International Herald Tribune said it destroyed Saint George's Hall and the Waterloo Chamber.

▶ **Exercise 3** Proofreading a Page to Correct Punctuation Errors Proofread these paragraphs, supplying missing punctuation and correcting errors in usage of end marks, commas, semicolons, quotation marks, hyphens, and apostrophes.

Neuschwanstein Castle in Germany is one of the worlds best known castles? With it's turrets and tall archways; it looks like a medieval castle As a friend of mine who visited it exclaimed This castle is a real fairy-tale fantasy come true

It sits high on a hilltop overlooking the Alps, and a deep gorge. The castle was built between—1869 and 1886—for King Ludwig II. The room's feature murals and detailed carvings. The woodcarving in Ludwigs bedroom took four-teen carpenters 4 1/2 years to complete Do you think you can pronounce *Neuschwanstein.*

▶ **Exercise 4** Proofreading to Correct Errors in Capitalization Revise the following sentences, adding the missing capital letters.

1. castles in europe developed from the ancient roman idea of walled cities.
2. from spain to transylvania, castles were almost always built for defensive purposes.
3. the word *castle* also refers to large residences like william randolph hearst's castle in san simeon, california.
4. the area of nairnshire in northern scotland is well known for cawdor castle.
5. segovia, spain, located on the eresma river, is known for the alcazar, a famous castle.
6. in torun, poland, there are the ruins of a castle of ancient knights.
7. the wittelsbach family, a german dynasty, took their name from their castle in bavaria.
8. one wittelsbach was count otto vi, who served the emperor frederick I; he was made a duke in 1180.
9. in 1020 bishop werner built habsburg castle on the aare river.
10. later divided into the austrian and spanish branches, the habsburg family ruled in europe for hundreds of years.
11. a result of world war I was the banishment of emperor charles I.
12. in england, king george III bought buckingham palace but sometimes lived at saint james's palace.
13. another castle, balmoral castle, is the british royal residence in scotland.
14. in central japan, the city of osaka features a park built on the site of a sixteenth-century castle.
15. on an island near tokyo, iwatsuki is a castle town that was founded in 1458.

▶ **Exercise 5** Revision Practice: Dialogue Write the following sentences as a dialogue, inserting the proper capitalization and punctuation, and beginning a new paragraph with each new speaker.

stan i just read a book about castles but im confused about the difference between a castle and a palace said rebecca
from what i remember from history class replied stan castles used to be the same as fortresses
kate added oh like the tower of london where they kept prisoners
right you must have read shakespeares *richard III* exclaimed stan
richard put prisoners in the tower added kate
thats true said stan however british royalty lived in the tower of london until the time of queen elizabeth I
wait a second kate said i saw the movie *elizabeth* but i dont remember the name of her castle
stan replied as time went on, *castle* came to mean the same thing as a large mansion
i think i see said kate some palaces were originally fortresses and were rebuilt as luxurious resorts
buckingham palace was built only as a residence but never to be a safe place during battle said stan

▶ **Exercise 6** Writing Application Write a brief dialogue in which you and a friend discuss your dream castle or palace. Be sure to follow all the rules of capitalization and punctuation.

Sentence Diagraming Workshop

Sentences can be diagramed to show how their basic parts are related. In a diagram, each word is positioned to show its use in the sentence. This section will show you how to diagram the basic parts of a sentence.

Subjects and Verbs

In a diagram, the subject and the verb are placed on a horizontal line, separated by a vertical line. The subject is placed to the left. The verb is placed to the right.

EXAMPLE: Snow fell.

$$\begin{array}{c|c} \text{Snow} & \text{fell} \end{array}$$

Names and compound nouns are diagramed in the same way as *snow* in the example above. Verb phrases are diagramed in the same way as *fell.*

EXAMPLE: Robert Stone has been selected.

$$\begin{array}{c|c} \text{Robert Stone} & \text{has been selected} \end{array}$$

▶ **Exercise 1** Diagraming Subjects and Verbs Each of the following sentences contains a subject and a verb. Diagram each sentence, using the preceding examples as models.
1. Rhonda phoned.
2. Smoke was rising.
3. Mick Bradley has arrived.
4. Everyone has been chosen.
5. Skyscrapers sway.

Adjectives, Adverbs, and Conjunctions

In addition to a subject and a verb, many sentences contain adjectives, adverbs, and conjunctions. These parts of speech are added to a diagram in the following ways.

Adding Adjectives An adjective is placed on a slanted line directly below the noun or pronoun it describes.

EXAMPLE:

Adding Adverbs Adverbs, like adjectives, are placed on slanted lines. They are placed directly under the verbs, adjectives, or adverbs they modify.

EXAMPLE:

Adding Conjunctions Conjunctions are placed on dotted lines drawn between the words they connect.

EXAMPLE:

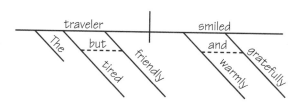

Exercise 2 Diagraming Sentences With Modifiers and Conjunctions Diagram each sentence below.

1. The red bus stopped suddenly.
2. A tall and excited stranger appeared.
3. Our new doctor listened very carefully.
4. A large but swift ship glided effortlessly and gracefully.
5. She spoke carefully but eloquently.

Compound Subjects and Verbs

To diagram a sentence with either a compound subject or a compound verb, you must split the main horizontal line.

Compound Subjects Each part of a compound subject is diagramed on a separate horizontal line. The conjunction that connects the subjects is placed on a dotted vertical line, as shown in the following example.

EXAMPLE: Red flags and blue banners appeared.

Compound Verbs The diagram for a compound verb is similar to the diagram for a compound subject.

EXAMPLE: Anne writes clearly and draws well.

Exercise 3 Diagraming Compound Subjects and Compound Verbs Diagram the following sentences.

1. Coffee and cake were provided.
2. Tom calls daily and writes occasionally.
3. A white horse and a beautiful gold carriage were hired.
4. Students, parents, and teachers applauded happily.
5. The new school band assembled, waited, and finally marched.

Imperative Sentences

Diagrams for sentences that give orders or directions follow a pattern similar to those you already know. The understood subject *you* is in the regular subject position, but in parentheses.

EXAMPLE: Go today.

Exercise 4 Diagraming Imperative Sentences Diagram the following sentences, placing the understood subjects correctly.
1. Read slowly.
2. Look closely.
3. Choose very carefully.
4. Try harder!
5. Stand up now!

Complements

The three kinds of complements—direct objects, indirect objects, and subject complements—are all diagramed in different ways.

Direct Objects A direct object is placed on the same horizontal line as the subject and verb. The direct object follows the verb and is separated from it by a short vertical line.

EXAMPLE:
      S   V   DO
   Steven bought a notebook.

```
  Steven  |  bought  |  notebook
                          \ a
```

Indirect Objects An indirect object is the only complement that is not placed on the main horizontal line. Instead, it is placed on a short horizontal line extending from a slanted line directly below the verb.

EXAMPLE:
      S   V   IO   DO
   Mother gave her a message.

```
  Mother  |  gave  |  message
           \ her       \ a
```

Subject Complements The subject complements—predicate nouns, predicate pronouns, and predicate adjectives—follow linking verbs. Like direct objects, they are placed on the same horizontal line as the subject and verb. They are positioned after the verb and separated from it by a slanted line that points back to the subject.

EXAMPLE:
$$\overset{S}{\text{Fred}}\ \overset{V}{\text{was}}\ \text{our last } \overset{PN}{\text{representative.}}$$

EXAMPLE:
$$\overset{S}{\text{Fred}}\ \overset{V}{\text{is}}\ \text{very } \overset{PA}{\text{talkative.}}$$

Exercise 5 Diagraming Direct Objects and Indirect Objects Diagram the following sentences.
1. The girls opened the carton.
2. I gave them the news.
3. They told us several scary stories.
4. The boys bought themselves new sneakers.
5. The troop leader gave us a difficult assignment.

Exercise 6 Diagraming Subject Complements Diagram the following sentences.
1. Dom is a fine swimmer.
2. The room is attractive.
3. The woman was once a powerful politician.
4. The redecorated kitchen looks absolutely sensational.
5. Alaska is the largest state.

> **Exercise 7** Writing and Diagraming Sentences Use the following instructions to write five sentences of your own. Then, correctly diagram each sentence.

EXAMPLE: Write a sentence that contains a compound verb.

ANSWER: The dog yawned lazily and stretched.

1. Write a sentence that contains a compound subject.
2. Write a sentence that contains two adjectives connected by *and*.
3. Write a sentence that gives an order.
4. Write a sentence that contains a subject complement.
5. Write a sentence that contains a direct object.

Prepositional Phrases

The diagram for a prepositional phrase is drawn under the word it modifies. The diagram starts with a slanted line for the preposition and continues with a horizontal line for the object of the preposition. Adjectives that modify the object are placed below it on slanted lines.

PREPOSITIONAL PHRASE: PREP   OBJ OF PREP
                      on a cold morning

Adjective Phrases An adjective phrase is placed directly under the noun or pronoun that the phrase modifies.

EXAMPLE: A teacher from our school spoke briefly.

Adverb Phrases The diagram for an adverb phrase is also placed directly under the word it modifies.

EXAMPLE: His family fled to the country.

▶ **Exercise 8** **Diagraming Prepositional Phrases** Each of the following sentences contains one prepositional phrase. Diagram the sentences, using the preceding examples as models.

1. She is a singer of great talent.
2. The room in the hotel was very warm.
3. This is the top to the plastic container.
4. They arrived after midnight.
5. The senator reached the city in the late afternoon.

Appositives

To diagram an appositive, place it in parentheses next to the noun or pronoun it renames. Any adjectives or adjective phrases that modify the appositive are placed below it.

EXAMPLE: Bill spoke about Countee Cullen, an American poet.

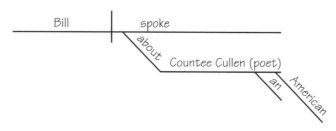

EXAMPLE: Albany, the capital of New York, is a river city.

> **Exercise 9** Diagraming Appositive Phrases Diagram the
following sentences, each of which contains an appositive
phrase.
>   1. Leslie, a friend of mine, phoned yesterday.
>   2. Alex sent me a postcard from Lagos, the capital of Nigeria.
>   3. You will like *White Fang*, a story about a dog.
>   4. Chris Evert Lloyd, winner of many matches, will be there.
>   5. Mother traveled to Istanbul, a city in Turkey.

Compound Sentences

A compound sentence consists of two or more independent
clauses. Each clause in a compound sentence is diagramed on
a separate horizontal line, one above the other. The clauses
are joined at the verbs with a dotted line in the shape of a
step. Place the conjunction or semicolon on the horizontal
part of the step.

EXAMPLE:
Jeff fixed the toaster, and then he began his
homework.

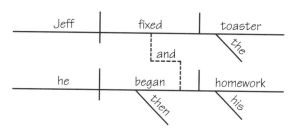

> **Exercise 10** Diagraming Compound Sentences Diagram
each of the following compound sentences, using the preceding
example as a model.
>   1. She enjoys all foods, but her husband is a vegetarian.
>   2. Agatha Christie wrote mystery stories; many of them are
now famous.
>   3. He bought an expensive coin, but it was a forgery.
>   4. Hammurabi was a Babylonian king; he enacted a famous
code of laws.
>   5. She has read many mysteries, but she dislikes spy stories.

Complex Sentences

A complex sentence contains one independent clause and one or more subordinate clauses. In diagraming a complex sentence, each clause is placed on its own horizontal line.

Adjective Clauses An adjective clause is placed on a separate horizontal line underneath the independent clause, with a dotted line connecting the two clauses. This line connects the noun or pronoun modified in the independent clause with the pronoun that begins the adjective clause.

EXAMPLE: She is the pupil who won the speech contest.

EXAMPLE: The antique car that you described is a Maxwell.

Adverb Clauses Like an adjective clause, an adverb clause is placed on a separate horizontal line underneath the independent clause. A dotted line connects the modified verb, adverb, or adjective in the independent clause with the verb in the adverb clause. The subordinating conjunction that begins the adverb clause is written on the dotted line.

EXAMPLE: I have known him since he was a boy.

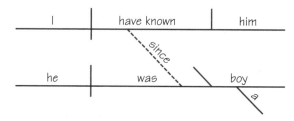

Diagraming Subordinate Clauses Each of the following complex sentences contains either an adjective clause or an adverb clause. Diagram each sentence.

1. Squids, which have ten arms, often swim in large groups.
2. If you buy a ticket now, you will get a discount.
3. Here is the book that you wanted.
4. The bus left the station before the storm began.
5. If you come on the trip, you certainly will enjoy the scenery.

Exercise 12 Writing and Diagraming Compound and Complex Sentences Use the following instructions to write five sentences of your own. Then, correctly diagram each sentence. (If you use contractions, spell them out before diagraming the sentence.)

EXAMPLE: Write a complex sentence in which an adjective clause modifies the subject of the main clause.

ANSWER: The house that we rented overlooks the beach.

1. Write a compound sentence connected by the conjunction *but.*
2. Write a compound sentence connected with a semicolon.
3. Write a complex sentence in which an adjective clause modifies a direct object in the main clause.
4. Write a complex sentence beginning with an adverb clause.
5. Write a complex sentence in which an adverb clause follows the main clause.

Academic
and *Workplace*
Skills

Speaking, Listening, Viewing, and Representing

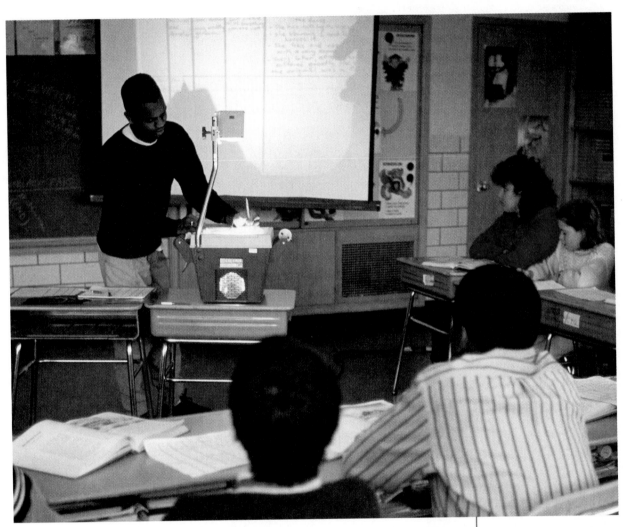

▲ **Critical Viewing**
This student is preparing to give a multimedia presentation. What different kinds of media would you use to make a presentation better? **[Analyze]**

Opening your ears and eyes is not enough. To understand information that is presented in a speech, for instance, or as a graph, you must use special skills. These are listening and viewing skills. Similarly, when it is your turn to communicate—to speak before a group or to draw up a chart—you need other sets of skills. These are speaking and representing skills. Along with writing, speaking, listening, viewing, and representing are all part of one process: communicating. In this chapter, you will learn to improve these skills and use them to improve your ability to communicate with others.

Speaking and Listening Skills

By developing good speaking and listening skills, you will be able to get more out of conversations, class discussions, and class presentations. Developing good speaking skills will enable you to contribute more effectively to class discussions, give formal presentations with greater confidence, and communicate your feelings and ideas to other people more easily. By developing good speaking and listening skills, you will be able to get more out of conversations, class discussions, and class presentations. The more fully you participate in class, the more profitable—and enjoyable—your classroom time will be.

Using Informal Speaking Skills

Informal speaking skills include talking with friends or family, speaking in class, giving directions, and making introductions.

▶ **KEY CONCEPT** Develop informal speaking skills to build confidence about participating in class discussions, giving clear and accurate directions, and introducing people properly. ■

How to Participate in Class You can improve your speaking skills by taking part in class discussions. If you plan what you want to say before you say it and participate in class often, you will become more fluent, comfortable, and confident in your speaking. The following chart offers some suggestions for improving your participation in class discussions.

TAKING PART IN CLASS DISCUSSIONS

1. Set a goal for yourself about taking part in class.
2. Do whatever homework and reading assignments are required so that you are well prepared.
3. Decide on the points you would like to make before class begins.
4. Do not wait for the teacher to call on you. Raise your hand, and volunteer to contribute your thoughts.
5. Listen to the discussion carefully, and make sure that your points are relevant to the discussion.
6. Observe other students who make meaningful contributions to the class, and learn from their example.
7. Ask questions about what you do not understand or what you want to know more about.

How to Give Directions You may be asked to give directions for how to get somewhere or how to do something. If you can give clear and accurate directions, people will be able to follow them easily.

The following chart offers some suggestions for giving clear and accurate directions.

SUGGESTIONS FOR GIVING DIRECTIONS

1. Think through the directions carefully before you speak.
2. Speak slowly so that your listeners can follow your directions without difficulty.
3. Choose your words carefully, being as specific as you can.
4. Use short sentences, so your listener can remember each one. Give only one step of the directions in each sentence.
5. Remember to give the most important details, but do not confuse your listener with unnecessary information.

How to Make Introductions How do you make a good introduction? The most important thing to remember is to pronounce the person's *full* name correctly. You should also include some interesting details about the person you are introducing.

Note the difference between these two introductions:

INTRODUCTIONS: Mom, this is David. I know him from school.

Mom, I'd like to introduce my friend, David Lawrence. He lives right down the street. We're in the same English class. David, this is my mother, Mrs. Joyce.

▶ **Exercise 1** Improving Class Participation Skills For each of your classes, keep a record of your contributions to class discussions for two weeks. Try to increase the number and the quality of your comments.

▶ **Exercise 2** Writing Directions and an Introduction Write clear and accurate directions to your house from school. Write an introduction presenting a famous person to your class. Then, give the directions and your introduction to a classmate, and have him or her evaluate them.

More Practice

Academic and Workplace Skills Activity Book
• pp. 1–2

Using Formal Speaking Skills

Formal speaking generally refers to speaking in front of an audience, such as giving a class presentation or a speech.

Recognize Different Kinds of Speeches There are three main kinds of speeches: explanatory speeches, persuasive speeches, and entertaining speeches.

KEY CONCEPT Choose the kind of speech you will give by considering the purpose of the speech and your audience:

- An **explanatory** speech explains an idea or an event.
- A **persuasive** speech is used to get your audience to agree with your point of view or to take some action.
- An **entertaining** speech is given to amuse the audience. ■

Plan Your Speech Preparation is the most important part of a speech. When you are asked to give a speech, begin by thinking carefully about the purpose of your speech and your audience. This will help you determine the kind of speech to give, the topic of the speech, and the way to present the material.

KEY CONCEPT Choose a subject that you know or like, in order to interest your audience. ■

Choose your topic and gather information about it. Then, organize it in outline form. Next, write the main ideas and major details for your speech topic on note cards. You can refer to your note cards quickly and easily as you deliver your speech.

The following chart offers suggestions for preparing note cards for a speech.

PREPARING NOTE CARDS FOR A SPEECH

1. Print all information neatly on 3" x 5" index cards.
2. Write out quotations or facts that you want to remember.
3. Write out beginning and ending statements.
4. Rely mainly on key words and phrases or clear abbreviations to jog your memory.
5. Use a clear outline form, and indent all the details under the ideas they support.
6. Use underlining and capital letters to make important information stand out.
7. Number your cards to help keep them in order.

Deliver Your Speech Practice giving your speech just as you plan to give it in class. Using the note cards you have prepared, deliver your speech several times alone, in front of a mirror, and then to your parents or a friend. The more practice you get, the more confidence you will have when you deliver your speech in class.

▶**KEY CONCEPT** Practice your speech to gain confidence. ■

Use the suggestions in the following chart while practicing and delivering your speech.

FIVE THINGS TO REMEMBER WHEN DELIVERING A SPEECH

1. Do not read to your audience. Refer to your note cards, and speak in a natural, relaxed way.
2. Pronounce your words clearly, and do not speak too hurriedly or too slowly.
3. Use nonverbal language—such as movements, posture, facial expressions, and gestures—effectively while you practice and deliver your speech.
4. Stay within the time limit you were given for your speech.
5. Be prepared to answer questions from your audience.

▶**Exercise 3** Planning and Delivering a Speech Prepare a short speech on a topic you enjoy or would be interested in researching. Gather information on this topic, and organize it in outline form. Next, write the information on note cards, following the suggestions in the chart on page 671. Then, practice giving the speech several times, following the suggestions in the chart above. As a final step, deliver your speech in class.

▶**Exercise 4** Giving and Getting Feedback After delivering a speech or after listening to a speech, sit down with a group of your classmates and critique the speech. Discuss all aspects of the speech—content, presentation, body language, organization— and tell how the speech could be better.

▶ **More Practice**

Academic and Workplace Skills Activity Book
• pp. 3–5

▶ **Critical Viewing** Barbara Jordan, member of the House of Representatives from 1973 to 1979, delivers a speech at the Democratic National Convention in 1992. Describe her nonverbal language. **[Describe]**

Listening Effectively

A good deal of your time in school is spent listening. To listen well, you must give the speaker your complete attention, and you must learn to identify and remember the speaker's main ideas and major details.

KEY CONCEPT Focus your attention on the speaker, and pay attention to the speaker's main points and details. ■

The ability to concentrate and pay attention is a skill that has to be learned. The chart below provides seven rules that will help you build your listening skills.

SEVEN RULES FOR LISTENING EFFECTIVELY
1. Pay attention and concentrate on what is being said. Avoid daydreaming by actively trying to listen, understand, and remember.
2. Do not look around at your friends in class, out the window, at books on your desk, or at anything else that would distract you from the speaker. Focus your eyes and ears on the speaker.
3. Concentrate on what the speaker is saying, and try not to be distracted by his or her looks or manner of speaking.
4. Block out any distractions, such as noises inside or outside the classroom, or any concerns or thoughts you had earlier in the day. Put all your energy into listening and taking in what is being said.
5. Put away anything that may detract from your paying attention to the speaker, such as books, magazines, and homework schedules.
6. Keep a pencil and paper handy so you can take notes, but avoid writing things unrelated to the discussion.
7. Try to find out in advance what main topic will be discussed. That way, you will have some idea of what to focus on while you are listening.

As you listen, identify the speaker's main idea and major details. These will help you decide what information you want to remember after the speaker has finished. Use the questions in the chart on the next page to help you identify this information.

IDENTIFYING MAIN IDEA AND MAJOR DETAILS

1. What is the opening sentence about? This is often the topic sentence that tells you the general topic.
2. What is the last sentence about? This is often a restatement of the main topic.
3. What important points are being made about the topic?
4. What needs to be remembered about each point?
5. What clues is the speaker giving about something's importance? For example, does he or she begin by saying "Remember . . . ," "Most of all . . . ," or "To sum up . . . "?
6. Does the speaker repeat an idea or phrase a number of times, or emphasize its importance by his or her tone of voice or gestures?
7. What is written on the blackboard? What do the visual aids or supporting materials (if any) say about the main idea and major details?

> **Exercise 5** Developing Your Listening Skills Read through the rules for listening, and try to practice them in one particular class. At the end of the class, grade yourself on how well you listened by placing check marks in your notebook next to all the rules you followed. Continue to practice the rules in the same class until you have placed check marks next to all of them. Repeat the strategy for the rest of your classes.

More Practice

Academic and Workplace Skills Activity Book
• pp. 6–7

> **Exercise 6** Practicing Listening Skills Work with another student on this exercise. One of you should read aloud the first announcement below, while the other listens for the main idea and major details, writing them down after the reading is completed. Then, switch roles and repeat the process with the second passage.

1. There will be a special performance of *You're a Good Man, Charlie Brown* on Friday night, October 21, in the Hayes Auditorium. Student tickets, priced at $4.00, will be available tomorrow only from 8:30 to 1:30 in Room 242. There will be no student tickets available at the time of the performance.
2. The Explorers' Club will have its first meeting on Wednesday, April 6, at 3:30 P.M. The registration fee is $3.00, and you must have a permission slip signed by a parent. Come to the school gym, and bring any suggestions or ideas for outings.

Viewing *and* Representing Skills

Section 28.2

Visual representation is an important way to communicate. Television programs, textbooks, and works of art are common types of media that use images to expand your view of the world. Graphic organizers, multimedia presentations, and performances are ways in which you can express yourself to the world. In this section, you will learn how to receive—and provide—information through visual representations.

Interpreting Maps, Graphs, and Photographs

Any map, graph, or photograph can provide a wealth of information. The key to the information these representations hold is your ability to interpret them.

KEY CONCEPT Use your knowledge of the features of maps, graphs, and photographs to get information visually. ■

Follow these general guidelines when reading a visual aid:

- **Determine Your Purpose** Knowing your purpose helps you focus on the information you need.

- **Read the Title, Caption, and Labels** The title or caption tells you what kind of information to expect.

- **Decode Symbols** Symbols are sometimes used to give information. Find out what they represent.

- **Look for Notable Features** Areas that stand out usually contain important information.

- **Link Information to Text** Determining the relationship between the visual elements and the text allows you to use the text to understand the visual elements better and vice versa.

Maps A map can do more than simply indicate the location of a state capital. For example, maps can identify population clusters, clarify wartime battle activities, and report weather forecasts.

Use these steps when interpreting maps:
1. Familiarize yourself with the map.
2. Find out which way is north on the map.
3. Look at the distance scale (usually found at the bottom of the map).

Graphs There will be times when you have to get information from graphs. Graphs provide a quick and easy way to compare several pieces of related information.

Different kinds of graphs are used to show different kinds of information. The following discussion of the three main types of graphs you are likely to find in your reading provides steps to help you interpret each type.

A **line graph** shows changes that occurred over time. It features a line that connects points. The points, which may appear as actual dots, represent numbers or amounts of something.

Use these steps to interpret a line graph:

1. Read the labels. The labels tell you what the data represent and the time interval over which the data are being reported.
2. Read each axis of the graph. The axes are the main vertical line and the main horizontal line that make up the graph.
3. Compare and contrast the data.

A **bar graph** compares and contrasts amounts. In a bar graph, you read the "heights" or "lengths" of bars to see what numbers they represent.

Use these steps to interpret a bar graph:

1. Look at the heights or lengths of the bars.
2. Match the subject that goes with the bar to the number the bar reaches.
3. Compare and contrast the heights or lengths of the bars.

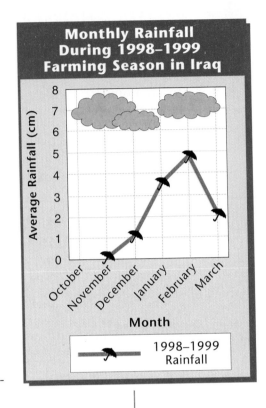

Monthly Rainfall During 1998–1999 Farming Season in Iraq

Ancient Mesopotamian Empires (3500–330 B.C.)

A **pie graph** shows the relationship of parts to a whole. It is in the shape of a circle that is divided into parts. The circle stands for 100 percent of something. Each part stands for a certain portion, or percentage, of the whole.

Use these steps to interpret a pie graph:

1. Look at the numbers that go with the individual parts.
2. Match the parts to the key.
3. Use the numbers and parts to make comparisons.

Photographs A photograph conveys meaning in a single, vivid burst. Whether it shows last year's solar eclipse or the facial expression of yesterday's home-run hero, a photograph allows you to be a witness to the event represented. Still, there is more to interpreting a photograph than just responding to its power. Use the caption and the main image of the photograph to identify what it is about—its main subject. Ask yourself these questions when you interpret a photograph:

• Which details are of particular interest?

• What do these details tell me about the main subject?

• What do other details tell me about the main subject?

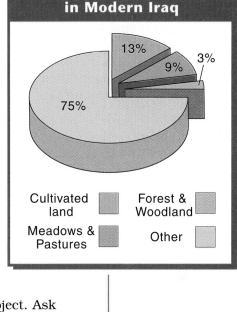

Types of Land in Modern Iraq

13%
9%
3%
75%

Cultivated land
Forest & Woodland
Meadows & Pastures
Other

Exercise 7 Reading Information Visually Find an example of each type of visual aid (maps, graphs, and photographs). Using the general guidelines and steps for interpretation, describe each visual aid, and indicate the kinds of information you can learn from it.

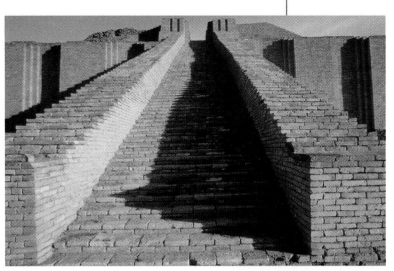

▶ Critical Viewing Look at this stair detail of a Sumerian ziggurat (a temple tower) at ancient Ur, now in Iraq. What details are of particular interest to you? **[Analyze]**

Viewing and Representing Skills • **677**

Viewing Information Media Critically

When you view information media critically, you think carefully about what you see and hear. Because the media distribute large amounts of information, it is important to learn how to differentiate among various media, as well as to evaluate the information presented.

Kinds of Information Media Television, documentary films, and other media provide news and other information. The quality and importance of the information you get depend on the kind of program or film you are watching.

The chart that follows describes several forms of nonprint information media.

NEWS MEDIA CHART			
Form of News Media	Topic(s)	Coverage and Content	Point of View
Television News Program	Focuses on current events or critical news	Summaries of events illustrated by video clips, graphics, and interviews	Recounts information objectively
Documentary	Focuses on one topic of current or historical interest	In-depth stories presented through narration, interviews, and illustrations	Sometimes expresses opinions and viewpoints
Television Newsmagazine	Covers a variety of current topics	In-depth stories or short features illustrated by video clips and interviews	Presents some information objectively and other information with an opinion
Interview	Addresses current topics of social, political, or cultural interest	Questions to find out more about the subject	Presents the opinions of the person being interviewed
Editorial	Addresses current controversial topics	Commentary by a single person sometimes supported by statistics or facts	Presents the opinions of a single individual
Commercial	Advertises products— things, people, places, or ideas	Message of engaging images and catchy slogan used to present a product in a memorable way	Designed to make people want to purchase something

Evaluating Information From the Media After having determined the kind of program you are watching, it is helpful to go a step further and evaluate both the images represented and the language spoken in the program.

▶ **KEY CONCEPT** Learn to evaluate the images and language in the media to enhance your critical viewing skills. ■

Learning the following concepts will help prepare you to evaluate information from the media:

- **Facts and opinions** are important to separate when watching the media. A *fact* is a statement that can be proven to be true. An *opinion* is a viewpoint that cannot be proven to be true.
- **Loaded language and images** are emotional words and visuals used to persuade you to think a certain way.
- **Bias** is a tendency to think in a certain way. As you watch, consider whether the information is being presented in a one-sided way, or whether it takes all viewpoints into account.

Use the following strategies to increase your grasp of information from the media.

EVALUATING INFORMATION FROM THE MEDIA
1. Be aware of the kind of program you are watching, its purpose, and its limitations.
2. Listen and watch carefully.
3. Sort out facts from opinions.
4. Be aware of any loaded language or sensationalist images that might cause you to react in a certain way.
5. Listen for bias, and note any points of view not discussed.
6. Check surprising or questionable information in other sources.
7. View the complete program before reaching a conclusion.
8. Develop your own views about the issues, people, and information presented.

▶ **Exercise 8** Analyzing Information Media Watch a program that provides news or other information, including the commercials during the program. In an essay, identify the kind of program and describe the topics covered. Also, identify what each commercial is selling. Then, evaluate the information on each topic in the program and in the commercials, using the strategies listed above.

▶ **More Practice**

Academic and Workplace Skills Activity Book
• p. 8

Viewing Fine Art Critically

When you look at a painting, you may not find much information about the world. Instead, you will find a mood, a movement of color, or the drama of an event. Paintings, drawings, and photographs are all examples of visual fine art. Visual art uses line, shape, color, and motion to take your imagination on a journey. By interpreting these elements, you can travel farther on the journey that a work of art inspires.

▶ **KEY CONCEPT** Interpret the elements of art to understand the devices used to enrich your enjoyment of it. ■

To help you interpret a work of art, answer the following questions on the formal elements of art:

1. Is the work a painting? Is it a photograph? Is it a drawing?
2. Does the work depict a scene or tell a story? Is it abstract—using lines, colors, textures, and patterns to create a mood or to release energy, but without representing people or objects?
3. What is your response to the work? Do you find it joyful or sad, calm or energetic?
4. Do objects represented seem ordinary-sized, gigantic, or tiny?
5. How is space defined? Is there a lot of space between objects, only a little, or are both large and small distances represented?
6. Are the colors neutral (black, white, grays, and browns), cool (blues and greens), or warm (reds, oranges, and yellows)?
7. What kinds of lines are used? Are they thick or thin, straight or curvy? Are they bold or faint? In a painting, what kind of brushstrokes does the painter use?
8. Which areas are darkest and which are lightest? What mood does the contrast create?
9. The outlines or arrangements of objects can create "lines" that guide your eye through a work. In what directions do the lines in the work invite your eye to travel?
10. What elements of the work contribute to your reaction to it?

▲ **Critical Viewing**
What personal experiences or memories does this painting bring to mind? **[Connect]**

▶ **Exercise 9** Interpreting Fine Art Interpret the formal elements of the painting *The Farmyard*, by Russian-born artist Marc Chagall, by asking and answering the questions given above. Write your answers in your notebook.

Creating Graphic Organizers for Comprehension

When you need to comprehend a great deal of information or read an article with long descriptions, it is helpful to organize what you read.

KEY CONCEPT When you have a lot of information or technical data to present, consider putting that information into a visual form that is easy to view and comprehend. ■

Use the following strategies to construct graphic organizers:

- **Use Text Descriptions** Some types of writing give lots of descriptive information, often organized with headings and subheadings to indicate various sections. To help you understand all the information, create a graphic organizer, such as a concept map, that displays the information visually. For text with detailed descriptions, you may want to create a drawing to clarify the details. For example, a graphic image would help to visualize an architectural concept.

- **Look at Text Structure** The organization of a text can help you create graphic organizers. First, identify the text structure. Is it presented in comparison-and-contrast, cause-and-effect, main-idea-and-details, or chronological order? For comparison and contrast, a Venn diagram or a comparison chart can show similarities and differences. A flowchart can help you understand cause-and-effect relationships. An outline is one way to organize a main idea with many supporting details. One way to visualize chronological order is by creating a timeline.

- **Identify Your Purpose** Consider which parts of the text you want to present. Then, decide which type of graphic organizer will help you to present this information effectively. For instance, you might want to show what two story characters have in common, or chart three possible outcomes of a character's actions. Or you might want to compare and contrast the percentages of people who own mountain bikes and racing bikes.

More Practice

Academic and Workplace Skills Activity Book
- p. 9–11

Charts, Graphs, and Tables To present columns of numbers, survey statistics, or other complex information, create a chart, graph, or table. A chart can be any shape or color and contain any type of information, such as the seating arrangement in your classroom. A graph, such as a bar or line graph, is a good way to show changes that take place over time. Tables enable you to present scientific and statistical information clearly and logically.

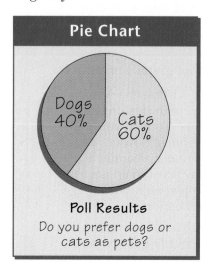

Diagrams and Illustrations Diagrams and illustrations are line drawings that indicate the features of something. If you were describing an airplane, for example, you might create a diagram and label the plane's parts—the rudder, the landing gear, the wing—on the diagram.

Maps If you are writing directions to someone's house or explaining the geography of several regions, it's probably best to present that information in map form. In fact, maps can show almost any type of information—for example, highway routes, geological formations, air currents, or hotel locations.

▶ **Exercise 10** Using Graphic Organizers and Aids Answer the following questions on a sheet of paper.
1. If you wanted to give a history of your town's population figures over the past century, what form of graphic organizer or aid would you choose to create? Why?
2. What forms of writing most typically contain graphic organizers or aids?

▶ **Exercise 11** Creating Graphic Organizers and Aids Complete each of the following assignments, using a sheet of paper of the appropriate size and kind. Use pens, pencils, or markers of different colors when necessary.
1. Draw a map of the route from your house to a friend's house. Show important landmarks and turns, but do not overload your map with unnecessary details.
2. Outline a section of your social studies or science textbook with a graphic organizer.
3. Take a poll of your class. Get their opinion on an issue or a question. Use a type of graph to present your data.

Formatting to Create Effect

Any written work can be enhanced by using basic word-processing formatting features such as boldface, italics, capitals, and numbered and bulleted lists. Following are some tips for making the most of these features:

1. Capitals in heads call out important ideas and topics.
2. Boldface can direct the reader's attention to key concepts or ideas within a written work.
3. Italics give special emphasis to a written line or word.
4. Numbered lists can be used when you have steps to be followed in sequence.
5. Bulleted lists can be used for items that do not follow a particular order.

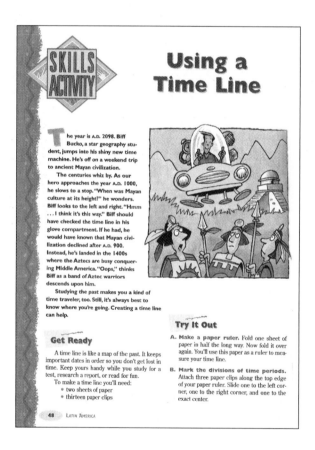

SKILLS ACTIVITY

Using a Time Line

The year is A.D. 2098. Biff Bucko, a star geography student, jumps into his shiny new time machine. He's off on a weekend trip to ancient Mayan civilization.

The centuries whiz by. As our hero approaches the year A.D. 1000, he slows to a stop. "When was Mayan culture at its height?" he wonders. Biff looks to the left and right. "Hmm ...I think it's this way." Biff should have checked the time line in his glove compartment. If he had, he would have known that Mayan civilization declined after A.D. 900. Instead, he's landed in the 1400s where the Aztecs are busy conquering Middle America. "Oops," thinks Biff as a band of Aztec warriors descends upon him.

Studying the past makes you a kind of time traveler, too. Still, it's always best to know where you're going. Creating a time line can help.

Get Ready

A time line is like a map of the past. It keeps important dates in order so you don't get lost in time. Keep yours handy while you study for a test, research a report, or read for fun.

To make a time line you'll need:
* two sheets of paper
* thirteen paper clips

Try It Out

A. **Make a paper ruler.** Fold one sheet of paper in half the long way. Now fold it over again. You'll use this paper as a ruler to measure your time line.

B. **Mark the divisions of time periods.** Attach three paper clips along the top edge of your paper ruler. Slide one to the left corner, one to the right corner, and one to the exact center.

48 LATIN AMERICA

▶ **Exercise 12** **Using Formatting to Create a Flyer** Using the tips on formatting listed above, create a flyer advertising a special event at your school. Then, give reasons for your formatting choices.

▶ **More Practice**

Academic and Workplace Skills Activity Book
• p. 12

Developing a Multimedia Presentation

In most multimedia presentations, the presenter gives an oral report, illustrating the main points with media selections. This type of presentation can be effective and memorable if it is well planned and executed.

KEY CONCEPT Multimedia presentations supply information through a variety of media, including text, slides, videos, music, maps, charts, and art. ■

Tips for Preparing a Multimedia Presentation

- Create an outline of your report first, and then decide which parts to illustrate through the use of media.

- Choose a medium that is suited to your topic. For example, if you were discussing the art of Leonardo da Vinci, reproductions of his artwork and music selections from his time would enhance your presentation.

- Evenly space the media within your presentation. Don't bunch them up at the beginning or end of your presentation.

- Check to ensure that the media you've selected will be able to be seen or heard by everyone. A postage stamp, for example, is too small to be held up in front of a large audience. It would be better to photocopy it and enlarge the image.

- Before the presentation, check your equipment—slide projectors, overhead projectors, microphones, cassette players—to be sure that they are in working condition.

- Always have a backup plan in case anything goes wrong with the equipment.

- Plan to rehearse with the equipment the day before the presentation. Be sure you know the location of all controls—for focus or for volume, for example—and understand their use.

▲ **Critical Viewing**
What media is this student using to enhance her oral report? **[Interpret]**

Exercise 13 Preparing a Multimedia Presentation Read through the saved writings in your portfolio. Select one that could be made into a multimedia presentation. Then, using an outline, select the media you'd like to include, and decide on the sequence of your presentation.

More Practice

Academic and Workplace Skills Activity Book
• p. 13

Creating a Video

Video allows viewers to see the world as you see it. A video can communicate a message, entertain, or do both.

▶**KEY CONCEPT** Create a video to inform or entertain your audience. ■

Although a video can last from seconds to hours, and subjects can range from the serious to the ridiculous, certain rules of thumb apply to all videography:

Basic Steps

1. Write out the story or message in the form of a shooting script. A shooting script contains lines to be spoken, or the dialogue among characters. It also contains directions about camera angles and descriptions of settings, costumes or wardrobe, and props.
2. Create a storyboard to show a clear sequence of events. A storyboard looks like a cartoon strip, with each important shot planned out.
3. Select locations for shooting, and get permission to use them.
4. Cast the roles or parts, and rehearse.
5. Write out a shooting schedule (the order in which scenes will be shot and who will be involved in each), and distribute it to all the characters.
6. Tape the scenes.
7. Edit the video. Store the video in a safe place.

▲ **Critical Viewing**
What tips for shooting a video are these students paying attention to? How could they improve their video shooting? **[Speculate]**

Tips for Taping

- Hold the camera steady.
- Select a quiet location for shooting. Keep in mind that outdoor locations can be unpredictably noisy.
- When in doubt, shoot more. It's easier to cut scenes than to have to reassemble the cast and crew to refilm.
- Keep scenes simple and short.

▶**Exercise 14** Create a Video Create a three-minute documentary. Write out the information you want to include in your documentary in the form of a shooting script. Next, create a storyboard. Select the location and actors for your documentary. Then, film and edit your work. Use the Tips for Taping to help you in your presentation.

Performing or Interpreting

Communication through performance is an art that has existed since the dawn of history, if not before.

KEY CONCEPT Performers use a variety of techniques to convey the meaning of a text or song. ■

Prepare to Perform

1. Write the text in a notebook, and highlight its most important words and ideas.
2. Read the text aloud several times, experimenting with the tone and pitch of your voice.
3. Practice using body language, including hand gestures and posture, to convey meaning.
4. Consider background music to enhance the mood.
5. Establish a mood through your choice of setting, costumes, and music.
6. Rehearse.

Keep in Mind

- Always speak more slowly than you think is necessary.
- Don't fidget.
- Periodically make eye contact with your audience, unless you are representing a character in a scene.

Exercise 15 Preparing to Perform Select a poem you would like to interpret. Copy it, highlighting its key ideas and words. Then, jot down performance notes, planning the effect you'd like your reading to have and the mood you'd like to set.

▲ Critical Viewing
Actor Albert Finney here plays Shakespeare's Hamlet. What mood does his body language convey? **[Infer]**

More Practice

Academic and Workplace Skills Activity Book
- pp. 14–16

Reflecting on Your Speaking, Listening, Viewing, and Representing Skills

Review all the different kinds of speaking, listening, viewing, and representing purposes discussed in this section. Write a journal entry discussing these experiences. Begin your inquiry by asking yourself these questions:

- What experiences did I find the most enjoyable?
- What experiences were the most difficult?
- What experiences gave me the most information?
- What experiences presented the most information?
- What skills would I most like to improve? Why?

Standardized Test Preparation Workshop

Interpreting Graphic Aids

Some standardized tests contain questions testing your ability to gather details, draw conclusions, and interpret from the information provided in maps, charts, graphs, and other graphic aids. The sample item that follows will help you become familiar with these types of questions.

Test Tip

As you look at each graphic aid, examine legends, keys, and titles before drawing conclusions from the information.

Sample Test Items

Read the passage, study the graphic aid, and answer the questions that follow.

Before 1950, television was a novelty. As technology advanced and prices fell, television sets became more accessible. By the end of the decade, they were a common feature in American homes.

1 For each two-year period, consider how many times greater the number of homes with television sets was at the end of the period than at the beginning. During which period did the largest proportional growth occur?

   A 1950–1952
   B 1954–1956
   C 1956–1958
   D 1958–1960

2 What logical conclusion could you draw about the increase in television purchases?

   F Televisions were not as large as before.
   G Televisions became more affordable for the average family during the decade.
   H There was more advertising of televisions toward the end of the decade.
   J Television created new celebrities.

Homes With Television Sets

Answers and Explanations

The correct answer is *A, 1950–1952*. During those years, the number of homes with television sets tripled.

The correct answer is *G. Televisions became more affordable for the average family during the decade.* This is the most logical conclusion to draw, based on the information provided in the passage and the chart.

▶ **Practice 1** **Directions:** Read the passage, study the map, and answer the questions that follow.

Egypt was first united in 3200 B.C. It was ruled by pharaohs during three great kingdoms: Old, Middle, and New. It developed along riverbanks, where great cities were built and civilizations developed.

Ancient Egypt

Old Kingdom	Middle Kingdom	New Kingdom
ca. 3200–2200 BC	ca. 2000–1800 BC	ca. 1600–1000 BC

1 Which statement best describes how Egypt changed between 3200 and 1000 B.C.?

A The area of land Egypt ruled grew.
B The area of land Egypt ruled shrank.
C The Egyptian navy grew more powerful.
D The area of desert in Egypt grew.

2 Throughout the three kingdoms, where did the rule of the pharaohs remain strong?

F along the northern part of the Nile
G in the Sahara
H along the Mediterranean
J from Syria to Upper Egypt

3 Which of the following geographical features encouraged the rise of early civilizations?

A a good ocean harbor in a region with a cool climate
B a large river in a region with a warm climate
C a large desert surrounded by numerous mountains
D a good ocean harbor near a large jungle

4 Along which bodies of water did ancient civilizations in Egypt develop?

F Red Sea and Nile River
G Nile River, Atlantic Ocean, and Red Sea
H Mediterranean Sea
J Nile River

5 What direction would one take to travel from Thebes to Giza?

A north
B south
C west
D east

6 Approximately how many miles lie between Memphis and Thebes?

F 600 miles
G 30 miles
H 300 miles
J 10 miles

Vocabulary and Spelling

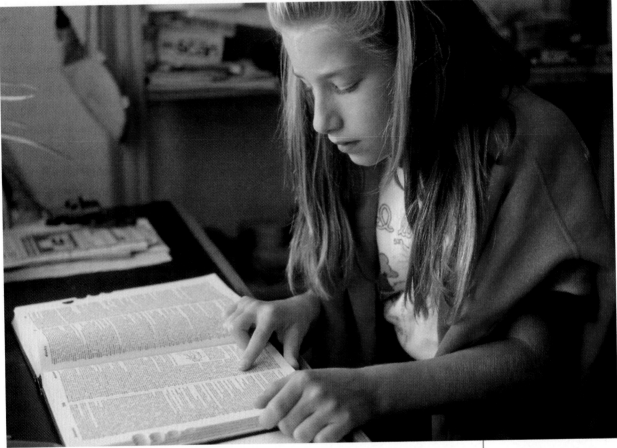

An unfamiliar word can be like a roadblock. When you hear or read the word, your understanding of what's going on may grind to a halt. At the same time, hearing or reading an unfamiliar word can be like coming to a bridge. It is your chance to learn the word and cross over into new understanding. By learning a new word, you increase your ability to grasp the ideas of others and to communicate your own thoughts effectively. This chapter includes a number of methods for learning and remembering the new words you encounter. Choose the methods that you find most useful.

▲ **Critical Viewing**
What language tool is this student using? How can it help increase her vocabulary?
[Analyze]

Developing Your Vocabulary

What would we do without words? We could draw complicated pictures. We could grunt and point. But we are lucky enough to have inherited a well-developed written and spoken language complete with a wide variety of words. Human beings use language to communicate with each other. By building your vocabulary, you can communicate with others more effectively.

KEY CONCEPT The most common ways to increase your vocabulary are listening, reading, and taking part in conversation. ■

Conversation You've been building your vocabulary since the day you were born! The words you learned as a toddler were ones you heard in conversation. By first listening to and then taking part in conversations, you learned the meanings and pronunciations of new words. Use the same strategy in your life today. Listen for unfamiliar words whenever you talk to teachers, people from different places, and people with interests that are different from your own. Find out what the words mean by asking or by looking the words up in a dictionary.

▲ Critical Viewing Do you think this student is listening to someone speak or thinking about something he just read? Explain. [Analyze]

Works Read Aloud Another way to build your vocabulary is to listen to works of literature read aloud. Many works are available on audiocassette or CD. By listening, you will hear how unfamiliar words are pronounced and how they are used in context. You may even choose to read along while the work is being read so that you can see and hear new words.

Wide Reading The more you read, the more new words you will encounter. Soon, new words will become familiar words as you encounter them again and again. Read from a wide variety of sources to encounter the widest variety of words and to learn how the same word may be used in a variety of contexts.

Recognizing Context Clues

If you carefully analyze the sentence or paragraph containing an unfamiliar word, you can sometimes determine the word's meaning.

> **KEY CONCEPT** The **context** of a word is the other words and the ideas that it is connected with. For instance, the rest of the sentence in which a word appears is part of its context. ■

USING CONTEXT CLUES

1. Read the sentence, concentrating on the unknown word.
2. Look for clues in the surrounding words.
3. Guess the possible meaning of the new word.
4. Substitute your meaning for the word. If the sentence does not make sense, try another guess.
5. Check the word's meaning in the dictionary.
6. Add it to your notebook.

Figurative Language *Figurative language*, which is language that is not meant to be taken literally, often uses familiar words in unfamiliar ways. For example, you might encounter the sentence, "The leaves pirouette in the wind." You might know the literal meaning of *pirouette*: "a dance movement in which the dancer spins on one toe." The context of the sentence shows, however, that leaves, not human dancers, are being referred to. Using your knowledge of the context, you can see that *pirouette* here means "spinning about like a dancer."

Idioms An *idiom* is an expression used with a special meaning, one different from what the words literally mean. For instance, "easy as pie" is an idiom meaning "extremely easy." Often, idioms used by people from an area or time other than your own will be unfamiliar. Use context clues to figure out the meaning. Compare unfamiliar idioms to expressions that you use for similar meanings.

Grammar and Style Tip

Use figurative language to add interest to stories and poems. Use idioms to make dialogue sound realistic.

> **More Practice**

Academic and Workplace Skills Activity Book
• pp. 17–18

> **Exercise 1** Using Context Clues Explain how context clues help you determine the meaning of each underlined word or group of words.

1. The arts <u>flourished</u> because patrons encouraged and supported artists.
2. Knowing this was a rare opportunity, the coach decided to <u>seize the moment</u>.
3. The <u>kaleidoscope</u> of autumn leaves filled the woods with color.
4. The baby sitter tried to <u>placate</u> the outraged child.
5. I prefer natural fabrics to <u>synthetic</u> ones.

Studying Meanings in the Content Areas

Use a Notebook and a Glossary

Learning words from context helps you incorporate them into your working vocabulary. This method takes time, though. To master a subject such as social studies or science, you need to have the meanings of special words right at your fingertips. Keep a special section of your notebook in each subject area to write the meanings and pronunciations of new words you encounter. Use the glossary at the back of your textbook to find the subject-specific meaning of unfamiliar words.

Social Studies In social studies, you are likely to encounter words that deal with types of government, political activity, and physical features of an area. Use categories such as these to group words based on what they name or describe. Make notes concerning similar or opposing ideas. For instance, you might note that democracy and dictatorship name opposite forms of government.

Science Unfamiliar words in science often have Latin origins. Categorize science words by their prefixes, suffixes, or roots. For example, you could group *photosynthesis* with *phototropism* because they both begin with *photo-*. Once you have learned that *photo-* means "of or produced by light," you will more easily remember the meanings of both words.

Current Events By listening to the news or reading a news-paper, you increase the likelihood that you will encounter the words you learned in science and social studies. The more times you hear or see a word used, the better you will understand its meaning. Use current event topics as a source of vocabulary reinforcement.

▶ **Exercise 2** Studying Words in the Content Areas Work with a partner to come up with a list of unfamiliar words in a chapter from your social studies or science book. Write the words on index cards, look up their definitions, and group the words in various ways. When you are satisfied that the words are logically grouped, record them in your notebook.

▼ **Critical Viewing** This student may be writing unfamiliar words in his notebook. How will that help him to increase his vocabulary? **[Infer]**

Using "Possible Sentences"

You can experiment with unfamiliar words by using the Possible Sentences strategy. This method increases your vocabulary and your understanding of words in context.

STEPS FOR USING POSSIBLE SENTENCES
1. Find an unfamiliar word in your reading, and use context clues to figure out its meaning.
2. Write a sentence for the unfamiliar word in your vocabulary notebook.
3. Check the actual meaning of the word in a dictionary.
4. Evaluate your sentence to see whether you have used the word correctly.
5. Revise your sentence to make it correct.

Exercise 3 Using Possible Sentences Using the steps mentioned above, apply the Possible Sentences strategy to increase your understanding of five vocabulary words from a novel, short story, or textbook you are reading.

◀ Critical Viewing Each of these people has a different set of vocabulary words. Why is it important for people to learn as many words as they can? [Analyze]

Section 29.2 — Studying Words Systematically

Keeping a Vocabulary Notebook

▶ **KEY CONCEPT** A vocabulary notebook will help you to learn new words. You can use the notebook, flashcards, and a tape recorder to help you review. Study and review new words a few times each week. ■

Create a Vocabulary Notebook Keep a notebook available to list new words, along with a dictionary. On the top of each page in your notebook, write the chapter or book title. Divide your page into three sections, listing the word, its definition, and some examples of how to use it.

Chapter 5: The Early Nation		
Words	**Definitions**	**Examples**
anticipate (an tis' ə pāt)	look forward to; expect	Did the British anticipate an early end to the war?
repeal (ri pēl')	withdraw officially or formally; revoke	Congress decided to repeal the law.
embargo (im bär' gō)	a government order prohibiting the entry or departure of commercial ships to its ports	What is the purpose of imposing an embargo?

▶ **Exercise 4** Setting Up a Vocabulary Notebook Select one of the subjects you are studying this year or one of the books you are reading for pleasure. As you read, jot down any unfamiliar words. When you have finished a chapter, look up unfamiliar words in a dictionary, and record the meaning in your notebook.

▶ **More Practice**

Academic and Workplace Skills Activity Book
• p. 19

Studying Words Systematically • **695**

Studying New Words

Set a regular time to review new vocabulary words. Use one or more of the following methods to review:

Use Your Notebook Study the words you have recorded in your notebook. As you review, cover the definition of each word, and try to remember the meaning by looking at the word and the example sentence. Then, uncover the definition and read it. Create a new sentence using the word.

Write Sentences With Vocabulary Words Create sentences using the words in your notebook. Use the definition of the word, along with the word itself, in each sentence.

EXAMPLE: He *anticipates* a good party because he is *looking forward* to getting expensive gifts.

Use Flashcards On the front of an index card, write a word you want to remember. On the back, write the definition, the pronunciation, and a sentence that uses the word. Use these flashcards to test yourself or ask others to test you.

Front	Back
aptitude	natural ability or talent ap'tə tōōd' I'm afraid I have no <u>aptitude</u> for creative writing.

Use a Tape Recorder Record a vocabulary word. Pronounce the word carefully. Then, after a pause, record its definition. To review, play the tape. During the pause, recall the word's definition. Listen to the recorded definition to check yourself.

▶ **Exercise 5** Making Flashcards or Tapes Make a set of flashcards or tapes to study these words. Add words from your own reading or from assigned vocabulary lists.

1. prodigy   3. uncanny   5. eminent
2. conspired   4. intrigue

Using a Dictionary

A variety of resources can help you clarify the meaning, pronunciation, and correct usage of an unfamiliar word.

To find the exact meaning of a word, look it up in a dictionary. Record in a notebook the words you look up. Words in a dictionary are listed alphabetically. The dictionary entry will tell you the pronunciation of the word, the parts of speech it functions as, and its various meanings. In addition, most dictionaries provide the origins of the word—the words from which it grew. Reading the origins of a word can help you make associations with other words that share the origin.

Using Other Reference Aids

Thesaurus A thesaurus lists a word's synonyms (words with similar meanings) and sometimes antonyms (words with opposite meanings). Words in some thesauruses are listed alphabetically. In others, words are arranged by categories. The categories are listed in an alphabetical index. Remember to always check the meaning of an unfamiliar word in a dictionary before using it.

Synonym Finder Many word-processing programs have synonym finders in their menus. If you are drafting on-line, highlight a word for which you want to find a synonym and use the finder to check alternative words. Again, remember to always check the meaning of an unfamiliar word in a dictionary before using it.

Glossary A glossary is a list of terms and definitions specific to a field of study. Each of your textbooks probably has a glossary that lists the words you need to know and learn in that subject area.

Software Like most references, dictionaries and thesauruses are available in electronic form. Some can be purchased and loaded onto your hard drive; others are available on the Internet.

▶ **Exercise 6** Using Vocabulary Reference Aids Look up each of the following words in the references indicated. Compare and contrast the information found in each source.
1. respiration (science textbook glossary, dictionary)
2. pioneer (dictionary, thesaurus)
3. preeminent (dictionary, synonym finder)
4. rotation (science textbook glossary, on-line dictionary)
5. resource (social studies textbook glossary, thesaurus)

◑ Learn More

To see an annotated dictionary entry, go to Chapter 31, Study, Reference, and Test-Taking Skills.

◉ Technology Tip

Almost any reference available in print is also available on-line. Ask a reference librarian to show you how to find and use on-line dictionaries and thesauruses. Find out what other vocabulary-building tools are available on-line.

▶ **More Practice**

Academic and Workplace Skills Activity Book
• pp. 20–21

Studying Word Parts and Origins

Using Roots

Learning roots, the most basic parts of words, will help you learn the meanings of groups of words. For example, if you know that the root *-gress* means "to step or move forward," you have a key to the meaning of the following words: *regress, progress, retrogress, transgress, egress,* and *digress.*

KEY CONCEPT A **root** is a word part that determines an important part of the meaning of a word. ∎

FIVE COMMON ROOTS		
Root	Meaning	Example
-mit- (-mis-)	to send	*dismiss* (to *send* away)
-mov- (-mot-)	to move	*motion, movement*
-ven- (-vent-)	to come	*convene* (to *come* together)
-vert- (-vers-)	to turn	*reversal* (*turning* around)
-vid- (-vis-)	to see	*vision* (ability to *see*)

Exercise 7 Learning Word Roots Match the words in the first column with the words in the second column that appear to have the same root. Look up each pair of words in a dictionary. Identify the root they share, and write its meaning.

1. reflect
2. motivate
3. dimension
4. pedal
5. hapless
6. model
7. manufacture
8. picture
9. distance
10. sentence

a. manuscript
b. deflect
c. centipede
d. immense
e. modify
f. happiness
g. motion
h. circumstance
i. assent
j. depict

Exercise 8 Using Roots to Determine the Meaning of Words Match each word in the first column with its definition in the second column. Explain how the roots you learned in the previous exercise helped you to determine each answer.

1. motility
2. pedestrian
3. manual
4. module
5. mishap

a. person walking
b. by hand
c. one of a set of units
d. unfortunate accident
e. ability to move on one's own

Using Prefixes

▶ **KEY CONCEPT** A **prefix** is one or more syllables placed at the beginning of a word to change its meaning or to create a new word. ■

FIVE COMMON PREFIXES		
Prefix	**Meaning**	**Example**
ex-	from, out	*ex*change (to change *from* one thing to another)
mis-	wrong	*mis*place (to put in the *wrong* place)
re-	back, again	*re*call (to call *back*)
trans-	over, across	*trans*port (to carry *over a* distance)
un-	not	*un*seen (*not* seen)

▶ **Exercise 9** Analyzing Prefixes Write each numbered word. Circle the prefix, and underline the base word. Then, write the letter of the definition for each word.

1. prepay
2. disassemble
3. uncooperative
4. exhale
5. retort

a. breathe out
b. pay before
c. not helpful
d. answer back
e. take apart

▶ **Exercise 10** Finding the Meanings of Prefixes Use a dictionary to find words beginning with the following prefixes. Give an example of a word beginning with each prefix. Define the word in a way that incorporates the meaning of the prefix.

1. ante-
2. hyper-
3. sub-
4. in-
5. tele-

▶ **Exercise 11** Using Prefixes to Determine Word Meanings Use what you have learned about prefixes to match each word in the left column with its probable definition in the right column. Check your answers in a dictionary.

1. preamble
2. misappropriate
3. transpose
4. unassailable
5. revive

a. change the places of two things
b. not able to be attacked
c. take for the wrong reason
d. bring back to health
e. introduction

Using Suffixes

> **KEY CONCEPT** A **suffix** is a letter, syllable, or group of syllables added to the end of a word to change its meaning or function or to form a new word. ■

FOUR COMMON SUFFIXES			
Suffix	**Meaning**	**Example**	**Part of Speech**
-able (-ible)	capable of being	vis*ible*	adjective
-ly	in a certain way	swift*ly*	adverb/adjective
-ment	the result of	content*ment*	noun
-tion (-ion, -sion)	being the act or state of being	predic*tion*	noun

> **Exercise 12** Analyzing Suffixes Write each numbered word. Circle the suffix, and examine the root or base word. Then, write the letter of the definition for each word.
>
> 1. gratitude   a. to make categories
> 2. verbose   b. quality of being grateful
> 3. heroism   c. especially verbal or talkative
> 4. sensory   d. quality of being a hero
> 5. categorize   e. of the senses

> **Exercise 13** Identifying How Suffixes Change Word Function
> Write each numbered pair of words. Then, write the part of speech for each word in the pair.
>
> 1. art, artistic
> 2. excite, excitement
> 3. fresh, freshen
> 4. quick, quickly
> 5. assist, assistant

More Practice

Academic and Workplace Skills Activity Book
• pp. 24–25

▶ Critical Viewing The artist is expressing herself in a nonverbal way. Using details from the picture, identify the tools and materials the artist uses to express herself. [Connect]

Examining Word Origins

English is part of the Indo-European family of languages. Within that family, the closest relatives to English are other Germanic languages, such as Dutch and German. English is the most widely spoken language in the world. It has also borrowed the most from other languages. More than 70 percent of the words we call English are borrowed from other languages.

Understanding Historical Influences If English had developed in isolation, it would have fewer borrowed words. No language develops in complete isolation, however. Battles, travels, new inventions and technologies—each of these events or circumstances contributes to the growth and change of a language.

HISTORICAL INFLUENCES ON ENGLISH

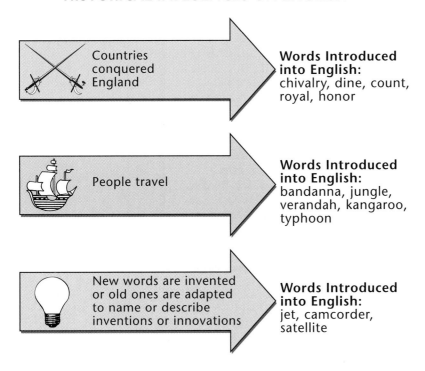

Countries conquered England → **Words Introduced into English:** chivalry, dine, count, royal, honor

People travel → **Words Introduced into English:** bandanna, jungle, verandah, kangaroo, typhoon

New words are invented or old ones are adapted to name or describe inventions or innovations → **Words Introduced into English:** jet, camcorder, satellite

▶ **Exercise 14** Analyzing Word Origins Look up each of the following words in a print or electronic dictionary. Then, write the language from which it comes.

1. camel
2. molasses
3. kosher
4. canoe
5. honor

Improving Your Spelling

Starting a Personal Spelling List

▶ **KEY CONCEPT** Select the words the spelling of which you want to learn, enter them in your notebook, and study them regularly. ■

Record Frequently Misspelled Words Create a section just for words that you frequently misspell. Review corrected tests, essays, and homework to find your problem words. Add to the list any words that sound the same but have different spellings for different meanings, such as *they're*, *their*, and *there*. Each entry should include the word's spelling, pronunciation, and definition, and either a sentence or a memory aid.

Word	Pronunciation	Definition	Sentence
audience	ô′dē əns	a group assembled to see and hear a play or concert	Debbie saw her mother and father in the audience.
decision	di sizh ′ən	the act of deciding something	Jack had a difficult decision to make.
license	lī′səns	formal or legal permission to do something specified	Does your sister have a driver's license?

Include Derivatives A derivative is a word that is formed from another word. Once you know how to spell a base word—the word from which the others are formed—you can more easily learn to spell its derivatives.

BASE WORD: decide
DERIVATIVES: decision, decisive

BASE WORD: caution
DERIVATIVES: cautionary, cautious

Include derivatives in your spelling notebook. Underline the parts of the word that are always spelled with the same letters. Circle any parts that change.

EXAMPLE: regul(ar) regul(ate) regul(ation)

Studying Your Spelling Words

Study your words regularly. Divide your list into groups of five or ten words, and study each group for a week. As you become more comfortable with this study method, you can test yourself on larger groups of words that include those you have learned and those you are in the process of mastering.

KEY CONCEPT Review your words several times a week. ■

A METHOD FOR STUDYING YOUR SPELLING WORDS

1. *Look* at each word. Notice any unusual features about the spelling of the word. For example, in the word *argument*, the *e* in *argue* is dropped before the ending is added. Concentrate on the part of the word that gives you the most trouble. Then, cover the word and try to picture it in your mind.

2. *Say* the word aloud. Then, sound the word out slowly, syllable by syllable.

3. *Spell* the word by writing it on a sheet of paper. Say each syllable aloud as you write it down.

4. *Compare* the word that you wrote on the paper with the word in your notebook. If you spelled the word correctly, put a small check in front of the word in your notebook. If you misspelled the word, circle the letter or letters on your paper that are incorrect. Then, start over again with the first step.

Exercise 15 Checking Spelling Skills Fill in the missing letter(s) in the words below. Add any words you misspelled to your personal spelling list.

1. accident__?__y
2. annivers__?__ry
3. cur__?__ous
4. di__?__appear
5. exer__?__
6. famil__?__r
7. n__?__ghbor
8. prob__?__bly
9. simil__?__
10. tomo__?__ow

Exercise 16 Identifying Commonly Misspelled Words
Look through your writing portfolio and through tests that have been returned to you. Find misspelled words and record them in your notebook. Study them. Have a partner test you on the words.

More Practice

Academic and Workplace Skills Activity Book
• pp. 26–27

Applying Spelling Rules

In addition to studying words that give you particular trouble, study rules that apply to groups of words.

Using *ie* or *ei*

There are basic rules for *ie* and *ei* words. You will need to memorize certain exceptions to these rules.

▶**KEY CONCEPT** Remember this rule: *i* before *e* except after *c* and when sounded as *ay*, as in *neighbor* and *weigh*. ■

When a word has a long *e* sound, use *ie*.
When a word has a long *a* sound, use *ei*.
When a word has a long *e* sound preceded by the letter *c*, use *ei*.

COMMON *ie* AND *ei* WORDS		
Long e Sound—Use *ie*	**Long a Sound—Use *ei***	**Long e Sound Preceded by c—Use *ei***
achieve	eight	ceiling
believe	freight	deceive
field	neighbor	perceive
grief	reign	receive
piece	vein	
thief	weigh	

Some of the exceptions to the preceding rules are listed in the next chart.

SOME EXCEPTIONS TO THE RULE		
either	neither	seize

▶**Exercise 17** Spelling *ie* and *ei* Words Fill in the blanks below with either *ie* or *ei*. Check the spellings in a dictionary. Add difficult words to your personal spelling list.
1. Samantha went to the doctor to get her ears p__?__rced.
2. R__?__ndeer live in the colder regions of the world.
3. The bride wore a shoulder-length v__?__l.
4. The soldiers were ready for another s__?__ge.
5. The cashier stapled the rec__?__pt to the bag.

Technology Tip

When you are working on a word processor, set the spelling checker to alert you immediately when a word is misspelled. The sooner you correct the word, the more likely you are to remember its correct spelling.

▶**More Practice**

Academic and Workplace Skills Activity Book
• p. 28

Adding Suffixes

SPELLING CHANGES WHEN ADDING SUFFIXES		
Word Ending	**Rule**	**Examples**
-*y* preceded by a consonant	Change *y* to *i*.	beauty, beautiful EXCEPTIONS: Most suffixes beginning with *i*: try, trying baby, babyish
-*y* preceded by a vowel	Make no change.	joy, joyous EXCEPTIONS: day, daily gay, gaily
-*e*	Drop the final *e* if suffix begins with a vowel.	love, lovable use, usable EXCEPTIONS: change, changeable peace, peaceable agree, agreeable
-*e*	Make no change if suffix begins with a consonant	hope, hopeful late, lately EXCEPTIONS: true, truly argue, argument
One-syllable word ending in a single consonant preceded by a single vowel	Double the final consonant if suffix begins with a vowel.	drop, dropped grin, grinned EXCEPTIONS: Words ending in *x* or *w*: mix, mixing blow, blowing
Word ending in a single consonant preceded by a single vowel and having the accent on the final syllable	Double the final consonant if suffix begins with a vowel.	permit, permitted EXCEPTIONS: Words in which the accent shifts when the suffix is added: refer´, ref´erence

▶ **Exercise 18** Working With Suffixes Make new words by combining words and suffixes. Check the spellings in a dictionary, and add difficult words to your list.

1. run + -er
2. value + -able
3. stop + -ed
4. hungry + -ly
5. dry + -ing
6. sleepy + -ly
7. mystery + -ous
8. commit + -ed
9. nerve + -ous
10. easy + -ly

Adding Prefixes

▶ **KEY CONCEPT** When a prefix is added to a word, the spelling of the word stays the same. ■

EXAMPLES: un- + noticed = unnoticed
              dis- + solve   = dissolve

▶ **Exercise 19** Working With Prefixes Make new words by combining the prefixes and words below.

1. dis- + appear
2. un- + necessary
3. mis- + behave
4. re- + entry
5. in- + experienced
6. dis- + satisfied
7. de- + press
8. im- + movable
9. co- + operate
10. re- + elect

Using Memory Aids

Because English contains words that come from many different languages, spelling rules do not always apply. Some words must be memorized. Help yourself remember the correct spelling of difficult words by making up a sentence that is a memory aid for spelling the word correctly.

▶ **KEY CONCEPT** Use memory aids to help remember difficult spelling words. ■

You can associate the troublesome part of a word with a word you know or find a short word within a longer word.

EXAMPLES: It is *wise* to *exercise*.
              Will you *hand* me a *handkerchief*?

▶ **Exercise 20** Making Memory Aids Make up a memory aid for each of the following words.

1. believe
2. curious
3. familiar
4. calendar
5. cemetery
6. committee
7. knowledge
8. laboratory
9. misspell
10. secretary

▶ **Exercise 21** Writing Your Own Memory Aids Select five words from your personal spelling list that contain a shorter word. Write a memory aid in your notebook for each.

▶ **More Practice**

Academic and
Workplace Skills
Activity Book
• p. 30

Understanding the Influence of Other Languages and Cultures

Most languages have a set of rules for spelling and pronunciation that are very predictable and constant. More than 70 percent of English words, however, have been borrowed from other languages. A borrowed word may come with traces of its spelling and pronunciation in the original language. For this reason, English uses a wide variety of letters to spell the same sounds: One sound may have been spelled different ways in different languages. For related reasons, English words often contain "silent letters"—letters that are not pronounced. Read widely and study often to overcome the difficulties these inconsistencies present. When you are writing, use a print or electronic dictionary to confirm the spelling of any word about which you are unsure.

KEY CONCEPT Because other languages and cultures contribute to the spelling and pronunciation of words in English, different letters might be used in different words to spell the same sound. ■

EXAMPLES:

puff	cough	fuel	phone
giraffe	jump	page	
call	keep	pack	hike

▲ **Critical Viewing** Many of our words for foods come from other languages. Speculate what you think these people might be ordering. Use the names of foods from other countries. **[Connect]**

Exercise 22 Choosing the Correct Spelling Select the correctly spelled word from each group. Check your answers in a dictionary. Enter misspelled words on your personal spelling list, and note the language from which each word originates.

1. spagetti   spaghetti   sphagetti
2. skunck   scunk   skunk
3. cayack   kyak   kayak
4. resteraunt   restaurant   restauraunt
5. scool   skool   school

Forming Plurals

The plural form of a noun indicates that more than one person, place, or thing is being named. For instance, the plural form of *dog, dogs,* refers to more than one dog. Plural forms are either *regular* or *irregular.*

▶ **KEY CONCEPT** Regular nouns form their plurals by adding *-s* or *-es.* Most nouns have regular plural forms. ■

Some regular nouns change their spelling in the plural form. Check the chart below for examples that change slightly.

FORMING REGULAR PLURALS		
Word Ending	**Rule**	**Examples**
-s, -ss, -x, -z, -zz, -sh, -ch	Add *-es.*	bus, buses mass, masses fox, foxes buzz, buzzes crash, crashes punch, punches
-o preceded by a consonant	Add *-es.*	tomato, tomatoes EXCEPTIONS: solo, solos (and other musical terms)
-o preceded by a vowel	Add *-s.*	radio, radios
-y preceded by a consonant	Change *y* to *i* and add *-es.*	party, parties discovery, discoveries
-y preceded by a vowel	Add *-s.*	day, days monkey, monkeys
-ff	Add *-s.*	bluff, bluffs staff, staffs
-fe	Change *f* to *v* and add *-es.*	knife, knives
-f	Add *-s.* OR Change *f* to *v* and add *-es.*	chief, chiefs calf, calves leaf, leaves

KEY CONCEPT Use a dictionary to look up the correct spelling of irregular plurals. Memorize them. ■

FORMING IRREGULAR PLURALS	
Rule	**Examples**
Add -en.	ox, oxen
Add -ren.	child, children
Change vowels.	goose, geese woman, women
Change vowels and one other letter.	mouse, mice
Use singular form as plural.	sheep, sheep deer, deer
Use plural form only.	clothes scissors

Most one-word compound nouns have regular plural forms. If one part of the compound noun is irregular, the plural form will also be irregular.

EXAMPLES: flashlight, flashlights (regular)
             snowman, snowmen (irregular)

Most compound nouns written with hyphens or as separate words form the plural by making the modified word—the word being described—plural.

EXAMPLES: son-in-law, sons-in-law
             suit of armor, suits of armor

More Practice

Academic and
Workplace Skills
Activity Book
• p. 31

Exercise 23 **Writing Plurals** Write the plural form for each of the following words. Use a dictionary if you need to. Add any difficult words to your personal spelling list.

1. class
2. valley
3. circus
4. sister-in-law
5. shelf
6. story
7. moose
8. potato
9. sheriff
10. diary

▶ **Critical Viewing** The best way to remember irregular plurals is to memorize them. Using this photograph for inspiration, think up a memory aid that you can use to remember that the plural of *moose* is *moose*. [**Connect**]

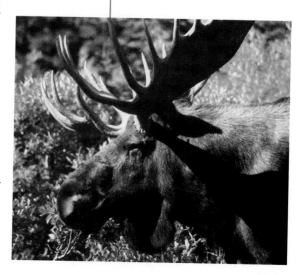

Spelling Homophones

> **KEY CONCEPT** **Homophones** are words that sound the same but have different meanings and may have different spellings. ■

Be especially careful to use and spell the following homophones correctly.

EXAMPLES:

their: a possessive pronoun that means "belonging to them"
they're: a contraction for *they are*
there: a place word or sentence starter, as in "There are five cookies."

tail: a part of an animal
tale: a story

piece: a portion
peace: the condition of not being at war

write: to put words on paper
right: correct

to: begins a prepositional phrase or infinitive
too: also
two: a number

> **Exercise 24** Spelling Homophones Select the correct word from each pair in parentheses. Check your answers in a dictionary. Enter misspelled words on your personal spelling list, and review them.
> 1. (Their, They're) party is Saturday.
> 2. Would you like a (piece, peace) of pie?
> 3. I don't believe that (tail, tale) for a minute.
> 4. My sister wants to help, (to, too).
> 5. We were asked to (right, write) a letter.

> **Exercise 25** Writing Sentences With Homophones Write a sentence for each lettered word in each numbered pair. Check a dictionary to make sure you are spelling and using each word correctly.
> 1. (a) sum   (b) some
> 2. (a) whole   (b) hole
> 3. (a) site   (b) sight
> 4. (a) reel   (b) real
> 5. (a) meet   (b) meat

Technology Tip

Spelling checkers will not catch places where you have misused a homophone. Proofread all your work, even if you have used an electronic spelling checker.

> **More Practice**
>
> Academic and Workplace Skills Activity Book
> • p. 32

Proofreading and Using References

Proofread your written work thoroughly to make sure that you have eliminated all spelling errors. Keep a dictionary or glossary, with you as you proofread. Place a red checkmark on any words for which you want to check the spelling. Then, look up each word and correct the spelling if necessary.

▶ **KEY CONCEPT** Use dictionaries, electronic spelling checkers, and glossaries to check spellings. ■

▶ **Exercise 26** Proofreading Sentences Copy and proofread the following sentences. Correct any words that are written incorrectly. Use a dictionary, spelling checker, or glossary to confirm the spelling of any words about which you are unsure.
1. Sally goes to an excercise class three times a week.
2. I need a pair of scissers to open this package.
3. The soccer team worked hard to acheive its goal of a winning season.
4. Is it neccessary to make reservations ahead of time?
5. Jane didn't want to dissappoint her brother by missing his swim meet.

▶ **Exercise 27** Proofreading a Paragraph Copy and proofread the following paragraph. Write the corrected paragraph on a separate sheet of paper.

The student awards diner was planed for Thusday night. Everyone was very exsited. Sum of the clases preparred posters and decorasions. Others were in charje of music. Althogh it had been on the calender for months, it still seemed as if the date arrivved to soon. The scool secretery made an announcemant in the morning. She gave the time that each comitte was expected to arrive. We couln't beleive that the big night was finaly hear.

Technology Tip

Most word-processing programs can alphabetize a list. Enter electronically your personal list of frequently misspelled words. Sort it alphabetically. Keep the alphabetized list in your folder as a "quick-check" list for proofreading.

Reflecting on Your Spelling and Vocabulary

Think about what you have learned by answering the following questions:

• Which technique do you find most effective for studying spelling words?

• Which do you find most helpful for studying vocabulary words?

• What do the techniques have in common? In what ways are they different?

Standardized Test Preparation Workshop

Using Context to Determine Word Meaning

The questions on standardized tests often require you to figure out the meaning of a word using the context of a passage. Using the group of words surrounding an underlined term or phrase will help you determine the meaning of idioms, expressions, words with multiple meanings, figurative language, and specialized and technical terms. Use the following strategies when answering these types of questions:

- Read the sentence carefully, focusing on the underlined word or words.

- Look for clues in the surrounding words.

- Use these clues to guess which answer choice best defines the meaning of the new word.

- Reread the passage, substituting your meaning for the new word to see whether it makes sense.

Test Tip

Just because you recognize an underlined word does not mean you know its definition. Some words have multiple meanings. Read the passage carefully and choose a word that best defines the underlined word in the context of the passage.

Sample Test Items	Answers and Explanations
Read the passage. Then, read each question that follows the passage. Decide which is the best answer to each question. In order to install your program on this system, you must first make sure your computer has enough memory.	
1 In this passage, the word *system* means— A a method of organization B a procedure C a computer program D the workings of a computer	The correct answer is *D*. Although both *A* and *B* are correct definitions of the word, the only meaning that applies, using the context of the passage, is *the workings of a computer.*
2 The word *memory* in this passage means— F the storing of things past learned G the capacity for storing information H remembering an event J the power of recalling	The correct answer is *G*. The word *memory* has a technical meaning. To fit the context of this passage, the word must refer to the capacity a computer has to store information for use at a later time.

Practice 1 **Directions:** Read the passage. Then, read each question that follows the passage. Decide which is the best answer to each question.

The campaign trail to the presidency always proves to be exciting for all. Beginning with the first primaries held to decide upon candidates to the day in November when you choose the president, voters are constantly bombarded with political tactics aimed at getting their support. Voters must learn to discern between information and promises that have value and those that are last-ditch attempts at winning their votes.

1 In this passage, the word *trail* means—
- **A** dragging behind
- **B** aftermath
- **C** a track through the wilderness
- **D** a course to be followed

2 In this passage, the word *primaries* means—
- **F** group of colors
- **G** elections
- **H** first occurrences
- **J** celestial bodies

3 In this passage, the word *bombarded* means—
- **A** bombed
- **B** repeatedly giving
- **C** subject to rapidly moving particles
- **D** attacked

4 The word *discern* in this passage means—
- **F** disapprove
- **G** identify differences
- **H** dislike
- **J** collect

Practice 2 **Directions:** Read the passage. Then, read each question that follows the passage. Decide which is the best answer to each question.

During the dog days of summer, when the heat is most intense, a tree starts storing nutrients in its roots and trunk and cuts off the leaves. The green leaves start to fade as they stop producing chlorophyll. As the chlorophyll starts to break down, a turning leaf remains partly green with splotches of red and yellow. The colors were always present on the leaves, but the green pigment camouflaged them. Soon, the green fades away to reveal beautifully colored leaves as vibrant as flames.

1 In this passage, the expression *dog days of summer* means—
- **A** days dogs don't have enough to drink
- **B** time between July and September
- **C** earliest days of summer
- **D** final days of summer

2 The word *chlorophyll* means—
- **F** green pigment
- **G** chlorine
- **H** a leaf's waxy coating
- **J** oxygen

3 Here, the word *turning* means—
- **A** thinking over
- **B** rotating
- **C** causing prejudice
- **D** changing

4 In this passage, the expression *as vibrant as flames* means—
- **F** as dangerous as fire
- **G** as brightly colored as flames
- **H** as toxic as fire
- **J** as hot as flames

Hobb Green Breakfast by Richard Schmid ©1999

Part of being a good reader involves adapting your reading style to fit the material you are reading and your purpose in reading it. For example, the right reading style for research may involve identifying and focusing on the most important information in the text. You must also know how to evaluate its reliability.

In this chapter, you will learn how to use a variety of reading skills to improve your comprehension of the materials that you read in school and on your own.

▲ **Critical Viewing**
What can you tell about the type of material this woman is reading and about her approach to reading? Explain.
[Analyze]

Reading Methods and Tools

To understand more fully the contents of a book or article, you have to be able to identify and understand the main ideas it presents. Through the use of the special sections and features of your textbooks, reading techniques, and graphic organizers, you can improve your comprehension of the material.

Using Sections in Textbooks

Knowing how your textbook is organized will help you to apply your reading skills to it. Most textbooks have special sections to help you use them effectively. It is important to become familiar with these sections so that you know what they are and how to use them.

▶ **KEY CONCEPT** Use the special sections of your textbook to become familiar with the book's content. ■

Table of Contents The table of contents is located at the front of a textbook. It lists the order in which sections and chapters appear and indicates the pages on which each section begins. It can be used to locate general information or a particular section.

Chapter Introduction and Summary A chapter introduction tells you the main ideas of a chapter. A chapter summary, often appearing at the end of a chapter, reviews the main points and other important information.

Glossary The glossary, located at the back of a book, is a list of terms with definitions. Generally, the glossary includes specialized terms that are used within the textbook. These terms are listed alphabetically.

Appendix Appendices are found at the back of a textbook. They contain useful additional, or supplementary, material.

Index The index is found at the back of a book. It lists alphabetically all the subjects covered in the book and indicates on which pages they are discussed. In an index, people are listed by their last names first. Titles or topics that begin with *a* or *the* are listed by the first main word.

▶ **More Practice**

Academic and Workplace Skills Activity Book
• p. 34

Index of Authors and Titles

D
Da... ..., A,
...a Mare, Walter,
...emeter and Persepho...
Dickens, Charles, 428,
Dickey, James, 554, 557, 544
Dickinson, Emily, 28, 31
Dillard, Annie, 564, 576
Dineen, Jacqueline, 623,
Djuha Borrows a Pot, 83...
Down by the Salley Ga...
...le, Sir Arthur Co...
Dyi.. Cowboy, The, 328

E
Emerson, Ralph Waldo, 134, 136
Enemy, The, 235
Essoyan, Susan, 342

F
Fable, 136

Henry V, from, 232
Herriot, James, 380, 382
Highwayman, The, 300
Hippopptamus, The, 420
His Just Reward, 833
Hoch, Edward D., 416, 418
Holler, Richard, 773
Hoose, Phillip, 344, 346
Horovitz, Israel, 644
How the Snake Got Poison, 424
How to Enjoy Poetry, 557
Howard, Johnette, 178
Hughes, Langston, 166, 168
Hummingbird That Lived Through Winter, The, 172
Hurston, Zora Neale, 416, 424

I
I am a Native of North America, 615
Icarus and Daedalus, 864
Iceman, The, 223
If—, 138
I'm Nobody, 31

Using Features of Textbooks

In addition to using the special sections of your textbooks, you should use the textbook's special features to help you read and study the material.

> **KEY CONCEPT** Use the special features of your textbook to aid your reading and study of the material. ■

Titles, Headings, and Subheadings The material in textbooks is usually divided into manageable sections. The sections are labeled with titles, headings, and subheadings. The headings are usually larger than the rest of the text and appear in bold type. Often, they are printed in color. Main topics usually have larger headings; subtopics, smaller ones.

Questions and Exercises Questions and exercises are often provided at the ends of chapters or units. To help direct your reading, look over the questions before you begin. After you finish reading, use the questions to check your understanding.

Pictures and Captions The pictures that accompany the written text can often help you grasp meaning as you read. Look carefully at the photographs and the captions that accompany them, and think about how they relate to what you're reading.

> **Exercise 1** Examining the Sections in a Textbook
Examine two textbooks to become acquainted with their special sections. For each book, answer the following questions:
> 1. According to the table of contents, how many units and chapters does the textbook have?
> 2. Does the textbook have a glossary or an appendix? What are two pieces of information you can learn from each?
> 3. Pick one subject covered in the textbook. Then, using the index, list all the information dealing with this topic.

> **Exercise 2** Examining the Features of a Textbook Answer the following questions about one of your other textbooks.
> 1. How many headings and subheadings does the first chapter contain? Explain how the size of the headings helps you figure out the relationship between topics.
> 2. Does the chapter have an introduction, a summary, or questions and exercises? What information can be learned from each?
> 3. Find three pictures with captions in the textbook. How do the captions explain the picture? What information in the text does the picture help to explain?

Using Reading Strategies

There are a number of different strategies you can use to increase your understanding of the material you read. Three important ones are varying your reading style, learning Question-Answer Relationships, and using the SQ4R method.

 KEY CONCEPT Use a variety of reading strategies to gain a more complete understanding of the material you read. ■

Vary Your Reading Style The three types of reading styles are *skimming*, *scanning*, and *close reading*. Before you begin reading any material, consider your purpose, and then decide which reading style is the most suitable.

Skimming refers to looking over a text quickly to get a general idea of the information it contains. Look for highlighted or bold type, headings, and topic sentences.

Scanning involves searching through a text until you find a specific section or piece of information. Look for words related to the topic for which you are searching.

Close reading is the most deliberate, careful style of reading. The goal of a close reading is to thoroughly comprehend all of the information in the piece you are reading.

Use Question-Answer Relationships (QAR) One strategy for improving your reading ability is to ask and answer questions as you read. The first step in answering your questions is determining how and where the answer can be found. Following are four different methods for finding answers to different kinds of questions:

QUESTION-ANSWER RELATIONSHIPS
(How and Where to Find Answers)

RIGHT THERE
The answer is right there in the text, usually in one or two sentences. To answer this question, scan the text to locate information.

THINK AND SEARCH
The answer is in the text, but you need to think about the question's answer and then search for supporting evidence.

AUTHOR AND YOU
The answer is not only in the text. Answer this question by thinking about what the author says, what you know, and how these fit together.

ON YOUR OWN
The answer is, for the most part, not in the text. To answer this question, you need to draw from your own experiences. You can, however, use examples from the text.

🖥 Internet Tip

You can use each of these reading styles when you are using the Internet. *Skim* to get an overall sense of a site. *Scan* to find specific pieces of information on a site. Use *close reading* to read articles and other extended passages that interest you.

▶ More Practice

Academic and Workplace Skills Activity Book
• pp. 35–36

▶ **Exercise 3** Varying Reading Style and Using QAR Using the description of QAR on page 717, create and answer the four types of questions for your next reading assignment. Use the various reading styles to answer your questions: *Scan* the text to answer the Right There question, *skim* the text to answer the Think and Search question, and *closely read* the text to answer the Author and You question.

Use the SQ4R Method Another reading strategy that is especially appropriate for reading textbooks is called the SQ4R method, a systematic approach to reading that involves the six steps below. This method not only helps guide you as you read but also helps you retain information.

THE STAGES OF SQ4R

Survey — Preview the material you are going to read for these features: chapter title, headings, subheadings, introduction, summary, and questions or exercises.

Question — Turn each heading into a question about what will be covered under that heading. Ask the questions *who, what, when, where,* and *why* about it.

Read — Search for the answers to the questions that have been posed in the step above.

Recite — Orally or mentally recall questions and their related answers.

Record — Take notes to further reinforce the information. List the main ideas and the major details.

Review — Review the material on a regular basis, using some or all of the steps above.

▶ **Exercise 4** Using the SQ4R Method Use the SQ4R method to read a chapter in one of your textbooks. Write an explanation of how the method helped you learn and remember the information.

Using Graphic Organizers

A graphic organizer can be an effective tool for thinking and learning because it visually organizes information so you can review it more easily. A graphic organizer helps you arrange the material that you have read to show the relationships among various ideas and to prepare information for use in writing. The graphic organizer that you use depends on the nature of the material that you need to understand and learn.

KEY CONCEPT Use graphic organizers to understand how ideas in a text are related. ■

Sunburst A sunburst organizer can help you break down a broad topic into key ideas and details. To create a sunburst organizer, draw a circle. Write the topic or idea that you want to describe inside the circle. Then, draw rays coming from that circle. At the end of each ray, draw a box. Write the ideas or details that explain, describe, or are associated with the larger idea or topic inside each box.

🖱 Research Tip

Use graphic organizers to organize material from newspaper and magazine articles when you are preparing information from those sources for reports and presentations.

More Practice

Academic and Workplace Skills Activity Book
• p. 37

SUNBURST DIAGRAM

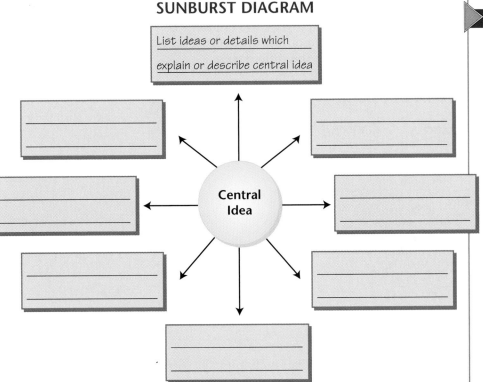

List ideas or details which

explain or describe central idea

Central Idea

Grid A grid can help you sort information from nonfiction texts. Create a series of boxes, as in the example below. In the box in the upper left corner, write the topic of the section you are reading. In the three boxes to the right, note subtopics or main points into which the topic is divided in the text. In the boxes directly below the topic box, list characteristics or key details of each subtopic.

GRID ORGANIZER

Topic you are studying	Subtopic	Subtopic	Subtopic
Characteristic			
Characteristic			

Venn Diagram Use a Venn diagram to look at similarities and differences between two subjects. Draw two overlapping circles. In the area where the circles overlap, write the characteristics that the two subjects have in common. In the sections of the circles that do not overlap, list the differences.

VENN DIAGRAM

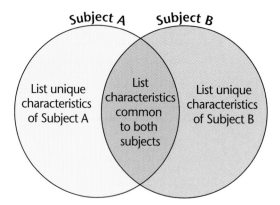

Exercise 5 Using Graphic Organizers Read a chapter from a textbook. Use one of the three graphic organizers described in this section to organize the information from that chapter. Explain why you chose the graphic organizer that you did.

Reading Nonfiction Critically

Section 30.2

Nonfiction is writing that is based on fact. When you read nonfiction critically, you examine and question the ideas the author presents. You learn to distinguish between fact and opinion, to identify the author's purpose, and to recognize when language is being used to distort your understanding of the text. This section will guide you through a number of reading strategies that you can use to become a critical reader.

Comprehending Nonfiction

Before you begin to read a text critically, you need to have a general understanding of it. This process involves finding and interpreting important information, identifying the author's purpose, and understanding the relationship the material has to what you are studying.

▶ **KEY CONCEPT** Comprehending nonfiction involves understanding the author's purpose as well as the information presented in the writing. ■

Locate Main Ideas and Major Details The main ideas are the key points an author wishes to convey. The major details explain and support these main points.

Interpret What You Are Reading Paraphrase, or state in your own words, the information in the text, starting with the main ideas and major details. This technique will help you to remember ideas and their relationship to each other.

Identify the Author's Purpose for Writing After you have a general idea of the content, examine the writer's choice of words and details to determine the author's purpose. As you continue to read, look for additional information that supports this purpose.

Reflect on What You Have Read After you have finished reading, take a moment to think about what the author has written. Consider the following questions: How does the information relate to what you are studying? How does this information relate to your life?

▶ **Exercise 6** Comprehending Nonfiction Use the strategies mentioned above to read a chapter from one of your textbooks. Then, answer these questions: What main points and major details did you locate? What was the author's purpose? What details did you use to identify it? What is the importance of the information you read?

🕖 **Learn More**

These critical reading skills are also helpful when revising the ideas in your own writing. See Chapters 1, 2, and 3.

▶ **More Practice**

Academic and Workplace Skills Activity Book
• pp. 38–39

Distinguishing Fact From Opinion

One of the keys to being a critical reader is being able to separate statements of fact from statements of opinion.

Facts A statement of fact can be *verified*, or proved to be true, using a written source (such as a dictionary, encyclopedia, or other reference book), an authority, a scientific experiment, or direct personal observation.

STATEMENT
OF FACT: The sun rises in the East and sets in the West.

The statement is a fact because it can be verified by a written source, such as an encyclopedia or a science textbook, or by direct personal observation.

Opinions A statement of opinion expresses a person's feelings, judgments, or predictions about a given situation. An opinion statement cannot be proved to be true or false. When you come across an opinion in a piece of writing, you should look to see whether the writer has supported the opinion with facts. Opinions that are backed up by facts are more worthy of acceptance than those that are not.

SUPPORTED   Solar energy is the most logical form of energy
OPINION: to develop because the sun will continue to
                release energy for another 5 billion years.

UNSUPPORTED: Solar energy is the best kind of energy, and in
                a few years, everyone will use solar energy
                instead of fossil fuels.

The first opinion statement is *worthy of serious consideration* because it is based on related facts. The second opinion statement, however, is *not* worthy of acceptance because it is not supported by facts.

▶ **Exercise 7** Distinguishing Between Fact and Opinion
Identify the first sentence in each numbered item as *fact* or *opinion*. If the statement is an opinion, tell whether it is *supported* or *unsupported*.
1. George Washington was a United States president.
2. George Washington was brave and honorable.
3. George Washington was a leader in the Revolutionary War.
4. He owned a great deal of land.
5. Mount Vernon, Washington's estate, is quite impressive. It covers about 500 acres of land and includes a mansion and fifteen smaller buildings.

🔲 **Research Tip**

Knowing the difference between fact and opinion will help you judge the accuracy of written material in such sources as editorials.

▶ **More Practice**

Academic and
Workplace Skills
Activity Book
• pp. 40–41

Identifying the Author's Purpose

Another part of being a critical reader is knowing how to determine the author's reason for writing. As you read, you should look for clues to help you identify the author's purpose. When you think you know what the author's purpose is, you should confirm this idea by linking it to details from the text.

KEY CONCEPT Learn to identify the author's purpose by using clues found in the material. ■

Following are some common purposes:

- **To Inform** The writer presents a series of factual statements.

- **To Instruct** The writer provides a step-by-step explanation of an idea or process.

- **To Offer an Opinion** The writer presents his or her viewpoint on an issue and attempts to convince readers to accept that viewpoint.

- **To Sell** The writer uses persuasive techniques to convince readers to buy something.

- **To Entertain** The author tells an engaging, often amusing story, or looks at a subject in an amusing way.

Exercise 8 Determining the Author's Purpose Read the following sentences, and determine the author's purpose. Explain your answer.

1. This manual will guide you through the steps for cooking a dinner for seven people.
2. Due to its smaller mass, the moon's gravity is one sixth of the gravity on Earth.
3. I'm going to tell you about three unconventional ways to relieve stress.
4. It is easy to avoid failure—simply never try anything.
5. Our modems are the quickest and easiest to use in today's market.

▼ Critical Viewing What clues can you identify in the picture that the girl is reading text meant to inform? [Analyze]

Applying Forms of Reasoning

As a critical reader, you should also use forms of reasoning —logical ways of thinking—to grasp underlying meaning and to make connections that extend beyond the text.

Make Inferences Sometimes, an author states his or her main ideas directly. In other cases, however, main ideas are implied, or conveyed indirectly. It is left up to you to piece together details to figure out what they mean or what message they convey. This is called **making inferences.**

INFORMATION: Stephen has been published in three different magazines.

INFERENCE: Stephen is a talented writer.

Make Generalizations You should also make generalizations, when appropriate, as you read. A **generalization** is a broad statement based on a large number of facts and examples.

INFORMATION: It rained on 25 out of 30 days this May.
GENERALIZATION: This May was a rainy month.

A *hasty generalization* is one based on too few examples, or one that fails to account for exceptions. Use these questions to make valid generalizations:

- What examples are presented, and how are they connected?
- Will the generalization hold true for all—or most—examples? Are there any exceptions to this statement?
- Are enough examples given to make a valid generalization?

▶ **Research Tip**

When you are conducting research on a topic, be careful to avoid making hasty generalizations based on a single source. Confirm your generalizations by consulting additional sources.

▶ **Exercise 9** Making Inferences and Generalizations Read the following passage. Then, answer the questions that follow.

According to Health and Human Services tests, American youth have gotten heavier than they were in the 1960's. Young people spend an average of thirteen hours a week at sports or other exercise. They spend three to four times that watching television and playing video games. Schoolchildren's scores are now declining for strength, power, speed, agility, and cardiovascular fitness. The tests also report that less than half of the young population meets the required standards of physical conditioning. Just a few years ago, the number was much higher.

1. What can you infer about the effect of physical activity on a person's strength and fitness?
2. What generalization can you make about the habits of schoolchildren?

▶ **More Practice**

Academic and Workplace Skills Activity Book
• pp. 42–43

Analyzing the Text

Analyzing a text involves looking at the language a writer uses and examining how the writer organizes the information that is presented.

▶ **KEY CONCEPT** Identify and understand the different uses of language, and recognize the various text structures. ■

Examine Authors' Language Authors sometimes use language in ways that can suggest how you should feel about a particular subject or issue. *Denotation, connotation,* and *jargon* are three ways that authors use language to affect your opinions and ideas about what you are reading.

Denotation and Connotation The exact meaning of a word is called its *denotation. Connotation,* on the other hand, refers to the feelings that a word stirs up. Often, writers carefully choose words with certain connotations. For example, if a writer is trying to convey a negative impression of a subject, he or she is likely to choose words with a negative connotation. Look at the different connotations of the words in the examples below:

EXAMPLES: Their furniture is *cheap.*
Their furniture is *inexpensive.*
The man was *dressed* in a *formal black suit.*
The gentleman was *outfitted* in an *elegant black tuxedo.*

Jargon *Jargon* is the use of specialized vocabulary intended for a specific audience— for example, sportswriters or doctors. Jargon is meant to have a very precise meaning, but it often hides, rather than reveals, meaning. The opposite of jargon is *direct language.*

▶ **Exercise 10** Analyzing Uses of Language
Look through magazines and newspapers. Find three examples of words with positive connotations, three examples with negative connotations, and three examples of jargon.

▶ Critical Viewing Describe this man's outfit in two ways—one using words with positive connotations, the other using words with negative connotations. [Describe]

Identify Text Structure Writers structure their texts in different ways depending on their topic, form, and purpose for writing. Learn to recognize how an author structures a text so that you can understand the relationship among ideas and locate information easily. Following are some of the common types of organization:

Cause and Effect In a cause-and-effect structure, the writer presents a series of interrelated events or situations. One or more events or situations cause another event or situation to occur, which can then lead to other events or situations.

Chronological Order Chronological order is the arrangement of events in the order in which they occurred. Writers frequently use chronological order when telling a story or describing an event.

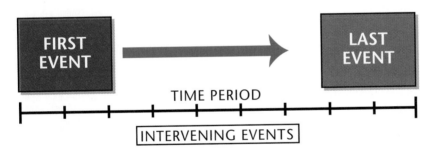

▶ **Speaking and Listening Tip**

Speakers also use these organizations when delivering public speeches. Think about the types of speeches for which each organization would be most appropriate.

Order of Importance When writers create a persuasive argument, they often arrange their evidence in order of importance. One effective way to use order of importance is to begin with your second-best argument to capture audience interest. Then, build your other support in increasing order of importance, finishing with your most powerful point.

Spatial Order When writers are describing something, they often arrange details as they appear in space. For example, they might move from top to bottom.

▶ **Exercise 11** Analyzing Text Structures Conduct research, either in the library or on the Internet, to find four pieces of nonfiction, each following one of the organizations described above. Explain why each organizational pattern was used.

Section 30.3 Reading Literary Writing

Literary writing refers to fiction, drama, and poetry. You can use some of the same strategies to read literary writing that you use to read nonfiction. However, there are some special strategies that will help you with these genres, or forms.

Reading Fiction

The following strategies will help you to increase your comprehension of short stories and novels.

Predict Read closely to find hints about what will happen next, and make predictions about these future events based on the clues that you find. As you read, check your predictions.

Identify With Characters When you imagine yourself as a character in a story or place yourself in the character's situation, you increase your understanding of the character's feelings and thoughts. As a result, the story comes alive.

Ask Questions Become involved in the story by asking questions about the characters, setting, and events. As you read, look for answers to your questions.

ACTIVE READING QUESTIONS

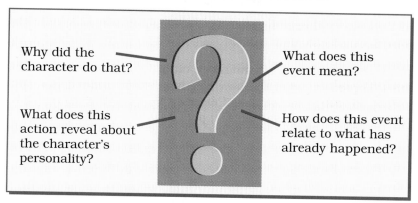

Why did the character do that?

What does this event mean?

What does this action reveal about the character's personality?

How does this event relate to what has already happened?

Make Inferences The theme, or central message, of a work of fiction is usually implied, or conveyed indirectly. To grasp this message, you need to make inferences, or draw conclusions, based on the characters' comments and actions, the outcome of events, and other details the writer provides.

▶ **Exercise 12** Reading Fiction Read a short story, and apply the strategies above. After you've finished, write an explanation of how the strategies affected your response to the story.

▶ **More Practice**

Academic and Workplace Skills Activity Book
• pp. 44–45

Reading Drama

Drama is a story designed to be performed on the stage. It is told mostly through what the actors say and do. Stage directions in the script contain instructions about how actors should move and how they should speak their lines. Sometimes, these stage directions contain information about the sets, costumes, lighting, and sound effects. Use the following strategies to increase your understanding of drama:

Read the Cast of Characters
Before the dialogue begins, there is usually a list of the characters who take part in the action. Reading this list can tell you the various relationships among the characters. It may also give a brief description of the characters to help you imagine who they are.

Use Stage Directions to Envision the Play
Use the information in the stage directions to create a mental picture of what is happening during the play, as well as a picture of what people look like and how they behave.

Review Events After Scenes or Acts
Dramas are often broken into acts or scenes. These breaks in the play give you a chance to review what has happened in the play. Pause at the end of each scene or act, summarize what has happened up to that point, and make predictions about what will happen in the next scene or act.

▲ **Critical Viewing**
What stage directions would you expect to find in a written version of this scene? **[Deduce]**

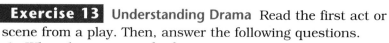

Exercise 13 Understanding Drama Read the first act or scene from a play. Then, answer the following questions.
1. What three pieces of information can you learn from reading the cast of characters?
2. Explain the significance of three stage directions. How do they contribute to your understanding of a mood, an action, or a character?
3. Summarize the events that occurred in the act or scene.
4. Predict what will happen in the next act or scene. Explain the basis for your predictions.
5. Read the next act or scene and check to see whether your predictions come true.

Reading Poetry

Poetry is a unique type of writing in which ideas are presented in verse. Poems are generally briefer than other forms of writing, and sound plays a more important role than in most other writing. Use the following strategies to help you understand and appreciate poetry:

Identify the Speaker The speaker is the imaginary voice that the poet uses to present the poem. Occasionally, the speaker is the poet. At other times, the speaker is a character invented by the poet. As you read, look for clues to help identify the speaker's personality, experiences, and perspective on life.

Experience Images Through Your Senses Poetry usually contains images, or word pictures, that appeal to one or more of your five senses. To experience these images more fully, use your senses to see, hear, smell, touch, and feel what the poet describes.

Read Lines According to Their Punctuation
Sometimes, readers make the mistake of pausing at the end of each line of a poem. Instead, you should read according to punctuation. When you see a comma, dash, or semicolon, pause before continuing with the poem. Stop longer at periods, question marks (remembering to read the material as you would a question), and exclamation points (remembering to stress the statements or exclamations).

Read the following excerpt from Walt Whitman's *Leaves of Grass*, pausing at the commas (shaded yellow), stopping longer at the periods, dashes, semicolons, and exclamation marks (shaded red), and continuing to read where it is shaded green.

> Poets to come! orators, singers, musicians to come!
> Not to-day is to justify me and answer what I am for,
> But you, a new brood, native, athletic, continental,
>   greater than before known,
> Arouse! for you must justify me.
>
> I myself but write one or two indicative words for➡
>   the future,
> I but advance a moment only to wheel and hurry ➡
>   back in the darkness.
>
> I am a man who, sauntering along, without fully➡
>   stopping, turns a casual look upon you and then➡
>   averts his face,
> Leaving it to you to prove and define it,
> Expecting the main things from you.

▶ Speaking and Listening Tip

One of the best ways to truly understand and appreciate a poem is to read it aloud. Listen to the sounds of the words and the rhythms of the lines. How does the poet use sound to enhance the poem's meaning?

More Practice

Academic and Workplace Skills Activity Book
• pp. 46–49

Paraphrase the Lines Paraphrase, or restate in your own words, what you think each part of the poem is communicating. Putting the ideas into your own words will help you clarify and remember the meaning.

> **Exercise 14** Reading Poetry Reread the poem on page 729. After you have read the poem, answer the following questions.
> 1. Who is the speaker of the poem?
> 2. How did the punctuation (or lack of it) help you to understand the poem?
> 3. What sensory details did the poem have? Describe the images that these details created in your mind.
> 4. Paraphrase the poem.

Reading Myths, Legends, and Folk Tales

Myths are fictional tales that explain the actions of gods or heroes, or explain natural occurrences. **Legends** are widely told stories about the past that may or may not be based on fact. **Folk tales** are entertaining stories about heroes, adventurers, or mischief-makers. Like myths, folk tales often offer fictional explanations for natural occurrences. Although these stories are retold in writing, they come to us from the oral tradition—the passing along of stories by word of mouth. Each story reveals something about the values and traditions of the culture from which it comes.

◀ Critical Viewing Does this look like a good setting for reading a piece of literary writing? Why or why not? **[Evaluate]**

Identify the Cultural Context Understanding the culture from which a myth, legend, or folk tale comes will help you to understand the ideas presented in it. Read any notes that accompany a story to find out more about the culture. While you read the story, look for details that tell you about the culture. Record these ideas in a chart like the one below.

Clues to Culture in "All Stories Are Anansi's"	
Clue	**What this clue says about the culture**
Anansi, spider Mmoboro, hornets Onini, python	shows a variety of animals and plant life in Ghana
Anansi wants to own stories	suggests storytelling is valued
conflict resolved by Nyame, the sky god	shows the religious beliefs of the culture

Predict Look for clues to help you make educated guesses about what will happen next. As you read ahead, revise your predictions as new details unfold, and check to see whether your predictions come true.

Recognize the Storyteller's Purpose Knowing why a legend, myth, or folk tale was told will help you understand why the characters in it behave in certain ways. It will also help you learn more about the culture itself. For example, knowing that a legend deals with how a terrible blizzard affected the land might lead you to conclude that its purpose is to find a way to explain changes in the weather.

 Technology Tip

Locate the Web site of a local cultural organization. What does it teach about this culture? How is this culture different from your own?

> **Exercise 15** Reading Myths, Legends, and Folk Tales

Read a myth, legend, or folk tale from your literature textbook, and answer the following questions.
  1. List details from the chart in this section, and explain what they suggest about the culture presented in the piece.
  2. What predictions did you make about events in the piece? Were you correct? Why or why not?
  3. What is the purpose of this piece? What does the purpose suggest about the culture's values or beliefs?

Reading From Varied Sources

You have a wide variety of sources from which you can choose reading material. You can read newspapers, magazines, advertisements, manuals, handbooks, textbooks, Web pages, or anthologies—collections of short works. What you read depends on why you are reading. Select material that is best suited to your purpose for reading.

Forms and Applications One of the most practical purposes for reading is to fill out forms and applications. Look over these texts carefully. Understanding what information is being requested and where you are expected to write it will help you fill out forms accurately. Look at the sample form below, and decide what information is being requested in each section. Follow any additional directions about how to fill out the form. Use the spaces and directions in italics to help you decide.

SAMPLE FORM

FORM A

Please print in blue or black ink.

Name (*last name first*)

Street

City   State

Date of Birth
MO   DAY   YR

Phone Number

Newspapers When you want to know what's going on in your community or the world, you can find out by reading a newspaper. Some newspapers are local—they cover events that affect a town, city, county, or region. Other newspapers are national—they cover events and issues that affect the entire country. If you are looking for news about a specific event, consider whether the event has local, national, or global impact. Choose the newspaper that will give the most thorough coverage to that particular type of event. Except for sections that are intended to offer a viewpoint, such as the editorial page, newspapers should report the news objectively, without including opinions.

⊙ Vocabulary Tip

When filling out a form or an application, use language as precisely as possible. Provide only the information asked for in the directions.

▶ **More Practice**

Academic and Workplace Skills Activity Book
• p. 51

Magazines When you want to read about a specific area of interest, such as a hobby or sport, you can find information and ideas in a magazine. Some magazines deal with current events, but many magazines focus on attracting a specific audience with specific interests. You can find magazines on camping, computers, crafts, cooking, woodworking, and celebrities. Unlike newspapers, magazines usually offer an opinion or a point of view on the topic they present. Even magazines that cover current events or celebrities set a tone or take an attitude toward the subjects they cover.

Electronic Texts Electronic texts such as Web pages provide detailed, specific information on a wide variety of topics. Web pages may offer objective information, or they may present one person's opinion about a topic. Because Web pages come from such a wide variety of sources, it is vital that you evaluate the authority and background of the source before using or accepting any of the information presented. Some electronic texts are provided by retailers—companies that want to sell you something—and should be viewed as advertisements rather than as informational texts.

▲ **Critical Viewing**
What kinds of information would you expect these students to find? **[Deduce]**

Anthologies If you discover that you enjoy a particular type of literature or a particular author, you might select an anthology or collection that focuses on your preference. There are anthologies that focus on a single author's work; on specific types of literature, such as poetry or drama; and on literature from certain periods, such as early American literature or modern short stories.

Reflecting on Your Understanding of Reading Strategies

Using the questions below as a guide, write a journal entry in which you reflect on what you have learned in this chapter.

- What strategies best helped me to study from my textbook? Why were they so helpful?
- How has my understanding of the uses of language changed?
- Which graphic organizers were most useful to me? Why?
- What are my most common purposes for reading?
- From what sources do I read most often?

Standardized Test Preparation Workshop

Make Inferences and Predictions

The reading sections of standardized tests often measure your ability to make inferences. You can make inferences, or draw logical conclusions, about what you have read, about characters and stories, or about the author's purpose or point of view. Some questions require you to make a prediction or anticipate future actions or outcomes from the material you have read. Some tests will ask you to read a passage, think about it by responding to a question, and explain your response in writing.

The following sample test items will help you prepare for answering these types of questions on standardized tests.

Test Tip

Before answering difficult questions, first mark them. Then, answer all the easy questions. Finally, go back and use the majority of your time to work on those questions that you have marked.

Sample Test Items

Read this passage from "The All-American Slurp" by Lensey Namioka. Then answer the questions that follow the passage.

We had been invited to dinner by our neighbors, the Gleasons. After arriving at the house, we shook hands with our hosts and packed ourselves into a sofa. Our family of four sat stiffly in a row; my younger brother and I stole glances at our parents for a clue as to what to do next.

1 The narrator feels—

   A comfortable in this setting.
   B uncomfortable.
   C happy and excited.
   D sad.

Answer the following question. Base your answer on the passage from "The All-American Slurp."

How does the narrator feel about her surroundings? Support your answer with details from the story.

Answers and Explanations

The answer is *B*. By using the information provided in the passage, you conclude that the narrator was uncomfortable with her surroundings.

Your answer should consist of a paragraph that includes a topic sentence and details from the passage that support it. One possible response:

The narrator is uncomfortable in her surroundings. She describes how her family withdrew to the safety of the couch but were not relaxed and sat stiffly. She and her brother don't know how to act and are looking to her parents for help.

> **Practice 1** **Directions:** Read the passage. Then, answer the questions that follow the passage.

The following excerpt from "Suzy and Leah" by Jane Yolen is a diary entry of a young girl who lived in a concentration camp and is now living in a refugee camp in the United States.

August 5, 1944

My dear *Mutti* (Mommy),

I have but a single piece of paper to write on. And a broken pencil. But I will write small so I can tell all. I address it to you, Mutti, though you are gone from me forever. I write in English, to learn better, because I want to make myself be understood.

Today another girl came. With more sweets. A girl with yellow hair and a false smile. Yonni and Zipporah and Ruth, my friends, all grabbed for the sweets. Like wild animals. Like . . . like prisoners. But we are no longer prisoners. Even though we are still penned in.

I stared at the yellow-haired girl until she was forced to look down. Then I walked away. When I turned to look back, she was gone. Disappeared. As if she had never been.

Leah

1 The author writes the story as diary entries—
- **A** to share the characters' personal thoughts and feelings.
- **B** to use a traditional story form.
- **C** to keep the reader guessing.
- **D** to create suspense.

2 Where is the girl's mother?
- **F** on a trip
- **G** living in another country

- **H** dead
- **J** in prison

3 The girl needs to learn English—
- **A** because it is required as her second language.
- **B** so she can work at her job.
- **C** so she can communicate in a new country.
- **D** because it is her hobby.

4 What is the best way to describe Leah's feelings toward the girl with the yellow hair?
- **F** dislikes her
- **G** admires her
- **H** believes she is kind
- **J** wants to be like her

5 If the girl with the yellow hair and Leah meet, they will—
- **A** instantly like each other.
- **B** become roommates.
- **C** probably not like each other at first.
- **D** not be able to communicate at all.

6 Leah stares at the girl because—
- **F** she is not in a regular home.
- **G** she thinks the girl is treating her like an animal.
- **H** she is jealous.
- **J** she doesn't like her hair.

> **Practice 2** **Directions:** Answer the following question. Base your answer on the passage from "Suzy and Leah."

READ, THINK, EXPLAIN What do Leah's reactions to the girl with the yellow hair (Suzy) tell you about Leah? Use details from the story to explain your answer.

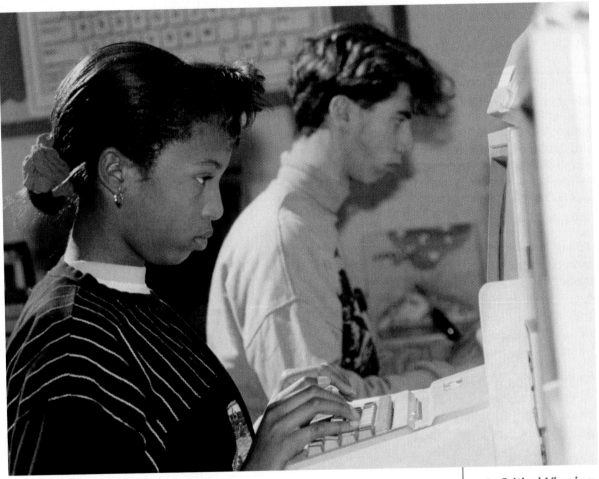

Studying, researching, taking tests—all are vital skills to develop as you progress through your years at school. In this chapter, you will learn how to make the most of your study time. You will also learn more about retrieving information from print and electronic sources. Finally, you will receive valuable tips that can help improve your test scores.

▲ **Critical Viewing**
On what types of assignments might these students be working? On what do you base your answer? **[Speculate]**

Section
31.1

Basic Study Skills

Developing good study habits is an important first step toward success in school.

Forming a Study Plan

A study plan is a consistent, well-thought-out approach to studying that includes where and when you study.

▶ **KEY CONCEPT** Establish a study area that works well for you, and set aside regular periods for studying. ■

Choose a Study Setting Even though you can probably get some studying done at school, you should set up a study area at home. Make a habit of studying in the same place every day. Keep everything you need in your study area, so you will not have to interrupt your studies to hunt for pencils, paper, and so on. A good study area is

- free from distraction.

- equipped with a chair, desk, and reading lamp.

- well-organized and neat.

Create a Study Schedule You will have enough time to complete all of your homework and still have time for other activities if you plan your time carefully. At the beginning of each week, plan how you will use your study time each day. Vary the amount of time you spend on each subject, based on tests, projects, and long-term assignments that are scheduled.

▲ **Critical Viewing** Judging from this photograph, is this girl working in a good study area? Why? **[Analyze]**

▶ **More Practice**
Academic and Workplace Skills Activity Book
• p. 52

		SAMPLE STUDY SCHEDULE	
		3:00–4:30	Sports Practice
◯	Mon	5:00–6:00	Daily Assignments
		7:30–8:00	Review for Science Test (Weds)
		8:00–8:30	Work on Social Studies Paper
	Tue	5:00–6:00	Daily Assignments
		7:30–8:30	Study for Science Test
	Wed	5:00–6:00	Daily Assignments
		7:00–8:00	Work on Social Studies Paper
		8:00–8:30	Review for Math Test (Next Tues)

Basic Study Skills • **737**

Keep an Assignment Book It is important to keep track of the papers, reading assignments, and tests due in each class. Do this by keeping an assignment book or a special assignment section in your notebook. Write down each assignment as you get it. This will help you plan what to work on in your scheduled time. Keeping an assignment book will help you to complete each assignment on time and to be prepared for any in-class discussions or tests.

▶ **KEY CONCEPT** Use an assignment book to record homework assignments and due dates. ■

Use the following model to set up your assignment book:

Date	Subject	Assignment	Due	Completed
10/15	History	Read Ch. 6, pp. 55–75	10/18	✔
10/16	Math	Answer problems 1–20 on p. 42	10/17	
10/17	English	Answer questions on pp. 76 & 77	10/19	

▶ **Exercise 1** Describing Your Study Area If you already have a study area, write a brief description of it, and explain any ways it can be improved. If you do not, choose one. Then, write a short explanation of why you selected this place.

▶ **Exercise 2** Preparing a Study Schedule Create your own study schedule, using the sample schedule as a model. Follow the schedule for a week. Then, evaluate it and make any needed changes. Keep a copy in your notebook.

▶ **Exercise 3** Setting Up an Assignment Book In a special section of your notebook or in a separate notebook, set up an assignment book. Use it for a week. Then, if you find it necessary, revise it. You may want to make changes, such as leaving more room for writing assignments or using a red marker to indicate tests.

Technology Tip

Computer software is available to help you keep track of your assignments. Consult with your teacher or technology coordinator to consider databases or management programs you might use for this purpose.

Taking Notes

Taking good notes is an important and useful study skill. Taking notes in class helps you remember what you heard, and taking notes while reading helps you remember what you read. Later, you can use your notes to study for a test or just to review the information you have learned.

TIPS FOR TAKING NOTES

- Don't record every word; focus on capturing main ideas.
- Label your notes with the topic and date.
- Keep notes for different subjects in separate notebooks or in separate sections of a general notebook.

Modified Outlines One note-taking device that you can use to sort out main ideas and major details is a *modified outline*. List each main idea, and underline it. Place major details below the main idea, and number them. Jot down supporting details under each major detail.

SAMPLE MODIFIED OUTLINE

Solar System —————— Main idea
1. Sun —————————— Major detail
    A star ——————————— Supporting details
    Center of the solar system
2. Planets
    Nine planets
    Orbit the sun in west to east direction
    Most have moons or satellites
3. Asteroids, Meteoroids, and Comets
    Asteroids—fragments of rock
    Meteoroids—the result of asteroid collisions
    Comets—solid nucleus surrounded by
        frozen gases and dust particles

Summaries Writing a *summary* is another way of organizing information you've learned. After reading a chapter or attending a class, write one or more paragraphs stating the key points covered and explaining how the ideas are connected.

> **Exercise 4** Making a Modified Outline and a Summary
> Create a modified outline and a summary of a chapter in your science or social studies textbook.

Speaking and Listening Tip

Spoken summaries can also be an effective study tool. With a classmate, take turns summarizing a lecture or a piece you have read. Check to see that you both have the same understanding.

More Practice

Academic and Workplace Skills Activity Book
- p. 53

Reference Skills

The information explosion of recent years makes it possible to obtain more and more information on your own. Just about every major form of printed reference now has its electronic equivalent on CD-ROM, on-line, or both. Many of the works, in both printed and electronic form, are available at school or public libraries.

Using the Library

Whether you want to know the date of a president's birth or of the first space-shuttle flight, your best source of information will generally be the library. Both your school and public libraries hold a vast amount of knowledge.

Most school and public libraries contain some or all of these resources: fiction and nonfiction books, audiocassettes and videocassettes, periodicals (newspapers, magazines, and journals), information on microfilm, reference works in printed and electronic form, and computer access to the Internet.

Use the Library Catalog Whether you seek books for casual reading or for research, your search usually begins with the *library catalog*. The catalog will show you whether the library owns a particular book. It can also help you find

- books by an author when you don't know the titles.
- books on a subject when you don't know titles or authors.

▶ **KEY CONCEPT** Use the library catalog to identify and locate the books that a library contains. ■

The library catalog will be in one of these three forms:

Card Catalog A card catalog lists books on index cards. Each book has a separate *author card* and *title card*. If the book is nonfiction, it also has at least one *subject card*. Cards are filed alphabetically in small drawers, with author cards alphabetized by last names and title cards alphabetized by the first words of the titles, excluding *A*, *An*, and *The*.

▲ **Critical Viewing**
What are the key pieces of information listed on the spines of these books? **[Analyze]**

▶ **More Practice**
Academic and Workplace Skills Activity Book
• pp. 54–55

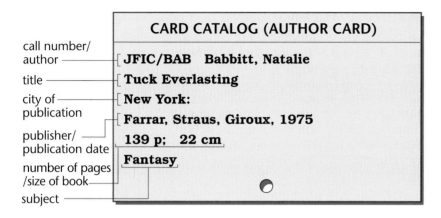

Printed Catalog A printed catalog lists information in printed booklets, with each book listed alphabetically by author, by title, and—if nonfiction—by subject. Often, there are separate booklets for author, title, and subject listings.

Electronic Catalog An electronic catalog lists entries in an on-line database that you can access from computer terminals in the library. Usually, you can find a book's catalog entry by typing in its title, key words in the title, its author's name, or an appropriate subject. Entries usually tell you

- whether the book is available or has been checked out.
- whether the book is available from other local libraries and may be obtained through an interlibrary loan system.

Technology Tip

Some electronic catalogs can be accessed remotely through a computer in your home or school. Ask your librarian if this feature is available and, if so, how to use it.

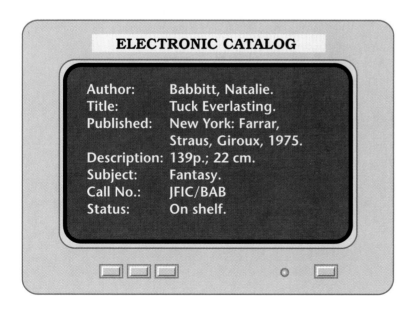

Finding Books on Library Shelves

Libraries need a special method of organizing their books so that people can find them. The library distinguishes between two kinds of books—*fiction* and *nonfiction.*

Fiction Books In most libraries, fiction books are shelved in a special section, alphabetized by the authors' last names. In the library catalog and on the book's spine, a work of fiction may be labeled *F* or *FIC*, followed by one or more letters of an author's last name—for example, *FIC Paul* may appear on a novel by Gary Paulsen.

▶ **KEY CONCEPT** Find fiction arranged alphabetically by the authors' last names. Find nonfiction on the shelves by using the call numbers. ■

Nonfiction Books Nonfiction books have call numbers. In most school and public libraries, the call numbers are based on the Dewey Decimal System. Books are arranged in number-letter order on the shelves—for example, 619.1, 619.2, 619.31A, 619.31D, 619.32A, 619.32P, 620.1. The system is named for an American librarian, Melvil Dewey, who suggested that books could be classified into ten main groups, as shown in following chart:

🔲 Research Tip

Through your library research, you may learn about authorities in the area you area researching. You may want to consider interviewing one or more of these authorities, either on the telephone or in person. Ask your librarian for help in locating information about such individuals.

General Works	Philosophy	Religion	Social Sciences	Languages	Pure Sciences	Technology	The Arts	Literature	History
000–099	100–199	200–299	300–399	400–499	500–599	600–699	700–799	800–899	900–999

MAIN CLASSES OF THE DEWEY DECIMAL SYSTEM

Locating Biographies and Other Special Materials Most libraries have separate sections for biographies and autobiographies, reference books, and young-adult books.

Biographies A *biography* is a factual account of a person's life. If that person wrote his or her own story, it is called an *autobiography*. In the library catalog and on the book's spine, a biography may be labeled *B* or *BIO*, or *921* (its Dewey Decimal number), followed by one or more letters of the subject's last name. For example, *BIO Lin* may appear on a biography of Abraham Lincoln.

Reference Materials Most libraries also have a special section for *reference books*. Frequently, the sources in the library's reference section are labeled *R* or *REF.*

Young Adult Books Books that are of interest to teenagers may be placed in a *young-adult section*. The letters *YA* or *J* (*Juvenile*) in front of the call number show that the book is in this section.

Nonprint Materials In addition to books, most libraries contain a variety of nonprint materials, including videos, audiotapes, audio CDs, CD-ROMs, and more. Libraries use a variety of symbols in catalog entries to indicate nonprint material, and these materials are usually kept in special sections of the building. Ask your librarian for help locating such materials.

▲ **Critical Viewing** How would you tell which one of these drawers to look in for a particular book or subject area? **[Analyze]**

▷ **Exercise 5** Using the Library Catalog and Finding Books on Shelves When you visit your school or local library, use the catalog to answer the following questions.

1. What kind of catalog does the library use—card, printed, or electronic? Where is it located?
2. What are the titles, subjects, and call numbers of the books that your library carries by author Laurence Yep?
3. What are the titles, authors, and call numbers of three books about the solar system?
4. Arrange these fiction authors in the order in which you would find them on the library shelves: Louise Erdrich, Elizabeth Enright, Ralph Waldo Emerson.
5. Using the Dewey Decimal System, indicate the general subject matter you would expect to find in nonfiction books with these call numbers:

   a. 973.7G   **b.** 613.5A   **c.** 423F   **d.** 746R

Using Periodicals and Periodical Indexes

Newspapers, magazines, and other printed materials that are published at regular intervals, or periods, are called **periodicals.** They may be issued daily, weekly, monthly, or at any other regular interval.

When to Use Periodicals Periodicals provide the most recent information about a wide variety of subjects. A book provides more detailed information, but will not include information, events, or developments that take place after its publication.

> **KEY CONCEPT** Use periodicals when you are researching a current event or development, or when you want to learn how an event was reported at the time it happened. ■

Using Periodical Indexes **Periodical indexes** contain *citations* that tell you precisely where and when an article was published. They may also contain *abstracts,* or brief summaries, of the articles. Indexes can be in print or electronic form. Many electronic indexes provide the full text for some or all of the articles cited.

> **KEY CONCEPT** Use a periodical index to find articles published in newspapers and magazines. ■

The most frequently used periodical index is the *Readers' Guide to Periodical Literature.* The *Readers' Guide* covers all types of periodicals. A sample entry from the *Readers' Guide* appears on the next page. Other periodical indexes focus on specific subjects, such as art and business.

Locating Periodicals If the periodical index does not provide the full text of an article, you need to find the article itself. Most libraries subscribe to many periodicals to which all library users have access. Current issues can usually be found on shelves in a special section of the library. Older issues may be available on CD-ROM or on microfilm.

▲ **Critical Viewing** What is this student doing with the information she gathers from a periodical index? Why? [Analyze]

SAMPLE *READERS' GUIDE* ENTRY

Fruit ——————————————————— Main subject heading

  See also ———————————————— Cross-references
  Cooking—Fruit
  individual names of fruit

Fruit for all seasons. E. W. Stiles il *Nat Hist* —— Author of article / Title of article
93:42–53 Ag '84

Fruit selection. N. Nevins. il *South Living* 19:144
Ag '84 ——————————————————— Magazine

Sweet summer sensations. il *Glamour*
82:188–99 Jl '84

Winter temptations. il *Glamour* 82:302–5+ N '84

    Diseases and pests ——————— Subheading

  See also
  Codling moths
  Fruit flies

      Drying

Stretch summer flavor with dried produce. M.
Chason. il. *South Living* 19:188+ Je '84 —— Volume: page numbers and date

    Preservation

Keeping fruit fresh [polyethylene film wrap]
Consum Res Mag 67:2 F' 84 ——————— Illustrated

      Ripening

Ripe promises. E. W. Stiles. *Nat Hist* 93:51
Ag '84

      Varieties

Have you grown new fruit varieties? *Sunset*
172:256 Je '84

Exercise 6 **Using Periodicals** Visit your school or local library to answer the following questions.

1. What newspapers does the library carry?
2. Name two newsmagazines the library carries. How far back does each go, and in what format(s) are they given?
3. Use a periodical index to find citations for articles on a subject you are studying in science or social studies. Then, find at least one of the articles in your library.
4. Using a periodical index, locate a newspaper or magazine article about someone you admire in sports or another field. Read the article, and then write a summary.
5. Using a periodical index, find two recent articles on a current event.

Using Vertical Files Pamphlets containing current information on topics such as local government, educational programs, and local parks can also be a valuable research tool. Most often, pamphlets are stored in a vertical file—a file cabinet with large drawers. Ask your librarian whether the library's vertical files contain any pamphlets that might aid you in your research.

Internet Tip

Many leading newspapers and magazines now have free Internet Web sites where you can read current editions at no cost. The older articles are usually stored in a section called the *archives.*

More Practice

Academic and Workplace Skills Activity Book
• p. 56

Using Dictionaries

A dictionary is the first place you should look to find the spelling and meaning of words. Dictionaries also contain other information about words, such as their pronunciations.

Distinguishing Types of Dictionaries Like most references nowadays, dictionaries are available in both print and electronic forms. They also come in various types and sizes.

THREE TYPES OF DICTIONARIES	
Unabridged	Exhaustive study of the English language containing over 250,000 words
Abridged	Compact editions containing listings from 55,000 to 160,000 words
Specialized	Limited to words of a particular type or field, such as foreign languages or mathemathics

Finding Words in Dictionaries In *printed dictionaries,* all the items are listed in strict alphabetical order—that is, letter by letter, starting with *a* and finishing with *z.* To help speed a word search, use *guide words,* the large words at the top of each page that indicate the first and last words listed. In *electronic dictionaries,* you usually find a word simply by typing the word and having the computer search the dictionary database.

Understanding Dictionary Entries The information contained in a dictionary entry varies from dictionary to dictionary. Following are some of the elements you will find:

1. **Entry Word** A word and the information about it are called a *main entry.* The word itself is called an *entry word.* From it, you can confirm the word's spelling and learn how to break it into *syllables.* Dashes, dots, or spaces show the syllables.

2. **Pronunciation** Pronunciation is indicated by symbols that show how to say the word and which syllable to stress. To understand the symbols, consult the dictionary's *pronunciation key.* The syllable that gets the most emphasis usually has a heavy *primary stress,* which is shown by a heavy mark after it ('). Words of more than two syllables may also have a shorter, lighter, *secondary stress* mark (').

 Spelling Tip

Some words have more than one acceptable spelling. These will all be listed in a dictionary.

3. **Part-of-Speech Labels** These labels tell you how a word is used. This information is given in abbreviated form. When a word can be used as more than one part of speech, the meanings are grouped under each part-of-speech label.

4. **Plurals and Inflected Forms** The dictionary may also show the *plural forms of nouns* and *inflected forms of verbs*—past tense and participle forms—if there is anything irregular about their spelling.

5. **Etymology** The word's history, or etymology, usually appears in brackets near the start or end of the entry. Abbreviations used are explained in a key.

6. **Definitions** When a word has more than one definition, the dictionary will give the definitions a number and group them according to their part of speech.

7. **Idioms and Derived Words** The end of an entry may list and define *idioms*, or expressions, that contain the word. It may also list *derived words* formed by adding suffixes, such as *-ly* or *-ness*, to the entry word.

Usage labels indicate words that are rarely used in formal English. For example, (*Arch.*) indicates that a word is archaic and no longer used. *Field labels* indicate words used in certain fields, such as math.

> **◎ Vocabulary Tip**
>
> Etymologies can help you extend your vocabulary. Knowing a word's origin can help you remember its meaning. It will also help you figure out the meaning of related words.

SAMPLE DICTIONARY ENTRY

①　②　③　④　⑤

ear|ly (ur′lē) *adv., adj.* **-li|er, -li|est** [ME *erli* <OE *ærlic,* adv. (> *ærlic,* adj.) <*ær,* before (see ERE) + *-lice,* adv. suffix (see -LY², LIKE¹] ⑥**1** near the beginning of a given period of time or of a series, as of events; soon after the start **2** before the expected or customary time **3** in the far distant past; in ancient or remote times **4** in the near future; before much time has passed — ⑦**early on** at an early stage; near the beginning —**ear′li ness** *n.*

▶ **Exercise 7** **Working With a Dictionary** Use a dictionary to answer the following questions.

1. Which word is not spelled correctly?
   a. lollipop   b. gasoline   c. kindergarden   d. judgment
2. How many syllables are in the word *extravagance*?
3. What part of speech is the word *before*?
4. What is the origin of the word *silhouette*?
5. What are two definitions of the word *place*?

▶ **More Practice**

Academic and Workplace Skills Activity Book
• p. 57

Using Other Print and Electronic References

A library's reference section includes other books and electronic resources that can help you in your studies. Listed below are a few of the resources you will find.

Print Encyclopedias When you are investigating an unfamiliar subject, one of the best places to start is a *general encyclopedia.* A general encyclopedia is a collection of articles that provide basic information on many subjects.

Most encyclopedias consist of several volumes. The spine of each book is marked with letters covering a part of the alphabet. Each volume contains articles on subjects that begin with those parts of the alphabet. At the top of each page, guide words show the subjects covered on that page.

CD-ROM Encyclopedias Encyclopedias on CD-ROM provide photographs, artwork, video, and audio to enhance the information on various topics. Generally, they have an alphabetical search feature that you can use to find topics.

WHEN TO USE AN ENCYCLOPEDIA

- Encyclopedias are a great source when you need information quickly for general interest or for a topic you're studying.

- Encyclopedias are a good starting point for research on a topic. However, they should *never* be your primary source of information for research papers.

Biographical References These books provide brief life histories of a variety of famous people. Some—such as *Current Biography, Merriam Webster's Biographical Dictionary,* and the *Biography Resource Center*—cover people from many walks of life; others, such as *Contemporary Authors* or *The International Who's Who of Women,* cover people in specific fields or areas.

Almanacs When you want to find specific facts quickly, you can check an *almanac.* These yearly publications are a source of facts and statistics in many areas. These include business, entertainment, government, population, sports, and current as well as historic events. They provide little background information. Most facts are represented in tables or charts.

Print Atlases Books of maps, called *atlases,* give information about geography. Maps show Earth's division into continents and countries, as well as the locations of cities, mountains, and oceans. Through the use of symbols and color, maps may also show climate, crops, and population. To find a specific map or location, use the index at the back of the atlas.

Technology Tip

There are CD-ROM encyclopedias on a wide range of specialized topics, from baseball and football to visual arts and music.

More Practice

Academic and Workplace Skills Activity Book
- p. 58

CD-ROM Atlases Atlases are also available electronically on CD-ROM. The maps may be interactive, allowing you to see how to get from one place to another or to see changes over time. Generally, they include a search feature that makes it easy for you to find a specific location.

Thesauruses A thesaurus is a specialized dictionary that gives extensive lists of *synonyms,* or words with similar meanings, and may also list *antonyms,* or words with opposite meanings. Some thesauruses show words arranged by categories according to an alphabetical index. Others are arranged in strict alphabetical order, as a dictionary is.

Electronic Databases Electronic databases provide large collections of data on specific topics. Using one or more search features, you can easily access any piece of the data, piece together related information, or look at the information in different ways. Electronic databases are available both on CD-ROM and on the Internet.

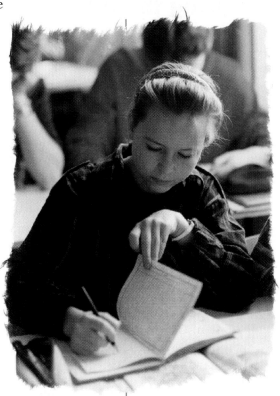

▲ **Critical Viewing**
What types of references might this girl be using? On what do you base your answer? **[Speculate]**

Exercise 8 **Using Other Reference Works** Use printed or electronic reference works to find the following information. Indicate the type of reference you used.

1. the three largest cities in Texas and their population
2. three countries that border Switzerland
3. the first astronaut to walk on the moon and the date he landed there
4. the birthplace of English author Aldous Huxley and the names of two books that he wrote
5. five synonyms for the adjective *cold*

Exercise 9 **Using All Types of Reference Works** Explain at least two specific uses for each of the following types of references.

1. the encyclopedia
2. newspapers
3. almanacs
4. nonfiction books
5. pamphlets

31.2

Using the Internet

The Internet provides access to an almost unlimited amount of information through a personal computer. Web sites consist of text, graphics, and sometimes audio or video displays, which you can download.

Locating Appropriate Web Sites Following are some strategies for finding information on the Internet:

- If you know a reliable Web site and its address (URL), simply type the address into your Web browser. Often, television programs, commercials, magazines, newspapers, and radio stations provide Web site addresses where you can find more information about a show, product, company, and so on.

- Consult library journals to learn addresses of Web sites that provide useful and reliable information.

- If you don't know particular Web sites, you can do a general search for a key term on a search engine. Try several search engines to discover which are best for each type of search. Some search engines are best for finding academic information. Others are best for hobbies and general interests.

- Remember to bookmark (or save to Favorite Places) the interesting and reliable sites you find while searching the Web.

Evaluating Web Sites Don't just assume that information is reliable because it is posted on the Web. Anyone with a computer can set up a Web site on any topic, regardless of that person's beliefs or how much that person knows about the topic. Critically evaluate a Web site by asking these questions:

1. Who or what is the source of the information on the site? Does that source have credentials, such as expertise in the field?
2. Does the source reflect a particular point of view on the topic? If so, you should consider this point of view before accepting any information that is presented.
3. Is the information up-to-date?
4. How does it compare to other information on the topic?

▼ **Critical Viewing** Does this student look interested in what he is finding on the Internet? On what do you base your answer? **[Speculate]**

> **Exercise 10** Using the Internet to Write an Essay On a library, school, or home computer, use the Internet to research the following topics. Record the names and addresses (URLs) of the Web sites you use as sources, and evaluate the effectiveness of each site.
> (1) Edgar Allan Poe (2) Russian czars (3) Yellowstone National Park (4) soccer (5) Egyptian pyramids

750 • Study, Reference, and Test-Taking Skills

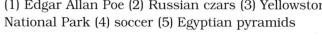

Section 31.3 *Test-Taking Skills*

Strategies for Taking Tests

Over the years, you will take a wide range of tests. These will include standardized tests, as well as the ones you take in school. Some will follow a multiple-choice format; others will require you to write an essay. Regardless of the type of test you take, there are strategies you can use to help you succeed. The most important strategy is to prepare thoroughly. Good time management and a familiarity with the types of questions you'll encounter will also contribute to your success.

KEY CONCEPT Budget your time between previewing the test, answering the questions, and proofreading. ■

PREVIEW THE TEST

1. Put your name on each sheet of paper you will hand in.
2. Look over the entire test to get an overview of the types of questions and how they are arranged.
3. Find out whether you lose points for incorrect answers. If you do, do not guess at answers.
4. Decide how much time you want to spend on each section of the test.
5. Plan to devote the most time to questions that are hardest or worth the most points.

ANSWER THE QUESTIONS

1. Answer the easy questions first. Put a check next to harder questions, and come back to them later.
2. If permitted, use scratch paper to jot down your ideas.
3. Read each question at least *twice* before answering.
4. Supply the single best answer, giving only one answer to a question unless the instructions say otherwise.
5. Answer all questions on the test unless you are told not to guess or there is a penalty for wrong guesses.
6. Do not change your first answer without a good reason.

PROOFREAD YOUR ANSWERS

1. Check that you have followed directions completely.
2. Reread test questions and answers. Make sure that you have answered all of the questions.

Answering Different Types of Questions

If you are familiar with the different kinds of questions that are frequently asked on tests, you may improve your performance. It is also important to know various strategies for answering the different kinds of questions.

Answering Multiple-Choice Questions This kind of question asks you to choose from several possible responses.

EXAMPLE:

What is a URL?

a. an Internet service provider   c. a universal reference

b. an Internet Web site address   d. a periodical index

In the preceding example, the answer is *b*.

ANSWERING MULTIPLE-CHOICE QUESTIONS
1. Try answering the question before looking at the choices. If your answer is one of the choices, select that choice.
2. Eliminate the obviously incorrect answers, crossing them out if you are allowed to write on the test paper.
3. Change a question into a statement by inserting your answer to see whether the statement makes sense.

Answering Matching Questions Matching questions ask that you match items in one group with items in another.

EXAMPLE:

__ 1. negligible   a. causing fear or dread

__ 2. formidable   b. difficult to understand

__ 3. inscrutable   c. small or unimportant

In the preceding example, the answers are *c*, *a*, and *b*.

ANSWERING MATCHING QUESTIONS
1. Count each group to see whether items will be left over. Check the directions to see whether items can be used more than once.
2. Read all the items before you start matching.
3. Match the items you know first. If you can write on the paper, cross out the items when you use them.
4. Match remaining items about which you are less certain.

Internet Tip

You can find additional information, strategies, and practice on test-taking on the Internet.

More Practice

Academic and Workplace Skills Activity Book
• p. 59–60

Answering True/False Questions True/false questions require you to identify whether a statement is accurate or not.

EXAMPLE:

__ You should study only when you have a test.

__ You should proofread your answers on a test only when you think you made some mistakes.

__ If permitted, you should use scratch paper to write down ideas when taking a test.

In the preceding example, the answers are *F, F,* and *T.*

ANSWERING TRUE/FALSE QUESTIONS

1. If a statement seems true, be sure the entire statement is true.
2. Pay special attention to the word *not,* which often changes the meaning of a statement.
3. Pay special attention to the words *all, always, never, no, none,* and *only.* They often make a statement false.
4. Pay special attention to the words *generally, much, many, most, often, sometimes,* and *usually.* They often make a statement true.

Answering Fill-in Questions A fill-in question asks you to supply an answer in your own words. The answer may complete a statement or it may simply answer a question.

EXAMPLE: An ___?___ in a periodical index summarizes the article.

OR: In a periodical index, what is a summary of an article called?

In the preceding example, the answer is *abstract.*

ANSWERING FILL-IN QUESTIONS

1. Read the question or incomplete statement carefully.
2. If you are completing a statement, look for context clues (such as *an*) that may signal the answer.
3. If you are answering a question, change it into a statement by inserting your answer to see whether that makes sense.

Answering Short-Answer Questions Short-answer questions require you to write briefly to demonstrate what you know about a specific topic. Make your answers as brief and direct as possible. However, be sure to include supporting facts and examples to back up your points.

Answering Analogies An analogy asks you to find pairs of words that express a similar relationship.

EXAMPLE: REDWOOD : TREE :: BEAR :

a. cave   b. mammal   c. honey

In the preceding example, the answer is *b*. The relationship between the pairs of words is *type*. A redwood is a *type* of tree, and a bear is a *type* of mammal. The following chart lists common analogy relationships:

COMMON ANALOGY RELATIONSHIPS	
Relationship	**Example**
synonym	enormous : gigantic
antonym	love : hate
part-to-whole	receiver : telephone
type	boat : yacht
cause-effect	question : answer
function	telescope : magnify

Once you have learned the different analogy relationships, use these strategies to answer an analogy:

ANSWERING ANALOGIES
1. Create a sentence that describes the relationship between the given word pair.
2. If more than one choice seems to express the relationship, go back to the given word pair, and restate its relationship.
3. If you are unable to establish a relationship between the given word pair or to find a parallel relationship among the answers, look for a second meaning to a word.

Writing Essays for Tests On many tests, you will also be called on to write one or more essays. See Chapter 13, Writing for Assessment, for detailed, step-by-step instruction on writing in a test situation.

▶ **Exercise 11** Answering Different Types of Questions
Using a subject you are studying in a class, prepare a short objective test on the material. Write five multiple-choice questions, five matching questions, five true/false questions, and five fill-in questions. Exchange papers with another student, and take the other student's test, writing your answers on a separate sheet of paper. Then, exchange again, and grade the test.

Learn More

For more instruction and information on answering the various types of questions, consult the table of contents to see the topics covered in the *Standardized Test Preparation Workshops.*

▶ **Exercise 12** Answering Analogies For each analogy, identify the relationship between the given word pair. Then, use the strategies you have learned to determine each answer.

1. WRITER : AUTHOR :: HERO :
   a. villain   b. scribe   c. champion

2. PIANO : MUSIC :: CANDLE :
   a. light   b. sound   c. wax

3. DALMATIAN : DOG :: TULIP :
   a. spots   b. field   c. flower

4. GRACEFUL : AWKWARD :: WORDY :
   a. eloquent   b. clumsy   c. speechless

5. CHAPTER : NOVEL :: ACT :
   a. character   b. play   c. stage

▶ **Exercise 13** Analyzing a Test Essay Analyze an essay that you wrote for a recent test. Come up with at least two suggestions on how you could improve it.

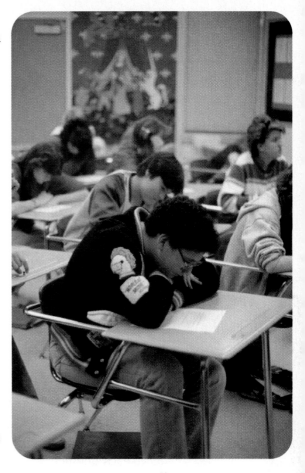

▶ **Critical Viewing** What details in this photograph indicate that the student in the front is carefully studying the questions before getting started? **[Analyze]**

Reflecting on Your Study Skills

Think about the various methods you have learned for improving your study, reference, and test-taking skills. Decide which methods you will need to work on most. Use these questions to help you reflect:

• What changes do I need to make in my study area or study schedule?

• What changes do I need to make in my assignment book?

• Which area of the library is most unfamiliar to me? How could becoming more familiar with that part of the library improve my reference skills?

• Which type of test question do I prefer answering? Why?

• With which type of test question do I most frequently have problems?

• What can I do to improve my performance with these types of test questions?

Standardized Test Preparation Workshop

Constructing Meaning From Informational Texts

When you take a standardized test, you often must answer questions about a passage you have read. These questions test your ability to construct meaning from the information provided in the passage. When answering these types of questions, you will be required to do the following:

- Identify the main idea, stated or implied, of a section of the passage.
- Identify the best summary—a concise restating of the key points of the passage.
- Distinguish between facts and opinions.

The following sample item will give you practice answering these types of questions.

Test Tip

When answering a main-idea question, make sure your choice is entirely correct and includes as much relevant information as possible.

Sample Test Item	Answer and Explanation
Read the passage. Then, read each question that follows the passage. Decide which is the best answer to each question. Mercury is the smallest of planets and the one closest to the sun. It is not visible from a basic telescope. Because it is so close to the sun, Mercury experiences extremely hot temperatures. These hot temperatures have led scientists to believe that life does not exist on the planet. 1 What is the main idea of this passage? A The planet is not visible from the novice astronomer's telescope. B Mercury is the smallest and hottest planet. C It is close to the sun. D Mercury is a small planet.	The correct answer is *B*. This is the only statement that includes all of the most relevant information from the passage.

▶ **Practice** **Directions:** Read each passage. Then, read each question that follows the passage. Decide which is the best answer to each question.

Venus is the closest planet to Earth and is a near twin in size. Venus provides scientists with a much more interesting subject for study than Earth. The average surface temperature on Venus is 887 degrees Fahrenheit, eight times hotter than any region on Earth. In addition, its atmosphere is dramatically different from that of Earth, consisting mostly of sulfuric acid and sulfur dioxide. Venus rotates only once every 243 days, in contrast to Earth, which rotates once every 24 hours.

1 What is the main idea of this passage?

   A Although Venus is near to Earth and is also close in size, it differs in temperature, atmosphere, and rotation patterns.

   B Venus rotates only once every 243 days, in contrast to Earth, which rotates once every 24 hours.

   C Venus is hotter than Earth and also has a different atmospheric makeup.

   D There are few similarities between Venus and Earth.

2 Which of the following is an OPINION expressed in the passage?

   F Venus is the closest planet to Earth and is a near twin in size.

   G The average surface temperature on Venus is 887 degrees Fahrenheit, eight times hotter than any region on Earth.

   H Its atmosphere is dramatically different from that of Earth, consisting mostly of sulfuric acid and sulfur dioxide.

   J Venus provides scientists with a much more interesting subject for study than Earth.

Early in its history, Mars was much more like Earth. Although both Earth and Mars used most of the carbon dioxide in their atmospheres to form carbonate rocks, Mars could not recycle it back into its atmosphere to sustain a significant greenhouse effect. Therefore, the surface of Mars is much colder than the surface of Earth would be at that distance from the sun. The thin atmosphere of Mars does produce a greenhouse effect, but it is only enough to raise the surface temperature by five degrees. It is unlikely that any life forms similar to humans could survive there.

3 What is the main idea of the passage?

   A Mars was at one time more like Earth because both atmospheres had carbon dioxide.

   B The surface of Mars is much colder than that of Earth.

   C The atmosphere of Mars cannot produce as significant a greenhouse effect as the atmosphere of Earth can.

   D Mars could not sustain life forms similar to humans.

4 Which of the following is the best summary of this passage?

   F The greenhouse effect on both Earth and Mars is caused by the recycling of carbon dioxide into the atmosphere.

   G Both Earth and Mars had carbon dioxide in their atmospheres that was used to form carbonate rocks.

   H Because of its cold temperature, Mars could not sustain any life forms similar to humans.

   J Because Mars cannot recycle the carbon dioxide from carbonate rocks, it cannot sustain a greenhouse effect as strong as Earth's.

Styles for Business and Friendly Letters

Business Letters

From a letter requesting information about a product to a letter asking for charitable donations, business letters are a common form of formal writing, writing intended for readers with whom the writer is not personally acquainted. Whatever the subject, an effective business letter

- includes six parts: the heading, the inside address, the salutation or greeting, the body, the closing, and the signature.

- follows one of several acceptable forms: In *block format*, each part of the letter begins at the left margin; in *modified block format*, the heading, the closing, and the signature are indented to the center of the page.

- uses formal language to communicate respectfully, regardless of the letter's content.

The **heading** indicates the address and business affiliation of the writer. It also includes the date the letter was sent.

Model Business Letter

In this letter, Yolanda Dodson uses modified block format to request information.

The **inside address** indicates where the letter will be sent.

A **salutation** is punctuated by a colon. When the specific addressee is not known, use a general greeting such as "To whom it may concern:"

The **body** of the letter states the writer's purpose. In this case, the writer is requesting information.

The **closing** "Sincerely" is common, but "Yours truly" and "Respectfully yours" are also acceptable. To end the letter, the writer types her name and provides a **signature**.

Students for a Cleaner Planet
c/o Memorial High School
333 Veterans' Drive
Denver, Colorado 80211

January 25, 20 – –

Steven Wilson, Director
Resource Recovery Really Works
300 Oak Street
Denver, Colorado 80216

Dear Mr. Wilson:

Memorial High School would like to start a branch of your successful recycling program. We share your commitment to reclaiming as much reusable material as we can. Because your program has been successful in other neighborhoods, we're sure that it can work in our community. Our school includes grades 9–12 and has about 800 students.

Would you send us some information about your community recycling program? For example, we need to know what materials can be recycled and how we can implement the program.

At least fifty students have already expressed an interest in getting involved, so I know we'll have the people power to make the program work. Please help us get started.

Thank you in advance for your time and consideration.

Sincerely,

Yolanda Dodson

Yolanda Dodson

Friendly Letters and Social Notes

When you write a letter telling news to a friend or thanking a relative for a gift, you are writing a friendly letter or a social note. A friendly letter is any informal letter based on a personal relationship with the reader. A social note includes a semiformal thank-you note written to someone you do not know quite well. Friendly letters and social notes typically feature the following elements:

- a heading, a salutation or greeting, a body, a closing, and a signature; they generally do not include an inside address

- a comma after the greeting

- paragraphs with indented first lines

- the use of a version of semiblock style, in which the heading, closing, and signature align to the right of center

- informal or semiformal language, often featuring the lively expression of feelings or amusement

How careful you need to be in following appropriate format depends on your relationship with the reader: The less well you know the person, the more careful you should be to follow the correct format. Consult the model below for proper formatting.

> The **heading, closing,** and **signature** are aligned, semiblock style, to the right of the center of the page. (In very informal letters, writers may choose to omit their own address in the heading.)

Model Social Note

In this letter, Mayra Gonzalez thanks her aunt for a gift.

> A comma is used after the **greeting;** Mayra addresses her reader semiformally.

> The first line of each paragraph in the **body** is indented. The writer uses informal language and gives details that are of personal interest.

> A friendly letter may use or adapt a **closing** such as "Love," "Yours," and "Best," followed by a comma. As is customary when writer and reader know each other well, Mayra signs her first name only and does not add her name written out.

1111 Main St.
Mayfair, OH
November 11, 20 - -

Dear Aunt Margie,

   Well, as you predicted, the trip to the amusement park was a lot of fun. I had a great time! The rides were more thrilling than any I've ever been on before. Even the twins were impressed——I don't think they had a single fight during the entire trip, and you know that's saying a lot!

   The only part I wouldn't visit again was the spooky House of Chills. Ugh! I didn't mind the visuals: skeletons, scary pirates, and that sort of thing. But there's one part of the ride that takes place in complete darkness, with very quiet sound effects, and while you sit there wondering what will happen next, a cold, clammy THING runs slithering across your back or your hand! I nearly jumped out of my skin. I wasn't that frightened even when we told scary stories the night the lights went out at your house.

   Thanks very much for the tickets and the fun day. We all loved the trip. I hope you'll come to visit again soon.

Your tallest niece,
Mayra

Citing Sources and Preparing Manuscript

The presentation of your written work is important. Your work should be neat, clean, and easy to read. Follow your teacher's directions for placing your name and class, along with the title and date of your work, on the paper.

For handwritten work:

- Use cursive handwriting or manuscript printing, according to the style your teacher prefers. The penmanship reference below shows the accepted formation of letters in cursive writing.
- Write or print neatly.
- Write on one side of lined $8\frac{1}{2}$" x 11" paper with a clean edge. (Do not use pages torn from a spiral notebook.)
- Indent the first line of each paragraph.

- Leave a margin, as indicated by the guidelines on the lined paper. Write in a size appropriate for the lines provided. Do not write so large that the letters from one line bump into the ones above and below. Do not write so small that the writing is difficult to read.
- Write in blue or black ink.
- Number the pages in the upper right corner.
- Do not cross out words on your final draft. Recopy instead. If your paper is long, your teacher may allow you to make one or two small changes by neatly crossing out the text to be deleted and using a caret [^] to indicate replacement text. Alternatively, you might make one or two corrections neatly with correction fluid. If you find yourself making more than three corrections, consider recopying the work.

PENMANSHIP REFERENCE

Aa Bb Cc Dd Ee Ff
Gg Hh Ii Jj Kk Ll
Mm Nn Oo Pp Qq
Rr Ss Tt Uu Vv Ww
Xx Yy Zz 1 2 3 4 5 6 7 8 9 0

For word-processed or typed documents:

- Choose a standard, easy-to-read font.
- Type or print on one side of unlined $8\,1/2$" x 11" paper.
- Set the margins for the side, top, and bottom of your paper at approximately one inch. Most word-processing programs have a default setting that is appropriate.
- Double-space the document.
- Indent the first line of each paragraph.
- Number the pages in the upper right corner. Many word-processing programs have a header feature that will do this for you automatically.

- If you discover one or two errors after you have typed or printed, use correction fluid if your teacher allows such corrections. If you have more than three errors in an electronic file, consider making the corrections to the file and reprinting the document. If you have typed a long document, your teacher may allow you to make a few corrections by hand. If you have several errors, however, consider retyping the document.

For research papers:

Follow your teacher's directions for formatting formal research papers. Most papers will have the following features:

- Title page
- Table of Contents or Outline
- Works-Cited list

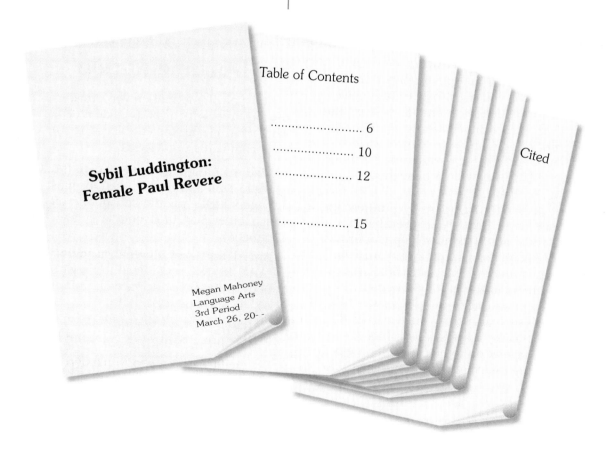

Table of Contents

.... 6

.... 10

.... 12

.... 15

Sybil Luddington:
Female Paul Revere

Megan Mahoney
Language Arts
3rd Period
March 26, 20- -

Cited

Incorporating Ideas From Research

Below are three common methods of incorporating the ideas of other writers into your work. Choose the most appropriate style by analyzing your needs in each case. In all cases, you must credit your source.

- **Direct Quotation:** Use quotation marks to indicate the exact words.
- **Paraphrase:** To share ideas without a direct quotation, state the ideas in your own words. While you haven't copied word-for-word, you still need to credit your source.
- **Summary:** To provide information about a large body of work—such as a speech, an editorial, or a chapter of a book—identify the writer's main idea.

Avoiding Plagiarism

Whether you are presenting a formal research paper or an opinion paper on a current event, you must be careful to give credit for any ideas or opinions that are not your own. Presenting someone else's ideas, research, or opinion as your own—even if you have rephrased it in different words—is *plagiarism*, the equivalent of academic stealing, or fraud.

You can avoid plagiarism by synthesizing what you learn: Read from several sources and let the ideas of experts help you draw your own conclusions and form your own opinions. Ultimately, however, note your own reactions to the ideas presented.

When you choose to use someone else's ideas or work to support your view, credit the source of the material. Give bibliographic information to cite your sources of the following information:

- Statistics
- Direct quotations
- Indirectly quoted statements of opinions
- Conclusions presented by an expert
- Facts available in only one or two sources

Crediting Sources

When you credit a source, you acknowledge where you found your information and you give your readers the details necessary for locating the source themselves. Within the body of the paper, you provide a short citation, a footnote number linked to a footnote, or an endnote number linked to an endnote reference. These brief references show the page numbers on which you found the information. To make your paper more formal, prepare a reference list at the end of the paper to provide full bibliographic information on your sources. These are two common types of reference lists:

- A **bibliography** provides a listing of all the resources you consulted during your research.
- A **works-cited list** indicates the works you have referenced in your paper.

Choosing a Format for Documentation

The type of information you provide and the format in which you provide it depend on what your teacher prefers. These are the most commonly used styles:

- **Modern Language Association (MLA) Style** This is the style used for most papers at the middle-school and high-school level and for most language arts papers.
- **American Psychological Association (APA) Style** This is used for most papers in the social sciences and for most college-level papers.
- *Chicago Manual of Style* **(CMS) Style** This is preferred by some teachers.

On the following pages, you'll find samples of MLA citation and documentation formats for the most commonly cited materials.

MLA Style for Listing Sources

Book with one author	Pyles, Thomas. *The Origins and Development of the English Language.* 2nd ed. New York: Harcourt Brace Jovanovich, Inc., 1971.
Book with two or three authors	McCrum, Robert, William Cran, and Robert MacNeil. *The Story of English.* New York: Penguin Books, 1987.
Book with an editor	Truth, Sojourner. *Narrative of Sojourner Truth.* Ed. Margaret Washington. New York: Vintage Books, 1993.
Book with more than three authors or editors	Donald, Robert B., et al. *Writing Clear Essays.* Upper Saddle River, NJ: Prentice-Hall, Inc., 1996.
A single work from an anthology	Hawthorne, Nathaniel. "Young Goodman Brown." *Literature: An Introduction to Reading and Writing.* Ed. Edgar V. Roberts and Henry E. Jacobs. Upper Saddle River, NJ: Prentice-Hall, Inc., 1998. 376–385. [Indicate pages for the entire selection.]
Introduction in a published edition	Washington, Margaret. Introduction. *Narrative of Sojourner Truth.* By Sojourner Truth. Ed. Washington. New York: Vintage Books, 1993. v–xi.
Signed article in a weekly magazine	Wallace, Charles. "A Vodacious Deal." *Time* 14 Feb. 2000: 63.
Signed article in a monthly magazine	Gustaitis, Joseph. "The Sticky History of Chewing Gum." *American History* Oct. 1998: 30–38.
Unsigned editorial or story	"Selective Silence." Editorial. *Wall Street Journal* 11 Feb. 2000: A14. [If the editorial or story is signed, begin with the author's name.]
Signed pamphlet	[Treat the pamphlet as though it were a book.]
Pamphlet with no author, publisher, or date	*Are You at Risk of Heart Attack?* n.p. n.d. [n.p. n.d. indicates that there is no known publisher or date]
Filmstrips, slide programs, videocassettes, DVDs, and other audiovisual media	*The Diary of Anne Frank.* Dir. George Stevens. Perf. Millie Perkins, Shelley Winters, Joseph Schildkraut, Lou Jacobi, and Richard Beymer. 1959. DVD. Twentieth Century Fox, 2004.
Radio or television program transcript	"Washington's Crossing of the Delaware." Host Liane Hansen. Guest David Hackett Fischer. *Weekend Edition Sunday.* Natl. Public Radio. WNYC, New York City. 23 Dec. 2003. Transcript.
Internet	"Fun Facts About Gum." NACGM site. National Association of Chewing Gum Manufacturers. 19 Dec. 1999. <http://www.nacgm.org/consumer/funfacts.html>. [Indicate the date of last update if known and the date you accessed the information. Content and addresses at Web sites change frequently.]
Newspaper	Thurow, Roger. "South Africans Who Fought for Sanctions Now Scrap for Investors." *Wall Street Journal* 11 Feb. 2000: A1+ [For a multipage article that does not appear on consecutive pages, write only the first page number on which it appears, followed by a plus sign.]
Personal interview	Smith, Jane. Personal interview. 10 Feb. 2000.
CD (with multiple publishers)	Simms, James, ed. *Romeo and Juliet.* By William Shakespeare. CD-ROM. Oxford: Attica Cybernetics Ltd.; London: BBC Education; London: HarperCollins Publishers, 1995.
Article from an encyclopedia	Askeland, Donald R. "Welding." *World Book Encyclopedia.* 1991 ed.

Sample Works-Cited List (MLA)

Carwardine, Mark, Erich Hoyt, R. Ewan Fordyce, and
    Peter Gill. *The Nature Company Guides: Whales,*
    Dolphins, and Porpoises. New York: Time-Life
    Books, 1998.

Ellis, Richard. *Men and Whales.* New York: Knopf,
    1991.

Whales in Danger. "Discovering Whales." 18 Oct. 1999.
    <http://whales.magna.com.au/DISCOVER>

Sample Internal Citations (MLA)

Author's last name

It makes sense that baleen whales such as the
blue whale, the fin whale, the bowhead whale, the
humpback whale, and the sei whale (to name just
a few) grow to immense sizes (Carwardine 19–21).
The blue whale has grooves running from under its
chin to partway along the length of its underbelly.
As in some other whales, these grooves expand
and allow even more food and water to be taken in
(Ellis 18–21).

page numbers where information can be found

Internet Research Handbook

Introduction to the Internet

The Internet is a series of networks that are interconnected all over the world. The Internet allows users to have almost unlimited access to information stored on the networks. Dr. Berners-Lee, a physicist, created the Internet in the 1980's by writing a small computer program that allowed pages to be linked together using key words. The Internet was mostly text-based until 1992, when a computer program called the NCSA Mosaic (National Center for Supercomputing Applications at the University of Illinois) was created. This program was the first Web browser. The development of Web browsers greatly eased the ability of the user to navigate through all the pages stored on the Web. Very soon, the appearance of the Web was altered as well. More appealing visuals were added, and sound was also implemented. This change made the Web more user-friendly and more appealing to the general public.

Using the Internet for Research

Key Word Search

Before you begin a search, you should identify your specific topic. To make searching easier, narrow your subject to a key word or a group of key words. These are your search terms, and they should be as specific as possible. For example, if you are looking for the latest concert dates for your favorite musical group, you might use the band's name as a key word. However, if you were to enter the name of the group in the query box of the search engine, you might be presented with thousands of links to information about the group that is unrelated to your needs. You might locate such information as band member biographies, the group's history, fan reviews of concerts, and hundreds of sites with related names containing information that is irrelevant to your search. Because you used such a broad key word, you might need to navigate through all that information before you find a link or subheading for concert dates. In contrast, if you were to type in "Duplex Arena and [band name]" you would have a better chance of locating pages that contain this information.

How to Narrow Your Search

If you have a large group of key words and still don't know which ones to use, write out a list of all the words you are considering. Once you have completed the list, scrutinize it. Then, delete the words that are least important to your search, and highlight those that are most important.

These **key search connectors** can help you fine-tune your search:

AND: narrows a search by retrieving documents that include both terms. For example: *baseball AND playoffs*

OR: broadens a search by retrieving documents including any of the terms. For example: *playoffs OR championships*

NOT: narrows a search by excluding documents containing certain words. For example: *baseball NOT history of*

Tips for an Effective Search

1. Keep in mind that search engines can be case-sensitive. If your first attempt at searching fails, check your search terms for misspellings and try again.

2. If you are entering a group of key words, present them in order, from the most important to the least important key word.

3. Avoid opening the link to every single page in your results list. Search engines present pages in descending order of relevancy. The most useful pages will be located at the top of the list. However, read the description of each link before you open the page.

4. When you use some search engines, you can find helpful tips for specializing your search. Take the opportunity to learn more about effective searching.

Other Ways to Search

Using On-line Reference Sites *How* you search should be tailored to *what* you are hoping to find. If you are looking for data and facts, use reference sites before you jump onto a simple search engine. For example, you can find reference sites to provide definitions of words, statistics about almost any subject, biographies, maps, and concise information on many topics. Some useful on-line reference sites:

On-line libraries
On-line periodicals
Almanacs
Encyclopedias

You can find these sources using subject searches.

Conducting Subject Searches As you prepare to go on-line, consider your subject and the best way to find information to suit your needs. If you are looking for general information on a topic and you want your search results to be extensive, consider the subject search indexes on most search engines. These indexes, in the form of category and subject lists, often appear on the first page of a search engine. When you click on a specific highlighted word, you will be presented with a new screen containing subcategories of the topic you chose. In the screen shots below, the category *Sports & Recreation* provided a second index for users to focus a search even further.

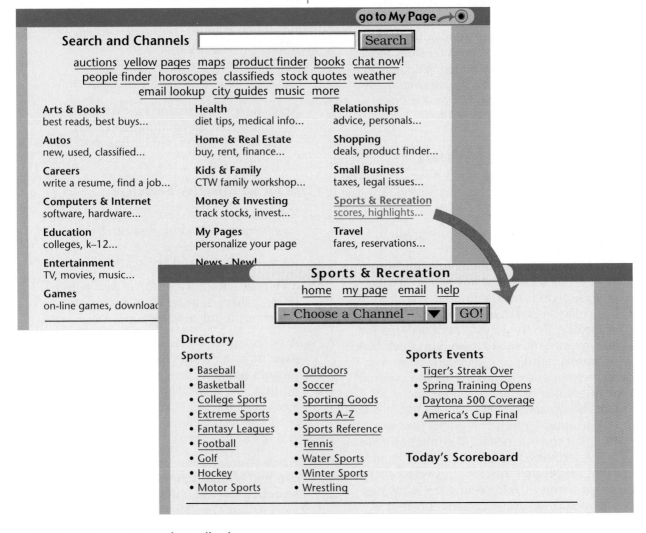

Evaluating the Reliability of Internet Resources

Just as you would evaluate the quality, bias, and validity of any other research material you locate, check the source of information you find on-line. Compare these two sites containing information on the poet and writer Langston Hughes:

Site A is a personal Web site constructed by a college student. It contains no bibliographic information or links to sites that he used. Included on the site are several poems by Langston Hughes and a student essay about the poet's use of symbolism. It has not been updated in more than six months.

Site B is a Web site constructed and maintained by the English Department of a major university. Information on Hughes is presented in a scholarly format, with a bibliography and credits for the writer. The site includes links to other sites and indicates new features that are added weekly.

For your own research, consider the information you find on Site B to be more reliable and accurate than that on Site A. Because it is maintained by experts in their field who are held accountable for their work, the university site will be a better research tool than the student-generated one.

Tips for Evaluating Internet Sources

1. Consider who constructed and who now maintains the Web page. Determine whether this author is a reputable source. Often, the URL endings indicate a source.

   - Sites ending in *.edu* are maintained by educational institutions.
   - Sites ending in *.gov* are maintained by government agencies (federal, state, or local).
   - Sites ending in *.org* are normally maintained by nonprofit organizations and agencies.
   - Sites with a *.com* ending are commercially or personally maintained.

2. Skim the official and trademarked Web pages first. It is safe to assume that the information you draw from Web pages of reputable institutions, on-line encyclopedias, on-line versions of major daily newspapers, or government-owned sites produce information as reliable as the material you would find in print. In contrast, unbranded sites or those generated by individuals tend to borrow information from other sources without providing documentation. As information travels from one source to another, the information has likely been muddled, misinterpreted, edited, or revised.

3. You can still find valuable information in the less "official" sites. Check for the writer's credentials and then consider these factors:

   - Don't let official-looking graphics or presentations fool you.
   - Make sure the information is updated enough to suit your needs. Many Web pages will indicate how recently they have been updated.
   - If the information is borrowed, see whether you can trace it back to its original source.

Respecting Copyrighted Material

Because the Internet is a relatively new and quickly growing medium, issues of copyright and ownership arise almost daily. As laws begin to govern the use and reuse of material posted on-line, they may change the way that people can access or reprint material.

Text, photographs, music, and fine art printed on-line may not be reproduced without acknowledged permission of the copyright owner.

Glossary of Internet Terms

attached file: a file containing information, such as a text document or GIF image, that is attached to an e-mail message; reports, pictures, spreadsheets, and so on transmitted to others by attaching these to messages as files

bandwidth: the amount of information, mainly compressed in bits per second (bps), that can be sent through a connection within a specific amount of time; depending on how fast your modem is, 15,000 bits (roughly one page of text) can be transferred per second

bit: a binary digit of computerized data, represented by a single digit that is either a 1 or a 0; a group of bits constitutes a byte

bookmark: a feature of your Web browser that allows you to place a "bookmark" on a Web page to which you wish to return at a later time

browser: software designed to present material accessed on the Web

bulletin-board system: a computer system that members access in order to join on-line discussion groups or to post announcements

case-sensitivity: the quality of a search engine that causes it to respond to upper- or lowercase letters in different ways

chat room: informal on-line gathering sites where people share conversations, experiences, or information on a specific topic; many chat rooms do not require users to provide their identity, so the reliability or safety of these sites is uncertain

cookie: a digitized piece of information that is sent to a Web browser by a Web server, intended to be saved on a computer; cookies gather information about the user, such as user preferences, or recent on-line purchases; a Web browser can be set to either accept or reject cookies

cyberspace: a term referring to the electronic environment connecting all computer network information with the people who use it

database: a large collection of data that have been formatted to fit a certain user-defined standard

digerati: a slang term to describe Internet experts; an offshoot of the term *literati*

download: to copy files from the Internet onto your computer

e-mail: electronic mail, or the exchange of messages via the Internet; because it is speedier than traditional mail and offers easier global access, e-mail has grown in popularity; e-mail messages can be sent to a single person or in bulk to a group of people

error message: a displayed communication or printout that reports a problem with a program or Web page

FTP site (file transfer protocol): a password-protected server on the Internet that allows the transfer of information from one computer to another

GIF (Graphic Interchange Format): a form of graphics used on the Web

graphics: information displayed as pictures or images instead of text

hits: items retrieved by a key word search; the number tracking the volume of visits to a Web site

home page: the main Web page for an individual or an organization, containing links to subpages within

HTML (HyperText Markup Language): the coding text that is the foundation for creating Web pages

interactivity: a quality of some Web pages that encourages the frequent exchange of information between user and computer

Internet: a worldwide computer network that supports services such as the World Wide Web, e-mail, and file transfer

JPEG (Joint Photo Experts Group, the developers): a file format for graphics especially suited to photographs

K: a measurement of file size or memory; short for "Kilobyte," 1,000 bytes of information (see *bit*)

key word: search term entered into the query box of a search engine to direct the results of the search

link: an icon or word on a Web page that, when clicked, transfers the user to another Web page or to a different document within the same page

login: the procedure by which users gain access to a server or a secure Web site; usually the user must enter a specific user name and password

modem: a device that transfers data to a computer through a phone line. A computer's modem connects to a server, which then sends information in the form of digital signals. The modem converts these signals into waves, for the purpose of information reception. The speed of a modem affects how quickly a computer can receive and download information

newbie: jargon used to describe Internet novices

newsgroup: an on-line discussion group, where users can post and respond to messages; the most prevalent collection of newsgroups is found on USENET

query box: the blank box in a search engine where your search terms are input

relevance ranking: the act of displaying the results of a search in the order of their relevance to the search terms

search engines: tools that help you navigate databases to locate information; search engines respond to a key word search by providing the user with a directory of multiple Web pages about the key word or containing the key word

server: a principal computer that provides services, such as storing files and providing access to the Internet, to another computer

signature: a preprogrammed section of text that is automatically added to an e-mail message

surfing: the process of reading Web pages and of moving from one Web site to another

URL (Uniform Resource Locator): a Web page's address; a URL can look like this:

http://www.phwg.phschool.com or
http://www.senate.gov/~appropriations/ labor/testimony

usenet: a worldwide system of discussion groups, or newsgroups

vanity pages: Web sites placed on-line by people to tell about themselves or their interests; vanity pages do not have any commercial or informational value

virus: a set of instructions, hidden in a computer system or transferred via e-mail or electronic files, that can cause problems with a computer's ability to perform normally

Web page: a set of information, including graphics, text, sound, and video, presented in a browser window; a Web page can be found by its URL once it is posted on the World Wide Web

Web site: a collection of Web pages that are linked together for posting on the World Wide Web

W3: a group of Internet experts, including networking professionals, academics, scientists, and corporate interests, who maintain and develop technologies and standards for the Internet

WWW (World Wide Web): a term referring to the multitude of information systems found on the Internet; this includes FTP, Gopher, telnet, and http sites

zip: the minimizing of files through compression; this function makes for easier transmittal over networks; a receiver can then open the file by "unzipping" it

Commonly Overused Words

When you write, use the most precise word for your meaning, not the word that comes to mind first. Consult this thesaurus to find alternatives for some commonly overused words. Consult a full-length thesaurus to find alternatives to words that do not appear here. Keep in mind that the choices offered in a thesaurus do not all mean exactly the same thing. Review all the options, and choose the one that best expresses your meaning.

about approximately, nearly, almost, approaching, close to

absolutely unconditionally, perfectly, completely, ideally, purely

activity action, movement, operation, labor, exertion, enterprise, project, pursuit, endeavor, job, assignment, pastime, scheme, task

add attach, affix, join, unite, append, increase, amplify

affect adjust, influence, transform, moderate, incline, motivate, prompt

amazing overwhelming, astonishing, startling, unexpected, stunning, dazzling, remarkable

awesome impressive, stupendous, fabulous, astonishing, outstanding

bad defective, inadequate, poor, unsatisfactory, disagreeable, offensive, repulsive, corrupt, wicked, naughty, harmful, injurious, unfavorable

basic essential, necessary, indispensable, vital, fundamental, elementary

beautiful attractive, appealing, alluring, exqui-site, gorgeous, handsome, stunning

begin commence, found, initiate, introduce, launch, originate

better preferable, superior, worthier

big enormous, extensive, huge, immense, massive

boring commonplace, monotonous, tedious, tiresome

bring accompany, cause, convey, create, conduct, deliver, produce

cause origin, stimulus, inspiration, motive

certain unquestionable, incontrovertible, unmistakable, indubitable, assured, confident

change alter, transform, vary, replace, diversify

choose select, elect, nominate, prefer, identify

decent respectable, adequate, fair, suitable

definitely unquestionably, clearly, precisely, positively, inescapably

easy effortless, natural, comfortable, undemanding, pleasant, relaxed

effective powerful, successful

emphasize underscore, feature, accentuate

end limit, boundary, finish, conclusion, finale, resolution

energy vitality, vigor, force, dynamism

enjoy savor, relish, revel, benefit

entire complete, inclusive, unbroken, integral

excellent superior, remarkable, splendid, unsurpassed, superb, magnificent

exciting thrilling, stirring, rousing, dramatic

far distant, remote

fast swift, quick, fleet, hasty, instant, accelerated

fill occupy, suffuse, pervade, saturate, inflate, stock

finish complete, conclude, cease, achieve, exhaust, deplete, consume

funny comical, ludicrous, amusing, droll, entertaining, bizarre, unusual, uncommon

get obtain, receive, acquire, procure, achieve

give bestow, donate, supply, deliver, distribute, impart

go proceed, progress, advance, move

good satisfactory, serviceable, functional, competent, virtuous, striking

great tremendous, superior, remarkable, eminent, proficient, expert

happy pleased, joyous, elated, jubilant, cheerful, delighted

hard arduous, formidable, complex, complicated, rigorous, harsh

help assist, aid, support, sustain, serve

hurt injure, harm, damage, wound, impair

important significant, substantial, weighty, meaningful, critical, vital, notable

interesting absorbing, appealing, entertaining, fascinating, thought-provoking

job task, work, business, undertaking, occupation, vocation, chore, duty, assignment

keep retain, control, possess

kind type, variety, sort, form

know comprehend, understand, realize, perceive, discern

like (adj) similar, equivalent, parallel

like (verb) enjoy, relish, appreciate

main primary, foremost, dominant

make build, construct, produce, assemble, fashion, manufacture

mean plan, intend, suggest, propose, indicate

more supplementary, additional, replenishment

new recent, modern, current, novel

next subsequently, thereafter, successively

nice pleasant, satisfying, gracious, charming

old aged, mature, experienced, used, worn, former, previous

open unobstructed, accessible

part section, portion, segment, detail, element, component

perfect flawless, faultless, ideal, consummate

plan scheme, design, system, plot

pleasant agreeable, gratifying, refreshing, welcome

prove demonstrate, confirm, validate, verify, corroborate

quick brisk, prompt, responsive, rapid, nimble, hasty

really truly, genuinely, extremely, undeniably

regular standard, routine, customary, habitual

see regard, behold, witness, gaze, realize, notice

small diminutive, miniature, minor, insignificant, slight, trivial

sometimes occasionally, intermittently, sporadically, periodically

take grasp, capture, choose, select, tolerate, endure

terrific extraordinary, magnificent, marvelous

think conceive, imagine, ponder, reflect, contemplate

try attempt, endeavor, venture, test

use employ, operate, utilize

very unusually, extremely, deeply, exceedingly, profoundly

want desire, crave, yearn, long

Commonly Misspelled Words

The list on these pages presents words that cause problems for many people. Some of these words are spelled according to set rules, but others follow no specific rules. As you review this list, check to see how many of the words give you trouble in your own writing. Then, read the instruction in the "Vocabulary and Spelling" chapter in the book for strategies and suggestions for improving your own spelling habits.

abbreviate	athletic	catastrophe	curious
absence	attendance	category	cylinder
absolutely	auxiliary	ceiling	deceive
abundance	awkward	cemetery	decision
accelerate	bandage	census	deductible
accidentally	banquet	certain	defendant
accumulate	bargain	changeable	deficient
accurate	barrel	characteristic	definitely
ache	battery	chauffeur	delinquent
achievement	beautiful	chief	dependent
acquaintance	beggar	clothes	descendant
adequate	beginning	coincidence	description
admittance	behavior	colonel	desert
advertisement	believe	column	desirable
aerial	benefit	commercial	dessert
affect	bicycle	commission	deteriorate
aggravate	biscuit	commitment	dining
aggressive	bookkeeper	committee	disappointed
agreeable	bought	competitor	disastrous
aisle	boulevard	concede	discipline
all right	brief	condemn	dissatisfied
allowance	brilliant	congratulate	distinguish
aluminum	bruise	connoisseur	effect
amateur	bulletin	conscience	eighth
analysis	buoyant	conscientious	eligible
analyze	bureau	conscious	embarrass
ancient	bury	contemporary	enthusiastic
anecdote	buses	continuous	entrepreneur
anniversary	business	controversy	envelope
anonymous	cafeteria	convenience	environment
answer	calendar	coolly	equipped
anticipate	campaign	cooperate	equivalent
anxiety	canceled	cordially	especially
apologize	candidate	correspondence	exaggerate
appall	capacity	counterfeit	exceed
appearance	capital	courageous	excellent
appreciate	capitol	courteous	exercise
appropriate	captain	courtesy	exhibition
architecture	career	criticism	existence
argument	carriage	criticize	experience
associate	cashier	curiosity	explanation

extension	library	particularly	restaurant
extraordinary	license	patience	rhythm
familiar	lieutenant	permanent	ridiculous
fascinating	lightning	permissible	sandwich
February	likable	perseverance	satellite
fiery	liquefy	persistent	schedule
financial	literature	personally	scissors
fluorescent	loneliness	perspiration	secretary
foreign	magnificent	persuade	siege
forfeit	maintenance	phenomenal	solely
fourth	marriage	phenomenon	sponsor
fragile	mathematics	physician	subtle
gauge	maximum	pleasant	subtlety
generally	meanness	pneumonia	superintendent
genius	mediocre	possess	supersede
genuine	mileage	possession	surveillance
government	millionaire	possibility	susceptible
grammar	minimum	prairie	tariff
grievance	minuscule	precede	temperamental
guarantee	miscellaneous	preferable	theater
guard	mischievous	prejudice	threshold
guidance	misspell	preparation	truly
handkerchief	mortgage	prerogative	unmanageable
harass	naturally	previous	unwieldy
height	necessary	primitive	usage
humorous	negotiate	privilege	usually
hygiene	neighbor	probably	valuable
ignorant	neutral	procedure	various
illegible	nickel	proceed	vegetable
immediately	niece	prominent	voluntary
immigrant	ninety	pronunciation	weight
independence	noticeable	psychology	weird
independent	nuclear	publicly	whale
indispensable	nuisance	pursue	wield
individual	obstacle	questionnaire	yield
inflammable	occasion	realize	
intelligence	occasionally	really	
interfere	occur	recede	
irrelevant	occurred	receipt	
irritable	occurrence	receive	
jewelry	omitted	recognize	
judgment	opinion	recommend	
knowledge	opportunity	reference	
laboratory	optimistic	referred	
lawyer	outrageous	rehearse	
legible	pamphlet	relevant	
legislature	parallel	reminiscence	
leisure	paralyze	renowned	
liable	parentheses	repetition	

Abbreviations Guide

Abbreviations, shortened versions of words or phrases, can be valuable tools in writing if you know when and how to use them. They can be very helpful in informal writing situations, such as taking notes or writing lists. However, only a few abbreviations can be used in formal writing. They are: *Mr., Mrs., Miss, Ms., Dr., A.M., P.M., A.D., B.C., M.A, B.A., Ph.D.,* and *M.D.*

The following pages provide the conventional abbreviations for a variety of words.

Abbreviations of Common Titles

Ambassador	Amb.	Lieutenant	Lt.
Attorney	Atty.	Major	Maj.
Brigadier-General	Brig. Gen.	President	Pres.
Brother	Br.	Professor	Prof.
Captain	Capt.	Representative	Rep.
Colonel	Col.	Reverend	Rev.
Commander	Cmdr.	Secretary	Sec.
Commissioner	Com.	Senator	Sen.
Corporal	Cpl.	Sergeant	Sgt.
Doctor	Dr.	Sister	Sr.
Father	Fr.	Superintendent	Supt.
Governor	Gov.	Treasurer	Treas.
Honorable	Hon.	Vice Admiral	Vice Adm.

Abbreviations of Academic Degrees

Bachelor of Arts	B.A. (or A.B.)	Esquire (lawyer)	Esq.
Bachelor of Science	B.S. (or S.B.)	Master of Arts	M.A. (or A.M.)
Doctor of Dental Surgery	D.D.S.	Master of Business Administration	M.B.A.
Doctor of Divinity	D.D.		
Doctor of Education	Ed.D.	Master of Fine Arts	M.F.A.
Doctor of Laws	LL.D.	Master of Science	M.S. (or S.M.)
Doctor of Medicine	M.D.	Registered Nurse	R.N.
Doctor of Philosophy	Ph.D.		

Abbreviations of States

State	Traditional	Postal Service	State	Traditional	Postal Service
Alabama	Ala.	AL	Montana	Mont.	MT
Alaska	Alaska	AK	Nebraska	Nebr.	NE
Arizona	Ariz.	AZ	Nevada	Nev.	NV
Arkansas	Ark.	AR	New Hampshire	N.H.	NH
California	Calif.	CA	New Jersey	N.J.	NJ
Colorado	Colo.	CO	New Mexico	N.M.	NM
Connecticut	Conn.	CT	New York	N.Y.	NY
Delaware	Del.	DE	North Carolina	N.C.	NC
Florida	Fla.	FL	North Dakota	N.Dak.	ND
Georgia	Ga.	GA	Ohio	O.	OH
Hawaii	Hawaii	HI	Oklahoma	Okla.	OK
Idaho	Ida.	ID	Oregon	Ore.	OR
Illinois	Ill.	IL	Pennsylvania	Pa.	PA
Indiana	Ind.	IN	Rhode Island	R.I.	RI
Iowa	Iowa	IA	South Carolina	S.C.	SC
Kansas	Kans.	KS	South Dakota	S.Dak.	SD
Kentucky	Ky.	KY	Tennessee	Tenn.	TN
Louisiana	La.	LA	Texas	Tex.	TX
Maine	Me.	ME	Utah	Utah	UT
Maryland	Md.	MD	Vermont	Vt.	VT
Massachusetts	Mass.	MA	Virginia	Va.	VA
Michigan	Mich.	MI	Washington	Wash.	WA
Minnesota	Minn.	MN	West Virginia	W. Va	WV
Mississippi	Miss.	MS	Wisconsin	Wis.	WI
Missouri	Mo.	MO	Wyoming	Wyo.	WY

Common Geographical Abbreviations

Apartment	Apt.	National	Natl.
Avenue	Ave.	Park, Peak	Pk.
Block	Blk.	Peninsula	Pen.
Boulevard	Blvd.	Point	Pt.
Building	Bldg.	Province	Prov.
County	Co.	Road	Rd.
District	Dist.	Route	Rte.
Drive	Dr.	Square	Sq.
Fort	Ft.	Street	St.
Island	Is.	Territory	Terr.
Mountain	Mt.		

Abbreviations of Traditional Measurements

inch(es)	in.	ounce(s)	oz.
foot, feet	ft.	pound(s)	lb.
yard(s)	yd.	pint(s)	pt.
mile(s)	mi.	quart(s)	qt.
teaspoon(s)	tsp.	gallon(s)	gal.
tablespoon(s)	tbsp.	Fahrenheit	F.

Abbreviations of Metric Measurements

millimeter(s)	mm	liter(s)	L
centimeter(s)	cm	kiloliter(s)	kL
meter(s)	m	milligram(s)	mg
kilometer(s)	km	centigram(s)	cg
milliliter(s)	mL	gram(s)	g
centiliter(s)	cL	Celsius	C

Other Commonly Used Abbreviations

about (used with dates)	c., ca., circ.	manager	mgr.
and others	et al.	manufacturing	mfg.
anonymous	anon.	market	mkt.
approximately	approx.	measure	meas.
associate, association	assoc., assn.	merchandise	mdse.
auxiliary	aux., auxil.	miles per hour	mph
bibliography	bibliog.	miscellaneous	misc.
boxes	bx(s).	money order	M.O.
bucket	bkt.	note well; take notice	N.B.
bulletin	bull.	number	no.
bushel	bu.	package	pkg.
capital letter	cap.	page	p., pg.
cash on delivery	C.O.D.	pages	pp.
department	dept.	pair(s)	pr(s).
discount	disc.	parenthesis	paren.
dozen(s)	doz.	Patent Office	pat. off.
each	ea.	piece(s)	pc(s).
edition, editor	ed.	poetical, poetry	poet.
equivalent	equiv.	private	pvt.
established	est.	proprietor	prop.
fiction	fict.	pseudonym	pseud.
for example	e.g.	published, publisher	pub.
free of charge	grat., gratis	received	recd.
General Post Office	G.P.O.	reference, referee	ref.
government	gov., govt.	revolutions per minute	rpm
graduate, graduated	grad.	rhetorical, rhetoric	rhet.
Greek, Grecian	Gr.	right	R.
headquarters	hdqrs.	scene	sc.
height	ht.	special, specific	spec.
hospital	hosp.	spelling, species	sp.
illustrated	ill., illus.	that is	i.e.
including, inclusive	incl.	treasury, treasurer	treas.
introduction, introductory	intro.	volume	vol.
italics	ital.	weekly	wkly
karat, carat	k., kt.	weight	wt.
left	L.		

Proofreading Symbols Reference

Proofreading symbols make it easier to show where changes are needed in a paper. When proofreading your own or a classmate's work, use these standard proofreading symbols.

insert	I proofred.
delete	Ip proofread.
close up space	I proof read.
delete and close up space	I proofreade.
begin new paragraph	¶ I proofread.
spell out	I proofread (10) papers. (sp)
lowercase	I Proofread. (lc)
capitalize	i proofread. (cap)
transpose letters	I proofraed. (tr)
transpose words	I only proofread her paper. (tr)
period	I will proofread.
comma	I will proofread and she will help.
colon	We will proofread for the following errors.
semicolon	I will proofread she will help.
single quotation marks	She said, "I enjoyed the story The Invalid."
double quotation marks	She said, I enjoyed the story.
apostrophe	Did you borrow Sylvias book?
question mark	Did you borrow Sylvia's book ?/
exclamation point	You're kidding !/
hyphen	online /=/
parentheses	William Shakespeare 1564–1616

Student Publications

To share your writing with a wider audience, consider submitting it to a local, state, or national publication for student writing. Following are several magazines and Web sites that accept and publish student work.

Periodicals

Creative Kids P.O. Box 8813, Waco TX 76714-8813

Merlyn's Pen merlynspen.org

Skipping Stones P.O. Box 3939, Eugene, OR 97403 http://www.skippingstones.org

Teen Ink Box 30, Newton, MA 02461 teenink.com

On-line Publications

Kid Pub http://www.kidpub.org

MidLink Magazine http://www.ncsu.edu/midlink

Stone Soup http://www.stonesoup.com

Contests

Annual Poetry Contest National Federation of State Poetry Societies, Contest Chair, Kathleen Pederzani, 121 Grande Boulevard, Reading, PA 19608-9680. http://www.nfsps.com

Paul A. Witty Outstanding Literature Award International Reading Association, Special Interest Group for Reading for Gifted and Creative Students, c/o Texas Christian University, P.O. Box 297900, Fort Worth, TX 76129

Seventeen Magazine Fiction Contest Seventeen Magazine, 1440 Broadway 13th Floor, New York, NY 10018

The Young Playwrights Festival National Playwriting Competition Young Playwrights Inc. Dept WEB, 306 West 38th Street #300, New York, NY 10018 or webmaster@youngplaywrights.org

Glossary

A

accent: the emphasis on a syllable, usually in poetry

action verb: a word that tells what action someone or something is performing (*See* linking verb.)

active voice: the voice of a verb whose subject performs an action (*See* passive voice.)

adjective: a word that modifies a noun or pronoun by telling *what kind* or *which one*

adjective clause: a subordinate clause that modifies a noun or pronoun

adjective phrase: a prepositional phrase that modifies a noun or pronoun

adverb: a word that modifies a verb, an adjective, or another adverb

adverb clause: a subordinate clause that modifies a verb, an adjective, an adverb, or a verbal by telling *where, when, in what way, to what extent, under what condition,* or *why*

adverb phrase: a prepositional phrase that modifies a verb, an adjective, or an adverb

allegory: a literary work with two or more levels of meaning—a literal level and one or more symbolic levels

alliteration: the repetition of initial consonant sounds in accented syllables

allusion: an indirect reference to a well-known person, place, event, literary work, or work of art

annotated bibliography: a research writing product that provides a list of materials on a given topic, along with publication information, summaries, or evaluations

apostrophe: a punctuation mark used to form possessive nouns and contractions

appositive: a noun or pronoun placed after another noun or pronoun to identify, rename, or explain the preceding word

appositive phrase: a noun or pronoun with its modifiers, placed next to a noun or pronoun to identify, rename, or explain the preceding word

article: one of three commonly used adjectives: *a, an,* and *the*

assonance: the repetition of vowel sounds in stressed syllables containing dissimilar consonant sounds

audience: the reader(s) a writer intends to reach

autobiographical writing: narrative writing that tells a true story about an important period, experience, or relationship in the writer's life

B

ballad: a song that tells a story (often dealing with adventure or romance) or a poem imitating such a song

bias: the attitudes or beliefs that affect a writer's ability to present a subject objectively

bibliography: a list of the sources of a research paper, including full bibliographic references for each source the writer consulted while conducting research (*See* works-cited list.)

biography: narrative writing that tells the story of an important period, experience, or relationship in a person's life, as reported by another

blueprinting: a prewriting technique in which a writer sketches a map of a home, school, neighborhood, or other meaningful place in order to spark memories or associations for further development

body paragraph: a paragraph in an essay that develops, explains, or supports the key ideas of the writing

brainstorming: a prewriting technique in which a group jots down as many ideas as possible about a given topic

C

case: the form of a noun or pronoun that indicates how it functions in a sentence

cause-and-effect writing: expository writing that examines the relationship between events, explaining how one event or situation causes another

character: a person (though not necessarily a human being) who takes part in the action of a literary work

characterization: the act of creating and developing a character through narration, description, and dialogue

citation: in formal research papers, the acknowledgment of ideas found in outside sources

classical invention: a prewriting technique in which writers gather details about a topic by analyzing the category and subcategories to which the topic belongs

clause: a group of words that has a subject and a verb

climax: the high point of interest or suspense in a literary work

coherence: a quality of written work in which all the parts flow logically from one idea to the next

colon: a punctuation mark used before an extended quotation, explanation, example, or series and after the salutation in a formal letter

comma: a punctuation mark used to separate words or groups of words

comparison-and-contrast writing: expository writing that describes the similarities and differences between two or more subjects in order to achieve a specific purpose

complement: a word or group of words that completes the meaning of a verb

compound sentence: a sentence that contains two or more independent clauses with no subordinate clauses

conclusion: the final paragraph(s) of a work of writing in which the writer may restate a main idea, summarize the points of the writing, or provide a closing remark to end the work effectively (*See* introduction, body paragraph, topical paragraph, functional paragraph.)

conflict: a struggle between opposing forces

conjugation: a list of the singular and plural forms of a verb in a particular tense

conjunction: a word used to connect other words or groups of words

connotation: the emotional associations that a word calls to mind (*See* denotation.)

consonance: the repetition of final consonant sounds in stressed syllables containing dissimilar vowel sounds

contraction: a shortened form of a word or phrase that includes an apostrophe to indicate the position of the missing letter(s)

coordinating conjunctions: words such as *and, but, nor,* and *yet* that connect similar words or groups of words

correlative conjunctions: word pairs such as *neither . . . nor, both . . . and,* and *whether . . . or* used to connect similar words or groups of words

couplet: a pair of rhyming lines written in the same meter

cubing: a prewriting technique in which a writer analyzes a subject from six specified angles: description; association; application; analysis; comparison and contrast; and evaluation

D

declarative sentence: a statement punctuated with a period

demonstrative pronouns: words such as *this, that, these,* and *those* used to single out specific people, places, or things

denotation: the objective meaning of a word; its definition independent of other associations the word calls to mind (*See* connotation.)

depth-charging: a drafting technique in which a writer elaborates on a sentence by developing a key word or idea

description: language or writing that uses sensory details to capture a subject

dialect: the form of a language spoken by people in a particular region or group

dialogue: a direct conversation between characters or people

diary: a personal record of daily events, usually written in prose

diction: a writer's word choice

direct object: a noun or a pronoun that receives the action of a transitive verb

direct quotation: a drafting technique in which writers indicate the exact words of another by enclosing them in quotation marks

documentary: nonfiction film that analyzes news events or another focused subject by combining interviews, film footage, narration, and other audio/visual components

documented essay: research writing that includes a limited number of research sources, providing full documentation parenthetically within the text

drafting: a stage of the writing process that follows prewriting and precedes revising in which a writer gets ideas on paper in a rough format

drama: a story written to be performed by actors and actresses

E

elaboration: a drafting technique in which a writer extends his or her ideas through the use of facts, examples, descriptions, details, or quotations

epic: a long narrative poem about the adventures of a god or a hero

essay: a short nonfiction work about a particular subject

etymology: the history of a word, showing where it came from and how it has evolved into its present spelling and meaning

exclamation mark: a punctuation mark used to indicate strong emotion

exclamatory sentence: a statement that conveys strong emotion and ends with an exclamation mark

exposition: writing to inform, addressing analytic purposes such as problem and solution, comparison and contrast, how-to, and cause and effect

extensive writing: writing products generated for others and from others, meant to be shared with an audience and often done for school assignments (*See* reflexive writing.)

F

fact: a statement that can be proved true (*See* opinion.)

fiction: prose writing about imaginary characters and events

figurative language: writing or speech not meant to be interpreted literally

firsthand biography: narrative writing that tells the story of an important period, experience, or relationship in a person's life, reported by a writer who knows the subject personally

five W's: a prewriting technique in which writers gather details about a topic by generating answers to the following questions: *Who? What? Where? When?* and *Why?*

fragment: an incomplete idea punctuated as a complete sentence

freewriting: a prewriting technique in which a writer quickly jots down as many ideas on a topic as possible

functional paragraph: a paragraph that performs a specific role in composition, such as to arouse or sustain interest, to indicate dialogue, to make a transition (*See* topical paragraph.)

G

generalization: a statement that presents a rule or idea based on particular facts

gerund: a noun formed from the present participle of a verb (ending in -*ing*)

gerund phrase: a group of words containing a gerund and its modifiers or complements that function as a noun

grammar: the study of the forms of words and the way they are arranged in phrases, clauses, and sentences

H

helping verb: a verb added to another verb to make a single verb phrase that indicates the time at which an action takes place or whether it actually happens, could happen, or should happen

hexagonal writing: a prewriting technique in

which a writer analyzes a subject from six angles: literal level, personal allusions, theme, literary devices, literary allusions, and evaluation

homophones: pairs of words that sound the same as each other yet have different meanings and different spellings, such as *hear/here*

how-to writing: expository writing that explains a process by providing step-by-step directions

humanities: forms of artistic expression including, but not limited to, fine art, photography, theater, film, music, and dance

hyperbole: a deliberate exaggeration or overstatement

hyphen: a punctuation mark used to combine numbers and word parts, to join certain compound words, and to show that a word has been broken between syllables at the end of a line

I

I-Search report: a research paper in which the writer addresses the research experience in addition to presenting the information gathered

image: a word or phrase that appeals to one or more of the senses—sight, hearing, touch, taste, or smell

imagery: the descriptive language used to recreate sensory experiences, set a tone, suggest emotions, and guide readers' reactions

imperative sentence: a statement that gives an order or a direction and ends with either a period or an exclamation mark

indefinite pronoun: a word such as *anyone, each,* or *many* that refers to a person, place, or thing, without specifying which one

independent clause: a group of words that contains both a subject and a verb and that can stand by itself as a complete sentence

indirect quotation: reporting only the general meaning of what a person said or thought; quotation marks are not needed

infinitive: the form of a verb that comes after the word *to* and acts as a noun, adjective, or adverb

infinitive phrase: a phrase introduced by an infinitive that may be used as a noun, an adjective, or an adverb

interjection: a word or phrase that expresses feeling or emotion and functions independently of a sentence

interrogative pronoun: a word such as *which* and *who* that introduces a question

interrogative sentence: a question that is punctuated with a question mark

interview: an information-gathering technique in which one or more people pose questions to one or more other people who provide opinions or facts on a topic

intransitive verb: an action verb that does not take a direct object (*See* transitive verb.)

introduction: the opening paragraphs of a work of writing in which the writer may capture the readers' attention and present a thesis statement to be developed in the writing (*See* body paragraph, topical paragraph, functional paragraph, conclusion.)

invisible writing: a prewriting technique in which a writer freewrites without looking at the product until the exercise is complete; this can be accomplished at a word processor with the monitor turned off or with carbon paper and an empty ballpoint pen

irony: the general name given to literary techniques that involve surprising, interesting, or amusing contradictions

itemizing: a prewriting technique in which a writer creates a second, more focused, set of ideas based on an original listing activity. (*See* listing.)

J

jargon: the specialized words and phrases unique to a specific field

journal: a notebook or other organized writing system in which daily events and personal impressions are recorded

K

key word: the word or phrase that directs an Internet or database search

L

layering: a drafting technique in which a writer elaborates on a statement by identifying and then expanding upon a central idea or word

lead: the opening sentences of a work of writing meant to grab the reader's interest, accomplished through a variety of methods, including providing an intriguing quotation, a surprising or provocative question or fact, an anecdote, or a description

learning log: a record-keeping system in which a student notes information about new ideas

legend: a widely told story about the past that may or may not be based in fact

legibility: the neatness and readability of words

linking verb: a word that expresses its subject's state of being or condition (*See* action verb.)

listing: a prewriting technique in which a writer prepares a list of ideas related to a specific topic. (*See* itemizing.)

looping: a prewriting activity in which a writer generates follow-up freewriting based on the identification of a key word or central idea in an original freewriting exercise

lyric poem: a poem expressing the observations and feelings of a single speaker

M

main clause: a group of words that has a subject and a verb and can stand alone as a complete sentence

memoir: autobiographical writing that provides an account of a writer's relationship with a person, event, or place

metaphor: a figure of speech in which one thing is spoken of as though it were something else

meter: the rhythmic pattern of a poem

monologue: a speech or performance given entirely by one person or by one character

mood: the feeling created in the reader by a literary work or passage

multimedia presentation: a technique for sharing information with an audience by enhancing narration and explanation with media, including video images, slides, audiotape recordings, music, and fine art

N

narration: writing that tells a story

narrative poem: a poem that tells a story in verse

nominative case: the form of a noun or pronoun used as the subject of a verb, as a predicate nominative, or as the pronoun in a nominative absolute (*See* objective case, possessive case.)

noun: a word that names a person, place, or thing

noun clause: a subordinate clause that acts as a noun

novel: an extended work of fiction that often has a complicated plot, many major and minor characters, a unifying theme, and several settings

O

objective case: the form of a noun or pronoun used as the object of any verb, verbal, or preposition, or as the subject of an infinitive (*See* nominative case, possessive case.)

observation: a prewriting technique involving close visual study of an object; a writing product that reports such a study

ode: a long formal lyric poem with a serious theme

onomatopoeia: words such as *buzz* and *plop* that suggest the sounds they name

open-book test: a form of assessment in which students are permitted to use books and class notes to respond to test questions

opinion: beliefs that can be supported but not proved to be true (*See* fact.)

oral tradition: the body of songs, stories, and poems preserved by being passed from generation to generation by word of mouth

outline: a prewriting or study technique that allows writers or readers to organize the presentation and order of information

oxymoron: a figure of speech that fuses two contradictory or opposing ideas, such as "freezing fire" or "happy grief"

P

parable: a short, simple story from which a moral or religious lesson can be drawn

paradox: a statement that seems to be contradictory but that actually presents a truth

paragraph: a group of sentences that share a common topic or purpose and that focus on a single main idea or thought

parallelism: the placement of equal ideas in words, phrases, or clauses of similar types

paraphrase: restating an author's idea in different words, often to share information by making the meaning clear to readers

parentheses: punctuation marks used to set off asides and explanations when the material is not essential

participial phrase: a group of words made up of a participle and its modifiers and complements that acts as an adjective

participle: a form of a verb that can act as an adjective

passive voice: the voice of a verb whose subject receives an action (*See* active voice.)

peer review: a revising technique in which writers meet with other writers to share focused feedback on a draft

pentad: a prewriting technique in which a writer analyzes a subject from five specified points: actors, acts, scenes, agencies, and purposes

period: a punctuation mark used to end a declarative sentence, an indirect question, and most abbreviations

personal pronoun: a word such as *I, me, you, we, us, he, him, she, her, they,* and *them* that refers to the person speaking; the person spoken to; or the person, place, or thing spoken about

personification a figure of speech in which a nonhuman subject is given human characteristics

persuasion: writing or speaking that attempts to convince others to accept a position on an issue of concern to the writer

phrase: a group of words without a subject and verb that functions as one part of speech

plot: the sequence of events in narrative writing

plural: the form of a word that indicates more than one item is being mentioned

poetry: a category of writing in which the final product may make deliberate use of rhythm, rhyme, and figurative language in order to express deeper feelings than those conveyed in ordinary speech (*See* prose, drama.)

point of view: the perspective, or vantage point, from which a story is told

portfolio: an organized collection of writing projects, including writing ideas, works in progress, final drafts, and the writer's reflections on the work

possessive case: the form of a noun or pronoun used to show ownership (*See* objective case, nominative case.)

prefix: one or more syllables added to the beginning of a word root (*See* root, suffix.)

preposition: a word that relates a noun or pronoun that appears with it to another word in the sentence to indicate relations of time, place, causality, responsibility, and motivation

prepositional phrase: a group of words that includes a preposition and a noun or pronoun

presenting: a stage of the writing process in which a writer shares a final draft with an audience through speaking, listening, or representing activities

prewriting: a stage of the writing process in which writers explore, choose, and narrow a topic and then gather necessary details for drafting

problem-and-solution writing: expository writing that examines a problem and provides a realistic solution

pronoun: a word that stands for a noun or for another word that takes the place of a noun

prose: a category of written language in which the end product is developed through sentences and paragraphs (*See* poetry, drama.)

publishing: a stage of the writing process in which a writer shares the written version of a final draft with an audience

punctuation: the set of symbols used to convey specific directions to the reader

purpose: the specific goal or reason a writer chooses for a writing task

Q

question mark: a punctuation mark used to end an interrogative sentence or an incomplete question

quicklist: a prewriting technique in which a writer creates an impromptu, unresearched list of ideas related to a specific topic

quotation mark: a punctuation mark used to indicate the beginning and end of a person's exact speech or thoughts

R

ratiocination: a systematic approach to the revision process that involves color-coding elements of writing for evaluation

reflective essay: autobiographical writing in which a writer shares a personal experience and then provides insight about the event

reflexive pronoun: a word that ends in -*self* or -*selves* and names the person or thing receiving an action when that person or thing is the same as the one performing the action

reflexive writing: writing generated for oneself and from oneself, not necessarily meant to be shared, in which the writer makes all decisions regarding form and purpose (*See* extensive writing.)

refrain: a regularly repeated line or group of lines in a poem or song

relative pronoun: a pronoun such as *that, which, who, whom,* or *whose* that begins a

subordinate clause and connects it to another idea in the sentence

reporter's formula: a prewriting technique in which writers gather details about a topic by generating answers to the following questions: *Who? What? Where? When?* and *Why?*

research: a prewriting technique in which writers gather information from outside sources such as library reference materials, interviews, and the Internet

research writing: expository writing that presents and interprets information gathered through an extensive study of a subject

response to literature writing: persuasive, expository, or narrative writing that presents a writer's analysis of or reactions to a published work

revising: a stage of the writing process in which a writer reworks a rough draft to improve both form and content

rhyme: the repetition of sounds at the ends of words

rhyme scheme: the regular pattern of rhyming words in a poem or stanza

rhythm: the form or pattern of words or music in which accents or beats come at certain fixed intervals

root: the base of a word (*See* prefix, suffix.)

rubric: an assessment tool, generally organized in a grid, to indicate the range of success or failure according to specific criteria

run-on sentence: two or more complete sentences punctuated incorrectly as one

S

salutation: the greeting in a formal letter

satire: writing that ridicules or holds up to contempt the faults of individuals or of groups

SEE method: an elaboration technique in which a writer presents a statement, an extension, and an elaboration to develop an idea

semicolon: a punctuation mark used to join independent clauses that are not already joined by a conjunction

sentence: a group of words with a subject and a predicate that expresses a complete thought

setting: the time and place of the action of a piece of narrative writing

short story: a brief fictional narrative told in prose

simile: a figure of speech in which *like* or *as* is used to make a comparison between two basically unrelated ideas

sonnet: a fourteen-line lyric poem with a single theme

speaker: the imaginary voice assumed by the writer of a poem

stanza: a group of lines in a poem, seen as a unit

statistics: facts presented in numerical form, such as ratios, percentages, or summaries

subject: the word or group of words in a sentence that tells whom or what the sentence is about

subordinate clause: a group of words containing both a subject and a verb that cannot stand by itself as a complete sentence

subordinating conjunction: a word used to join two complete ideas by making one of the ideas dependent on the other

suffix: one or more syllables added to the end of a word root (*See* prefix, root.)

summary: a brief statement of the main ideas and supporting details presented in a piece of writing

symbol: something that is itself and also stands for something else

T

theme: the central idea, concern, or purpose in a piece of narrative writing, poetry, or drama

thesis statement: a statement of an essay's main idea; all information in the essay supports or elaborates this idea

tone: a writer's attitude toward the readers and toward the subject

topic sentence: a sentence that states the main idea of a paragraph

topic web: a prewriting technique in which a writer generates a graphic organizer to identify categories and subcategories of a topic

topical paragraph: a paragraph that develops, explains, and supports the topic sentence related to an essay's thesis statement

transition: words, phrases, or sentences that smooth writing by indicating the relationship among ideas

transitive verb: an action verb that takes a direct object (*See* intransitive verb.)

U

unity: a quality of written work in which all the parts fit together in a complete, self-contained whole

V

verb: a word or group of words that expresses an action, a condition, or the fact that something exists while indicating the time of the action, condition, or fact

verbal: a word derived from the verb but used as a noun, adjective, or adverb (*See* gerund, infinitive, participle.)

vignette: a brief narrative characterized by precise detail

voice: the distinctive qualities of a writer's style, including diction, attitude, sentence style, and ideas

W

works-cited list: a list of the sources of a research paper, including full bibliographic references for each source named in the body of the paper (*See* bibliography.)

Index

Note: **Bold numbers** show pages on which basic definitions and rules appear.

A

Abbreviations, 580, 584, 632, 774–777
  academic degrees, 774
  commonly used, 777
  geographical, 776
  metric measurements, 776
  states, 775
  traditional measurements, 776
Abstracts, **195**, **744**
Accent, **780**
accept, except, 479
Action shots, as image type, **69**
Action verbs, **87**, 314, **316**–319
  adverbs located after, 567
  direct objects follow, 411
  grammar exercises on, 319
  intransitive, **316**–317, 319
  mental, 318
  review exercises on, 319
  transitive, **316**–317, 319
Actions, 171, 254
  parts of speech and, 61, 314, 426, 504
  visible, 318
Active reading, 727
Active voice, **780**
Actors, as pentad category, 254
Addresses, 595, 750
Adjective clauses, **439**–440, 445, 593, **780**
  diagraming, 664
Adjective phrases, **426**–427, 434, 436, **780**
  diagraming, 661
Adjectives, **113**, **336**, **780**
  commas and, 114, 588–589
  compound, **342**, 620
  cumulative review exercises on, 371, 388
  demonstrative, 345
  diagraming, 657
  endings of, 352, 561
  forms of, 560–561
  help for troublesome, 567–570
  infinitives as, 430, 432–433
  interrogative, 346
  linking verbs and, 567
  modified by other parts of speech, 348–349, 428, 441–442
  as modifiers, 336–337, 352, 434
  nouns as, 340–341

  participles as, 237, 430
  possessive, **343**–344
  predicate, 417–418, 451
  pronouns as, 305
  proper, **341**, 619, 622, 634, 643–644, 651
Adjectives and adverbs, 334–359, 558–575
  degrees of comparison, 558, **560**–566
  diagnostic tests on, 335, 559
  distinguishing between, **352**–353, 355
  grammar exercises on, 566, 571
  as modifiers, 334
  multiple functions of, 352
  review exercises, 356–357, 572–573
  test preparation on, 358–359, 574–575
  usage of, 358, 567–571
  See also Adjectives; Adverbs
Adventure stories, 73
Adverb clauses, **441**–442, 445, **780**
  diagraming, 664
  sentence combining using, 32
Adverb phrases, **428**–429, 436, **780**
  diagraming, 662
  sentence combining using, 32
Adverbs, **211**, **348**, **780**
  cumulative review exercises on, 371, 388
  diagraming, 657
  distinguishing, from prepositions, 367, 369, 370
  endings of, 352, 561
  forms of, 560
  functions of, 348–350
  grammar exercises on, 355
  help for troublesome, 570
  infinitives as, 430, 432–433
  locations of, 351, 567
  modified by other adverbs, 348, 350
  modified by other parts of speech, 428, 441–442
  as modifiers, 348, 352
  as parenthetical expressions, 592
Advertisements, 45, **144**–145, 678
advice, advise, 479
Aerial view shots, as camera technique, 121
affect, effect, 479
Agencies, as pentad category, 254

Agreement errors, 576–577
Agreement rules. *See* Making words agree; Pronoun-antecedent agreement; Subject-verb agreement
ain't, 508
Aircraft, capitalization and, 615, 641
Allegory, **780**
Alliteration, **780**
Allusion, **780**
Almanacs, 748
Analogies, **312**–313, 754–755
Analysis, skills for, 94, **105**, 147
  analyze as key word, **156**
  media and technology, 95, 245
  nonfiction text and, 725–726
  peer review and, 113, 138
  for visual arts, 195, 675, 680–681
  writing purpose, 55, 157, 260
Annotated bibliography, **780**
Antecedents, **302**–303, 305–306, 343–344
  See also Pronoun-antecedent agreement
Anthologies, 733
Antonyms, **697**, 749
Apostrophes, 580, 618, 623–628, **780**
  contractions and, 525, 626–628
  grammar exercises on, 629
  showing ownership with, 623–624
Appendixes, 715
Applications
  filling out, 732
Appositive, **434**–435, 437, 593, **780**
  diagraming, 662
Appositive phrases, **434**–435, 437, 593, **780**
  diagraming, 663
apply, as key word, 105, 156
Archives, **745**
argue, as key word, **277**
Arguments
  end marks for, 139
  persuasion and, 125–127, 137
  pro or con, 105, 156
  refutation and, 143, 148–149
  rhythm and organization of, 132
  standardized tests and, 148–149
  types of, **127**, **131**–133
  See also Evidence
Art, fine. *See* Responding to Fine Art and Literature; Spotlight on the Humanities

Art, visual
  choosing subjects for, 195
  interpreting, 271, 675–677, 680–683
  multimedia forms of, 271, 685
  See also type of, e.g., Movies
Articles, published, 616
  in periodicals, 115, 265, 745
Articles (parts of speech), **780**
  as adjectives, 338–339, 347, 356
  pronunciation of, 338
  in titles, 647, 715
Artistic works
  evaluating, 44, 146, 170, 288
  titles of, 614, 616, 647
Assessment, **274**
  See also Artistic works, evaluating; Rubrics for Self-Assessment; Standardized Test Preparation Workshops; Tests; Writing for assessment
Assignments, class, 738
Associate, 105, 156
Assonance, **780**
at, 479
Atlases, maps in, 748–749
Attached file, **768**
Audiences, **55, 80,** 130, 171, 671, **780**
  appropriate writing for, **16,** 148–149, 204
  considering, 104, 204, 215, 220, 255
  writing affected by, 55, 80, 141, 181, 231
  See also Reader interest
Audio elements. *See* Sounds
Audiovisual equipment, 9, 685
Authors, 249, 257
  library catalogs and, 740–741
  main points of, 152–153
  purposes of, 126–127, 721, 723
  strategies of, 19, 49, 73, 99, 125, 151, 175, 199, 223, 249
  See also Spotlight on the Humanities
Autobiographical writing, 48–71, **49, 780**
  drafting, 56–57
  editing and proofreading, 63
  photo essays as, 68
  prewriting, 52–55
  publishing and presenting, 64
  purpose of, 48–49
  revising, 58–62
  test preparation for, 70
  types of, **49**
Awards, capitalization and, 641

B
bad, badly, 567, 570
Balance in writing, 160, 209, 324
Ballad, **780**
Balloon help, computers and, 219
Bandwidth, **768**
Bar graphs, 676, 682
Basic sentence parts, 390–423
  complements, **410**–419
  compound parts as, **400**–404
  diagnostic test on, 391
  function of, 392–395
  grammar exercises on, 395, 399, 404, 409, 419
  review exercises on, 420–421
  subjects, **392,** 396–399, 405–409
  test preparation on, 422–423
  verbs, **392**
Bays, names of, 638
be, 626
  forms of, 21, 320, 326, 422, 535
because, 479
beside, besides, 480
Bias, **147, 679, 780**
Bibliography, 760–763, **780**
Biographies, **743,** 748, **780**
  firsthand, **67**
  sketches as, 223, 229, 232, 240
  See also Autobiographical writing
Bit, **768**
Block method, organization by, 158, 160, 173, 279
Blueprinting, **52,** 178, **780**
Body, in compositions, **39,** 182, **780**
Boldface, function of, 684
Bookmarks, electronic, 750, **768**
Books, 738
  finding, in libraries, 742–743
  reviews of, 249, 265
  titles of, 614, 616, 647
  See also Textbooks
Brainstorming, 6, 178, 179, 254, **780**
Brand names, capitalization and, 643
Broadcast media, **45**
Browsing, 252
Bulletin board system, electronic, **768**
Building elements of writing, 84, 251, 260, 268
Building your portfolio, **23**
  autobiographical writing, 64
  cause-and-effect essay, 190

comparison-and-contrast essay, 166
description, 115
how-to essay, 215
persuasive essay, 140
research report, 240
response to literature, 265
short story, 89
using technology for, 25
writing for assessment, 284
See also Portfolios, work to include in
Buildings, capitalization and, 641
Businesses, names of, 639–640
BUT Charts, 154

C
Call numbers, 742
Cameras
  techniques and, 69, 86, 104, 121
  video, and uses, 157, 685–686
Candid photographs, **195**
Capitalization, 634–653
  diagnostic test on, 635
  in direct quotations, 608–609
  errors, proofreading for, 22, 290–291, 652–653
  function of, 634, 684
  proper adjectives, **643**–646
  proper nouns, 63, 298, **637**–642, 647–648
  review exercises, 650–651
  sentence requirements for, 283, 636
  state abbreviations and, 632
  on tests, 290–291
Captions, **195,** 229, 675
Careers, 301–311, 374–387
Carets, revising with, 71, 149
Caricatures, **244**
Cartoons, storytelling devices in, 95
Case, **780**
Case-sensitivity in search engines, **768**
Catalogs, library, 740–741
Causal connections, types of, **183, 190**
Cause-and-effect essay, 174–197, **175, 780**
  drafting, 182–183
  editing and proofreading, 189
  how-to essays and, 201
  order in, 38
  prewriting, 178–181
  prompts for, 279

publishing and presenting, 190
purposes of, 174
relationships in, 209, 275, 726
revising, 184–188
test preparation for, 196–197
transitions in, 38
types of, 175
Celestial bodies, capitalization and, 641
Chains, expository, 190, 209, 275
Characterization, **781**
Characters, **96**, 727, **780**
  describing, 50, 57, 85, 251, 257
  exposition of, 74, 82, 90, 261
  as literature element, 73, 83, 272, 728
Charts, 154, 682
  T-charts, 131–133, 181
Choosing a form for writing
  extensive, 12
  focus on form, 18
  modes, 12
  reflexive, 12
Choosing your topic, **14**
  blueprinting, 14, **52**, 178
  brainstorming, 178–179
  BUT charts, 154
  drawings, 102
  freewriting, **52**, 78, 102, 202–203
  interviewing yourself, 228, 252
  invisible ink, 202
  journals, 416
  listing, 128, 154, 202, 228
  media flip-through, 78, 128, 178
  newswatch, 228
  photograph reviews, 24
  quicklists, 128, 154
  round-table discussions, 128
  timelines, 102
  writing prompts on tests, 276
  writing round, 78
  See also Topic Bank ideas
Chronological order, **38**, 209, 279, 726
  how-to essays and, 199, 206
  as organizational method, 71, 106, 232
  for series of causes and effects, 182, 191–192
  See also Standardized Test Preparation Workshops
Citations, **781**
  APA style, 760, 762
  CMS style, 760, 763

examples of, 226, 239, 241, 242, 760–764
  internal, 226, 239, 764
  MLA style, 760–761, 764
  periodical indexes and, 744–745
  in reports, 223, 239, 242, 760–764
Cities, names of, 638, 642
Clarifying your writing, 185, 238
  with effective sentences, 235, 267, 426, 454
  elaboration and, 232–233
  organization in, 249, 268, 272–273
Classical Invention, 230, **781**
Classification, 232
  classify as key word, **277**
  by noun types, **296**
  by order type, 241
  by preposition types, 365, 371
  by sentence function, 456–459
  by sentence structure, 443–446
Clauses, **424**–425, 438–449, **452**, **781**
  adjective, **439**, 445, 593
  adverb, 211, **441**–442, 445
  conjunctions and, 376–377
  cumulative review exercises on, 488
  dependent (*see* Subordinate clauses)
  fragments of, 471–472
  grammar exercises on, 449
  independent, 211, 263, 438, 441, 443–445, 462, 600–601, 603
  introductory, set off by commas, 590–591
  main (*see* Independent clauses)
  review exercises on, 451
  revising sentences with, 86
  subordinate, 263, **438**–439, 463
  test preparation on, 452–453
Clichés, avoiding, 336
Cliffhangers, as storytelling device, **95**
Climax, **76**, **82**, 84, 90, 92, **781**
Clocking process, 63
Close reading, **717**
Close-up shots, as camera technique, 121
Clubs, names of, 639–640
Coding
  revising with, 59, 60, 135–136, 185
  See also Color-coding; Highlighting

Coherence, **781**
Collaborative writing, **6**
  See also Cooperative Writing Opportunities; Peer review
Collective nouns, **297**, 388
Colons, 264, 580, **600**, 603–605, 631, **781**
  grammar exercises on, 605
  between independent clauses and lists, 603
  special uses for, 604
Color-coding, 19, 114
  ideas, 137, 260
  specific problems, 20, 111
  words to reconsider, 61, 237, 263
Combining sentences, 29–32, 460–463
Commas, 214, 434, 445, **580**, **585**–597, **781**
  adjectives and, 114, 588–589
  adverb clauses and phrases with, 211
  basic rules for, 632
  conjunctions with, 444, 475, 585–586, 600
  grammar exercises on, 599
  independent clauses with, 600
  interjections and, 381
  introductory material and, 381, 590–591
  items in series with, 214, 587, 591
  parenthetical expressions and, 592–593
  quotation marks and, 608–609, 611–612
  quotations and, 264, 612
  review exercises on, 630
  run-on sentences with, 473, 475
  set-off, 381, 590–597
  special material and, 594–597
Commercials. *See* Advertisements
Common expressions, as parentheticals, 592
Common nouns, **298**–299, 388
Commonly misspelled words, 772–773
Commonly overused words, 770–771
Communication skills, 686–687
  the arts and, 8, 68–69, 95, 121, 687
  formal speaking, 671–672
  of ideas, 45, 390
  informal speaking, 669–670
  sentences and, 390, 454
  storytelling, 95, 731

visual representation as, 675–687
See also Listening skills; Reading
skills; Speaking, listening,
viewing, and representing;
Viewing skills
Comparative degree, 560–566
forming, with *-er* or *more,*
560–562
memorizing, of irregular
modifiers, 563–564
spelling rule for, 561
using, of irregular modifiers,
565–566
compare, as key word, **156,**
164, **277**
Comparison, 249, 257, 259
avoiding double, 565, 574
degrees of, 558, **560**–566,
574–575
Comparison-and-contrast essay,
150–173, **151, 781**
comparison, 257
contrast, **277**
cross-media character assessment in, 288
descriptions in, 280
drafting, 158–159
editing and proofreading, 165
prewriting, 154–157
prompts for, 279
publishing and presenting, 166
requirements for, 275
revising, 160–164
test preparation for, 172–173
types of, **151**
Complements, **410**–421, 430–432,
781
cumulative review exercises on,
488
diagraming, 659–660
direct objects as, 410–413, 430
grammar exercises on, 419
indirect objects as, 414–415
phrases and, 431–432
subject, and linking verbs,
416–418
Complete sentences
editing and proofreading, 283
fragments and, 469–473
subjects and verbs in, **392**–395,
410, 422
verb as requirement of, 314
Complete subjects, **396**–399
Complete thoughts, **410**
sentences as expressions of,
392–395
Complex sentences, **263,**
445–446, 449, 463
diagraming, 664

Compositions, **28,** 37–43, **195**
Compound modifiers, **342,**
620–621
Compound nouns, **297**–298,
388, 619
Compound numbers, 618
Compound objects
combining sentences with, 412,
415, 460–461
direct, **411**–413, 443
indirect, **414**–415
pronoun cases and, 530
Compound prepositions, **362,**
364–365, 443
Compound sentences, **137,**
444–445, **781**
combining sentences into, 31,
462
commas with, 585–586
conjunctions and, 462
diagraming, 663
grammar exercises on, 446, 449
Compound subject complements,
418
Compound subjects, **163, 538**
combining sentences and, 30,
163, 460–461
diagraming, 658
grammar exercises on, 404
pronoun cases and, 530
recognizing, **400**–401, 403–404
in simple sentences, 443
subject-verb agreement with,
163, 538–540
Compound verbs
combine sentences with, 30,
460–461
diagraming, 658
grammar exercises on, 404
recognizing, **402**–404
in simple sentences, 443
Comprehension, 681–683, 721,
727–731
Computer technology
browsers, 245
glossary of Internet terms, 768–
769
how-to help with, 219
Internet Research Handbook,
764–767
research help using, 222
search engines as, 231, 245
software for reference works,
697
test-taking with, 289
tracking class assignments with,
738
writing tools, 9, 25
See also Word processors

Conclusions, **39,** 153, **781**
conflict resolution in, 66, 77
drawing, 176, 251, 268,
688–689
expression of, 608, 610
restatement in, 242, 286
revising and, 161, 281
Conflict, **56, 80, 781**
describing, in autobiographies,
49–50
details and, 51, 58, 91
establishing, in openings,
73, 75
resolution of, 51, 56, 66, 73,
82, 92
short stories with, 73, 82, 92
Conjugation, **502**–503, **781**
Conjunctions, **376**–380, 540, **781**
in compound sentences, 462
in compound subjects, 163,
538–540
coordinating, 86, **376,** 379,
444, 462, 475, 585–586
correlative, **377**–380
cumulative review exercises on,
389
diagraming, 657–658
functions of, 374, 376–377, 379
grammar exercises, 380
independent clauses and, 462,
600
revising sentences with, 86, 475
subordinating, 86, 441, 463
in titles, 647
usage test on, 387
Conjunctions and interjections,
374–387
conjunctions, **376**–380
diagnostic test on, 375
interjections, **381**–384
review exercises, 385–386
See also Conjunctions;
Interjections
Connecting ideas
different media used for, 120,
218, 288
in written work, 209, 217, 387
See also Standardized Test
Preparation Workshops
Connections, 58, 257
coding, 59, 136, 185
making, 137, 251, 254, 262, 268
types of, **183, 192**
See also Cross-Curricular
Connections; Reading-Writing
Connections; Spotlight on the
Humanities
Connotation, **725, 781**

Considering your audience and purpose. *See* Audiences; Purposes for writing
Consonance, **781**
Consonants, 338, 561, 705, 708
Consumer reports, as product comparisons, 151, 166, 169
Contests, writing, 6, 779
Context, **692**, 731
Continents, names of, 638, 642
Contractions, **626**–628, **781**
  apostrophes with, 626–628
  common, with verbs, 626
  possessive forms versus, 525
  usage of, 627
contrast, as key word, **277**
Contrast, 45, 49, 56, **105**, **156**, 164, 209
  persuasion and, 127, 142
  See also Comparison-and-contrast essay
Conversation, 669, 691
convince, as key word, **277**
Cookie, electronic, **768**
Cooperative Writing Opportunities
  aquarium display research and captions, 229
  cause-and-effect pamphlet, 179
  collaborative story, 79
  how to organize games, 203
  panel talk, 253
  possibilities for, 6
  radio documentaries, 129
  school-year autobiography, 53
  travel brochures, 155
Coordinating conjunctions, **376**, 475, **781**
  combining sentences with, 379, 462
  in compound sentences, 444, 462, 585–586
  See also Conjunctions
Correlative conjunctions, **377**–379, **781**
Counties, names of, 638
Countries, names of, 638, 642
Couplet, **781**
Crediting sources, **760**
Critical reading. *See* Nonfiction, critically reading
Critical Viewing
  analyze, 4, 6, 24, 31, 44, 57, 76, 81, 86, 100, 104, 116, 132, 142, 176, 182, 187, 195, 204, 222, 227, 238, 241, 257, 301, 314, 321, 322, 327, 334, 337, 350, 374, 390, 393, 405, 427,

474, 490, 494, 532, 537, 548, 552, 558, 622, 668, 677, 714, 723, 737, 740, 743, 744, 755
  apply, 106, 141, 143, 152, 160, 167, 243, 259, 274, 277, 281, 287, 565, 648
  assess, 344, 501
  classify, 440
  compare, 5, 92, 117, 218, 244, 543, 562, 645
  compare and contrast, 117, 150, 168, 194, 328, 339, 432, 497, 522
  connect, 28, 98, 101, 174, 198, 307, 363, 377, 379, 414, 472, 539, 603, 634, 680
  contrast, 367, 407, 480
  deduce, 153, 288, 728, 733
  describe, 349, 360, 400, 424, 435, 601, 619, 620, 624, 672, 725
  distinguish, 346, 439
  draw conclusions, 48, 286, 397, 461, 524, 544
  evaluate, 93, 209, 411, 412, 454, 477, 541, 567, 730
  hypothesize, 62, 191, 193, 233, 288, 610
  identify, 340, 586
  infer, 74, 234, 279, 429, 462, 518, 581, 589, 687
  interpret, 8, 68, 83, 94, 174, 188, 248, 251, 267, 268, 270, 275, 285, 685
  make a judgment, 568
  question, 224, 457
  relate, 12, 90, 112, 164, 169, 213, 294, 298, 317, 324, 343, 353, 364, 403, 503, 526, 597, 642
  respond, 24, 582
  speculate, 2, 72, 94, 124, 158, 192, 200, 255, 266, 269, 298, 302, 366, 381, 467, 469, 510, 578, 595, 606, 609, 637, 646, 686, 736, 749, 750
  summarize, 77
  support, 444, 581, 586, 589
Criticism, expressing, 62
Cross-cultural influences, 94, 707
Cross-Curricular Connections
  humanities, 438–451, 465–468 (*See also* Spotlight on the Humanities)

physical education, 454–459, 460–464, 518–529, 618–631, 632–633
science, 294–300, 301–311, 334–347, 348–355, 360–373, 374–386, 388–389, 390–409, 410–419, 426–437, 465–468, 490–499, 606–617, 693
social studies, 314–331, 469–485, 500–515, 534–547, 548–552, 558–573, 578–599, 600–605, 634–651, 693
Cross-cutting, as storytelling device, 95
Cross-media activities
  comparing, 218–219, 289
  comparing and contrasting, 155, 170–171, 244, 288
  connecting ideas, 120, 218, 288
  evaluating, 45, 288
Cubing, 105, 156, **781**
Culture
  cross-cultural influences, 94, 707
  identify cultural context, 731
  reading myths, legends, and folk tales, 730
Cumulative review exercises. *See subheading under subject, e.g.,* Parts of speech, cumulative review exercises on
Curricular topics. *See* Cross-Curricular Connections
Cutting and pasting, as revision strategy, 108
Cyberspace, **768**

D

Databases, electronic, **768**
Dates (calendar numbers), commas and, 594–595
Days, names of, 639
Deadlines, budgeting time for, 5
Declarative constructions
  grammar exercises on, 584
  sentences, **456**, 580, **781**
Definite articles (parts of speech), **338**–339, 347, 356
Definitions, 237, 348, 692, 699, 747
Deities, names of, 640
Demonstrative adjectives, 345
Demonstrative pronouns, **305**, 345, **781**
Denotation, **725**, **781**
Dependent clauses. *See* Subordinate clauses
Depth-charging, technique, 107, **781**

Derivatives, dictionaries for, 747
describe, as key word, **105**, 156
Description, **99**–123, **781**
  comparing, in different media,
    120–121
  details and, 49, 99–101,
    104–105, 107–109
  drafting, 18, 106–107
  editing and proofreading, 114
  elaboration in, 259, 280
  examples of, 100–101,
    116–117, 119
  focus on, with graphic aids,
    681–683
  modifiers and, 334
  precise words preferred, 563
  prewriting, 102–105
  publishing and presenting, 115
  revising, 108–113
  scoring, 115
  test preparation for, 122–123
  types of, **99**
  as writing mode, 12
Deserts, names of, 638, 642
Desktop-publishing programs, 9
Details, **35**, 225, 232, 721
  assessment of, 70, 215
  characterizing with, 50, 57, 76,
    83
  confirming, 22, 231
  conflict and, 51, 58, 91
  describing, 49, 99–101,
    104–105, 107–109, 211
  how-to essays and, 199,
    205–208, 220
  listening for main, 673–674
  making connections with, 51,
    58, 254
  purpose of, 55, 80, 91, 106,
    116, 231
  techniques used for, 55, 104,
    254
  use of supporting, 249, 281
  See also Gathering details;
    Providing elaboration
Dewey Decimal System, 742–743
Diagraming sentences, 656–665
  adjective, adverbs, and conjunc-
    tions, 657
  appositives, 662
  clauses, 665–666
  complements, 659–660
  complex sentences, 664
  compound sentences, 663
  compound subjects and verbs,
    658
  orders (imperatives), 659
  phrases, 661–663
  subjects and verbs, 656

Diagnostic Tests
  adjectives and adverbs, 533, 559
  capitalization, 635
  conjunctions and interjections,
    375
  nouns, 295
  phrases and clauses, 425
  prepositions, 361
  pronouns, 295, 519
  punctuation, 579
  sentences, 391, 455
  verbs, 315, 491
  word agreement, 533
Diagrams, 190
  as graphic aids, 82, 682,
    719–720
  Venn, 157, 173, 720
Dialect, **781**
Dialogue, 40, 43, **781**
  interjections in, 381–382
  punctuating, **88**, 613
Diaries, **781**
  reflexive writing in, **12**
Diction, as style element, **42**, **782**
Dictionaries, 61, 560
  checking spelling with, 619,
    708–709, 711
  definitions in, 692, 699,
    747
  entries in, 746–747
  types of, **746**, **748**
  vocabulary development and,
    692, 697
did, done, 508
different from, different than, 480
Digerati, **768**
Direct objects, **411**–413, 509–511,
    782
  action verbs and, 411
  as complements, 410–413, 430
  compound, 412, 443
  cumulative review exercises on,
    451
  modified by adjective phrases,
    427
  pronouns as, 520, 523–524
  verb usage problems and,
    509–511
  word order of, and verbs, 413
Direct quotations, **606**–610, **760**,
    782
  capitalization in, 608–609
  distinguishing indirect and,
    607
  quotation marks around, 606
  set off by commas, 596
Directions, giving informative.
    See Instructions
Directives, end marks of, 139

Discussions, 128, 188, 248, 284,
    669
Dividing words, 621–623
  rules for, 622
Documentaries, 129, 193, 195,
    678, 686, **782**
Documentation, **762**
  APA style, **762**
  CMS style, **762**
  MLA style, **762**, 763–764
Documented essays, 223, **782**
Documents, names of, 639
done, did, 508
Double comparisons, 565, 574
Double negatives, **478**, 480
Double quotation marks, 264
Downloading, **768**
Drafting, **13**, **782**
  providing elaboration, **18**, **207**
    with causal connections, 183
    with descriptions, 280
    with details, 50, 57, 83
    with examples, 280
    with explanations of main
      idea, 153
    find points to clarify, 232–233
    heightening tension by, 66
    self-assessment of, 215
    techniques for, 18, 133, 159,
      207
    telling and showing as, 83
    test preparation for, 221
    types of support for, **259**
  shaping your writing, **18**
    create a main impression, 106
    create a plot, 82
    develop a main idea, 232
    focus in, 258, 279, 285
    make an outline, 232
    organize details, 206, 232
    organize for emphasis, 132,
      251
    organize logically, 182
    plan your organization, 279
    select an effective organization,
      158, 232
    tension for reader interest, 56
    thesis statements, 132, 141,
      232, 241
  See also Standardized Test
    Preparation Workshops
Drama, 64, 93, 194, 728, **782**
  plays as, 614, 647
  reading, 728
  as theater medium, 170, 244,
    288
Dramatic interpretation,
  presenting, 271
Drawings. *See* Graphic aids

E

E-mail, 9, **768**
Editing and Proofreading, 13, **22**
  capitalization, 63, 652–653
  citations, 239
  commas, 88, 114, 214
  complete sentences, 283
  dialogue, 88
  end marks, 88, 139
  error detection on tests, 290–291
  prepositions, 189
  pronouns, 165
  quotations, 88, 264
  See also Standardized Test
    Preparation Workshops
Editorials, 129, 678, 722
effect, affect, 479
Effective sentences, 454–489
  avoiding problems in, 469–482
  combining, 29–32, 460–464
  communicating clearly with,
    454
  cumulative review exercises on,
    489
  diagnostic test on, 455
  functions of, 456–459
  grammar exercises on, 459,
    464, 468, 483
  review exercises on, 484–485
  test preparation on, 486–487
  varying, 465–468
Elaboration, **18**, **207**, **782**
  with causal connections, 183
  with descriptions, 280
  with details, 50, 57, 83
  with examples, 280
  with explanations of main idea,
    153
  find points to clarify, 232–233
  heightening tension by, 66
  self-assessment of, 215
  techniques for, 18, 133, 159,
    207
  telling and showing as, 83
  test preparation for, 221
  types of support for, **259**
Electronic texts
  building portfolios with, 25, 140
  databases as, 749
  on-line publishing oppor-
    tunities, 6, 140, 779
  reference works as, 740–741,
    746, 748–749
  test-taking with, 289
  See also Internet resources
Emotion, 195, 381
  exclamation marks and, 139,
    582

expressions of, 456, 458, 722
  persuasion and, 125, 127
  supported by explanatory
    details, 268
Emphasis, creating, 40, 132, 251
Encyclopedias, 722, 748
End marks, **139**, **474**
  basic rules for, 632
  grammar exercises on, 584, 617
  location of, in direct quotations,
    608–609
  review exercises on, 630
  sentences and, 139, 283,
    456–458, 474
  See also Exclamation marks;
    Periods; Question marks
Endings of words. *See* Suffixes
English language, 456, 560, 578
  formal versus informal, **43**
  standard, usage, 43, 332, 358,
    574, 747
  word origins of, 701, 706–707
Entertain, as communication
    purpose, 43, 157, 671
Epic, **782**
Episodes, titles of, 616
Error message, electronic, **768**
Errors, 7, 290–291, 652–653
Essays, **782**
  extensive writing in, **12**
Essays, types of
  cause-and-effect, 174–197
  comparison-and-contrast,
    150–173
  compositions, 28, 37–43
  how-to, 198–221
  persuasive, 124–149
  photo, 69
  plan evaluation, 151
  product comparisons, 151
  reflective, 49
  research report, 223
  response to literature, 249
Etymologies, **782**. *See also* Word
    origins
Evaluating media, 245, 679
  literature, 257, 267
  points to consider, 84, 147, 204
Evaluating writing. *See* Peer
    review; Reflecting on your
    writing; Rubrics for Self-
    Assessment
Events, 186, 639
  in autobiographical writing, 49,
    53
  historical accounts of, 175, 179
  natural phenomena as, 229, 730
  using pentads with, 254, 261

Evidence, 135, 177
  descriptions as, 250–251
  facts as, 126, 131, 280
Examples, **35**, 280
except, accept, 479
Exclamation marks, 580,
    582–583, **782**
  basic rules for, 632
  location of, with quotations,
    611–612
  sentences and, 139, 381, 457,
    582
Exclamatory statements, 456,
    458, 582, 584, **782**
Experiences, relating, 257, 727
Experiments, science, 223, 722
explain, as key word, **277**
Explanations, 225, 262, 671
  elaborating with, 153, 183
  how-to essays and, 199, 203,
    723
  supporting with, 268, 286
  topic ideas for, 179, 276,
    730
  See also Exposition
Exploding the Moment technique,
    207
Exploring topics, 225, 230, 289
  See also Choosing your topic;
    Details; Prewriting; Providing
    elaboration
Exposition, 74, 82, 90, 150–221,
    175, **199**, **782**
  gathering details for, 157, 173,
    205, 278
  prompts for, 275, 279
  requirements for, 275
  topics for, 154–155, 202–203,
    218, 276
  types of, **151**, **175**, **199**, **223**
  as writing mode, 12
  See also Cause-and-effect essay;
    Comparison-and-contrast
    essay; Essays, types of;
    Explanations; How-to essay
Expressions, 267
  concluding, 608, 610
  idioms as regional, **692**
  interrupting, 608–610
  introductory, 607, 610
  parenthetical, **592**–593
  quotation marks and, 607–610
  sentences as, 390, 392–395,
    410
Expressive writing. *See* Description;
    Journals; Narration; Poems
Extensive writing, **12**, **782**

F

Facts, **35**, **722**, **782**
  checking, as true, 22, 722
  as evidence, 126, 131
  opinions and, 147, 679, 722, 756–757
  reference sources for, 226, 748
  statements of, 139, 456
  uses of, 18, 280, 721, 730
Fairy tales, 194
Family relationships, titles for, 645–646
Fantasy stories, 73, 79
Farcical rhythm, as storytelling device, **95**
farther, further, 480
Feelings. *See* Emotion
fewer, less, 567
Fiction, 727, 742, **782**
  folk tales, 194, 288, 452–453, 730–731
  legends, **730**–731
  myths, 270, 640, **730**–731
  science, characteristics, 73, 218
  strategies for reading, 727–731
  See also Drama; Poems; Short story
Figurative language, 257, 272, **692**, **782**
Figures of speech, **118**, 261
Film. *See* Media and Technology Skills workshops
Fine Art. *See* Responding to Fine Art and Literature; Spotlight on the Humanities
First-person narration, **165**, 303–304, 502
Firsthand biography, **67**, **782**
Five *W*'s, **16**, **782**
Flashbacks, as storytelling device, **95**
Flashcards, 696
Flip-through process, 78, 128, 178, 228
Focus, 241, 258, 266, 279, 285
  See also Main points
Folk tales, 194, 288, 452–453, 730–731
Formal English, **43**
Formats, presentation, 193, 226, 684, 686
Fractions, with hyphens, 618
Fragments, **469**–**473**, **782**
  clause, 471–472
  correcting, 482
  paragraph, 473

  phrase, 470
  sentence, 469
  test preparation on, 486–487
Frame questions to direct research, 228–231, 244
Free verse, 119
Freewriting, **52**, 78, 102, **782**
FTP site, **768**
Functional paragraphs, **40**, **110**, **782**
Funneling, narrowing topics with, 130
further, farther, 480
Future perfect tense, 500, 502, 504, 506, 516–517
Future tense, **492**, 626
  basic form of, 500, 502
  progressive verb form of, 504, 506
  usage test on, 516–517

G

Gathering details, **16**–**17**
  cubing, 105
  doing research, 181, 192, 231
  five *W*'s for, **16**
  hexagons for, 17, 256–257
  itemizing, 55, 81, 205
  listing and itemizing, 55, 81
  T-charts for, 131, 181
  Topic Webs for, 278
  See also Evidence; Providing elaboration
Generalizations, 147, **724**, **782**
Generating topics. *See* Choosing your topic
Genres, reading a wide variety of, 715–733
Geographical sites. *See* Names, geographical; Places
Germanic languages, 701
Gerund, **782**
Gerund phrase, **782**
GIF, **768**
Glossaries, 693, 697, 711, 715
gone, went, 508
good, well, 567
Government bodies, names of, 639–640
Government titles, capitalization and, 644
Grammar, definition of, **782**
Grammar exercises
  on chapter sections (*see sub-heading under subject,* e.g., Using punctuation marks, grammar exercises on)

  on entire chapters (*see subheading under subject,* e.g., Using punctuation marks, review exercises on)
Grammar in Literature
  adjectives, 339, 564
  adverbs, 352
  articles and other adjectives, 339
  capitalization, 644
  commas, 591
  common and proper nouns, 299
  conjunctions, 378
  contractions, 627
  forms of irregular adjectives, 564
  interjections, 382
  linking verbs, 324
  number agreement of pronouns and verbs, 545
  prepositions, 363
  pronoun cases in, 525
  quotation marks, 612
  sentence effectiveness, 457, 465
  sentence parts, 397, 401
  sentence structures, 447
  verbs, 505
Grammar in Your Writing
  adjectives, 113–114
  adverb clauses, 211
  adverb phrases, 211
  commas and items in series, 214
  commas with two or more adjectives, 114
  complete sentences, 283
  complex sentences, 263
  compound sentences, 137
  compound subjects, 163
  confirming, as proofreading task, 22
  end marks, 139
  nouns, **61**
  participial phrases, 237
  prepositions, **189**
  pronoun-antecedent agreement, 165
  punctuating dialogue, 88
  punctuating quotations, 264
  quotation marks with titles, 239
  sentences, 137, 263, 283
  underlining with titles, 239
  verb tense, **187**
  verbs, 87
  See also Hands-on Grammar; Number; Objects

Grammatical agreement. *See* Making words agree; Pronoun-antecedent agreement; Subject-verb agreement
Graphic, electronic, **768**
Graphic aids, 102, 675, 681–683
  diagrams as, 682, 719–720
  grids, 720
  illustrations as, 682
  interpreting, on tests, 688–689
  types of, **682–683**
Graphic organizers,
  creating, 681
    charts, 682
    diagrams, 682
    formatting, 684
    graphs, 682
    illustrations, 682
    look at text structure to, 681
    maps, 683
    set a purpose for, 681
    tables, 682
    using text descriptions, 681
  interpreting, 688
    graphs, 675
      bar, 676
      line, 676
      pie, 677
    maps, 675
    symbols, 675
Graphs, 675–677
  types of, **676–677**
Group work. *See* Brainstorming; Cooperative Writing Opportunities; Peer review

H

Habits, as causal connections, 183
Haiku, **119**
Hands-on Grammar
  action verb showdown, 318
  adjectives and adverbs, 354
  agreement flip book, 546
  capitalization, 649
  interjections wheel, 383
  nouns and pronouns, 308
  preposition pop-up, 368
  pronoun case checker, 527
  punctuation circles, 598
  sentence break-up and make-up, 482
  sentence structures, 448
  troublesome modifiers fold-up, 570
  verb fortune teller, 506
have, of, 508
"Help" files, computer, **219**

Helping verbs, **326**–329, **782**
  forms of *be* as, 326
  grammar exercises on, 329
  with main verbs, 326–327
  with past participles, 511
  separation of, in verb phrase, 328
  verb phrases with, **326**–327, 492
here, functions of, 408
Hexagonal writing, 17, 256–257, **783**
Highlighting, 19, 134, 136, 254, 262
  See also Coding
Historical accounts, 175, 179
  names of events in, 639
  names of periods in, 639
Holidays, names of, 639
Home pages, electronic, **768**
Homophones, **710, 783**
How-to essay, 198–221, **199, 783**
  cause and effect in, 200–201
  comparisons of, 217, 218–219
  directions given in, 199, 201
  drafting, 206–207
  editing and proofreading, 214
  prewriting, 202–205
  prompts for, 279
  publishing and presenting, 215
  revising, 208–213
  scoring, 215
  test preparation for, 220–221
  types of, **199**
HTML, **768**
Humanities, **783**
  See also Responding to Fine Art and Literature; Spotlight on the Humanities
Hyperbole, **783**
Hyphens, 580, 618–623, **783**
  compound modifiers and, 620–621
  compound words and word parts, 619–621
  dividing words and, 621–623
  function of, 618
  grammar exercises on, 629
  review exercises on, 631

I

I-Search report, 243, **783**
Ideas, 3, 4, 140, 224, 604
  communicating, with sentences, 390, 456
  keeping track of, 3, 137, 160
  layering, 133, 159

listening, 673–674
  main, 33–34, 162, 185, 756–757
    (*see also* Main points)
  parts of speech and, 296, 500
  persuasion and, 137, 279
  See also Topic Bank ideas
Idioms, **692,** 747
Illumination
  as revision strategy, 85
Illustrations (line drawings)
  See Graphic aids
Illustrations (examples), **35,** 36, 162
Imagery, **783**
Images, 69, 729, **783**
  evaluating media, 147, 171, 679
  as evidence, 131–132
  vivid, 131–133, 147, 161
Imperative sentences, **457, 783**
  end marks for, 457, 580, 582
  function of, 456–457
  grammar exercises on, 584
  implied *you* in, 406
Importance, order of, **38,** 106, 251, 726
  conclusions and, 161, 268, 286
  formatting for, 279, 604
Impressions, creating, 106, 116
Improving your work, 5
  See also Peer review; Revising; Revising overall structure; Revising paragraphs; Revising sentences; Revising word choice
in, into, 480
Indefinite articles (parts of speech), **338**–339, 347, 356
Indefinite pronouns, **306**–307, 543–545, 551–553, 625, **783**
Independent clauses, **137, 438,** 441, 443–445, **783**
  adverb phrases and, 211
  colons following, 603
  complex sentences and, 263, 445–446
  compound sentences and, 137, 444, 462
  semicolons with, 600–601
  simple sentences and, 443
Indexes, 131, 697, 715, 740–741, 744–745
Indirect objects, **414**–415, 451, 520, 523–524
Indirect quotations, **606**–607, **783**
Inferences, 100–101, **176**
  making, 177, 724, 727
  test preparation on, 734–735

Infinitive phrases, **432**–433, **783**
Infinitives, 430, **432**, 436, **783**
Informal English, **43**
Information media, 45, 678–679
  analyzing, 679
  and bias, 679
  commercial , 678
  comparing and contrasting
    newscasts, 45
  comparing different media,
    120, 170–171, 218, 288
  documentary, 678
  editorial, 678
  evaluating varieties of, 679
  facts and opinion in, 679
  interview, 678
  loaded language and images,
    679
  newsmagazine, 678
  nonprint materials as, 675–677,
    740–741, 743, 749
  purposes of, 679
  television news program, 678
  See also Media and Technology
    Skills workshops
Informative writing. *See* Exposition
Insight, **56**
Inspirational arguments, 127
Institutions, names of, 639–640
Instructions
  in how-to essays, 199, 201
  imperative sentences as,
    456–457
  informative purpose of, 157, 723
  recognizing subjects in, 406
  revision strategy with, 184, 209
  speaking skills for giving,
    669–670
  for test taking, 289
  writing prompts as, **275**
Interactivity, electronic, **768**
Interjections, **381**–384, **783**
  cumulative review exercises on,
    389
  function of, 374
  grammar exercises on, 384
  help on, 383
  punctuation used with,
    381–382, 582
Internet resources, 140, 239,
  733, **765**, **768**
  and copyright, 767
  evaluating, 245, 750, 767
  glossary of terms, **768**–**769**
  key word search on, **765**
  narrowing a search on, 765
  nature of, 9, 45
  on-line reference sites, 766

  searching, 222, 231, 245, 564,
    603, 750
  subject searches, 766
  Web sites, 240, 731, 745,
    750
Interpreting, **74**, 77, 721
Interrogatives
  adjectives, 346
  grammar exercises on, 584
  pronouns, **306**, 346, **783**
  sentences, **456**, 581, **783**
Interrupting expressions,
  608–610
Interviews, 222–223, 228, 252,
  678, 742, **783**
into, in, 480
Intransitive verbs, **316**–317, 319,
  783
Introductions, spoken, 670
Introductions, written, **783**
  See also Openings
Inverted word order, **407**–409,
  413, 467, 542
Investigations, 175, 193
Invisible-ink technique, 202, **783**
Irony, **783**
Irregular parts of speech
  adjectives, 564
  modifiers, 563–564, 566
  verbs, 492, 495–498, 505
Islands, names of, 638
Italics, 614, 684
Itemizing, 55, 81, 205, **783**

J

Jargon, **725**, **783**
Journals, 3, 8, 12, 416, **783**
JPEG (Joint Photographic Experts
  Group) format,
  768
Judgment, 249, 722
just, 567–568

K

Key elements, as topic sentences,
  35, 41
Key words, **784**
  as search tool, 765, **769**
  in writing prompt, 277
kind of, sort of, 480

L

Labels, 604, 675, 747
Lakes, names of, 638
Land craft, names of, 615, 641
Landscapes, **195**

Language, 21, 94, 130, 138, 390
  conventions of written, 22, 43,
    290–291, 725
  figurative, 257, 272, **692**
  loaded, 131, 133, 142, 147,
    679
  variety used in, 213, 324
Language variety checker, 213
Languages, 578, 639–640,
  647–648, 701
  See also English language
lay, lie, 509
Layering process, 133, 159, **784**
Leads, 18, **39**, 208, **784**
  expository, **161**
Learning logs, 3, **784**
Legal issues, as topics, 129
Legends, 730–731, **784**
Legibility, **784**
  cursive *vs.* print, 758
  manuscript preparation,
    758–759
  proofreading and, 22
less, fewer, 567
Letters
  business, 43, 604, 758
  friendly, 43, 759
  sending, to build portfolios, 140
  writing, 249, 253, 596
Letters (alphabet), silent, 707
Library resources, 9, 265, 745
  catalogs of, 740–741
  librarians as, 131, 741–742
  reference skills and, 222–223,
    740–750
  reference works as, 181, 697,
    722, 744–749
  using, to confirm details, 22,
    261
lie, lay, 509
like, 480
Line graphs, 676, 682
Link, electronic, **769**
Linking verbs, **320**–325, **784**
  action verbs distinguished from,
    323–325
  adjectives located after, 567
  examples of, 320–322
  forms of *be* as, 422
  grammar exercises on, 325
  subject complements and,
    416–418
List-serves, creating, 140
Listening skills
  comparing and contrasting
    newscasts, 45
  comparing different media,
    120, 170–171, 218, 288

comparing personal interpretations with that of others, 253, 670

distinguish between fact and opinion, 147

effective listening, 673

eliminating barriers to listening, 673

evaluating objectivity, 147

evaluating speeches, 45, 147

for problems, 164, 413, 473, 521

generating criteria for evaluations, 671–672

monitoring listening, 674

preparing to listen, 673

peer review and, 238, 672

identifying main idea and details, 674

set a purpose for, 673

taking notes, summarizing and organizing, 673

vocabulary development through, 691, 693

Listing, **784**

generating topics by, 202, 228

itemizing and, 55, 81, 205

with symbols, 603, 684

Literary logs, 253

Literary writing, **727**

reading, 727–731

See also Drama; Fiction; Poems

Literature. *See* Grammar in Literature; Literary writing; Models From Literature; *Readers' Guide to Periodical Literature;* Responding to Fine Art and Literature; Response to Literature; Spotlight on the Humanities

Logical arguments, 131, 133, 149, 192, 268

thinking for, 734

Logical order, 224

checking structure of, 184

in how-to essays, 199, 201, 220

organizing paragraphs in, 28, 37–41, 46, 182

test preparation and, 122, 285

Login, **769**

Looping, **784**

narrowing topics with, 54

Lyric poem, **784**

M

Magazines

articles from, 3, 744

as presentation opportunity, 64, 115

reading, 45, 78, 228, 733

titles of, 614, 647

Main clauses, **784**

See also Independent clauses

Main points, 142

coding, as revision strategy, 134, 136, 260

focus statement of, 279

identifying, 152–153, 195, 673–674, 721

organization of, 36, 142, 162, 242

in paragraph structure, 36, 162

types of support for, 153, **259**, 281

See also Ideas, main

Making words agree, 532–557

diagnostic test on, 533

grammar exercises, 547, 553

indefinite pronouns and verbs, 543–545

review exercises, 554–555

subjects and verbs, 534–545

test preparation on sentence construction, 556–557

See also Pronoun-antecedent agreement; Subject-verb agreement

Manuals, computer, **219**

Manuscript, preparing, 758

handwritten work, 758

research papers, 759

word-processed or typed documents, 759

Maps, 56, 675, 683, 748–749

Meaning, 74, 328, 410

communicating, through the arts, 8, 686, 729

constructing, from informational text, 232–233, 280, 756–757

using dictionaries for, 692, 747

visual art and, 68–69, 95, 121

word order and, 567–568

See also Definitions

Media and Technology Skills workshops

analyzing camera techniques, 121

analyzing cartoons, 95

analyzing photographs, 195

building an electronic portfolio, 25

comparing and contrasting newscasts, 45

comparing book and movie versions, 171

creating multimedia interpretations, 271

creating photo essays, 69

evaluating objectivity, 147

exploring electronic texts, 289

finding and evaluating on-line sources, 245

getting on-line help, 219

identifying appropriate technology, 9

supporting learning with, 9, 25, 219, 289

See also Computer technology; Word processors

Media flip-throughs, 78, 128, 178, 228

Memoirs, **49, 784**

Memorials, capitalization and, 641

Menu bars, computer, 219

Metaphors, **118, 784**

Meter, **784**

Military titles, capitalization and, 644

Misspelled words, recording, 702–703, 707

Models From Literature

autobiographical writing, 50–51

cause-and-effect essay, 176–177

comparison-and-contrast essay, 152–153

description, 100–101

how-to essay, 200–201

persuasive essay, 126–127

research report, 224–227

response to literature, 250–251

short story, 74–77

Modem, **769**

Modifiers

adjective phrases, 426–427, 434

adjectives, 334, 336–337, 352, 434

adverb clauses, 441–442

adverb phrases, 428

adverbs, 334, 348–350, 352

compound, 434, 620–621

irregular, 563–564, 566

misplaced, 476–477, 486–487

regular, 560–562, 566

See also Adjectives; Adverbs; Using modifiers

Monologue, **784**

Months, names of, 639

Monuments, capitalization and, 641

Mood, **784**
   as literature element, 272
Motives, as causal connections, 183
Mountains, names of, 638
Movies, 121
   as broadcast media, 45, 218
   compared and contrasted to different media, 155, 170–171
   reviews of, 269
   titles of, 614
Multimedia presentations, 271, 685, **784**
Music, 171, 199
   multimedia projects and, 271, 685
   titles of, 614, 616
   writing activities on, 94, 120, 146, 170, 270
Myths, 270, 640, **730**

N

Names, geographical, 594–595, 638, 642, 651
Names, object, 615
Names, personal, 592, 715
   capital letters and, 634, 637, 651
   as nouns, 61, 296, 637
   titles of, in family, 645–646
Narration, 48–97, 193, **784**
   elements of, 80, 93, 96
   personal, 49–51, 56, 79
   test preparation on, 70–71, 96–97
   as writing mode, 12, 21
   See also Autobiographical writing; Short story
Narrative poem, **784**
Narrowing an Internet search, **765**
Narrowing your topic, **15**
   asking questions, 180
   circling key words, 277
   cubing, 156
   evaluating its scope, 204
   "funneling," 130
   identifying topic and purpose, 277
   listing, 15
   looping, 54
   using a pentad, 254
   using Classical Invention, 230
   zooming in, 104
Nationalities, names of, 639–640
Nations. *See* Countries

Natural phenomena, 183, 229, 730
Newsgroup, electronic, **769**
Newspapers, 45
   articles from, 745
   generating topics with, 3, 128, 178, 228
   reading, 228, 693, 732
   student work in, 7, 115, 265
   titles of, 614, 647
Nominative case, 520–522, 528, 530, **784**
Nonessential expressions. *See* Parenthetical expressions
Nonfiction, critically reading, 721–726
   analyzing the text, 725–726
   applying reasoning, 724
   comprehending, 721
   distinguishing fact from opinion, 722
   finding books for, 742–743
   identifying the author's purpose, 723
Nonprint media, 675, 681–683, 719–720, 743
Nonverbal language, 672
Normal word order, 413
Notebooks, personal, 3, 693–696, 702, 706, 738
Notes, 231, 671–672, 739
Nouns, **61**, **294**–300, **296**, **784**
   adjectives as, 340–341, 343–344
   in analogies, 312–313
   appositives as, 434
   classification of, 296
   clauses, **784**
   collective, **297**
   color-coding, 61
   common, **298**–299
   compound, **297**–298, 619
   conjunctions and, 376–377
   contractions with, 626
   cumulative review exercises on, 331, 357, 371, 388
   grammar exercises on, 300
   infinitives as, 430, 432–433
   modified by other parts of speech, 336–337, 426–427
   as objects, 411, 414, 426
   plural, 534–535, 610, 708–709
   possessive, 343–344, 623–624
   predicate, 416, 418, 451
   proper, 63, 290–291, **298**–299, 341, 619, 622, 634, 637–642, 644, 651
   singular, 534–535
   test preparation on, 312–313

Nouns and pronouns, **294**–313
   diagnostic test on, 295
   examples of, in circle books, 308
   nouns, 296–300
   pronouns, 301–307
   review exercises on, 310–311
   See also Nouns; Pronouns
Novels, **784**
   reading, 727
Number, **165**, 303–304, 534–537
Numbers, 682, 742
   punctuation and, 596, 604, 618
Numerals, Roman and Arabic, 644

O

Objective case, 520, 523–524, 528–529, 530, **784**
Objectivity, bias versus, 147
Objects
   compound, 460–461
   cumulative review exercises on, 451
   diagraming, 659
   direct, 410, **411**–413, 427, 430, 443, 509–511, 513
   indirect, **414**–415
   nouns as, 426
   of prepositions, 366–367, 426–427, 520, 523–524, 530
   pronouns as, 426, 520, 523–524
Observations, 99, 131, 135, 222–223, 722, **784**
Occasions, in autobiographical writing, 53
Oceans, names of, 638, 642
Ode, **784**
of, have, 508
On-line sources. *See* Electronic texts; Internet resources
Onomatopoeia, **784**
only, 568
Open-book test, **287**, **784**
Openings, 161
   effective, 18, 50, 65
   focus statements in, 224, 266, 279, 285
   punctuation and, 590–591, 607, 610
   purpose of, 73–74, 250
Opinions, **722**, **784**
   expert, 131, 222
   expressing, 263, 267, 723
   facts and, 147, 679, 722, 756–757

Oral tradition, 94, 730–731, **784**
  finding clues to culture, 730
Orders (arrangement)
  types of, **106**, **199**, **232**
  See also Word order
Orders (directions)
  diagraming, 659
  See also Instructions
Organization, **7**, 145, 203
  analyzing, 134, 260, 725–726
  applying, 55, 106, 108, 122,
    134, 217, 279
  chronological order, **38**, 71,
    106, 182, 191–192, 199, 206,
    209, 232, 279, 726
  clear, 249, 268
  comparison-and-contrast essays
    and, 151–152, 158, 160, 167,
    172–173
  creating emphasis through,
    132, 250
  logical order of, 28, 38–39,
    122, 182, 184, 199, 201,
    217, 220, 224, 285
  methods of, 71, 152, 158, 160,
    167, 173, 232, 279
  spatial order, 38, 106, 726
  test preparation on, 46, 122,
    272–273
  textbook, and reading skills,
    715–716
  types of, **38**
  See also Classification; Structure
    in writing
Organization, revising. *See*
    Overall structure, revision
    strategies for
Organizations, names of,
    639–640
Outlines, 257, **785**
  adding details to, 280
  making, 232, 279, 739
  matching, to written work, 234
Overall structure, revision
    strategies for, **19**
  analyze your organization, 108,
    134, 160, 260
  build to a point, 84, 260
  check structure, 160, 184, 281
  circle details and points for
    strength, 109, 260
  code details and points for
    support, 135, 160, 260
  connect the steps, 58, 184
  cut and paste for order, 108
  evaluate pacing, 84
  highlight main points, 134, 161
  identify connections, 58, 185

  match draft to outline, 234
  tag high points, 134, 161
  write a strong lead, 208
Oxymoron, **785**

P

Pacing, as climax building, 84
Page, electronic, **769**
Page numbers, 596
Paintings, titles of, 614, 647
Pamphlets, 179, 745
Pan shots, as camera technique,
    121
Parables, **785**
Paradox, **785**
Paragraphs, **28**, 33–36, **785**
  blocks of, 41
  coherence and, **38**
  compositions and, **39**
  depth-charging technique and,
    107
  endings of, 66, 77
  fragments in, 473
  functional, **40**, **110**
  "glue," together with *however*,
    225
  layering process in, 133
  main idea statements, 185
  middle, purpose, 73
  models of, 33, 37, 40
  openings of, 39, 65, 74
  organization of, 38–39, 46, 182
  sentences in, 33–36
  structure of, 36–39, 46, 74–77,
    162, 182
  test preparation on, 46–47
  topical, **40**, **110**
  transitions between, 235
  types of, **40**
  unity in, **37**, 39
  word processors and, 108
  writing effective, 33–41
  writing styles and, 42–43, 46
Paragraphs, revision strategies for,
    20
  adding functional paragraphs,
    110
  adding support, 261
  checking support, 281
  checking unity, 136
  coding connections, 59, 136,
    185
  finding the "tug," 185
  illuminating for improvement,
    85, 261
  making applications, 20
  marking patterns, 162

  using steps, stacks, chains, and
    balances, 209
  using transition words, 235
Parallelism, **785**
Paraphrasing, **721**, **760**, **785**
Parentheses, **785**
Parenthetical expressions,
    592–593
Participial phrases, **237**, **431**, 593,
    785
Participles, **237**, **430**–431, 436,
    785
Parts of speech, 390, 747
  actions in, 314
  connected with conjunctions,
    376–377
  cumulative review exercises on,
    421
  irregular, 492, 495–498, 505,
    563–564, 566
  See also Diagnostic Tests
Parts of speech, cumulative
    review exercises on
  action verbs, 357
  adjectives, 371, 388
  adverbs, 371, 388
  agreement errors, 576–577
  conjunctions, 389
  interjections, 389
  linking verbs, 357
  modifiers, 577
  nouns, 331, 357, 371, 388
  prepositions, 388–389
  pronoun cases, 576
  pronouns, 331, 357, 388, 529
  verb tenses, 576
  verbs, 331, 357, 371, 388, 529,
    576
  word usage errors, 577
Passive voice, **785**
Past participles
  as *-ed* or *-d* verbs, **237**
  end irregularly with *-en, -n,* or *-t,*
    430
  helping verbs with, 511
  of irregular verbs, 495–497
  of regular verbs, 492–493
Past perfect tense, 500, 502, 504,
    506, 516–517
Past tense, **492**
  basic form of, 500, 502
  progressive verb form and
    principal part in, 504–506
  usage, 505, 516–517
  as verb principal part, 492–493,
    495, 496
Patterns in writing, 36, 82, 162
peace, piece, 710

Peer review, 6, **21**, 62, **785**
  analytic talk as, 113, 138
  asking for specifics, 21
  giving feedback as, 188, 213, 238, 672
  highlighting afterward, 62, 87
  marking paragraph patterns, 162
  "say back" discussions as, 188
  sharing in, 162, 263
  summarizing as, process, 164, 238
  trying out your directions, 213
Peer revision. *See* Peer review
Penmanship reference, **758**
Pentads, 254, 261, **785**
Performance arts, 614, 686
  evaluating, 44, 146, 171, 288
Periodicals, 744–745
  See also Magazines; Newspapers
Periods, 580–581, **785**
  basic rules and exception for, 632
  end declarative sentences, 456
  as end marks of sentences, 139
  end some imperative sentences, 457
  location of, inside quotation marks, 611–612
  one space after, 445
Personal experiences, 257
Personal narratives, 49–51, 56, 79
Personal observations, 131, 133, 222–223, 722
Personal pronouns, **303**–304, 518–531, **785**
  antecedent agreement with, 548–550
  capitalizing word *I*, 634, 637, 650
  cases of, 518, **520**, 527–530
  diagnostic test on, 519
  nominative, 518–522
  objective, 518–520, 523–524
  possessive, 518–520, 525–526, 625
  as possessive adjectives, 343–344
  singular and plural, 165, 303, 502
Personification, **118**, **785**
Persons
  in grammar, 165, 303–304, 502, 535, 549
  historical, as topics, 223, 276, 748
  names of, 61, 296–297, 592, 634, 637, 645–646, 651, 715

nonspecific, and *a* or *an*, 338
  specific, and *the*, 338
  as story characters, 73
  titles of, 644–646, 651
  as visual art subjects, **195**
  writing about, 48–71, 99–101, 223, 229
Persuasion, 276, 280, **785**
  evaluating, 138, 144, 147
  key word for, **277**
  prompts for, 275, 279
  purpose of, 125, 157
  speeches as, 671
  as writing mode, 12
  See also Persuasive essay
Persuasive essay, 124–149, **125**
  argument in, 131–133, 137, 139, 143
  drafting, 132–133
  editing and proofreading, 139
  formal English for, 43
  prewriting, 128–131
  publishing and presenting, 140
  purpose of, 124, 130
  revising, 134–138
  test preparation on, 148–149
  types of, **125**, **129**, **144**–**145**
Photographs, 24, 45, 195
  interpreting, 675, 677
  meaning and, 68–69
Phrases, **424**–437, **426**, **452**, 470, **785**
  adjective, 426–427, 434
  adverb, **211**
  appositive, **434**, 593
  cumulative review exercises on, 488
  grammar exercises on, 436–437
  infinitive, **432**–433
  introductory, 590–591
  participial, **237**, **431**, 593
  prepositional, **366**–367, 369, 372, 376–377, 426, 443, 537
  review exercises on, 450–451
  sentence combining using, 29, 463
  test preparation on, 452–453
  transitions and, 153, 286
  using, 262, 267
  verb, **326**–328, 492
  verbal, **430**
Phrases and clauses, **424**–453, **452**
  clauses, **424**–425, 438–449
  diagnostic test on, 425
  phrases, **424**–437
  review exercises, 450–451

sentence combining using, 29, 31–32, 462–463
  test preparation on, 452–453
  See also Clauses; Phrases
Physical processes, as causal connections, 183
Pie graphs, 677
piece, peace, 710
Places
  capitalization and, 641
  names of, 61, 638, 642, 651
  nonspecific, and *a* or *an*, 338
  as nouns, 61, 296
  specific, and *the*, 338
  as visual art subject, 195
  writing about, 98–99, 103, 155
Plagiarism, **762**
Planning for studying, 737–739
Plays, 614, 647
Plots, **82**, **94**, **96**, 272, **785**
Plural, **785**
Plural nouns, 534, 610, 708–709, 747
Plural number, **165**, 502, **534**–537
  apostrophes and possessives, 623–624
  spelling, 534–535, 610
Poems, **118**–**119**, 257, 270, **785**
  reading, 729–730
  rhyming, 118–119
  titles of, 614, 616, 647
  as writing mode, 12
Poetry, reading. *See* Poems
Point-by-point method, organization by, 152, 158, 160, 167, 173, 279
Point of view, 49, 56, 122, 272, 729, **785**
Political parties, names of, 639–640
Political speeches, 125
Portfolios, 23, 25, **785**
  work to include in
    autobiographical writing, 166
    consumer watchdog essays, 166
    demonstrations given with handouts, 215
    graded essays, 284
    illustrated booklets, 115
    letters written, 64, 140
    magazine materials, 64, 89, 115, 190
    newspaper materials, 115, 265
    notes, drafts, finished work, 3
    posters, 215, 265

preparations for brief skit, 190
presentation diagrams, 190
reading events and occasions,
64, 89
"Wall of Fame," 240
Web site of your design, 240
See also Building your portfolio
Portraits, **69, 195**
Positive degree, 560–564
basis for comparative and
superlative degrees, **560**–562
using, of irregular modifiers,
563–564
Possessive adjectives, 343–344
Possessive case, 520, 525–526,
529–530, **785**
Possessive nouns, 343, 623–624
Possessive pronouns, 165, 625
"Possible Sentences" strategy, 694
Posters, 215, 265
Practice tests, across media, 289
Precise nouns, **61**
Precise words, 61, 138, 188, 263,
267, 282, 500, 725
Predicate adjectives, 417–418
Predicate nouns, **416**, 418
Predicate pronouns, **416**, 418
Predicates
cumulative review exercises on,
451, 488
grammar exercises on, 399
nominative pronouns as,
520–522
as subject complements,
416–417
Prediction, 722
as reading strategy, 727, 731
as reading-writing connection,
50–51
test preparation on, 734–735
Prefixes, **619, 699, 706, 785**
Prepositional phrases, **366**–367,
369, 372, 426, **785**
compound, in simple sentences,
443
connected with conjunctions,
376–377
diagraming, 661
subject-verb agreement not
affected by, 537
Prepositions, **189,** 360–373, **362,**
785
capitalization of, in titles, 647
classifying, 365, 371
compound, **362,** 364–365
cumulative review exercises on,
388–389
diagnostic test on, 361

distinguishing, from adverbs,
367, 369, 370
functions of, 362, 366
grammar exercises, 365, 369
learning aids for, 368
objects of, **366**–367, 426, 520,
523–524, 530
phrases with, 366–367, 369,
372, 376–377, 426, 443, 537
preferred number of, 189
review exercises, 370–371
usage test on, 372–373
Present participles
as -*ing* verbs, **237**
end with -*ing,* 430
of irregular verbs, 495–497
of regular verbs, 492–493
Present perfect tense, 500, 502,
504, 506, 516–517
Present tense, **492**
basic form of, 500, 502–503
progressive verb form and
principal part in, 504, 506
usage test on, 516–517
as verb principal part, 492–493,
495–497, 500, 502–503
Presentations
evaluating 45, 94, 121, 146–
147, 170–171, 194, 218
multimedia, 271, 685, **784**
speech, 671–672
Presenting, **13, 23, 785**
See also Publishing and Presenting
Prewriting, **13, 14**–17, **785**
See also Audiences; Choosing
your topic; Gathering details;
Narrowing your topic; Purposes
for writing; Standardized Test
Preparation Workshops
Print media, **45,** 253
applying conventions of,
290–291
comparing and contrasting, with
visual media, 155, 171, 288
as electronic texts, 746, 748
flip-through process and, 78,
128, 178, 228
library catalogs as, 740–741
Problem-and-solution essay, 217,
785
Problems
avoiding, with sentences,
469–485
listening for, 164, 413, 473, 521
subjects as special, 405–409
word usage, 479–481,
508–512, 529, 567–569
Product comparisons, writing,
151, 166, 169

Professional titles, capitalization
and, 644
Prompts for responding to
media. *See* Critical Viewing
Prompts on tests, 10, **275**–277,
279
choice of, 276
expository, 172, 196, 220
key words as, 277
responding to, 26, 70, 148
test preparation on, 272–273
See also Standardized Test
Preparation Workshops
Pronouns, **165, 296, 301**–309,
786
antecedents of, **302**–303, 305–
306, 343–344 (*See also*
Pronoun-antecedent agree-
ment)
apostrophes and, 625
appositives as, 434
conjunctions and, 377
contractions and, 626
cumulative review exercises on,
331, 359, 388, 529
demonstrative, **305,** 345
as direct objects, 411
functions of, 164, 305
grammar exercises on, 309
indefinite, **306**–307, 543–545,
551–553, 625
as indirect objects, 414
interrogative, **306,** 346
modified by other parts of
speech, 336–337, 426–427
as objects of prepositional
phrases, 426, 520, 523–524,
530
personal, 303–304, 343–344,
518–531, 548–550, 551–553,
625, 634, 637, 650
plural, 502, 534–535
possessive, 343–344, 520,
525–526, 529, 625
predicate, 416, 418, 520–522
singular, 502, 534
types of, **165, 303**–307
See also Using pronouns
Pronoun-antecedent agreement,
532, 548–553
grammar exercises on, 553
indefinite and personal, 551–552
person and number, 165, 549
personal pronouns and, 548–550
See also Antecedents; Pronouns
Pronoun cases, 520–526, 528–530
cumulative review exercises on,
576
nominative, 518–522, 528, 530

objective, 518–520, 523–524, 528–530
possessive, 520, 525–526, 529, 530
Pronunciation, 338, 746
Proofreading, **13, 22**
See also Editing and Proofreading
Proofreading symbols, 778
Proper adjectives, **341**, 622
capitalization and, 634, 643–646, 651
hyphens and, 619–620
Proper nouns, 63, **298**–299, 341, 622
capitalization of, 298, 634, 637–642, 644, 651
cumulative review exercise on, 388
hyphens and, 619–620
standardized test questions on, 290–291
Prose, **786**
Providing elaboration, **18, 207**
with causal connections, 183
with descriptions, 280
with details, 50, 57, 83
with examples, 280
with explanations, 153
find points to clarify, 232–233
heightening tension by, 66
self-assessment of, 215
techniques for, 18, 133, 159, 207
telling and showing as, 83
test preparation for, 221
types of support for, **259**
Provinces, names of, 638, 642
Public-service announcements, 125
Publishing and Presenting, 4, 7, **13, 23**, 147, **786**
desktop-publishing programs for, 9
See also specific writing modes; Building your portfolio; Reflecting on your writing; Showing and telling
Pull-away shots, as camera technique, 121
Punctuation, 729, **786**
in dialogue, 88, 264
proofreading for, errors, 22, 290–291, 652–653
sentences and, 283, 444, 473
test preparation on, 220, 290–291, 633
See also specific marks, e.g., Commas; End marks; Using punctuation marks

Purposes for writing, **16, 157,** 171, **786**
analysis of, 55, 157
audiences and, 148–149, 181, 255
details affected by, 80, 231
identifying, 126–127, 277, 721, 723
persuasion as, 125, 130, 255, 723
types of, **157, 723**

Q
QAR Strategy, for reading skills, 717
Qualities, names of, 61
Question marks, 139, 456, 580–582, 611–612, 632, **786**
Query box, electronic, **769**
Questions, 141, 244
finding parts of speech in, 407, 413
interrogative pronouns and, 306
in interrogative sentences, 456
inverted word order in, **407**–409
strategy, for reading fiction, 717, 727
types of, on tests, 46, 122, **752–755**
Quicklists, 128, 154, **786**
Quotation marks, 580, 606–614, **786**
around direct quotations, 606–607
brief quotations and, 264, 612
with dialogue, 613
double versus single, 264
grammar exercises on, 616–617
location of other punctuation with, 607–612
review exercises on, 631
rules for, 264, 606–612, 632
titles and, 239, 614, 616
Quotations, 259, 261
capitalization and, 634, 650
direct, 596, **606**–610, 760
indirect, **606**–607, 760
punctuating, 264, 606–612

R
Races, names of, 639–640
Radio, 45, 128–129, 228

raise, rise, 510
Ratiocination, **19, 786**
"Read Me" files, computer, 219
Reader interest, 90, 130
balance for, 209, 324
strategies for, 39, 72, 141, 225, 255
tension for, 56, 73, 92
Readers' Guide to Periodical Literature, 744–745
Reading, 691, **717,** 732–733
active, 727
Reading aloud, 238, 691, 729
listening during, to detect problems, 164, 413, 473, 521
readings as events, 64, 89
Reading skills, 714–735
critical, for nonfiction, 721–726
graphic organizers for improving, 719–720
for literary writings, 727–731
methods and tools for, 715–720
question-answer relationships, 717
reflecting on strategies for, 733
strategies for improving, 717–718
SQ4R (survey, question, read, recite, record, review), 718
test preparation on, 734–735
textbook organization and, 715–716
varied sources and, 732–733
Reading-Writing Connections
author's main points, 152–153
author's purpose, 126–127
cause-and-effect, 200–201
evidence, 250–251
inferences, **176**
prediction, 50–51
questions, asking and answering, 224, 226
Realistic stories, 73
Reasoning, 724
See also Conclusions; Logical arguments
Record albums, titles of, 614
Reference skills, 222–223, 740–750
See also Internet resources; Library resources
Reference works, 697, 743
almanacs, 748
atlases, 748–749
dictionaries, 61, 328, 560, 619, 687, 692, 697, 699, 708–709, 711, 722, 746–747
electronic catalogs, 741
electronic databases, 749

encyclopedias, 722, 748
glossaries, 693, 697, 711
indexes, 697, 744
nonprint material, 743
periodicals, 744
thesauruses, 138, 697, 749
Reflecting on your writing, 7, **27**
autobiographical writing, 64
cause-and-effect essay, 190
comparison-and-contrast essay, 166
how-to essay, 215
persuasive essay, 140
research report, 240
response to literature, 265
short story, 89
writing for assessment, 284
Reflective essays, 49, **786**
Reflexive pronouns, **786**
Reflexive writing, **12**, 686, **786**
Refrain, **786**
Refutation, 143, 148
Regular modifiers, 560–562, 566
Regular verbs, 492–494, 505
Relationships, 235, 257, 645–646, 754–755
Relationships, types of
cause-and-effect, 209, 275, 726
part-to-whole, 312
preposition-and-noun, 189, 362
question-and-answer, 717
step-by-step, 209
whole-to-part, 312
Relative pronouns, **786**
Relevance ranking, in Internet searches, **769**
Religion, capitalization and, 639–640, 644
Remembrances, descriptions of, 99, 103
Repetition, as problem, 86, 163–164, 212
Reporter's Formula, 16, **786**
Reports, 43, 241, 243
citations in, 239, 242, **760**
product comparisons as, 151, 166, 169
science and, 175, 223
See also Research report
Requesting information, 193, 243
See also Interviews; Reference skills
Research, **786**
access prior knowledge for, 230
doing, 181, 192, 222, 231, 724
as writing mode, 12, **786**
See also Reference skills

Research report, 222–247, **223**
detailed notes for, 231
drafting, 232–233
editing and proofreading, 239, 246
generating questions for, 228–231
manuscript preparation, 759
prewriting, 228–231
publishing and presenting, 240
revising, 234–238, 246
test preparation for, 246–247
types of, **223**
Responding to Fine Art and Literature
autobiographical writing, 53
cause-and-effect essay, 179
comparison-and-contrast essay, 155
description, 103
how-to essay, 203
interpreting fine art, 680–681
interpreting literature with multimedia, 271
persuasion, 129
research report, 229
response to literature, 253
short story, 79
See also Spotlight on the Humanities
Response to literature, 248–273, **249**, **786**
drafting, 258–259
editing and proofreading, 264
prewriting, 252–257
publishing and presenting, 265
revising, 260–263
test preparation on, 272–273
types of, **249**
as writing mode, 12
Review exercises
on chapter sections (*see subheading under subject, e.g.,* Verbs, grammar exercises on)
on entire chapters (*see subheading under subject, e.g.,* Verbs, review exercises on)
Reviewing work. *See* Reflecting on your writing; Peer review; Revising
Revising, 13, **786**
Revising overall structure, strategies for, **19**
analyze your organization, 108, 134, 160, 260
build to a point, 84, 260
check structure, 160, 184, 281
circle details and points for strength, 109, 260

code details and points for support, 135, 160, 260
connect the steps, 58, 184
cut and paste for order, 108
evaluate pacing, 84
highlight main points, 134, 161
identify connections, 58, 184
match draft to outline, 234
tag high points, 134, 161
write a strong lead, 208
Revising paragraphs, strategies for, **20**
adding functional paragraphs, 110
adding support, 261
checking support, 281
checking unity, 136
coding connections, 59, 136, 185
finding the tug, 185
illuminating for improvement, 85, 261
making applications, 20
marking patterns, 162
using steps, stacks, chains, and balances, 209
using transition words, 235
Revising sentences, strategies for, **20**
add adjectives and adverbs, 353
add transitions, 282
circle repetitious sentences, 163
circle verbs in inconsistent tense, 186
code for connections, 137
code for problems, 20, 111
code for transitions, 60
combine pairs with phrases, 450
combine short sentences, 236
combine to show connections, 137, 262
find cluster of main action, 236
highlight connections, 262
use "spy camera," 86
vary sentence beginnings, 210, 466–467
vary sentence length, 236, 465–466
Revising word choice, strategies for, **21**, 86, 209
circling verbs, 21, 87
color-coding nouns, 61, 237, 263
highlighting, 188, 212
marking "empty" words, 112, 138, 188, 297
reading aloud, 164
showing instead of telling, 282

Revising work with others. *See* Peer review
Rhyme, **786**
Rhyme scheme, **786**
Rhyming poems, **118–119**
Rhythm, 42, **95**, 132, 729, **786**
right, write, 710
rise, raise, 510
Rivers, names of, 638, 642
Roots, word, **698**, **786**
Round-table discussions, 128
Rubrics for Self-Assessment, **23**, **786**
  autobiographical writing, 64
  cause-and-effect essay, 190
  comparison-and-contrast essay, 166
  description, 115
  how-to essay, 215
  persuasive essay, 140
  research report, 240
  response to literature, 265
  short story, 89
  writing for assessment, 284
Run-on sentences, **111**, **473**, **786**
  correcting, 283, 474–475, 482
  test preparation on, 486–487

S

Salutation, **786**
Satire, 218, **786**
saw, seen, 511
"Say Back" discussions, 188
Scanning, **717**
Scenes, 93, 254, 686
Scenic spots, names of, 638
Schedules, for studying, 737
School life, 43, 53, 129, 647–648, 669, 738
Science fiction, 73, 218
Science reports, 175, 223
Sculptures, titles of, 614
Sea craft, 615, 641
Search engines, 765–766, **786**
Seas, names of, 638, 642
Second person, **165**, 303–304, 502
Sections of a country, names of, 638
seen, saw, 511
SEE technique. *See* State, Extend, Elaborate (SEE) Technique
Self-assessment. *See* Rubrics for Self-Assessment
Self-interviews, 228, 252
Semicolons, 580, **600–602**, **786**
  avoiding confusion with, and serial commas, 602

  correcting run-on sentences with, 475
  grammar exercises on, 605
  joining independent clauses with, 600–601
  review exercises on, 630
Sentence combining, 29–32, 460–463
Sentence diagraming, 656–665
  adjective, adverbs, and conjunctions, 657
  appositives, 662
  clauses, 663–665
  complements, 659–660
  complex sentences, 664
  compound sentences, 663
  compound subjects and verbs, 658
  orders (imperatives), 659
  phrases, 661–663
  subjects and verbs, 656
  writing and, 661
Sentences, 3, 35, **392**, 414, 469, 694, **787**
  appropriate construction of, 422–423, 556–557
  beginnings of, 210, 408, 465–467, 634, 636, 650
  classifying, 443–446, 456–459
  combining, 29–32, 86, 163, 236, 262, 435, 465–466
  complete, 283, 314, 392–395, 422
  complex, 263, **445**–446, 463, 489
  compound, **444**–445, 462, 489
  cumulative review exercises on, 451, 488–489, 529
  declarative, **456**, 580, 584
  exclamatory, 456, **458**, 582–584
  imperative, 457, 580, 582, 584
  interrogative, 581–582, 584
  punctuation in, 139, 457, 580–584, 590–591
  run-on, **111**, **473**–475
  simple, **443**–444, 489
  structure of, 215, 217, 225, 236, 443–448, 451, 460–468
  test preparation about, 220
  topic, **33**–34, 36, 162
  variety of, 24, **42**, 86, 210, 225, 236, 460–468, 542
  word order in, 351, 542
  See also Basic sentence parts; Compound sentences; Effective sentences; Sentence combining

Sentences, revision strategies for, **20**
  add adjectives and adverbs, 353
  add transitions, 282
  circle repetitious sentences, 163
  circle verbs in inconsistent tense, 186
  code for connections, 137
  code for problems, 20, 111
  code for transitions, 60
  combine pairs with phrases, 450
  combine short sentences, 29–32, 236
  combine to show connections, 31–32, 137, 262
  find cluster of main action, 236
  highlight connections, 262
  use "spy camera," 86
  vary sentence beginnings, 210, 466–467
  vary sentence length, 29–32, 236, 465–466
Sequential relationships, 209
Serial commas
  function of, 214, 587, 591
  grammar exercises, 599
  semicolons and, 602
Serial numbers, 596
Server, electronic, **769**
set, sit, 511
Settings, 90, **96**, 171, 737, **787**
  details for, 76, 83
  as literature element, 93, 272
Shaping your writing, **18**
  create a main impression, 106
  create a plot, 82
  develop a main idea, 232
  focus in, 258, 279, 285
  make an outline, 232
  organize details, 206, 232
  organize for emphasis, 132, 251
  organize logically, 182
  plan your organization, 279
  select an effective organization, 158, 232
  tension for reader interest, 56
  thesis statements, 132, 141, **232**, 241
  See also Providing elaboration; Standardized Test Preparation Workshops
Sharing your work, 4
  See also Publishing and Presenting
Short story, 72–97, **73**, **787**
  climax in, 76
  developing narrative elements, 80

folk tales, 288, 452–453
oral tradition, 94
plot diagram to organize, 82
reading, as fiction, 727
storytelling devices of, 95
structure of, 73
timing in, 257
titles of, in quotation marks, 616
types of, **73**
Showing and telling, 83, 282
See also Publishing and Presenting
Showing differences. *See* Contrast
Showing similarities. *See* Comparison
Signature, electronic, **769**
Simile, **118**, **787**
Simple sentences, **443**–444, 446, 449
Simple subjects, 397
Single quotation marks, 264
Singular number, **165**, **534**–537
sit, set, 511
Sketches, written
autobiographical, and their purpose, 49
biographical, 223, 229, 232, 240
Skills assessments. *See* Rubrics for Self-Assessment; Standardized Test Preparation Workshops
Skimming, **717**
Social titles, capitalization and, 644–645
Songs, 270, 616
Sonnets, **787**
sort of, kind of, 480
Sounds
article, before consonants or vowels, 338
background, in multimedia projects, 271, 685
homophones, 426, 525, 551, 707, 710
long *a,* spelling, 704
long *e,* spelling, 704
poetry and, 729
recording equipment for, 129, 696
s, to avoid, 504
spelling of, 426, 476, 525, 704
See also Music
Spacecraft, 615, 641
Spatial order, **38**, 106, 726
Speaker, **787**

Speaking, listening, viewing, and representing, 668–689
listening skills, 673–674
representing skills, 681–687
speaking skills, 338, 668–672, 726, 746
test preparation for, 688–689
viewing skills, 675–680
Speaking skills 669–672
class participation and, 669
formal, 671
giving directions, 670
informal, 669
making introductions, 670
nonverbal language, 672
planning a speech, 671
preparation for, 669
preparing note cards for, 671
taking part in class discussions, 669
varieties of speech, 671
Special events, names of, 639
Special places, capitalization and, 641
Special things, capitalization and, 641
Specific groups, capitalization and, 640
Speech, 726
audience and, 271, 687
delivering, 672
evaluating speeches, 45, 147
giving and getting feedback, 672
nonverbal language, 672
planning a speech, 671
preparing note cards for, 671
providing main idea and details, 671
varieties of, 671
volume, pitch, and tone, 271, 687
Spelling, 702–711
-c endings of verbs and added *k,* 504
-tion, for *shun* sound, 476
adding prefixes, 706
adding suffixes, 705
apostrophes and, 623–624
commonly misspelled words, 772–773
dropping letters when, 351, 441, 466
ei words, 704
exceptions to, rules, 525, 561, 704–705, 708
homophones, **710**
hyphens and, 619
ie words, 704

influence of language and cultures on, 707
personal notebook for, words, 378, 702, 706
plural, 534–535, 610, 708–709
proofreading for errors in, 22, 290–291, 652–653, 711
recording errors in, 702–703, 707
Roman numerals in, 644
rules, 704–706
sounds and, 426, 476, 525, 704
studying, 703, 706
test preparation on, 220, 290–291
word usage and, 328, 426, 479, 481, 551
See also Dictionaries; Vocabulary and spelling
Spelling plurals
add *-es* to singular nouns, 534
add *-s* to singular nouns, 534
add *-ves* to singular nouns ending in *-fe,* 534–535, 708
change *-f* of singular nouns to *-v* and add *-es,* 610, 708
learn special forms, 534–535, 709
Spotlight on the Humanities
art, 270
dance, 44
drama, 194
forms of self-expression, 8
motion pictures, 120
opera music, 146
operettas, 170
oral tradition, 94
painting, 120, 270
photography, 28, 68
science fiction, 218
theater, 244, 288
Spy camera, revision technique, 86
SQ4R Method, reading skills and, 718
Stacks, explanatory, 209
Standardized Test Preparation Workshops
adjectives and adverbs, 358–359
agreement, 556–557
basic sentence parts, 422–423
capitalization, 652–653
cause-and-effect essay, 196–197
comparison-and-contrast essay, 172–173
conjunctions, 387

constructing meaning, 756–757
effective sentences, 486–487
general strategies, 10–11
how-to essay, 220–221
inferences and predictions, 734–755
interpreting graphic aids, 688
narrative writing, 70–71
nouns in analogies, 312–313
persuasive writing, 148–149
phrases and clauses, 452–453
prepositions, 372–373
proofreading, 290–291
research report, 246–247
response to literature, 96–97, 272–273
strategy, organization, and style skills, 46–47, 122–123
using context, 712–713
using modifiers, 574–575
using pronouns, 530–531
using punctuation marks, 632–633
using the writing process to respond to prompts, 26–27
using verbs, 516–517
verbs, 332–333
Stanzas, **118, 787**
State, Extend, Elaborate (SEE) technique, 18, 133, 159, **786**
State of being, 314, 320, 326
States (government organizations), names of, 638, 642
Statistics, **35,** 126, 131, 133, 682, 760, **787**
Step-by-step relationships, 209
Steps, explanatory, 209
Still lifes, as image type, **69**
Stories, 73, 95, 647, 731
See also Short story
Storyboards, 686
Storytelling, 95, 731
Streets, names of, 638, 642
Structure in writing, 50, 73, 171, 726
focus on, with graphic aids, 681–683
patterns and, 36, 82, 162, 414
sentences and, 215, 217, 225, 236, 443–448, 451, 460–468
See also Organization; Overall structure, revision strategies for
Student publications, 779
Student Work in Progress, drafting
adding characterizing details, 57, 83

adding supporting details to outline, 280
depth-charging, 107
elaborating causal connections, 183
exploding the moment, 207
finding points to clarify in, 233
providing elaboration, 133
providing support, 259
using layering, 159
Student Work in Progress, final drafts of
autobiographical writing, 65–66
cause-and-effect essay, 191–192
comparison-and-contrast essay, 167–168
description, 116–117
how-to essay, 216
persuasion, 141–143
research report, 241–242
response to literature, 266–268
short story, 90–92
writing for assessment, 285–286
Student Work in Progress, prewriting
asking questions to narrow a topic, 180
blueprinting, 52
browsing, 252
classical invention as, 230
conducting a self-interview, 228
cubing to gather details, 105
cubing to narrow topics, 156
itemizing the details, 205
listing to discover a topic, 202
looping, 54
media flip-through, 178
using a BUT Chart for choosing topics, 154
using hexagonal writing, 256
using a pentad, 254
using a personal experience timeline, 102
using a quicklist, 128
using a T-chart, 131
using a Topic Web to gather details, 278
writing round, 78
See also Choosing your topic
Student Work in Progress, revising
adding support, 135, 261
adding transitions, 136

circling details to strengthen main impression, 109
circling verb tense, 186
coding for transitions, 60
color-coding pauses to eliminate run-ons, 111
combining short sentences, 236
connecting the steps, 184
eliminating repeated words, 212
finding the glue between paragraphs, 235
highlighting empty words, 112
highlighting sentences that explain why, 262
identifying connections to conflict, 58
improving word choices, 138
marking paragraph patterns, 162
tagging high points, 161
using points to illuminate, 85
varying sentence beginnings, 210, 466–467
writing a strong lead, 208
See also object being revised, e.g., Sentences, revision strategies for
Study, reference, and test-taking skills, 736–757
basic study skills, 737–739
question-answer relationships, 717
reference skills, 740–750
reflecting on, 755
SQ4R method, 717
test preparation on, 756–757
test-taking skills, 751–755
See also Reference skills; Standardized Test Preparation Workshops; Summaries
Style in writing
audiences and, 55, 181
elements of, **42**–43
test preparation and, 46, 122
titles and, 239, 614–615
Styles in reading, types of, **717**
Subject complements, **416**
compound, 418
linking verbs and, 416–418
predicates as, 416–418
Subject-verb agreement, 532–547
compound subjects, 163, 538–540
grammar exercises on, 545
prepositional phrases and, 537
singular and plural subjects, 536–537

test preparation on, 556–557
See also Subjects; Verbs
Subject-verb order, 422, 542
　inverted, **407**–408, 467, 542
　normal, **405**–407
Subjects, 195, **787**
　complete, 396–399
　in complete sentences,
　　392–395, **422**
　compound, 30, **400**–404, 443,
　　460–461
　cumulative review exercises on,
　　451, 488
　diagraming, 656
　modified by adjective phrases,
　　427
　pronouns as, 520–522
　recognizing, 400–409
　sentence requirements for, 283
　simple, literature model, 397
　in simple sentences, 443
　special problems with, 405–409
　using library catalogs to find,
　　740–741
　See also Subject-verb agreement;
　　Subject-verb order
Subordinate clauses, **438, 787**
　adjective clauses as, **439**
　in complex sentences, 263,
　　445–446, 463
　diagraming, 664–665
　sentence combining using, 32
Subordinating conjunctions, 86,
　　441, 463, **787**
Suffixes, **619, 700, 787**
　-ch, add *-es* for regular plurals,
　　708
　-e, drop or keep, 705
　-en, add for irregular plurals, 709
　-en, -n, or *-t,* of past participles,
　　430
　-ff, add *-s* for regular plurals,
　　708
　-ing, of present participles, 430
　-ly, 352, 561, 620
　-o, adding letters for regular
　　plurals, 708
　-ren, add for irregular plurals,
　　709
　-s, add *-es* for regular plurals,
　　708
　-s on personal pronouns without
　　apostrophe, 525
　-sh, add *-es* for regular plurals,
　　708
　-x, add *-es* for regular plurals,
　　708

　-y preceded by consonant, 561,
　　705, 708
　-y preceded by vowel, 705, 708
　-z, add *-es* for regular plurals,
　　708
　change two-letter, for irregular
　　plurals, 709
　drop letters when spelling, 466,
　　705
　hyphens with, 619
　single consonant, doubling final
　　letter, 705
　spelling rules for, 561, 705, 708
Summaries, **787**
　content of, 257, 259, 268
　in research, **760**
　note-taking, 739
　summarize as key word, 164,
　　238, **277**
　test question on, 756–757
　writing, 249, 739, 744
Superlative degree, **560**–566
　forming, with *-est* or *most,*
　　560–562
　memorizing, of irregular
　　modifiers, 563–564
　spelling rule for, 561
　using, of irregular modifiers,
　　564–566
Support for arguments.
　See Evidence; Gathering details;
　　Providing elaboration
Supporting your writing, **259**
　for arguments, 142
　with chronological order, 71
　citations for facts as, 226
　with comparisons, 259
　with descriptions, 259
　with details, 249, 280–281
　with elaboration, 259
　with evidence, 135
　with explanations, 268, 286,
　　444
　with illuminating points, 261
　with quotations, 259
　with summaries, 259
　See also Evidence; Gathering
　　details; Providing elaboration
Surfing, electronic, **769**
Suspense, 56, 66, 92
Syllables, 560–562, 622, 746
Symbols, 578, 746, **787**
　caret, in revisions, 71, 149
　coding and, 136, 675
Synonyms, 213, 238, **697**
　thesauruses and, 138, 697, 749

T

Tables, as graphic aids, 682
Tables of contents, 715
tail, tale, 710
Tape recorders, 129, 696
T-charts, 131–133, 181
Technology skills
　and the writing process, 25,
　　219, 245, 289
　See also Media and
　　Technology Skills workshops
Telephone numbers, 596
Television, 193, 614
　as broadcast medium, 45, 128,
　　228, 678
　video cameras for, 157, 686
　See also Media and Technology
　　Skills workshops
Telling and showing, **83**, 282
　See also Publishing and
　　Presenting
Tension, 56, 66, 92
Test-taking skills, 289, 751–755
　analogy questions, 754
　essay questions, 754
　fill-in questions, 753
　matching questions, 752
　multiple-choice questions, 752
　short-answer questions, 753
　strategies for, 751
　true/false questions, 753
Tests, 277, 284, 287, 289
　See also Diagnostic Tests;
　　Prompts on tests;
　　Standardized Test Preparation
　　Workshops
Tests, preparation for. *See* Rubrics
　　for Self-Assessment;
　　Standardized Test Preparation
　　Workshops; Writing for assess-
　　ment
Textbooks,
　appendix, 715
　chapter introduction and sum-
　　mary, 715
　glossary, 693, 697, 715
　index, 715
　pictures and captions, 716
　questions and exercises, 716
　tables of contents, 715
　titles, headings, and subhead-
　　ings, 716
Text organizers, using to locate
　　information,
　glossary, 693, 697, 715
　graphic features, 716
　headings, 716

tables of contents, 716
textbook sections, 715
that, which, who, 480
Theater, 170, 244, 288
their, 408, 481, 525, 710
their, there, they're, 481, 710
Themes, **96, 257, 787**
  cause-and-effect, 194
  cross-curricular subjects as *(see* Cross-Curricular Connections)
  discovering, as response to literature, 257
  implied, in fiction, 727
  as literary element, 272
  as narrative element, 94–95
  personal interest, 297, 301, 454–464
  summary of, in conclusions, 268
  using pentads with, 261
there, they're, their, 408, 481, 710
Thesaurus, 138, 697, **749**
Thesis statements, **39**, 132, 141, **232**, 241, **787**
they're, their, there, 481, 710
Things
  capitalization and, 641, 647–648, 651
  nonspecific, and *a* or *an,* 338
  as nouns, 61, 296–297
  as prepositions, **189**
  specific, and *the,* 338
  titles of, 647–648, 651
Third person, **165**, 303–304, 502, 535, 549
Time, 10, 682
  budgeting, 5, 737
  periods of, 639, 733
  verb tense and, 186–187, 492
  See also Chronological order
Timelines, 102, 221, 279, 280
  details and, 20, 206
Timing, as author technique, 257
Titles, 614–617
  capitalization and, 644–648
  for family relationships, 645–646
  finding, in library catalogs, 740–741
  in indexes, 715
  interpreting visual aids from, 675
  for people, 644–646, 651
  punctuating, 614, 616–617, 632
  social and professional, 644–645

for things, 647–648, 651
  underlining, 614–615, 617
to, too, two, 481, 710
Tone, as style element, **42, 787**
too, two, to, 481, 710
Topical paragraphs, **40, 110, 787**
Topic Bank ideas
  biographical sketch of admirable person, 229
  causes of victory or defeat, 179
  compare and contrast a book and movie with same title, 155
  compare and contrast historical leaders, 276
  compare and contrast Saturday and Monday mornings, 155
  events or occasions, 53, 79, 103, 155, 179
  explain a cycle, 179
  explain a process, 276
  fantasy or futuristic stories, 79
  how-to improve a skill, 203
  how-to make a gift, 203
  legal or school issues, 129
  letters based on literary logs, 253
  natural phenomenon report, 229
  persuade a historical figure, 276
  remarkable places, 103
  review a favorite or hated printed work, 253
  special moment or vignette, 103
  your own life or community, 79
  See also Cooperative Writing Opportunities; Responding to Fine Art and Literature; Spotlight on the Humanities
Topics, 14, **277**
  See also Choosing your topic; Narrowing your topic; Topic Bank ideas
Topic webs, 278, **787**
Towns, names of, 638, 642
Trademarks, capitalization and, 641
Transitions, 38, 142, **787**
  adding, as revision strategy, 136, 282
  coding for, as revision strategy, 60
  between paragraphs, 225, 235, 242
  phrases for, 153, 286
  test preparation and use of, 215, 221
  word choices for, 153, 225

Transitive verbs, **316**–317, 319, **787**
two, to, too, 481, 710

U

Underlining text, 239, 614–615, 617
Unity, **787**
URL, **769**
Usenet, **769**
Using modifiers, 558–577
  cumulative review exercises on, 577
  degrees of comparison, 558, **560**–566
  diagnostic test on, 559
  fold-up help for, 570
  grammar exercises on, 566, 571
  review exercises on, 572–573
  test preparation on, 574–575
  See also Modifiers
Using pronouns, 518–531
  cases and, 518, **520**, 527–530
  diagnostic test on, 519
  review exercises on, 528–529
  test preparation for, 530–531
  See also Pronouns
Using punctuation marks, 578–633, **580**
  apostrophes, 623–629, 631
  basic rules for, 632
  colons, 603–605, 631
  commas, 585–599, 630
  common, 580
  diagnostic test on, 579
  exclamation marks, 582–583
  grammar exercises on, 584, 599, 605, 617, 629
  hyphens, 618–623, 629, 631
  periods, 580–581
  question marks, 581–582
  quotation marks, 580, 606–614, 616–617, 631
  review exercises on, 630–631
  semicolons, 600–602, 605, 630
  test preparation on, 632–633
  See also Punctuation
Using verbs, 490–517
  basic verb forms, 500–503
  common problems with, 508–512
  conjugating basic verb forms, 502–503
  diagnostic test on, 491
  grammar exercises on, 499, 507, 513
  irregular verbs, 495–498

principal parts of, 492–506
progressive verb forms,
    504–505
regular verbs, 493–494
review exercises, 514–515
test preparation on, 516–517
troublesome verbs, 508–512
See also Verbs

V

Valleys, names of, 638, 642
Value, 249, 263, 730
Vanity page, electronic, **769**
Variety
    balancing action and linking
        verbs for, 324
    inverting word order for, 467,
        542
    sentence, as style element, **42,**
        86, 225, 236, 460–468
    in sentence beginnings, 20,
        210, 466–467
    using, of research sources, 231
    using synonyms for, 213
Venn diagrams, 157, 173, 720
Verb phrases
    grammar exercises on, 329
    helping verbs and, **326**–329,
        328–329, 492
    usage test on, 516–517
Verb tenses, **187, 492**
    consistent, with exceptions, 186
    cumulative review exercises on,
        529, 576
    in dictionaries, 747
    future, 492, 500–502
    future perfect, 500–502, 504,
        506
    past, 492–493, 495, 496, 500,
        502
    past perfect, 500, 502, 504,
        506
    present, 492–493, 495, 497,
        500, 502, 503
    present perfect, 500, 502, 504,
        506
Verbal phrases, **430, 787**
    grammar exercises on, 436–437
Verbals, 430
    infinitives, **432**
    participles, **430**–431
Verbs, 91, **314**–333, 542, **787**
    action, **87,** 314, **316**–319, 411,
        567
    circling, as revision strategy, 21,
        87, 186
    common problems with,
        508–512

in complete sentences,
    392–395, **422**
compound, 30, **402**–404, 443,
    460–461
conjugating, 502–503
conjunctions with, 377,
    538–540
contractions with, 626
cumulative review exercises on,
    331, 359, 371, 388, 451, 576
diagnostic tests on, 315, 491
diagraming, 656
forms of, in dictionaries, 747
grammar exercises on, 499,
    507, 513
helping, **326**–329, 492, 511
linking, **320**–325, 416–418,
    422, 567
main, 326–327
modified by other parts of
    speech, 348, 428, 441–442
participial forms of, 237, **430,**
    492–498
plural, 163, 502, 538–539
principal parts of, 492–506
review exercises on, 330–331,
    514–515
revision strategies for, 21, 87,
    187–188
sentence requirements for, 283
in simple sentences, 443
singular, 163, 502, 538
with singular and plural subjects,
    536–537
test preparations on, 332–333,
    516–517
See also Subject-verb agreement;
    Subject-verb order; Using
    verbs; Verb phrases; Verb
    tenses
Vertical files, 745
Viewing skills
    comparing and contrasting
        newscasts, 45
    comparing different media,
        120, 170–171, 218, 288
    fine art, analyzing elements 680
    graphs, 675
        bar, 676
        line, 676
        pie, 677
    information media, 678
    link information to text, 675
    maps, 675
    notable features, 675
    photographs, 675, 677
    set a purpose, 675
    symbols, 675
    title caption and labels, 675

See also Critical Viewing,
    Information media,
    Responding to Fine Art and
    Literature
Viewpoints, 49, 56, 122, 272
Vignettes, 99, 103, **787**
Virus, electronic, **769**
Visual media
    comparing and contrasting,
        with print, 155, 171
    formatting scripts for, 193, 686
    graphic organizers as, 681–683
    meaning and, 68–69, 95, 121
    See also type of, e.g.,
        Photographs
Vocabulary, 690–701, 711
    development of, 691–694
    listening and, 691, 693
    notebooks for, words, 693–696
    "Possible Sentences" strategy,
        694
    reading and, 691
    studying word parts and origins,
        698–701
    studying words systematically,
        695–697
    in subject content areas, 693
    using context, 692
Vocabulary and spelling, 690–713
    reflecting on, 711
    spelling improvement, 702–711
    study tools for, 695–701
    test preparation for, 712–713
    vocabulary development,
        690–694
    See also Spelling; Vocabulary
Voice in writing, **7,** 729, **787**
    See also Point of view
Vowels, 338, 705, 708

W

Waterfalls, names of, 638
Web page, **769**
    See also Internet resources
Webs. *See* Topic webs
Web site, **769**
Weeding, as revision strategy, 59
well, good, 567
went, gone, 508
when, where, why, 481
which, who, that, 480
Word agreement. *See* Making
    words agree; Pronoun-
    antecedent agreement;
    Subject-verb agreement
Word choice, 153, 212
    audiences and, 204
    for cause and effect, 209

clichés, 336
double comparisons, 565, 574
double negatives, 478, 480
persuasion and, 130, 131, 133
precise, 7, 61, 138, 188, 263, 267, 282, 297, 563
repetition in, 86, 164, 212
revising (*See also* Revising word choice, strategies for)
systematic study of, 695–697
test preparation on, 122, 149, 221
vivid, 7, 76, 83, 91, 161, 282, 336, 349
Word choice, revision strategies for, **21**, 86, 209
circling verbs, 21, 87
color-coding nouns, 61, 237, 263
highlighting, 188, 212
marking "empty" words, 112, 138, 188, 297
reading aloud, 164
showing instead of telling, 282
Word endings. *See* Suffixes
Word order
of adverbs in sentences, 351
inverted, **407**–409, 413
inverted, of persons' names in indexes, 715
inverting subject-verb, for variety in sentences, 467, 542
location of adverb phrases, 428
location of participial phrases, 431
meaning and, 567–568
normal, **405**–407, 413
of subjects and verbs in sentences, 542
Word origins, 701, 706, 707, 747
Word parts. *See* Prefixes; Roots, word; Suffixes
Word processors
features of, 56, 134, 138, 684
grammar checkers on, 476, 480
keyboarding with, 445
spell checkers on, 704, 710, 711
synonym finder on, 138, 697
tracking changes with, 85, 260
as writing tool, 9, 29, 108
Word usage, 26, 725
common problems, 479–481, 508–512, 529, 567–569
cumulative review exercises on, 529, 577
pronouns and, 518–531

same sound as different words, 525, 551, 707, 710
same word as different parts of speech, 305
Working in groups. *See* Cooperative Writing Opportunities; Peer review
Works-cited list, **239**, 242, **761**, **762**, **787**
APA style, 762
CMS style, 762
MLA style, 762, 763–764
write, right, 710
Writer in You, The, 2–11
available technologies for, 9
develop, with different approaches, 3–7
planning to write, 5
publishing opportunities for, 7
purposes of your writing, 2–3, **16**
qualities to strive for, 7
working with others, 6
writing for standardized tests, 10–11
Writers. *See* Authors
Writing, types of, **12**
using writing technologies, 25
See also Autobiographical writing; Cause-and-effect essay; Comparison-and-contrast essay; Narration; Persuasive essay; Problem-and-solution essay; Research report; Response to Literature; Short story; Writing for assessment
Writing activities, ideas for
See Cooperative Writing Opportunities; Media and Technology Skills workshops; Spotlight on the Humanities; Topic Bank ideas
Writing for assessment, 10–11, 274–291, **275**
computerized tests, 289
drafting, **11**, 279–280
editing and proofreading, 283, 290–291
open-book tests, 287
prewriting, 276–278
publishing and presenting, 284
revising, 281–282
test preparation for, 290–291
types of, **275**
Writing Process, A Walk Through the, 12–27
drafting, **13**, 18
editing and proofreading, **13**, **22**

prewriting, **13**, 14–17
publishing and presenting, **13**, **23**
revising, **13**, 19–21
stages of, 13
test preparation on, 26–27, 46, 122
using writing technology, 25
See also entries beginning with Student Work in Progress
Writing-Reading Connections. *See* Reading-Writing Connections
Writing-round process, 78
Written works
developing your own style for, 42–43
titles of, 614–616, 647
verifying facts in, 722
See also Print media

Y

you, 406
Young adults, library section for, 743

Z

ZIP Codes, 596
Zip, electronic, **769**
Zoom shots, as camera technique, 104, 121

Acknowledgments

Staff Credits

The people who made up the *Prentice Hall Writing and Grammar: Communication in Action* team—representing design services, editorial, editorial services, electronic publishing technology, manufacturing and inventory planning, marketing, marketing services, market research, on-line services and multimedia development, product planning, production services, project office, and publishing processes—are listed below. Bold type denotes the core team members.

Ellen Backstrom, Betsy Bostwick, Evonne Burgess, **Louise B. Capuano**, **Sarah Carroll**, **Megan Chill**, Katherine Clarke, Rhett Conklin, Martha Conway, Harold Crudup, **Harold Delmonte**, Libby Forsyth, Maggie Fritz, Ellen Goldblatt, Elaine Goldman, Jonathan Goldson, **Rebecca Graziano**, **Diana Hahn**, Rick Hickox, Kristan Hoskins, Raegan Keida, Carol Lavis, **George Lychock**, Gregory Lynch, William McAllister, Loretta Moser, Margaret Plotkin, Maureen Raymond, Julie Tomasella, Gerry Schrenk, **Melissa Shustyk**, Annette Simmons, Robin Sullivan, **Elizabeth Torjussen**, **Doug Utigard**

Additional Credits

Ernie Albanese, Diane Alimena, Susan Andariese, Michele Angelucci, Penny Baker, Susan Barnes, John Carle, Cynthia Clampitt, Ken Dougherty, Angelo Focaccia, Kathy Gavilanes, Beth Geschwind, Michael Goodman, Jennifer Harper, Evan Holstrom, Leanne Korszoloski, Sue Langan, Rebecca Lauth, Dave Liston, Maria Keogh, Vicki Menanteaux, Gail Meyer, Artur Mkrtchyan, LaShonda Morris, Karyl Murray, Omni-Photo Communications, Kim Ortell, Brenda Sanabria, Carolyn Sapontzis, Mildred Schulte, Slip Jig Image Research Services, Sunnyside, NY, Debi Taffet

Grateful acknowledgment is made to the following for permission to reprint copyrighted material:

Addison-Wesley Educational Publishers
"Hans Christian Andersen" from *Children & Books* by Zena Sutherland. Ninth edition. Copyright © 1997 Addison-Wesley Educational Publishers, Inc. Reprinted by permission.

Bantam Books
"The Eternal Frontier" from *Frontier* by Louis L'Amour, copyright © 1984 by Louis L'Amour Enterprises, Inc. Used by permission of Bantam Books, a division of Random House, Inc.

The Estate of Gwendolyn Brooks
"Pete at the Zoo" by Gwendolyn Brooks. Reprinted by permission of The Estate of Gwendolyn Brooks.

Curtis Brown, Ltd.
From "Suzy and Leah" by Jane Yolen. Copyright © 1993 by Jane Yolen. Originally published by *American Girl Magazine*. Reprinted by permission of Curtis Brown, Ltd.

Hodder and Stoughton Limited
From *Wildlife at Risk: Pandas* by Gillian Standring. Reproduced by permission of Hodder and Stoughton Limited.

John Wiley & Sons, Inc.
"Moving Mountains" from *Earth Science for Every Kid* by Janice VanCleave. Copyright © 1991 by John Wiley & Sons, Inc. Reprinted by permission of John Wiley & Sons, Inc.

The Poynter Institute
"House of Memories" by Kaitlin Crockett (student model). The Poynter Institute, St. Petersburg, Florida.

The Reader's Digest Association
"How Do Rainmakers Make It Rain?" from *How in the World?* Copyright © 1994 by The Reader's Digest Association Limited. Used by permission of The Reader's Digest Association, Inc., Pleasantville, NY, www.rd.com.

The Saturday Evening Post
From *Luke Baldwin's Vow* by Morley Callaghan. Reprinted with permission of The Saturday Evening Post. © 1947 (renewed) BFL & MS, Inc.

Scholastic Inc.
From "Bat Attacks" by Laura Allen from *Scholastic Science World*, May 11, 1998. Copyright © 1998 by Scholastic, Inc. Reprinted by permission.

St. Martin's Press
"Cat on the Go" from *All Things Wise and Wonderful* by James Herriot. Copyright © 1977 by James Herriot. Reprinted by permission of St. Martin's Press, LLC.

University Press of New England
Gary Soto, "The Bike" from *A Summer Life*. Copyright © 1990 by University Press of New England.

Walker and Company
From "Sarah Tops" from *The Key Word and Other Mysteries* by Isaac Asimov, copyright © 1977 by Isaac Asimov. Reprinted with permission from Walker and Company, 435 Hudson Street, New York, NY 10014, 1-800-289-2553. All rights reserved.

Note: Every effort has been made to locate the copyright owner of material reprinted in this book. Omissions brought to our attention will be corrected in subsequent editions.

Photo Credits